W9-ADS-955

Images of the Medieval Peasant

Figurae

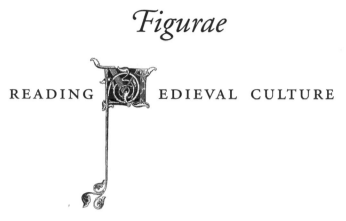

READING MEDIEVAL CULTURE

*I*mages
of the Medieval
Peasant

Paul Freedman

Stanford University Press, Stanford, California, 1999

Stanford University Press
Stanford, California
© 1999 by the Board of Trustees of the
Leland Junior University
Printed in the United States of America
CIP data appear at the end of the book

*F*or Bonnie, as always

Preface

In preparing a study of how peasants were represented in the Middle Ages, I have solicited and exploited the advice and knowledge of many scholars. My experience with Iberian rural history was the stimulus to ask questions about how peasants might be simultaneously despised and yet thought of as particularly close to God. In expanding the scope of my inquiry to the rest of Europe, and in attempting to use literary, religious, and artistic sources, I have trespassed, probably rather awkwardly, on new fields. I have been saved from many errors; but, insofar as mistakes persist, they are my fault rather than the fault of those who so generously shared their expertise with me. This formulation of gratitude, although conventional, is particularly meaningful to me in attempting a larger subject than those I had previously undertaken.

I would first like to thank Gabrielle Spiegel, David Nirenberg, John Friedman, Yuri Bessmertny, Peter Haidu, and Teófilo Ruiz, who read through the manuscript at various stages and offered suggestions to change not only particular passages but the order in which the argument of this work is constructed. My Vanderbilt colleagues Larry Crist and Joel Harrington also read substantial portions in manuscript. Professor Crist pointed me toward more up-to-date use of French literary evidence, and Professor Harrington offered me extremely valuable advice in the areas of German history and the history of spirituality. Helmut Smith and Michael Bess, also of Vanderbilt's History Department, provided comparative information and insights.

An especially large debt is owed to Yuri Bessmertny, whose work on the peasants as viewed by the chivalric class was an early inspiration to me. Giles Constable introduced me to many key works on the subject, including especially those of Bessmertny and Jonin. This project was first conceived during the academic year 1986–87, which I spent at the Institute for Advanced Study, and I retain not only happy memories of that period but a strong sense of gratitude for Professor Constable's advice and encouragement then and over the intervening years.

I thank David R. L. Heald of the University of Kent for his permission to use and to cite his University of London dissertation *The Peasant in Medieval German Literature: Realism and Literary Traditionalism, c. 1150–1400*, which was invaluable to me for its discussion of favorable and unfavorable representations of peasants. Elizabeth Traverse generously allowed me to see her doctoral dissertation on the Neidhart poems in advance of its publication, as well as a conference paper on peasant violence in these poems. In my presentation of the complex questions of attribution and interpretation she corrected numerous mistakes that arose from the popularity of Neidhart and the consequent proliferation of his imitators.

For their help with material from Hungary I owe a large debt to János Bak and Gábor Klaniczay. Their work on the Hungarian rebellion of 1514 and its background has been of vital importance to me. They shared their knowledge and pointed me in the direction of understanding a literature with which I was previously entirely unfamiliar. The late Father Gedeon Gál, O.F.M., Paul Spaeth, and Rega Wood also helped me with the sermons of Oswald of Lasko, the head of the Hungarian Franciscans in the period leading up to the Hungarian peasant war. For material regarding medieval Bohemia, I thank Lisa Wolverton.

In the fields of art and English literature, and for all manner of medieval lore involving peasants, I am greatly indebted to Michael Camille and John Friedman. They offered me aid at several points in this long project. It will become quickly obvious to the reader how much I owe to their books and articles on representations of peasant labor and character and on connections among the various ways of describing outcast peoples and their origins. I am also very grateful to John Plummer, Steven Justice, Thea Summerfield, and Douglas Moffatt for their insights and advice with regard to English literary and historical texts and to Liana Vardi, whose work on peasant labor in early modern art has been inspirational. Ellen Kanowitz and Robert Baldwin made several important suggestions and referred me to other studies of sixteenth- and seventeenth-century art and the styles of portraying rural life.

For assistance with Hebrew texts, especially those concerned with Noah's curse against Ham, I thank Alexandra Cuffel, Steve Benin, and Benjamin Braude. The latter was also kind enough to share with me his research on medieval travelers and geographers. Philippe Buc aided me with regard to Biblical commentaries and their political and social implications. Phyllis Roberts helped me greatly with sermons and the work of Stephen Langton. Susan Reynolds has offered useful advice and careful reading of my work over many years, but I am especially grateful for her generous help with the myths of origin of peoples and nations. Tom Scott and Peter and Renate Blickle led me to understand something of the ideas behind the German Peasants' War of 1525. John Baldwin encouraged me and read several parts of this project.

I owe a great debt for the advice, expertise, and enthusiasm of Nancy Young, my copy editor, and to Victoria Velsor, who drew up the index for this book.

Research on the images of peasants was made possible by grants from the Vanderbilt University Research Council and the American Philosophical Society in the academic year 1990–91 and from the John Simon Guggenheim Memorial Foundation in 1994–95. I am also grateful to the Ecole des Hautes Etudes en Sciences Sociales for supporting a one-month visit to France in 1995 that allowed me to consult manuscripts in Paris and Troyes, and to the Spanish Ministry of Foreign Affairs for a research fellowship in 1994.

Aspects of this project were presented at a number of conferences, and the comments of many people who attended shaped my research and corrected dubious interpretations and outright errors. I thank those who heard papers given at the Russian Academy of Sciences, Moscow, in 1992; at the medieval congresses at Kalamazoo, in 1993 and 1995, and at Leeds, in 1994; at the French Historical Studies meeting of 1994; and at the Institute for Historical Research, London, in 1995. I also presented papers on the medieval peasantry at Yale's Program in Agrarian Studies (1993), at the University of California at Santa Barbara (1994), and at Harvard (1995). I am very grateful to Jim Scott, Sharon Farmer, Thomas Bisson, Jan Ziolkowski, and their colleagues for these invitations.

Finally, I wish to express my deep gratitude to Vanderbilt University, where I taught from 1978 until 1997. My work was always generously supported by the Vanderbilt administration, and I benefited immensely from the learning and company of my colleagues.

P.F.

Contents

꧁

List of Illustrations   xv
A Note on Translations   xvii
Abbreviations   xix

Introduction: Marginality and Centrality of Peasants   1

Part 1. PEASANT LABOR AND A HIERARCHICAL SOCIETY

Chapter 1. Peasant Labor and the Limits of Mutuality   15

Chapter 2. The Breakdown of Mutuality: Laments
over the Mistreatment of Peasants   40

Part 2. THE ORIGINS OF INEQUALITY

Chapter 3. Equality and Freedom at Creation   59

Chapter 4. The Curse of Noah   86

Chapter 5. National Myths and the Origins of Serfdom   105

Part 3. UNFAVORABLE IMAGES OF PEASANTS

Chapter 6. Representations of Contempt and Subjugation   133

Chapter 7. Peasant Bodies, Male and Female   157

Part 4. PEASANT AGENCY, PEASANT HUMANITY

Chapter 8. Peasant Warriors and Peasant Liberties   177

Chapter 9. Pious and Exemplary Peasants   204

Part 5. THE REVOLT AGAINST SERVITUDE

Chapter 10. The Problem of Servitude: Arbitrary
Mistreatment, Symbolic Degradation 239

Chapter 11. Peasant Rebellions of the Late Middle Ages   257

Conclusion: Harmony and Dissonance   289

Notes   307
Bibliography   403
Index   451

Illustrations

1. A representation of the Three Orders of Society.   21

2. Adam being taught by an angel to work. Thirteenth-century painting on the ceiling of the Monastery of Sigena, Aragon.   29

3. Work after the Fall: Adam digging, Eve spinning. Another thirteenth-century painting from the Monastery of Sigena.   65

4. Mistreatment of serfs. Woodcut engraving by the so-called Petrarch Master.   68

5. A tree representing the social estates. Woodcut engraving by the Petrarch Master.   70

6. Captured fugitive serfs with horns. Early-fourteenth-century illustration to Codex 6.1, "De fugitivis servis."   90

7. Cain shown with horns and kinky hair. From an English Psalter, ca. 1270–80.   92

8. The labors of the months, August, wheat harvest. From the Queen Mary Psalter, early fourteenth century.   145

9. A scene from Neidhart's scatological misadventure, the "Violet Prank" (*Veilchenschwank*). Mural painted between 1360 and 1380, from the "Zum Grundstein" house, Winterthur, Switzerland.   152

10. Peasant tournament, drawing by Hans Burgkmaier, early sixteenth century.   180

11. Christ with a spade. English alabaster sculpture, fifteenth century, now in the Victoria and Albert Museum.   225

12. The world turned upside down: a peasant at the altar and a priest plowing. Woodcut engraving from Joseph Gruenbeck, *Spiegel der naturlichen, himelischen und prophetischen sehungen* (Leipzig, 1522).   233

13. The execution of György Dózsa. Woodcut illustration from Stephanus Taurinus, *Stauromachia* (Vienna, 1519).   270

14. The execution of György Dózsa. Woodcut illustration from the pamphlet *Die auffrur so geschehen ist im Ungelandt mit den Creutzern* (Nuremberg, 1514).   271

A Note on Translations

English translations of passages cited from original-language editions are my own. Other translations are from the cited published English editions. Full information on original and English editions is provided in the bibliography.

Abbreviations

The following abbreviations are used in the notes and bibliography.

BLVS   Bibliothek des litterarischen Vereins in Stuttgart
CC   Corpus Christianorum
CSEL   Corpus Scriptorum Ecclesiasticorum Latinorum
GAG   Göppinger Arbeiten zur Germanistik
LCL   Loeb Classical Library
MGH   Monumenta Germaniae Historica
PG   Patrologia cursus completus. Series Graeca, ed. J. P. Migne,
        161 vols. (Paris, 1857–66).
PL   Patrologia cursus completus. Series Graeca, ed. J. P. Migne,
        221 vols. (Paris, 1844–55).

Images of the Medieval Peasant

Introduction

Marginality and Centrality of Peasants

Medieval Europeans of the upper classes, like their modern descendants, regarded rural life as appealingly simple and admirably productive, but above all as strange, a tableau populated with alien beings of a lower order. Jean de La Bruyère described a countryside whose inhabitants appeared at first glance to be ferocious animals, dark, burnt by the sun, attached to the soil that they worked with stubborn persistence. Yet they could speak, and indeed, when they raised themselves up, they had a human countenance. In fact, they *were* human.[1] A more poignant oscillation between the human and not-human is voiced by the peasants themselves in Carlo Levi's memoir of exile in an impoverished part of southern Italy:

> "We're not Christians," they say. "Christ stopped short of here, at Eboli."
> "Christian," in their way of speaking means "human being," and this almost proverbial phrase that I have so often heard them repeat may be no more than the expression of a hopeless feeling of inferiority. "We're not Christians, we're not human beings; we're not thought of as men but simply as beasts, beasts of burden, or even less than beasts, mere creatures of the wild."[2]

To be Christian meant to be fully human, in the European Middle Ages as well as in twentieth-century Lucania. Thus being treated as less than human clashed with the dignity and equality, however minimal, conferred by being a Christian. The bitter proverb of the peasants cuts two ways: it both recognizes how they were regarded by their superiors and protests their humanity against this dominant image.

This book considers the different images of the peasant in the Middle Ages. These images formed an extensive vocabulary of contempt, but at the same time they portrayed the peasant as closer to God than those who oppressed him. On the one hand, the peasant was lowly, even subhuman: ugly, dull-witted, coarse, materialistic, and cowardly. Such depictions did not simply present the supposed physical characteristics of rustics but explained their subordination, their separation from the rest of humanity. While nothing so elaborate as modern pseudobiological theories of inferiority existed, representations of the peasant as naturally lowly excused his relative lack of freedom and justified his exploitation.

The language of subordination was applied as well to many groups alien to Christian Europe in the Middle Ages. Some of the opprobrious language used for peasants spilled over into hostile characterizations of Jews, Muslims, heretics, lepers, and strange foreign peoples, including the fantastic "monstrous" or "Plinian" races thought to inhabit the East. All these could be regarded as unclean, dishonest, savage, or cursed, and their religious, physical, or geographic differences viewed as fearsome.

Peasants differed from these marginal or outcast peoples in three important respects, which made their representation as alien more problematic: they constituted the overwhelming majority of the European population; as their superiors acknowledged, they were necessary to feed the rest of society; and they were Christians. An array of unfavorable images indeed characterized peasants as debased, even subhuman, but these stereotypes were tempered by the fact that peasants were not "marginal" in the same way as outcast peoples, foreigners, or the destitute poor.[3]

As the largest segment of the Christian population, the peasantry was a pervasive and familiar presence in the medieval European landscape and thus could hardly be viewed as alien in the same way as the teeming infidels of the immense non-European world "out there," beyond the borders. Furthermore, to the extent that the peasants supported those placed above them, they appeared dutiful and necessary. They fulfilled, perhaps reluctantly, the duties laid upon them by the dominant model of society that saw it divided into functional orders: those who fight, those who pray, and those who work. Finally, the nature of Christianity itself gave pause to the dominant elements of society: might the degradation of the peasantry bode a future reversal? would God reward their meekness and implicit closeness to Him in the world to come?

Although the largest number of images in literature and art depicted peasants as unpleasant and boorish, a series of favorable images also gained currency, especially in didactic and sermon literature, ranging from praises of their labors, to laments of their unjust exploitation, to sentimental exemplifications of their fortitude, simplicity, and piety. The vocabularies of both hostile and laudatory representations, their interaction, reconciliation, and opposition, form the subject of the following chapters. Rather than simply collecting and contrasting "favorable" and "unfavorable" images, I will show how they could be combined or held simultaneously in a certain tension to deal with a vast segment of society regarded as "other" but also as immediately necessary.

The seemingly inconsistent images of peasants have been often remarked, particularly by students of the various national literatures. Historical treatments of literature in relation to society have drawn up catalogues, analyses, and typologies of the presentation of peasants. Thus Wilhelm Blankenburg in 1902 described how peasants appeared in the French *fabliaux*, and Oskar Reich in 1909 used literary sources to discuss the life and culture of the peasantry in France.[4] A dissertation written by Stanley Leman Galpin in 1905 listed the base characteristics of peasants in contrast to the favorable ones of the knights.[5] In 1934 another dissertation, this one concerning German medieval literature, discussed both harsh antipeasant satires and writings in praise of peasants.[6] G. G. Coulton, dedicated to exploding the romantic image of medieval harmony, offered in 1925 a thoroughly researched catalogue of attacks on peasants and peasant resentment.[7] Hilde Hügli (1929) and, more exhaustively, Fritz Martini (1944) described the variations in the peasant's appearance in the several genres of medieval German literature.[8] Martini's book is especially important because of both its detail and the author's desire to present as much of the favorable imagery as could be discovered. More recently David Heald, Helga Schüppert, and Herwig Ebner have demonstrated the shifts and ambivalence of portrayals of peasants in literary and historical works.[9]

It is not my intention to show that peasants were more favorably depicted than has been conventionally assumed.[10] As will become apparent, I have profited greatly from the works mentioned above, but I am more interested in the connections among images than in whether one sort outweighed the other. I contend that language concerning the peasant was not simply a collection of positive and negative representations. The vocabulary describing peasants formed itself into a variegated discourse, a grammar, by which peasants could be regarded *both* as degraded and as exemplary, as justly subordinated yet as close to God. Such ideas were not synthesized into a consistently articulated doctrine, but literate observers at least occasionally worried about why peasants were subordinated, and especially why many of them were unfree (serfs) and at the mercy of their lords, a condition that could be reconciled with Christian doctrine and social assumptions, but not complacently or automatically.

In addition, I examine common themes of peasant labor, productivity, and exploitation that fit into both positive and negative imagery. However debased the peasants were in the eyes of the dominant orders of society, their labor was recognized as providing sustenance for all. Labor might be regarded as expiation rather than a positive activity in itself, but even if peasants were uniquely afflicted by the Fall or by some biblical event such as Noah's curse upon his son Ham, their labor was necessary.

Such labor, it could be argued, repaid some service, such as protection and prayer in accord with the functional division of society into the Three Orders. If, however, agricultural labor was coerced (either by servitude or by a general pattern of seigneurial domination) and was not in fact matched by any real benefit, then society's conformity to divine will was called into question. The doubt nagged especially in that the peasants were not paradigmatically alien or infidel. Enslaving Saracens captured in battle created few moral problems according to the prevailing view. But degrading Christian rustics exercised quite another prerogative, one requiring more elaborate justifications.

These justifications lie behind the proliferation of images of the peasantry, both negative and positive, and are expressed in the images themselves. In such representations we find the rustic's position explained in terms of an innate character that fits him for toil and ill-treatment, or in terms of some negation of original equality transmitted hereditarily (such as Noah's curse), or in terms of an admitted secular injustice that is part of a larger scheme, to be overcome in a heavenly reversal of fortune.

A collection of images organized according to a pattern conforms to the definition of ideology as "the imaginary relationship of individuals to their real conditions of existence."[11] The images cannot be divorced from their social context. Moreover, they form a program more active and self-interested than a mere pattern of thought (mentality or collective imagination) that is unpremeditated and unexamined. Paul Zumthor regards ideology as "an ensemble of intellectual and discursive schemes" whose function is to legitimate the ruling order as natural and unquestionable.[12] Ideology is both a "fossilization" in its historical terms and active as a coercive device. Yet, as I will argue in concluding this investigation, images of peasants did not form an uncontested or "hegemonic" discourse that serenely justified how peasants were treated. Historians reading literary sources are often tempted to reduce them to ideological statements at the expense of their specificity as essentially imaginative works. I hope to show that, doctrinaire though such texts may be, they possess an individuality, seriousness, and inner tension that resists ideological simplification.

The forms that discourse about the peasants took unequivocally reflect the material conditions of medieval society. To understand the dynamic of that society, however, requires knowledge of what Michel Vovelle calls the "complex mediators" between real life and representation.[13] Such mediators in this context include notions of labor, human dignity, and mutuality, to be discussed in the following chapters. I will not treat the images and their peculiar evolution and interaction either as free-floating inventions apart from society, or as narrow rationalizations of the way of the world. The history of mentalities explores the relationship between objective conditions of human life and the way people narrate and live it. Shaped as they are by these paired forces, mental constructs do not necessarily point in only one direction (such as bolstering the hegemonic view of the powerful), nor can they be related mechanically to the structures of social organization. They have a certain amount of play or autonomy, and in addition, as thought patterns with a certain power, they influence the material basis of society. For example, as I have pointed out elsewhere, jurists and historians in a particular region of medieval Europe, in their efforts to categorize and explain servitude, effectively promoted defining formerly free peasants as serfs, yet undermined serfdom by their doubts: articulating these doubts, peasants of the region mounted a successful rebellion against servile status.[14]

Images of medieval peasants were varied, even contradictory, but not irreconcilable. They could be fit into an intelligible pattern, even forming an ideology of exploitation, but it was a pattern with enough internal points of contestation to require constant reinforcement in rebuffing challenges both from within elite circles and from outside, from the peasants themselves. Even though contemptuous images of rustics seem a constant in Europe across the centuries, regarding the peasant as an object of contempt was not inevitable. In the Byzantine Empire, for example, it was artisans, not peasants, who figured as the opponents of saints, as boorish scoffers. Peasants were viewed as virtuous when they were not simply unnoticed.[15]

To the extent that images in the medieval West were oriented around certain ideas—that peasants are like animals, that rustics are equal in the sight of God, that they are the progeny of Ham—they were inscribed in social reality but have to be described according to a certain internal logic and coherence not limited to specifics of time or place. My attempt to articulate this logic and coherence is what, I hope, justifies the organizing principles of what follows. Rather than moving chronologically from the Carolingian era to the German Peasants' War of 1525, I examine the conceptions of peasants in society synchronically, thematically.

The two chapters in the first part of the book concern what might be considered the idealized model of the peasants' social position and the admitted flaws in that vision. The need for peasants who nourish society was joined to a justification of their subordination by an appeal not only to hierarchy but also to mutuality, particularly through the image of the three functional orders of society: those who fight, those who pray, and those who work (Chapter 1). Yet from its beginnings, the Three Orders model was recognized not to benefit the rustics in fact. This flawed mutuality provoked a series of complaints and challenged the justification of a system that in reality depended on unrecompensed, exploited labor (Chapter 2).

The subsequent group of three chapters examines the attempts to address the unequal relations among the Three Orders. Chapter 3 describes how the original equality of humanity at the time of Creation was seen as opposing the manifest inequality of condition in the world. Writers disagreed about how far original equality and freedom still held as moral imperatives for contemporary society and about the legitimacy of subverting them, especially among Christians. While authorities agreed on humanity's common descent from our first parents, they also posited some event, not merely fortune, that differentiated not only rich from poor but free from unfree. One popular candidate for such an event, as noted above, was the curse of Noah upon his son Ham (Genesis 9:25), whose descendants, through his own son Canaan, would have to serve their brethren. Although this biblical passage would later be put to various uses, notably in defending the enslavement of Africans in the New World, its medieval exegesis focused on European serfs, in an effort to explain their bondage and subordination to arbitrary lordship (Chapter 4). Secular historical legends served a similar purpose. Myths of national origin, especially in Catalonia and Hungary, identified a moment when the ancestors of peasants preferred a timid safety to the choice of bellicose freedom. The moment of foundation differentiated nobles—the free and the brave—from those licitly held in subjugation for their ancestors' cowardice (Chapter 5).

The two chapters in the third part of this book consider the well-known panoply of negative images of the peasant. While in many genres the ostensible force of such images was merely comedic, the base, coarse, bestial rustic they presented sometimes served as a naturalistic argument tending to condone, if not actually justify, the bad treatment of peasants. Rather than attempting to account for some past cause of inequality, farcical imagery suggested that the rustic was simply inferior by nature and so fitted to toil and exploitation (Chapter 6). The seventh chapter looks particularly at the difference between caricatures of male and those of female peasants. Peasant men represented a peculiarly gross, dull materialism, but one that involved only a torpid sexual instinct. Peasant women, until the end of the Middle Ages, were less grotesque than the men in literary renditions, but more libidinous.

The fourth part of the book discusses the forms of retaliation against or rebuttal to negative imagery of peasants. Chapter 8 studies the ability of at least some peasants to constitute themselves as autonomous and to defend themselves by military force. Chapter 9 examines countervailing representations of rustics as sanctified by their suffering and their labor. Here the failure of mutuality in the Three Orders system is regarded as secular and temporary, something that could and should be overcome (Chapter 9).

The chapters in the fifth part consider how the disparate views of the peasantry outlined above affected the social problems that lay at the heart of the peasant rebellions that erupted between the Black Death of 1348–49 and the German Peasants' War of 1525. Theoretical efforts to reconcile servitude with the necessary social role of the peasantry and their status as Christians are dealt with in Chapter 10. That these were not merely abstract discussions but were appropriated by peasants in their grievances and programs is considered in Chapter 11.

A thematic (as opposed to chronological) treatment of the highly complex issue of medieval conceptions of peasants runs the risk of disengaging observations from their contexts, both their immediate historical situation and their role in certain genres. My approach has the advantage, however, of highlighting the frequency and longevity of certain themes and images. Moreover, the social meaning of such texts must be understood not only in relation to their historical moment but also in relation to a symbolic tradition that influenced thought about peasants. Images, symbols, and representations do not have a completely arbitrary or independent life, but they must be studied over a long period of chronological development even when they might seem to have become merely repetitious and empty. A central thesis of the last chapter (Chapter 11) is that late-medieval dissent and rebellion, even well into the sixteenth century, was shaped by earlier discourse about the peasant. Not only were such ideas as the value of labor, the failure to compensate it, and the original equality of all humanity appropriated by peasants as late as 1381 and 1525, but such ideas also created doubts and dissension within the elite circles that discussed the peasant as an object or problem in these centuries.

Looking at images across a variety of genres threatens to violate distinctions among rules and forms that differed from one national literature to another, from written to pictorial depiction, and from poetry and romance to didactic works such as histories or sermons. What is significant, as I hope to show, is that within the conventions of various genres certain representations were shared: the military incapacity of rustics, for example, figured not only in the romance but in historical and legal accounts of nations; the dependence of society on rustic labor appears in descriptions of the Three Orders, in thirteenth-century sermons, and in the plaints of peasants at the end of the Middle Ages.

Much of the imagery concerning peasants occurs in literature. In Germany, where a whole genre of satire against the peasant (*Bauernschwank*) developed, peasants often figured as ludicrous protagonists. Elsewhere, as in French romances, they played comic or grotesque minor roles. I have tried not to approach literature as if it were a realistic mirror of society. Literary conventions, exaggerations, and stylizations make such an approach a very dubious enterprise. Yet literature, an imperfect mirror, nevertheless reveals, as Jacques Le Goff noted, something about the makers of the mirror.[16] Literary obsessions, distortions, and stereotypes entertained their audiences but also represented and categorized peasants according to certain norms. Even in the most hostile genres, however, these categories were unstable and could, by their very exaggeration, undermine and call into question the subordination of the peasantry.[17]

Although seldom a protagonist, the peasant is ubiquitous in medieval texts, but of course not in the sociologically descriptive fashion that might be most helpful to us. It is also obvious that such documents as peasant memoirs and diaries are in short supply.[18] Nevertheless, as Jean-Claude Schmitt remarked, "it is not so much the documents that are lacking as the conceptual instruments necessary to understand them."[19] I do not claim any particular methodological advance, but I have attempted to look at a large and varied array of texts regarding peasants to discern repeated themes in the discourse about them. In doing so I am most concerned with persistence over time but will discuss to some extent what seems to have changed over the first five centuries after the millennium.

Certain kinds of texts proved less fruitful than I had hoped. Cistercian and Franciscan literature might be expected to offer many reflections on rustic labor, but this turned out not to be so. The Cistercians had uneducated lay brethren (*conversi*) who worked in agriculture rather than prayer, but despite the status of these toilers as members of the community, and despite the obedience and piety that their agricultural role presumably required, their labor was only occasionally regarded as sanctifying. Furthermore, their spiritual role as brethren was downgraded even further by the end of the twelfth century. For their part, the Franciscans were concerned more with poverty than with work—and as will be seen, the medieval peasant, even if starving, only partially qualified as "poor" from the Franciscan point of view. Franciscan attention was devoted to the marginal and the destitute, especially in the cities, rather than to the poor holding land. In the accounts of Francis himself, the boorish interlocutors whom the saint treats with astonishing meekness and whose abuse he embraces often conform to stereotypes of rustics. Serfdom was often evoked by Francis and his followers as a model of humility and devotion, but this did not in itself imply any particular attention to worldly serfs.[20]

The subject of this book and the object of so much medieval discussion, the peasant needs to be defined before looking at the various modes of description.

The definition of peasants in modern agrarian studies focuses on several points: peasants are family farmers who produce a large part of what they consume but are tied to a wider economy (producing or laboring for a market). They have access to the use of land and usually to a specific, hereditarily transmissible unit of property, but they are not its owners. They pay rent in the form of produce, money, labor, or a combination of these, and their dependence on the landlord (private or state) is more than merely economic or contractual.[21] Peasants are thus neither independent, self-sufficient small farmers nor sharecroppers in the fashion of the American South in the nineteenth and early twentieth centuries (sharecroppers did not grow their own food and moved frequently). Nor are peasants like slaves, who were also likely to be moved around, did not have particular pieces of property that they could transmit to their heirs, and could not legally form permanent family units.[22] But peasants do have a tie to the land and its masters that binds them by means of a certain loss of freedom, or debt, or taxation.

Use of the word "peasant" to describe medieval agriculturalists has been called "a confession of weakness" that fails to grapple with a more complex reality.[23] The modern definition of a peasant does, in my opinion, possess sufficient precision in itself and is applied accurately to the system of land tenure that existed in the Middle Ages. The medieval peasant was a tenant farmer who, at least in theory, could sustain himself and his family while paying a substantial rent (labor service, produce, and/or money) that supported his lord. The extra-economic power exerted on him was usually that of a private landlord (most obviously the members of the military elite, that is, the knights) or the Church. In this overwhelmingly agrarian society, the vast majority of the population were peasants, and the ultimate source of its wealth and economic expansion was peasant labor.

Some peasants were free, while others were serfs, defined by custom or law as constrained either by being deprived of redress through public law, by rights over their persons and property exerted at the discretion of their lords, or by an inability to remove themselves from the land. Although serfdom was widespread and varied in the Middle Ages, at no time was a majority of the rural population legally defined as unfree. Nevertheless, a substantial proportion of that population consisted of serfs; moreover, medieval law, terminology, and the very image of the peasant encouraged a tendency to regard all rustics as at least potentially or essentially servile. Indeed, with few exceptions, peasants of all conditions were constrained by a system of economic exploitation and social subordination.[24]

In the medieval period a number of terms were used to denote peasants. The most common Latin word until the eleventh century was *colonus*, originally a late-Roman term for a person of semifree condition (that is, not a slave) who was attached to a particular property.[25] It lost its particular legal meaning upon the collapse of the Western imperial authority and seems to have been applied thereafter to rural cultivators but with a connotation of servitude, close to the Roman term for slave, *servus*. *Rusticus* and *agricola* were also popular and carried pejorative connotations of stupidity and barbarism (especially *rusticus*).

In the high and late Middle Ages, the most common term in Latin was *rusticus*, which meant any country-dwelling laborer, landless or landed, free or serf. *Servus* and other Roman terms (*adscripticius* or *colonus* in a more restrictive meaning) were applied to serfs but in theoretical works rather than in everyday documents. The use of *servus* thus gave to serfdom an even more degraded set of implications, in that jurists tended to apply the Roman law of slavery to medieval serfdom.[26]

In the vernacular, terms such as *Bauer*, *vilain*, and "villein" carried different shadings of meaning. In Germany, *Bauer* denoted a person of fairly extensive property but carried, as did *rusticus*, at least a certain implication of unfree, servile status.[27] The image of the *Bauer* was set off against that of the knight, so that the former was associated most of all with agricultural productivity and military incapability.[28]

In France and England, such words as *vilain* and "villein" had more implications concerning legal standing than did the German word *Bauer*, but their meanings changed. The English villeins were distinct from the slaves (*theows* and a host of other terms) in the Anglo-Saxon and Norman periods, but became assimilated to a less differentiated class of servile though not enslaved rural tenants in the high and late Middle Ages.[29] A similar change took place in the definition of *vilain* in northern France, although in common parlance, the word continued to mean rustic (with connotations of base behavior) rather than specifically serf.

Medieval discourse about the peasant is entangled with changes in the concept of "the poor." This fluctuating entanglement was of more than sociological interest, reflecting as it does medieval concern about biblical solicitude for the poor, as expressed by Old Testament prophets and in particular by the New Testament. The word "poor" continues today to have a certain ambiguity in the United States, for example, where a distinction is often made between "the working poor" and "the underclass," the former being seen as worthy but unfortunate by reason of low wages; the latter as marginal, criminal, unstable in their manner of life. In general during the Middle Ages, the peasant, however impoverished, held a parcel of land and could in some measure sustain himself. He was not considered among the poor because he was not utterly destitute or without means of support. By the thirteenth century, especially with the rapid growth of cities, the poor, unlike the peasants, seemed to pose an urgent problem of social control, much as would be the case in the modern era.[30] At the same time, by their visibility, rootlessness, and lack of property, the urban poor were more obvious objects of charity than the peasants, who were regarded as avaricious even if their "property" was miserable and their labor exploited.

At various times and in several contexts, however, peasants and *pauperes* were regarded as similar or identical. This was especially true in the early Middle Ages, when *pauper* meant something close to the modern word "poor," covering both the destitute and the lower-level agricultural worker.[31] In the late Merovingian and Carolingian era, a *pauper* was conceived as anyone who, although free, lacked power and substantial property. The *pauperes* (who included independent free men) were contrasted with the powerful (*potentes*), who owned extensive lands and servile laborers. *Pauperes* were those who needed to be protected by the kings, although their freedom and autonomy would come under pressure from the powerful as state authority waned in the ninth and tenth centuries.[32]

With the growth of the European economy after 1000 and with the impress of new religious movements, "the poor" became much more sharply distinguished from the peasantry. The poor were differentiated from those with property, not from the tiny elite of the *potentes*. The reasons for this were twofold. On the one hand, the example of the apostolic life stirred the powerful to convert themselves into *pauperes Christi*.[33] The spectacle of wealth effaced power as the emblem of worldliness, and especially with Saint Francis, a literal poverty was exalted as a graphic form of humility. Francis understood poverty in terms of begging, the most obvious act connoting destitution and lack of property.[34] On the other hand, beginning with the thirteenth century and accelerating after 1348, the poor were regarded as a problem, and attempts were made to police them and to distinguish between worthy and un-worthy poor.[35]

Thus in the later Middle Ages, the peasants and the poor alike figured as both exemplary and base, even dangerous. Yet at the same time, the peasants were distinguished quite clearly from the poor in that, as emphasized above, the peasants were seen not as economically marginal but rather as productive. In reality, however, the peasants were fundamentally divided between those who actually were self-sustaining and those who did not possess a tenancy sufficient for their support. The latter had to labor for others to supplement a meager living and lived closer to the margins of society.[36]

As well as being internally differentiated between those holding full tenures and those in a more precarious position, the peasantry was also di-vided between those who were legally of free condition and those who were serfs. At different times and places these divisions appeared of greater or lesser importance and affected the image of peasants accordingly. In German litera-ture, for example, the peasants appear extremely coarse in their manners but not impoverished. In fact, their boorishness is exemplified by, among other things, an inappropriate and foolish display of weapons, fine clothes, glut-tony, and other marks of an ill-managed prosperity. In the French *fabliaux* the peasant (*vilain*) is often too well-off for his own good, while in the romances, poetry, and didactic literature of France he is a more wretched character.

Whether servile or free, prosperous or indigent, the medieval peasants were above all defined as unprivileged and lowly, yet as productive. Elite re-gard of the peasantry displayed a fundamental ambivalence, conceiving of rustics on the one hand as inhabiting a completely different and lower world—if not literally "other," at least constructed as alien—and on the other hand as ur-human, exemplarily Christian, conforming most closely to what God had intended for humanity, people whose worthy labor supports all of humanity. This ambivalence shapes the following chapters.

Part I

Peasant Labor and a Hierarchical Society

Chapter I

Peasant Labor and the
Limits of Mutuality

Medieval observers could not consistently maintain that peasants were marginal. Peasants were not a minority of the population, as Jews and lepers were, nor could they easily be presented as "Other," like the Saracens or the Plinian races. Peasants formed a majority, a *Christian* majority moreover. They were thus central, not peripheral; they cultivated the land to which they were born and sustained the whole society from generation to generation.

Above all, in the eyes of their superiors, peasants were necessary. Without them, asks a late-fifteenth-century German poem entitled "The First Nobleman,"

> Who would produce for us the wheat,
> And also the good wine
> By which we are often gladdened?[1]

More pointedly, Ordericus Vitalis in the twelfth century questioned how the clergy (*oratores*) could survive without the labor of plowmen (*aratores*).[2] Thomas of Wimbledon remarked in a sermon in 1388 that if there were no laborers, priests and knights would have to work the land and herd animals, or perish.[3]

That the whole population depended ultimately on agricultural labor was acknowledged by those of a practical turn of mind as well. In enacting a new tax in 1298, the councilors of Siena claimed they would limit its impact on the rural poor, who nourished the entire urban population. We may doubt that the councilors' generosity flowed from sincere concern for the poor, but if we are right, the fact that the councilors worried about the rural poor even absent altruism shows all the more emphatically the force of the image of the ultimate basis for wealth.[4]

That the higher orders of society depended on the toil of the peasantry was a commonplace that did not require a sophisticated appreciation of economics. Yet it was a commonplace with a number of more complex implications. A society's dependence on agriculture did not necessarily imply that those engaged in it could, by virtue of their economic importance, lay claims upon those who were not. In societies built on slave labor, for example, it was perfectly possible to recognize the dependence without thereby conferring any dignity upon or conceding any obligation to the slaves. The medieval peasant, however, was usually regarded as at least partially free, and he was after all a Christian.

The hard lot of semi-free, Christian peasants and their role as subordinate producers of wealth for others were explained and excused in two ways. For one, the peasant's condition could be regarded as merited punishment for some primordial sin (either biblical or pseudo-historical); we will examine this idea in chapters 4 and 5. For another, if the peasant's essential nature fit him for little more than brutish, docile labor, if he were naturally lowly, dull, coarse, and stupid, then his labor and subordination could be viewed as simply appropriate, and no explanations based on sin or history would be needed. This supposed debased character is an important implication of the myriad derisive and hostile representations of peasants to be discussed below in chapters 6 and 7.

To the extent that the peasant was, despite his "fallen" condition or his "lowly" nature, nevertheless partially free and a Christian, he could not simply be dismissed as subhuman, and the question of the purpose of his labor remained complicated by the degree to which it appeared unremunerated. It is this question of recompense that troubled medieval authors to whom, on first glance at least, peasants seemed to be exploited. In this chapter, I will discuss two medieval responses to this concern. The prevailing model of society—its division into the Three Orders of clerics, knights, and (agricultural) laborers—addressed the problem of recompense by positing the relationships among the orders as mutually beneficial rather than as exploitative. Peasants worked for the other two orders and in exchange received the prayers of the one and protection from the other. The second response was to ascribe a degree of spiritual worth to peasant labor in itself, regardless of whether it was adequately compensated in a material way. Such a valuation of labor as more than just penitentially beneficial might counsel quietism (the reward would be conferred in the next world), but could also carry subversive import: it could imply that human beings *should* toil, and that those who do so might be entitled to make present demands on the basis of its merit. Mutuality (the Three Orders) and the intrinsic virtue of labor will be treated in this chapter following a discussion of the basic observation underlying them: the indispensability of the peasant's work.

The Dependence of the Elite: Peasants as the Support of Society

Explicit statements that agricultural labor supports the rest of society first appeared near the year 1000. In his *Liber apologeticus* (ca. 994), addressed to Hugh Capet and his son and coruler Robert, Abbo of Fleury divided lay society into agriculturalists (*agricolae*) and warriors (*agonistae*). The former sustained the Christian populace by their sweat and rustic skills, while the latter fought the enemies of the Church.[5] In this, apparently the sole mention of rustics in Abbo's works, there is no reciprocal obligation among the Three Orders of society; rather, both groups of laymen uphold the Church.[6] For Aelfric, abbot of Eynsham (died 1020), the different functions are explicitly joined to a theory of the Three Orders in mutual relation (Aelfric was the first to term the functional categories "orders").[7]

In his *Colloquy*, a Latin schoolbook, Aelfric answers the question "which among the secular arts is the most important?" Without directly referring to the scheme of the Three Orders, Aelfric cites the activity of the plowman (*arator*) who feeds everyone else.[8] Archbishop Wulfstan of York, to whom Aelfric had addressed a letter on the Three Orders, paraphrased Aelfric, observing that the entire population is supported by those who labor (the *woercmen*).[9] In the *Colloquy* the plowman describes his difficult travail in cold weather for an exigent master, lamenting, "the work is hard, because I am not free."[10] Elsewhere Aelfric reiterates the role of the *laboratores*, who nourish everyone but who are aided by the *bellatores*, fighters of earthly foes, and the *oratores*, battlers of spiritual enemies. Here the reciprocity that is clouded in the *Colloquy* by the plowman's servitude is more confidently asserted.[11]

Bishop Gerard of Cambrai, in his *Gesta episcoporum Cameracensium* (written probably in 1036), asserts that those who pray and those who fight (*oratores* and *bellatores*) are nourished by those who labor.[12] This dependence was also emphasized by Adalbero, bishop of Laon, whose *Carmen ad Rotbertum regem* (ca. 1025), it is now thought, dates from shortly before Gerard's work rather than after (as Claude Carozzi, the work's editor, and Georges Duby, in his discussion of the orders, believed).[13] Although Adalbero exalts the notion of mutuality among the social orders, he expresses a frankly pessimistic view of the dependence of the wealthy on agricultural labor and exploitation. The way in which lords live and rule requires that those who labor receive only the barest rewards.[14]

Two aspects of the commonplace that the peasant supports all as it appears in Adalbero's *Carmen* would persist in later centuries. On the one hand it is a simple statement of fact, intended as a reminder to the powerful, or simply as a recognition of the paradox that those who are great are ultimately at the mercy of those they dominate. Adalbero points out that no free man can live without servile dependents (*servi*) and that even the powerful depend on their servants.[15] Behind this is Augustine's wry observation that those who seem to command are in fact ruled by those who serve them.[16] On the other hand, the statement that all are supported by agricultural labor could contain a reproach that the peasant does not receive a reward for his labor, neither the actual wealth produced nor any reciprocation from society. Adalbero calls the *servi* an "afflicted race" who have nothing except sorrow and toil.[17]

In these two aspects of the commonplace we thus find what might be called a "complacent" version of the dependence of the clergy and knights on rustic labor and a more uneasy, even apologetic concern with society's evident failure to realize the ideal of mutuality. The complacent tendency is exemplified in *Helmbrecht*, a satirical didactic poem written before 1290 by Wernher de Gartenaere. Its moral is the folly of the peasant who tries to rise above his place. The young peasant Helmbrecht, disdaining the warnings of his father, leaves the family farm to become a marauding knight. Although Helmbrecht is quite a competent fighter, his reckless and savage career is eventually ended by maiming and death.

In attempting to dissuade his son from becoming a knight, Helmbrecht's father extols the useful labor of the plowman, who supports all other orders of society. Helmbrecht should take pride in agricultural work, not scorn it. Many a king owes his crown to the plowman's toil, a sentiment that the author endorses but that the wicked Helmbrecht rejects.[18] Similarly in the *Buch der Rügen*, rustics are advised to be cheerful, for by their "pure" labor they feed all Christendom.[19] In contrast to Adalbero, who acknowledges the coercion of peasants, these thirteenth-century writers claim rustic labor is rewarded. The recompense is primarily spiritual, to be sure, and requires a certain docility. The author of the *Buch der Rügen* counsels diligence and acceptance on the part of the peasants, for the "purity" of their productive labor confers a degree of sanctity upon them.

Late medieval German literature bitterly satirized rustic stupidity and faithlessness but simultaneously praised peasants as the uncomplaining bulwark of the social order. Hans Rosenplüt, a Nuremberg artisan best known for his Carnival plays that featured ludicrously crude rustics, was also author of a poem in praise of the "noble, pious peasant" who feeds the entire world with his plow. In this poem, written in about 1450, Rosenplüt acknowledges that he has no better friend than the "noble plowman" who has fed both him and his parents.[20] A late-fifteenth-century German song in the form of a dialogue has a peasant point out to a knight that without the plow the knight could not survive.[21] A poem by Heinrich "der Teichner" (ca. 1350) praises the peasant whose plow feeds the world.[22] The mutual benefit conferred by the three-fold division of society is invoked by an entry in the fifteenth-century Colmar Song Collection likening the "pious peasant" to the priest. His plow relieves us of physical hunger as the priest ministers to our spiritual needs.[23]

Similar sentiments can be found in English texts. The late-medieval song-poem whose modern title is "God Speed the Plow" begins by acknowledging that "the merthe of alle this londe maketh the gode husbonde [i.e., husband-man] with erynge of his plowe."[24] Several stanzas end "God speed the plow all day" (or "all way"). Having described the various labors of the seasons, the poem concludes by wishing long good life to those who pray for the plow-man and who benefit from his work.

Such praises of peasants as the sustainers of all avoid close examination of reciprocity by emphasizing the virtue of agricultural labor. Virtue inheres not in the work itself but in its benefit to others, although agricultural work is re-garded as more "real" and productive than any other form of labor. The vi-sion of the "noble" peasant is an aspect of the paradox of medieval concepts of physical labor: while lowly and despised, such labor was acknowledged as necessary and even meritorious.

Alongside these relatively serene assertions of the benefits of peasant ef-forts we find laments over the breakdown of mutuality and the difficulty of peasants' lives. The next chapter looks at reactions to this failure of the Three Orders model, but here we should note where the theme of the peasant feed-ing all others is joined to an acknowledgment that peasant labor is exploited rather than compensated.

The German Franciscan preacher known as Brother Ludovicus, a fol-lower of Berthold von Regensburg active in the late thirteenth century, sur-veyed different callings and observed that the labor of rustics nourishes the entire populace, but not by a benign process. Their lords simply take from the peasants what they produce and devour it.[25] More than a hundred years earlier, Stephen of Fougères (bishop of Rennes, 1168–78) had complained that those who produce the best-quality bread for their lords (and for "us" as well) are forced to sustain themselves on a meager and wretched diet.[26] Mon-strelet's *Chronicle* for the year 1422 describes a rhymed petition supposedly delivered by the desperate peasants of France to the king, which begins by re-minding the privileged orders that they live off the toil of the laborers.[27]

Even those who regarded the peasant as unworthy, bestial, or cowardly were willing, at least on occasion, to recognize their dependence on rustic la-bor, although one finds in such acknowledgments no concession to mutuality nor any semblance of concern for the well-being of the peasantry. In the course of a hysterical denunciation of the English Rising of 1381, John Gower likened the rebels to all manner of verminous and destructive animals, but feared that without their productive activity, famine would stalk the land. The suppression of the revolt relieved his fears: "When the peasantry had been bound in chains and lay patiently under our feet, the ox returned to its yoke and the seed flourished beneath the plowed fields, and the villain ceased his warning."[28] The Tyrolean poet Oswald von Wolkenstein (died 1445) frankly conceded that he lived off the peasants' labor and that their taxes supported him. Their role was to produce their own food and that of their masters. Oswald contemned them as deformed, black, and ugly, but they were, he admitted, productive.[29]

Legendary accounts of the origins of Catalonia attributed the existence of serfs to the failure of their ancestors to aid Charlemagne's conquest of Islam in the Spanish March. According to one popular version of the tale, Charlemagne triumphed against the Saracens even without the help of the timid Christian populace, whom his nobles then advised him to kill as punishment for their cowardice and virtual apostasy. Charlemagne, however, spared the captive peasants, because after all, his knights could not cultivate the land.[30] Once again the peasants were rendered as both contemptible and necessary.

A similar portrayal appeared in the aftermath of the Hungarian Peasant Rebellion of 1514. While issuing a general pardon to all but the rebel leaders, King Vladislav acknowledged that as a matter of justice all peasants who revolt should be executed as traitors. Nevertheless, to avoid exterminating the entire peasant population, "without which the nobility would not fare very well," he spared them—a grudging but for that very reason telling admission of the basic facts of the premodern economy.[31]

That the world depended on the peasant was an unimpeachable fact. But the fact could carry moral implications concerning the value of agricultural labor, and opinions differed as to what the peasant deserved in return and whether he was receiving anything.

Mutuality: The Three Orders

Since Georges Duby, Otto Gerhard Oexle, and most recently Giles Constable have written important studies on the origins and permutations of the Three Orders theory, it is hardly necessary to dwell on its content and elaboration.[32] This durable and much-reworked theory presented a hierarchical model of society incorporating a recognition of the importance of agricultural labor into an overall notion of mutual service. According to this model, the

1. A representation of the Three Orders of Society. From *Image du Monde*, British Library MS Sloane 2435, fol. 85r. Reprinted by permission of the British Library, London.

function of the majority of the population—thus the function preeminently of peasants—was to labor in return for the prayers of the clergy and the protection of the knights (Fig. 1). A text attributed to Peter the Chanter, for example, divides society into clergy and laity but further distinguished the *oratores*, who pray for all Christians; the *bellatores*, who fight the opponents of the Church; and the *agricolae*, *pauperes*, and *operarii*, "by whose labor everyone eats and lives."[33]

The words "mutuality" and "reciprocity" in the context of the Three Orders model refer to the idea of a functional interdependence among social orders. Medieval scholars divided society according to a number of different schemes. Their systems were often organized around the various manners of Christian life (virgins, continent persons, and married persons) or ecclesiastical roles (monks, secular clergy, laity).[34] The three-fold division by social function into those who fight, those who pray, and those who labor was, therefore, merely one among many ways of imagining society, but it would outlast its medieval clerical origins.

It has been claimed that the Three Orders model is predicated on certain fundamental Indo-European mental structures, but this perhaps exaggerates and mystifies continuity.[35] Although the idea of hierarchical and functional division was found in antiquity, the specific roles and supposed reciprocity envisioned in the Three Orders model were medieval creations. The ideal of this interrelation among the orders would characterize medieval thought not only in France but throughout Europe, and would endure into the twentieth century.[36]

In connection with the Three Orders, more attention has been given to the emergence of knighthood than to the position of peasants. Duby in his pioneering work was concerned to show the ideology of knighthood and nobility whose legitimation was a key step in the social upheavals of the formative eleventh century. It was at this time that mere ternarity (three separate ways of life) yielded to a more powerful idea of mutuality that transcended earlier notions of common subordination to the ruler. Society was defined by diversified aristocratic and clerical orders rather than by a unifying royal or imperial rulership. Even with the revived power of kings in the twelfth century, royalty made an accommodation with aristocratic power, whose legitimation and sacralization were perpetuated and elaborated.

The Three Orders in Duby's work are presented as an adaptable fantasy of permanence and reciprocity that shored up and prettified a society whose real bases were noble violence and seigneurial exploitation. Recent work has called into question Duby's belief that the theory emerged in the early eleventh century, precisely coinciding with the breakdown of the French monarchy and the rise of the knights. The theory of three interdependent orders existed as early as the School of Auxerre in the ninth century.[37] It was also more important for Anglo-Saxon thinkers such as Aelfric and Wulfstan than Duby and other French observers allowed.[38]

The existence of earlier full-fledged concepts of mutuality tends to divorce the beginning of the Three Orders theory from a putative feudal crisis of the eleventh century. This is important because it allows us to regard the theory's origins as something more than an artificial, self-serving thought system devised to justify the knightly class that emerged as dominant from that

crisis. To the extent that the theory existed before the eleventh-century upheaval, it is less tied to an exclusively aristocratic view of society.

Duby considered the Three Orders an imagined ideological construct
elaborating a compelling but insincere rhetoric of mutuality that cloaked predation with piety.[39] He draws a dichotomy between a "real" social world and
an "imaginary" idealized and ideological one, typifying the Three Orders as a
thought system mobilized to serve those in whose interests the theory was
cynically elaborated. As a legitimation of power, the Three Orders system
could not be used effectively to complain about the dereliction of knights or
the oppression of the lower orders. Anything that looks like such a complaint
was dismissed by Duby as insincere or irrelevant.

Aaron Gurevich and Otto Gerhard Oexle have disputed the supposed
contrast of "real" versus "ideological," warning against imposing modern concepts on medieval thought patterns that did more than rationalize an arbitrary ordering of society exclusively for the benefit of those in power. Gurevich emphasizes that many of the elements of trifunctionality were found in
popular culture, that the Three Orders was not an elite fantasy imposed on
an inarticulate mass.[40] Oexle criticizes the assumption that ideas exist complete outside society or that medieval mental representations constituted ideologies in the sense of invented legitimation.[41] This is not to argue that the
Three Orders schema was a sociologically accurate portrait of medieval society but that it represented a believable ideal outside the clerical world, that it
might be referred to and manipulated by warriors, even peasants.[42] It was
marshaled to deal with real problems, such as the role of the clergy in the
Peace of God movement, or the defense of Anglo-Saxon England against the
Scandinavians, or the need for justifications of the crusades.[43]

The Three Orders theory was thus more than a form of mystification. It
was a vehicle for justifying but also for criticizing exploitation, for one could
protest the failure of social reality to live up to the model. The accusation that
the nobles exploit without protecting carries force only if there is an idea
of reciprocity (rather than mere domination) to appeal to. We should not
imagine late-medieval peasant rebellions as proceeding according to the patterns laid out by clerical writers, but clerical complaints over the dereliction
of lords and the virtue of peasant labor would figure in justifications of peasant protests.

The dereliction of lords—their failure to live up to the credo of mutuality—appears in the writings of those who elaborated the Three Orders and
those who pointed to its shortcomings. Adalbero of Laon was the first since
John Chrysostom to discuss not only the productive labor of those who till
the fields but also their miserable and exploited condition. Who, he asks, can

count their innumerable labors that furnish riches to their masters?[44] Others, such as Benedict of Sainte-Maure, Stephen of Fougères, and Stephen Langton, would also lament the oppression of those whose toil supports society. But Duby regarded these as complacent acknowledgments of worldly injustice that did not detract from confidence in the trifunctional model.[45] Despite his belief in their fundamental insincerity, a view I do not share, Duby assembled a useful dossier of laments over the failure to live up to the ideal of mutuality.[46]

The Three Orders system was perceived nearly from its inception as flawed in practice, but this did not, of course, render it weaker as a theory or ideal. The disparity between ideal and practice, the failure of mutuality, opened up the question of the nature and value of peasant labor. That peasants supported society was, as we have seen, a truism. That they did not receive an adequate recompense was also widely recognized. The need to explain this provoked discussion of the value of work and the origins of human inequality (particularly of servitude). If genuine reciprocity had obtained (or were thought to exist), there would have been no need to explain exploitation.

The Value of Work

The emergence of the Three Orders model coincides with a more positive evaluation of work. Although late antiquity regarded work as demeaning and early Christian writers viewed it as penitential at best, thinkers of the Carolingian era began to emphasize the profit and necessity of labor.[47] Implicit within the idea of mutuality is the notion that labor has a merit at least comparable to that of spiritual and physical protection. Beyond the mere fact of society's dependence on peasant labor, the trifunctional theory gives work a particular (if not quite contractual) value. This is different from saying that the lower orders toil because that is what they are fit for, or because they are thereby justly punished for some transgression, or because they are simply unfortunate, victims of the way of the world.

The development of the notion that work has a certain positive value did not necessarily signal a revolution in attitudes of the sort identified by Max Weber or, more recently and with regard to the Middle Ages itself, by Jacques Le Goff. We are not trying to examine the origins of capitalism, the monetary economy, or the commodification of time. Acknowledging the utility of labor is not the same thing as lauding it. Adalbero of Laon, in his *Carmen ad Rotbertum regem*, expressed an early appreciation for the necessity of rustic labor, but he cannot be said to have viewed labor as especially virtuous or creative, and, as has been seen, he evinced a pitying contempt for the struggles of the benighted *laboratores* to meet the demands of their oppressors. The necessity of labor was universally recognized in the High Middle Ages, but labor never lost its lowly representation as "servile."

Such continuity of negative associations notwithstanding, the trifunctional scheme did amount to a change in the value and visibility accorded to work. Indeed the most important novelty of the Three Orders is the presence and function of the *laboratores*.[48]

The shift toward a more positive opinion of work coincided with increased agricultural production beginning before the tenth century. The growth of the medieval economy raised society above the level of subsistence, eventually providing immense and unsettling wealth. Economic expansion was disturbing because of its subversive effect on what had previously appeared to be a stable hierarchy, but also because of its deleterious moral effect on those who benefited most from it.

At the same time, once labor resulted in something more substantial than mere survival, its accomplishments came to be estimated differently. It is well known that Cistercian criticism of Cluny in the twelfth century contrasted the parasitic splendor of the Benedictine foundations with the austere industry of the White Monks. The Cistercians presented themselves as uniquely faithful to Saint Benedict's insistence on manual labor rather than as the authors of a new movement. In the *Dialogue Between a Cluniac and a Cistercian*, by the monk Idungus, the Cistercian claims that his order devotes itself to rustic labor as ordained and established by God Himself. Work and contemplation were thus joined as a path to ascent, not opposed.[49] Having rejected receiving properties with ties to the donors and having accepted poverty, the White Monks had to work. According to Isaac of Stella, the Cistercians labored in accord with God's command to Adam (Genesis 3:19). Like other men, they fittingly worked and sweated at their labors.[50]

Yet "labor" in Cistercian writings is not simply physical toil. After all, libertines and thieves strain themselves, for example by staying up all night, but are hardly engaged in activity pleasing to God. Bernard exalted work resulting from voluntary poverty as opposed to labor resulting from necessity. Bernard also included under the rubric of labor such monastic practices as fasting, keeping vigils, and prayer.[51] The same contrast between voluntary and involuntary poverty is drawn by Aelred of Rievaulx, who regarded the latter as "the curse of the peasants," imposing upon them the urgent physical necessity to work.[52]

The Cistercians were sufficiently devoted to agricultural labor to establish a form of monastic life for lay brethren who were illiterate and so might accomplish their vows through work in the fields with only occasional atten-

dance at religious ceremonies.[53] The labor of these *conversi*, along with the often inept efforts of the choir monks, allowed the Cistercians to free themselves partially from dependence on tenancy and seigneurial exploitation.[54]
During the early years of the order, stories were recounted in praise of lay
brethren sanctified by their struggles with the land. According to Conrad of
Eberbach, for example (writing ca. 1190), a *conversus* dreamed that Christ
walked beside him as he plowed, goading the ox for him.[55]

More often, however, the *conversi* were praised for their humility and obedience, qualities that figure in most of the eighteen stories included in Conrad's *Exordium magnum* and in other Cistercian miracle collections.[56] Arnulf
of Villers, a lay brother recognized as a saint, is described in his *vita* composed by Goswin of Villers as exemplary by virtue of self-mortification more
than by work. True, he is praised for his obedient labor for the monastery in
Villers, but Goswin notes with approval that Arnulf obtained permission to
abstain from manual tasks in order to devote his time to prayer and contemplation.[57] Those lay brethren granted access to direct spiritual experience
could dispense with the relatively paltry blessings of work.

The *conversi* themselves may have held a more positive concept of sanctification conferred by work, but this is impossible to reconstruct. There is an
interesting miracle story about a *conversus* of Clairvaux (described as a "rustic") whom Saint Bernard visited on his deathbed. The *conversus* displayed an
inappropriate confidence that he would shortly be in paradise. Bernard rebuked him, reminding him that he had entered the community with little in
the world to give up and thus motivated more by necessity than by the fear of
God. The dying *conversus* accepted the rebuke but explained that heaven is
gained by obedience rather than by wealth or a noble body, and that his own
obedience might serve as an example to others. At this Bernard praised him
as blessed, for the truth he spoke was inspired by God Himself.[58] A degree of
assertiveness is also demonstrated by a revolt of *conversi* at Schönau in 1168,
occasioned by an unequal distribution of shoes.[59] There is thus evidence for
independent thought, but nothing directly concerning estimates of the value
of labor.

Ultimately the Cistercians cannot be credited with exemplifying a dramatic change of attitude toward work. Labor remained firmly anchored to
penitential rather than positive good in their writings and was not joined to
the functional idea that agricultural work feeds the other orders. To the extent
that labor provided spiritual benefit, the latter derived from the voluntary
self-deprivation involved, according to Cistercian opinion, not from any
value inhering in the work itself. In any event the Cistercians rather early on
lost their fondness for manual labor. The order therefore does not seem to

have influenced substantially the estimation of value or dignity placed on the daily tasks performed by the peasant masses.

The Franciscans and Dominicans, with their emphasis on begging and (for the Franciscans) exaltation of poverty, raised questions about wealth and property but also implicitly about work. The secular master Guillaume de Saint Amour, for example, initiated a controversy at the University of Paris when he questioned the utility of the mendicant orders who lived off the rest of society. Their defense was that preaching constituted an arduous form of work, a response that did not dispute the positive image of labor. Even when economic motives were denounced (as in ecclesiastical censure of usury), the condemnation took place against a background distinguishing profitable useful ventures from sterile or passive enterprise.[60] By this time, the late thirteenth and fourteenth centuries, the activities of the urban classes were sufficiently visible to undermine earlier assumptions that labor meant exclusively or essentially the tasks of rustics.

Clearly the idea that until the Reformation work was treated with disdain—which owes most of its force to Max Weber's *Protestant Ethic*—is no longer tenable. Few aspects of the understanding of medieval society have been as thoroughly changed by twentieth-century historiography. Yet the medieval image of productive work did not grow uniformly and smoothly out of urban prosperity. Le Goff notes the complexity of the medieval attitudes that moved away from unmitigated deprecation but continued to hold manual labor in low regard.[61] It is worth examining this ambivalence a bit more, because it affected the variety of opinions about the utility and moral position of the peasantry expressed by the other elements of society and by the peasants themselves.

We should first distinguish among different meanings of "labor." During the High Middle Ages labor certainly became a more visible topic. Although agricultural work is seldom mentioned in sources from the fifth to eighth centuries,[62] beginning in the tenth century agricultural production as the source of worldly wealth was recognized and discussed. This is not to say that estate management or economic rationalism of a modern sort resulted, but to say that even in a discourse concerning exploitation, such as Adalbero's *Carmen*, work was credited with a fruitful energy beyond that of a pitiful subsistence. Adalbero's use of the word *servi* notwithstanding, an exploitable peasant was different, and more difficult to assess, than a none-too-productive slave.

Of course it is one thing to acknowledge the benefit accruing from labor and another to endow labor with actual merit. Moreover, such merit as it has might be construed negatively—as a penance—or positively—as a good in itself—or as a combination of the two. For Adalbero, the harsh toil of the *servi* is necessary but neither especially meritorious nor beneficial to the laborers themselves. For Humbert of Romans and Jacques de Vitry two centuries later, peasant labor is pleasing to God and supports the *res publica* as well as the destitute poor dependent on alms, but is nevertheless a penance enjoined on Adam and his progeny.[63] Within the monastic orders as far back as Saint Benedict labor was valued as an expression of discipline and piety, retaining a penitential significance rather than assuming an unequivocal virtue. The peasants themselves argued at various times that work is a moral good and a moral necessity, and that all should labor in obedience to the commands of God to Adam, commands that affected all rather than merely part of humanity.

In addition to this diversity of attitude among different classes, varying intellectual legacies from the past also created certain inconsistencies with regard to the value and dignity of labor. Jacques Le Goff describes three lines of transmission: Judeo-Christian (primarily biblical), classical, and "barbarian."[64] The Bible offered conflicting suggestions in this as in many other matters. God labored over His creation and rested from His toil on the seventh day. Adam and Eve were supposed to work to maintain the Garden of Eden (Genesis 2:15–16); thus, contrary to what is often thought, paradise was not intended to be experienced in complete leisure, nor was work in itself a consequence of the Fall. Before his disobedience, Adam learned from an angel how to labor, as depicted in illustrations to Aelfric's Pentateuch and in thirteenth-century wall paintings formerly at the female monastery of Sigena, in Aragon (Fig. 2). Michael Camille, who assembled these and other examples, also notes that the Book of Jubilees (from the Pseudepigrapha) has the angel instructing Adam how to work the land before the expulsion from paradise.[65]

The sin of Adam was punished by the difficulty of toil, not by the necessity to labor as such. Adam and his descendants would face a difficult struggle with a resisting, unbountiful nature, a situation worsened by Cain's fratricide, after which the earth would no longer "yield unto thee her strength" (Genesis 4:12). Instead of an easy custodianship, the relation of humanity to the land was transformed into harsh (although still productive) labor, just as pain would now accompany childbirth (the dual meaning of "labor" is found in several languages).

Human toil after the Fall involved not only sweat and pain but the brutal domination of nature, as God promised to Noah and his offspring at the opening of Genesis 9.[66] Nature would not "naturally" produce of its free, effortless beneficence but would have to be tamed. The biblical image of domination is twofold, for the statement regarding human power over other

2. Adam being taught by an angel to work. Thirteenth-century painting on the ceiling of the Monastery of Sigena, Aragon. From a photograph taken before the Spanish Civil War, when the monastery was burned. A restoration is now at Museu Nacional d'Art de Catalunya, Barcelona. Reprinted by permission of Arxiu Mas, Barcelona.

earthly things is immediately followed by that regarding mastery of one man over another, the story of the origins of slavery in Noah's curse against his son Ham. Human power over nature originates in divine command, while the subjugation of other human beings results from the first postdiluvian transgression, but they are located at the same point in biblical history.

In the New Testament labor appears virtuous, as in Luke 10:7, where Christ remarks, "the labourer is worthy of his hire." Paul's Second Epistle to the Thessalonians contains the famous distillation of the thinking of *homo economicus*: "if any man will not work, neither let him eat" (3:10). More often cited in the Middle Ages, however, was the disdain for material preoccupations expressed by Christ's praise of the lilies of the field that flourish without effort (Matthew 6:28).

The classical heritage also praised cultivated leisure and deprecated manual labor, associated as it was with slavery. The value of *otium* (leisure) could be grafted onto Christianity, as in the case of Mary's superiority over Martha, the former signifying the Christian contemplative life, the latter the active life.[67] The Roman era also produced texts in praise of rustic simplicity (such as Virgil's *Georgics* and Horace's *Odes*) that were well known in the Middle Ages, but these works observe the obvious distinction between the careful husbandry of the landowner and the forced labor of his slaves.

What Le Goff refers to as the "barbarian legacy," that of the Germanic and Celtic worlds, placed a high value on craftsmen such as swordsmiths, even crediting particularly skilled artisans with magical powers. But the exaltation of war in these cultures, and their identification of wealth with plunder rather than productivity, assured the celebration of the warrior over the mere toiler.

In the Middle Ages, therefore, it was possible to hold conflicting opinions of labor and to praise or belittle it for different reasons. From the aristocratic view, the value of labor was that it produced what was necessary for consumption and display. For the knight to engage in manual or commercial labor was sufficiently demeaning to amount to abandoning any claim to noble status, an attitude that would endure as long as the European aristocracy itself.

While disdain for work may have been encouraged by the barbarian preference for war over agriculture, the aristocracy also inherited an ideal of leisure from the Greco-Roman world (although medieval ideals of freedom from work were of a more bellicose sort than the calm philosophical atmosphere of the Stoics). The elaboration of chivalric ceremony reinforced the already powerful antithesis between labor and war, turning it toward an opposition between boorish productivity and refined courtesy. Even when the military function of the nobility diminished, noble status would endure and continue to depend on immunity from remunerative work.

The sociologist Norbert Elias, relying on the drawings collected in the so-called *Mittelalterliches Hausbuch* (composed 1475–80), posited a certain ease and comfort experienced by the nobility as they observed their dependents' toil. According to Elias the peasants are part of the background scene, scarcely human and certainly not individually important. They exhibit less personality and distinction among themselves than the master's hounds.[68] Elias argues that it was impossible for the privileged classes to imagine that the peasants might have grievances or be fully human; but even if we assume that rustics were most often regarded with contempt, the serene enjoyment of the results of other people's toil did not necessarily imply the invisibility of those people.

It is true that in the romances, beginning with Chrétien de Troyes, a series of splendid castles seem to exist with no labor to support them. Their luxurious if sometimes dangerous accommodations are maintained without much in the way of visible servitors, whose absence makes the setting all the more magical. Such rustics as occasionally appear are deformed, solitary, strange, and not engaged in activity of immediate benefit to the chivalric world.

A somewhat different attitude is reflected by the *Très Riches Heures*, the Book of Hours created for Jean, Duke of Berry, by the Limbourg brothers (left incomplete in 1416 and finished by Jean Colombe in 1489). Here the aristocracy is complacent (as Elias imagined) but not unaware of where its wealth originates. The juxtaposition of castles and scenes of aristocratic leisure with toiling peasants shows that the work of one class makes the ostentation of another possible.[69]

Of all the intellectual legacies of the past, the Christian attitude toward work was the most complex and dealt most directly with the peasantry. It is possible to exaggerate the supposed antipathy of the Church Fathers to secular labor.[70] Nevertheless, the Christian tradition exhibited a consistent mistrust of the world that combined with the classical praise of philosophical leisure. Isidore of Seville transmitted to the High Middle Ages a disparagement of those who labored and the results of their efforts. Isidore's *Etymologies* contains no word for work other than the mindless toil associated with slavery.[71] Saint Benedict asserted the value of labor, but as a form of expiation and service to God.

Agricultural labor was accorded spiritual value because of its penitential quality but also, under certain circumstances, because of its benefit to the order and prosperity of society. The fact that his labor supports all gives the peasant a certain advantage in the next world, according to the theological compendium by Honorius Augustodunensis, the *Elucidarium*, written about 1100. Discussing the various estates, the master in this dialogue states that most rustics will be saved because they live simply and feed the people of God by their sweat. Honorius paraphrases Psalm 127:2: "For thou shalt eat the labours of thy hands: blessed art thou, and it shall be well with thee."[72] Yet in Honorius's work some penitential attributes of work remain, notably in his acceptance of the common opinion that *servi* are descended from Noah's cursed son Ham.[73] Labor does confer spiritual benefit but is presented as the activity of a morally tainted population. Its undoubted merits are set alongside an accumulated spiritual deficit.

As will be seen in later chapters, the suffering of peasants was regarded as meritorious more commonly than their productivity. To the extent that God might be said to favor the peasants, it was because of their poverty and unjust treatment rather than the utility of their efforts. Nevertheless, at least an occasional attempt was made to praise peasants and to exalt their spiritual condition because of the results of their work. Sermons written by (or under the influence of) the German Franciscans Berthold von Regensburg and Brother Ludovicus praise the peasants on whom all society depends and whose labor earns them merit in God's eyes. If all peasants became knights, who would then produce wheat and wine for "us" (a statement echoed by the fifteenth-century poem cited at the beginning of this chapter)?[74] According to Brother Ludovicus, rustic labor, on which all depend, pleases God. Ill-usage at the hands of their lords makes the peasants all the more God's chosen children, a favorable condition not fully realized since they persist in laziness and iniquity. Were it not for their thievery, dishonesty, and perjury, peasants would be saints.[75] The *Buch der Rügen*, mentioned earlier in connection with the idea that the "pure" labor of rustics supports Christendom, states that their work will bring them to God's kingdom.[76]

A German poetical narration and gloss of the Book of Daniel written by a member of the Teutonic Order in the mid–fourteenth century lists various plants that might have grown on the Plain of Dura where Nebuchadnezzar set up the golden idol (Daniel 3:1), and likens the peasants to grass. As in the *Buch der Rügen*, here peasants are the foundation of all society; kings, popes, knights, and townsmen depend on their labor. The peasant's toil affords him spiritual benefit and an eternal crown if he remains a faithful laborer.[77]

Thus a nexus of ideas depicts labor as worthy but penitential, an expiation of Adam's sin. It confers spiritual rewards, but they depend on patience and meek devotion. Peasants are unfortunate because they must work, yet blessed because of its supernatural effects; but then again they are in peril of losing this benefit because of their materialism and spiritual torpor.

Jacques de Vitry, in one of his *Sermones vulgares*, touches on each of these points succinctly. The statements do not contradict one another but rather unfold in succession. Their interrelationship outlines the fundamental dimensions of the peasant's image in the Middle Ages. Taking as his text Zachariah 13:5, "I am a husbandman" (*homo agricola ego sum*), Jacques remarks:

> Literally, the Holy Scriptures truly praise agriculture and manual labor, without which society would not be able to survive. After the sin of Adam, God enjoined penance on him and his sons. . . . Therefore, those who labor with this intention that they fulfill their penance ordered by God will be praised more and not less than those in the entire church who sing God's praises or keep vigil from night to morning. For we see many poor tillers of the soil who by the labor of their hands sustain a wife and children: and they work more than monks in their cloister or clerics in their churches. If the intention of peasants is to fulfill the penance enjoined on them by God's injunction, then they act in love; they will acquire their temporal sustenance and attain eternal life. If, however, they are like the brute animals and their intention is not penance but merely to eat and drink, then they will lose grace in this life and their labor will be for nought.[78]

The Symbolic Plow

Ecclesiastical writers, as I have attempted to demonstrate, offered a qualified approbation of peasant labor. Peasants engaged in productive toil that fed all of society. They fulfilled God's commands to work and suffered not only physical exhaustion but unjust exploitation. Yet such effort was penitential, the paying off of a spiritual debt, rather than an unalloyed good, and the peasants themselves, by their grasping and debased character, risked forfeiting the spiritual benefits of their situation.

The activities of clerics were endowed with more uniformly positive connotations, but during the High Middle Ages, their prayers, service, and preaching were presented as a form of spiritual labor that borrowed metaphors from the agricultural world. The plow in particular served as the emblem of religious effort, as a symbol of preaching for example, as early as the works of Saint Eucherius, bishop of Lyons, in the mid–fifth century.[79]

The plow as a sign of fruitful and virtuous labor is found in the Book of Proverbs, where its literal meaning is clearly secular. Those who work (plow) will have food, while the idle will languish.[80] In the New Testament, agricultural labor (and plowing in particular) was used to represent the diffusion of the word of God. Christ is the sower of "the good seed," with the entire world as his field (Matthew 13:37–38). Saint Paul, writing about his apostleship, likens his task to that of an agricultural laborer, even an ox. Paul depends on the flock that he nourishes, partaking of their faith, for "he that plougheth should plough in hope" (1 Corinthians 9:10). Preaching was likened to the work of plowing and threshing.

Gregory the Great used the ox and plow to mark the arduous but productive duties of the preacher. The image of the "plowshare of the tongue" would influence the way in which preaching was viewed throughout the Middle Ages, connoting the vigorous activity that cuts the hardness of minds that fail to respond to intellectual methods (reading) and require the furrows of voluntary affliction to receive the seeds of exhortation.[81]

Stephen Barney identifies Gregory as the most important source for the image of the righteous plowman in William Langland's masterpiece. Piers is a literal plowman engaged in meritorious labor, but also a figure for the spreading of God's word. The early-medieval coupling of preaching and plowing eventually affected the image of the plowman, who formerly had been regarded as below fisherman or shepherds (apostolic figures) within the class of laborers.[82] Elizabeth Kirk regarded Langland as more of an innovator, arguing that his virtuous plowman contrasted with a longer tradition of negative images.[83] Plowmen had their origins with Cain, the first to till the land, whereas the spiritual ancestor of the shepherds was Abel. It had been shepherds, not plowmen, who received word of the birth of Christ.[84]

Although Langland was not the first to regard the activity of plowing with favor or to use it as a metaphor for spiritual labor, his era saw the proliferation of more literal images of virtuous plowing. The plow represented piety and worthwhile labor in the late Middle Ages, but these remained conceptually distinct despite their many points of contact. One might praise the diligence of the laborer without thereby crediting him with spiritual dignity. It was quite possible to maintain an image of the plowman as a worthy and patient worker while considering physical toil itself the punishment for Adam's sin. The artistic representation of labor depicted the virtue of work as opposed to the sin of laziness without thereby necessarily ascribing to the laborer a dignified spiritual or social status.[85] Diligent agricultural toil could symbolize the wickedness of Cain. In artistic representations the efforts of this supposed progenitor of peasants were a negative and literally fruitless activity. He is depicted in the Holkham Bible (1315–21) behind a mixed team of animals (an anticipatory violation of Deuteronomic laws), furiously but futilely plowing.[86]

What at one time were regarded as quaint or nostalgic evocations of rural simplicity in art and literature are now viewed in conjunction with the degraded status applied to those who work, a status perfectly in keeping with their productivity.[87] The modern tendency to equate productivity with moral character makes it difficult to see how medieval observers might acknowledge the utility, necessity, and even *virtue* of agricultural labor while expressing a frank contempt for those engaged in it. The peasants laboring for the Duke of Berry in the *Très Riches Heures* are productive but coarse and risible. Engaged in tedious labor, they are poorly dressed, graceless, and shameless, showing their sexual parts.[88] Nevertheless, they are hardly marginal, for they support the extravagant wealth of the duke. This picture contrasts with the early-modern depiction of grand estates as innately bountiful, as in the world of Jonson's Penhurst or Carew's Saxham, "rear'd with no man's ruine, no mans grone," from which dull labor is missing (along with its practitioners).[89]

Plowing, therefore, could be ascribed with a positive, productive value without necessarily being said to confer spiritual benefit. It could symbolize religious activity without endowing the laborers themselves with virtue; its spiritual benefits could even be essentially negative. Adam was sometimes shown behind a plow, or engaged in an even more difficult agricultural labor, digging with a spade.[90] Plowing might be presented as appropriate to the human condition while still partaking of a penitential aspect from which the higher orders were exempt.

The late Middle Ages exhibited a wide register of possible valuations of plowing, from the unproductive and wicked efforts of Cain to the useful subordination of peasants in the *Très Riches Heures* of the Duke of Berry, to Langland's virtuous protagonist. At least in some cases, not only the metaphorical activity but the actual plowman as well was endowed with sanctity. Chaucer's plowman (the upright brother of the parson in the *Canterbury Tales*), or the earnest peasant who argues with death in Johannes von Tepl's *Ackermann aus Böhmen* are examples. By this time, the late fourteenth century, it was possible to imagine the plowman as holy in himself. I will defer discussion of the symbolism of the pious plowman and the representation of Christ as a plowman until representations of peasant sanctity are considered (Chapter 10). Here I would like to focus on a less transcendent use of plowing as a metaphor for virtuous productivity.

As argued earlier, productivity was not necessarily regarded as implying the rectitude of those engaged in labor. Nevertheless, if medieval understanding of the dependence of society on the toil of the lowly was ambivalent, it did at least include the possibility of endowing symbols such as plowing with favorable moral connotations. The virtuous plowman would symbolize peace, diligence, and obedience well beyond the Middle Ages. Bruegel's *Fall of Icarus* is perhaps the most famous of many images that exalt the orderliness of the industrious peasant. A plowman is tilling the fields in the foreground while the reckless Icarus, who sought to change how things in the world are arranged, plunges unnoticed to his doom.[91]

In what we can reconstruct of the discourse of peasants themselves, labor was unequivocally the measure of piety and social worth. Richard Landes, examining the heresies that arose in eleventh-century France, pointed to the positive religious valuation placed on work as one of the unifying features of these otherwise diverse movements.[92] The heretical movements of the eleventh century at Arras, Monteforte, and elsewhere taught that everyone should gain his bread by the sweat of his own brow.[93] Whether or not one accepts Landes's crediting of Jewish thought with influencing a Christian sacralization of work, a case can be made for linking teachings of heretical movements against hierarchy and the sacraments to a disdain for the clergy, who claimed exemption from work on the basis of proximity to God and the saints.

One cannot prove a continuity of such beliefs among the common people from the eleventh century to the fifteenth, when they became more evident, but there are some hints at the endurance of such ideas. Emmanuel Le Roy Ladurie offers a fascinating collection of what amount to proverbial statements among the followers of the Cathars at Montaillou in the early fourteenth century. Pierre Authié told Sybille Pierre that he worked not to avoid poverty but to save his soul. Jean Maury boasted of eating only what he had earned with his labor because Christ himself said that man must live by the sweat of his brow. Two *parfaits* were overheard agreeing that priests ought to live by their own labor in accord with God's commandment rather than living off the toil of others.[94]

In the fifteenth and early sixteenth centuries the notion that all should work surfaced and proliferated. During the later years of the extended revolt in Forez (which ended in 1431), the peasants apparently reworked the theme of the Fall as the origin of manual labor by arguing that all were included in this expiation of Adam's sin (a version of the argument that all humans are descended from Adam and hence are equal). Since the consequences of Adam's misdeed were transmitted to all equally, nobles should work just as peasants do in order to feed themselves.[95] Similar ideas were expressed among certain Bohemian reformers of the fifteenth century. Peter Chelčický, a follower of the Hussite movement but a pacifist and so isolated from its most radical currents, wrote treatises in the 1420s against the idea that the Three Orders had been instituted by divine decree. God could not have intended for the two higher orders to live in idle luxury off the labors of the lowly. The theory never functioned for the benefit of all, Chelčický claimed, and amounted to nothing more than an excuse for violent exploitation.[96] Chelčický here dissents from John Wyclif, whom he and others in Bohemia followed in so many other respects, by rejecting any division of society into orders.[97] He argues that Christ's body is not (as commonly proposed) a metaphor for higher and lower functions of a hierarchical society; rather, those who work (and they alone) form the true body of Christ. The apostles worked with their hands, and accordingly Chelčický cited 2 Thessalonians 3:10–11, to argue that no one should be idle in the manner of courtiers; all should labor.

Such radical ideas were also expressed in 1476 on the occasion of the abortive pilgrimage led by Hans Behem, a Franconian shepherd (and probably a serf) who was later derisively known as the "Piper of Niklashausen."[98] Behem was one of many uneducated German rustics of the pre-Reformation era credited with gifts of prophecy and inspirational preaching. He claimed to have spoken with the Virgin Mary, who told him that she would perform miracles and reveal herself to those who followed him to Niklashausen. The three basic teachings of the movement, according to a contemporary observer (Lorenz Fries of Würzburg) were the end of all lordship, universal brotherhood, and a requirement that all should earn their sustenance with their own hands.[99] Repeated recommendations that all clerics be killed accompanied the fervid devotion to Mary.[100] In a sermon delivered on July 2, 1476, Hans Behem advised that priests be killed, but also noted that if spiritual and worldly princes shared what they had, there would be enough for all. More than this redistribution of property, Behem preached that work is a universal obligation, to be undertaken even by princes and lords.[101]

On the eve of the German Peasants' War, the image of the peasant as the exemplar of piety was still a powerful element of the movement for Church reform. Andreas Bodenstein von Karlstadt (who at this time actually wore peasant garb) wrote in a letter to Luther that he wished he were a real plowman, peasant, or craftsman. To farm was an honest mortification of the flesh, a labor pleasing to God.[102] In a pamphlet written in 1525, near or at the time of the revolt, a peasant in a dialogue with a friar condemns the parasitism of the clergy, who live off the labor of others. The peasant quotes the common saying "man was born to work like the bird to fly"; all should earn their bread by the sweat of their brows, like Adam, and, moreover, like Christ.[103] Another *Flugschrift* recalled the happy former times when nobles went out to the fields with their serfs.[104]

That all should work was a theme of the early reform pamphlets. All, including clerics and nobles, were included in the requirement that bread be earned with the sweat of one's brow; thus what some inaccurately interpreted as a curse falling on one part of the population was rather a divine command applicable to all. The peasant was regarded as the exemplar of obedience to God, for, as many popular tracts argued, he feeds all, unlike Jews and shopkeepers, who live off the impoverishment of others. Craftsmen, pastors, and the rest must at least aid the plowman, whose labor is the most important.[105]

At the same time, the late Middle Ages witnessed the most virulent attacks on peasants, in which they were no longer regarded as even useful, let alone necessary, but instead viewed as unredeemably wicked. A common negative image of peasants portrayed them as having to be beaten or otherwise coerced into working. At a further extreme, rustics came to be regarded as almost without purpose. The canon of Zurich, Felix Hemmerli, writing in the mid-fifteenth century, recommended that peasant farms be destroyed every 50 years to tame rustic arrogance.[106] Hemmerli, in his own voice, interrupts his imagined dialogue between a knight and a rustic to recall an occasion when he passed through the Duchy of Baden during the "Hussite" uprisings. At an inn he was forced to listen to an insolent group of rustics denouncing clerical immorality. He answered by saying that outside of Oppenheim he had seen 24 wheels upon which criminals had been executed. Not one of the dead was a cleric or noble: they had all been rustics. Had even just one of higher rank been among them, however, there would be no end of denunciation of the upper classes for their infamy. After this observation, Hemmerli recalls, he told his clerical companion that it would be best to leave the inn immediately.[107]

A fifteenth-century poem, the "Edelmannslehre," recommends that nobles pillage peasants, rob them of their money, and strangle them.[108] Clearly they are not useful for anything other than to be plundered. In the literary tradition of the satiric poet Neidhart, who placed his hapless eponymous knight in a peasant village, the peasants were impudent, pretentious, and violent and never engaged in any sort of productive activity. This would be elaborated in the late Middle Ages, when Neidhart became a more aggressive trickster, the "Enemy of the Peasants" (*Bauernfeind*) who enjoyed victimizing the boorish villagers.[109]

In fifteenth-century German-speaking regions, therefore, the peasant was imagined simultaneously as useless and as the provider of wealth; as bestial and as human exemplar; as an object of derisive or fearful contempt and as sanctified. For most of the Middle Ages, however, the opinions of articulate members of the higher orders occupied a narrower range. They agreed, in large measure, that rustic labor fed and supported the leisure of the rest of society. Peasants' subordination might be explained by positing an intrinsic character that rendered them apt for work. More often, some moral credit attached to this labor, although this was not to be paid off in any worldly context.

The utility and spiritual worth of agricultural labor made it difficult consistently to represent the peasants as subhuman or their exploitation as natural. Religious and didactic writers differed as to what recompense, if any, the peasantry received for their toil. The most widely diffused explanation was the idea of reciprocal obligations embodied in the theory of the Three Orders, but it was obvious almost from the inception of this model that practice did not conform to prescriptive mutuality. Such a contradiction might simply be lamented or entered in the ledger of sinful humanity's common shortcomings. Nevertheless, as will be discussed in the next chapter, the failure of mutuality was disturbing to many and carried with it implications that might call for explanations less complacent than the Three Orders, or even serve as the basis for justifying revolt.

Chapter 2

The Breakdown of Mutuality

Laments over the Mistreatment of Peasants

The previous chapter described certain inherent difficulties with the theory of the Three Orders, in particular the small recompense received by the peasants in return for their labors. It was also argued that the theory, whatever its visible limitations, was more than a fantasy. It enunciated an ideal that could be defended and whose failure was cause for reproach. Here we are concerned with the nature of this reproach and the reaction of medieval observers to the perceived waning of mutuality, especially their laments over the mistreatment of peasants. I hope to show that these complaints, although delivered from a certain fatalistic distance, were not only sincere but significant in influencing how peasant grievances were articulated.

Almost from its medieval origins, the image of the Three Orders was considered more an ideal than a reality, but this hardly means that it was an ineffective or hypocritical theory of society. In neither the Middle Ages nor the contemporary world have political and social ideologies been discarded simply because they were impossible to put into practice. The inevitability of falling short of the ideal did not excuse those who subverted it. Lords were warned that if they treated their tenants with excessive cruelty, they would lose the labor that supported them. This is the point of much of the didactic literature cited in the previous chapter as well as such literary works as the "Combat des Trente" (which argues that if the poor are mistreated, the nobles themselves will have to work the fields and suffer poverty) and the "Dit des Avocats" (which condemns the rich who mock the workers on whom their way of life depends).[1]

The Three Orders constituted both a description of society and an idealized vision. On the first level, the scheme demarcated and justified social reality, and on the second, it established a standard by which to measure one's own time. Many critiques of society's insufficient adherence to the model of mutuality suggested that during some earlier era humanity had been harmoniously united in mutual service. As early as the *Life of Saint Dagobert* (dating probably to the ninth century), an idealization of the Three Orders was credited to the past, when everyone performed his duty and remained in his order. Under King Dagobert the priests supplicated God, the warriors served the king, and the rustics obediently cultivated the land.[2] Unfavorable estimations of the present contrasted with a better past—what the Hungarian historian Jenő Szűcs characterized as the "*sed-modo* reaction"—underlay attacks on those who exploited the service of other ranks of society without recompensing them. Such attacks were of course directed primarily against the knights.[3] At one time, it was claimed, the military class protected the populace, *but now* they exploit them. Felix Hemmerli's virulent antipeasant *De nobilitate et rusticitate dialogus* (Dialogue on nobility and rusticity), written in 1443, has the rustic argue that the nobles have abandoned their role as warriors in order to live for pleasure. Even Hemmerli is induced to denounce "modern" nobles for their exactions and banditry, a charge that the knight in the dialogue reluctantly accepts.[4] Such a contrast could also be drawn for other orders, as part of a perceived general decline. Late-medieval observers such as John Gower contrasted the impudent and disobedient peasants of their day with an unspecified past when service was performed without complaint, the tithe was paid, and order reigned.[5]

But complaints about deviation from mutual service among the Three Orders were more than a nostalgic evocation of a happier past. It was recognized that the scheme had a built-in flaw: the likelihood of inordinate exploitation of the laborers by the knights (and often by the clergy as well). Adalbero of Laon, while outlining the Three Orders, acknowledged quite frankly the drudgery and torment borne by the *servi* of the countryside. As noted in Chapter 1, Adalbero saw that the laborers were absolutely necessary to the survival of the other orders but that they clearly received little or nothing for their toil.[6]

For Georges Duby, Adalbero's *planctus* expresses only the most superficial sympathy. Its intent was to obtain submission of the oppressed to their lot, and the lament thus forms part of Adalbero's overall "reactionary" ideology designed to serve the dominant classes.[7] Adalbero assuredly did regard the status of the *servi* with more equanimity than remorse, but Duby's reading seems contradictory, arguing on the one hand that Adalbero emphasized their humiliation and on the other that he attempted to convince them that mutuality did indeed reign.[8]

Some resolution was possible by emphasizing the penitential value of suffering, and we shall see that later authors would urge peasants to bear their admittedly unjust lot in the expectation of a future heavenly reward. But this is not, in fact, what Adalbero argues. He unabashedly states that no fair exchange of benefits obtains for the laborers in the world as it is constituted. His tears may indeed be sanctimonious, and clearly Adalbero is preoccupied more with the disruption of the orders (including the terrifying vision of a "deformed" and "vile" peasant wearing a crown while clerics follow the plow) than with the injustice of exploitation.[9] Nevertheless, the passage describing the lot of the *servi* reads neither as a counsel to patience nor as a vindication of mutuality. As Otto Gerhard Oexle has quite effectively argued, embedded in Adalbero's *Carmen ad Rotbertum regem* (especially in the above-cited passage) is an assertion of the value of labor, whose lack of reward is therefore not simply part of the order of fallen humanity but rather more immediately unjust.[10] If labor were simply an expiation of Adam's sin, or if servitude were the merited punishment for those who lack discipline (the Isidorian formulation), then the oppression of the toiling *servi* would be acceptable and unremarkable. The whole point in positing mutuality, however much it had the effect (and purpose) of exalting the prerogatives of the dominant classes, was that labor amounted to a real service, not a purely expiatory act. The absence of recompense was therefore at least mildly disturbing.

Adalbero was by no means the last clerical observer to recognize seigneurial exploitation, and the same mixture of lamentation and defense of the established social hierarchy can be observed in successive generations of clerical comments. Duby is reluctant to credit clerical complaints as sincere (or really significant), and regards it as anachronistic to see in them any sort of attack on the seigneurial regime.[11]

Despite his belief in their insincerity, Duby assembled a useful group of complaints over the lot of laborers, complaints that can be approached somewhat differently. The question to ask is not so much whether one finds them "sincere" or "insincere" as how one understands medieval social and political thought. Those who criticized kings and lords in the twelfth and thirteenth centuries were attempting to describe and judge the exercise of power, which they considered neither totally legitimate nor absolutely inexcusable. That they proposed no consistent program of political action does not make their ruminations irrelevant, and in fact such inconsistency shows that their writings did not amount to a complacent defense of how the world was ruled. Not only did writers differ in their opinions from other writers, but a single author might express a series of attitudes within his own opus.

As has been often observed, this variability follows from the dialectical style of medieval reasoning, which attempted to bring order from disorder, harmony from dissonance. That a consistent opinion might not emerge from a series of ideas does not mean the author was hypocritical. It was possible, for example, to denounce the order of society while calling for passivity on the part of those afflicted. As Philippe Buc has elegantly pointed out, the medieval biblical commentators in particular searched for an *equilibrium* more than a *synthesis* between conflicting images or opinions. This was not an equilibrium of compromise but a range of responses to social and political conditions of temporal reality. As the divine and human nature of Christ formed a model of government, so coercion and mercy were both inevitably present in its exercise.[12] The equality of all humanity was not contradicted by a need for hierarchy or the presence of sin that made hierarchy necessary. Equality formed one pole of a discourse accommodating notions of resistance to authority and its simultaneous legitimation.

If we examine some of the authors whose lamentations are cited by Duby, we find certain common images and ways of explanation. Benedict of Sainte-Maure translated (with some notable additions) Dudo of Saint-Quentin's *On the Character and Acts of the First Dukes of Normandy*. In recounting a visit of Duke William to the monastery of Jumièges and his conversation with its abbot, Martin, Benedict digresses from Dudo to acknowledge, in a speech put in William's mouth, the oppression of the rustics who sustain the other orders but suffer severely themselves:

> They endure the great scourges
> Snow, rain, and wind
> Working the earth with their hands.
> Terribly uncomfortable and hungry,
> Their lives are most bitter,
> Poor, destitute, and beggarly.[13]

Benedict alters Dudo of Saint-Quentin in reporting a question asked by Duke William of the abbot: who will be most likely to enter heaven—knights, clerks, or peasants? (Dudo had listed monks, canons, laymen.) The abbot responds that those who have served God will receive their reward, but he does not contradict William's fears that the knights, having committed so many offenses against Him, will be punished.[14]

Later in his chronicle, Benedict, here relying on Wace as his source, denounces the Norman peasant rebels of 997, who, inspired by the devil, undertook the great "folly" of trying to be equal to their masters and to throw off their subordination.[15] Benedict and Wace devote considerable attention to enumerating peasants' grievances over oppressive levies and prohibitions on the use of forests and other common lands. Benedict cites their conviction that it is better to die or flee than live in misery. He also recalls Wace's statement of their belief in their equality with their masters.[16]

Benedict and Wace can hardly be called social reformers, nor (writing more than 150 years after the event) are they accurate sources for whatever the Norman rebels actually claimed. Their reported laments, however stylized, display what peasant grievances were thought to express in the twelfth century. The chronicles implicitly acknowledge that the laborers do not enjoy material benefits from the functioning of the orders in practice.

In the *Livre des manières*, written in the late twelfth century, Stephen of Fougères bewailed the oppression of the peasantry but more explicitly than Adalbero or Benedict attributed it to the immoderate demands of their lords. It is not by reason of the order of creation but rather through a deliberate series of acts that the peasants suffer. While clergy and knights live off of what peasants produce, the toilers receive no reward. Here the poor diet of the peasants (a common theme in antipeasant satire) is an involuntary deprivation, not an attribute of low-born nature:

> They don't eat the fine bread;
> We have the best grain,
> The most pleasant and sound;
> The dross is left for the *vilain.*
>   . . .
> If his lord knows he has wine from his vines,
> He tricks and traps the *vilain*
> By flattery or menace;
> At any rate, he carries it off unjustly.[17]

Duby says that Stephen merely "pretends" to sympathize with these exploited creatures.[18] Stephen is hypocritical, according to Duby, for promising the peasant a conveniently otherworldly reward on condition of meek fortitude and then denouncing the peasants' unwillingness to accept this advice. If the rustic bore his lot patiently, he would merit salvation before his wicked social superiors in this life ("the more his life is impoverished, so much the greater is his merit"). But, Stephen complains, this is precisely what the *vilain* refuses to do. Mired in impiety, he resists paying tithes, renders no thanks to God, and is no more grateful than a dog.[19] Stephen's real intention, according to Duby, is to "consolidate the class barrier."[20] Certainly to modern eyes the invocation of the life to come and prescription of obedience seem transparently self-serving. Nevertheless, Stephen's description of the condition of the rustics is neither insincere nor complacent, but rather reflects a recurrent problem of justification. The claim that physical labor provides spiritual benefit could be used as something more activist than a recommendation for quiescence.

The last of the lamenting clerics dealt with by Duby is Stephen Langton, the indefatigable commentator on the Bible whose denunciations of the oppression of the *abjecti* are worth considering in some detail. Given his eloquent and repeated statements, Langton is more difficult for Duby to dismiss as sanctimonious or hypocritical. Langton is rather more brutally honest than his contemporaries, Duby acknowledges, but his reaction to the plight of the rustics is one of horror rather than sympathy, the product of pessimism more than outrage.[21]

Stephen Langton

Langton, a Parisian master, archbishop of Canterbury, and the author of an extraordinary mass of biblical commentaries, was reputed to have glossed the entire Bible perhaps two or even three times in separate treatises. Friedrich Stegmüller's *Repertorium* contains over 200 entries for Stephen, encompassing overlapping disquisitions.[22] Very little of this oeuvre has been edited, and the study of the manuscripts (numbering over 120) and their interrelation is exacting. There are, for example, several versions of Langton's commentary on Isaiah alone. In some of them, those that deal exclusively with the moral form of interpretation, he eloquently and repeatedly condemns the conduct of those, especially the clergy, who oppress the poor (*pauperes*). Others, such as those encompassing the complete fourfold scheme, do not directly invoke contemporary society.

In an article published in 1930, Beryl Smalley and Gilbert Lacombe explained the variety and overlapping of the extant commentaries by arguing that most employed a single interpretive method (such as the moral) that formed segments of a larger complete gloss encompassing the range of interpretive possibilities.[23] What are most often preserved are literal or moral interpretations of Scripture, portions of a master commentary encompassing the fourfold ways of approaching the Sacred Page (literal, moral, allegorical, and anagogical).

Smalley and Lacombe disclaimed any sweeping assertion of priority, leaving it open whether the complete gloss was an amalgam of earlier separate treatises or the reverse: that the much more common single interpretations were sectioned off from an original compendium. More important is the relationship among the separate aspects of the composition of Langton's work that might explain the state of the manuscripts we now possess. Smalley and Lacombe drew three conclusions. First, Langton probably wrote at least two separate, complete biblical commentaries. Second, what survive include complete as well as literal or moral commentaries. Third, the manuscripts reflect their origin as lectures given at Paris between 1180, when Langton began his teaching career, and 1206, when he was named archbishop of Canterbury.

This brings some order to the apparent chaos of the manuscripts, but M.-B. de Vaux de Saint-Cyr showed that at least for Isaiah (which particularly concerns us since it occasioned commentary on the iniquity of the powerful), the hypothesis of related complete and partial glosses is not particularly helpful.[24] There are 28 manuscripts of Langton's commentaries on Isaiah, of which some offer only the moral analysis. None contain solely a literal interpretation, nor has any "complete" gloss survived (assuming it ever existed). Moreover, there is an entirely different group of Paris manuscripts that seem to be glosses of glosses on Isaiah, of which in turn there are long and short versions. Paris, Bibliothèque Mazarine, manuscript 177, for example, contains a short version of the "gloss to the gloss" (fols. 113–26) and a moral commentary (fols. 128–56). Paris, Bibliothèque National, 8874 and 14417 are long versions of the second-order gloss.

The gloss to the gloss has nothing concerning the oppression of the poor. The theme is characteristic only of the moral commentaries on Isaiah, but these too are by no means simple, for they fall into what are certainly different recensions, probably different versions altogether.[25] Langton's commentaries on the minor prophets, especially Hosea, Amos, and Malachi, also are laced with condemnations of the oppression of the poor and the arrogance of the nobility and clergy.[26]

Despite the extremely complicated textual state of Langton's commentaries, certain themes can be discerned that bear on the present study. In his moralized Isaiah commentaries and in comments on other prophets, Langton was concerned in the first instance to direct the attention of the clergy to their pastoral obligations and to warn against greed and covetousness. Pastors who out of selfishness fail to guard their sheep anger God, he asserts in discussing Hosea.[27] Such ministers, who glory in the things of this world, are not shepherds but beasts who devour their sheep (commenting on Isaiah 13:20).[28]

The Troyes and Vienna moralized commentaries on Isaiah are somewhat more elaborate in their criticism of prelates. Although Langton customarily refers to the common people in general terms as *pauperes* (thus following the Vulgate text of Isaiah), he clearly means not the marginal but those whose exploited labors support the great princes and prelates. Langton tells us that it is not the ignorant or stupid poor whose ingratitude toward God Isaiah denounces with the words "The ox knoweth his owner and the ass his master's crib, but Israel hath not known me . . . " (Isaiah 1:3). It is rather the powerful (*optimates*) who are being castigated. God will judge the depredations of those who have appropriated the goods of the poor (Isaiah 3:14).[29] Citing Ezekiel 22:27, Langton argues that God accuses the princes, who are like wolves, shedding the blood of the poor and destroying their souls. Princes and prelates are the intended targets of Isaiah 3:15: "Why do you consume my people and grind the faces of the poor." This reminds Langton of Jeremiah 2:34: "in thy skirts is found the blood of the souls of the poor and innocent." Clerics and nobles should defend and support their subjects but prefer to bleed the population, not even bothering to hide their misdeeds, beating and grinding up the poor.[30] The metaphor is elaborated by a distinction between the prelates who give the orders and their savage underlings who fulfill them, the former resembling the teeth of lions, while the petty officials are the molars of lion cubs (taken from Joel 1:6).[31]

Similar language appears in the English manuscripts of the moral interpretation of Isaiah. In a different comment on the same passage in Isaiah (3:15), Langton castigates the prelates (the lions). What they do not manage to seize, their officials (the lion cubs) extort.[32] In Lambeth Palace manuscript 71, the passages of Isaiah 3 (especially verse 12) evoke denunciations of those "prelati moderni" who violently despoil the goods of their subjects. The image of tearing and eating again appears, but now from the prophet Micah, as Langton bitterly condemns those who mislead the populace, biting them with their teeth while preaching peace.[33]

The Peterhouse and Corpus Christi manuscripts speak even more graphically of those who drink blood, grind the faces of the poor (*pauperes*), and adorn their horses via the sweat of the poor.[34] The image of drinking blood also appears in the Lambeth Palace commentary on Amos 1:3, where Damascus refers to blood while Gilead signifies the poor. Damascus signifies the rich and powerful who drink the blood of the poor, despoiling them and oppressing them.[35] The previously discussed commonplace that the laborers feed all the other orders is here graphically illustrated. Not only do the poor feed the rich indirectly by their labor, they are consumed by their oppressors; it is their blood that nourishes the strong.[36]

The dietary laws of Leviticus served Langton as another occasion for likening the conduct of the oppressors of the poor to the thirst for blood. The tyrants who drink the blood of the poor symbolically violate Leviticus 7:26, "Moreover, you shall not eat the blood of any creature whatsoever." One meaning of blood here, according to Langton, is the labor and sweat of the poor, which the powerful of this world drink. This is followed by a reference to the grisly passage of Micah 3:3, "Who have eaten the flesh of my people, and have flayed their skin from off them: and have broken and chopped their bones as for the kettle and as flesh in the midst of the pot."[37] Discussing Leviticus 3:17 ("neither blood nor fat shall you eat at all"), Langton states that the reference to eating blood means homicide or the desire to pillage (an interpretation he supports with a citation from Lucan). Even those who do not actively rejoice in plunder and destruction are in some measure guilty of the same blood-lust, specifically the powerful who afflict the poor (again citing Jeremiah 2:34) and are stained with their blood.[38]

Langton is perhaps unusually insistent and dramatic in his lamentations, but he is by no means unique. Philippe Buc has recently shown the significance of eating as a metaphor for both good and bad forms of governance. The king nourishes the populace or consumes it.[39] Beneficent rule is that exercised by the Church, according to a tradition based on Genesis 9:2–3. When God gave dominion over the earth to Noah and his heirs, he permitted them to exploit its animal and vegetable life. In Gregory's *Moralia on Job*, this form of subjugation is contrasted to domination of other human beings in violation of our original equality, a theme we shall return to in the following chapter.[40] Good government, according to medieval glosses on Genesis 9, is limited to control over the animal nature of human beings.[41] Clerics receive their subsistence from the laity, but this form of eating is also an allegory of the Church's transformation of worldly goods and even sin into a spiritual form of nutrition. The work of preachers, according to a Dominican tradition based on earlier commentaries, is a form of "spiritual manducation" or a "sacrament of manducation."[42]

A more physical and obviously brutal manducation is that of secular domination, in particular the exploitation of the poor by the powerful. Walter Map likened the forest keepers of King Henry II (who was responsible for enforcing the punitive regulations concerning hunting and poaching) to those who "eat the flesh of men in the presence of Leviathan, and drink their blood."[43] Langton bases his denunciations on Peter the Chanter, for whom the eating of blood in Leviticus 7:26 meant in the first place those *raptores* who plunder the helpless. "Blood" is the labor and sweat of the *pauperes* that is drunk by the rich and the tyrants of this world.[44] In his *De miseria condicionis humane*, Lotario dei Segni (later Pope Innocent III) laments the degraded and exploited condition of the unfree (*servi*), quoting Ecclesiasticus 13:23, "the wild ass is the lion's prey in the desert: so also the poor are devoured by the rich."[45]

Langton, unlike Stephen of Fougères, issues no accompanying instruction to the poor to bear their lot patiently, except by implication insofar as Langton claims their misery will be transferred to their oppressors in the world to come.[46] The poor (*pauperes*) are the equals of the powerful. In the course of his discussion of Amos 1:9 (the transgressions of Tyre, which "remembered not the brotherly covenant"), Langton cites Malachi 2:10: "Have we not all one Father? hath not one God created us?"[47] But not only are the poor endowed with ordinary human dignity; they are also blessed, the people of God. Commenting on Hosea 1:5, Langton observes that while the rich and powerful have shut the poor out of any share in the wealth of this world, they should take care lest the poor eject them from *their* realm, that of heaven. "We" must befriend the poor in order that they might receive us in heaven.[48] Oppressive conduct will come back to haunt the wealthy in the world to come, where they will become the victims of the poor, crying out for God to hear them (Hosea 5:1).[49]

Metaphors of cannibalism and of drinking blood would persist beyond Langton into the late Middle Ages and beyond. The verses Micah 3:2–3 served in the Dominican biblical commentaries organized by Hugh of Saint-Cher between 1236 and 1239 to describe the brutal exploitation of the poor in a lurid series of images of boiling, cooking, serving, and eating.[50] Jacques de Vitry, in his *Historia occidentalis*, imagined the servants of the powerful shouting to each other to pull apart their victims, crucify, burn, and eat them![51] The Franciscan James of Lausanne, commenting on Leviticus in the early fourteenth century, likened clergy who live luxuriously off the poor to those who eat bloody meat. Rulers and clergy are like eagles with the blood of the poor under their wings (Jeremiah 2:34 and Isaiah 40:3).[52] A villager of Montaillou, Bélibaste, observed that the pope "swallows the sweat and blood of the poor." Another, Pierre Maury, scoffed at the Franciscans and their claims to humility. They are wolves who would like nothing better than to devour "us" dead or alive.[53] The rich eat the poor, according to a sermon by Thomas of Wimbledon written in 1388.[54] The Czech Hussite pacifist Peter Chelčický near the middle of the fifteenth century likened the clerical and noble orders to gluttons drinking the blood of those who labor while treating them as little better than dogs.[55]

Langton was perhaps the most eloquent high-medieval critic of the exploitation of the poor, but complaints over their condition were quite common, usually divorced from an explicit lament over the failure to observe the Three Orders' mutuality of service, but always implicitly contrasting oppression with what were supposed to be the obligations of prelates and nobles. An important category of denunciations concerned servitude. That certain peasants were held by their lords as serfs was a particularly graphic emblem of subordination in violation of mutuality and, arguably, of Christian equality. I shall postpone discussing servitude and condemnations of servile institutions until Chapter 10, where I will bring together the topics of equality and explanations (and refutations) of subordination that remain to be explored. Serfdom would be attacked in the late Middle Ages and would provoke or at least influence many of the insurrections of the two centuries before 1525. Beyond specific complaints over status, medieval laments concerning the oppression of the peasants repeat and develop certain themes: warnings of the consequences of mistreatment (in terms of God's eternal judgment but also in this life); comparisons with the wicked behavior of infidels; and comparisons with the treatment meted out to animals, with a corresponding reassertion of the peasants' humanity.

Consequences of Mistreatment

Two royal dreams concern the sense of guilt over tyrannical conduct, including that toward the peasantry. Benedict of Sainte-Maure describes a nightmare of King William II of England on the eve of his mysterious death while hunting in the New Forest. William dreamt that he was hunting alone, nearly starving with hunger. Desperately looking for food, he entered a chapel in which a freshly dressed deer seemed to be lying upon the altar. William started to devour the carcass, raw as it was, and did not cease even when it was transformed into a man. The dream as interpreted by the bishop of Winchester symbolized the king's misdeeds against the people and the Church.[56] The story also appears in Gerald of Wales and Walter Map, with some variations, notably that it was immediately obvious that the body on the altar was human.[57]

John of Worcester tells of a dream King Henry I experienced (probably in 1131) in which the king found himself threatened by successive representatives of the estates of society, including a group of peasants who denounced his oppressive rule, menacing him with their agricultural implements.[58]

God heeds the groans of the oppressed and punishes their oppressors. As early as 900, in a collection of the miracles of Saint Bertin, the sighs and prayers of the helpless, unwarlike common people are heard by God, leading to the downfall of the powerful.[59] In Lambert of Ardres's *History of the Counts of Guines* (written near the end of the twelfth century), the evil Count Rudolph encounters a group of wretched shepherds who do not know who he is. He asks them about the count, and they bewail their lot, cursing their ruler. Rudolph shortly after dies in a tournament.[60] At the end of the Middle Ages, Werner Rolevinck, in his *De laude veteris Saxoniae* (1478), said that the clamor of the downtrodden rises to heaven asking revenge against cruel lords.[61]

It was also possible to imagine that the peasants might themselves inflict punishment on their oppressors. The anger of the peasants destroys and burns the lord's castles, according to the thirteenth-century German poet known as Der Stricker.[62] An explicit warning of the consequences of the nobles' failure to fulfill their role as protectors of the poor is given in an anonymous fifteenth-century German poem. Not only will God punish the wicked, but the peasant will kill the evil nobles.[63] Johannes de Rupescissa, writing in 1356 after the capture of King John II at Poitiers, warned of the impending wrath of the people against the "tyrannical noble traitors," a catastrophe allegorized as the triumph of the lowly worms against great beasts such as lions and wolves. Rupescissa, an apocalyptic Franciscan visionary imprisoned by the papacy in Avignon, foresaw something resembling the *Jacquerie*, which would occur two years later. Although the insurrections in his prophetic account are among a host of horrific visitations of divine chastisement, he specifically calls the future slaying of the lords by the "afflicted populace" an act of "popular justice."[64] Rupescissa's prophecies would find resonance in Bohemia, where an even more bitter denunciation of the oppression of the peasantry was interpolated into a revised text of the *Vade mecum* drawn up in 1422 in the apocalyptic atmosphere of Hussite Bohemia.[65]

More frequently, laments over mistreatment of rustics were joined to a future, otherworldly reordering in which the meek would be admitted to paradise and the wicked punished in the manner of the forest keepers in Walter Map's anecdote. Invoking divine redress in the life to come constituted a warning to the powerful but also to the victims, lest in their impatience they should be tempted to exact a more immediate vengeance. We have seen that in Langton the powerful need the assistance (prayers) of the weak in order to be saved. The Carinthian author of the poem "Vom Rechte" (written between 1130 and 1150) states flatly that the lord who is unjust will appear before God as a serf while the serf will be free if he fulfills the divine ordinances.[66] English preachers of the fourteenth century condemned the rich, who would burn in hell while those they ground under them would be blessed. In *Literature and the Pulpit*, G. R. Owst cited the Augustinian John Waldeby, the Franciscan Nicholas Bozon, and especially the Dominican preacher John Bromyard, whose *Summa Predicantium* (early fourteenth century) vividly imagines the rich confronted in heaven by those whom they starved, beat, and extorted. The sufferers will air their complaints at length before God, demanding vengeance for the absence of recompense for their labors, the failure of mutuality: "O just God, mighty judge, the game was not fairly divided between them and us. Their satiety was our famine; their merriment was our wretchedness."[67] The demands of the poor for justice are the inverse of their earthly prayers for those who give them charity. In both cases the poor are heard by God because of their wretchedness. In the world to come, those "who here on earth are called nobles" shall blush in shame at their transgressions and fearfully await their punishment.

On this issue, as on many topics, the German didactic poet Hugo von Trimberg most exhaustively reproduces the range of common attitudes. In *Der Renner* (ca. 1300), a long compendium of moral and scientific learning (with particular reference to the vices), Hugo complains about the tyrannical lords who force the poor to work for them, an act worse than diabolical, for even the devil himself stops short of demanding service against one's will.[68] Hugo returns to the theme of the violence and pillaging committed by knights against the poor. How does it happen that the Jews, according to Leviticus, incurred such severe punishment from God for relatively minor transgressions while wicked Christians seem to be able to despoil peasants with impunity? To the extent that their crimes are allowed to wax on earth, their ultimate punishment will be greater.[69] The robber-knights will burn in hell for their conduct.[70] Hugo also remarks that they are worse than pagans, who indeed would not treat a dog thus. So gravely have these nominally Christian oppressors jeopardized their souls that they need preaching more than the infidel overseas.[71]

The invidious contrast between pagan and Christian conduct would also figure in the *Reformatio Sigismundi* (1439). Here servitude rather than plunder or direct exploitation is the object of the writer's anger. The man who calls another his serf is not a Christian but resembles an infidel in his defiance of God's law.[72] In fact, he is worse than a "pagan," as the author demonstrates by a story about a Turkish "duke" who supposedly visited the Council of Basel. Exhorted to convert by those he met at the gathering, the wise Turk acknowledged the appeal, even the truth of Christianity as set forth in Scripture, but reproached Christians' propensity to wicked actions such as perjury and the oppression of other Christians as serfs. The Crusade (*merfart*) is unfavorably compared to the more useful task of redeeming those already supposed to be Christians.[73]

The Hungarian peasant insurrection of 1514 actually began as a crusade against the Turks, but self-serving opportunism on the part of the nobles, compounding the longstanding misery of the peasants' living conditions, induced the peasant crusaders to turn upon their masters. Why should they fight the Turks when their own nobles treacherously refused to sacrifice for the common effort, continuing their extortionate (and unchristian) conduct?[74] In a chronicle of the Hungarian rebellion written in 1576, the Italian religious exile Gian Michele Bruto rebuked the Hungarian nobles for falling on their own populace with arms that should have been directed against the

Turks. The peasants, he lamented, suffered not from Turks or Scythians but from those of their own nation.[75] A similar accusation in a Swiss war-song of 1495 directed against the Swabian League attacks the nobles for seeking to conquer Christians when they should be upholding their responsibility to fight the Turks.[76] The idea of mutuality could be used to justify not simply the castigation but even the destruction of a noble class that had not upheld its duties to protect the other orders. Chroniclers of the French *Jacquerie* (notably Jean Froissart and Jean de Venette) have the peasants justifying their revolt by condemning the nobility for betraying the country and the military obligations of their rank.[77]

Thus, although it was a hegemonic ideology that could serve to justify social domination, the theory of the Three Orders could be turned against those in whose favor it was elaborated in situations where their dereliction was clear. One way to appropriate mutuality in favor of the peasants was to join it to invidious distinctions between pagans and Christians (the argument of the *Reformatio Sigismundi*). Not only would pagans not behave as wickedly as putatively Christian nobles, but peasants were treated by their fellow Christians as if they were pagan. Stephen of Fougères had observed in the twelfth century that those whom the knights pillage rather than defend are Christians, not pagans or "Syrians."[78] In the Crown of Aragon, where arbitrary lordship was symbolized by the treatment doled out to local rural and urban Muslim populations, some Christian tenants lodged a complaint in 1323 against their lord, accusing him of treating them "worse than Muslims."[79]

But the image of the treatment meted out to animals would become the most common (and vivid) statement of the injustice of the lords' exploitation. Antipeasant satire and diatribe commonly likened peasants to wild or domesticated animals as a way of demonstrating their stupidity, their subordination, and, most of all, the appropriateness of their mistreatment. The greater the distance between them and what might be considered full humanity or equality with their social superiors, the less disturbing their subordination.[80] The association of subhuman and, in particular, bestial characteristics with the peasantry could, however, be taken in the reverse direction: that they *were* humans but treated as badly as animals (or worse). Thomasin von Zerclaere, a Friulian who wrote a didactic poem in German (ca. 1215), lamented that free men were enserfed and dealt with as livestock.[81] More matter-of-factly, Robert of Courçon distinguished three sorts of *servi*, the lowest being those (such as were supposedly found in Apulia and Sicily) who were bought and sold like sheep and cattle (*sicut oves et boves*).[82] A text attributed to the Franciscan preacher Berthold von Regensburg remarked that lords made sure their animals were better nourished than their peasants.[83]

The peasants of the era of the German peasant wars complained that they were treated like animals. The eighth article of the Salzburg peasants' demands (1525) condemns serfdom, likening the oppression of the serf to that of an animal led around by the nose. Serfs were treated as cattle only more tyrannically.[84] A declaration of the peasants of the abbey of Ochsenhausen (in Upper Swabia), also from 1525, said they should no longer be sold like cattle or sheds, "for we all have one lord, that is God in heaven."[85] The peasants of the abbey of Kempten, who had long struggled over their rights and status with their monastic lords, claimed their condition was worse than that of serfs or dogs.[86]

The animal-like subjugation of rustics represented the logical outcome of the breakdown of the Three Orders. If they were deprived of what was owed them by the rule of mutuality, the peasants ceased to have any standing or dignity and were ultimately deprived of their humanity. Tomàs Mieres, a Catalan jurist of the early fourteenth century, in a marginal note to one of the basic Roman law treatments of servitude, wrote that serfs must be treated humanely. They are men and so should not be killed, dismembered, or otherwise mistreated. This was not a vague theoretical statement but an important declaration in a territory that recognized a legal right of seigneurial mistreatment.[87] Towards the end of the Middle Ages, Peter Chelčický argued (against Wyclif) that the threefold division of society had never worked for mutual benefit. The lords and priests "ride the working people as they will." If the three orders really did represent the body of Christ, the lower order would have the greatest honor, but this is visibly not the case; peasants, shepherds, and beggars are scorned and insulted by the powerful, who refer to them as "blisters," "screech-owls," "hornets," "louts," or simply (as sufficient insult) "peasant."[88]

The complaints of peasants varied from place to place. In some areas servitude was a major issue, in others, taxes or free access to forests or a host of local economic issues. At times, what now appear to be rather specific grievances were couched in a grandiose rhetoric of human dignity and Christian truth, but that rhetoric is of interest in itself. However we may regard the import or background of peasant demands, they tended to center around a reiteration of humanity and of piety (in which Christianity is a proof or manifestation of humanity).

Even those, like Froissart, who regarded the peasants with contempt and hostility could imagine their complaints of bondage on the basis that they were men, like their lords, not beasts. Froissart portrays the English rebels of 1381 as arguing that servitude had not existed at the beginning of the world (the original equality of humanity proven by its common origin). Servitude should punish those, like Lucifer and his rebel angels, who defied God, but the rustics were men, formed like their lords. Why should they then be kept under like beasts?[89] The chronicler Wace, writing in the twelfth century about the Norman peasants' revolt of 997, has them claim that they are men just as their masters are, with the same members, hearts, and sensitivity to pain.[90]

Laments over mistreatment were directed against the perceived failure of mutuality. The peasants fed the other orders, and even the least realistic of chivalric writers grasped this basic dynamic of the medieval economy.[91] If the peasants were indeed oppressed, it could be argued, this was owing to some merited punishment—for Ham's sin against Noah, for example—or their inferior or even subhuman nature. In some sense, however, the humanity of the peasants, their status as Christians, and especially the moral and rhetorical force of statements of human equality made it difficult consistently to place them outside society as objects of a thoroughly deserved exploitation.

Part 2

The Origins of Inequality

Chapter 3

Equality and Freedom at Creation

Complaints over mistreatment and exploitation found warrant in an ostensible common humanity that such conduct violated. No one claimed that all people should enjoy the same rank, but many commentators believed that degrading peasants to the condition of beasts or objects negated an underlying equality of the most basic sort. What follows examines the forms and implications of this notion of fundamental equality.

Adam and Eve

A poem by Walter von der Vogelweide asks who could tell a serf from a lord if he found their skeletons? Even had he known them both while they lived, their worm-devoured remains would demonstrate their underlying equality.[1] Death is the ultimate proof of our essential resemblance regardless of status. The Dance of Death, an evocation of pessimism and materialism that was very popular in the late Middle Ages, presented the overwhelming impress of mortality but was also a reminder of the imminent obliteration of worldly distinction.[2]

Acknowledging the common fate of humanity hardly constitutes a revolutionary egalitarian assertion. Johan Huizinga observed that late-medieval egalitarian statements were devoid of social import since they did not propose to mobilize cosmic equality in an effort to level worldly hierarchy. Huizinga quotes from a ballad by Eustache Deschamps that joins human equality in the face of death to an even more ubiquitous *topos* of equality, the common ancestry of all people. Deschamps has Adam asking his distant offspring how noble and villein differ, for they are all "covered by the same skin"; they are all his descendants. Death holds the reins for princes and the poor alike.[3] In the thirteenth century the jurist Philippe de Beaumanoir began his discussion of servitude by noting that in the beginning all were free, for we are all the offspring of a single father and mother. This does not materially affect the institution of servitude, which arose through a variety of historical factors according to Beaumanoir, but nonetheless it is generally a bad thing to hold Christians in bondage and a good thing to free serfs.[4]

Stylized and politically empty as such statements might be, they formed a conventional repertoire concerning equality that could be shaped in a number of practical directions. If universal helplessness before death manifested the fundamental equality of all, the single origin of humanity did so even more polemically because it implied a wicked deviation from a better, earlier practice. "Have we not all one father? hath not one God created us?" Commenting on this passage from the prophet Malachi (2:10), Stephen Langton denounced the avaricious who refuse charity and despise the poor.[5] Ultimate equality in death may mock current pretensions to superiority, but original equality at creation renders such pretensions potentially unjust usurpations.

The best-known medieval statement concerning human equality and common descent is a couplet associated with the English Peasant War of 1381: "When Adam dalf and Eve span, Who was thanne a gentelman?" (When Adam delved and Eve spun, who was then a gentleman?) According to Thomas Walsingham, writing in 1390, the *verba proverbii* of the couplet furnished the text for a sermon given by John Ball to the rebels assembled at Blackheath.[6] A similar poetic proverb was commonly recited in England during the decade before the Peasants' War:

> When Adam delf and Eve span,
> Spire [*i.e., "ask"*], if thou wil spede,
> Whare was than the pride of man,
> That now merres his mede?
> Of erth and slame, als was Adam,
> Maked to noyes and nede,
> Ar we, als he, maked to be
> Whil we this lyf sal lede.[7]

Adam as universal father, an undeniable tenet of Christian belief, could be used to buttress three related assertions: fundamental equality, the illicit nature of servitude, and the hollowness of pretensions to innate nobility. These statements are not quite interchangeable, since it would, for example, be perfectly possible to attack the perquisites of noble status without thereby advocating the abolition of serfdom. It is also one thing to assert the primordial equality of humanity and quite another to demand its restoration. The shaded meaning of the couplet as well as its pointedness gave it a certain currency in the late Middle Ages (the rhyme works in several languages), but not always in the context of the same argument.

The proverb could be linked to the idea that all should labor, that work was the common obligation of humanity on the model of Adam and Eve. As a rallying cry it demanded the end of servitude, which violated the basic human equality implicit at Creation. After invoking the Adam and Eve couplet, John Ball's Blackheath sermon continued with the statement that all were equal by nature and that serfdom was a form of oppression introduced against the will of God, who, if He had wished to create serfs, would have separated them from lords at the moment of creation.[8]

Other orders of society, however, did not draw such radical conclusions from the proverb. Creation merely established an original favorable situation, after which the elaboration of privilege and its opposite, servitude, took place. Fortune, character, or human law might be said to modify fundamental equality (the *ius gentium* as opposed to *ius naturalis*); or some specific occurrence in the past (the Fall, Noah's curse upon Ham, or a historical event) might be claimed to have destroyed the egalitarian happiness of paradise. An ur human equality did not necessarily remain valid throughout history, nor did it inevitably accord with divine will as played out in secular time.

The propositions that God created human beings to be equal and that all are descended from Adam and Eve were not in themselves complex or even really debatable. The real challenge was to explain what had happened to undermine equality. Was the falling away from equality natural and licit, or the result of sin and force? Should or could actions in the present restore the pristine balance? Answers varied according to how durable (or renewable) the first form of society was supposed to be: whether human equality perished irretrievably with Adam's Fall (or Ham's mockery of Noah), or whether Christ had restored it in something more than a spiritual sense.

The couplet about Adam and Eve is found in Latin and several vernaculars.[9] Although it became a proverbial statement in written sources only in the late Middle Ages, some evidence suggests that Adam and Eve were invoked in earlier assertions of equality, as in the movement known as the *Capuciati*, or "White Capes," in central France of the 1180s.[10] Even earlier, in Adalbero of Laon's *Carmen ad Rotbertem regem* (ca. 1025), the disorderly society, the world-upside-down, is symbolized not only by peasants wearing crowns but by undressed bishops and monks following the plow "singing the songs of the first parents," possibly an allusion to an ancestor of the couplet.[11]

Whatever its precedents, the couplet really became widely current only in the late Middle Ages, but it then appeared everywhere. Sylvia Resnikow demonstrated in 1937 how widespread was the use of this "democratic proverb."[12] It emerges in a German poem of the fifteenth century known as "Das Gedicht vom ersten Edelmann," which praises the peasant and skeptically questions the basis for nobility, since both wicked and pious are descended from Adam and Eve.[13] A fifteenth-century manuscript written in Nuremberg (presumably for an urban audience) phrases the couplet somewhat differently: "Wo was ein graff, ritter und edelman, / do Adam hackt und Eva span?"[14] A Swedish adaptation of the chess-game allegory of Jacobo de Cessolis, written between 1476 and 1492, states: "ho war tha een ädela man / tha adam groff ok eua span?"[15] There were also Dutch, Czech, and Polish versions of the couplet, according to Resnikow.[16]

A more recent discussion by Albert B. Friedman takes issue with Resnikow's rather literal interpretation of the couplet as a program for social change.[17] Although invented relatively late in the Middle Ages, the couplet expresses an opinion common long before the spate of major peasant rebellions: that all are descended from one set of ancestors. Boethius, in *The Consolation of Philosophy*, asserted that all humans are born in the same way and through the same Creator who fashioned them from noble seed.[18] Indeed, positing a universal ancestor or a common creation is an ancient commonplace directed against excessive pride in noble origins. The corollaries, that true nobility does not depend on blood and that noble birth does not guarantee noble conduct, are found in Boethius and earlier, in the Greek philosophers (e.g., the Sophists and Aristotle) and playwrights (Euripides and Menander).[19] The notion that deeds or virtuous conduct rather than blood are the true markers of nobility does not mean equality of legal standing, still less literal economic egalitarianism. Melanchthon reported the riposte to the couplet made by the emperor Maximilian in the form of another rhyme, which acknowledged that the emperor was a man, like other men, different only in that God had given him high rank.[20] The subversive implications of the Adam and Eve argument could be answered by reference to diversity in human fortunes, all of which must accord with the will of the all-powerful deity.

The couplet did not necessarily, then, imply a program of absolute social equality. It might simply encapsulate the complaint against excessive pride in ancestry. One finds the lines "Als Adam grab und Eva spann, Wo war denn da der Edelmann?" in the Augsburg weavers' guildhall, where it was clearly aimed by townsmen against the nobility, without implying a demand for the emancipation of rural serfs.[21] The poet John Gower, whose denunciation of the English Rising of 1381 is among the most vitriolic antipeasant documents of the entire Middle Ages, nevertheless (both before and after 1381) belittled claims to nobility or "gentilesce" by invoking the common descent of all from Adam and Eve.[22] Resnikow cites a poem by Hans Rosenplüt of Nuremberg that uses the image of Adam digging and Eve spinning not as proof of equality but to depict labor as the consequence of sin:

> When Adam tainted himself by eating [the apple]
> Then God commanded him to win his bread
> By tilling the soil and Eve by spinning
> In sweat, their faces turned towards the earth.[23]

Resnikow considers Rosenplüt's lines a "misinterpretation," but in fact it does not inevitably follow from common parentage that our present condition must be equal.

Yet this statement of original equality was both sufficiently well known and sufficiently subversive in its implication to be consistently put into the mouths of lower-class characters by learned observers. Andreas Capellanus has his "plebian" would-be lover argue with a noble lady that since all come from Adam, no one can claim unique aptitude for love on the basis of rank.[24] Chroniclers and didactic writers depict peasant rebels as trotting out Adam and Eve to justify their grievances. Original equality was the one peasant argument with which noble, urban, and clerical observers were familiar. We find the couplet about Adam and Eve in Walsingham's description of John Ball's sermon, and Froissart reports that arguments from equality at Creation were promulgated during the English rebellion.[25] In imagined peasant discourses, the didactic poet Hugo von Trimberg, the political controversialist Felix Hemmerli, and the satiric poet Heinrich Wittenwiler have their peasant spokesmen argue their equality with the nobles on the basis of common descent from Adam and Eve only to be refuted. The refutations do not deny original similarity but posit subsequent distinctions deriving from Noah's curse or some other hereditary basis for social differentiation: whatever the origin, from that point on there have been nobles and subordinates, an inevitable result of history after the Fall.[26]

The fifteenth-century *Book of St. Albans*, a miscellaneous collection of lore best known for its catalogue of collective nouns for animals, imagines "bonde men" as arguing that all come from Adam, a view that is contemptuously dealt with.[27] Machiavelli, in his account of the Ciompi uprising in Florence (1381), has the rebels argue that boasts of noble blood are vain since all men come from equally ancient lineage, having as they do a common beginning. If rich and poor exchanged garments, they would reverse the appearance of nobility and baseness; poverty and wealth differentiate men, not nature.[28]

Thus the couplet was used to justify equality in both radical and commonplace observation, but it was regarded by the articulate classes as the quintessential lower-class argument against privilege and for equality here and now.

Original Equality

That originally all were equal and that common descent from Adam confers a single human character are sentiments and assertions that can be found in medieval writers long before the invention of the Adam and Eve couplet. One could cite Adam's ancestral role to underscore the folly of human pride without thereby proposing any revision of the social order. Thus in two *chansons de geste* of the mid–fourteenth century the nature of true nobility is said to amount to something other than lineage. The father of the hero of *Hugues Capet* is a knight, but his grandfather is a wealthy Parisian butcher.[29]

This version of the Capetians' ancestry is first found explicitly in Dante's *Purgatorio* (20.49–52), completed in 1315. Here it has a distinctly unfavorable connotation, and the legend of the Parisian butcher, which probably goes back to the mid–thirteenth century, was regarded as an anti-Capetian slur. This legend of the lowly origins of the Capetians, including a variant that has Philip the Fair rescued (by reason of his handsome appearance) from a butcher's shop, was brought to England and popularized at the time of the Hundred Years' War.[30] In France itself, the *Chanson de Hugues Capet* (mid–fourteenth century) alludes to the butcher shop as an example of the moral superiority of character over birth. High lineage is all very well, but in fact we all are descended from Adam, the author remarks, so that true nobility cannot be by blood alone.[31] In *Baudouin de Sebourc*, written at the same time and in the same milieu as *Hugues Capet* but by a different author, "gentle" nature is from good character, not birth, since we all come from Eve and our common father is Adam.[32]

What was Adam's social rank? While he could hardly have been a tenant farmer, he was logically an agricultural laborer, for the Book of Genesis describes him after the Fall as destined (or cursed) to toil, to gain his bread by the sweat of his brow. This applied to human beings generally; thus in commenting on Zachariah 13:5, Peter the Chanter describes Adam as the exemplar of the human species, for all of us, like the *agricola*, eat our bread by the sweat of our brow.[33]

While many regarded Cain as the first peasant (because of the nature of his rejected offerings to God), his father could also be depicted as an agricultural worker. In a fifteenth-century Nuremberg Carnival play entitled simply *Ein Spil von der Vasnacht*, the mockery of peasants, a usual feature of such plays, is condemned, for no one ought to mock his parent, and Adam was a peasant who called all of us "my children."[34] In the stained glass of the clerestory at Canterbury and the nave at Chartres, Adam is shown digging

3. Work after the Fall: Adam digging, Eve spinning. Another thirteenth-century painting in the Monastery of Sigena. From a photograph taken before the Spanish Civil War, when the monastery was burned. A restoration is at Museu Nacional d'Art de Catalunya, Barcelona. Reprinted by permission of Arxiu Mas, Barcelona.

with a spade, muscular, miserably half-clothed, but at the same time resembling Christ with his long hair and facial type. He uses something more like a pick or mattock in the mural formerly at the Sigena monastery in Aragon (Fig. 3) and in mosaics at Monreale and the Palermo Palatine Chapel.[35] Late-medieval German songs asserted that the first man God created was a peasant.[36] In late-medieval Scandinavia, rather exceptionally, Adam was shown plowing.[37] Just as Christ was the new Adam, restoring humanity to spiritual life, He also might be represented with a plow or a spade, and the peasant could assume a symbolic significance for spiritual labor.[38]

As discussed earlier, the plow and the activity of plowing could serve as either favorable or unfavorable symbols. The plowman represented piety, productive labor, even preaching. At the same time plowing denoted debased status and earthly toil.[39] Adam's labor could be regarded as a productive model for virtuous conduct in the world or, as in Rosenplüt's poem cited above, a punishment that most immediately affected those who perform manual (especially agricultural) work. One could also regard this form of toil as not only valuable but of higher moral worth than any other lay calling, arguing from common descent and from Adam's duties that all people, regardless of condition, should work with their hands.[40]

In didactic literature treating the estates of society, however, the common descent of humanity did not invalidate the hierarchical ordering of society. Equality in Adam was used to argue that one should be content in the rank one was allotted.[41] Far from violating original equality, mutual service among the Three Orders might be regarded as its legacy in a sublapsarian world of diverse conditions. To the extent that mutuality was perceived not to work in practice, however, the question of common descent became more critical. If the nobility did not fulfill its duty of defense, then should not society revert to its earlier egalitarian form?[42]

The unitary origin of humanity did not necessarily mean that all should subsequently remain *equal*. It might mean that all should work, or again that all should be *free*, that slavery and servitude are illicit. Shared ancestry might also mean that humanity shared a perhaps minimal but inviolable dignity. Such interpretations fostered a potentially radical turn to one of the most venerable of learned clichés, the vanity of pride in noble birth. Behind the almost banal statements of common origin or the superiority of virtuous conduct to noble status could be discerned, at various times, the program of John Ball. Crucially, the presence or absence of peasants determined the force of the statement.

We might take as an example of the argument of fundamental equality the German translation of Petrarch's *On the Remedy of Both Kinds of For-*

tune, a series of parallel dialogues consoling those who lament their misfortunes and correcting those whom fortune for the moment has favored. The German version, *Von der Artzney bayder Glück*, was printed in 1532, but its woodcut illustrations by the so-called "Petrarch Master" were created about 1517, before the German Peasants' War of 1525 and so during the years when peasants were commonly imagined and portrayed as long-suffering and holy.[43]

The illustrations often elaborate on, significantly sharpen, or even change the points of the text. Petrarch was not especially favorably disposed toward rustics. He has Reason dispute those who rejoice in fertile land by observing that although formerly virtuous, rustics are now wicked and of classes of society the least likely to recover the good customs of the past.[44] The Petrarch Master, however, was outraged at the oppression of the peasantry, and his woodcut engravings show the cruelty of judges, stewards, and lords. Petrarch had stated in rather general terms that there was no such thing as a "good lord" because lordship limited one's freedom and property, and because the only true lord was God Himself, but the Petrarch Master exemplifies the notion more vividly, showing bedraggled rustics brought with their wrists tied before a group of richly clad magnates.[45] Petrarch's consolation to a serf in the Book of Misfortunes repeats the Stoic and patristic distinctions between the inner and outer man, but under this heading the Petrarch Master depicts (Fig. 4) a peasant being flogged.[46] In another example, what for Petrarch was a comic instance of bad fortune—being importuned by impudent servants—becomes in the German version the cruel punishment of underlings. The complaint of "Sorrow" about his unruly servitors is accompanied in the German translation by a scene in which two men are being whipped while a third is about to have his tongue cut out.[47] In a woodcut for a translation of Cicero's *De officiis*, the Petrarch Master imagines a cosmic judgment in which a balance scale holds a bound and gagged peasant on one side and an armed knight kneeling in prayer on the other. Despite (or because of) their postures, the peasant in the balance outweighs the knight. His suffering in this life confers spiritual benefit, whereas the knight's conduct condemns him, no matter what his professed piety.[48]

To return to the German version of Petrarch's *De remediis*, one of the dialogues concerning good fortune discusses noble birth ("De origine genrosa", translated as "Von adelichem Ursprung").[49] "Joy" (*Freud*) is chided by "Reason" (*Vernunft*). Joy delights in his noble origins while Reason ridicules his pride. Petrarch's text pointedly, elegantly, and quite conventionally begins by deriding the supposition that noble blood is in itself virtuous.[50] The question of whether birth, feats of arms, or virtue conferred true nobility was charac-

Von Dienstparkeyt / Das
Sybendt Capitel.

Chmertz. Jch bin ein knecht / oder leybaigen inn
dise welt kommen. Vernunfft. Haß keinen schmertzen / du wyrdest
frey / wiltu anderst selbs / gleicher weyß als vil frey in die welt gan
gen / werden darauß dienstpar geen. Schmertz. Jch bin zü dienen
geporn. Vernunfft. Leß frey / mylt / dann nichts verhindert das du an deinem
besten tail nit frey seyest / allein dienstparkeit / der sünd ist die schwerest / aber sye
mag die nit wöllenden nit zwingen / wyrff von dir die sünd / so wyrdest du frey
sein. Schmertz. Das gelück hat gewölt mich einen knecht sein. Vernunfft. Es
mag auch wöllen das widerspyl / vnnd wie wol es sich seiner sytten gepraucht /
Waist du wol was zü hoffen sey / du hast kennnet dises wunderzeichen schimpf
vnd gaugkelwerck / magst nicht allein frey / sonder deines hertzen herr werden /
wie wol es nichts zum handel dienet / was das glück wöll oder nicht wöll / Jch
setze / es sey vnerpyttlich (wie beyweylen geschicht) hat doch kaynen gewalt v
ber das gemüt / du müst aber in allem krieg wider es dein hilff von dem seynde
foroeren. Offt den das gelück eynenn knecht geporn / hat dye tugendt frey ge
macht. Schmertz. Noch trucket schwerer dienst. Vernunfft. Wer das
soch willigklichenn tregt / dem wirdt es leicht / Jch will dir anzeigen / ein ainige
leychterung / vnnd vntödlichenn erbtheyl / auch auß der wale deynes hertzen
wye wol mächtigenn entnommen / das dich frey vnnd reycher dann dein hert
ist / machen wirdet / leg fleiß auff weißheit / die wirt dich zü freyheyt berüffen /
Der

4. Mistreatment of serfs. Woodcut engraving (1517) by the so-called Petrarch Master. From Petrarch, *Von der Artzney bayder Glück* (Augsburg, 1532), fol. 8v. Reprinted by permission of the New York Public Library, Astor, Lenox, and Tilden Foundations, Spencer Collection, New York City. Photo credit: Robert D. Rubic, New York City

teristic of chivalric and humanist discussions throughout the late Middle Ages.[51]

Petrarch notes that all blood is the same color and that a renowned father is seldom followed by an equally worthy son. Nobility depends on the way one's life and death unfold; it is not a matter of birth. Petrarch then states that all mankind has a common origin. Over time the same blood has produced individuals of high and low rank, so that, quoting Plato's *Theaetetus,* "there is no king who did not come of slaves, and no slave who did not come of kings."

The woodcut (Fig. 5) is directed to this part of the text, but provides a more puzzling image. It represents the estates of society as a tree, but with a paradoxical configuration. The different orders are hierarchically arranged in reference to the roots and branches of an immense larch tree. Two rustic laborers suffer at its base, enmeshed in the root system, groaning as they clutch their implements of toil. They support above them first merchants and artisans, then bishops and kings, and then the pope and the emperor. At the top, however, are two rustics identical to the crushed pair at the base, one perhaps a shepherd playing his bagpipes and the other sleeping, his pitchfork held at rest. The humble men at the top seem to be enjoying an ostentatious, even contemptuous ease: the foot of the bagpipe player rests casually on the pope's shoulder.

There are several possible interpretations of this woodcut, none of them completely satisfactory. Like the Adam and Eve couplet, it conveys a truism but with a certain potentially subversive edge. Indeed, a later edition of *Von der Artzney* (1539), with a different translator, reproduced the estates-tree illustration accompanied by the German version of the couplet.[52] According to Walter Scheidig and Herbert Zschelletzschky, who wrote in East Germany, the Petrarch Master sounds a call to revolution, exalting the struggle of the oppressed for justice.[53] This view is opposed by the Renate and Gustav Radbruch, who demonstrate that the estates-tree was a popular theme illustrative of social reciprocity. The decoration of the town hall at Überlingen (from 1494), for example, features a tree very much like the later design of the Petrarch Master. Trees were used as metaphors for the varieties of love and military service (e.g., Honoré Bonet's influential *L'Arbre des batailles*) as well as the estates of society.[54] The Petrarch Master's illustration, according to the Radbruchs, follows Plato's suggestion that kings are descended from rustics (if not literally slaves), and rustics from kings.[55] The tree thus has a genealogical purport, resembling the Tree of Jesse or other depictions of lineage, such as the *arbor consanguinitatis,* showing the degrees of consanguinity barring marriage.

Von Adelichem vrsprung /
Das XVI. Capitel.

Freud. Ich haß einen adelichen vrsprüg. Vernunfft. Geestu widerumb narzen wercke nach/was geets dich an. Freud. Mein stam ist alt vñ erwirdig. Vernunfft. Ein lächeriger Rome ist / sich aß frembden dingen zü gloryeren/der Anherren wol verdienst sind vngeratner kind marck zaiche/nichts anders eröffnet mehr der absteygē des mackeln/dann der voreltern schein vnd eere / Offt hat einem die tugennt eines andern nutz zütragen/du ne mest dañ wares lob vō dem so eigen dein ist/bedarffestu von kainem andern wartē. Freud. Groß ist ð Adel meiner vozeltern. Vernunfft. Ich wolt vil lieber/das andere durch dich/dañ du durch andere erkant werest/darumb thün du auch etwas/deßhalb du Edel seiest/ dañ wo dise nichts lobwirdiges gethon hetten/weren nimmer mehr Edel worden. Freud. Vil ist der klarheyt meines plüts. Vernunfft. Ein yedes plüt/ist gar nahent ein färbig / ob aber villeicht eins dañ das ander klärer erfunden würdet/thüt nicht der Adel / sonder die gesuntheyt. Freud. Groß ist die klarheyt meiner eltern. Vernunfft. Wie wann dein dunckelheit grösser were:ihr nemet den leib allwegen/vnnd den erbthail offt vonn den eltern/Ein vatter aber/oß der die schon hat/pringt seltenn die klarheit inn dem sone / Der so sye aber nicht hatt /sichts bey weylenn im Sun/Wie fürtreffennlicher was Cesar /dann sein vatter /

Wievil

5. A tree representing the social estates. Woodcut engraving (1517) by the Petrarch Master. From Petrarch, *Von der Artzney bayder Glück* (Augsburg, 1532), fol. 17r. Reprinted by permission of the New York Public Library, Astor, Lenox, and Tilden Foundations, Spencer Collection, New York City. Photo credit: Robert D. Rubic, New York City.

The Radbruchs see the Petrarch estates-tree in relation to the early-sixteenth-century tendency to identify simple virtue, even sanctity, with rustics.[56] In this sense, its message might resemble that of the Cicero judgment: piety makes the peasants closer to God than the proud and worldly.

Hans-Joachim Raupp agrees with the Radbruchs in relating picture to text, although he sees the paradoxical position of the peasants at the top of the tree as indicating the caprice of fortune, or perhaps the moral superiority of the peasants. The idealizing of the peasants in religious controversial literature of the early sixteenth century may be reflected here, and this popular imagery might even have indirectly inspired peasant rebels in 1525.[57] In this sense the tree represents not lineage but a moral statement.

The estates-tree illustration may have chronological as well as genealogical import. The peasants and shepherds are oppressed in this life, and their drudgery supports the luxury of the other estates (all of whom are richly dressed and accompanied by symbols of wealth), but in the world to come, the weak and the subjugated will lord it over the other estates.[58] This interpretation encounters the same difficulty as the Radbruchs' theory of peasant piety: the posture and activities of the rustics do not convey an image of holiness, for neither napping nor bagpipes can be termed positive iconographic symbols.[59] Nevertheless, the woodcut makes some statement about labor and ease, whether as a point of divine history or as a warning to the privileged. Without deviating completely from the text, the artist goes beyond Petrarch's caution against excessive pride in noble birth to depict a reversal of fortune more lasting than the temporal ups and downs of family histories. A conventional statement directed against noble pride in Petrarch is turned in a more unsettling, even subversive direction by the Petrarch Master when he figures peasants both as the basis of society (another commonplace) and as obtaining an eventual compensation for their ill-treatment and inequality.

Classical and Medieval Theories of Essential Equality

The Adam and Eve couplet, Petrarch's discussion of true nobility, and the illustration of the estates-tree accompanying the German translation of Petrarch are elaborations on an essential equality underlying distinctions in the secular order. These assertions were understood by a wide spectrum of the population and would come to possess a proverbial character. Behind such compact formulations, however, are generations of philosophical and theological debate about nature, natural law, and society. The moralizing didactic and sermon literature that served as the proximate source for what might be considered "popular" ideas of equality and difference had as their foundation a tradition of commentary on inequality within both the classical and Christian worlds.

Human society was thought to be appropriately divided into different levels of wealth, privilege, and labor. According to Plato and Cicero, as well as Saint Paul and Saint Augustine, the cooperation among unequal social orders was required for the survival of society. This meant not only that inequality was useful, but that to blur the hierarchical division of society in any way was to undermine its moral as well as practical basis.[60] Inequality was necessary rather than merely excusable.

Slavery presented something of a problem since it could not immediately be fit into a pattern of mutual cooperation. Slavery was prominent in Greco-Roman discussions of social order, natural law, and inequality not only because it undergirded the classical economy but because slavery represented an absolute inequality, less easily explicable than simple differences in wealth or fortune. I would reiterate the distinction between equality in a literal, economic sense (in which, for example, property would be equally divided, or not exist at all), which was seldom advocated, and minimal equality of condition in which what requires justification is not that some people are rich and others poor, or even that a few are rich and many are poor, but that some are relegated to a subhuman condition. Although equality is obviously not the same thing as freedom, the two are entwined because slavery is the most obvious and least immediately explicable form of subordination, a form enforced moreover by law and coercion, and not to be explained away as the result of haphazard circumstance.[61]

One way to approach the problem of slavery was simply to repudiate equality and to suppose that some are naturally fit for slavery while others are naturally capable of profiting from freedom. The denial of fundamental human equality and the idea of natural slavery were enduringly presented in Aristotle's *Politics*.[62] Certain people are slaves by reason of their lack of intelligence or physical strength. It is better for them to be subordinated to those who are their superiors, who are "upright." Aristotle does not deny that enslavement might result from conventional circumstances rather than nature, from the practice of enslaving captives taken in war, for example (which as far back as Heraclitus was an explanation for the origin of slavery).[63]

For Aristotle the superiority of Greeks to barbarians was demonstrable evidence for the limits of human equality.[64] The sense that slavery was natural is similar to the sense that the state, the family, and the superiority of men to women and animals are natural. These are all postulates of what Aristotle regarded as civilized (Greek) social order and are found closely joined in the opening sections of the *Politics*.

Greek and Roman Stoicism, however, regarded slavery as contrary to nature, the result of human convention and a certain coarsening of human character and institutions following an earlier golden age. For the Stoics, living in a larger, more cosmopolitan world that included other civilized, even Greek-speaking peoples, the barbarian/Greek distinction was no longer dominant, nor was the enslavement of foreigners regarded as an axiom of natural law. In Cicero and Seneca, human beings are by nature equal, and freedom is defined as a condition more of mind than of body. Only the wise are truly free, according to Cicero.[65] Seneca stated that slavery does not affect the entire being but only the lower part (the body), while the superior faculty (the mind), remains free.[66] This contrasts with Aristotle, for whom a feeble or potentially corrupt spirit (along with a strong body) characterizes slaves.

The Stoic conception of an eternal law joining human institutions to universal harmony meant that slavery violated nature and the cosmic order. Slavery was a salient aspect of the corruption of human life, which had declined from a primordial period of happiness when human beings lived in peace with the gods and coercion was unknown. Nevertheless, slavery was ultimately not terribly important to the Stoics since it was essentially a matter of body rather than spirit.[67]

In Roman law the contrast between nature and convention was described in terms of natural law versus the law of nations. The jurists were less interested than the Stoics (and certainly less than Christian authors) in how slavery had come about, although the theory of captivity in battle held a certain prominence.[68] Slavery was the classic example of an institution contradictory to natural law but nevertheless widespread among the nations of the earth. The jurist Ulpian was the author of two canonical formulations of human equality and freedom according to the law of nature: that "with respect to natural law, all men are equal," and that "by natural law all are born free." These appear in Justinian's *Digest* among general statements about slavery and manumission.[69] It should be emphasized again that equality and freedom are not the same thing, but they are related, for the most obvious example of inequality is enslavement, the deprivation of freedom, of one set of people by another. The conceptions of the Roman jurists would be taken over in the Middle Ages, but with some changes.[70]

The distinction between natural law and the law of nations in connection with slavery would find its way into Gratian's *Decretum* and Aquinas's discussion of law, but for the early Christian period these types of law mattered less than divine law in understanding how to think about a practice seemingly in violation of Christian doctrine. The Stoic idea of a golden age could be annexed to the doctrine of the Fall, with the result that the existence of equality at creation did not mean that equality extended in time beyond the catastrophe of Adam's disobedience. The next chapter will look at some of the explanations offered by the Church Fathers for the origins of slavery, especially Noah's curse on his son Ham (Genesis 9:25). What is certainly clear is that patristic writers were willing to acknowledge slavery as licit, if unfortunate, within the order of things following from the sinful condition of humanity after the Fall, whether or not this was reinforced by a specific imposition of social distinction in biblical time. From its beginning, Christian thought exhibited a tendency to posit what the Scholastics would call a "relative natural law" that modified or diminished the rules that had obtained in paradise.[71] Although at the Creation human beings were equal, through sin humanity had become divided. The Fall, Cain's murder of Abel, Ham's mockery of his father, or some combination of events made coercion and subordination unfortunate necessities. Force in the form of state power and the maintenance of social inequality was licit although not in every respect harmonious with natural and divine law.[72]

It is not entirely surprising, therefore, that Christianity did not significantly undermine the practices of ancient slavery. The venerable idea that a more humane legislation resulted from the conversion of Constantine is contradicted by the bland savagery of later Roman and Romanized Germanic law.[73] Nevertheless, Christian writers carefully described the discrepancy between slavery and God's present intention, not just the contradiction of slavery by some earlier state of grace. God granted an immortal soul to all, slave as well as free. Acceptance of the secular order, most obvious in Romans 13, does not quite confer moral legitimacy on slavery. The writer known as Ambrosiaster (fl. 366–84) states that God created all men free. While Ham, Noah's accursed son, appears as the progenitor of slavery, he functions in Ambrosiaster as a symbol of sinfulness and stupidity who incurs subordination upon his posterity. But this condition affects the body only, not the soul, so control over the body by the master must be just and temperate.[74]

In Ambrosiaster, as in Lactantius,[75] slavery has no validity in God's eyes, but aside from this personalization of divinity, their view is thoroughly compatible with the Stoics' mild laments about the falling away from the standards of a vanished egalitarian era.

How vividly original equality might be said to persist in the physical world is a matter about which the Fathers differed in important ways. According to Ambrose, for example, it is sin that truly enslaves, so that the slave can surpass the free man in virtue. In such a case it is the supposedly free man who is truly enslaved. This resembles Seneca's thinking on the matter, except that what underlies the common nature is Christ, in whom we are all one.

For Ambrose, equality was not limited to the happy past but in some sense continued in the present.[76]

Augustine discussed original human equality in describing the limited purposes of the state in book 19 of *The City of God*. No longer was the Roman Empire to be understood in classical terms as established to further human virtue; rather, it existed for the negative but necessary task of controlling by force the consequences of sin. Government was natural neither in the Aristotelian sense of promoting the good nor in the Stoic and Ciceronian sense of harmonizing with natural law. The state, like human inequality, was the result of sin.

In an extremely influential passage, Augustine said that God created rational man not to rule over other rational men but to rule the earth's irrational creatures (as God instructed Noah and his sons in Genesis 9:2–3).[77] Slavery quite obviously violated the original plan of creation, but its biblical origin (Genesis 9:21–27, Noah's curse upon Ham and Canaan) appears just after God's statement of human dominion over animals. We have seen the first passage from Genesis cited in medieval biblical commentaries to contrast legitimate with tyrannical dominion, and will come across it again in connection with the injustice of serfdom.[78]

In the evolution of Augustine's thought, of course, confidence in the present power of a harmonious natural law working for earthly good gave way to a more pessimistic conception of the enduring consequences of sin. This affected Augustine's teachings concerning grace, the nature of state authority, and slavery, which now became an inevitable accompaniment to the social order of fallen humanity. Domination of men by their fellows, the enduring consequence of sin, was manifested by public and private coercion: by the state and by slavery. Augustine regarded both as unfortunate necessities.[79]

In another passage that would be frequently repeated, Augustine more specifically ascribed slavery to two forces: iniquity and adversity.[80] Iniquity here means the moral guilt of those who become enslaved. Its archetype is Ham, who laughed at his father's nakedness and whose son Canaan would be the first postdiluvian slave. We will look subsequently at the uses made of Noah's curse in justifying slavery, but here it should be remembered that Genesis 9 was read as establishing not only human domination over the earth but also a more unfortunate order resulting from sinfulness—a differentiation within humanity, the origin of slavery with Ham.

By adversity, Augustine meant a general condition of fallen humanity in which misfortune rather than a specific cause leads to enslavement.[81] This resembles Aristotelian resignation in instances of simple bad luck (such as capture in battle) that lead those not naturally fit for slavery into servile status.

This did not mean that Augustine unswervingly acquiesced to unjust enslavement. In one of his later letters he condemned the buying and selling of free men and children as slaves in North Africa. Additionally, in a letter to a jurist, he attempted to find grounds to oppose the degradation into slavery of someone born of a free mother and unfree father.[82] Slavery was a social reality but was not for that reason to be accepted in all circumstances as merely a chance misfortune. For Augustine, original equality was obscured by the unpredictability of this world, but more pointedly by sinfulness in two aspects: a general disorder that makes harsh measures necessary, and weak character and misconduct that is fittingly chastised by subordination. If a portion of humanity was not *created* with an inferior character (contrary to what Aristotle said), nevertheless some people are appropriately restrained by slavery even if their subjugation came about by accident of fortune.

The author who most clearly presents original equality as a present reality is Gregory the Great. In his *Moralia on Job*, Gregory relied on Augustine for the assertion that all men are equal and the unfortunate contrast between God's command to rule the earth's animals and the fact of human subjugation.[83] It is important to see how Gregory differs from Augustine, however, with regard to the present implications of an original equality. Augustine was concerned with the origins of state authority, while for Gregory this was of less intrinsic interest. If Augustine did not share Ambrose's confidence in the mission of the Roman Empire, he still had before him a classical idea of governmental power, whereas for Gregory, deferential though he might be to the imperial authorities in Constantinople, political ideas were outweighed by personal, pastoral, and contemplative matters. The cultural autonomy of the secular world was considerably reduced in the period between Augustine and Gregory. Less attention needed to be devoted to problems of civil law and custom and more to pastoral concerns.[84] On the other hand, Gregory did not share Augustine's opinion that the existence of state power was directly related to sin as a divinely sanctioned punishment for disobedience, a view that would be prominent in Isidore of Seville. The prince should rule justly and mercifully, in accord with a fundamental, subsisting human equality, not simply dominate.[85]

Augustine had ascribed slavery to an overarching sinfulness that affected humanity in general as a result of the Fall. Although equality persisted in a certain providential sense, and would be fully restored when the Two Cities were definitively separated, it was shadowed by an inevitable result of sin in historical time. Gregory diverged from Augustine in having a much firmer sense of the immediate continuing equality of humanity. In the passage from *Moralia* 21, Gregory stated, *Omnes namque homines natura aequales sumus*: we are all equal by nature. This was not contradicted by his subsequent Augustinian formulation that all are *born* equal by nature, *omnes homines natura aequales genuit*. For Gregory, a mysterious dispensation of God, along with individual human sins, had brought about the "diversity" of conditions and character because of which some must rule and others be ruled. For Augustine, it was a universalized sin resulting from Adam that brought about subordination.

In the *Regula pastoralis* Gregory recalled his statement in the *Moralia* but acknowledged that social inequality bore a relation to vice and virtue and that humanity was not intended to live in equality. Here the domination of animals is linked to licit human rule by the necessity of controlling the bestial part of human nature, but the rule so necessitated is that of prelates, not of secular power.[86] This text would be used to buttress medieval assertions that differences in rank and privilege are sanctioned by God and that absolute human equality is now impossible.[87] However, as Robert Markus points out, for Gregory, nature (by which all are equal) has not been as thoroughly deformed by sin as it has for Augustine. An original human equality still underlies the present order.[88]

Another *locus classicus* for human equality and its limitations comes in a letter of Gregory's to the bishop of Syracuse, defending the authority of the papacy while acknowledging that insofar as sin (*culpa*) does not obtain, all are equal according to the rule of humility.[89] Gratian would cite this in his *Decretum*, and Peter the Chanter would slightly rework it into a frequently repeated formula: *Ubi non delinquimus pares sumus*. This statement contrasts with what might be called the Isidorian interpretation that justified servitude by reason of the necessity to repress sin. *Ubi non delinquimus*, quoted repeatedly throughout the Middle Ages, was an egalitarian statement of a *still valid* underlying equality, obscured but not effaced by human failings.[90]

The two themes from Gregory could be combined: that human beings were given dominion over animals, not over one another, and that setting sin aside, we are equal. Genesis 1:26 begins with God's statement "Let us make man to our image and likeness," after which God confers dominion over all creatures of earth, sea, and sky. In a commentary on these lines, Nicholas of Tournai cites Gregory's *Moralia* regarding dominion over animals and joins to it the formula of Gregory's Syracusan letter by way of Peter the Chanter: *ubi non delinquimus, pares sumus*.[91]

Gregory also had a higher estimation of the effects of the Incarnation on subsequent liberty than did Augustine. In a letter of manumission addressed to two *famuli ecclesiae Romanae*, he writes that Christ assumed human flesh in order to release us from the servitude in which we were held captive. He restored to us our original liberty and canceled the effects of the *ius gentium* that had disrupted our original freedom. Nature made the two manumitted men free, while *ius gentium* enslaved them. Gregory cancels the effects of the law of nations just as Christ broke a chain (of sin) to restore humanity to its pristine liberty.[92]

Restoration of freedom is joined to underlying human equality. To be sure, this does not mean in and of itself the end of slavery as a human institution. Once more, the contrast between inner and outer liberty could be deployed to excuse (render irrelevant) actual social status. Gregory did not advocate, nor was he interested in, the abolition of slavery. Yet the passage from his letters quite clearly referred to human subjugation and not some metaphorical servitude. Christ liberated us from sin and has thus restored our original nature, a thesis that the Augustine of the *City of God* would not quite so literally have agreed with.

In later centuries, the image of Christ as the destroyer of bondage would serve to answer arguments that posited a biblical or historical basis for servitude. Even if Adam or Ham was the unwitting author of subjugation, Christ had canceled that debt, restoring our original liberty. The delivery of the children of Israel from "Pharaoh's thralldom" betokens Christ's passion that redeems us from the devil, according to Aelfric. In this we are alike before God, the slave as well as the king.[93] The passage from Gregory's letter to the Roman church would appear explicitly in Gratian (C.12 q.2 c.68) but also in a prologue to peasant demands in fifteenth-century Catalonia. It would inspire remarks by Adam of Eynsham in England and by the author of the *Reformatio Sigismundi*, and it stands behind legal texts and sermon literature in Germany, Bohemia, and Hungary.[94]

Gregory is thus to be distinguished from Augustine, but also from his near contemporary Isidore of Seville, with whom he is often closely associated in descriptions of Christian theories of inequality.[95] Isidore was more confident than Gregory that servitude was necessary to restrain the will of those likely to behave sinfully. Isidore acknowledged that baptism cleansed the original sin of Adam but nevertheless believed that the domination of potential malefactors by their masters accorded with the will of God.[96] This interpretation would be frequently reproduced in legal and didactic works of the ninth through twelfth centuries.[97] Isidore thus explained slavery more by iniquity (in Augustine's terms) than unfortunate circumstance. This fits in with Isidore's emphasis on the necessity for the coercive power of the state and its institutions, which follows immediately his justification of servitude.[98]

There is a tendency to introduce medieval discussions of social division with a quick run through the thought of the Church Fathers, especially Augustine, Gregory, and Isidore. I have followed that practice but would like to go beyond it somewhat by underlining differences among the Fathers that would become increasingly important as their formulations concerning slavery became canonical. It is often said that all three explain slavery by reference to human sinfulness. This is true as far as it goes, but what is of consequence is that they differ with regard to the precise relationship between sin and subordination. All might agree that the Fall had ended absolute human freedom and equality and ushered in the domination of sinfulness, but they differed on how to apportion responsibility within a generally sinful world order. For Isidore it was most clearly the actual or potential conduct of those enslaved that represented human sinfulness. Slavery existed to punish or prevent the wickedness or weakness of those who are subjugated. Sin in Augustine was more general. While some were rightfully punished for their iniquity (Ham), others were unfairly enslaved. Sin thus brings about an unequal distribution of fortune's favors, and there is usually no appropriate gradation of temporal suffering to fit varying degrees of sinfulness. In Gregory, although slavery accorded with God's hidden purposes, sin did not destroy human liberty or equality. Diversity and inequality came into the world through sin, and it was necessary for some to rule others, but Gregory was less confident than Augustine and Isidore that coercion was necessary or that slaves had a greater propensity to sin.

Slavery and Serfdom

Patristic texts would be influential in an age in which the distinction between free and unfree was no longer as clear as it had been in the late Roman Empire. Beginning with the Carolingian period it becomes difficult to say whether the dependent tenants on the great estates were slaves or serfs, although probably their condition was further from that of Roman slaves than the reigning school of historians of medieval slavery believes.[99] Whether or not the actual institutions of society resembled the social structures of late antiquity, the writers of the ninth and tenth centuries used the term *servus* to mean slave.

These authors invoked the Augustinian/Gregorian distinction between human dominion over the earth, which accorded with God's direct instructions, and subordination of one class of men by another, which might not be in harmony with God's intentions. For Alcuin, God created man in His image, and gave him dominion over irrational animals. Citing Augustine's commentary on Genesis 9, he noted that some fell into slavery because of iniquity, others through misfortune. Finally, Alcuin added the Roman-law derivation of *servus* from *servare*, a term referring to war captives who were "preserved" rather than being killed.[100] Hrabanus Maurus repeated Alcuin's text but stated at the outset that servitude was just. Hrabanus approaches an Aristotelian theory of slavery when he says that some excel in reason while others are deficient. Hrabanus was willing to admit that this did not always prove true in practice, but counseled patience and the expectation of a heavenly reward, so that, for him as for Augustine, slavery is explicable by a combination of moral failing and misfortune.[101] In the context of an argument against Jews holding Christian *mancipia*, Agobard of Lyons offered a slightly sharper distinction between God's creation of human beings and the reality of slavery. He repeated Gregory's description of an original equality that was still valid despite sin and God's "most just and most hidden judgment" by which some were degraded to servitude. Agobard distinguished exterior liberty from an interior liberty by which people who were essentially (internally) equal might licitly hold one another in bondage—Christian might hold Christian—but which did not legitimate the holding of Christians by spiritual inferiors, namely Jews. As with Gregory, so for Agobard, slavery was sanctioned by God, despite our original condition of freedom and equality, because of what human nature now is.[102] Haimo of Auxerre states flatly that slavery is due not to natural law but to sin and guilt. As in Isidore, however, the sin is firmly that of the slave (or his ancestors). Slaves are not naturally subordinate but rather, as with Canaan, son of Ham, placed in servitude because of sin.[103]

While no Carolingian writer can be said to have denounced slavery consistently, there were those who upheld some original condition of equality that had not been destroyed by sin or misfortune. Jonas of Orléans speaks of the relationship of the powerful to those he refers to as *pauperes* as well as *servi*.[104] In the most general sense, he argues, the wealthy should not think that those placed below them are by nature inferior. They are equal in the sight of God and by nature even if (by the usual "hidden dispensation") there are various gradations of liberty and fortune. Jonas ends rather than begins this discussion with the Augustinian contrast between rule over the irrational animal world and subordination of humans. Instead of considering this distinction to be more or less abrogated, Jonas holds it to be still valid even if in the present world divers conditions of men exist.

Rather of Verona followed the order of Hrabanus's discussion when addressing those who are lords (*patroni*) but differed in his conclusion, rejecting the notion that normally those who rule are more fit to do so by nature. Human beings were given dominion over fish, birds, and beasts but not over men, who are equal in nature. Often those who are unworthy dominate those who are better than they: "Hence our ancestors preferred to call those who had dominion over the others fathers of their country, dictators, and consuls rather than kings, thinking it would be hateful if men were said to be ruled, like cattle, by anyone."[105] On the other hand, when addressing *servi*, Rather not only counsels patience but also quotes Isidore of Seville on the restraint of wicked license by servitude. Subjugation is providential, an aspect of the necessary fear of authority without which sin would have unrestrained power.[106]

For Smaragdus, human equality was *not* ended by events after the Creation, and domination is not readily excusable. Smaragdus urges Christians to free those enslaved to them.[107] Servitude is the result of sin, but the sin appears to be more the fact of domination than some general human condition.

This view is sharper in Atto of Vercelli's commentary on Paul's epistle to the Ephesians. *Servi* are admonished to be humble, but lords must not forget that *servi* are their equals under divine law and within the Church. The name *servus* is abhorrent, because servitude is the result not of nature but of iniquity. Moreover, this is not the Augustinian/Isidorian iniquity of those who were enslaved but rather the injustice and lust for power of those doing the subjugating.[108]

Complaints over the sale of slaves and other unfree men cited the distinction between humans and animals in defense of a basic Christian equality. At the Synod of Coblenz (922), the sale of Christians as slaves was deemed a crime similar to homicide. A letter written by Emperor Conrad II in the period 1027–29 denounced the sale of *mancipia* as if they were beasts, which violates canon law. Similar language appears in legislation of the Synod of Westminster in 1102 and in the *Chronicae Bohemorum*, by Cosmas of Prague.[109] Stephen Langton referred to the distinction in Gregory's *Moralia* between human dominion over animals, bestowed in Genesis 9:2, and the subjugation of men that was *not* conferred by God on other men and that violates human equality.[110]

The same sort of language appears occasionally in ordinances purporting to limit the buying and selling of slaves in the high and late Middle Ages. There can no longer be any doubt that slavery existed on a massive scale in the medieval Mediterranean.[111] Serfdom did not so much replace slavery as supplement it. In Catalonia, Saracens, Tartars, Circassians, and Sardinians were either bought or captured.[112] There was a reasonably clear distinction between slaves and unfree or semifree peasants, to the extent that the former were foreign peoples bought and sold as servants or laborers, not members of the native population hereditarily settled as tenants. The servitude of the Catalan peasantry might present a difficult moral problem (discussed below, Chapter 11), but slavery did not. Elsewhere one does find occasional implicit criticism of slavery. Much has been made of two laws passed by the Great Council of Ragusa (Dubrovnik) in 1416 and 1466 that invoke God's creation of man in His image and protest against treating human beings as if they were animals. These laws regulated rather than abolished traffic in slaves, however, and were at any rate ineffective.[113] Although slaves could be defined and recognized as different from serfs, nevertheless some blurring of these boundaries occurred. Discussions of natural law among the theologians and canonists still used Roman terminology of slavery but applied it to various classes of the unfree and semifree. Burchard of Worms, Ivo of Chartres, and Gratian taught the legitimacy of marriages between free and slave on the basis of the fundamental equality of human beings before God.[114] The decretal "Dignum est" of Adrian IV recognized as legitimate the marriages of *servi* undertaken without seigneurial permission.[115] The canonists in the twelfth century, beginning with Huguccio, defined servile condition as a perpetual obligation that could exist apart from personal status. Thus *servi*, like those of intermediate or ambiguous status in Roman law (*adscripticii, originarii, liberti*), could be considered free as persons but burdened by an irrevocable and perpetual servitude related to land more than status. The use of the term *servi* in canon and medieval Roman law therefore applied to tenants of rather different condition from that of ancient Roman slaves and so was less artificial than might at first appear. The border between freedom and unfreedom was important to canon law for such problems as defining who was ineligible to enter holy orders or defining the status of children of mixed marriages. Romanists and canonists assumed that the majority of those affected by the laws on unfree persons were rustics, but were less interested than theologians or even customary lawyers in explaining the origins of serfdom or the rural economy.[116]

With less concern than the jurists for technical definitions of status and more attention to problems posed by the ethics of slavery properly speaking, Aquinas considered slavery in trying to reconcile Aristotelian teachings regarding differences in human nature and the naturalness of government with Augustinian/Gregorian assertions of the fundamental injustice of domination and slavery's violation of human equality. He distinguished two sorts of dominion, one that deviated from original human equality (slavery), and another that was completely natural (the rule of free men by other free men—the state). Slavery itself (like private property) did not coincide absolutely with natural law, but might be an addition to it inasmuch as the *ius gentium* arises from human natural reason. Slavery, like property, answers certain necessities and bestows certain conveniences on human life.[117]

Commenting on the *Politics* of Aristotle, Aquinas acknowledged that the peasants of his era were not slaves and so not completely subsumed under the Aristotelian doctrine of natural slavery. Nevertheless, Aquinas agreed with Aristotle that some were fit for servile labor by their lack of natural reason and the strength of their bodies.[118] In his commentary on the *Nicomachean Ethics*, Aquinas accepted Aristotle's definition of the slave as a "living tool" (*instrumentum animatum*).[119] Agricultural labor was lower than any other work, and its practitioners should be ruled by their intellectual superiors. There was therefore a certain resemblance to classical slavery in Aquinas's thoughts concerning the peasants of his time, but he never discussed their situation with any great interest or detail.

The work of Thomas's followers, such as Giles of Rome and Ptolemy of Lucca, shows more clearly how Aristotelian natural inferiority might cover more than actual slavery. They explicitly embraced Aristotelianism to the extent that they agreed with the Philosopher that some men lack reason by nature and cannot rule themselves and so are appropriately given servile tasks. Nicholas of Oresme argued in this manner commenting on Aristotle's *Politics*.[120] All the neo-Aristotelians refer to "servile" work, but Nicholas includes under this rubric agricultural, artisanal, and commercial employment.

When one turns from the highest levels of university culture to sermons and other didactic literature, it becomes clear that serfdom rather than slavery provoked the question of the violation of natural equality. Classical and patristic teachings concerning the origin and nature of slavery could be applied to the more familiar forms of medieval dependence. Thus, for example, didactic writers such as Hugo von Trimberg and Konrad von Ammenhausen, satirists such as Heinrich Wittenwiler, and even Chaucer explained *eigenshaft* or "thralldom" by reference to Noah's curse.[121] The Roman-law explanation for slavery as punishment for treason was adopted for theories of the origins of serfdom in Hungary, while deriving slavery from captivity in battle was used in Catalonia.[122]

Serfdom was, of course, less clear-cut than slavery as a violation of a fundamental natural order. Without invoking Aristotle on natural difference among humans, it could be argued that serfdom was no more a unique form of bondage than anything else in a society built around mutual obligations, a society, moreover, in which everyone shared in the privation of absolute freedom resulting from sin.[123] Indeed serfdom as a status was sufficiently imprecise that much of the discourse of lamentation as well as counsels to patience were addressed to the peasantry in general, irrespective of their specific condition.

What was seen as violating natural equality was not, therefore, a dramatic difference in social condition but arbitrary and unjust lordship. This aspect of serfdom was vividly resented by those it afflicted and lay behind demands for the abolition of serfdom, such as those made by the peasants assembled at Blackheath to hear John Ball. Even in lands such as the Tyrol, where the agricultural population was technically free, revolt centered around "servitude" because what were perceived as oppressive and arbitrary conditions of lordship placed tenants in a de facto servile condition.[124]

The nature of serfdom was encapsulated in Bracton's saying that the serf does not know today what his lord might order him to do tomorrow. In fact, as R.W. Southern observes, this is unlikely to have been true and, if anything, describes the unstable life of the knight more than the rather predictable routine of the agriculturalist.[125] Nevertheless, it was the potential for a lord to order what he wished, including degrading or violent treatment, that defined a subjugation that included serfs but could also affect those not legally deprived of free status.

The arbitrary nature of lordship over medieval peasants was a major grievance motivating rebellions, a grievance that conceptually joined two arguments: one concerning natural equality, the other natural liberty. The antithesis of equality was the lack of freedom or subjugation to the arbitrary will of another, whence much of the polemical force of denunciations of lords treating their serfs or other dependents as "animals" and the significance of symbolic demonstrations of subjugation by yoke or mutilation.

The argument of equality was formulated as the assertion of a fundamental liberty that sin and subsequent events had not obliterated. This could rely on the simple physical fact of human resemblance. In Wace's often-cited account of the rebellion of Norman peasants at the end of the tenth century, the peasants protest that they are as much men as their oppressors, formed in the same fashion and equally capable of experiencing pain.[126] It could appear as an argument that all people, nobles as well as peasants, were obligated to labor (thus if manual work was in some sense the result of sin, it affected everyone). Finally, the argument of basic liberty could deny that human sin explained or justified subjugation. According to the *History of the Bishops of Auxerre*, the peasant rebels known as the "White Capes" (Capuciati), active in the diocese of Auxerre and elsewhere in the middle of France between 1182 and 1184, demanded that they be restored to that primordial liberty enjoyed by our original parents, Adam and Eve. Specifically, the Capuciati demanded freedom from seigneurial taxes and recognition of their status as free men. The author of this section of the History, after describing the formation of sworn associations, denounces their diabolical inspiration. He adds that in justifying *libertas* by reason of common descent from our primordial parents, they seemed unaware that servitude was the price of sin.[127] Later denunciations of servitude and peasant revolts against serfdom would turn ideologically on the permanence of a measure of human dignity and liberty, obscured by sin but restored by Christ's Incarnation.

Original equality meant original freedom. To the near unanimity concerning equality we can add the general agreement that in the beginning all were free. The names of serfs freed by the city of Bologna in 1256 were entered into a book called the *Paradisus*. Two preambles to this record declared that God created men to be perfectly free but the Fall had brought about servitude. Bologna, which had always struggled for liberty (*semper pro libertate pugnavit*), would now lift the yoke of servile condition imposed by the *ius gentium* and restore that original freedom in honor of Christ, who had broken the bonds of servitude by His sacrifice.[128] Marc Bloch observed that a model manumission document issued by the chancery of Alphonse of Poitiers also claims to restore the natural liberty that the *ius gentium* had taken away.[129] Bloch lists citations of this opposition of natural liberty and the law of nations from the canonists Paucapalea and Stephen of Tournai, the Roman lawyers Bulgarus and the author of *Brachylogus*, the customary lawyer Beaumanoir, the encyclopedist Vincent of Beauvais, and the theologian Thomas Aquinas.[130]

These scholars explained why the original condition of freedom had been vitiated, but there remained a problem of the degree to which original liberty could legitimately be weakened. On a theoretical level the difference revolved around absolute versus relative natural law. To the extent that natural and divine law can be modified, it was possible to excuse servitude, but if such ordinances were fixed and not capable of being weakened, then servitude (of Christians at least) became difficult to justify. As Peter Bierbrauer points out, this distinction lies at the heart of Wyclif's teachings concerning the "Lex Christi" as opposed to the administration of the Church. By limiting the ability of the Church to rule by reason of sin or to interfere with a now-immutable natural law, Wyclif questioned how the original liberty of human beings could be licitly obscured.[131] Radical thinkers such as Wyclif, however, were not the only ones who asserted the unchanging nature of natural and divine law, and this question would be a source of anxious controversy among jurists throughout the Middle Ages.[132]

The following two chapters will examine explanations for the origin of servitude that identified a particular moment in the biblical or historical past when the free were separated from the unfree. The necessity for such explanations reflects the limited utility of the simplest reason for servitude, Aristotelian "natural slavery," a limitation due to that concept's incompatibility with certain fundamental Christian doctrines.[133] It also demonstrates the problem posed by Gregory the Great's statement that Christ had freed all from servitude. Biblical and national myths of servitude answered the question posed by the Adam and Eve couplet by acknowledging common ancestry but identifying a licit division subsequent to Creation.

Chapter 4

The Curse of Noah

The starting point for medieval speculation concerning the origin of the world's different peoples was the biblical Flood and its aftermath. Genesis 9 describes the first settlement, made by Noah and his sons after the floodwaters had receded, while Genesis 10 provides the genealogy of Noah's sons, rather confusingly linked to various territories.

The biblical account of the repopulation of the earth would be used to explain human difference—not only the origins of different nations but the reasons for inequality, particularly why some human beings were held in bondage. The curse uttered by Noah upon the line of Canaan resolved the problem of the origin of despised or feared peoples, those whose outcast status seemed to *require* explanation. Noah's curse appears in several medieval contexts.[1] Among the many uses found for Ham's fateful laughter at his father's nakedness was to situate a biblical origin for unfree rustics. The institution of serfdom was thought to have arisen from Ham's sin and Noah's curse. No treatment of medieval theories of servitude can entirely divorce itself from the other uses made of the puzzling story of Noah's drunkenness. Not only were medieval serfs said to be descended from Ham, but at various times slaves, Africans, Saracens, and Mongols were fit into the same genealogical paradigm.

The ninth chapter of Genesis opens with God's blessing on Noah and his children along with the covenant not to send any future flood. Instructing them to be fruitful, God promised Noah's progeny that they would dominate the earth and its animal inhabitants (reiterating the blessing conveyed to the earth's first human inhabitants, Genesis 1:28). After the ark reached land, Noah planted a vineyard and at some unspecified time thereafter became drunk. His son Ham saw his stupefied father naked and told his brothers Shem and Japheth, who hastened to cover Noah without looking at him by walking backwards toward him with a cloth. Upon awakening, Noah "learned what his younger son had done to him" and uttered the curse: that Ham's son Canaan should henceforth be a servant of his brethren.

The Bible is replete with interpretive conundrums, and this episode provided several difficulties that prompted ingenious efforts to address them. What exactly had Ham done to deserve such a punishment, and why was the penalty levied on Canaan rather than on his father, the author of the crime, whatever it was?

The Talmud and Midrash provide a number of speculations concerning the nature of the transgression and its punishment. The relevant passages in these texts are difficult and subtle as regards their original meaning and long-term significance.[2] It has been something of a misleading commonplace to suppose that the Jewish commentaries began an unbroken tradition of denigrating black Africans by attributing slavery and black skin color to the curse of Noah. The supposed talmudic origins of this version of the curse and its consequences is asserted in such standard works as the latest edition of *The Oxford Companion to the Hebrew Bible.* In a more sinister fashion this claim of talmudic origin has also become part of a campaign to "prove" that Jews bear a particular burden of guilt for the enslavement of Africans.[3] What David Aaron calls the "myth about the myth" (i.e., the putative Jewish origins of black subordination) makes it more urgent to see how a complex edifice has been built on the shaky foundations of a few poorly translated passages collected by untrained scholars from a voluminous and variegated textual tradition.[4]

Here I am not concerned directly with Ham in relation to Africans but rather with the history of thought about him before he was cast as the progenitor of European serfs. Although medieval Christian writers assumed the justice of Noah's curse and were not especially concerned about the Ham/Canaan conundrum, early rabbinic commentators labored over this question. According to a passage in the Babylonian Talmud, Ham was punished because he sodomized his father while he was inebriated, or because he castrated him (or both).[5] Elsewhere in the same tractate it is said that three creatures were punished for violating God's penitential order to abstain from sexual intercourse during the voyage: Ham, the dog, and the raven.[6] Why was the punishment meted out to Canaan and not Ham? Either because Canaan was himself the guilty party, or because this was an appropriate means of punishing his father. Perhaps Canaan rather than Ham had actually been the first to see Noah's drunkenness and had told Ham, so that they both merited punishment; or perhaps Ham castrated Noah, rendering Noah unable to "perform in the dark" (i.e., perform sexual intercourse) and sire a fourth son, so Noah cursed Ham's fourth son with dark skin.[7]

But it was the nature of the punishment that was to be of most consequence. According to Talmud, Sanhedrin 108b, Ham was punished by being
"smitten in his skin" (which may or may not have meant that he turned
black). The Jerusalem Talmud, at one point, says that Ham came out of the
ark "charcoal colored."[8] Nowhere in the Talmud, however, is there anything
typifying blackness as a hereditary taint, nor was there yet any connection
drawn between black skin and Canaan or servitude.

Within the Jewish tradition, consideration of Ham as the originator of
blacks amounted to little more than occasional speculation. The role of Ham
as the unwitting originator of slavery is more significant, because Genesis 9:25
says that Canaan would be "a servant of servants unto his brethren."[9] Nevertheless, before the eleventh century no Jewish commentaries ascribed any link
between Ham as progenitor of slavery and black skin. There is a faint correspondence in the works of Jewish travelers and geographers of the High Middle Ages. In the twelfth century, Benjamin of Tudela wrote of one of the peoples of Cush who are naked, eat wild herbs in the fashion of animals, and are
easily taken captive by the inhabitants of Aswan and sold into slavery in
Egypt: "these are the black slaves, the sons of Ham." Although the slaves are
black, so too, apparently, are those who capture them, for they form another
part of the people of Cush.[10]

How influential Jewish commentaries might have been on Christian understanding of Noah's curse is difficult to determine, partly because of problems in dating rabbinic and Christian commentaries. Certain aspects of talmudic speculation certainly were absorbed by early Christianity. Justin Martyr states in his *Dialogue with Trypho* that the curse of Noah foretold the
Hebrew conquest of the Canaanites and also the Roman conquest of Pales-
tine, while Origen said that Canaan had been the first to see Noah's disgrace.[11] Considerably later, a thirteenth-century gloss to Peter of Riga's *Aurora* borrowed from Jewish notions of Ham's sexual undiscipline, although
here Ham merely summoned a demon to enable him to lie with his wife in
the ark without leaving footprints in the ashes Noah had strewn about to prevent such an occurrence.[12] On the whole, however, there is little evidence for
Christian knowledge of (let alone borrowing from) the Talmud before the
twelfth century, and even after this point, its influence on Christian speculation was small.[13]

In medieval Christian exegesis, Ham's particular sin was laughter. Not
only did he behold his father's nakedness and not do anything about it, he
was thought to have mocked Noah, and it was for this that he deserved to be
cursed.[14]

Like Judaism, early Christianity only very tentatively joined race to the exegesis of the curse.[15] It was in the Islamic world that slavery and blackness were first closely joined, for unlike the Jews or Christians of the period before the High Middle Ages, the Muslim populations of North Africa and the Near East actually did own and traffic in black slaves.[16] Although nothing is said in the Koran about Ham at all (let alone about any connections between him and Africa, slavery, or blackness), beginning with Ibn Qutayba in the ninth century a current of Islamic opinion held that Africans were descendants of Ham, whom God had turned black.[17] Shortly thereafter, Tabari, in his massive *Ta'rikh*, made explicit the crucial connections among the three elements: Ham, blackness, and slavery. He attributed to Noah a prayer that Ham be turned black and that his progeny serve the offspring of Shem and Japheth.[18] A similar theory was offered by the eleventh-century traveler Ibrahim ben Wasif Sah.[19] By the time of Ibn Khaldun (died 1406), it was widely thought that blacks were Ham's descendants cursed as slaves by Noah.[20] Despite the dissents of Ibn Khaldun and others, this commonplace would frequently be adduced into modern times to excuse trading in African slaves.[21]

For medieval writers, the curse of Noah showed why there were nations of people whose apparent strangeness might otherwise be inexplicable.[22] The curse was extremely useful taken in conjunction with the genealogies that followed. Isidore of Seville combined the lore of classical ethnography with biblical suggestions to produce a taxonomy of the world's peoples. Although he discussed neither the curse of Noah nor slavery in this context, Isidore attributed 31 peoples of the world to the line of Ham, including Ethiopians and Africans, among whom were numbered cannibals (*Anthropophagi*) and other fantastic savages.[23] According to an Irish account, horse-headed people, two-headed people, "maritime" leprechauns, and "the merry blue-beaked folk" were all of the line of Ham, as were Saracens according to Pseudo-Aethicus Ister, and Mongols according to the older versions of John de Mandeville's *Travels.*[24]

Genesis 9–10 was not the only text in the Bible that could be used to explain difference. Cain was commonly thought to be the progenitor of the monstrous races, the ancestor of Grendel in *Beowulf,* for example. Another elaborate tradition invoked Hagar, the servant of Sarah who bore Ishmael by Abraham (Genesis 16). According to Josephus, Hagar fled to the desert twice, the second time with Ishmael at Sarah's insistence after the birth of Isaac. Abraham gave the unprepossessing land of Arabia to Ishmael by way of compensation. That the Arabs sprang from Ishmael was a Jewish commonplace, repeated by Jerome and given new currency by Bede writing in the wake of the dramatic expansion of Islam.[25]

A certain amount of crossover is evident in the typology of despised peo-

6. Captured fugitive serfs with horns. Early-fourteenth-century illustration to Codex 6.1, "De fugitivis servis." Tübingen, Universitätsbibliothek MS Mc 295, fol. 153r. Reprinted by permission of the Universitätsbibliothek Tübingen.

ples and their supposed origins. Thus, the eleventh-century Vienna Genesis made Cain rather than Ham the progenitor of blacks.[26] Ham was, in any event, commonly thought to be descended from Cain, so that to some degree he reinforced an earlier cause of subjugation.[27]

Cain served as the originator of a number of outcast peoples, from giants to the Plinian races.[28] The mysterious "mark of Cain" was interpreted as some species of physical deformity (even horns); hence the mythical misshapen peoples of the Indies or of Africa were thought to be his offspring.

The malformed Cain could also be regarded as the first peasant. We have already seen Adam in this role, especially in the discourse concerning equality. Cain functioned as one of several possible points of separation, the beginning of inequality. Cain was suggested in part because of the common representation of peasants as physically deformed. A peculiar example of the application of the mark of Cain to rustics occurs in an early fourteenth-century Roman-law manuscript now in the Tübingen University Library, which shows captured runaway slaves (or serfs) being led by cords before a judge. They have horns on their heads, in keeping with a conventional iconography of the mark of Cain (Fig. 6).[29] A manuscript at St. John's College, Cambridge University, combines several negative iconographic themes in portraying Cain with kinky hair, horns, and a peasant's scythe (Fig. 7).[30]

Cain was thought to be the ur-peasant because of other inferences drawn from Genesis. Cain offered to God the "fruit of the ground," which was rejected (Genesis 4:3), while Abel's offering from his flocks was accepted. Prudentius (died ca. 405) began his poem on the origin of sin—*Hamartigenia*, which is in fact a denunciation of the heretic Marcion—with an evocation of Cain, a tiller of the soil (*fossor*) who slew his brother Abel, a virtuous shepherd. Death entered the world through Cain, a *rusticus*.[31] Cain was a plowman, a German medieval sermon states, and Abel a herdsman.[32] Cain is associated with "the devil's plow" in Hugo von Trimberg's *Der Renner*.[33]

Cain was the first peasant, and his wicked character was sometimes said to have been transmitted to his rustic progeny, for example, in Petrarch's *De remediis* and a fifteenth-century satiric denunciation of rustics attributed to Cecco d'Ascoli.[34] But it is Ham, not Cain, who is the direct cause of bondage. Although he would at first be thought of as the ancestor of slaves rather than agriculturalists as such, the nature of serfdom made Ham the father of the lower orders of medieval rural society. In the numerous vernacular adaptations of Jacobo de Cessolis's allegorical treatise on the game of chess, Cain is presented as a negative rustic model or image but not as progenitor of all peasants. In Konrad von Ammenhausen's *Schachzabelbuch* (completed in 1337), Cain is the first peasant, but Konrad goes beyond Cessolis in mak-

7. Cain shown with horns and kinky hair. From an English Psalter, ca. 1270–80. St. John's College, Cambridge, MS K.26, fol. 6v. Reprinted by permission of the Master and Fellows of St. John's College, Cambridge.

ing Noah's curse the origin of rustic servitude.[35] In John Gower's dream-vision of the English rebellion of 1381, the rebels are described as the accursed progeny of Ham, turned into beasts, as Circe transformed the servants of Ulysses.[36]

After the murder of Abel, God promised that the earth would not yield its produce bountifully for Cain (Genesis 4:12), who could therefore be regarded as an emblem of fruitless agricultural labor.[37]

Western medieval writers thus showed a tendency to mix theories of origins, but not just at random. A rough correspondence was established between cursed biblical figures and the taxonomy of outcasts. Hagar and Ishmael were primarily considered the ancestors of Muslims. Cain functioned as the originator of the monstrous races and also of peasants, whether free or unfree. Ham had two medieval roles: as the father of a number of peoples, including black Africans, and as the ancestor of European serfs. If Cain was an archetype of the peasant regardless of status, Ham was the progenitor of the unfree of whatever race. In the Islamic Middle Ages and in modern Europe and America, the symbolic linkages were fused. Ham was the ancestor of black slaves, as commonly argued from the sixteenth to the nineteenth century.

For the Christian Middle Ages, however, Ham was not exclusively associated with Africa, Africans were not thought of as exclusively black, and blacks were not thought of primarily as slaves. Although they could be symbols of frightening savagery (as in *The Song of Roland*), black people since antiquity had been thought of more favorably as exotic, for example the Ethiopians in the Isis cult and in Origen's commentaries. Later, black Africans were depicted as the purveyors of the golden treasure mined south of the Sahara.[38] In 1324 the spectacular pilgrimage to Mecca of Mansa Musa, king of Mali, dazzled not only the Islamic but the European Christian world with a magnificent display of gold and slaves. The Catalan Atlas of 1381, designed by Cresques in Majorca, shows Mansa Musa holding a gold nugget. He is described as the wealthiest and most noble lord in Africa because of the gold that abounds in his territory.[39]

The portrayal of a luxuriously bedecked black Caspar in paintings of the Three Kings was especially popular in the late fifteenth century, but the identification of Caspar as king of India and Ethiopia is found earlier in Otto of Freising and has been traced to sixth-century Armenia.[40] Blacks sometimes appeared as grotesques in illustrations, and characteristics such as kinky hair could appear as part of an iconography of contempt, but whether exotic or despicable, blacks in European eyes before the advent of the African slave trade were not usually considered the victims of biblically sanctioned servitude.[41]

Ham was cited to explain a more familiar phenomenon, the subordination of European peasants. Ham represented servitude and proved useful for explaining inequality among the Christian population. Cain could not genealogically be distinguished from Abel as an ancestor because of the intervention of the Flood; thus he served more as a negative type in sermons and other didactic literature than as originator of the peasantry. Because of the Flood and the genealogy presented in Genesis 10, Ham via Canaan could be regarded as the literal father of the unfree. What is more, the curse of Noah could excuse the violation of divine and natural law that serfdom otherwise appeared to commit.

The invidious use of Noah's malediction in the modern era to explain slavery is well known. Among the many theories devised to explain the origins of the New World peoples were those connecting them to Ham and thus casting them as cursed or at least lowly races meriting servitude. Speculation about Ham as the progenitor of the American indigenous peoples was especially popular in sixteenth-century Spain and France, countries that had previously evinced little interest in Ham as the originator of serfdom.[42]

The discovery of the New World also led to a vast increase in the slave trade, and because Africans rather than Indians were enslaved and brought to the new colonies, the curse of Noah was applied most frequently to Africans and became a ubiquitous excuse for their captivity. In the mid–fifteenth century, well before Columbus, Gomes Eannes de Azurara, under the patronage of Prince Henry the Navigator of Portugal, described a group of West African captives sent to the prince, distinguishing the Muslim nobles among them ("cavaleiros") from the subordinate "black Moors" who were slaves because of Noah's curse.[43] In the later part of the sixteenth century, the English explorer George Best invoked Ham's sexual undiscipline as the origin of the curse and its perpetuation through Cush to the Africans.[44] In all of these works, however, the connections between the curse, slavery, and race remained tenuous, and the curse itself was presented gingerly and offhandedly as the allegation of unidentified persons other than the author.

The seventeenth century saw more explicit assertions of the curse as joined with race and enslavement. The Spanish Creole savants Buenaventura de Salinas y Cordova and León Pinelo, writing near 1650, justified both the conquest and the slave trade by the curse of Noah, which, they argued, affected Indians and black Africans alike. Attempting to defend enforced subordination and at the same time extol the favorable conditions of the New World, these proponents of the colonies used the curse to explain why the indigenous and involuntary African inhabitants were inferior while the land itself was not; to disassociate the territory from its subjugated population.[45]

At about the same time, in England the fragments of an ambivalent tradition were put together to form a biblical justification for the enslavement of Africans, while in Germany Johann Ludwig Hannemann devoted an entire book to the question of the origin of the Ethiopians' skin color, adducing Noah's curse but also naturalistic explanations such as climate and alchemical notions of human generation.[46]

Before the eighteenth century, therefore, Ham as the progenitor of African slaves had become a commonplace. A peculiar example is Jacobus Capitein, a missionary preacher ordained in the Dutch Reformed Church in 1742 (the first black Protestant minister anywhere), who defended slavery as a vehicle for the salvation of Africans to make up for the sin of Ham, progenitor of slaves.[47] The Dutch settlers in southern Africa also made use of the curse against Ham to justify harsh rule over the Khoikhoi during the early nineteenth century, but did not elaborate this into pseudoscientific or evangelistic arguments in the manner of intellectuals of the southern United States.[48]

Apologists for slavery in the English colonies of the New World made use of the association of Ham with Africa and slavery. In New England, Samuel Sewall in 1700 questioned whether the curse remained valid even if it were true that blacks were descended from Ham. Although this would seem to show that the curse against Ham was already a common defense of the African slave trade, most apologists in the eighteenth-century colonies preferred to argue on the more practical basis of economic utility or the frightening specter of what would happen if slavery were ended, especially in the Caribbean sugar colonies.[49]

In the course of the demands for the abolition of slavery in the southern United States, demands which became heated after 1830, the curse against Ham was sometimes invoked by the proslavery side. As it did in medieval arguments, the curse answered assertions of human equality by denying the perpetuation of original likeness beyond the primal divide after the Flood.[50]

American apologists for slavery were largely unaware of (or uninterested in) medieval or patristic speculation. Their attempts to reconcile slavery with Christianity purport to be original disquisitions on biblical texts, often combining fanciful etymologies with pseudoscientific or neo-Aristotelian assertions of the natural inferiority of Africans (their fitness for labor, their frivolity, their need for guidance) or with peculiarly American ideas of evangelism and Manifest Destiny.

Ethnological studies purporting to demonstrate that blacks formed a separate species were more popular than medieval or Renaissance speculation and lent themselves to theories of the refoundation of humanity after the Flood.[51] The curse against Ham was also tailored to the prevalent idea of

America's mission as the latest revelation in the unfolding of God's intentions, so that not only was Ham's role as servant most clearly fulfilled in the contemporary South, but Ham was depicted as a willing subordinate, recognizing his place in a divine plan in which his labor served the mighty task of clearing the American wilderness, an enterprise conceived and directed by the sons of Japheth that might eventually result in the lifting of the curse.[52]

Scientific theory and assertions of American destiny placed Noah's curse against Ham in a conceptual setting for which medieval or patristic precedents were irrelevant (even had they been familiar). What in nineteenth-century Europe had become dubious antiquarianism would be fashioned in America as religious, moral, and even scientific proof texts.[53]

The one important instance of a justification for American slavery that at least indirectly referred to the Middle Ages was the so-called "Corner-Stone Speech" given in Savannah by the Confederate vice president Alexander Stephens on March 21, 1861, the eve of the American Civil War. Past governments had been based on serfdom and other methods of oppressing members of the same race. Subordination of Europeans by their brethren, Stephens argued, violated both natural law and Providence. The enslavement of blacks, on the other hand, was licit, for either by nature or by the curse upon Canaan they were suited for slavery.[54] In the course of defending racial subordination, the "cornerstone" of the Confederate foundation, Stephens rhetorically exemplifies the perceived moral difference between subjugating those who appeared alien ("other") and subjugating those who were not manifestly marginal or different.

Understandably, historians of the United States have tended to share the nineteenth-century Protestant lack of interest in the earlier uses of Noah's curse. But in the absence of such investigation it has been too easily assumed that there was simply an unbroken tradition joining together Ham, Africans, and slavery, traceable ultimately to a supposed Jewish rabbinic consensus. Not only did no such consensus exist, but the curse of Noah was malleable and for centuries could apply to various problems of difference, including those that had nothing to do with Africa or skin color. The Mongols and Tartars, who forced themselves on the attention of Europe in the thirteenth century, were thought to be members of the enclosed nations of Gog and Magog descended from "Cham." Such speculation was encouraged by the similarity between the Mongol title "khan" and the biblical name "Cham," a putative connection emphasized especially by John de Mandeville.[55] Saracens and cannibals were also occasionally related to Noah's curse.[56]

In the Middle Ages it was commonly assumed, and often explicitly asserted, that rustics, and serfs in particular, were descended from Ham. Ham was more useful in justifying subjugation of Christian inhabitants of Europe than explaining the existence of foreign peoples. The Vienna Genesis, as we have seen, made Cain the forefather of blacks, but Ham's guilt was cited by that text's author (in what was by this time standard fashion) to explain European serfdom, a more immediate problem.[57] In those parts of Europe where serfdom persisted or grew in strength after the Middle Ages, Ham continued to denote the serf, and by extension the peasant, boor, lowly person, a meaning it retains today in Lithuanian and a number of northern Slavic languages. In a Chekhov story a wretched prisoner exiled in Siberia protests with pathetic pride that he is a deacon's son, "not a mere peasant of Ham's condition."[58] In modern Polish, "Cham" remains a common term of opprobrium, denoting a boorish, loutish character.[59]

Medieval commentaries on the curse of Noah were based on patristic theories of the origin of slavery, apart from anything to do with Africa or Asia. Such speculation abounded since doctrines of Christian liberty and equality had to be reconciled with the realities of social subordination. Slavery resulted from sin, sin of that persistent kind that still infected the world after Christ's Incarnation and Sacrifice.

Saint Basil and Saint Ambrose in the late fourth century were the first Christian writers to fit Noah's curse to servitude, justifying slavery by reference to the unfortunate necessity to subordinate the intellectually weak and the undisciplined.[60] While no one is by nature a slave (Basil), and while Saint Paul does call us from servitude into liberty (Ambrose), nevertheless, the fathers agreed, citing Noah's curse upon Canaan as a pertinent example, a chronic lack of wisdom and of discipline made subjugation necessary.[61] Ambrose regarded Ham's punishment for his laughter as proof of an unbalanced nature that merited enslavement.[62] Finally, in a treatise on fasting, Ambrose adduced the misdeeds of Noah himself, whose primordial drunkenness might be said to have led to servitude: "there would be no servitude today if there had been no drunkenness," a locution that would be absorbed into medieval canon and civil law.[63] Ham thus appears at the outset of the Christian tradition as an emblem of culpable lack of discipline more than deliberate wickedness. In the exegesis of Colossians (4:1) by the so-called Ambrosiaster, servitude is the result of Ham's foolish behavior, his "stupidity."[64] John Chrysostom was the first to emphasize the deliberate, sinful nature of Ham's offense and to identify slavery as punishment for a past transgression, applied in the present to those with a propensity to sin. Like Ambrose, Chrysostom stated that servitude entered the world through Noah's drunkenness, but he added that it also entered through Ham's sinfulness in calling attention to his father's condition.[65] Ham's willful depravity (rather than some natural defect) corrupted the nobility of his character.[66] Chrysostom explains the punishment meted out to Canaan and his descendants by their sinful character. Servitude is a consequence and reflection of sin.[67] Just as the subordination of women to men results from Eve's transgression, according to Chrysostom, so slavery results from Ham's laughter. Both punishments stem from the necessity of controlling those incapable of self-discipline.[68]

Saint Augustine perfected the Christian understanding of the consequences of the Fall and original sin, placing Noah's curse in the context of the nature and origins of civil order and repression.[69] In book 19 of *The City of God*, Augustine described slavery as a particular aspect of the general rule of sublapsarian sin and the need for countervailing force. Elsewhere (as discussed in the previous chapter) he argued that servitude could arise from two kinds of sin: active human iniquity (as in Ham's case) or a more circumstantial adversity (as with Joseph and his brothers).[70] Once again, servitude was the outcome of sin, of this world's wickedness, but part of a necessary social order. Augustine's use of the curse against Ham would influence the formulations of Alcuin and Hrabanus Maurus in the Carolingian era.[71]

A less specific location for the beginning of domination is given in Gregory's *Moralia on Job*, in which sin remains important in rationalizing slavery but no single event stands as its cause. Sin, brought into the world by the Fall and affecting the generality of humankind, served to explain force and inequality. There is no quasi-historical moment in which slavery figured as the punishment for a specific offense.[72] Ham also does not appear in Isidore of Seville's influential explanation for slavery, namely that it is necessary to restrain the desire to commit wrong on the part of those unsuited to freedom. The propensity to commit evil deeds is the result of the Fall, a more fundamental event than Ham's misdeed, which split humanity genealogically.[73] The Isidorian formulation would be repeated by Rather of Verona, Burchard of Worms, and Ivo of Chartres and paraphrased in the *History of the Bishops of Auxerre* in reference to peasant rebels (the *Capuciati*) of the late twelfth century.[74]

The curse of Noah, therefore, was useful as a justification for slavery, but a less pointed, more generalized theory such as that found in Isidore of Seville, referring to the Fall, could also serve the same purpose. Ham's offense became most important in the Middle Ages when it was mobilized to excuse serfdom, a condition of partial subordination that affected those who were, unlike slaves, recognized in some sense as part of the Christian and local communities. In such a setting, alternative genealogies might be preferable to the universal law of sublapsarian domination.

It is not easy to determine at what point the curse was applied to serfs rather than slaves, largely because of the problem already alluded to of situating a particular moment in which slavery suddenly gave way to serfdom. This difficulty is exacerbated by the use of *servus* by medieval authors to cover both forms of servitude. Thus a group of proverbs and riddling dialogues dating from the ninth to eleventh centuries answer the question of whence came *servi* by making Ham responsible, but who exactly is meant by *servi* depends on our interpretation of the status of unfree rural inhabitants of the post-Carolingian world.[75]

A certain ambiguity concerning the meaning of *servi* is present also in Honorius Augustodunensis. Describing the world's Second Age, Honorius linked knights (*milites*) with Japheth, freemen (*liberi*) with Shem, and *servi* with Ham. While the pairing of *liberi* and *servi* indicates that the latter were unfree, Honorius in all his works was firmly cognizant of the circumstances of his own society. Writing in about 1100 (probably in England), he was most likely thinking of the lower level of agricultural tenants rather than literal slaves.[76]

Noah's curse against Ham became more the preserve of didactic than high theological discourse after the twelfth century, although Alexander of Hales, justifying servitude by the need to teach humility, notes its introduction through Ham.[77] Saint Antoninus (+1439), the Dominican archbishop of Florence, said that servitude was sanctioned by divine law, not merely by the law of nations, as evidenced by Noah's curse against Ham.[78] The curse also circulated among jurists as at least a stylized explanation for the origin of servitude. Thus in the course of elucidating the English common-law action of naifty, the early-fourteenth-century *Mirror of Justices*, acknowledging that serfdom violates natural law, traced it either to Noah and Canaan or to the subjugation of the Philistines by Israel.[79] A manumission document of 1301 from Berne liberated a serf "from the curse of Noah." Similar language appears in an 1123 charter issued by Saint-Maur-des-Fossés.[80]

Generally, however, by the late Middle Ages Ham was a largely literary rather than juridical figure, a symbol of foolishness, inappropriate mockery, and lack of sexual control.[81] He was also identified as the progenitor of servile rustics rather than of slaves narrowly defined. The early-fourteenth-century English poem *Cursor mundi* adopted the model offered by Honorius Augustodunensis:

> Knyht, and thral and fre man
> of these thre britheren bigan;
> Of Sem fre mon, of Iapheth kniht,
> thral of Cam, waryed wihte.[82]

The early-fifteenth-century dialogue *Dives and Pauper* made Ham's mockery and disrespect for his father the origin of bondage and thraldom.[83] Along with Gower's invocation of Ham in the *Vox clamantis*, the best-known English example is that in the "Parson's Tale" where, in the course of pointing out that conquerors make thralls of those born of royal blood, Chaucer says that the institution of thralldom was unknown before Noah made his "son" Canaan subject to his brethren. In Chaucer this comes in connection with a discussion of equality in God's eyes ("As wel may the cherl be saved as the lord"), and no genealogy of servitude is posited. Canaan is the first slave but not the lineal ancestor of all who are unfree.[84] In the Miller's Tale the curse against Ham is given an anticlerical turn when the mocking and lascivious clerk Nicholas makes John the Carpenter play the role of a ludicrous Noah. According to Lee Patterson, the Miller, as a member of the peasantry, answers the courtly myth of peasant degradation by manipulating the image of Ham as astrologer and seeker after forbidden knowledge to apply it to the arrogant clerk. Here again Ham is more a type than the literal father of servility.[85]

Ham's general responsibility for the invention of servitude amounted to something of a cliché in the Middle Ages, but its use was selective. The curse of Noah was especially brought forward in works by German authors, notably didactic poems, such as Hugo von Trimberg's *Der Renner* (ca. 1300) and Konrad von Ammenhausen's reworking of Jacobus de Cessolis's chess allegory, completed around 1337.[86] The curse was also employed in the chronicle by Jansen Enikel in the late thirteenth century, in a satire by Pamphilius Gengenbach in the sixteenth, and in Felix Hemmerli's antipeasant diatribe of the mid–fifteenth century.[87]

On the other hand, Noah, Ham, and Canaan do not figure in discussions of serfdom in Spain, Italy, or (with one exception that I know of) France.[88] Within the German tradition of didactic poetry and antipeasant satire, the curse of Noah was more than a merely conventional symbol. It answered the question of how inequality, more especially servitude, could exist within a community that included neither captives, strangers, nor manifest aliens. The curse is one answer to the conventional observation that all humans were originally (and therefore essentially) equal. By locating a moment in the past such as the subordination of Canaan to his brethren, medieval writers legitimated serfdom by means of the biblical origins of nations.

To whom were such arguments addressed? In satires of peasants or in descriptions of estates the curse reassured townsmen and nobles that the rural inhabitants were degraded justly. They were immediate and genealogical successors of Ham and Canaan. In his one-sided dialogue between a rustic and a knight, Felix Hemmerli has the rustic argue that Noah's curse could not affect indefinite future generations. The noble denies this, demonstrating the persistence of the distinction and reasserting the permanent effect of Canaan's misfortune without directly refuting his interlocutor.[89]

More extensively, Hugo von Trimberg's long poem *Der Renner* recounts a confrontation with a group of inebriated village louts, one of whom asks Hugo why "you lords are so much better off than us poor peasants," and further whether some people are owned while others are free? The reply to the latter query, a simple "yes," angers the rustic, who counters with the familiar argument that all are born of one original mother.[90] It is against this already standard assertion of original equality that Hugo recounts the history of Noah and his sons, rendering the curse thus: "Accursed be Canaan and all his race. They will be the serfs [*eigen knehte*] of my two sons."[91] One of his befuddled interlocutors misunderstands and exclaims "Only now I understand that we must always be an apostate [*vernoyert*] people," thinking that the name Noah (*Noye*) is etymologically related to *vernoyert* and that Noah was the one who was cursed.[92] After correcting this error, Hugo assures the villagers that not only serfs but also Jews, witches, and heathens are offspring of Ham. Nevertheless, unlike these outcasts, the unfree peasants, while cursed on earth, will find their entry into heaven easier than that of their oppressors, for the freedom of the privileged is not of long duration.[93]

While it is unlikely that such a conversation took place in quite this fashion (especially in view of the suspicious alacrity with which the peasants accept Hugo's reasoning), Hugo von Trimberg's poem affords at least an imagined response to familiar denunciations of servitude based on the common origin of humanity in Adam and Eve.

In his mock epic *Der Ring* (written ca. 1400), the Swiss poet Heinrich Wittenwiler imagines a similar conversation but in an exclusively peasant setting, a discussion among the men of the benighted village of Lappenhausen, who are assembled for a war council.[94] When someone points out that according to imperial law a military expedition must be led by a prince, an especially unruly peasant asks whence princes derive their right to rule, for are we not all Adam's children? A relatively wise village elder responds that although all come from Adam and Eve, some are more worthy and have been appointed by the people to rule, just as one of Noah's sons was punished for his ridicule by becoming a bondsman and the others were honored for their virtue and remained free men: "Therefore we are not equal. One is poor, the other rich, one a peasant, the other noble."[95] Once again, the curse of Noah annuls primordial equality. The villagers in *Der Ring* ultimately decide that they constitute their own empire and so can make war, but the poet offers this folly as further proof of their inferiority and hence of the validity of the curse.

By the time of Wittenwiler's poem the connection between contemporary human inequality and scriptural genealogy was venerable and well established. The late-fifteenth-century *Book of St. Albans* invoked the Bible's answer to the assertion of equality at Creation in a discussion of both Cain and Ham as the progenitors of rustics: a "bonde man or a churle" will say we all come from Adam, but one might just as well assert that Lucifer and his followers all came from heaven (and were therefore somehow worthy).[96]

A current of resistance to theories attributing the origins of servitude to Noah's curse did spring up fairly early on, however. Basing his critique on Augustine's *City of God* and Gregory's *Moralia on Job*, Jonas of Orléans in the ninth century denounced the powerful who forget that their subordinates are their equals by nature and that they share the same God. Noah and his sons received dominion over the earth's animal inhabitants, not over other men.[97] Here the opening of Genesis 9 implicitly counters the uses made of verse 25 ("Cursed be Canaan; a servant of servants shall he be unto his brethren"). In the mid–tenth century, Atto of Vercelli, although counseling *servi* to be humble, specifically rejects attributing their status to Ham, who was, after all, the ancestor of kings. Masters and servants are equal by nature, distinguished only by mere names. Servitude comes from worldly iniquity rather than divine precept. The good *servus* is the friend of God, and the wicked master is the servant of the devil.[98]

A similar reassertion of equality and refutation of the genealogy of servitude appeared in a thirteenth-century legal collection, the *Sachsenspiegel.* Here the fundamental texts by which an indelible human equality is affirmed are taken from Gregory the Great. The author of the *Sachsenspiegel,* Eike von Repgow, asserted that human beings were created equal after God's own image, and were all saved equally by Christ's death.[99] Human equality was therefore not erased by either Adam's Fall or Noah's curse. Speaking in the first person, the jurist states that he cannot accept that one man can licitly belong to another. This is preceded by four refutations of attempts to legitimate servitude by biblical authority, specifically by the cases of Cain and Abel; Ham, Shem and Japheth; Ishmael; and Jacob and Esau. All of Cain's descendants, Eike von Repgow points out, perished in the Flood. And the Bible says nothing about any curse or serfdom pertaining to either Ishmael or Esau, even if they were looked upon unfavorably by God. The curse of Noah is irrelevant, according to Eike (here making some crucial alterations to his immediate source, Petrus Comestor), for the Bible does not say Ham was subordinated, and at any rate since his descendants settled in Africa, while Shem remained in Asia, and Japheth came to Europe, the offspring of one do not serve the descendants of the other.[100] Thus what would later appeal to apologists for slavery, namely Ham's migration to Africa, *refuted* serfdom in the thirteenth century, when the problematic of subordination involved Europeans alone and when Africa appeared exotic and remote.[101]

Wyclif contemptuously rejected any effort to trace oppressive lordship to punishment for Cain's or Ham's sin. In his tract "De servitute civili et dominio seculari," written in 1378, he ridicules the notion that Cain was the progenitor of servile orders, for all his descendants perished in the deluge (and Abel is not reported as having any offspring). Some progeny of Shem and Japheth have been unfree, while conversely (as Atto of Vercelli had noted) the line of Ham includes rulers (specifically, according to Wyclif, the Pharaohs).[102] Less upset about the existence of serfdom than Eike von Repgow, however, Wyclif went on to repeat the Pauline assurance that physical servitude does not affect the liberty of the spirit.[103]

Luther, in his commentary on Genesis, has Ham taking over Asia, the largest share of the world, and ruling from Babylon. Canaan, his accursed son, occupied the land later given to the people of Israel, the land in which paradise was located. Luther asserted this in order to show that the righteous may be afflicted while the wicked are, for a time, allowed to prosper. The curse has been "deferred but not removed, in order that the ungodly might fill their measure and feel more smug."[104] Nothing is said here about serfdom, and Ham is situated in Asia rather than Africa, but Luther makes use of the paradox of curse and rulership as found in Wyclif. For Eike von Repgow, Wyclif, and Luther, Ham and his offspring were independent of the favored brothers, so the curse could not mean a literal enslavement nor justify later literal enslavement.

Against such arguments, it may seem surprising that the curse of Noah proved so hardy, outliving the Middle Ages to find new vigor in the American South of the nineteenth century. In part, it endured because it served handily as a sweeping, biblical counter to the sweeping, biblical egalitarian argument of common descent from Adam. It does not have what might be considered an effective legal or constitutional force (as it is rather sweeping and not specific to a particular polity). The curse is found casually and only infrequently in the works of jurists. Its appeal was strongest among didactic writers for whom it answered the best-known peasant argument against exploitative lordship.

The following chapter looks at another refutation of equality, more effective than Noah's curse in the eyes of jurists and historians, but applicable only to certain individual nations: the attribution of serfdom to a secular form of the curse, an event in relatively recent (i.e., nonbiblical) history that conferred liberty and power on those who would subsequently form the nobility and condemned to hereditary servitude those who failed the moment of testing. The event or test was always of a military nature and was linked to what was regarded as the formative period of the nation. It annexed the idea of a single, neat origin for the deprivation of liberty to the deeply held idea by which military capability or the defense of religion gave rise to subsequent privileges. Failure to defend oneself or the true faith placed the timid and insufficiently pious in hereditary servitude.

Chapter 5

National Myths and the Origins of Serfdom

Bravery, Freedom, and Inequality

The curse of Noah might have served to exculpate servitude from the charge of violating divine law and proved useful for explaining the origins of outcast peoples in a general way, but it was too sweeping to be easily applied to specific subordinate groups. One could assert that peasants descended from Ham or Canaan, but this did not address the particular causes of debasement within a given nation or explain why some members of a single polity were unfree.[1]

As medieval kingdoms developed powerful identities, myths of origin proliferated, stories that glorified the epoch of foundation. Such accounts could also manipulate the past to explain why some members of a nation enjoyed privileges while others were deprived of freedom. Myths of origin exalted a national community while defining its social boundaries. Such quasi-historical accounts of national formation were more specific than the universal biblical origins of peoples.

Proclaiming the grandeur of a people, these stories raised and answered questions about inclusion and exclusion: they explained why, within a populace sharing the same language and other apparent marks of identity, there were free and unfree, aristocrats and serfs. In certain medieval realms an invented genealogy served better than biblical precedent to devise an origin for serfdom, for the problem was not the abstract one of how subjugation came into the world, but specifically the reasons for division *within* France, Catalonia, or another nation. It was relatively easy to explain on the basis of Roman law or biblical precedent why Saracens, Africans, or even captive subjugated foreign Christians should be unfree, but unlike slavery, serfdom generally affected those who at least appeared to be of similar origin to their masters.

Moreover, the very act of extolling a nation as favored by God prompted the question of why some members of that glorious community were nevertheless subjugated. If Catalans, Hungarians, or Franks had descended from heroes, why were they not equal, or at the very least all free? The work of building a corporate identity had to address these questions, and did so most frequently by creating myths of exclusion to justify division.[2]

One strategy in such mythologizing was to type the original conquered population and their descendants as servile by emphasizing right of conquest or by arbitrarily creating an ethnic difference. Such explanations were promulgated in ninth- and tenth-century Saxony, gained at least slight currency in England, enjoyed considerable sway in medieval (and for that matter modern) Ireland, and accompanied the Catalan conquest of parts of Greece in the fourteenth century.[3]

Theories of this sort worked where a clear linguistic difference existed or where a conquest had taken place relatively recently. They were less effective in countries without radical internal language differences, or where such differences did not mirror distinctions of status.[4] The most interesting approach to exclusionary myth-building, from our point of view, sought a moment in the legendary past to serve as the point of original differentiation among the particular nation's social strata, much as the moment of Noah's malediction functioned for universal history. The chosen moment, however, would be situated in relatively recent historical rather than biblical time. Moreover, it would be founded on a believable event particular to that nation.

With the exception of England, one tends to find *either* mythical origins of servitude *or* biblical origins but not both in any given nation. In Germany, as has been seen, Noah's curse enjoyed considerable popularity. In Catalonia and Hungary, where national mythologies of servitude were strongest, the curse was unremarked if not literally unknown. France created the form that national legends of the origin of serfdom would take, although Catalonia and Hungary gave them more elaborate life, for in these countries serfdom flourished during the late Middle Ages rather than waning as it did in France. All three countries, however, preferred Charlemagne to Noah as the author of privilege and subjugation.

In England one finds the curse associated with the peasantry in literature,[5] but in the actual discussion of serfdom in the fourteenth century, or in justifications of later revolutionary or reform movements (in the seventeenth and nineteenth centuries, for example), the Norman Conquest was held far more responsible than biblical events for oppression (the "Norman Yoke" theory) or for the subsequent wicked concealment of liberty (by appeals to Domesday Book and the royal demesne).[6]

Myths of Legitimation

The Middle Ages had a notorious predilection for historical fabrications. Until recently historians were inclined to dismiss them as amusing examples of credulity, ahistoricity, or talent at forgery. The medieval fondness for fantasy and invention used to be contrasted to the Renaissance's supposed penchant for demythologizing and unmasking historical forgeries. The reality of temporal distance and cultural difference replaced Gothic anachronistic manipulation of the past: Lorenzo Valla at work demonstrating that the Donation of Constantine was forged.

It is now evident that the sixteenth century, its philological advances notwithstanding, yielded to no other period in its fondness for ingenious, circular, and spectacularly erroneous historical theorizing.[7] Historians of our own day are interested in the creation of useful pasts, viewed as products not of naiveté but of the appeal and malleability of the so-called "imagined community," an artifice of national sentiment.[8] Another somewhat over-used term, "the invention of tradition," takes its name from an influential collection of articles demonstrating that modern and contemporary states devised plausible rituals and iconographies to legitimate monarchy, nationalism, or colonial rule.[9] If putative Trojan origins of superior persons or populations were no longer likely to be swallowed, then credible "ancient traditions" such as Scottish clan tartans or the English coronation rite could be created nearly ex nihilo, demonstrating that recent centuries too permitted and even encouraged historical fantasies.

Artificial traditions and invented histories usually amount to something more than erudite musings. Above all, they are fantasies of legitimation, attempting to read back into the authoritative past an assertion of privilege and domination or (as with such minority nationalities within modern nation-states as the Welsh) of cultural uniqueness. They arise to prove specific images of collective identity: who constitutes a people or kingdom, where they came from, and what their imputed character may be.

The decline of historiographic positivism has turned attention to the process of historical invention and given it the status of a narrative not to be easily separated from "reliable" history. As the boundaries between literature and history have become permeable, it is easier to view the latter as a rhetorical strategy, a discourse of contingency and manipulation, rather than a science.

A respect for what is at stake in contested versions of history has produced important studies of how historical legends were formed and used. Susan Reynolds has shown the significance of medieval myths of the origins of peoples.[10] Miquel Coll i Alentorn and Thomas Bisson have described legends concerning the foundation of Catalonia and their uses.[11] Peter Linehan has not only collected medieval Spanish historiographic forgeries and pieties but shown how they were perpetuated into contemporary times.[12] The uses of dynastic saints and the identification of kingdom with conversion in east central Europe has been studied by Gábor Klaniczay.[13] The legends underlying the identity of the French nation have been elaborated by Colette Beaune, while Gabrielle Spiegel has depicted the struggles between royal and noble history writing and the role of genre and language in political controversy.[14]

The authors of these impressive works differ as to how annoying or how useful they find the accretion of unreliable tradition, rather as different viewers react differently to exuberant architectural styles such as the flamboyant Gothic or Sicilian Baroque. For Linehan, there is fakery and there is truth. The former is to be stripped away to reveal the austere bare wood of reliable fact. According to this view historical fictions may be amusing, and what prompted them is worth exploration, but they interfere with an accurate vision of medieval reality. For Spiegel, on the other hand, historical manipulation *is* the fact. There are no innocent or objective readings of the past to be restored.

From a vast body of historical invention, as well as the varied recent studies of it, I wish to extract a small group of ideas relating to the subjugation of peasants. Their subordination cannot be completely separated from what medieval writers were most concerned with: praising the nobility and demonstrating the supposed moral and historical basis for their privileges. Texts describing the establishment of a nation, kingdom, or people justified the polity by means of antiquity, genealogy, or some set of foundational acts. Classical antecedents (Aeneas's grandson Brutus in England, Hercules in Spain) provided illustrious origins by reason of high birth, learning (taking the polity back beyond the barbarians), and connection with the sources of literary and philosophical heroism. Biblical searches for ancestors were encouraged by the genealogies of nations in the Book of Genesis. Biblical and classical figures could be blended, as in Spain, where both Noah's grandson Tubal (Genesis 10:2) and Hercules supposedly figured in the settlement of Iberia.[15] The English chronicler Robert Mannyng "proved" that Brutus, founder of England, was directly descended from Noah.[16]

The prevailing myths therefore justified occupation of the land and extolled its current inhabitants. They also tended to legitimate the privileges of the nobles. For this task events with some recognizable historical specificity were more useful than biblical or classical antecedents. In Catalonia, where the foundational era was identified with Charlemagne, the French literary figure of Ogier le Danois was transformed into "Otger Cataló," who, with his nine noble companions, fought the Moors south of the Pyrenees *before* the arrival of Charlemagne. Otger Cataló gave his name to the newly liberated land, and the progeny of his comrades became the high nobility of Catalonia; hence Catalonia was presented as essentially a nobles' creation. This challenged a comital myth ascribing the foundation of Catalonia to the historically genuine Guifré "the Hairy."[17] In France, the nobility rejoined royal historiography with "truer" accounts of French history not only by proving their ancestors' independence of the monarch but by subsidizing vernacular prose chronicles.[18]

Aristocracy, genealogy, and fanciful history have certain natural affinities and are found in many medieval historical narratives. More unusual is the corollary explanation for the *privation* of liberty, why some members of the collectivity did not share what was won at the crucial moment of origin. At a particular historical moment a genealogy of privilege and servitude was established by a test of bravery and martial skill. Military success and courage were crucial to winning hereditarily transmissible high status, while timidity or desertion justified the imposition of a heritable *loss* of freedom. A trial of courage and valor had to be situated at the real or mythical establishment of the nation whose political birth included its hierarchical differentiation.

Legitimation was built into any narrative that exalted a people. Celebrating the accomplishments of a population required explaining who really was included in this supposedly superior nation. For an abstract theory of social order, mutual service and the tripartite division might illustrate why lordship and servitude were providential. Within a nation whose virtue and vigor (*strenuitas*) were surpassing, however, servitude could not so easily be justified. Aristocracy needed to stem from a violent assertion of right, not develop as a functional category within an organic metaphor. This violent assertion was legitimate and virtuous but expressed aggression rather than reasonableness.[19] The aristocracy proved through their character that they possessed indelible moral strength, so that this class alone represented the virtue of the nation.

Bravery and freedom were conjoined in something more violent than the uplifting generalities common to modern national pieties such as the American national anthem, which describes the United States as the "land of the free and the home of the brave," or "Rule Britannia," in which naval supremacy is joined to liberty and national character. In a society with a multiplicity of special, chartered liberties, privileges, and exemptions, hierarchical difference was not submerged in equality of citizenship or patriotic solidarity (except within local communities such as a particular valley). Liberty resulted from an act of bravery, not just constitutionally (through a declaration or war of independence) but as a moral reward for valor hereditarily transmissible into posterity. The political existence of Catalonia did not have to be traced to a formal act of the fictional Otger Cataló and his noble companions. Their successful wars against the Saracens began decades before Charlemagne could be thought to have validated titles to nobility. The moral and political order of Catalonia were symbolized by a made-up etymology, not by a particular document or moment of institutional foundation.[20] The legitimating significance of bravery was not exclusively the prerogative of the nobility. Not only did medieval cities boast of their (usually fictitious) origins, but (as we shall see), such peasant communities as managed to achieve independence from seigneurial domination elaborated their own stories of heroic resistance (such as the legend of William Tell) or of military victories that secured freedom.[21] In Hungary, a nobles' myth of servitude as the result of failure to perform military service was answered by the reproaches of peasant crusaders in the fifteenth and early sixteenth centuries, who insisted that they fought against the Turks (and even occasionally won) while the nobles failed to fight the common enemy and continued their extortionate lordship over fellow Christians.

France and the 'Pseudo-Turpin Chronicle'

If nobles' ancestors demonstrated courage at the foundation of the polity, serfs were the unfortunate descendants of those found wanting in the military emergency. Their crime was timidity rather than treason, refusal to fight rather than some wicked but violent deed such as Ganelon's. In keeping with the image of the peasant as militarily incapable and essentially harmless (despite his frightening and distorted appearance), an original act of cowardice condemned peasants to servitude. The timidity of *vilains* was a well-established literary theme especially in France.[22] The emasculation of rustics was therefore not a natural condition in an Aristotelian sense, nor the result of a separate ethnogenesis, but the outcome of a historical moment of testing. Failure resulted in a licit and appropriate punishment: the perpetuation of servitude as a concomitant of military incapability.

The first explanation of serfdom based on a supposed historical lack of nerve appears in the story of Charlemagne's Spanish campaigns in the *Historia Karoli Magni et Rotholandi*, more commonly known as the *Pseudo-Turpin Chronicle*, first composed in Latin probably in the early twelfth century. It purports to be an account composed by the bellicose Archbishop Turpin, who figures memorably in *The Song of Roland*.[23] No fewer than six separate translations into French were made by scholars working for various Flemish aristo-crats in the early thirteenth century. The most popular of these translations, accomplished before 1206, was that of a certain "Master Johannes." The Jo-hannes version subsequently was added to as well as abbreviated. Pierre de Beauvais joined to the already eclectic Turpin narrative a translation and reworking of an earlier text, the *Descriptio qualiter Karolus Magnus clavum et coronam Domini a Constantinopoli Aquisgrani detulerit*, an account of Charlemagne's supposed expedition to liberate Jerusalem and receive the im-perial crown from Constantinople.[24] Pierre de Beauvais's adaptation of the Jo-hannes version was itself abbreviated in a form referred to as the "Descriptio-Turpin."[25]

The Pseudo-Turpin material mentions both a foundational liberation of those previously serfs and the enserfment of those previously free. In the "Descriptio-Turpin," Charlemagne offers freedom to serfs (as well as prison-ers and other lowly people) who will aid his expedition to fight King Agolant of Pamplona.[26] The obverse of this act of enfranchisement is taken from a re-lated *Descriptio* of Charlemagne's journey to the East found only in the Pierre de Beauvais and modified Johannes accounts (which were, however, widely diffused). In Pierre de Beauvais, Charlemagne orders that those who are ca-pable of bearing arms but do not accompany him to Constantinople will owe the four *deniers* that denote the servile payment of *chevage*. Not only will they have to make this payment during their lifetimes but it will be an obligation incumbent on their descendants as well.[27] In the "Descriptio-Turpin" debase-ment to servitude is more explicit: those who did not respond to the sum-mons were to be serfs, they and their heirs in perpetuity.[28]

Also in the early thirteenth century, shortly after 1211, the *Chanson de Gui de Bourgogne* traced the origins of serfdom to a form of early retirement from Charlemagne's army.[29] After 27 years of fighting the Moors, his troops com-plained of fatigue. Charlemagne grudgingly allowed anyone who wished to do so to return to his lands, but only on condition that he and his posterity henceforth be considered serfs:

> But I want them to know one thing in truth
> By the faith that I owe to holy Christianity
> It is that all their lineage will be unfree serfs
> All the days of their life they will be known as serfs.[30]

The offer was accepted by 4,700 soldiers, all of them Gascons and Angevins (an evident display of regional prejudices). The author goes on to observe that these were the first recorded serfs.[31]

A century later the *Roman de Renart le Contrefait* returned to the suggestion of Pseudo-Turpin by making the original crime cowardice rather than desertion.[32] In the first redaction of the *Roman*, the primal serfs were those who refused to follow Charlemagne's armed pilgrimage to Santiago to battle the Saracens. The author claimed (this time motivated presumably by anti-bourgeois sentiment) that in Paris there were now a thousand of their descendants.[33]

The second redaction offers a more extensive and peculiar account. At confession, Renart bewails the pride and rapacity of knights and acknowledges that he has himself extorted servile payments (*mainmorte, formariage, taille*). Posing the question of the origin of serfdom, Renart locates it, as was by now customary, with Charlemagne. Followers were summoned to accompany him to Santiago. The muster was held at a then-deserted valley known as Apremont, site of the future town of Provins. Many among the host were reluctant to fulfill their obligations and wished to stay and settle Apremont. These "cowards of Apremont," some 16,000 souls, preferred to pay tallage rather than to risk their lives. Charlemagne allowed this (and added to their number the *ribauds* and dice-players expelled from his army), but they were "condemned" to pay the tallage, another indication of servitude.[34] Tacked on to this was the account of the city built by these serfs, Provins, and the etymology of its name. When Charlemagne returned, he remarked with amazement how well set up the town appeared:

> The king remarked, "They have worked well,
> And by God they've shown themselves [*prouvé*] well."
> And because of this, the place is called Provins.

Here the object of aristocratic disdain was not Paris but one of the Champagne Fair towns.[35]

What had begun as a literary-historical formulation found its way into legal theories of the beginning of serfdom. In Beaumanoir's late-thirteenth-century *Customs of Beauvaisis*, which would have authority as a legal compilation well outside the region, several origins are advanced for the deprivation of liberty characteristic of serfdom: serfs are descended from those captured in battle (an account based on Roman law), or from those forced into servitude by wicked lords, or from those who placed themselves in voluntary servitude (for reasons of poverty or piety), or from those who had failed to heed a royal call to arms (or had fled from a battle).[36]

By the time of the last Capetians, the association of servitude with a historical crime was sufficiently well established for it to be referred to offhandedly. The preamble to the royal letters of commission for administering the enfranchisements of 1315 and 1318 speaks of the "misdeed" of the ancestors of contemporary serfs meriting privation of liberty but observes that such privation contradicts natural law and the very name of Frank ("free").[37]

As Marc Bloch has pointed out, the eloquence of this document does not disguise the fact that enfranchisements were a means of raising money rather than acts of gracious beneficence. Nevertheless, the grouping of ideas in the preamble demonstrates the transformation of a literary into a legal assumption, and the peculiar interplay of juridical, literary, and religious sources.

In Roman as well as Carolingian laws, one finds precedents for the notion that treason, desertion, or other military dereliction should be punished by servitude (in these instances slavery). Servitude is what traitors deserve, according to several chapters of the *Digest*.[38] In late Frankish law, the failure to answer a military summons (*heribannum*) could lead to enslavement if the offender could not pay the normal fine; ignoring a general levy in the event of an invasion (a crime called *lantweri*) was punishable by death or enslavement.[39] For desertion (*herisliz*), the normal punishment was death, although this could also be commuted to perpetual slavery.[40] But these legal sanctions do not completely explain the appeal of associating cowardice with serfdom, an association suggested by the theological idea of a sin committed in the past that continues to affect morally the descendants of the sinner. Thus the cowardice of peasant ancestors is a secular, "national" version of the Curse of Noah, if not of the Fall itself. The association also results from consideration of freedom and privilege. It is not surprising that the *Pseudo-Turpin Chronicle* is both the first place in which military failure explains serfdom and the first source to identity the etymology of "France" as "terre franche," land of the free.[41]

The alliance of bravery with freedom and of cowardice with servitude plays itself out in both legal and pseudohistorical literary texts. The paradigm has certain limitations; thus Louis X and Phillip V seem to indicate in the preambles to their enfranchisements that even if servitude was merited for the original misdeed, its eternal perpetuation was not. In Catalonia, where the Pseudo-Turpin material would be adapted to a more dangerous and disputed situation, the king of Aragon in 1388, desiring the freedom of the servile population, seemed prepared to argue that the sentence of degradation had a limit, that "the time of servitude has already passed," and ordered his archivist to find the documents to prove it (presumably in the form of original records enacting the sentence).[42] If the medieval period for the most part did not share the tendencies of modern racism to posit literal biological distinction, it placed the moment of division far enough back in the historical past to account for the marked, physical difference of the servile population. The historical moment, however, was not so removed as to erase all trace of original equality. The peasant and the lord were still in some fundamental sense equal, especially where there was no obvious or relatively recent conquest to encourage a theory of "ethnic" differentiation.

~~~

In Catalonia and Hungary, the French myth of an original act of cowardice was appropriated in the context of an extension and hardening of servile tenurial arrangements. Whereas thirteenth and fourteenth-century France saw widespread emancipation of serfs in return for payments to the royal treasury, Catalonia and Hungary gradually inflicted servitude on previously free populations, restricted freedom of movement, and defined a subordinate legal status out of what had been miscellaneous seigneurial exactions.[43] Historical myths were elaborated to defend the extension of servile institutions and so are found in chronicles and legal writings rather than in religious, didactic, or literary works, the habitat of Noah's curse.

Medieval jurists eagerly consumed opportunistic reworkings of national history.[44] In France, as previously noted, Beaumanoir was content to cite ancestral cowardice as one of several possible explanations for a social condition that was becoming less widespread. For Hungarian and Catalan jurists, however, a fairly urgent problem presented itself: how to explain and justify a seemingly anomalous condition contradicting the supposed liberties of the *gens*, a condition that, far from dying out, continued to define lordship and its economic perquisites. In both territories, legends of heroic foundations already existed, so not only did serfdom have to be fit retrospectively into a glorious epic of foundation, but the jury-rigging had to be accomplished without shaming or tainting all the heirs of the imagined past. To paraphrase the Hungarian jurists' formulation: how could nobles and serfs emerge within one nation, from one historical moment?

Catalonia

I have elsewhere tried to describe the Catalan explanations for servitude and how they were shaped by jurists to suit older foundation myths.[45] The inspiration for linking serfdom to an original act of cowardice seems to have come from the *Pseudo-Turpin Chronicle*. The Latin version of Pseudo-Turpin was known in Catalonia as early as 1173, when a copy was made at the monastery of Ripoll.[46] The Carolingian era was always an ambiguous foundational period for Catalonia. On the one hand, the Franks had freed the core territory from Islam. On the other hand, the Franks ruled as oppressors and were useless in fighting Islam, according to the first and most widely diffused legend: the independence from the Franks won by Count Guifré "the Hairy." At some point between 1160 and 1184, the *Gesta comitum Barcinonensium* made Guifré the Hairy—a real ninth-century count of Barcelona—the founder of Catalan independence. The *Gesta* claimed that Guifré's father had been murdered by Franks who were supposed to escort him to the royal court to stand trial for killing a noble who had insulted him. When he grew up, Guifré was able to return to his home and overthrow the Frankish count. Still obedient, however, Guifré effected a reconciliation with the king of France. When the Saracens invaded the county of Barcelona, Guifré received from the king, who was unable to help him, a promise that if he could drive the Saracens out unassisted, he might have the county free of any tie to France.[47]

Charlemagne therefore did not figure in the earliest Catalonian narratives of foundation. This was in part because the *Gesta* reflected the memory of the events in 985 and the years immediately following, when Barcelona was sacked and burned by forces of the rulers of Muslim Córdoba and the feeble last Carolingian and first Capetian monarchs failed to come to the aid of the beleaguered count of Barcelona.[48] The *Gesta* thus conflated an embroidered version of the career of the ninth-century Guifré I with the last recognition of Frankish lordship in 985–87, when Count Borrell asked for military aid to no avail. The retreat of Islam and subsequent victories against it were annexed to an earlier achievement of de facto independence. The heroic legendary foundation of Catalonia partakes of the common pairing of courage and liberty by means of a test in which endurance and victory in military adversity establishes a permanent right to privileged independence.

Beginning in the thirteenth century, the foundational moment was extended further back to Charlemagne, while two complementary legends were created to offer a basis for both nobles' privileges and peasants' subjugation. In the *Crònica de Espanya*, written in 1268 by Pere Ribera of Perpignan, it was Charlemagne who began the task of liberating Spain from the Saracens. Charlemagne's work was followed up by Guifré, who was unaided by the emperor's weaker successors (from this point the *Crònica* follows the course laid out by the *Gesta*).[49] Although Charlemagne in fact never set foot in the future Catalonia, the Christian conquest of the Marca Hispanica did take place during his reign. His exalted reputation made it difficult to ignore his role in the establishment of Catalonia and also placed Catalans in the grand narrative of European chivalric history.[50] While from the point of view of the counts of Barcelona it was important to distance Catalonia from its Frankish antecedents (France would continue to make claims on Catalonia intermittently to the time of Napoleon), Charlemagne and his immediate successors sanctioned Catalan institutions far more effectively than could recherché, local tenth-century events and personages.

Two legal comments on the origins of servitude demonstrate how the Frankish era could be used in defense of the enserfment of one group of Catalans by another. They are contained in a fifteenth-century Escorial manuscript of the enactments of the Catalan parliament (*Corts*). The first is a gloss to the constitution "Item quod in terris sive locis" of the Barcelona parliament of 1283, which restricted movement of servile seigneurial and ecclesiastical tenants to royal land. The anonymous jurist explains why these tenants are subject to "redemption," a manumission payment necessary for them to leave the lord's jurisdiction, which served as a key index of servile status. He does so by means of a historical excursus.[51] When the Saracens occupied Spain, they held the Christian population captive (*quasi captiuos*), forcing them to make redemption payments and other services. "Christian princes" (not at this point further specified) came to restore this territory to the Faith, but the timid captive population ignored the call to help the liberating armies.[52] The Christian princes conquered anyway, and although they had the right simply to kill the peasants who were now *their* captives, they mercifully chose instead to perpetuate the servile conditions first imposed by Muslims.[53] The gloss evidently dates from the very late thirteenth or early fourteenth century, for it appears to be prior to another gloss by Bertran de Ceva, datable to the early fourteenth century (see below).

Clearly this theory derives from Roman law, according to which being taken captive in battle was one of the few ways in which free men could be degraded into slavery.[54] The gloss also refers to the Roman legal commonplace that *servus* is derived from *servare*—that the captives were "preserved" rather than being killed.[55] In common with most medieval lawyers, the anonymous author of this gloss willingly and indiscriminately applied the law of slavery to the situation of serfs, even though Catalonia harbored a substantial slave population (comprising North Africans, Tartars, Sardinians, Greeks, and Caucasians), so that the difference between the two forms of dependence was in practice obvious.[56] The author, however, was not content simply to refer in general to captivity in battle as the origin of serfdom, but rather situated it at a precise (if vaguely defined) moment of testing in which failure to heed the summons to battle amounted to treason or apostasy, punishable by means reminiscent of the Fall or Noah's curse.

The same Escorial manuscript contains a short commentary on certain customary laws of Catalonia, which offers another version of the legend that is more precise as to the foundational event. The author of this brief work, the *Consuetudines Cathaloniae*, was Bertran de Ceva, a jurist active in the early fourteenth century.[57] Here Charlemagne appears specifically as the liberator of the territories up to the Llobregat River (corresponding to medieval Old Catalonia). Responding to the proposal simply to kill the captives, Charlemagne points out that nobles cannot be expected to cultivate the land (a backhanded acknowledgment that peasants labor for the benefit of the entire society, which could not survive without them).[58]

The legendary account of the origins of serfdom would be transmitted from legal to historical works in the fifteenth century, and survive as a believable explanation into the nineteenth century.[59] This should not obscure the more immediate usefulness it enjoyed as a bulwark against attacks on seigneurial rights in the late Middle Ages. From the time of King Joan's efforts to obtain the end of serfdom on church lands in 1388 to the end of the successful peasant rebellion in 1486, which led to the abolition of peasant servitude, Catalonia was bitterly divided over serfdom. Members of the royal court in the early fifteenth century denounced it as bringing infamy to Catalonia, and peasant agitation combated serfdom even before the outbreak of open war in 1462. The cowardly-peasants legend would be popularized by the historian Pere Tomich in his writings of 1438, where he made Louis the Pious (who, unlike Charlemagne, had actually campaigned in the future Catalonia) the author of the punishment and dated it to 814.[60] The influential jurist Joan de Socarrats, commenting in 1476 (during the Catalan peasant uprising) on the primary collection of Catalan law governing lords and vassals, restated Bertran de Ceva's formulation of the origins of serfdom.[61]

The heightened atmosphere of the fifteenth-century Catalan conflicts over serfdom (and between the crown and the nobles) encouraged the formation of a parallel legend of the origins of noble privilege. The legend of Otger Cataló and his nine barons appears to have been developed from older material in the early fifteenth century to portray the nobility rather than the counts of Barcelona as the real founders of Catalonia.[62] After Charles Martel's victory at Poitiers, a group of nobles maintained a guerrilla war against the Saracens. After Charlemagne's invasion, the emperor rewarded the warriors by dividing the now conquered territory among them. This land was named "Catalonia" in honor of their fallen leader, Otger Cataló (an etymology frequently questioned but largely accepted until the nineteenth century). Not surprisingly, the names of Otger's captains corresponded to those of the great houses of the High Middle Ages.

The Otger legend did not say anything about the peasants, but by crediting the achievement of the first victories against the Moors to the nobles, it legitimated aristocratic privilege. Courage in the era of Charlemagne was rewarded while fear was punished. In 1438 the historian Tomich combined Otger and the cowardly-peasants legend to make explicit the simultaneous origins of privilege and subjugation. He gave much more attention to the heroic story, but the two legends together explained the internal divisions among Catalans.[63] Gabriel Turell's chronicle, *Recort*, written in 1476, derived a succinct constitutional statement from the two histories: that Charlemagne had established the liberties of Catalonia for the brave and highly born, not for the rustics or "the common mob."[64]

The question of how members of the same *gens* could be of such different social conditions was thus answered. Rather than inventing a racial or historical theory that would posit different ethnic origins for serfs and nobles, the Catalan account imitated biblical teachings by identifying the founding of social orders within the creation of the nation, orders distinguished by valor versus cowardice. A primordial act established a constitutional basis for differentiation of status and removed the subjugated from the definition of Catalan at least as regarded the liberties of Catalonia, thus excusing serfdom while saving Catalonia's military reputation.

That this was not ultimately morally acceptable is shown by the peasants' civil-war victory in alliance with the monarch, a victory eventually followed by the abolition sentence of 1486. Nevertheless, despite the bitterness of that conflict and the ideological strength of the nobles' resistance, there was a wide area of agreement about what constituted a basis for freedom and acceptance. All agreed that human beings were by nature equal. That the *ius gentium* excused subjugation of captives encouraged seigneurial apologists to call the ancestors of the serfs "captives," but more than this, they asserted the contingent nature of freedom as the result of courage and bondage as a consequence of timidity.

Hungary

A similar legend was elaborated in Hungary, where a series of peasant revolts and near-revolts would also take place, preceding a general insurrection in 1514. Suppression of the 1514 uprising would result in the enserfment of the Hungarian peasantry according to laws drafted in light of the same French historical justifications that were taken up less successfully in Catalonia.

As in Catalonia, in Hungary military failure set in a foundational past was used by historians and lawyers to account for social difference. It was supposed that the ancestors of the Magyars held an annual military muster and that failure to attend was punished by death, banishment, or hereditary servitude. Those who were of lower condition (later specifically serfs) descended from those Hungarians who had failed in this test of valor.

The introduction of the legendary origins of serfs can be pinpointed more precisely in Hungary than in Catalonia. Simon of Kéza, court chaplain to King Ladislas "the Cuman," composed a Hungarian history that elaborated a heroic pre-Christian past.[65] The *Gesta Hungarorum* was written between 1282 and 1285, at approximately the same time that the parliament meeting in Barcelona enacted the fundamental legislation for Catalan serfdom. Simon obtained some of his material from earlier Latin chronicles written in Hungary, but, as studies of the labyrinthine textual history of these early chronicles have shown, they do not represent any genuine folk tradition of the migration or conversion periods but are rather congeries of antiquarian learning.[66] Simon was original in attempting to explain the aristocratic privileges of his era by reference to a specific foundational practice.[67] He was most interested in explaining the prerogatives of the nobles; since serfdom was scarcely developed, his concern with the lower orders was minimal. Nevertheless, his distinction between nobles and everyone else would be useful in elaborating justifications for a sharper contrast between noble and unfree nearer to the end of the medieval period.

Simon was also the first Hungarian chronicler to celebrate the fictitious link between Magyars and Huns, a notion current in the West from shortly after the Hungarian invasions began at the end of the ninth century. By the time of the *Nibelungenlied*, written in Austria or Bavaria shortly after 1200, the inhabitants of Hungary were referred to as "Huns" and were confused with the real Huns, who had warred against the Burgundians in late antiquity. The *Nibelungenlied* depicted the Huns in positive terms. Their king, Etzel, was pagan, but they were chivalrous, wealthy, and hospitable. Their war with the Burgundians was caused by Kriemhild's revenge upon her Burgundian brothers for their murder of her husband, Siegfried, not by their aggression.[68]

Despite the changed image of the Huns, early Hungarian historians were reluctant to accept what still seemed an unflattering association. "Magister P.," an anonymous source for much of Simon's work, acknowledged the possibility of some institutional relationship with the Huns but was unwilling to make them the literal ancestors of the Magyars.[69] Simon, on the other hand, embraced the notion of barbarian ancestors. He took advantage of the established pivotal significance of the conversion of the Hungarians (conventionally dated from King Stephen's reception of a crown from Pope Sylvester II in 1000), an event contrasting with (but also in some sense preserving) the customs of warlike barbarian forebears. King Stephen became a saintlier version of Clovis, the leader of a successful barbarian people newly and fervently converted.

Much in the manner of the Catalans, the Hungarians made use of such possibilities as already existed in established literature (such as the *Nibelungenlied*) to connect themselves to the prestigious figures in the dominant cultural realms of medieval Europe. Of course Charlemagne really did have something to do with Catalonia, and the Catalan legends of social foundation were presented in a more or less recognizable historical setting. The Catalans also could produce a legend that made use of the Christian struggle against Islam. Although in both realms Christianity was joined to the establishment of the nation, the Hungarians had at one time been pagan, while the proto-Catalans were Christians who had liberated territory from Islam. Even if the Hungarian state, in common with others of east-central Europe, was thought of as coming into existence with the conversion of its kings, it was possible to imagine and invent a preconversion Hungarian past of permanent constitutional significance (as indeed was the case for the various Germanic tribes). The Catalans, in contrast, did not have a mythologized existence prior to Charlemagne (they rarely displayed any interest in their Visigothic antecedents).

Hence Hungarian serfdom would be located in a Hunnish past well before the arrival of Christianity. According to Simon of Kéza, following earlier authors, the Huns descended from Noah's son Japheth through Magog and more proximately from the brothers "Magor" (whence Magyar) and "Hunor" (Hun).[70] Simon, however, distinguished between "pure" and "mixed" Hungarians. The pure were descended from 108 original clans (108 being the number of noble families established in a tabulation of 1280).[71] The others were at least partially descended from foreign nobles and war captives. Although he seems here to establish a quasi-ethnic division into superior and inferior levels, Simon does not use the opportunity to propose a different ancestry for nobles and non-nobles. He specifically tells us that both are found among pure and mixed Hungarians, that both form part of the Hungarian *natio*.

In addition to the "pure" and "mixed" division, Simon of Kéza made use of the French theme of serfdom resulting from cowardice, transposing the moment of testing, however, into Hunnish customary times. In the year 700, we are informed, the Huns elected captains and began their movement westward from Scythia, selecting a leader, Kadar, who disciplined and shaped the army. At this time the Huns established the custom of sending emissaries to call the population to a military "muster" (literally, to attend, armed, a general council). Those who failed to obey the summons without good reason were subject to one of three punishments according to the "Lex Scitica": being cut in two with a plowshare, degraded by banishment, or degraded to servile status.[72]

Although Simon's reference to the year 700 confers some precision on his account, only by implication does his text date the supposed beginnings of degradation as a military penalty to this period. More importantly, to explain the origin of a servile population, he posited not an original act of cowardice corresponding to the failure of the Catalan "captives" to heed Charlemagne's call, but only a more general unwillingness to engage in military activity.

Bearing arms and fighting the enemies of the nation merited the privileges of liberty, while refusal to do so led to hereditary servitude, hence separation from the original egalitarian community. While the alleged laws of the Huns might not have been maintained intact in the period after the conversion, they nonetheless permanently identified the medieval kingdom and its society and served as constitutional myths. Simon concludes with a formulation of the problem answered by his history: it was one's own wicked actions that differentiated one Hungarian from another, "for how else, since one father and mother procreated all Hungarians, could one of them be called noble, another ignoble, unless he were held to be guilty of such a crime?"[73] Here Simon is interested in the contrast between the nobility and everyone else, rather than the specific origin of serfdom. Like all the other foundational myths we have noted, the Hungarian version aimed chiefly to laud noble origins and justify privilege rather than to theorize about the peasantry, but as we shall see, Simon's account would later be used as a historical explanation for the existence of the unfree.

Simon of Kéza's sources for the differentiation of estates were French and Italian, certainly not Hungarian. No single text had the specific influence that the *Pseudo-Turpin Chronicle* exerted in Catalonia. Jenő Szűcs has demonstrated Simon's familiarity with both literary and legal learning of France and Italy.[74] Simon visited Germany and France and served as an emissary to Charles of Anjou upon his arrival in Calabria from Tunis after the failed crusade and death of Louis IX (1270). Simon was the first Hungarian historian to use a French toponym (Châlons) and was eager to show how up-to-date he was. So he neither wrote in isolation nor shaped an already extant popular tradition. He placed Hungary in the mainstream of historical explanations for the differentiation of estates and privileges. The threefold punishments of his tale reflect the influence of Roman law (the *Lex Iulia maiestatis*) more than any "Lex Scitica." Next to the barbaric method of execution by colter is the technical formulation of banishment and an imitation of Roman degradation by enslavement in the mines.[75] The *Roman de Renart* as well as the older *Gui de Bourgogne* and *Pseudo-Turpin* were all in circulation at this time and must have suggested to Simon (much as to the anonymous Catalan jurist who commented on the 1283 parliamentary legislation) the possibility of ascribing to a formative historical era the contemporary social division.[76]

The enduring contribution of Simon of Kéza's history was to enshrine the supposed Hunnish origins of the Magyars. The separation of noble from non-noble on the basis of the military summons would also become canonical, but gradually and through reformulation over centuries. The 1358 *Chronica de Gestis Hungarorum* (known as *The Hungarian Illuminated Chronicle*) repeats almost verbatim the story and conclusion of Simon of Kéza.[77] There are a few differences, however. The penalty of execution is absent (only banishment and servitude appear), and the chronology has changed to place the invention of Hungarian institutions at the historically attested time of the Huns. Whereas Simon of Kéza had located the westward migrations and election of Kadar in the eighth century, the *Illuminated Chronicle* placed them in the reign of Valens, 373 A.D.

A more significant alteration occurred in the late fifteenth century, when the condition of the servile population and the privileges of the nobles with regard to the king were more contested than when Simon of Kéza wrote. In the *Chronica Hungarorum*, by János Thuróczy, the response to the military muster was the origin not merely of noble and non-noble but of noble and serf.[78] Most of the relevant chapter in Thuróczy repeats the history told by Simon of Kéza. It is now a specific edict from the era of Kadar as well as custom that mandated the three punishments for failure to obey the summons. Thuróczy records a picturesque detail: a bloody sword was brandished by the messenger who announced the armed assembly, a gathering that in Thuróczy is both a deliberative body and the muster for a military expedition.[79] In accord with earlier accounts, Thuróczy says that the custom of the three punishments persisted until the time of Géza (grandson of the dynastic founder Arpád, father of the Stephen who converted to Christianity). He added the observation that by means of this custom, many had been reduced to perpetual "rusticity."[80] The final rhetorical question is also changed: "For since they were of one and the same birth and came equally from Hunor and Magor, how else could it be that one could be made a lord, another a serf or peasant?"[81] Reflecting the seigneurial pressures of the late fifteenth century, the *Chronica* assumes that serf and rustic are equivalent and makes explicit the descent of contemporary serfs (rather than all non-nobles) from the customs and laws of the Huns.

During the reign of the ineffectual Jagiellonian king Vladislav II (ruled 1490–1517), the Hungarian nobles obtained official recognition of the "Doctrine of the Holy Crown" of Saint Stephen, according to which the nobility shared the exercise of royal power with the monarch. The doctrine formulated in the fourteenth century considered the nobility and higher prelates as equal parts of a corpus of an organic royal power along with the monarch.[82] At his election, Vladislav recognized his obligations to the noble and clerical estates, and acknowledged that the crown itself was in the custody of noble *conservatores* at the castle of Visegrad.[83] Equality within the noble estate was underscored by the common military service obligations ascribed to the Hunnish foundational era; thus by 1500 the nobility solidified against the foreign king and began to press their claims to subjugate the peasantry, and combined myths of privilege and constitutional domination coalesced.

The sudden and violent uprising in the spring and summer of 1514 terrified the Hungarian nobility and was put down only after considerable effort and extraordinary savagery.[84] The insurrection began when a crusade against the Turks authorized by the newly elected Pope Leo X and led by the archbishop of Gran-Esztergom became the occasion for peasants to air their grievances against nobles. According to the peasants, the nobles refused to cooperate with the crusade, preferring to oppress their tenants as usual at home rather than fight in defense of religion and the homeland. The peasants transformed the crusade into a holy war against the nobility, whom they denounced as infidels, worse than the Turks. The *nobles* were the rebels, according to the crusaders, rebels against God and against the responsibilities incumbent on members of the military caste. Later we will consider the program enunciated by the leaders of the peasant armies, but here it is worth indicating elements of propeasant agitation that responded to the legend of the Hunnish origins of nobles and serfs.

In condemning the nobles, the peasant crusaders in the first place contrasted their own willingness to fight with the indifference of the chivalric estates. In France and Catalonia, territories well removed from the frontiers with Islam in the late Middle Ages, the assumption that rusticity meant military incapacity was plausible. In Germany, the imperial laws governing who could carry weapons enshrined the symbolic privileges and responsibilities of nobles by restricting the ownership and display of swords and other chivalric weapons to members of the knightly classes.[85] In Hungary, however, peasants were often enlisted in armed campaigns against the Turks and were far from incompetent in the use of weapons.

After the rebellion was quashed in the late summer of 1514, punitive laws were enacted that further reflect the legendary origins of differentiation among Hungarians. As we have seen, the French legend could be read as punishing cowardice or treason. With the harrowing recent experience of peasant violence (real and imagined), the authors of legislation degrading virtually the entire rural population to servitude could not contemptuously assume that only nobles had martial skill or an affinity for violence. The prologue to the laws of November 1514 condemned the *plebs rustica* for the slaughter and destruction wreaked on the higher orders at a time when the kingdom was already beset by infidel armies.[86] Article 14, however, spares the majority of rustics from the penalty of death deserved by "traitors" who rebel against their lords.[87] The peasants are thus "unfaithful"—rebels rather than cowards—yet, as Richard Hoffmann has pointed out, Article 14, restricting the movement of servile tenants, repeats the formulation of Thuróczy, subjecting the rustic population to "perpetual servitude."[88] The article took particular vengeance on the leaders of the revolt, whose descendants were to be banned from ever holding any office or privilege of even the most local sort, so that they should endure perpetual servitude and bewail forever their ancestors' crimes. This evokes not only Thuróczy but the hereditary taint of Ham and of those who failed Charlemagne. The posterity of the instigators, particularly of those who encouraged the rape of noble women and girls, were to be treated as a "cursed generation."[89]

An even more graphic example of legislation borrowing from quasi-historical narrative is offered by the *Tripartitum*, a semiofficial collection of customary law compiled in the fateful year 1514 (and published in 1517) by István Werbőczy at the instance of the Hungarian parliament.[90] The *Tripartitum* uses Simon of Kéza and János Thuróczy to justify more explicitly the privileges of nobles with regard to the peasantry on the one hand and the king on the other. The relevant passage appears in order to show the origins of nobles' "liberty." Like the *Illuminated Chronicle*, the passage designates two rather than three punishments for ignoring the military summons, but they are now execution and servitude, bringing the penalties closer to both the "cowards of Apremont" model and the Catalan legend of Charlemagne, but more immediately referring to the "merciful" intent of the 1514 laws that present servitude as the commutation of a merited death sentence.

Werbőczy produces, as it were, a short-term and a long-term justification for serfdom. In a section of the *Tripartitum* that concerns the dependent peasantry (the *jobagiones*), their degraded legal status results simply from the recent insurrection against the nobility.[91] The specific consequence of their subjugation is an inability to move off their lords' land at will. Earlier in the *Tripartitum*, however, the privileges of nobles were explained by reference to the historical legend of the Hunnic military summons. The general lack of freedom and the subordination of the peasantry are thus of long standing, but the specific penalty of the 1514 insurrection is deprivation of the freedom of movement.

Discussing the contrast between noble liberty and rustic bondage, Werbőczy's *Tripartitum* repeats Thuróczy's conclusion, which is itself, of course, based on Simon of Kéza's rhetorical question. The distinction between lords and serfs, however, is slightly altered: the Huns' custom explains why descendants of Hunor and Magor include both lords and serfs, nobles and non-nobles or peasants.[92]

At this point the major concern for Werbőczy was not simply to explain and justify social distinction within the Hungarian nation but to determine true Hungarian identity—who could be considered Hungarian with the rights and privileges thereto appertaining? The answer was not an "ethnic" definition but a historical-juridical finding.

The peculiar political idea that the Hungarian monarchy ultimately resided with the noble estate was perfected by Werbőczy and joined to the explanation of peasant subjugation in what has accurately been described as a "Magna Carta" of aristocratic national identity.[93] Werbőczy grouped together the nobility, previously split between greater and lesser magnates, as a body representing the Hungarian crown and nation. Building on the doctrines already present in parliamentary legislation of 1505 (by which the Hungarian nobles required that in future a Hungarian rather than foreign monarch be selected), Werbőczy defined the Hungarian state in terms of the nobles, repositories of its national identity.[94] The *Tripartitum* neatly asserts that the *populus*, in whom resides the power of the Hungarian crown, consists of the secular and ecclesiastical nobility only, not the non-nobles.[95]

Like Gabriel Turell's *Recort*, which stated that Catalan liberties were for nobles, not rustics, Werbőczy's addition to the Doctrine of the Holy Crown removes the lower orders from consideration as members of the national community without actually inventing what could be called a "racial" or "ethnic" distinction. The *Tripartitum* defines the nation as an aristocratic polity against both king and commoner. The success of this formulation was due not only to the weakness of the Jagiellonian monarchs but to the crushing of the 1514 uprising. The contrast with Catalonia is quite obvious. The kings of Aragon-Catalonia emerged victorious from the Civil War of 1462–86 and servitude was abolished. Gabriel Turell, on the losing side, is no more than a minor curiosity recalling nobles' claims and ambitions, while Werbőczy's codification and supporting arguments would be authoritative for over three centuries.

The 1514 legislation and the *Tripartitum* did not enserf the countryside suddenly, for the extension of servitude antedates 1514.[96] In addition, the disastrous Battle of Mohács (1526) resulted in the conquest of most of the kingdom by the Turks and the secession of Transylvania, so that the local customs and tenurial relations of much of the former kingdom of Hungary were overturned. Nevertheless, serfdom remained in the remnant of western Hungary, and the disaster did not directly affect Hungarian constitutional development. Consequently, whereas serfdom was abolished in Catalonia in the fifteenth century, serfdom in Hungary continued into the modern era.

How can we classify the historical mythology developed in Catalonia and Hungary, two such different societies both heavily influenced by France and its official culture and historiography? Richard Hoffmann discusses Ireland, Spain, Hungary, and Poland as examples of medieval "racist ideologies," but this term does not accurately apply to societies that did not posit a literal distinction of blood or language. While the English could regard the conquered Irish as a separate and inferior people (by extension, an inferior "race"), the Catalans and Hungarians pointed to a moral and juridical moment in past history when a hereditarily transmissible curse was created. True, this curse was carried in the blood, but this does not constitute a racial theory, because it does not reflect either a real or an invented ethnogenesis. The difference between the curse of Noah and secular legends is a difference not merely of chronology but of geopolitical scope: the biblical curse affected entire peoples descended from Canaan, while Charlemagne, Kadar, and other quasi-historical figures established ordinances that drew a line *within* a linguistic and national community.

The affinity between historical myth and legislation is thus of crucial importance in Catalonia and Hungary. Not only did law receive historical and ethical justifications from literature in both realms, but discriminatory practice (i.e., serfdom) affected a population that was not self-evidently conquered, captive, or "outsider." In the absence of a historically attested subjugation (such as the Germans could claim in the East or Frederick II in Sicily), servitude would appear to be artificial. There was no obvious reason why a segment of the population should be unfree; thus an essentially arbitrary law would have to be buttressed by historical precedent placed at the moment of national origin.

England

One reason why the historical mythology of servitude never amounted to much in medieval England was that the rupture caused by the Norman military conquest disabled potential arguments defending servitude on the basis of continuity with an ancient arrangement. An image of servitude did color some accounts of the conquest and its consequences but was never brought to bear on discussions of the status of actual villeins. In fact, the matter of the origin of villeins was not much explored. Military victory and defeat correspond imperfectly to a free/servile distinction. Not that there was less agitation in England (which experienced its share of peasant rebellions directed against servile institutions), but the Norman Conquest was a more recent event than the supposed foundations of Hungary or Catalonia, and also it was amenable to quite contradictory interpretations.

Within the English setting it was conceptually *possible* to link servitude with a specific transgression. According to Roger of Wendover, King John ordered knights and foot soldiers to Dover to forestall a French invasion in 1213, threatening to degrade to servitude anyone failing to heed the summons.[97] But this was simply the same sort of thing as the Frankish *lantweri*, the failure to answer a general mobilization against invasion. Not only was King John's threat without substance, but only in the vaguest sense could it apply retrospectively to those already villeins.

The obvious moment of social formation for medieval England was the Norman Conquest. William's victory was sometimes attributed to the sins of the English. The Worcester version of the *Anglo-Saxon Chronicle*, in the entry for 1066, sought to explain the catastrophe by blaming, rather generally, the sinful conduct of the entire populace.[98] Henry of Huntingdon considered the Norman invasion the last of five plagues sent to punish the Saxons for their behavior.[99]

Ascribing the dramatic overthrow of a society to divine retribution for the sins of the defeated was, of course, nothing new. Gildas and Bede had attributed the Saxon invasion to the misdeeds of the British.[100] No element of society was singled out for blame; therefore the historical event of conquest amounted to a natural misfortune, a phenomenon like the comet that foretold the invasion—part of the inconstancy of fortune and regimen of change, not resulting from a single key transgression followed by a particular chastisement. The punishment of group sin by group disaster was predictable and reasonable according to the tradition reflected by historians of both the Saxon and Norman invasions.

There was at least an opportunity to connect conquest with servitude. Thorlac Turville-Petre, Douglas Moffat, and Thea Summerfield have called attention to three fourteenth-century chronicles that identify the conquered English as thralls or serfs to the Normans, seeming to imply a genealogy or ethnic origin for contemporary villeins.[101] According to Robert of Gloucester (writing in the late thirteenth century), the nobles ("heye men") of his era were of Norman origin while the lowly were the descendants of the vanquished Saxons.[102] The defeat and its consequences were God's will, a punishment for infidelity as well as for the deadly sins of gluttony, lechery, and sloth. If any part of the population bears a greater share of blame, however, it is the nobles and the clergy, the former for robbery, the latter for "hordom."[103]

Thomas Castleford (ca. 1337) offered an even grimmer view of the consequences of 1066: the English were permanently placed in "thraldum," "bondage," and "servage" by the victorious Normans.[104] Castleford, however, was less concerned than Robert of Gloucester to apportion guilt, content to depict King Harold as untruthful but not as the instigator of an exemplary moral chastisement. For Castleford, the dire results of the conquest were due to the *ius gentium*, not to divine vengeance. Peter Langtoft's chronicle (written in French), states simply that the English have lived under foreign rule, "in servitude and pain," since the conquest.[105]

Robert Mannyng's *Chronicle* (written before 1338 and based on Wace and Langtoft) emphasizes both sin and punishment. The sin was not that of the English as a nation but rather that of Harold's individual perjury. Yet, as in Thomas Castleford, the conquest led not to social differentiation but to the degradation of the entire English population: "Since he [*i.e., William*] and his have held the land in heritage, that the English have been forced to live in servitude, He placed the English in thralldom, who were formerly so free."[106] Mannyng elaborates on Langtoft and goes beyond him in emphasizing Harold and Godwin's breaking of their oaths.[107] They are forsworn, he reiterates, making the defeat of the Saxons closer to the model of Noah's curse (or Charlemagne's): permanent subordination stemming from particular but formative incidents in the past. Mannyng would therefore seem to have the elements necessary for a myth of the origins of servitude on the order of what would be developed for Catalonia and Hungary: a crime with serfdom as its hereditary retribution. But Mannyng was not interested in villeinage.

Like the other fourteenth-century chroniclers, he means by thralldom a political condition, not personal legal servitude. It is the entire nation of the English who have been held in bondage, and Mannyng employs the first-person plural to include himself among those subjugated. It was King William who "sette *us* in seruage." On the fateful day of the decisive battle "*our* fredom . . . for euer toke the leue."[108] As Moffat has pointed out, it could not be literally true that any of these authors were of unfree status; Robert Mannyng, for example, was a Gilbertine monk.

Turville-Petre's argument that the historians' laments were intended to denounce villeinage (for the self-interested purpose of alleviating the Gilbertines' labor shortage once villeins became free agents) is not convincing.[109] The fourteenth-century historians did have an image of conquest and captivity in relation to King William I, but it was not unique to them. Matthew Paris, writing at St. Albans in the mid–thirteenth century, describes the conquest and the Conqueror's oppressive customs as bringing about the "servitude" of the English, which he compares to the biblical tyranny of the Egyptians.[110]

The complaints of the later historians are connected to more immediate issues of their times, such as the barons' wars against Edward II, denunciation of "foreigners," and especially taxes. They have little to do with serfdom or its justification. In one of the above-cited passages, Mannyng talks of William "setting us in servitude," and of the fall of freedom, going on to complain about taxation ("borgh taliage"), which is clearly what in this context constitutes the true misery of "servage."[111] At its most bombastic, the Norman Conquest myth of origins is about language, privilege, and identity (Moffat refers to "race," which I think exaggerates even the perceived difference).

Arguments over villeinage did take place, but it was in the demands of peasants, not the apologetics of lords, that the Norman Conquest was invoked, and there only indirectly, by way of Domesday Book. The Norman Conquest, regarded as an unalloyed triumph of the aristocracy by seventeenth-century revolutionaries and nineteenth-century reformers, could serve as at least a notional basis for common liberty in the Middle Ages. On the eve of the English Rising of 1381, villeins in many parts of England claimed that their lands lay in the "ancient demesne" of the crown, so that they should be free tenants of the king rather than unfree tenants of ecclesiastical or aristocratic lords. Peasants looked back to the beneficent lordship of the Norman and early Angevin monarchs and beyond them to an original Anglo-Saxon freedom.[112] Appeals were made to Domesday Book, which peasants considered authoritative regarding what tenants on what lands were free and unfree. Rather than overturning earlier liberty, the Norman Conquest (and Domesday Book in particular) was regarded as enshrining it within the sphere of royal protection. A petition presented to Parliament in 1377 speaks of villeins who, abetted by unnamed agitators, have purchased exemplifications (official excerpts) of Domesday Book and withheld their required services in order to prove and demand exemption from seigneurial jurisdiction.[113] The "inaccuracy" of the peasants' perceptions ("ancient demesne," for example, was a relatively recent legal definition) is less important than the belief in written documents and Norman precedent as charters of peasant liberties. The idea was by no means far-fetched, in that it was accepted that land once in royal hands might continue to enjoy privileged status. In 1364, Edward III wrote to the convent of Saint Swithun remonstrating with them over the treatment of tenants in Crondall (Hampshire) who had complained that they were being made to perform services beyond the obligations rendered at the time the manor had belonged to Edward's forebears.[114]

English peasants demonstrated a peculiarly persistent faith in the possibility of achieving exemption from servitude by means of formal legal procedures. Although English peasants, like peasants elsewhere, burned documents during rebellions, the English villeins believed that somewhere there were ancient charters dating from an authoritative source that would prove their liberty. In the early fourteenth century villeins resident in the towns of St. Albans demanded rights to representation, borough status, and permission to grind grain at home on the basis of Domesday Book but also on the basis of a supposed charter of King Offa of Mercia that they believed the abbot was holding in secret. By 1381, faith in the existence of a venerable charter of liberties was so strong that the rebels demanded that the abbot produce it, and when he could not, they forced him to write out a new one.[115] That peasants considered Offa and Domesday Book to be compatible shows the degree to which the Norman Conquest could be shaped by positing an earlier tradition of liberty. The conquest had brought aristocratic lordship to England but had not destroyed a supposed earlier free status guaranteed by the crown.

History was therefore not exclusively the weapon of seigneurial apologists. As we shall see in connection with the late-medieval insurrections, an answering mythology of origins was presented from the peasant side. That we know more about legends justifying serfdom is due to the way in which records survive, reflecting the literacy of the upper orders and their greater opportunity to construct rationales for their domination. For them, history explained exceptions to natural law or deviations from social solidarity. If all humanity possessed equal dignity, the Bible at least afforded certain moments of consequential disgrace and certain primordial sinners such as Cain and Ham affecting disproportionately one sector of the future populations. If a more localized privilege seemed unfairly distributed, an event in the national past could be used to explain, again by means of a hereditary transgression, the privation of rights otherwise to be enjoyed. History, both sacred and secular, provided answers to the question of why divine, natural, or customary liberty had been infringed upon or destroyed. These answers might seem at first glance consistent to the point of becoming universally accepted truisms. The curse of Noah explained servitude, after all, from Saint Ambrose to the antebellum South. The suggestion of treachery or cowardice survived transplantation from France to such different realms as Hungary and Catalonia and persisted for centuries in both.

Part 3

Unfavorable Images of Peasants

Chapter 6

Representations of Contempt
and Subjugation

Previous chapters discussed the ways in which peasants were useful and necessary to society and explanations for why they did not receive the benefits
promised by the model of mutually dependent orders. Peasants produced not
only food but wealth for the nobility and clergy, but received little recompense for their toil, as was frequently acknowledged and lamented. By virtue
of their status as members of the Christian community, it was difficult simply
to categorize them as alien in order to excuse their oppression. We have examined biblical and pseudohistorical theories that posited some ancestral
crime or deficiency to explain the subsequent lack of freedom and justify exploitation. This chapter will consider another form of justification for the ill-
treatment of peasants, namely, the proliferation of images of peasants as base,
filthy, and stupid. While intended as amusing condemnations of the lowly,
the satiric literary representations of peasants may be read as an elaboration
of Aristotelian natural slavery. The peasant by nature is fit for toil and, moreover, toil that does not deserve a reward but rather is assured by coercion. To
the extent that he is naturally base, the peasant is appropriately exploited, and
there is no need to invent a temporal origin for inequality.

Parody and Satire

That the medieval peasant was usually regarded with contempt is hardly a
novel observation. The rustic or *vilain* was a literary type for the base, the
ridiculous. He served as a model of how *not* to act, epitomizing qualities opposed to the virtuous chivalry of the knight.[1] In the fourteenth century Jean
de Condé wrote a brief poem entitled "Des Vilains et des Courtois," in which
the two social types and their qualities are given as absolutely contrasting, the

one motivated to do evil, the other good. The etymological origin of the word *vilain*, according to Jean, is *vilenie*.[2]

Medieval literary genres such as the French *fabliaux* or German *Schwankliteratur* were devoted (in whole or in part) to the antics of rustics, their foolishness, murderous violence, or proclivities for the lower body functions. Mock "grammars" or taxonomies of rustics offer a précis of these themes. A Northern French text of the late thirteenth century divides *vilains* into no fewer than twenty-three varieties. Some are like animals (*vilains porcins, vilains chenins, vilains asnins*), others merely ferocious (*vilains ramages*). Others are odd in their appearance, while still others are associated with filth and excrement.[3] A fifteenth-century "Peasant Catechism" begins by defining *rusticus* as a "Hebrew noun" because a peasant is as inept and wicked as a Jew. It is of the third declension, for "before the cock had crowed twice, the rustic shat three times." Additionally, rustics are of the "asinine race."[4] A Goliardic text of the twelfth or thirteenth century offered a "complete" declension of *rusticus*: "this villein, of this rustic, to this devil, this thief, O robber!, by this plunderer." In the plural: "these accursed ones, of these gloomy ones, to these liars, these wicked people, O evil ones! by these infidels."[5]

There is a temptation to approach this vocabulary of negative characteristics either too literally or too symbolically, as if harsh depictions of peasants amounted to realistic social criticism on the one hand, or were merely literary forms of reference to an abstract lowliness on the other. The old historicist approach, which saw the representations of peasants in literature as unmediated commentaries on society, was certainly over-literal. At the beginning of the twentieth century Stanley Galpin distinguished the two worlds of peasant and knight according to a clear division of unfavorable and favorable. Galpin organized his thesis according to the negative qualities embodied by the peasants and the positive qualities of the chivalric order. The knight has fine manners, the rustic is rude; the knight is generous, the rustic miserly; and so forth. Comic denunciation of rustics amounts unproblematically to a hierarchical social statement.

It is easy to demonstrate that medieval writers by and large held peasants in contempt, but their purpose was often tangential to social criticism. The contrast between *vilain* and *courtois* was not necessarily structured with the peasant in mind as a direct target of satirical attack. Per Nykrog observed that the *fabliaux* use courtly verse forms and are intended as parodies, not as in any sense "realistic" depictions of rustics.[6] Using almost the same title as Galpin for a recent study of high and low in French literature, Kathryn Gravdal regards the contrast of *vilain* and *courtois* as a literary trope, a dichotomy with shifting borders affording opportunities for transgression. For Gravdal these medieval texts are self-reflexive parodies in which it is genre (such as the romance) that is mocked, not the peasant.[7] Gravdal argues that antirustic discourse amounts to an occasion for transgressing styles and forms, a parody of literary topoi rather than satire directed at the peasantry as a social class, a game (parody) instead of a lesson (satire).[8]

This divergence of literal and literary approaches affects the way in which literature is used as evidence for attitudes toward society. Pierre Bonnassie, in discussing the degraded condition of rustics at the mercy of the seigneurial regime, cites section (*branche*) 10 of the *Roman de Renart*—a series of versified animal fables of the twelfth century—as an example of seigneurial contempt. Here Renart refers to the *vilain* Liétard and his like as "disloyal villein . . . stinking serf . . . son of a whore, mangy villein . . . stinking villeins, filthy and thieving."[9] Gravdal, on the other hand, in discussing *Renart*, rejects a transparent reading of social attitudes against rustics. Not only are there heroic rustics in the other *Renart* stories, but the purpose of the work is to show the world as comically immoral. The frontiers between courtly and rustic (as between animal and human) are ambiguous and easily dismantled or redrawn. Thus the passage in *branche* 7b in which the peasants ineptly arm themselves against an attack of hungry animals is a parody of epic battle scenes, not a statement about the nature of peasants.[10]

Are the two interpretive tendencies focusing on literal contempt versus literary parody really so divergent? Could one even have a parody without a comical referent? After all, what makes the parody funny is that the *vilain* is already recognized as a ridiculous figure. Medieval compositions do indeed refer to prior traditions and conventions, often for the purpose of amusing distortion, but this does not vitiate their pointed significance as discourses about the peasantry.

The poems of Neidhart (who died between 1237 and 1245) and his followers made fun of the solemn conventions of the German *Minnesang* by transposing the setting from the court to a benighted village.[11] The high-flown sentiments of longing were directed not to delicate and distant noblewomen but, with comic inappropriateness, to assertive and lustful peasant lasses. Neidhart's hero and namesake is a knight who consorts with the peasants of a remote and impoverished village called Reuental ("Valley of Grief"). He is admired by the village girls (especially in the so-called Summer Songs), but frustrated by his male peasant rivals in his attempts at seduction (in the Winter Songs).

Although his initial intent may have been to parody the refined ceremony of court poetry, Neidhart would come to be known for his mockery of peasants. Later poetry purporting to be by Neidhart emphasized their violence and boorishness.[12] A group of *Schwanklieder* ("Prank-Songs"), another group of short plays about Neidhart, and a fifteenth-century cycle of poems with a comic protagonist named Neidhart Fuchs ("Neidhart the Fox") describe a veritable war between the knight and the rustics.[13] Neidhart thus moves from genre parody to antipeasant satire. He begins in the thirteenth century as a hapless and rather fainthearted lover but becomes by the mid–fourteenth century a cunning and sadistic Eulenspiegel-like figure whose sole aim is to torture and humiliate peasants. It is in this latter guise, not as a parody of courtliness, that Neidhart would remain popular until well into the sixteenth century. The peasants in Neidhart really *are* supposed to be contemptible rather than mere representations of generic lowliness. The poems were read by medieval audiences more as antipeasant satires than as parodies of *Minnesang*, so that by the fourteenth century any original intertextual purpose had been pushed aside by a less subtle antipeasant sentiment of unmistakable, direct social import.[14]

Peasants were contemptible and so could function both as symbols of reversal or inversion *and* as direct objects of disdain. Not only did they symbolize the dishonest, unchivalric, and lowly, they *were* dishonest, unchivalric, and lowly (it was supposed). It was their "real" baseness that made parodies explicable.

The general category of "unfavorable" depiction of peasants included a number of subdivisions. It is not just that peasants might be filthy in one work and appear as dishonest in another, but that there was a lexicon of negative images. Several major axes of pejorative discourse occur: the peasant as object of ridicule versus the peasant as dangerous; the lowly but useful peasant versus the completely base and useless; peasants as representative of human nature versus peasants as grotesque, semihuman, or bestial figures. Behind these oppositions lies a fundamental distinction between what might be regarded as "social" descriptions (peasants as avaricious) and fanciful hyperbole (peasants as savage animals). Bernard of Cluny's denunciation of rustics for evading the payment of tithes[15] is quite different from the comical accusation (found in the same Italian manuscript with the declension of *rusticus*) that rustics crucified Christ, or that they resemble asses, wolves, and dogs (from another, somewhat earlier Italian source).[16] Both social and typological condemnations, however, return to the same set of attributed characteristics, and of course, as modern racism has demonstrated, the establishment of grotesquely comical types and norms of behavior for subordinated groups is deadly serious business.

It is useful to explore these different forms of contempt since they reveal issues of social fear, degree of control, and the limits of the human. We should keep in mind, however, that we are not really looking at a set of uni-dimensional images about "outcasts," however hysterical the statements may at times be. Language describing peasants might be derived from or related to that applied to other despised peoples, as in the case of the "Hebrew etymology" of the word "rustic," or Chrétien de Troyes's description in *Yvain* of the grotesque herdsman who "resembled a Moor."[17] In an important recent compendium of artistic conventions for denoting outcast status, Ruth Mellinkoff has shown how traits such as kinky or red hair might cross over among various groups, including peasants.[18] Nevertheless, there was a significant difference between peasants and Saracens, Jews, or lepers in that peasants could not consistently be regarded as "other" or as marginal either to the social economy or to the Christian faith. Or rather, representations of peasants as other—as not human, as meriting no consideration as fellow Christians by the dominant elements of society—had to be exaggerated and grotesque. But this effort could never be completely successful as long as peasants were considered necessary for the survival of their superiors.

Rustics as Ignorant of Religion

One might expect medieval peasants to have been characterized as insufficiently Christian or as practitioners of superstitious (hence anti-Christian) rites. The Latin word *paganus*, meaning "rustic," began to be applied as a term of contempt by Christians to believers in the old religions in about 300 A.D., especially with the end of the urban Roman religion and the conversion of the empire.[19] Martin of Braga's "De correctione rusticorum," written in the mid–sixth century, has influenced our idea of the survival of pagan rituals in the countryside and the image of the rustic as eternal pagan.[20] In late antiquity "rustic" and "rusticity" referred to lower qualities of character, not just rural folk. The term *rusticitas* was often employed to mean a lack of appropriate understanding of or reverence for sacred persons, places, and events rather than literal lack of Christian belief, or "rural paganism."[21] In the twelfth and thirteenth centuries, chroniclers would describe heretics (such as the Waldensians or Cathars) as *rustici*, but here the word denotes ignorance without implications concerning the social status of the movements' followers.[22]

Frequently, however, *rusticus* actually did mean what it seemed to: a peasant, quite likely an ignorant or insufficiently reverent one, but in any case a member of a social category and not simply a type. For Saint Augustine *rusticus*, as opposed to *urbanus*, had the connotation of ignorant versus civilized, but for Martin of Braga "rustics" clearly meant the literal country dwellers who also engage in pagan practices.[23] Throughout the late antique period and beyond, *rusticus* rather more consistently denoted someone engaged in agriculture, with a connotation of ignorance and susceptibility to paganism.[24]

In the tenth book of his *Decretum*, Burchard of Worms (early eleventh century), like Martin of Braga, provides a catalogue of superstitious beliefs and ceremonies tied to agricultural life.[25] Our impression of an incompletely Christianized countryside persisting throughout the Middle Ages has been influenced by the studies of Jean-Claude Schmitt and Carlo Ginzburg concerning the appropriation of Christian rituals to serve local ends and the existence of practices traceable to pre-Christian ceremonies and outlook.[26] But if we look at even the harshest attacks against the peasants, the charge of paganism is much less common than typification of peasants as merely ignorant, materialistic, or negligent in their religious observance.

There are certainly examples of rustics who supposedly did not know a thing about the most basic tenets of Christianity. The English Dominican preacher John Bromyard cited the example of a shepherd who responded to the question of whether he knew of the Father, the Son, and the Holy Ghost by saying "The father and son I know well, for I tend their sheep; but I know not that third fellow; there is none of that name in our village."[27] The preacher wrings his hands over this ignorance, but does not lament an alternative religious practice. Rustics are much more commonly accused of stupidity or of preoccupation with their everyday concerns than of unbelief or heresy.

In his list of contrasting French examples of chivalric and lowly literary types, Stanley Galpin assembles a number of instances of rustic irreligion, but here too it is really their grossness or foolishness that is mocked. *Le Donnei des Amants* states that *vilains* have nothing to do with God and the angels, not because of some deficiency in their observance but because they are base.[28] According to the *fabliau* "Le vilain qui conquist Paradis par Plait," rustics are not admitted to heaven, as a result of unpleasant character rather than any defiance of Christian belief and practice.[29] The eleventh-century *Book of Sainte Foy*, which reports numerous miracles involving peasants, nevertheless characterizes a certain scoffer from the vicinity of Conques itself as an ignorant rustic. It is not surprising, according to the author, that such errors should arise from "a peasant, a stranger to all wisdom, completely unfamiliar with every divine virtue, and what is worse, a liar with a depraved and perverse mind."[30] This ignorant man had mocked the author, Bernard of Angers (who wrote the first two books of the miracle collection), for telling a story of a miraculous cure of a mule; hence the outraged tone. While individual rustics, objects of seigneurial robberies and violence, receive the help of the child Saint Foy, rusticity always remains in potential proximity to irreverence and lack of proper religious understanding, but not paganism.

The Appearance of the Rustic

More than religious ignorance or superstition, the clearest indication that rustics constituted a lower order of humanity was their physical form. Peasants were at best crudely made, coarse featured, ill-dressed, and graceless. In French literature especially, the peasant was endowed with comical or threatening qualities of subhuman grotesqueness. While the rustics in German literature before 1400 tended to act in a boorish, even frenzied way, they were usually of normal shape and appearance. Elsewhere, especially in France, they were often depicted as dark-skinned or "black," either by reason of their labor in the sun and their proximity to the earth, or as a sign of overall hideousness. Froissart describes the peasants of the *Jacquerie* as small, dark, and ill-armed.[31] In a dispute over servile condition that took place in Mantua in about 1200, a witness testified that the father of the man in question, a certain Bazelarius, had been well-formed, nearly white, and taller than the scribe writing the document. Another witness said he had been small and fat, but agreed that he had been white and reasonably good-looking.[32] In this instance stature and color were considerations in evaluating servile status.

Peasants were frequently presented as misshapen: deformed and unnaturally large or, occasionally, dwarfish. They were commonly said to resemble animals, an analogy that carried moral as well as physical implications. The spectrum of characterizations runs from mere ugliness to comical and unnatural extremes of grotesqueness. Some images depict the peasant as a familiar subordinate, lowly in a normal way (ill-dressed, bent over, dark), while others render him as a disturbing inhabitant of a world apart, subhuman. The first type of image reflects a complacent idea of rustic labor, of toil performed in a productive landscape by beings who perhaps need to be treated firmly (like domesticated animals), but whose distance from the courtly is (in our terms) cultural rather than biological. They occupy a position below, but not totally apart from those above them whom they sustain. The second, more exaggerated type of image emphasizes the strangeness of the rustic and his distance from humanity.

These images are not polar opposites. In both cases peasants can be represented as animals, although usually the grotesque peasant is rendered as a wild animal while the toiling peasant in the fields is likened to a draught animal. The images can also appear side by side. The Luttrell Psalter, for example, contains *bas-de-page* illustrations of rustics working away with various implements but also peculiar, semihuman grotesque forms known as *babewyns* (i.e., "baboons") that in this instance may also be intended as representations of peasants.[33]

Rustics could be depicted as impossibly malformed and bestial. The two guards to the chamber of Laris in the *Romance of Claris and Laris*, for example, are *vilains* of an ugliness "never before seen." They are covered with black hair, their nails are as long as snakes, their eyes fiery. Their teeth resemble those of a wild boar, their noses those of cats, their snouts (*hure*) those of wolves.[34]

Yet even the most bestial semblance could be transformed into a recognizable and human figure. A series of both literary and quasi-historical texts describes forest encounters between nobles and solitary rustics whose horrifying appearance transcends the "realistic" but who are, nevertheless, revealed to be human, capable of speech and even courtesy. The knight Calogrenant in Chrétien's *Yvain* describes a herdsman whom he came upon while lost in a forest. This rustic not only "resembled a Moor" but is like no fewer than six animals: horse, elephant, cat, owl, wolf, and boar.[35] In *Aucassin and Nicolette*, Aucassin encounters a cowherd with bestial physical traits: he is huge and hideous, with an immense black muzzle (again *hure*), red lips, and yellow teeth. Variations on the word "large" (*grand*) are repeated obsessively.[36]

According to John of Marmoutier's *Historia Gaufredi* (ca. 1180), Count Geoffrey of Anjou was lost while hunting (again in a sylvan setting). He met a charcoal burner, blackened, of hideous and intimidating appearance, who nonetheless helped him find his way and described to the count (who did not reveal his identity) the abuses committed by his officials on the hapless inhabitants of the countryside.[37] In a similar incident, the young Philip Augustus, on the eve of his scheduled coronation, lost his way in the forest of Compiègne during a hunt. In what appears to be an example of a historical narrative imitating a literary convention, the chronicler, Rigord, reported that a solitary rustic with a misshapen head and black face so frightened the young prince in the forest that the coronation had to be postponed.[38]

Yet another knight lost in the forest is the protagonist in a dialogue between a knight and a rustic written in 1443 by Felix Hemmerli, a ferocious hater of peasants. The rustic is black, hirsute, bestial. His head is overlarge, his face twisted, and his expression "asinine." Somewhat surprisingly, under the circumstances, the rustic speaks not only correct but florid Latin.[39]

All of these denizens of the woods are misshapen, large, hirsute, bestial, and frightening. As Jacques Le Goff has noted, the forest is the site of the strange, the savage. The knight who enters it, whether for adventure or by accident, places himself in a world opposite that of the court.[40] The forest, home of the wild man and other sinister humans and semihumans, is also removed from what might be considered the normal habitation of rustics, the fields closer to civilization in which labor of a less solitary, more obviously productive sort is performed.

Sylvan loneliness and danger accentuate the strangeness of the rustic, but it would be wrong simply to let this go as another example of an undifferentiated "medieval Other." The encounters mentioned above begin with the monstrous but evoke the possibility of the peasant's humanity. In response to Calogrenant's jocular but uneasy question, "Come, tell me if you are a good or evil thing," the herdsman responds that he is a man. Calogrenant then asks, "What sort of man are you," to which the herdsman responds with simple dignity, "Just as you see me and no different."[41] Count Geoffrey is praised for recognizing his interlocutor as a man rather than regarding him with the contempt usually felt by the rich for the poor. They converse earnestly about the common misery of fallen humanity, condemned by the sin of Adam to earn its bread by the sweat of its collective brow.[42] Felix Hemmerli's noble warrior, on his way to fight the heathen, is accosted insultingly by the rustic. The knight asks if the rustic is a devil or a man, and the rustic responds that he is a man, the same as the noble only better.[43] Their dialogue is certainly weighted in favor of the knight, but the rustic is reasonably adept in argument, and eventually, convinced of the wickedness of his tribe, he shows the knight the way out of the woods, and they part as friends.[44]

None of the rustics in these stories is the equal of the knights, but they come into focus as human from their original beastly semblance. They oscillate between the bestial and the human (or praiseworthy) in a way that is characteristic of medieval discourse about strange peoples. In *The Song of Roland*, for example, some of the Saracens (notably those from far away) are described as alien in appearance, especially blacks such as Abisme or the 50,000 troops faced by the dying Roland. The Saracens in general are vile, dishonest, accursed.[45] Nevertheless, not only do they share similar tastes in horses, armor, and ceremony with their Christian counterparts, but they can be wise and brave, as is Blancandrin, for example.[46] The poet describes the ruler of Balazuez as well-formed, clear-eyed, and courageous, lamenting that such a fine knight is not a Christian. It is now only faith and not nature that separates them.[47] In the famous entrance to the nave at the basilica of Vézelay, the apostles are sent out at Pentecost to the farthest reaches of the earth, where pygmies, dog-headed people, and those with ears reaching to their waists dwell. These monstrous races are nevertheless deemed sufficiently human to receive the Word of God.[48]

This is to argue not that the Middle Ages was actually "tolerant" but rather that images of humanity or animality were not fixed. There was a discourse of unease characterized by doubts over whether or not to consider a subordinate people fully human. One sees a reiterated recognition of difference alternating with its disavowal similar to that found in colonial discourse. An obsessive but inconsistent focus on the separation between cultivated and barbaric was accompanied by a nagging refrain of the notion of similarity. The view of "the Other" is more complex and internally contradictory than the simplified picture often given of absolute determination (by race or other criteria) of inferiority and superiority.[49] The peasants presented a problem because their subhumanity was even more difficult to maintain consistently than that of Muslims or other clearly outcast peoples, for the peasants were numerous, productive, and (most importantly) Christian.

Nonetheless, that it was logically difficult to argue the essential bestial character of the peasantry did not forestall attempts to make such a characterization. In the late Middle Ages, an era in which peasant revolts were a serious preoccupation of the higher estates, rustics were commonly likened to wild animals. In earlier times, rustics had been represented comically as animals without necessarily being regarded as rebellious. Thus a *fabliau* of the thirteenth century describes rustics as "unfortunate in every respect, hideous as wolf or leopard. They don't know how to live among people."[50] The humanist Maffeo Vegio wrote a savage antipeasant satire in 1431, the *Rusticalia*, in which the peasants are told to cease complaining about wolves or dogs stealing their animals, for it is *they* who are the real thieves and despoilers.[51]

In more serious (if overblown) rhetoric denouncing their insurrections, the savagery and unreason of the peasants were likened to uncontrolled bestial wildness. There was now little notion of utility; the peasants are threats to order, verminous even, to be thinned out if not altogether destroyed. Pope Gregory IX, in a Crusade letter of 1233 directed against the Stedinger rebels in northern Germany, said they are like beasts, only even *more* cruel.[52] The abbot of Vale Royal, in a dispute with the men of the villages of Darnell and Over in 1336, described the peasants who had attacked his entourage as "bestial men of Rutland."[53] The Swiss, exemplars of rebellious peasants, were referred to by their Austrian would-be overlords as "mountain beasts."[54] Felix Hemmerli denounced the Swiss as monsters, not human beings.[55] The most sustained hysterical attack on rebellious peasants, likening them to animals, is book 1 of John Gower's *Vox clamantis*, in which the rabble takes on the aspect either of domestic beasts that have escaped control (asses, oxen, swine, dogs) or of wild or verminous creatures (foxes, flies, frogs).[56] At the end of book 1, with the suppression of the revolt, the peasants have become draught animals, oxen, who have returned to the yoke after a terrifying episode in which they left the fields, forgot their nature, and turned into lions, panthers, and bears.[57]

The Domesticated Peasantry

Contrasting with the solitary, savage rustic and the wild rebellious mobs is the useful laborer whose ragged, dirty, hirsute appearance is a token of his natural subservience, a lowliness befitting the productive toil described above in the first chapter. *Eupolemius*, a Latin poem of the late twelfth century probably written in Germany, records a battle between the forces of God and the forces of Satan. The wicked scorn their opponents as peasant rabble, more fit for the plow than the sword as is proven by their hair, cropped like that of slaves; by their "necks designed for receiving blows"; and by their short tunics, which leave their limbs uncovered "so that you might think satyrs were frolicking." In keeping with an essential paradox of Christianity, it is the good who appear to be the lowly and subordinate and who are ultimately victorious.[58]

Cropped hair was a sign of subordination, but its inverse, extreme hairiness, was an even stronger indication of a more savage lowliness, a resemblance to the beasts. The wild man of the forests, a semihuman savage figure with a long history in literature, ceremony, and even heraldry, was covered with hair that grew from all parts of his body.[59] Rustics in *Garin le Loherain*, *Yvain*, *Aucassin et Nicolette*, and Hemmerli's *Dialogue* either have overgrown hair or are covered with hairy clothing.[60]

Rustics are also filthy. Even Rigaut, the doughty rustic fighter in *Garin*, is large and shaggy, and his face is blackened by dirt in that he has neglected to bathe for six months.[61] Their natural element is dirt and manure. So pervasive is the association of peasants with excrement that it merits a separate discussion.

Dirt indicates not only a lack of civilization but the nature of peasant toil, productive, useful, but unpleasant and so degrading as to remove the unfortunate victim from full consideration as human. The Franciscan bishop of Silves, Alvaro Pelayo (died 1352), accused rustics of dishonesty, refusal to pay church tithes, and a host of other vices. But lazy and uncooperative though they may be, they are so devoted to tilling the soil that they have become identified with it: "For even as they plough and dig the earth all day long, so they become altogether earthy; they lick the earth, they eat the earth, they speak of the earth; in the earth they have reposed all their hopes, nor do they care a jot for the heavenly substance that shall remain."[62] The archbishop of Zamora, Rodrígo Sánchez de Arévalo, expressed similar sentiments in a survey of estates and occupations written about 1465. He begins by praising agriculture but says that men exhaust themselves in tilling the soil, an activity that demeans the intellect. Again the laborers are greedy and disobedient, unlike the peasants of earlier times, but they are so devoted to the soil, "so utterly earthly, that we may truly say of them: They shall lick the earth and eat it."[63] The author of the poem "Despit au vilain" remarked, "Instead of eating meat, the *vilains* should graze the fields naked on all fours together with the cattle."[64] Here the peasants may be bestial, but the resemblance is to farm rather than forest animals.

Yet it was widely acknowledged that this labor, however degrading, was important, even vital. In the *Très Riches Heures* of the Duke of Berry, scenes of peasant labor are juxtaposed with those depicting the recreations of the nobles. Calendars showing the labors appropriate to each month have a long history antedating the fifteenth century, but the Berry Hours portray a particularly sharp contrast between aristocratic leisure and rustic work, exhibiting the nobles' profit from the docile, slightly comical toil of the laborers. Not only are leisure and labor "transformed into an antithetical characterization of divergent milieus," as Erwin Panofsky has noted,[65] but clearly the rustics' subordination is regarded as appropriate.[66] The January miniature shows the duke feasting by a roaring fire, while the February image depicts peasants trying to warm themselves outdoors in the snow. In the background a peasant cuts wood; another drives a donkey toward a village. The figures are not in themselves particularly distorted, but their attitudes and postures are unselfconsciously coarse. The distant man and woman show their sexual parts, while a woman in the foreground lifts her skirts before the fire. March shows the duke's castle of Lusignan in the background with rustics plowing and pruning vines. The peasants are bent over, and one shows his posterior. In September the vines are harvested in front of the towers of another castle of the duke, Saumur. At the center, adjoining draft animals, a peasant is again bent over displaying his rear end. The attitude here is not one of patronizing or nostalgic evocation of rustic simplicity but a harder-edged contempt.[67]

The Queen Mary Psalter, made in early-fourteenth-century East Anglia, also presents the labors of the month in a way that is in some respects charming and idealized. Nevertheless, in the scene of an August wheat harvest, not

8. The labors of the months, August, wheat harvest. From the Queen Mary Psalter, early fourteenth century. British Library, MS Royal 2 B VII, f. 78v. Reprinted by permission of the British Library, London.

only are the peasants bent over awkwardly to cut the wheat with their sickles, they are being supervised by a reeve or steward pointing with a stick (Fig. 8).[68]

The rustics inhabit a different space in terms of comfort, character, posture, and physique, but they are working in close proximity to the dwellings of their masters. They are not strange beings of the remote forest. Their labor is suited to their God-given nature, one completely different from that of the aristocracy, to be sure. If they are lower humans, they are, nonetheless, necessary. The splendid castles in the near background could not exist without their labor. The duke of Berry may have regarded his tenants with complacency and ease (as opposed to the discomfort felt by the wealthy before social inferiors typical of the modern era), but the lords did not delude themselves concerning the source of their wealth, a calculation requiring no particular economic sophistication.

The peasants of the Duke of Berry or in the Luttrell Psalter are docile, as opposed to the ravening animals evoked by accounts of peasant rebellions or the hopelessly disobedient rustics of the Spanish bishops cited above. There was, however, an intermediate category of *vilain* who was not naturally cooperative but could be forced to fulfill his lowly role as provider of extensive labors for his betters. The labors of the peasant were specified with derision in a poem written in 1247 and found within a fragment of a cartulary drawn up by Mont-Saint-Michel.[69] The verses are in the vernacular; the census accompanying it is in Latin. The poem is mocking while the census is serious (as such documents tend to be). They are in the same hand and clearly related. Both concern revenues extracted from the peasants of Verson, a village near Caen in Normandy. Thus the verses ridiculing the tenants stand alongside a routine and technical inventory of their payments and other obligations. The poem, written by a monastic official named Estout de Goz, begins by denouncing the peasants who have challenged the onerous services demanded by the monastery. The author accuses Viscount Osbert, lord of Fontenay-le-Pesnel, of inciting the peasants' complaint brought before the Norman Court of the Exchequer.

The tone is humorous and scornful. Near the beginning the *vilains* are described as "more rascally than mastiffs," and the author concludes by asserting that there are no more rascally folk than the *vilains* of Verson.[70] The 235-line poem enumerates the peasants' duties in connection with harvesting, cartage, the keeping of pigs, pasturage, and various labor services. Among other things, it includes the first authentic mention of something that looks like a seigneurial right to symbolic sexual humiliation, here termed *cullage* (vv. 159–74).

The text seems to resist analysis, as Alain Boureau points out.[71] It has long been considered a vernacular verse equivalent of what is enumerated in the census as owed to the monastery. Indeed there are many points that coincide: the extent of the hay-mowing obligation, the tax levied on pigs paid on the day of the Virgin's Nativity (September 8), and the digging and maintenance of ditches.[72] On the other hand, not only are most of the obligations less onerous in the census than in the poem, but according to Boureau, the poem is intended to show the degrading obligations that the viscount will impose if he accomplishes his attempts to take over the village. Boureau argues that it is hard to believe that the monastery would describe with such light-hearted cynicism the unfair and burdensome nature of its own demands.[73] The right of the lord to receive fines for young women marrying off the seigneurie (what would be referred to in other contexts as *formariage*) is here given a particularly degrading coloration that may indeed be an accusation against Viscount Osbert, or a warning to the *vilains* about what he is likely to demand. The author says that a certain "Rogier Adé" has told him "what shame the vilain might have escaped," namely the three sous *cullage* fine. The *vilain* would never have married off his daughter had he known how much would be demanded.[74] It is possible that the *vilain* "escapes" this obligation by remaining within the jurisdiction of the monastery.

Whether or not the poem concerns the monastery's rights (and at least a considerable part of it does), it is hard to see it as a complaint about secular

mistreatment of peasants, for after all, they are already regarded as disobedient dependents who *should* be coerced to work. Their duties, whether owed
to the monastery legitimately or claimed by the viscount illegitimately, are
seen as amusing precisely because they are onerous. It is characteristic of the
poem that it derides the peasants' labors while condemning their slackness
and "dishonesty." The multiplicity of services and the poem's gay contempt
show the lowliness of the tenants, their suitability for toil despite their reluctance. Their labor is coerced, whether by Mont-Saint-Michel or Viscount Osbert. No claim is made that this service is rendered in return for anything
such as protection or prayer. They labor because that is what being a *vilain*
entails.[75]

The inhabitants of Verson were not, in fact, unfree tenants,[76] nor were
they subject to quite the arbitrary mistreatment implied by the term *cullage*,
but the poem seems to distinguish itself from the careful enumeration of the
census, which recognizes a hierarchy or at least multiplicity of tenant categories owing different dues. In the poem they are indistinguishable, all *vilains*, all rascals.

Another example of what appears to our sensibilities as a cruel and inap-
propriately merry account of seigneurial exploitation is an Italian poem of the
late fourteenth century by an otherwise unknown Lombard writer named
Matazone de Calignano. This composition, translated by Paul Mayer into
modern French under the name "Dit sur les vilains," begins by mocking the
dishonesty and impudence of *vilani*.[77] They complain loudly to their lord of
their mistreatment, but it is right for the lord to imprison and constrain
them. They forget their origin. The first villein was born of the flatulence of
an ass.[78] From this it has been established that he should be nourished with
bread made of maslin and raw rye, with beans, garlic, and other humble
foods. He will have to wear dark and strange-looking clothes. He talks to his
animal as they work, for they are in fact related, sharing the same parent.
Thus far we have the conventions of the foul nature of rustics and their coarse
diet.

The lord, on the other hand, was born in a garden, of a rose and a lily, accompanied by seven allegorical maidens (of whom only six are mentioned:
Joy, Happiness, Prowess, Largesse, Beauty, and Bravery). They salute the
knight and describe for him the nature of his dominance over the *vilan* who
is to be given to serve him. At this point the various tasks of the rustic are
enumerated month by month along with various things the lord ought simply to take from him. In February, at Carnival, seize a capon from him every
day. In March, make him work in the vineyards and prohibit his wearing
shoes. In June demand a day of labor service each week. In sum, by making

him work in this fashion, one punishes the wicked rustic.[79] The tone is light-hearted, and the author, who describes himself as lowborn but wanting to associate with the knights rather than the rustics, intends the enumeration of arbitrary and humiliating obligations to be amusing but (with only slight exaggeration) fitting. Here is Marc Bloch's "essence profonde" of serfdom, a humiliating productivity.

Contemptuous images of subjugation were thus perfectly compatible with a certain understanding of where the wealth of the nobility came from. The peasant is "rascally," wicked, and uncooperative but responsive to coercion. A mixture of irritation and amused indulgence is conveyed in Leon Battista Alberti's brief discussion of how to deal with peasants in the course of his *Della Famiglia*. Rustic tenants are wicked, and their main purpose in life is to cheat their masters, pretending to be poor, constantly complaining and never rendering what they are obligated to. Yet even if one could provision an estate by simply buying goods in the market, it is better to rely on one's own agricultural laborers. With close supervision one can get something out of the rustics, and after all, their villainous tricks are amusing and good training for dealing with similarly inconsiderate urban citizens.[80]

For most late-medieval observers, the element of force had to be somewhat greater than that envisioned by Alberti. The peasants could be conceived as both necessary *and* bestial. This was linked to the imputed nature of their service: reluctant but productive, given a certain level of coercion. They could be held to resemble useful rather than threatening animals. A proverb held that a rustic was like an ox, the only difference being that he lacked horns.[81] But as with such domesticated beasts as oxen, he could not be relied on to labor of his own volition, but rather required discipline. Another proverb likened the rustic, the ass, and the nut, all of which must be struck in order to produce anything.[82] A Latin rhyming proverb states that rustics are best when weeping, worst when laughing.[83] Similarly, a French proverb holds that if you "anoint" a *vilain* (i.e., treat him with kindness) he will sting (or prick) you; sting *him* and he will behave well.[84]

In these examples, the rustic is like an animal that only responds to goading: ornery but ultimately tractable and useful. A more hostile view sees them as only barely tamed. According to the Catalan Franciscan Francesc Eiximenis, servile peasants are naturally inclined to evil and, like cruel and savage beasts, must be beaten and starved into submission.[85] Ruprecht von Freising's *Freisinger Rechtsbuch* (compiled in 1328) allowed lords to flog their peasants as long as the peasant did not die within a day of administration of this punishment (thus anything short of deliberate flogging to death was licit). This degree of power and its limitation was not especially unusual (it is ultimately derived from Exodus 21:20–21), but the rationale given by the lawbook is significant: "masters must keep them in fear or they'll never work."[86]

Exploitative discipline to be sure: a popular riddle asks "what do peasants most earnestly pray for?" The answer is: for the lords to have plenty of fine horses, for otherwise the lords will ride the peasants instead.[87] Beside such confidence in the peasants' haplessness must be set other images of rural insurrections in which the peasants were depicted as wild and dangerous beasts. Perhaps they had once been properly domesticated, but now they have run wild.

In the fifteenth century the Swiss epitomized impudent and rebellious rustics, and it was frequently argued that their success could have been prevented had they been supervised more harshly. A poem from the time of Appenzell's revolt against the jurisdiction of Saint Gall (1400–1404) says that one must "bleed" the peasants occasionally to get more work out of them.[88] The humorist Heinrich Bebel, in a poem written under the pseudonym Heintz von Bechwinden in 1499, recommended that the rebellious Swiss peasants be punished, just as a willow tree is trimmed with a knife to be made to produce more.[89] Peasants are impudent because they get to keep too much money. Hemmerli, writing during the Toggenburg War between Zurich and the rural cantons, proposed that to tame the arrogance of the rustics it would be best to destroy their farms every fifty years or so.[90]

The productive as opposed to bestial *vilain* is not so drastically physically distorted as the solitary rustic of the French romance, but posture, dress, and diet mark out and emphasize his subordination. A song written at the time of the Flemish peasant uprising of 1323–28 mocks the "Karls" for their long beards, torn clothes, tattered shoes, and peculiar hats. According to the chorus, curdled milk, bread, and cheese are their diet; anything more would dull their wits. All the peasant really needs is a thick slice of rye bread to hold as he heads for the plough. His raggedly dressed wife, her mouth full of fibers, works her distaff until it's time to prepare the supper porridge. The poem ends, "We shall know how to punish the Karls . . . we shall drag them to execution, we shall hang them, they must again submit to the yoke."[91] Once they *have* been subdued, they will return to their wretched but useful labor.

John Gower, in the *Mirour de l'omme*, contrasts the obedient rustics of past times, who were content with a diet of coarse bread, milk, and cheese, with the greedy and disloyal rabble of his own time.[92] A common story was told of a woman married to a wealthy peasant who found that her husband complained when she served him delicacies. Her mother advised her to give him beans and peas with soaked bread, which she did, whereupon her husband cheered up and ceased his carping.[93] In one of the German poems attributed to Neidhart, the peasant Berewolf, once the cynosure of the village lasses, marries the hectoring Trûte and has to look forward not only to a life of harsh labor but to a diet of horseradish and cabbage.[94] Peasants in Germany and the Low Countries were commonly referred to as "turnip-eaters," while those of France were sometimes typified as "pea-eaters."[95]

Peasants were supposed to be capable of (and even to require) large amounts of the unpleasant food appropriate to their station. While the knight managed to do battle on a light, elegant diet of game, fish, and exotic birds (swans, peacocks), rustic feasts were depicted as occasions for drunkenness and the consumption of immense quantities of crude provender.[96]

All these traits—ugliness, hairiness, bizarre or ragged clothing, coarse food—are essential characteristics of the peasant but in some sense acquired rather than the product of an entirely different species. The peasant's customs and instincts are certainly intrinsically base, but these characteristics are the result of neglect or habit, of debasement rather than "biological" difference.

Stupidity and Excrement

The peasant as stupid and his association with excrement (both animal and human) are two recurrent traits that indeed seem to mark off the peasant as possessed of a gross, inferior nature. Peasants were supposed to be stupid, an enduring image of the countryman common across boundaries and time. True, habit and habitat were thought to encourage and bring out this doltishness (Marx's "lunacy of rural life"). The peasant might not be biologically inferior in mind at the moment of birth, but his essential nature was credulous, slow, and dull-witted.

The *fabliaux* often depict rustics who are tricked and cuckolded. They are not the only victims, of course, but with townsmen or nobles it is greed, old age, or amorous fatuity that interferes with an otherwise natural sagacity (as with the elderly knight Januarie in Chaucer's "Merchant's Tale"), while the peasant is simply dumb in the first place. Peasants are portrayed as easy victims for all manner of swindlers.[97] Even when innocence is rewarded, it is a foolish innocence. In Jean Bodel's "Brunain, la vache au prestre," a peasant couple, taking literally the words of the Gospel from a sermon that God will repay twofold what is given in His name, donate their cow named "Blerain" to the priest. Pleased with this acquisition, the priest puts Blerain with his own animal, "Brunain," but Blerain leads her new companion from the priest's pasture back to the peasants, who indeed obtain thereby two beasts for one. Their simplicity is rewarded, but the animal is, in effect, smarter than its masters.[98]

In the later Neidhart material, the knight becomes a trickster who victimizes the extraordinarily credulous villagers.[99] He fools them into covering themselves with a malodorous salve, or drops them into a pit of manure. Disguised as a peddler, Neidhart leaves a basket of carved images of the villagers, and then, before the duke of Austria, denies having anything to do with what has the look of spell-casting. The villagers are fined by the duke for their "false" complaint. In the *Brautschwank* Neidhart poses as a bride for one of the boorish peasants, who is so entranced by love that even on the wedding night he fails to realize the deceit. Neidhart steals the customary gift to the bride (the *Morgengabe*) and departs.

Francesc Eiximenis tells a story about peasant stupidity in connection with Saint Bonaventura, who was reputed to have come from extremely humble origins (his father was, in fact, a doctor). According to Eiximenis, Bonaventura returned to his native village in the north of Italy after he had achieved fame for his sanctity, learning, and high office. At first he was greeted cordially by the villagers, but their attitude changed as the rumor spread that Bonaventura owed his intelligence to diabolical practices that had sucked out all the intellect of his fellow villagers and gathered it for his use and profit. This explained not only Bonaventura's extraordinary success but also the villagers' witlessness.[100]

Keeping animals and attempting to fertilize his fields, the peasant could be easily associated with manure and various other forms of animal waste, which served as an emblem of his distance from civilization. Neidhart's hatred of the peasants begins with a rustic prank in which symbols of chivalric delicacy collide with peasant baseness. In a *Schwanklied* that goes under Neidhart's name, and in the earliest surviving secular drama of the Middle Ages, the knight proposes a contest to the court of the duchess of Bavaria to find the first violet of spring. He himself finds the flower, and after marking the spot with his cap, runs off happily to alert his companions. But the discovery has been observed by a "filthy peasant" who lifts the hat, defecates onto the violet, and then carefully replaces the cap. Neidhart returns with the duchess, the court, and musicians to celebrate his victory, only to be disgraced when the cap is ceremoniously lifted to the sound of a trumpet fanfare. The villagers then take the turd-encrusted violet, hoist it on a pole, and dance around it. But Neidhart has his revenge, cutting off the left legs of no fewer than 32 of the dancers.[101]

The Violet Prank (*Veilchenschwank*) would be the most popular Neidhart

9. A scene from Neidhart's scatological misadventure, the "Violet Prank" (*Veilchenschwank*). Mural painted between 1360 and 1380, from the "Zum Grundstein" house, Winterthur, Switzerland. Reprinted by permission of the Stadtbibliothek Winterthur.

theme of the late Middle Ages and beyond.[102] Sometime before 1330, the moment of Neidhart's humiliation was painted on the wall of a patrician drinking hall in the town of Diessenhofen, on the Rhine in what is now the Swiss canton of Thurgau. The mural, now destroyed (a paper copy is in Zurich), showed Neidhart with the musicians while the duchess points to something now effaced. An onlooker delicately holds his nose. The early date of the mural shows the popularity of the *Veilchenschwank* even before the first Neidhart play appeared in 1350.[103]

Another depiction of the "Violet Prank" dating from between 1360 and 1380, adorned the house "Zum Grundstein" in Winterthur (Fig. 9). At the castle of Trautson in the Tyrol, a series of Neidhart pranks, including the *Veilchen* episode, was painted in the mid–fifteenth century.[104] In 1979, another cycle of Neidhart murals dating from about 1400 (including the *Veilchenschwank*, mirror theft, and peasant brawl) was discovered at a house in Vienna.[105]

I have already mentioned the Italian poem that attributed the origins of the *vilain* to the colossal fart of a barnyard animal. In accord with these circumstances, the *vilain* himself was credited with an extraordinary proclivity for flatulence. Rutebeuf's *fabliaux*, "Le pet au vilain," purports to explain why rustics are admitted neither to heaven nor to hell. There is no place in heaven for *vilains*, for they hate priests and are devoid of charity. Formerly, demons routinely awaited the separation of rustic souls from their bodies. In accord with this office, a demon attended a certain dying peasant's bedside with a sack. The soul exited not from the mouth (as with those of higher estate) but from the rear. Shortly before dying, the peasant had eaten a meal of beef seasoned with garlic. As he expired and his soul was put in the sack, the rustic broke a final, powerful wind. So powerful, in fact, that when the soul was released in hell, the unpleasant smell was enough to compel its expulsion. Henceforth no rustics would be allowed in hell, and so Rutebeuf advises them to sing with the frogs after death or seek the realm of excrement, the territory of Audigier (on which see below).[106]

The peasant is surrounded by excrement and dirt, symbols of unpleasant natural productivity and of the uncontrollable body. In common with other examples of the polymorphous body, the obsessive scatology may indicate not just the hostile regard of the superior orders but some element of the carnivalesque culture of the lower classes themselves. Excretion may also be akin to the making of fiction, a comical self-reference in the *fabliau* genre to the peculiar art of transforming the world into verse.[107] But the scatological image of the rustic shows him, as it were, in his native element and represents a statement about his nature, condition, and relation to the rest of the world. In the *fabliau* "Le vilain asnier," a rustic leading two asses loaded with manure through the crowded streets of Montpellier faints dead away, overcome by the unaccustomed sweet aromas of the spice market. He seems to be dead (and is blocking traffic), but is revived when a clever passer-by holds a pellet of dung under the peasant's nose. Brought back to life by the familiar odor, the peasant goes on his way completely restored.[108]

The rustic's natural setting consists not only of animal manure but of his own excrement. In a *fabliau* with the down-to-earth title "La crote" (The turd), a peasant and his wife play a semierotic game that involves tricking each other into eating feces.[109] Another story combines the theme of stupidity with defecation. In "Jouglet," the *jongleur* (poet or minstrel) is entrusted with educating a peasant named Robin in preparation for his marriage. His advice is to eat lots of green apples and to avoid defecating on his wedding day. The result is a frenzied production of excrement all over the house and its contents, even in the case holding the minstrel's viol.[110] The uncontrollable body is here indicated not by malformation but by a foolishly self-inflicted gastrointestinal crisis.

The mock epic *Audigier* tells the story of the prince of a "soft kingdom" of the intestine who courts a rustic girl. In its outline the piece follows a conventional story of war, marriage, and revenge, but its gastroenterological location is unforgettable. The dower consists of dog turds, the wedding meal is a stew with chicken droppings, the minstrels are paid with goat turds.[111]

～

What has been described above is a vocabulary of terms of subordination, a set of conventional representations of use to medieval comic and didactic writers about the peasantry. In most texts, various images are combined. Thus in 14 of the surviving 124 fifteenth-century Nuremberg Carnival plays (*Fastnachtspiele*), peasants are described in by-now familiar terms as obscene, scatological, gluttonous, and rowdy.[112] They are ludicrously unsuccessful in their wooing and susceptible to every sort of (usually self-inflicted) mishap. In a further 25 such plays, there are characters described simply as "fools," but they are clearly rustic fools or have comical rural names, such as "Heinz Molkenfass" (cheese-eater).[113] These plays, designed for the inverted social world of Carnival, entertained townspeople for the peasant was an emblem of the comically base. The costume of peasants was second only to devil's outfits in popularity during Carnival celebrations.[114]

A number of the themes concerning the wickedness and lowliness of rustics are also summarized conveniently in a fifteenth-century poem of mixed Italian and Latin contained within a medical treatise.[115] The "Life of the Infidel, Wicked, and Rustic Villeins" begins by rejoicing at the vexations afflicting the peasants. They are penniless, go about in bare feet, eat grass mixed with turds, and keep sickly livestock.[116] They subsist on garlic, onions, roots, and vegetables.[117] They labor and suffer while others receive the benefits of what they produce. They are stupid and bestial, infidels, "worse than Jews."[118] Their appearance provokes laughter. They are liars and robbers, rightly made to suffer in purgation for their wickedness.[119] The poem ends with a play on several Latin liturgical tags: "*Servi servorum*, Ass of Asses, God curse you for ever and ever, Amen. From the intrigues of the devil, the lordship of the villein, and the furor of the rustics release us O Lord."[120]

The rustic is thus wicked, bestial, and tamed only by coercion. But he *is* generally (although not always) regarded as being useful, even if coercion is required. In hostile texts such as the "Life of the Infidel, Wicked, and Rustic Villeins," they still labor while others profit. The late-medieval (or perhaps sixteenth-century) Italian "Alphabet Against the *Villani*" opens with the statement that the perfidious, wicked, and ungrateful rustic is destined to labor.[121] There follows another catalogue of evil characteristics, especially dishonesty.

The degraded condition of the rustic was demonstrated by an essential subhumanity, deformity, resemblance to animals, or other attributes setting him apart from civilization. In other cases, his separation from the fully human is the result of character, or baseness that does not necessarily render him completely unhuman. We have distinguished between the savage, solitary rustic and the more docile, productive peasant, but in both cases a debased character, a malformed (if powerful) body, and a subhuman nature demonstrate that subjugation is appropriate.

The *vilain* in literature thus amounted to more than a conventional sign for base behavior. He was an *exemplum a contrario* but not simply for the purpose of instruction by reverse example or to parody high-flown genres. Rusticity was not simply a vehicle to teach manners or displace and transgress the heroic. The convenience of stereotypical images is that they conform to perceptions and reinforce them. The assumption of a background of peasant filthiness or stupidity made it possible to build didactic and comical tropes on these themes.

At the same time it won't do to describe the rustic as simply the target of a hegemonic discourse of domination by which he is represented as "Other." Along with embodying certain negative qualities, the peasant was productive, important, necessary. He inhabited a world apart but could not be serenely or consistently regarded as a subhuman Other, because his lowliness was useful, more so than the supposed alien character of Jews, Saracens, or "monstrous races." There was a tension between regarding the peasant as excluded from human society and as necessary for its survival.

A resolution of this tension was to see the negative qualities as signs of a natural but domesticated lowliness. In a sense the entire discourse about the filthy, wicked, or bestial peasantry is an extended commentary on the theory of natural slavery, that some are fit by their nature for labor. They may fulfill this function docilely, or they may require coercion. The peasant's physical strength and intellectual debility may signal his aptitude for toil, as Aristotle says,[122] but such an explanation encounters certain problems with Christian notions of equality, humanity, and the relation of this world to the next. To the extent that the debasement of peasants was seen as violating their humanity, by arguing their infidelity or essentially subordinate nature one could begin to justify their status.

As we have seen, there were several other ways to deal with this problem: to attribute the rustic's condition not to biological or acquired subordination but to a hereditary taint, originating in an event such as Noah's curse against his son Ham, or in an act of betrayal in more recent national history, such as deserting Charlemagne. The advantage of these approaches was that they did not require setting the peasants apart from humanity, but rather made them heirs of a crime on the order of Adam's Fall and its consequences. In all such constructions, however, the peasant might be regarded in some sense as "naturally" debased, but insofar as he was productive, Christian, and not dwelling in some far-off fantastic realm but in proximity to those he supported, his condition remained a moral problem.

Chapter 7

Peasant Bodies, Male and Female

As has been shown, peasants were often depicted as filthy, subhuman, and comical, the reverse of the civilized and courtly. In medieval literature, the *vilain* was everything that the knight was not: lowly, servile, grossly materialistic, cowardly, malformed, and unfit for the service of love. Above all, the rustic, more specifically the *male* rustic, represented gross materiality. Peasants appeared in art and iconography as coarse and ill-favored.[1] Likened to domestic animals or even (by means of images of filth and excrement) to the land he tilled, the peasant was rendered as large, grotesque, and rather sluggish. He craved food, yawned, scratched himself, was partial to drink, and enjoyed sleeping.

Given these contemptuous depictions, oriented as they are around a disturbing physicality, one might expect the peasant to be portrayed as dangerous or as sexually threatening. Comical and frightening images readily coexist, as demonstrated by durable stereotypes of African-Americans. Both during and after the era of slavery, American blacks were simultaneously regarded as amusing and childlike on the one hand and as dangerous, savage, and sexually powerful on the other.[2]

In general, medieval peasants were not considered dangerous except in insurrections, when they formed a wild and murderous throng. The individual rustic was undisciplined, to be sure. The carnivalesque embodiment identified by Mikhail Bakhtin exalted a grotesque, hyperbolic physicality and a subversive disorder.[3] Lack of discretion also emblematized the lower orders. As noted previously, Noah's cursed son Ham, progenitor of the unfree, earned punishment for an undisciplined character that henceforth typified slaves.[4]

None of this, however, presented a threat to the knightly class. Rustic males appear in the French romances as grotesque but harmless. The herdsman in Chrétien's *Yvain* and the charcoal burner in *Aucassin et Nicolette* are frightening in appearance but hardly intimidating in character. They resemble the "wild man," a folkloric and literary figure who dwelled in the forest, a debased, semihuman being.[5] Like the wild man, they are timid and ungainly rather than fierce, with only crude weapons (such as clubs). The herdsman encountered by Calogrenant is powerful enough to grab his bulls by the horns, causing them to tremble, but presents no threat to the knight, who is in fact more worried about the bulls.[6]

In German literature the peasant men are less often rendered as misshapen, and they are also more aggressive, prone to internecine violence. In the poems of Neidhart and his later imitators, the male villagers kill and dismember each other in the course of celebrations that degenerate into comic brawls. The peasants exemplify the unchivalric, here by reason of stupidity rather than timidity. They quarrel over ridiculous pretexts, just as they dress foppishly in ludicrous imitation of courtly garb. They use swords, weapons that are too dangerous for their reckless lack of control, and so commit mayhem. In all this, however, they pose no danger to Neidhart, the knight-narrator, whose only fear is that he will be accidentally caught in the midst of their murderous rage.[7]

Only in exceptional contexts, therefore, was the peasant thought to be capable of violence toward his betters. Seigneurial accounts of late-medieval peasant revolts did reiterate stories of torture, murder, and rape of nobles by enraged rustics, but under normal circumstances peasants posed no physical, military, or sexual threat.

How dangerous could the peasant be, defined as he was in contrast to the knight as unwarlike? Chivalric prestige depended on military courage and skill with an overlay of courtesy and amorous sensibility. The peasants, on the other hand, were inept at war. Although sufficiently brutish to practice violence on members of their own class, peasants were laughable as any sort of military force (again apart from the exceptional occasion of mass rebellion). Nor were peasant men regarded as possessing any particular sexual energy or aggressiveness. It was a literary commonplace that rustic men are unfit for love, not merely because they lacked the necessary refinement but because they were too materialistic. Their concerns were land, work, money, all rendering them unable to experience the yearning that afflicts the brave and well-born.

Valor and skill at love were joined in the image of knighthood. Both love and chivalry required an elaborate set of rules but also a spiritual desire that raised the knight above an interest in mere physical comfort. Conversely, the peasant not only lacked the ability to master the complex rituals of love and war but wallowed in an innate, gross embodiment and materiality. The desire for safety, a reluctance to risk life for honor, made the peasant a ludicrous figure in any military context. He was suited for the plow, not the sword, and driven more by appetite than honor. In the *fabliau* "Berengier au lonc Cul," the lowborn "knight" prefers tarts and baked custards to such unsatisfactory intangibles as fame or chivalry.[8]

The rustic is also unlikely to experience more than a torpid sexual desire. He is certainly not about to engage in any sacrifice or quest for its sake. In several Old French pastourelles a rustic girl laments that she is saddled with a husband who is dull or who thinks only of money.[9] A story in Boccaccio's *Decameron* about the gardener of a convent who disports himself with its inmates begins by citing the common belief that "spade and mattock and coarse victuals and hard living do altogether purge away carnal appetites from the tillers of the earth." This opinion attributes to rural laborers both dulled wit and feeble sexual appetite, notions that the career of the crafty and sexually athletic gardener superficially disproves but actually reinforces precisely because he is exceptional.[10]

Lumbering, misshapen, and dull, peasants were, as a rule, supposed to be incapable of the passionate spiritual energy that drives chivalric male desire. In this chapter I want to explore this curious asexual materiality of the male peasant and to describe the rather different image of the female peasant, who could be physically alluring, even witty.

It was both a learned and a popular convention in the Middle Ages that women represented a principle of matter, generation, and embodiment. Medical, theological, and literary orthodoxy made women the vehicles of a natural, biological force complementing or opposing a spiritual, intellectual male principle.[11] The emblem of embodiment in medieval condemnations of women was their sexuality. Women were regarded as sexually insatiable and as temptations to male sinfulness.[12] In accord with Galen, the medical school of Salerno taught that women were more lustful than men, an opinion that was sometimes challenged but remained dominant throughout the Middle Ages.[13]

Stereotypes of peasant men in some sense resembled those attributed to women generally, in that the male peasant, too, represented embodiment. But the image of the male differed in portraying his body as oriented around the digestive system and as devoid of the sexual and procreative energy attributed to women. Peasant women, although sharing the supposedly common traits of all peasants, did not share the image of gross materiality associated with their male counterparts.

Ineptitude at Love

Peasant men might be affected by a crude form of desire but were thought to be devoid of amorous and certainly of chivalric yearning. In a Spanish eclogue written at the end of the Middle Ages by Juan del Encina, the allegorical figure of Love punishes the shepherd Pelayo by making him become painfully enraptured with the ugly peasant girl Marinella.[14] A passing squire, informed of Pelayo's malady, expresses incredulity at the idea of a rustic suffering amorous pangs. Juan del Encina wrote at the beginning of the revival of the ancient pastorale. During the Spanish "Golden Age," lovesick shepherds and other amorous *villanos* would litter the landscape, but the medieval opinion was that only the well-born can feel the sweet pain of love.

That peasants love in the manner of beasts was a medieval commonplace. A well-known passage from the handbook of love by Andreas Capellanus states that peasants are not servants of love but are merely urged to it by nature in the manner of horses or mules.[15] A thirteenth-century treatise states that peasants love as beasts do, with neither courtesy nor goodness. The author likens rustic lovemaking to "wildness" (*rage*), an animal instinct more pathetic than threatening.[16]

Peasants' sexual desire was either inept or unorthodox. An engraving by Cornelis Massys, *Market Peasants in a Brothel* (ca. 1540), comically depicts prostitutes fleecing peasants who had become temporarily affluent through the sale of their produce.[17] Within the print is a picture on the wall showing a peasant sitting on a pile of eggs; under the picture is the legend "It is a sorry house where the hen crows and not the rooster." The lecherous peasants at the brothel resemble the generality of male rustics who allow themselves to be dominated by their wives. Here the peasant is not immune to lust, but he cuts a figure more ludicrous than rakish.

In the course of his diatribe against the Swiss, Felix Hemmerli theorized that because Swiss men tended and milked animals, performing what is properly women's work, they were perhaps inclined to copulate with their cattle.[18] Their masculinity is put in doubt and their supposed proclivity to unnatural vice is mocked.

Rustic couples might occasionally be portrayed in the French *fabliaux* as enjoying what John Baldwin calls "robust, cheerful, marital sexuality,"[19] but more often the rustic man, among whose most prominent characteristics was stupidity, was rendered as the ridiculous victim of his wife's adultery. In a *fabliau* by Jean Bodel, the wife of an ugly, disagreeable, and foolish *vilain* plans to entertain her lover, the parish priest, but shortly before the rendezvous her husband returns unexpectedly. With a pretense of alarm, she exclaims that her husband looks as if he is dying. When the priest arrives on the scene, she convinces her husband that he is in fact dead. The amorous couple disport themselves, having assured the hapless *vilain* that since he is now dead, there is nothing he can do to stop them. Lying on a straw pallet, the foolish husband resignedly accepts this and closes his eyes.[20]

In a *fabliau* by Garin, another priest looks through the keyhole of a rustic house and sees a *vilain* having dinner with his pretty wife. The priest rushes in, denouncing them for fornication. The bewildered husband protests that they were simply having a meal. The priest asserts that the keyhole must be enchanted as it *looks* as if those innocently dining at the table are engaged in sexual play. The priest invites the peasant to see for himself. The rustic confirms this phenomenon as he views the priest and his wife enjoying each other while they assure him that they are merely sitting at the table.[21]

There are several factors that contribute to the vilain's lack of skill at love. His constitution and plodding stupidity fit him for toil, while his nature makes him prefer safety and dull material concerns to the risk and thrill of love and war. Such ignorance and lack of interest in love fit the hierarchical medical and ethical theories of desire. Knights were thought to be peculiarly susceptible to the sickness of love, a spiritual rather than purely bodily disorder. The *Viaticum*, a Latin translation of an Arab book of medical advice for travelers, included a diagnosis and treatment for lovesickness.[22] Twelfth-century Latin treatises based on this popular work identified lovesickness as a peculiarly aristocratic affliction.[23] In a gloss to the *Viaticum* by Gerard de Berry, love was joined to nobility by an etymological contortion. In keeping with established medical learning (including the *Viaticum*), Gerard referred to "the love that is called *heros*" (derived from eros) as a type of mental disorder. Cobbling together eros, heros (hero) and herus (noble), Gerard remarked that nobles are most likely to succumb to the disease, a susceptibility encouraged by their leisure and wealth.[24]

Even if the peasant is not biologically incapable of love, his manner of life makes him ill-equipped for love's demands. Leisure is the prerequisite for love. Idleness (*Oiseuse*) is the (female) allegorical gatekeeper of the enclosed garden at the beginning of *Le Roman de la Rose*.[25] Hard work, which defines the peasant, is not conducive to the cultivation and refinement of amorous sentiment. After likening peasants' desire to that of beasts, Andreas Capellanus concludes that toil with the plow and hoe is the sole "consolation" of these unfortunates. It would be an error to instruct them in love's mysteries since they would then abandon the fields, to the detriment of all society (invoking the theme of the plodding, usefully productive peasant).[26] Rustics were supposed to work, and knights were supposed to fight and to love. The practice of love required valor and a degree of self-sacrifice, a combination of pleasure and deprivation, characteristic noble attributes neither of which applied to male rustics. Knights should disdain comfort and be driven by the defense of honor and amorous passion. Peasants were immune to the disease of love, for they lacked both honor and the susceptibility to higher forms of spiritual suffering.

The clergy form something of a case apart. They were regarded as peculiarly given over to lust, their inordinate sexual desire amounting to a more urgent and less praiseworthy passion than that of the nobility. Among 50 *fabliaux* examined by Baldwin, 23 involve lustful clerics whose objects of desire, as seen in the examples mentioned above, are often peasant wives.[27]

The clerical members of the pilgrim company in Chaucer's *Canterbury Tales* exhibit less controllable, more sinister desires than does the young squire. A passage in the *Death Dance*, probably by Hans Hesse, published in 1490, parodies the scheme of the Three Orders by having the devil address the folly of each estate: he says to the priest, "tu fornicator"; to the knight, "tu praedor" (robber); and to the rustic, "tuque lecator," meaning "glutton" in this context.[28]

Even in literary genres that depict the peasant as more violent than hapless, notably the Neidhart and Neidhart-related poems, the peasant men are not suited for even an unrefined form of love. The men of the village of Reuental ("Valley of Grief") are violent and boorish rather than timid and physically grotesque as in the French tradition.[29] Within their own world they are certainly more assertive than the pathetic lowborn husbands of the *fabliau*. In the entire Neidhart corpus (and indeed in almost all the voluminous German antipeasant satirical texts), the peasants do not appear engaged in productive labor.[30] Unlike their French counterparts, therefore, they do have the idleness necessary for the pursuit of love. In fact they seem to have the economic wherewithal to sport foppish and absurd clothes and inappropriate weapons. These are not placid, dutiful rustics but rather violent, lazy, presumptuous, and, above all, boorish ones. It is their uncouth character that makes them ridiculous and absurd as lovers rather than poverty, work, or unprepossessing physique.

The unsuitability of the men of Reuental for love is manifested by their rough treatment of the village women. In the so-called Winter Songs, the village fête features dancing followed by an inevitable fight. During the dance the girls are manhandled by their partners, who step on their clothes, fondle them, and steal their adornments.[31] In 12 of the 36 Winter Songs, a mirror belonging to Vriderûn, the peasant lass for whom Neidhart longs, is stolen by the loutish Engelmâr, Neidhart's rustic rival.

The comic art of the Neidhart poems is such that the knight himself is sometimes pathetically unsuccessful at love. He is misplaced in this remote village, and his refined longings, appropriate to the habits of renunciatory longing in the *Minnesang*, are wasted even when he is admired. Although he is the object of the village maidens' ambitions in the Summer Songs, Neidhart displays a pathetic lassitude or impotent rage in the Winter Songs. The mirror theft is avenged only by the destructive brawling of the peasants themselves. Neidhart, while lamenting the theft in exaggerated terms (ultimately blaming it for the general decline of chivalry)[32] is helpless to do anything about it except to rejoice from a safe distance as the rustics proceed to kill and maim each other in the fight that ensues.[33]

The original Neidhart cuts a poor figure, but this is the result of his own misfortune and lack of decisiveness, not the work of his boorish rivals. In the late-medieval *Neidhartschwänke*, the knight has been transformed into an accomplished and sadistic trickster. His archrival is still Engelmâr, but the reason for their enmity is the Violet Prank, and the female villagers have dropped out of the story. By this time, the peasants are ignorant, credulous, and helpless before the pranks of the clever knight. They conform more closely to the general European image of the hapless rustic, but love is no longer at issue.

Rustic Women

Having stated that peasants experience desire in the fashion of beasts and are fit for labor rather than love, Andreas Capellanus, in his discourse on love, grudgingly admits that knights might possibly find peasant girls alluring. In such an event, seduction ought to be undertaken by force, preceded by a bit of flattery perhaps, but certainly without any elaborate courtesy.[34] Even more dismissively, Juan Ruiz, archpriest of Hita, the Castilian author of the fourteenth-century *Libro de buen amor*, has the wise counselor Don Amor remark that peasant women are too stupid to know anything about love.[35]

Yet there was a distinction between peasant men and peasant women. The former were at best awkward and slow, and more often misshapen and grotesque. The females (especially when young) were comely enough to be the objects of rather predatory seduction. A mock catechism directed against the rustics (preserved in several late-medieval manuscripts in company with the previously mentioned comic "declension of *rusticus*") includes the prayer: "God, thou who hast sown perpetual discord between lechers and rustics, give to us the use of their wives and daughters and allow us to rejoice in their [the male rustics'] death."[36] Chaucer's Miller depicts the attractive Alison as a peasant, notwithstanding her patina of urban sophistication. Although she tends dairy cattle, she is fair: fit for a lord to bring to his bed, or for a yeoman to wed.[37]

In the Neidhart poems, the village maidens are engaging, if not very dignified. Sharp and eager, they are altogether inappropriate if the standard is the remote aristocratic female, but they are desirable. Neidhart is foolish not because the girls lack charm but because he makes the mistake against which Andreas had cautioned, that is, ludicrously applying a language of longing to a situation that calls for more forthright lechery. Even in the ribald poem "Der Wengling" (The prick), a species of pastourelle by an imitator of Neidhart, the girl, although stupid ("dy tume"), is nevertheless a perfectly credible object of lust.[38]

The French and Provençal pastourelle, narrated by a knight or cleric who encounters a rustic peasant girl or shepherdess, may be considered a poetic gloss on Andreas Capellanus's advice on how to deal with peasant women.[39] The pastourelle is a fantasy based on desire sharpened by social subordination, "the eroticism of inequality."[40] The wellborn narrator, riding through the countryside in springtime, comes across a young rustic girl who is alone. They banter, and he attempts to win her by gifts and flattery. She rejects his advances, and several possible scenarios ensue: she continues to repulse him, he is driven off by her peasant companions, he convinces her, or he rapes her. Regardless of the "plot," the tone is lyrical and lighthearted. Although descended from the classical pastorale and eclogue, the medieval pastourelle presents a sharp social contrast between interlocutors and a more combative atmosphere than that of the Theocritan or Virgilian idyll.

The pastourelle is something of a vacation from the fatiguing courtship rituals undertaken by knights in the romances. That the suitor is noble while the object of his desires is a rustic might render the dalliance either insignificant in the chivalric scheme of things (as Gaston Paris, inventor of the term "courtly love," believed), or a satire of social class (perhaps by clerics against knights, as W. T. H. Jackson asserts).[41] The Neidhart poems also make use of the socially inappropriate juxtaposition of knight and peasant girl, but the knight lives in the village, and so his encounters are not the casual, unplanned opportunities of the pastourelle. Neidhart's melancholy contrasts with what William Paden has called the *jouissance* of the pastourelle.[42] Both the German and the French poems make fun of the ennobling renunciatory tone of courtly conventions by portraying sexual desire as undignified, whether quickly fulfilled or comically thwarted.

Mocking the customary deference of the knight to his lady, the pastourelle proposes rapidity and coercion. Not only is it appropriate for knights to take peasant girls by force, but that is what the victims themselves enjoy. In twelve of the Old French pastourelles, the shepherdess's initial reluctance turns to sighs of pleasure after she has been raped.[43] While only eighteen percent of the pastourelles, according to Kathryn Gravdal's calculation, involve an actual sexual assault, the acceptability of rape influences the entire genre. Taunting, or a pretense of resistance followed by eager consent, establishes the unreliable coyness of the shepherdess, legitimating rape by turning it into a game.[44] The "game of rape"—the lighthearted presentation of an assault on a resilient and compliant victim—asserted that women are avid, that their protestations to the contrary are insincere, and thus that the rituals of chivalric courtship are at least faintly ridiculous.

The pastourelles are at once lyrical and humorous; they are about rape *and jouissance,* the two not really distinct in the eyes of the authors. Such poems of amorous social transgression are celebrations of pliable women who are appealing, pert, and resilient. A certain allure is evoked by the spring landscape, the beauty of the girl, and the pleasure of an opportunity exploited. The poems are intended to show amusing erotic dalliances, but also parody refined sensibility by mixing up as well as fortifying social boundaries and compressing what might take thousands of lines in a serious love poem into a few brief verses.

The action of the pastourelle speeds along by comparison to the glacial progress of nobles' love. Meeting, compliments, offers of gifts, and sexual assault take place within an imagined time frame to be reckoned in minutes. In "A l'entrant del tanz salvage," by the thirteenth-century French poet Hue de Saint-Quentin, the clerical narrator encounters a girl with a flock of goats, asks her name, and then tells her to kiss him and become his sweetheart, offering an alms-purse or hood. He then proceeds to assault her, reporting the girl's reaction laconically: "I never heard such a fuss." After he "plays the game for her" three times, she assures him, "this is a pleasing tune," and quite contentedly returns to her goats.[45]

In an anonymous pastourelle of the early thirteenth century, a cleric offers a tunic, smock, clasp, and belt to a shepherdess who has lost her cloak. She first threatens to hit him, but when he asks for marriage, she agrees. After their embrace, she cries out:

> May any woman who refuses
> Such sport and such joy
> Be put to shame by God.

The narrator then boasts that he has fooled her, for he has no intention of marrying her. But she is unperturbed. After all, she has been deflowered by the handsomest man in the empire, and as a sporting gesture, she gives him a parting counter-gift of a collar clasp.[46]

In some examples of the pastourelle, the young woman is more thoroughly humiliated, an addition to the narrator's *jouissance*. In "Quant voi nee," another anonymous French poem of the thirteenth century, the shepherdess tries vainly to summon the male shepherds who should have protected her. After flattering her, the knight seizes the girl, enjoying her shame, and has his way with her. As he mounts his palfrey, he offers to take her with him. Clinging to a semblance of honor, she refuses unless he will marry her. He commends her to God and leaves her disheveled before the young men who have belatedly shown up (among them the rustic boyfriend Robin).[47]

There is a triangular relationship among the shepherdess, the knight, and the inept shepherd Robin in which the woman may be thought of as an object of exchange and competition between the two males. Viewed from the knight's vantage point, the eroticism of inequality here encompasses not only an attractive dalliance (the vacation from the ceremonies of the court) but an agreeable contest humiliating to the comical rustic males.[48] Not a very difficult contest, to be sure, but then again hunting and similar recreations did not require fair odds or great difficulty of execution on every occasion to be enjoyable.

It takes only a slight variation for the male rather than female rustic to be the principal object of humiliation. In the *Jeu de Robin et Marion*, a play with a pastourelle plot written circa 1300 by Adam de la Halle, the knight attempts to win Marion first with words, then with force, but she manages to free herself from his clutches. In this instance Robin arrives in time but is too frightened to intervene. Along with his companions, Robin timidly observes the struggle from behind some trees.[49] The cowardice of the male rustic, a venerable theme, is accentuated by the resourcefulness of the shepherdess. The male rustic is cowardly while the female is plucky; the male misshapen and the female winsome. The intention of the pastourelle is comic, but the peasant lass is not in herself an absurd figure. Within the lexicon of male desire she is a physically credible entry. What *would* be ridiculous would be for the knight to regard her with the same hesitant submissiveness that surrounds the higher forms of love. The poems of Neidhart play with precisely this absurdity. Even here, although the knight's longings are foolish, in purely physical terms the village girls are reasonable objects of yearning.

Inverting the Pastourelle

The insincerity of female claims to honor and the knight or cleric's high-handedness do not mean, therefore, that the young woman is always helpless or that the narrator always conquers. The parody of noble courtship is tuned to a new key by the ability of the girl to answer the knight's false courtesy with witty derision and to turn the game around. An early pastourelle by the Occitan poet Marcabru shows a series of attempts at flattery, all of them contemptuously rebuffed by the shepherdess. To the knight's affected solicitude to protect her from the wind, she avers that she is cheerful and healthy; she also declines his offer to keep her company while she guards her flocks. His compliments on her manners and beauty are likewise rejected, for the promise of his devotion is hardly sufficient recompense to tempt the shepherdess to surrender her virginity. The poem ends without a definitive resolution, but the shepherdess has the last word.[50]

Often the girl is simply too smart to be taken in by flattery or attempted intimidation. A poem by Simon d'Authie (fl. 1222–1232) ends with the shepherdess mocking the knight's unsuccessful efforts:

> You have tried your best with me
> But little have you won.
> Many another have you wooed;
> You didn't learn how here.
> Your heart is not so constrained
> As it seems by your words.
> Some men kiss women and embrace them
> Who don't love them at all.[51]

The witty and articulate response of the rustic girl is such that some authorities have argued that she is not really a rustic at all but rather a "sanitized" fantasy object suitable for chivalric desire,[52] or an aristocrat dressed up in peasant garb.[53] The young woman is, however, attractive because of her social subordination combined with innate physical beauty, a theme not altogether unfamiliar to modern literature. She is firmly set in a rustic world with rustic companions. The encounter is a social as well as a sexual trespass. Only with the Renaissance pastorale does one find something more like a masque of Arcadia, in which the shepherds are nobles in costumes.[54]

In certain examples of the pastourelle, the knight not only is thwarted but displays an unbecoming cowardice as he is chased away by the friends or lover of his intended conquest, those who in other poems were so timid. The knight is ludicrously frightened in Jocelin's "Quant j'o chantier l'aluete," declaring:

> I would have no use for a doctor
> If he had caught me that day,
> The peasant with his great strength

> Bent his crossbow and shot
> With a bolt he nearly killed me—
> And I mounted and fled.
> But I can assure you
> That I never had so great fear.[55]

The comic effect is heightened when the girl calls to him to return to her. Not for all the gold in the empire, he recalls, would he have done so! In two poems by Thibaut IV, count of Champagne (died 1253), the knight flees the scene. One concludes with a sarcastic postscript by the shepherdess: "indeed, knights are too brave."[56]

Comic inversion is augmented when the woman becomes the aggressor. Not only is the knight not brave, but he is the somewhat dazed victim of the girl's forcefulness. In "L'autre jour en un jardin," the knight initiates the dialogue with a pretty shepherdess in the usual fashion, but the poem concludes with the knight futilely trying to escape: "In truth, she had her way with me, stripped me naked / Trampled and abused me, more than I can say."[57]

The rustic girl of the pastourelle is sometimes shy, sometimes bold; often she is forced (but ultimately willingly) to submit, while on other occasions she escapes. Whatever her poetic attitude, she is always (until the fourteenth century) attractive, even dazzling in appearance—blond, slender, and with a fresh complexion (although sometimes deviating from the courtly ideal of paleness by reason of her outdoor life). She is often very young: fifteen and a half in one example, thirteen in another, and *parvula non nubilis* in a third.[58]

The peasant girl or shepherdess is thus not merely human but (within the conventions of the era) desirable. Unlike the male rustic, she is not rendered as grotesque, nor is she unskilled in the ways of love. If she is ignorant about love, it is a charming innocence fully in accord with an essentially eager and easily exploited sexuality. She is more clever than her awkward, boorish male companions. Young male peasants may be more aggressive than those of mature age (and in the German Neidhart poems, they are very aggressive indeed), but they are fumbling and inept, whereas the young female rustics are delightful in form and affect.

One should not mistake the articulate and witty responses of the shepherdess for genuine contestation, nor is the fact that she is pretty the mark of a fully realized humanity. The pastourelle cannot be said to provide a voice for its female victim merely because she is not always victimized. It is possible to present females as talking back within the rules of a discourse written and conceived by male authors, but of course the pastourelle is hardly subversive.[59] Her pleasing form differentiates the female from the male peasant, but as a different sort of seigneurial object. It is the labor of the male peasant that is exploited, so that he can be rendered as a more or less tractable domestic animal. The female peasant is an object of sexual exploitation, so she is presented with a different sort of body than that of generic peasants.

Grotesque Female Rustics

In the fourteenth and fifteenth centuries, the difference between representations of male and those of female rustics diminished. For the first time, peasant women were portrayed in shapes as unflattering and grotesque as were their male counterparts. This is in part due to the development of a further inversion or parodic level within the logic of the pastourelle. The usual bravery of the knight having been overturned, it was in some sense logical to experiment with an amusingly unattractive rustic girl. In an Occitan mock pastourelle of 1320, "Mentre per una ribiera," the narrator sees a girl herding pigs (rather than the canonical sheep). She is not only sexually voracious but wild, ugly, fat, and "black as pitch."[60]

Not all ugliness, however, was rustic. The Loathly Lady of Chrétien's *Perceval*, the grotesque lady Guote in Ulrich von Turheim's *Rennewart*, or Villon's decrepit prostitute "la belle Heaulmière" are burlesques of the conventions of female beauty.[61] Moreover, "Mentre per una ribiera" would remain exceptional within the corpus of the pastourelle. Even in the Neidhart poems the village girls are reasonably pretty, even if they are more scheming and materialistic than their counterparts in the pastourelle.

Juan Ruiz's *Libro de buen amor*, a miscellany of anecdotes and observations written between 1330 and 1343, is the first work involving a series of grotesque and comically ugly rustic women. Contained within it are a series of *serranillas* (songs of the *serranas*, the girls of the mountains). These lyric sections alternate with narrative in a verse style known as *cuaderna vía*. The setting, rules, and logic of the *serranilla* invert the conventions of the pastourelle.[62] We are in the barren and rugged landscape of the border of Castile and La Mancha rather than the lush meadows of France. It is winter, not spring. The narrator is timid, while the girl is repulsive and aggressive.

The narrator first encounters a shepherdess called La Chata (Snubnose), who collects tolls from unfortunate travelers in the remote Sierra de Guadarrama and boasts she can tie up men who are unable or unwilling to pay. The hapless poet is hardly on the prowl for sexual gratification. By the time he meets La Chata he is frozen, interested only in shelter and warmth. Hoisting him on her shoulder, she carries him back to her lair. She is "horrendous, wicked, and ugly," but hospitable (she plies the poet with rabbit, partridges, veal, smoked cheese, and trout), and amorous. She orders him to take off his clothes and suggests that they "wrestle together awhile" (*luche-mos un rato*).[63]

Next the narrator encounters Gadea de Riofrío, a "strong mountain girl" who is at least sufficiently prepossessing for the narrator to greet and casually threaten to have his way with if she does not give him directions. In reply, she whacks him on the ear with her staff, but she then takes the shaken poet to her hut, boisterously instructing him not to mind her little joke. Once again he seems more interested in food than loveplay. Having dined, he abruptly departs.[64]

Mengua Lloriente, the third mountain girl, is stupid and acquisitive. She is strong (like the rustic in *Yvain*, she can tame bulls) but more civilized than the others, for she can dance as well as wrestle. Alda, on the other hand, the *serrana* of the fourth *cuaderna vía*, is impossibly malformed, with immense breasts, ribs protruding out of her black chest, her wet hands covered with hair, her little finger bigger than the narrator's thumb.[65]

The strange savagery of the *serranas*, especially the grotesque Alda, differentiates the poems of the *Libro de buen amor* from other parodies of the pastourelle on the order of "Mentre per una ribiera." The *serranas* are not only unattractive but powerful figures, with perhaps some antecedents in folkloric representations of nature, such as the swaggering rustic women who guard mountain passes in the popular *villancicos serranos*.[66] But the *serranas*, like their counterparts in the German *Schwank* and French *fabliau*, are not quite wild or completely unhuman. They have names (unlike the usually anonymous girls in pastourelles). They herd animals and produce food. Although certainly forbidding, they are neither inarticulate nor mad. They possess the putative rural characteristics of coarseness, aptitude for unpleasant labor, and association with animals. These traits, formerly limited to male peasants, now cut across gender.

The *serranillas* of the *Libro de buen amor* invert the pastourelle, amounting to parodies of parodies.[67] To the extent that the pastourelle makes fun of high-minded courtship, it contains within its own logic the possibility for further levels of reversal: the girl is no longer innocent but the sexual aggressor, nor longer pliant but fierce, no longer winsome but abhorrent. The knight now displays the characteristics of the shepherd girl of the pastourelle. It is he who is seized and raped; he who is bribed by gifts. He comes also to resemble the conventional image of the male peasant, his interest turned more toward food and warmth than sexual gratification.

Later Castilian *serranillas* would go back and forth between lyrical praise of a beautiful rustic lass (in the manner of the pastourelle) and a reassertion of the barbarous mountain-girl image. The prevailing theme of the poems of

Carvajales (written in the mid-fifteenth century) is the amorous knight whose affections are roused by a socially dubious but physically appealing woman, but two of his poems include frightful female rustics.[68] The lyrical *serranillas* of the Marqués de Santillana, also dating from the mid-fifteenth century, involve assertive but attractive mountain girls.[69] The poet's assessment that each *serrana* is uniquely beautiful or *gentil* amounts to comic hyperbole and says more about the lovesick narrator than the rustic women, but the latter at least possess a certain coy dignity.

If the Spanish tradition draws back from the grotesque female rustic, German literature of the late Middle Ages thoroughly breaks down the earlier distinction between alluring female peasants and their brutish male companions. In the Neidhart poems (as well as the German equivalents of the pastourelle, such as in the *Carmina Burana*) the village girls are pretty if more willful and scheming than the protagonists of the French pastourelles. By the fifteenth century, however, the rustic women either have disappeared (as in the prank stories about Neidhart's persecution of the villagers) or are rendered as misshapen and grotesque. The peasant's image overall changes in late medieval Germany from exemplar of folly to malevolent and debased, with no distinction in this regard between men and women.

In later poems written in the manner of Neidhart, the male peasants are even more violent than in the thirteenth-century versions. Elizabeth Traverse has compared a song from two Neidhart manuscripts (MS R and MS c), one regarded as containing the earliest forms and the other including additional stanzas and poems.[70] The original is a series of gloomy meditations on the mirror theft and the stupidity of the peasants.[71] Neidhart complains that the peasants have taken his love from him. He threatens violence, but nothing actually happens other than a scuffle among the peasants over a wreath of red flowers. Neidhart wishes that "someone" would skewer his rival (here Enzemen, not Engelmâr), or that at the very least the peasants might beat each other up.

The c manuscript contains fourteen additional stanzas, including four that describe in gory detail a violent peasant brawl occasioned by the wreath. A group of peasants gloats over plans to disembowel their enemies, and in stanza 13 a lethal sword fight breaks out, which the poet regards with horror mingled with satisfaction because five rustics are slain.[72]

In the fourteen *Schwanklieder* dating from the late fourteenth and early fifteenth centuries (and assuredly not by Neidhart), the peasants are no longer violent. The cause of Neidhart's enmity is the excrement-covered violet, not the stolen mirror. Instead of making futile promises of revenge as in the earlier poems, Neidhart cuts off the left legs of 32 dancing villagers.[73] As a prankster, Neidhart consistently and successfully torments his enemies. The peasants have become more credulous and hapless than violent. Neidhart's enmity has nothing to do with frustrated love but with an innate hatred of these savages who are likened to all manner of animals: bears, cranes, swine, dogs, and so on.[74]

In *Der Ring*, by Heinrich Wittenwiler, written in about 1400, the grotesque female protagonist appears for the first time in German literature. The poem is some 9,700 lines long, the most extended German antipeasant satire, and is largely taken up with the comically unpleasant wedding of Bertschi Triefnas (Dripnose) and Mätzli Rüerenzumph (Touch-the-Cock).[75] Many of the Neidhart themes are echoed, including a cameo appearance by Neidhart himself. The reader is treated to a Neidhart prank, dancing ending in a brawl, and presumptuous peasants with ridiculous names foppishly dressed and sporting murderous weapons. The results, however, are cataclysmic: a war erupts between two peasant villages as a result of the brawl, and most of the villagers of Lappenhausen (Village of Fools) are killed.

The tone of the work is even more unremittingly harsh than the late Neidhart material or its other model, the short peasant-wedding poem of the fourteenth century, "Metzen Hochzit."[76] The peasant men are rendered as subhuman more by their actions than by their physical form. Here it is the bride Mätzli whom Wittenwiler depicts as impossibly ugly and malformed. While Bertschi is merely healthy and (foolishly) proud, Mätzli has a goiter that hangs past her belly, teeth and hands like coal, cheeks "rosy as ashes," and breasts "as small as sacks of lard."[77]

Only one manuscript copy of Wittenwiler's *Der Ring* exists, so the work's literary influence, at least at the outset, must have been fairly limited. The grotesque female rustic was not quite so elaborately described in later antipeasant satires, but from the fifteenth to eighteenth centuries, female and male peasants in equal measure were commonly rendered as crude, ugly, and disorderly, if not as deformed. In sixteenth-century woodcut engravings and paintings, the riotous peasant wedding or other festive occasion emblematized the low nature of rustics much in the manner of the Neidhart tradition but with less lethal violence and with more gluttony and vomiting (borrowed from the Carnival plays).[78] In one of Frans Verbeeck's peasant-wedding paintings, an inscription describes the bride as "an ugly, dirty, licentious beast," while the groom is merely sturdy and handsome (the pair is thus like the wedding couple in *Der Ring*).[79] In general, however, it is the behavior of rustics that is condemned, and their stocky, clumsy bodies exemplify a life given over to immediate gratification. Men and women alike represent a disgraceful (although amusing) material embodiment and lower nature. The genre of "Grobianism" (from the German *grob*, *Grobian* meaning coarse, gross, a boor) would be popular in Germany, Spain, and the Netherlands from the sixteenth to eighteenth centuries. Grobian art and literature catalogued the gluttony, violence, and boorishness of ill-favored rustics of both sexes, elaborating on the examples set by the festive representations of the sixteenth century whose roots, as we have seen, go back to Neidhart in the thirteenth century.[80]

While the proliferation of rustic scenes in visual art of the sixteenth to eighteenth centuries might indicate a feeling for realism and even a positive description of the life of the common people, there is usually an ideological and moral edge.[81] The peasant is a laughable, reverse moral typification of bad manners and gross customs. As they were in the Middle Ages, now rustics may be as much counterexample as specific target of ridicule, but this does not mean rustic life is in itself somehow appreciated more favorably than it was in the frankly averse Grobian genre. Even in works such as those by Bruegel, which are not primarily intended to show peasants as wicked, the rural folk eat, dance, indulge bodily whims, and succumb to instinct and materialism. The new element in Bruegel and the seventeenth century is the rediscovery of the productive labor of the peasant. After centuries of festive and useless peasants, the rustic as symbol of dutiful labor (as in *The Fall of Icarus*) returns.[82]

Part 4

Peasant Agency, Peasant Humanity

Chapter 8

Peasant Warriors and Peasant Liberties

Peasant men represented embodiment of a coarse and lowly sort. Appetite, cowardice, and an exclusive concern with the material and immediate rendered them inept and morally unfit for war, hence to be denied the perquisites of love or of freedom. Foundational legends explaining the origins of nobles and serfs focused, as we have seen, on a genealogy of courage and cowardice. The subordination of peasants shorn of the rhetoric of mutuality was traced to an authoritative historical moment. Common benefit yielded to a sharper distinction between those willing to fight, who deserved liberty, and those incapable of the moral force of character necessary for risking life in the field, condemned to unfree manual labor. Rather than recognizing a functional division of responsibility, in which the military order protects and the laborers feed, the legends enshrine the debased status of the latter.

This chapter looks at a notable response to the assertion of peasant timidity, based on the syllogism equating freedom (hence dignity) with courage and victory at arms. There were certain peasant communities that managed to preserve their autonomy, often by force, and these could accept and exalt the chivalric cult of bravery and its association with freedom, but now against the nobles who attempted to subjugate them.

Peasants Who Seek to Become Knights

Peasants constituted the *inerme vulgus* of the Carolingian world. From the ninth to eleventh centuries, as the nobility came to be identified with warfare, the free-unfree distinction among the lower orders became less significant than the division based on military competence. The nobility came to be regarded as the only truly free group, while all those incapable of making war were regarded as in some sense constrained, regardless of their legal status.

In the eleventh century, Andrew of Fleury, describing some of the miracles of Saint Benedict in connection with his monastery, referred to peasants (*agrestes*) as a multitude of the common unarmed folk. Andrew was scandalized by clergy and common people who confronted knights in military combat to uphold the Limoges peace ordinances of 1031. The peace armies, according to Andrew, owed any success they had to their turbulent pride and greed, which offset whatever moral superiority they might claim over the knights.[1] For Andrew, the military gap between knight and peasant remained immense, bridgeable only by exceptional mob violence. The helplessness of peasants before the onslaught of knights is graphically depicted in *Garin le Loherain* and celebrated in the violent fancies of Bertran de Born, who rhapsodized about rustics and their herds fleeing in terror as knights attacked them on the run.[2] The peasant is advised, in a French poem, to stay home and leave his rusty sword hanging at the foot of his bed.[3]

Insofar as peasants *could* acquire the military skills of knights, the prospect was disturbing. There were German *ministeriales*, knights who retained servile status while performing military and sometimes important administrative functions. Although they were personally and not contractually obligated to their lords, the *ministeriales* were full-fledged knights with no connection to agricultural labor, nor did they bear the same burdens (such as head taxes or exclusion from court) as unfree rustics.[4] The *ministeriales* may have had peasant ancestors, but if so, they were as distant and unknown as the ancestors of lesser free knights. Their lack of liberty was not conceptually joined to any agrarian background.[5] The Alsatian *Chronicon Eberheimense* (written in 1163) traced the establishment of *ministeriales* to Julius Caesar's campaigns in Gaul. Having defeated the Gauls with the help of the Germans, Caesar commended the German *minores milites* to their princes (now Roman senators), saying they should be treated no longer as *servi* but rather as their *ministeria*, whom they should protect.[6]

German military practice also offered opportunities for what Hugo von Trimberg referred to as "Halbritter" (half-knights), those who could fight in the manner of knights but who were clearly of rustic origin.[7] In attacking this class, Hugo repeated a long-standing complaint of other authors seeking to correct the disorderly estates and functions of the Holy Roman Empire. In the cycle of thirteenth-century didactic poems known as *Seifried Helbling*, a hapless peasant serving unwillingly in his lord's army begs to be allowed to return to his farm and plow, where he belongs.[8] Ottokar of Styria, author of a rhymed history of his region (written in the first years of the fourteenth century), ridiculed the folly of the abbot of Admont in summoning peasants to his army when they should be in the fields, performing useful ignoble activities.[9] For Ottokar, as for Andrew of Fleury, the assumption remains that peasants make poor soldiers.

Sancho Panza, exemplar of the rustic amusingly and unsuitably thrust into adventure, has an extensive ancestry. Yet in Spain, during the medieval centuries, there *had* been knights of non-noble social status, the *caballeros villanos*, whose rights and duties as guardians of the frontier settlements gave to medieval Castile much of its particular ethos and social character.[10]

In early-medieval Italy the military caste was not exclusively noble.[11] Rather of Verona, in the tenth century, offered a hypothetical typical lineage for the son of a count: his grandfather might have been a judge, but his great-great-grandfather a mere soldier. That soldier's father, in turn, could have been anything: a fortune-teller, wrestler, fishmonger, muleteer—a knight or a peasant.[12] Apart from the *ministeriales*, the late-medieval empire had low-born mercenaries and other formidable infantry forces such as the Swiss and Hussite armies. The Swiss emerged as the finest soldiers in Europe by the end of the fifteenth century, defeating mounted companies, as Charles the Bold's defeats at the end of his career demonstrate.

That the image of peasant helplessness and martial incompetence did not conform consistently to social reality provoked a number of reactions from contemporary observers and variations on the dominant conventions of history and literature. The seemingly unnatural intrusion of rustics from the realm of Demeter into that of Mars stirred derision or fear, but in some instances the possibility of a measure of admiration.

Peasants' attempts to imitate chivalric violence were often presented as comical. An early-sixteenth-century German drawing of a peasant tournament (Fig. 10) depicts a rustic "knight" charging at an unseen enemy. The would-be knight is armed with a rake rather than a lance. A straw basket functions as his shield, and a beehive topped with a heraldic shoe serves as his helmet.

There were several ways of denouncing peasant pretensions to military status besides simple ridicule. Perhaps the best-known account of the fatal consequences of a peasant seeking to become a knight is the German poem *Helmbrecht*, which has been mentioned in connection with the image of the productive peasant. In this late-thirteenth-century story, a young peasant of more strength than sense determines to leave the farm and become a knight. His father attempts to prevent this rebellion against his ordained station, remonstrating with his obstinate son that his place is at the plow.[13] Ignoring his father, Helmbrecht becomes a robber-knight and terrorizes the countryside,

10. Peasant tournament. Drawing by Hans Burgkmaier, early sixteenth century. Photograph by Städelsches Kunstinstitut und Städtische Galerie, Frankfurt am Main. Reprinted by permission of Städelsches Kunstinstitut und Städtische Galerie, Frankfurt am Main.

all the while ridiculously imitating the external attributes of chivalry. He comes to a bad end, maimed and then killed while his father looks on in grim satisfaction.

It is important to emphasize, however, that Helmbrecht is not portrayed as militarily inept. All the so-called knights in the poem are lowborn brigands, and Helmbrecht is as competent as any in performing violent deeds. While ludicrously unsuccessful at imitating chivalric manners and dress, he is able, for a time, to make a career of fighting. His is a moral rather than a military failure, and his father's warning is not literally true: it *is* possible at least temporarily to change one's status. Thus the poem does not imply a complacent encomium of the noble class but a more disturbing picture of a world given over to stupid violence.

Some examples of rustic warriors crop up in medieval romances, but they remain burdened with other characteristic peasant markers and so function as chivalric parodies. The eponymous hero of the scatological mock epic *Audigier* is manifestly comical, but even the honorable and militarily able *vilain* Rigaut in *Garin le Loherain* is filthy and hideous.[14] Neither circumstance nor even physical deficiency makes rustics incapable of war, but their nature. Perceval becomes an exemplary knight, but the whole point is that he is not really a rustic.

Germany had peasant knights, and they were on occasion acknowledged as important by their superiors. Otto of Freising, in his account of the deeds of Frederick Barbarossa, describes how a rustic soldier (*strator*) whom the emperor wished to elevate to knighthood for his valor during the siege of Tortona declined the honor, saying he was of humble status (*cum plebium se diceret*) and preferred to remain in that order.[15] More often, peasant ambitions for knighthood were denounced in the manner of *Helmbrecht* or the Neidhart poems. Peasants were perceived as dangerously close to breaching the frontier between them and the lower ranks of knights. The peace ordinance issued by Frederick Barbarossa in 1152 prohibited peasants from carrying lances or swords.[16] A Bavarian ordinance of 1244 allowed peasants to keep weapons to protect their houses but regulated what arms they could carry as well as the color and quality of their clothing.[17] Here the problems are the same as those addressed by *Helmbrecht*: the arrogant peasants who use swords and affect knightly dress and hauteur.

The concern with peasant weapons and ambitions is characteristic of the Hohenstaufen and Interregnum empires. The author of the (literally) censorious *Buch der Rügen*, written in Bavaria slightly before *Helmbrecht*, praises peasants' piety but condemns their senseless lust for spear and shield, which they prefer to keeping their hand on the plow as is proper.[18] The Franciscan preacher Berthold von Regensburg matched the sentiments of *Helmbrecht* by instructing his peasant audiences that they must not seek to change their divinely appointed status, since all men have been given their vocation by God.[19] Elsewhere Berthold is more anxious and forceful: "Even though you wish to become a knight, you must be a peasant and cultivate for us wheat and wine. . . . Who would then guide the plow if all of you were lords?"[20] For peasants to seek to become knights violates not only functional hierarchies but also Providential dispensation. The fourteenth-century allegorical interpretation of the Book of Daniel composed in the Prussia of the Teutonic Order urges peasants to return to their plows cheerfully, for which they will receive their proper place (and a crown) in heaven.[21]

Peasant Armies

Literate observers agreed fairly widely that insofar as peasants could actually acquire the equipment and privileges of knights, this was a lamentable thing. What if peasants who remained in their order should come to possess weapons and military force? Andrew of Fleury's criticism of the Limoges Peace of 1031 is typical of the anxieties evoked by the sight of armed peasants even if they were simply attempting to defend themselves from the depredations of knights. Indeed, as Georges Duby has shown, the ideological model of the three orders of society was shaped by the desire to discourage clergy and commoners from taking up arms. The identification of functional orders and the idea of mutuality arose from a process of exclusion of those who pray and those who labor from the world of military violence. The formulations of Adalbero of Laon and Gerard of Cambrai responded to disruption of appropriate and divinely ordained social boundaries perpetrated by the Peace of God.

If an armed rural populace represented disturbing proof of social disintegration in the eyes of Adalbero of Laon or Andrew of Fleury, it also raised the question of the knights' discharge of their responsibilities. This problem became clearer once knighthood was sacralized and noble status defined by military function. In Hungary in the fifteenth and early sixteenth centuries, the fact that peasants and clergy were conspicuous in armies mobilized against the Turks occasioned condemnation, but it was directed against the perceived dereliction of the nobles more than against the scandal of inappropriate activities by the other two orders.[22]

It was also possible within the normal terms of elite discourse to accord some sympathy and perhaps apprehensive respect to peasants not engaged in crusades (such as those against the Turks in Hungary) but simply defending themselves against nobles, even their own lords. The *Schwabenspiegel*, a German law collection of the thirteenth century, states that lords are charged with defending the land and its people, and that if they fail in this duty, they are not owed obedience.[23] This is not addressed to peasants as such, but it does go beyond the normal vassalic right to withdraw from the service of an unjust lord in that it treats the obligation to defend the territory and its inhabitants, not simply one's dependents.

In 1240 Bartholomaeus Anglicus admiringly described the Frisian peasants who formed free communities and preferred to sacrifice their lives than to live under the yoke of servitude.[24] In 1256, these peasant warriors would in fact defeat the army of William, count of Holland. They enticed the heavily armored and mounted count into frozen marshlands and easily dispatched him after he fell through the ice.[25] Such exceptional populations were acceptable as curiosities, but of course this did not mean that Bartholomaeus, or anyone else of the higher orders, recommended them as a general model.

That the peasants might take revenge on the lords for mistreatment was not as impossible to accept as we might think. Armed peasants participated in the Peace and the Truce of God against seigneurial violence in the late tenth and early eleventh centuries.[26] The Peace and the Truce eventually were taken over by secular authorities, and so an interlude of peasant agency was ended by the second half of the eleventh century.[27]

In addition to such temporarily sanctioned means of disputing seigneurial violence, there was a tradition of direct but somewhat clandestine peasant violence. In a surprising number of cases, peasants killed their lords without incurring the punishment one would expect (even in cases where it was punished, the crime did not give rise to sanguinary counterviolence). A study by Robert Jacob focusing on incidents in which lords were killed by collective and premeditated action is quite revealing.[28] He has found twelve such assassinations for northern France from 1040 to 1150, of which seven took place in Flanders and Artois. Included in this figure are deaths caused by rebellious vassals (such as the murder of Charles the Good, count of Flanders), but there are also at least three murders by peasants of unjust lords or of higher seigneurial functionaries, the best known of which was the death of Arnoul III of Ardres, who was strangled in 1140. Certain private grudges had a resonance beyond the immediate motive and perpetrator. At the end of the eleventh century, an ecclesiastical *advocatus* named Dudo was killed by a certain Gunter, but this essentially private act of vengeance was cheered by the local peasantry and commemorated as late as sixty years after the event.[29]

Seigneurial murder was not regarded as extraordinary, nor was it necessarily thought of as a terrible crime. The killing of lords was presented as either the martyrdom of a just ruler (Charles the Good) or, more commonly, the judgment of God against a local tyrant. Jacob finds that all of these incidents are in the nature of a revolt, and that far from indicating spontaneous lawlessness, they were structured according to certain patterns and rituals.

The lord of the Andalusian village of Fuenteovejuna, Fernán Gómez de Guzmán, commander of the Order of Calatrava, was murdered in 1476 to put an end to his abusive lordship. As immortalized by the poet and dramatist Lope de Vega in the seventeenth century, the villagers were united in claiming collective responsibility for the deed ("Fuenteovejuna, todos a una"). They escaped serious punishment, albeit not entirely because of their own courage but in part thanks to the support of the authorities of Córdoba.[30]

For Spanish Galicia, Carlos Barros has unearthed eight murders of lords resulting from social revolts between 1369 and 1527. Within an extremely violent environment in which both official and private rituals of vengeance were common, the violent disposal of an unjust lord even by peasants was neither unexpected nor regarded as a violation of divine law.[31] The seigneurial regime and aristocratic mentality could tolerate certain direct forms of peasant action. What was feared and violently denounced was mass movement on the order of the rebellions of the late Middle Ages.

The relatively discreet disposal of an oppressive lord is not the same as an armed peasant movement. Centuries before Courtrai or Agincourt, an undercurrent of opinion hinted that knights could be effectively combated by modestly equipped soldiers. The admittedly obscure narrative poem *Eupolemius*, a Latin work from twelfth-century Germany, offers several examples of poorly equipped soldiers mocked by better-armed opponents who nevertheless succumb to the well-placed dart or spear.[32] "Sometimes the spears of peasants can harm a knight," the author remarks.[33]

Other voices warned of the limits of oppressive conduct. The thirteenth-century poet known as Der Stricker wrote a short animal-metaphor story about a place (the "Gäu," meaning simply "district") inhabited by chickens (*die Gäuhühnern*), where knights tried repeatedly but unsuccessfully to build castles. They were constantly defeated by the forces of nature, but also by the legitimate authority of the ruler (the *Landesherr*). In warning of the consequences of erecting fortifications to exploit the countryside, the author refers to the power of peasants who know how to destroy castles no matter how strongly protected they may be. The inhabitants of "Kirchelinge" (Kirling, in Austria near Klosterneuburg) have already demonstrated this. Rustic anger (*zorn*) is not that of a rebellious or disorderly mass but of a formidable and reasonable populace.[34]

In Catalonia peasant militias were formed by King James I in 1258 to combat disorder. This legislation grew out of the royal Peace ordinances and the privilege given to Barcelona to enforce it. Throughout the fourteenth century these police forces, which were especially active in the rural territory surrounding Barcelona, earned the condemnation of nobles. They saw the peasants, with some justice, as mobilized against their interests, for the militias were empowered to arrest, and to enter and even destroy fortified places. At a parliament that met at Perpignan in the mid–fourteenth century, a noble spokesman referred to the legislation permitting such militias as a "wicked and terrible practice or law . . . contrary to God, the lord king, and good customs." He described the militias as "a riot of peasants who have neither reason, sense, nor understanding of what they do."[35]

The failure of lords to uphold the obligations incumbent on their order led to retribution from the peasants. A popular poem of the fifteenth century reflects currents of peasant as well as elite opinion, condemning the nobles for failure to protect the poor and threatening them with death at the hands of the peasants: "The nobility should protect the poor, as is its duty. But the nobles are disgraced and neglect their duty. God will not suffer this, he will torment the wicked. Some day they will be slain by the common peasant."[36]

Free Peasant Communities

ANDORRA

The clearest evidence for peasants rejoicing in their feats of arms comes from those places in Europe where free rural communities successfully defended their claims to freedom, often by resort to arms. In privileged valleys such as Andorra, rural inhabitants were able to preserve a substantial measure of self-government and free status amidst seigneurial power. These communities were vividly aware of their unusual good fortune. Explanations of such anomalous self-government referred to a combination of geographical determinism (isolation or mountain liberties), and the ability to fight off seigneurial incursions. In elaborating foundational myths or celebrating victories against the nobles, free rural communities exalted their exceptional fortune while accepting the conventional linkage of bravery with liberty.

In Andorra there was no heroic struggle with a seigneurial outsider that defined the moment of liberty and its meaning—no William Tell. The liberties of Andorra emerged gradually.[37] The principality was formed from six parishes in and adjoining the valley of the Valira River.[38] Referred to both as the "Valley of Andorra" and the "Valleys of Andorra," the territory was able to prolong the relatively free structure of land tenure that characterized Catalonia in the tenth century.[39] Although elsewhere seigneurial regimes were able to impose heavier and more arbitrary obligations on rural tenants after 1050, the Andorrans were able to preserve a measure of autonomy and representation that were eroded in most parts of Catalonia.[40] From 1278 to the present Andorra has been a coprincipality shared by the bishops of Urgell and the counts of Foix (the latter succeeded by the king of France near the end of the sixteenth century, and the king succeeded in turn by the subsequent heads of the French state). Andorra was able to play its co-lords off against each other, but its curious survival through an era in which small privileged communities were absorbed by nation states was due also to the difficulty of breaking up a shared jurisdiction. Above all, the Andorrans were able to convert what were originally arrangements to exploit them into effective charters of privileged liberty.

This does not mean that Andorra was free from exactions or the profits from lordship. Particularly in the late Middle Ages, the counts of Foix and bishops of Urgell obtained considerable revenue from justice, tithes, rents on land, and various aids and customary tributes in money and kind.[41] Andorra's privileged status consisted of recognition as a political entity, a measure of local government through a representative council of prominent men, specific rights regarding the pasturing of livestock, and exemption from the most degrading seigneurial dues.[42]

Originally subject to the counts of Urgell, Andorra became much more closely tied to secular lordship of the bishops of Urgell from the late tenth to the early twelfth centuries as the ambitions of the count turned toward the south. The bishop consolidated his power over the valleys by means of donations and the exercise of military and judicial authority. The noble family of Caboet reinforced the sway of the bishops of Urgell in the early eleventh to late twelfth centuries by providing military support in return for a share of Andorra's revenues. The Caboet performed homage to the bishops for their jurisdictional and fiscal privileges. The extinction of the male line of Caboet and the marriage of Arnaldeta de Caboet to Arnau de Castellbò in 1185 brought the more powerful and less deferential viscounts of Castellbò into rivalry with the bishops for control over various territories in the diocese of Urgell, including Andorra. The Castellbò were in turn merged into the comital family of Foix in 1226. The counts of Foix waged several wars with the bishops of Urgell over Andorra during the thirteenth century and refused to perform any meaningful homage for tributes they levied in the valleys.

The Andorrans profited from their ability to maneuver among rival lords. Already by the late twelfth century they had obtained recognition as a community capable of negotiating with the bishops of Urgell. They acknowledged episcopal rights to tithes, military service, and justice, but they asserted their agency and their legal standing in one agreement (of 1176) that was signed by every male head of household in Andorra, some 383 in all.[43] The struggle between the counts of Foix and bishops of Urgell was finally resolved in 1278 and 1288 by arbitration in two agreements known as *pariatges*.[44] The treaties provided for the sharing of lordship. This was not a partition but a joint exercise of seigneurial jurisdiction (*communiter et simul* or *communiter et indivisio*), something not unknown in Foix and other lands on the northern side of the Pyrenees, where similar agreements were made between nobles and various ecclesiastical entities from the eleventh to fourteenth centuries.[45] The bishop and count agreed to alternate year by year in collecting the general tribute of lordship (the *questa*). They both retained rights to summon the men of Andorra to military service, but not against each other. The count obtained a larger share of profits from the exercise of justice, while the bishop obtained the tithes and other ecclesiastical dues. The count acknowledged holding his rights from the bishop, but the *pariatges* elevated the status of the count with regard to Andorra to something more than a military subordinate. Before 1278 the bishops had been clearly the lords of Andorra, while their secular partners were obedient or rebellious vassals. The *pariatges* gave equal status to the representatives of each lord in the levying of tributes and the administration of justice, so that, in effect, the two powers were co-princes, a title they would adopt officially later.

The first *pariatge* recognized that Andorrans were exempt from seigneurial taxes on marriage and inheritance (*cugucia, intestia,* and *exorquia*), which had become indices of servile status in Catalonia. But the *pariatges* did not at the moment of their enactment establish an extraordinary degree of liberty or the peculiar status that Andorra would enjoy in later centuries. The *pariatges* were intended as a means of sharing the profitable exploitation of the valleys, not as charters of exemption. By the late Middle Ages Andorra clearly enjoyed privileged communal identity that was unusual if not yet unique, but it was never a peasant republic completely free of external lordship in the way that Dithmarschen or certain Swiss communities could claim.

Its reputation in modern times as a haven of happy, archaic liberty was due to the ability of the Andorrans to turn the two *pariatges* into effective constitutional documents. This was possible because the two lords could be played off against each other, but also because by the fourteenth century Andorra was recognized as exceptional within the Pyrenees, which at one time had many free communities. In the eleventh and twelfth centuries, and even at the time of the *pariatges*, Andorra was not so unusual. Other Pyrenean subregions, such as the Vall d'Aran and the Vall de Querol, enjoyed exemptions from various comital or seigneurial levies.[46] Mountain villages, such as Bescaran in the diocese of Urgell, held charters from the counts of Barcelona and for a time could repel seigneurial demands such as the military service claimed by the bishop of Urgell in 1085. Ten years later, the men of Bescaran had to place themselves under the bishop's "protection" but reasserted their status as *homines liberi*, although a document of 1097 shows them paying the servile dues in cases of death without direct heirs (*exorquia*) and cases of female adultery (*cugucia*).[47]

The exceptional nature of Andorra's status began to become clear in the century after the *pariatges*, when it was declared not to belong to any of the territorial or seigneurial powers of the region but to be ruled indivisibly by representatives of the co-princes.[48] The Andorrans managed to deflect attempts of the kings of Aragon and the Catalan estates in the late fourteenth and fifteenth centuries to tax or annex them.[49] In the fourteenth century the men of Andorra obtained recognition of their rights to defend themselves with weapons, appeared as litigants in matters involving pasture rights, and remonstrated with the co-princes concerning the administration of their land.[50] The *pariatges* were successfully used to resist annexation by territorial states and changes in the system of local levies and administration of justice. These limited but significant rights would come to be regarded as a puzzling anomaly, a curious survival, or a minor miracle during the ancien regime and in modern times. By the eighteenth century, when Andorra's official customary and administrative law treatise was drawn up, its author, Antoni Fiter, could attribute to a special providential dispensation the preservation of "a holy and honest liberty which is the envy and admiration of all nations that know of it."[51]

The privileged status of Andorra was underscored by the successful claim to neutrality. The first *pariatge* forbade the men of Andorra to take sides in the event of a quarrel between their co-princes. In 1515 the Andorrans argued before the Catalan parliament that this meant they were permanently neutral with regard to all conflicts, although in fact, as we have noted, the *pariatge* allowed either prince to summon the Andorrans to military service as long as it was not against the other prince.[52] Andorra's neutrality would be of crucial significance to the *Manual digest* and its supplement, the *Politar Andorrà*. Although Switzerland's neutrality was recognized by international law in 1815, Andorra has the unofficial (although admittedly impressive) authority conferred by centuries without invasion.[53]

In addition to the *pariatges*, Andorra claimed Charlemagne as a source of its legitimacy. A false privilege of the emperor (probably from the twelfth century) attributes the peopling of the valleys forming Andorra to an effort to settle inhabitants in lands wrested from the Moors. Although rights of high justice are granted to the count of Barcelona, the inhabitants are allowed to elect whatever lord they wish, whose responsibility will be to defend them (*senior defensor*).[54]

This document indicates the prestige of Carolingian origins during the twelfth century, although for Andorra (unlike most of the rest of Europe), Charlemagne would be invoked in modern times more than during the medieval era. Later authorities pointed to the Charlemagne charter as the basis for the equality of all the inhabitants of the valley.[55] Charlemagne is invoked in the Andorran National Hymn, with words by Joan Belloch Vivó, bishop of Urgell (hence co-prince of Andorra) from 1906 to 1918. The anthem begins: "Great Charlemagne, my father, freed me from the Arabs. . . . I remain alone the unique daughter of Charlemagne's empire, believing and free for eleven centuries, believing and free I want to remain."[56]

For Andorra, Charlemagne was the founder of liberty, while for Catalonia he legitimated servitude. No claim was made that the Andorrans served Charlemagne with extraordinary distinction. Their privileges were those of early settlers, able certainly to defend their land, but not soldiers in the vanguard of reconquest. According to a popular etymology, the name Andorra was bestowed by Charlemagne in reference to the biblical Valley of Endor, where the Medianites were defeated; no heroic battle is specifically recalled or invented.[57]

Another relatively modern notion used to explain the peculiar liberty of Andorra was its alleged geographical isolation and the resulting fortunate ignorance of outsiders. In Catalonia it is still common to indicate that someone has traveled widely by saying "he has been to the Mint [Venice], Mecca, and the Valley of Andorra."[58] Nevertheless Andorra is in fact not all that isolated and in certain respects was less so in the Middle Ages (when *all* roads were difficult) than it is today. The Pyrenees have tended to be a passage rather than a barrier.[59]

The idea of mountain liberties is closely related to the difficulty-of-terrain argument: it would seem self-evidently easier to preserve freedom when the land is difficult to invade. Switzerland immediately comes to mind in this connection, but difficulty is not the same thing as isolation (it was the importance of the mountain passes rather than remoteness that allowed the Swiss forest cantons to negotiate with princes and emperors). Moreover, isolation can work both ways. Mountain regions can display what Chris Wickham refers to as "the Count Dracula model" of oppressive lordship in which limited accessibility allows a local despot unusual opportunities.[60] Near Andorra lay the valley of Castellbò, which was harshly ruled by violent brigand-like viscounts and which had become terribly impoverished by the sixteenth century.[61] On the other side of the mountains were villages such as Montaillou, which was also poor but where serfdom (or really any sort of effective lordship) was unknown.[62] Also in the Pyrenees, one finds peasants in the county of Bigorre firmly subjugated to servile status in close proximity to communities such as Salies-de-Béarn, which lacked all formal ties of dependence.[63]

Andorra was clearly privileged and for reasons traceable neither to Charlemagne nor to geography. In Switzerland one finds a similar combination of imagery: virtuous poverty, isolation, and mountain liberties. There, however, freedom was conceived in terms of a martial tradition: liberties defended by force, a conception that Switzerland is only now abandoning. Andorra thought of itself in modern times as privileged by reason of detachment from the centers of power and oppression, protected by its co-princes, by its *pariatges*, and by neutral isolation, the "Brigadoon" or "Shangri-la" model, quietly opting out of rather than battling oppressive lordship or political annexation. Although in the mid–eighteenth century Fiter could describe Andorra as the envy of all nations familiar with it, he was not eager to have its fame spread too widely.

He appended to his legal treatise a list of moral and practical maxims for good political conduct. Maxim 26 recommended that peasants be favored by the government, citing the example of the Roman Republic.[64] Fiter tellingly reinforced the image of a poor but virtuous rusticity by instructing Andorrans never to boast of wealth or power but always to "preach the poverty and weakness of the valleys" (which is, he went on to observe, after all true).[65] Perhaps most revealingly, in his prologue Fiter stipulated that the *Manual digest* never be printed. It should be available only in manuscript copies kept within Andorra to avoid encouraging foreigners to learn how the valleys were governed.[66]

Only very recently, in 1993, did Andorra alter its status by adopting a constitution allowing it to claim sovereignty in accord with international law.[67] The co-princes remain the official heads of state, but Andorra is fully independent, is represented in the United Nations and so has shed at least some of its Ruritanian aura. The peculiar continuity of Andorra, its reputation as a vestige of a feudal agreement, has now ended.

SWITZERLAND

The most famous territory of liberty protected by military skill is Switzerland. In an embittered look at what he took to be the Swiss habit of complacent neutrality, Max Frisch chose the name *Andorra* for a play about Switzerland's indifference toward refugees from the Nazis.[68] Despite certain similarities to Andorra, Switzerland during the medieval and early modern period was more violent and heroic than the quietly neutral principality. Switzerland's contemporary reputation for peaceful standoffishness, reinforced by its fortunate evasion of the world wars, is not in fact sanctified by extremely long usage—its neutrality was recognized three centuries after Andorra's (albeit by a more official international body). Moreover, until very recently, Switzerland guarded its neutrality not through passive obscurity but by universal conscription and a sophisticated military defense.[69]

Switzerland generated cycles of myths of mountain liberties that were so well disseminated, through such works as Schiller's *Wilhelm Tell*, as to have become national, even commercial clichés. A logo for products made in Switzerland is the crossbow of William Tell. The statue of Tell and his son, which was erected at Uri in 1895, has been copied in everything from decorative handkerchiefs to advertisements.[70] So hackneyed is the Tell legend that the most extensive recent treatment of Tell's career and image began, its author says, as a joke.[71]

Another cliché of Swiss liberty is the argument from geographical determinism that equates rugged terrain with freedom. For Switzerland, as for Andorra, the assumption that mountains are difficult to conquer and so encouraged liberty does not weather examination. Not only were the actual conflicts over Swiss liberties determined in the woodland and lakeshore of the *Mittelland*, not in the Alps, but on those occasions when armies (such as Napoleon's) *did* invade, the mountains proved, in Christopher Hughes's words, "singularly penetrable."[72]

Switzerland also shares with Andorra (although the former case is much better known) a reputation for privileged happiness. In the eighteenth century the Alps suddenly seemed beautiful, but the people were still regarded as wretched. Beginning in the romantic era, the good fortune of the Swiss was related to landscape. Switzerland's exemption from war in recent centuries afforded it additional and unusual luck. In the twentieth century wealth was added to this agreeable picture.

Nevertheless, even for the earlier period, when Switzerland was poor, when the mountains were regarded as horrifying, when in addition the Swiss were famous soldiers, they were deemed privileged, not because of wealth, beauty of landscape, or peace, but because of their unusual liberty. This too is not quite all that it seems, since to speak of Switzerland as if it were at all a consistent, unified polity before 1815 is inaccurate. The Swiss Confederation included what may be considered free communities of shepherds and other herdsmen (the original Forest Cantons or Appenzell), but also oligarchical cities and seigneurial regions. What is now Switzerland would produce a folk literature celebrating triumphs over princes, but also some of the bitterest attacks on the peasantry, such as those written by Felix Hemmerli, of Zurich, or Heinrich Wittenwiler, who came from Toggenburg.

By the late Middle Ages, the valleys and forests that had obtained de facto rights by reason of their strategic position controlling access to mountain passes had defended those rights in battle and were regarded (by friends, enemies, and themselves) as free, which might mean without lords, or (to their enemies) without law.[73] They appeared to be exemplars of equality, and, not completely accurately, of *peasant* equality. According to an anti-Swiss poem written by Heinrich Bebel during the Swabian War (1499), the Swiss wanted to live free of all lordship. They refused to serve as anyone's serf (*knecht*), and wanted to be their own masters.[74]

In the fifteenth and early sixteenth centuries the Swiss (at least those in the rural cantons) saw themselves as representatives of peasant virtue against the nobles.[75] Songs, plays, and other political propaganda—constituting what Guy Marchal has dubbed the "Peasants' Answer"—praised the heroism of the Swiss resistance to the lords who sought to conquer them. These works should not be taken literally or ingenuously as the voices of the peasantry, and their context is often as much the defense of urban as of rural privileges.[76] Nevertheless, however artful and removed from genuine "folk" discourse, the dramatic, musical, and poetic celebrations of Swiss victories invoke the image of the pious peasant and put in the mouths of their adversaries great contempt for these insolent opponents of lordship and seigneurial domination.

The Swiss self-image combined piety and local or proto-national patriotism with celebration of the common man. The portrayal of William Tell, the hero of resistance to seigneurial oppression, is the most famous and enduring legend of the defense of liberty against seigneurial pretension.[77] The question of whether Tell existed and who he really was if he did exist is convoluted and the object of enough controversy to form an industry, albeit in many respects a discredited one. The authenticity of the story cannot be "proved" with contemporary documents. It first appears in the *White Book of Sarnen*, compiled in the decade of the 1470s and rediscovered in the nineteenth century.[78] Long before the *White Book* was unearthed, however, Schiller had made Tell an international hero. The earlier popularity of the legend was due to several texts dating from the late fifteenth and sixteenth centuries, especially a ballad (*Das Lied von der Entstehung der Eidgenossenschaft*), whose earliest parts were written in 1477, and an early-sixteenth-century play, *Das Urner Tellspiel*.[79] These were the most important sources for what would prove to be the classic account by the antiquary Aegidius Tschudi in the mid–sixteenth century.[80]

The Tell story is a constitutional myth in which the grievances of the people of the original cantons were mobilized by an act of insolence, cruelty, and symbolic subjugation imposed by the Hapsburgs. Gessler, the Hapsburg administrator for Uri and Schwyz, set up a hat in a prominent spot in the marketplace at Altdorf and required all who passed it to bow. Tell did not so much refuse the obeisance as simply not perform it, and when interrogated by Gessler, he politely (but implausibly) attributed the lapse to forgetfulness. By way of punishment, Tell, a noted marksman, was compelled to undergo the mock-chivalric ordeal of shooting an apple off his son's head with a crossbow. If he missed altogether, he would be put to death, but of course if he aimed carefully, he nevertheless risked killing his son. Gessler's punishment combined danger with the same element of comic humiliation implied by the setting up of the cap in the first place. Both were meant as graphic reminders of who was the ruler and who the object of arbitrary control, or more pertinently, who the peasant. In the *Urner Tellspiel* Gessler exclaims:

Say no more, Tell, you must do it,
For you shall have no mercy from me!
I desire my revenge from you peasants,
Even if it breaks your hearts.[81]

After Tell successfully shot the apple off his son's head, Gessler asked him why he had held two arrows in his hand. Tell boldly answered that had his first shot missed the apple or hit his son, he would have aimed his second shot at Gessler. This arrogation of chivalric rights of revenge enraged Gessler, and he ordered that Tell be shut up in a dungeon. Tell escaped from the boat carrying him on Lake Lucerne to captivity. He later assassinated Gessler with a crossbow while the steward traveled toward his castle at Küssnacht.

The Tell legend is not directly related to the establishment of the Confederation. The story ends abruptly, and at any rate takes place in 1307, after the date 1291, which has been elevated by another quasi-historical tradition to the status of foundational year. The Tell legend is, nevertheless, a response to a symbolic vocabulary of subordination involving cruelty, capriciousness, and the arbitrary exercise of power.

Another cycle of legendary explanations for the revolt appears along with the accounts of Tell. This is the story of the "Three Swiss," well-off peasants grossly insulted by boorish representatives of the nobility.[82] The several atrocities serve to explain and bring together the origins of the mutual oaths supposed to have been sworn in 1291 at the field of Rütli. One narrative begins almost in the manner of an antipastourelle. A lower-ranking Habsburg functionary riding through the countryside sees a pretty rustic woman alone, her husband off working in a nearby forest. The lecherous official orders her to prepare him a bath and then to share the bath with him. She rushes outside just as her husband is returning, and he avenges the insult by killing the surprised functionary. They flee to safety in Uri but strangely disappear from the rest of the history.[83]

In another instance, two peasants of Unterwalden have their oxen seized, and the father has his eyes gouged out because the son has the effrontery to resist the seizure. The son takes refuge in Uri. Another conspirator is a well-off peasant of Schwyz who owns a stone house, which the steward Gessler, regarding such property as inappropriate for a rustic, takes from him (or threatens to take in some versions). This peasant, too, departs for Uri, where he meets the young man whose oxen were taken and a native of Uri who is the third founder (thus one native of each of the founding cantons is included). They swear an oath at the field of Rütli and start the insurrection that will lead to the recognition of the liberties of the cantons while retaining their ties to the Holy Roman Empire. No date is supplied by the *White Book*.

Tschudi placed the oath in 1307, but it would be moved back to the consecrated date of 1291 when the document that established the Confederation was found.

The legend of the Three Swiss shares certain attributes with other foundational stories involving avenging of humiliation. The late-twelfth-century *Gesta comitum Barcinonensium* traced the independence of Catalonia from the Franks to the murder of the father of the dynastic founder, Guifré "the Hairy."[84]

The Swiss founders, however, are non-noble (Tell) or well-off peasants (the Three Swiss). The indignities that they avenge are what might be considered classic seigneurial abuses: sexual intimidation, arbitrary confiscation, physical violence. The Swiss heroes are punished for their independence or for possessing something regarded as fair game by their oppressors. The peasant with the stone house is most clearly violating the limits of his status.

For our purposes it is not necessary to argue that these legends contain a core of historically authentic material, nor that the medieval Swiss Confederation was in some constitutional sense a "peasant state." What we are concerned with is an image of the liberty of rural common people, their resistance to symbolic oppression by seigneurial authority, and some degree of justification and self-celebration.

The legends were extremely flexible. Tell appeared on the one hand as the upstanding protofounder of the state and on the other as a revolutionary protector of the common man. By the late fifteenth century his name was invoked by peasant rebels in Germany, as at Niklashausen in 1476 and during the several Bundshuh uprisings (1442–1517). The famous treatise on witchcraft, the *Malleus maleficarum*, depicts Tell as a male witch, the diabolical inspirator of rebellious peasants.[85]

The Swiss celebrated their courage and the defeat of their aristocratic opponents in a variety of genres. Popular songs (*Kampflieder*) that proliferated in the fifteenth and early sixteenth centuries extolled the victories of the rural cantons. While they are not battle songs in the sense of being spontaneous compositions on the occasions of such triumphs as Morgarten (1315) or Nancy (1477), they reflect, even in their artifice, the attributes of piety, courage, and skill claimed by the Swiss. The noble and pious peasant soldiers appear as fearless, valiant, stalwart, and determined to defend themselves to the death against all who would seek to subdue them.[86] As Marchal has pointed out, the songs respond to learned as well as vernacular denunciations of the Swiss. The attacks of Hemmerli and Jakob Wimpfeling, although written in Latin, were well known and infuriating to peasants.[87]

In the century leading up to the great rebellion of 1525, the image of

Switzerland in German-speaking lands was esteemed as the model of liberty for the common man and the defense of freedom by force. The Swiss became the object of scornful but apprehensive hatred on the part of urban and aristocratic observers. For Felix Hemmerli in the mid–fifteenth century, the Swiss embodied all the vices his exceptionally vituperative imagination could apply to peasants generally. They are not exactly peasants, since they herd animals rather than cultivate land, but insofar as "rustic" connotes gross and uncouth character, they are indeed rustics (*rusticus a ruditate*). Hemmerli was forced to admit, however, that they were savagely effective soldiers. They were impious, treacherous, evil, and not so much men as monsters.[88] According to Hemmerli the Swiss are descendants of the Saxons defeated by Charlemagne, who settled the wildest men of that nation to guard the Alpine passes. For a time they were faithful warriors, willing to sacrifice sweat and blood to defend the honor of the emperor, hence "Swiss" (*Schwitzer*) from "sweat" (*schwitzen*) and the red background to their flag.[89] This is a variation on the themes of liberty, bravery, and the origins of nations we have discussed above. Now, however, the Swiss peasants have become rebels against Church and empire, thoroughly bestial, their savagery exemplified by their sexual proclivities.[90]

For most hostile observers the Swiss were symbols of a more dangerous sort: they epitomized lordlessness. The Swiss are disobedient peasants, according to the above-mentioned poem from the Swabian War (1499).[91] Their desire to live free defies God and His governance of the earth; like the Turks they are enemies of Christendom.[92] In his edict of April 1499 (which effectively launched the Swabian War), Emperor Maximilian I vilified the Swiss as crude, lowborn, un-Christian peasants whose rebellious impiety threatened the survival of the German nation.[93] Fear of lordless subversion and infidelity were stimulated by the apparent military competence of the Swiss peasantry.

At the turn of the sixteenth century South Germany was seized with a fever of expectation that the Swiss example would lead to the end of nobles' domination. The Swiss came to represent not merely anomalous freedom but a contagious inspiration, fomenting the potential ability of peasants or townsmen to arm themselves against the nobles.[94] Their desire to defend their liberty had become a perilous ambition to free all peasants from lordship. A chronicler of the Carinthian peasant uprising of 1478 attributed the rebellion to the desire of the peasants to imitate "faithless Swiss customs."[95] The Swabian War song cited above puts in the mouth of the Swiss the ambition to establish a worldwide insurrection (*buntschuh*) so that everyone might be free.[96] Peasants of neighboring regions, in the words of a song of 1525, "tried to learn evil tricks from the Swiss and become their own lords."[97]

The Swiss themselves turned their reputation for lordlessness to their own honor. In *Das Spiel von den alten und jungen Eidgenossen*, written in 1514, the baseness of the nobles and the heroism of the Swiss have inverted the social order: "the nobles have become peasants and the peasants nobles." This is not a disordered social upheaval but a reflection of intrinsic moral character: "the Swiss are the true nobles: it is their virtue, above all, which gives them nobility."[98] The oppressed peasants of southern Germany admire the Swiss and long to emulate them:

> It would be better to be killed outright
> than to wear such a heavy yoke,
> Therefore you [Swiss] are the happiest of peoples
> that live in these days.
> And if you don't want any lords,
> watch out now, and never stop.[99]

It was in this era that Swiss mercenary companies were celebrated for their victories against Burgundy and for bravery in the Italian wars. The correlation of liberty with military prowess is explicit in a revolutionary pamphlet of 1525, *An die Versammlung gemayner Bauerschaft*, which praises the Swiss who fight and usually win because they struggle to protect their land, families, and freedom.[100] The author adopts a popular rhyming motto: "Wer meret Schwytz? Der herren geytz!" (What makes the Swiss grow? The lords' greed!)[101] "Swiss" meant the throwing off of noble exploitation and the formation of a unified political community that would withstand, with arms, seigneurial attempts to take back control.[102]

Anti-Swiss songs elaborated the theme of the heretical or un-Christian nature of this rebellious people. An Austrian song of 1443 (at the time of the Zurich War between an alliance of towns and the Hapsburgs against the Confederation) calls upon God, His angels, and the saints for aid against "such infamous people," whose success is an insult to Christianity.[103] The Swiss responded to specific antipeasant compositions by their enemies; thus a *Kampflied* in praise of the Swiss allies (*Eidgenossen*), also from 1443, answered an Austrian song that had denounced them as pagans and Turks.[104] In this song, as elsewhere, the Swiss describe themselves as *fromen Eidgenossen*, pious members of the common union. Although their enemies called them "Schwiz," after the name of one of the original cantons of the Confederation, the Swiss considered themselves part of a brotherhood united by a common oath of mutual defense. *Eidgenossenschaft* carried the meaning of being without a lord (which by the late fifteenth century also was implied by "Swiss").[105] This was the reproach of their enemies but also a source of pride and identity.

Repeatedly the Swiss apostrophize themselves in war songs as "You pious *Eidgenossen*," (rather than as "You Swiss"), invincible if they continue to obey God.[106] The conviction that they are God's people emerges in celebratory songs such as one for the victory at Murten in 1476 in which the Swiss are likened to the children of Israel crossing the Red Sea, having bested their noble and seemingly more powerful enemies.[107] The proof of God's particular love for the Swiss is their victory in battle; thus piety and bravery are joined, exalting peasants and herdsmen in a manner perfectly compatible with the aristocratic equation of Christian rectitude proven and defended by force.

A long composition commemorating the victory of the Forest Cantons and Lucerne against the Hapsburgs at Sempach in 1386 touches a series of heroic themes associating valor, piety, and the defense of peasant liberties. The song probably dates from the early sixteenth century and emphasizes not only the courage of the Confederation but also the Austrians' misplaced confidence that they could easily quell these peasants. Duke Leopold, who lost his life at Sempach, is mocked for his rashness in trying to subdue the peasants:

> Duke Leopold of Austria was quite a bold man,
> he didn't follow good advice,
> he wanted to fight with the peasants,
> he ventured forth in princely fashion
> but when he came upon the peasants,
> he met his death.[108]

The enemy underestimates the Swiss, thinking to compel them to accept lordship.[109] Overconfidence resoundingly chastised is a common theme of these songs, which depict mockery against the "rascally peasants" turning to lamentation as nobles and their mercenaries suffer defeat at the hands of the pious *Eidgenossen*.[110] In a *Kampflied* from the mid–fifteenth century, the nobles promise to subjugate the unruly Swiss as their serfs, but after the Swiss show their skill and courage, the nobles turn fearful, lamenting:

> The Common Man can't be beaten,
> For the Swiss take no prisoners.
> Therefore, let's get out of here,
> For they are wild with anger
> And will murder and despoil
> The nobles on the spot.[111]

The Swiss oppose the "princes, knights, and nobles" with strong hearts and virile skill, but this they receive through God's approval and their piety.

The Swiss pray before the battle, invoking Christ's sacrificial blood, which saved sinners so that it might protect the land and its people.[112] The fact that the Swiss had been consistently able to fight off seemingly superior enemies was proof of God's favor, as was constantly repeated in political addresses and popular literature.[113]

Festival plays were another form by which the virtues of the Swiss were announced. They constituted a riposte to the German fashion for low comedies about peasant stupidity, ugliness, and vulgarity (especially Carnival plays). In the *Spiel von den alten und jungen Eidgenossen* of 1514, not only are nobles denounced for their rapacity, but the true nobility of the Swiss peasants is said to be proven by their feats of arms, as at the Battle of Novara the previous year. God has willed that the peasants should become nobles and the nobles peasants, for the Swiss are God's chosen people, as proven by their success in battle. It is the Swiss who form the true nobility, by reason of their piety and valor.[114] Here the peasants defend their right to liberty and attack the failure of the nobles to live up to their calling. The nobility has perverted the social order by plundering rather than defending the common good. In response to accusations by Hemmerli and others that the peasants have overturned the mutual service of the traditional hierarchy, the Swiss invoke a theme we shall see recurring at the close of the Middle Ages: the justification of revolt or of peasant liberty by reference to a combination of piety and bravery against a military aristocracy accused of abandoning its function. Another *Kampflied* from 1495, the time of the Swabian Wars, nicely sums up the dichotomy of noble dereliction and Swiss righteousness. Addressing the nobles, the author, a certain "Brother Hans," castigates them for their effort to subjugate the "pious noble peasants" of Switzerland. It is disgraceful that the princes have abandoned their responsibility to protect Christendom against the Turks while they are shedding Christian blood in Swiss lands.[115]

Thus in praising themselves in the face of the fear and contempt of seigneurial Germany, the Swiss emphasized their skill at arms; their unexpected success must show God's favor. Piety and valor were conventionally allied, but applied to the common man rather than the knights. The peasant spokesmen reflect a different sort of valor (a communal defense of land and liberty rather than individual pride), but partake of assumptions similar to those of the nobles concerning piety: that it is a virtue proven in battle, not the product of meekness or acceptance. Such an understanding of piety responds not only to the seigneurial contempt for the unmilitary peasant but to the sermons and didactic literature that counsel passivity and obedience. The combination of heroism and defense of peasant liberties would be largely extinguished by the aftermath of the German Peasants' War of 1525 and the eclipse of the Swiss armies during the Hapsburg-Valois wars. The Confederation and its allies were not harmed, but their prospects for exporting communal ideas to Swabia, Alsace, and Baden were unrealized, and subsequently they were content to minimize their symbolic role as advocates of peasant freedom.[116]

DITHMARSCHEN

The marshes of Friesland (in the Netherlands), as well as the northeastern corner of Germany and southern Denmark, formed another region of peasant liberty against seigneurial power. As already noted, in 1240 Bartholomaeus Anglicus remarked on the exceptional freedom of the inhabitants of Frisia, who appeared to live without lords.[117] Just east of Frisia and slightly north along the North Sea coast, at Stedingen, peasants revolted against the archbishop of Bremen and the count of Oldenburg beginning in 1200.[118] They refused to pay oppressive dues (*tributa*) and, according to the *Rasted Chronicle*, sought to defend their "liberty" against all claims of lordship. They were eventually subjugated but only with great difficulty. It required the proclamation of a crusade against these "heretics" by Gregory IX to bring an end to their decades of successful resistance. The Stedingen peasants were decisively defeated at the Battle of Altenesch in 1234.

Among the indirect beneficiaries of this war was a federation of independent peasant communities in another small marshy territory, Dithmarschen in Holstein. Lying slightly north of Stedingen, Dithmarschen was protected by the Danes against the ambitions of the counts of Holstein and others who had expanded in the wake of the Wendish Crusade of 1147. The Dithmarschen peasants abandoned the alliance with the Danes and so profited from the military setback suffered by Denmark's King Waldemar in 1227 at the hands of the city of Lübeck, the counts of Holstein and Schwerin, and the archbishop of Bremen. Their autonomy under the lordship of the archbishop of Bremen was acknowledged in the aftermath of the Danish War. Dithmarschen supported the crusade against the Stedinger and found its nominal subordination to the archbishops convenient during the thirteenth century. The power of family clans grew at the expense of the lesser nobility, and the Dithmarschen peasants formed capable military forces that could defeat mounted knights on the swampy terrain of their homeland.[119]

The extended families of Dithmarschen established a confederation that would be defended against the claims of the counts of Schleswig and Holstein beginning in the early fourteenth century and the kings of Denmark in the late fifteenth and early sixteenth centuries. In 1559 the Danes at last successfully invaded Dithmarschen, defeating the peasants and massacring the inhabitants of the capital, Meldorp, whereupon Dithmarschen was annexed to Denmark.

Dithmarschen was, therefore, a free peasant community from the late thirteenth century until 1559, aware of itself as an anomaly and with a strong political cohesion born of military necessity. Dithmarschen litigated, signed treaties, and concluded agreements with Denmark, Holstein, and other neighboring powers.[120] It also successfully defended itself in battle.

A number of songs have survived that commemorate the Dithmarschers' surprising victories over the noble forces that came against them. Two battles were especially important as proof of the heroism of the peasant soldiers of Dithmarschen. In 1404, after repeated efforts, the men of Dithmarschen captured the Marienburg, a castle belonging to the counts of Schleswig at Delbrügge, near Meldorp. A war song probably intended to inspire the Dithmarschers to attack after an initial defeat commemorates a certain Rolf Boikensohn, "the best in our land," who had fallen in the siege. Addressing his people, Rolf exhorts them ("you proud Dithmarschers") to destroy the castle: "what hands have built, hands can destroy." The men of Dithmarschen answer that they are willing to die before submitting to the count of Holstein.[121] The castle fell on Saint Oswald's Day (August 4), which was to be observed as a holiday according to the *Landrecht* of Dithmarschen enacted in 1447.[122]

With the death of the last Schauenberg counts of Holstein, Denmark would become the chief opponent of Dithmarschen's peculiar liberty. Another victory fraught with both tactical and symbolic significance was won against the Danish King John at Hemmingstedt on Saint Valentine's Day, 1500.[123] Hemmingstedt would be celebrated in nineteenth- and twentieth-century German literature: a ballad by Theodor Fontane, for example, and a novel by the anti-Semitic nationalist journalist and literary historian Adolf Bartels.[124] Several contemporary poems about the war against Denmark and the Battle of Hemmingstedt were collected by the antiquary Johann Adolfi (known as "Neocorus"), who died in about 1630. The last lines of one of these poems warn against underestimating the strength of the peasants of Dithmarschen, in a tone similar to that used by the Swiss with reference to Leopold's defeat at Sempach:

> Whoever comes against Dithmarschen
> Had better come well-armed.
> Shouldn't Dithmarschen belong to the peasants?
> Surely they should be considered lords.[125]

Another poem boasts that many a proud nobleman lost his life in the battle.[126]

Other poems join bravery to piety, God's favor, and the overconfidence of their noble enemies, in a fashion again reminiscent of the Swiss examples. The Danish army boasted before the battle that they would kill all the peasants, while the Dithmarschers prayed to the Virgin, promising to build a church in her honor if they should gain victory. The Danish forces recoiled from the crucifix carried by the Dithmarschen army, and in a brief hour, seven thousand of the *Garde* (Danish troops) fell in battle: "This is what God did by means of the Dithmarschen peasants!"[127] The crucifix cheered the men of Dithmarschen on to slay as many Danes, Holsteiners, and Frisians (from the opposing army) as possible. Claims of miraculous intervention show how exceptional peasant freedom and military victory was. The first of the poems in Neocorus's collection calls the defeat of lords trying to destroy the common man (*Iderman*) a "wonder." The peasants' victory is made possible through piety and fearlessness.[128]

In another poem, the Virgin Mary is again invoked as the protector of the common people (*armen Volkes*). If the cause of the Dithmarschen peasants is unjust, they should die, but if they have right on their side, they will triumph through her patronage.[129] Their Danish enemies boast that they will slay the peasants like dogs, but the princes forget Christ's sacrifice. Rather than mocking the saints and seeking to subjugate the men of Dithmarschen, they should fight the infidels; "so says now the common man."[130] Fear of God and fearlessness before the enemy are thus joined.

Neocorus also reports a speech supposedly given on the eve of the Battle of Hemmingstedt in which bravery, specifically willingness to face death, was extolled as the price of freedom (here quite clearly opposed to the servitude that the Danes sought to impose): "If we had to die a thousand deaths, even without winning eternal fame, we should do it for the sake of our fatherland. . . . Even those who are born serfs long to be free. Are we, who are born free, to subject ourselves to servitude without resisting?"[131] In Dithmarschen as in Switzerland, the freedom of a community of peasants was associated with military ability and piety. The success of the free peasants against those who would subjugate them was recognized as exceptional, and attributed to courage and divine favor.

⁓

Peasants were capable of waging war, even before the advent of the Swiss and other formidable late-medieval infantry companies. The conventions of social description might portray peasants as militarily helpless, but they came to be regarded as dangerous beginning in the fourteenth century. It was also at this time, as we have seen, that the self-image of free rural communities focused on martial and religious virtue in the defense of autonomy.

Images of peasant bravery inverted and answered chivalric themes. The very fact that peasants defeated knights reversed what was supposed to be a military commonplace, namely the superiority of mounted warriors. Victories against Hapsburgs or Danes proved divine favor not only because God grants victory to whom he chooses in general, but because the peasants' triumphs were "wonders." The heroic portrayal of peasant armies served also as a response to seigneurial stereotypes of peasants as militarily incompetent and the symbolic construction of the peasant as gross embodiment, incapable of passion, sacrifice, or privation. Finally, the songs and plays served to answer accusations of infidelity with evidence of peasant piety and divine favor.

In one key respect the heroic images of peasants followed the seigneurial model rather than contesting it. The Swiss and Dithmarschen peasants accepted a relationship between bravery and liberty similar to that found in seigneurial myths of foundation. Peasants in free communities such as Dithmarschen or the Swiss cantons appropriated this association of liberty with military heroism. They justified their freedom not by reference to abstract or even religious arguments, but in the first instance by what must be seen as the common medieval political assumption that liberty is not inherent or "natural" but exceptional, the result of force.

Praising war and courage, the peasants of the best-known privileged communities did not offer a completely countervailing theory of liberty or human equality against the predominant chivalric values. They accepted a linkage not only between war and freedom but also between physical militancy and the crusade idea of piety. The victories of the Swiss forces and of the men of Dithmarschen evidenced God's favor, all the more so in that these victories were unusual within the context of normal peasant-lord encounters.

One must bear in mind, however, that there were really two basic and opposing images of peasant piety: that of the armed peasant who struggles for an idea of Christian liberty and that of the oppressed rustic laborer who will be rewarded by God for his quiescent suffering on earth. The former image, as we have seen in this chapter, reflected an understanding of fundamental human equality, a commitment to a more local communal struggle to protect privileged status (freedom from seigneurial domination), and an acceptance of a link between piety and testing in battle. This image took root particularly in certain peasant communities, especially toward the end of the Middle Ages, where the natural condition of the peasantry was seen as sanctifying: they toiled, their labor fed others, they were the redoubt of true Christianity in a corrupt world (corrupted especially in its clerical and noble estates). Their closeness to God was indicated not by acceptance of suffering but by victory in battle. But the opposing image, that of the piously enduring peasant, reflected quite a different belief, namely, that God favored the peasant only if the peasant accepted his lot. The following chapter looks at the image of the humbly suffering peasant, the patient emblem of Christian meekness, Jerome's *sancta rusticitas*, as glossed by the Middle Ages. In the concluding chapter I will discuss how these two essentially opposed images might combine in specific peasant uprisings of the fourteenth to sixteenth centuries.

Chapter 9

Pious and Exemplary Peasants

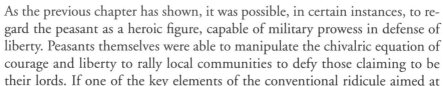

As the previous chapter has shown, it was possible, in certain instances, to regard the peasant as a heroic figure, capable of military prowess in defense of liberty. Peasants themselves were able to manipulate the chivalric equation of courage and liberty to rally local communities to defy those claiming to be their lords. If one of the key elements of the conventional ridicule aimed at the peasantry was its alleged cowardice and physical and moral unfitness for war, certain communities of peasants displayed a military competence that defied this typification while accepting the relation among prowess, honor, and freedom.

This chapter examines a number of other means by which the peasantry was exalted, especially the assertion that peasants possessed a special role in the divine plan, not despite their lowly condition but because of it. We have already discussed the background of this tendency: the necessity of peasant labor combined with the lack of mutuality rendered the peasant the beneficiary of the Christian language of reversal. If he was oppressed on earth, surely God would reward him in heaven, just as God would punish those who exert terrestrial power (considered at times almost by definition wicked). It is worth recalling Stephen Langton's observation, commenting on Hosea, that the poor will rule in heaven, hence we must befriend them in this life if we are to be admitted to bliss in the next.[1] The poor, according to Langton, are elected by grace.[2]

Of particular importance is the status of the peasant as Christian. As noted previously, it was one thing to "marginalize" groups that were outside the Church, such as Jews, Muslims, or distant mythical races, but quite another, more difficult task to construct peasants as subhuman. True, it could be argued that peasants were essentially lowly or bestial, or that whatever equality might have existed originally had been obscured by a biblical or historical taint hereditarily transmitted. But by their very ingenuity, such arguments recognized that the reason for the degradation of peasants was not self-evident. After all, not only were peasants the majority population, whose labor, moreover, supported all of society, but they professed Christianity and thus had to be acknowledged as in some sense fully human.

I do not mean to suggest that Christianity conferred what would now be understood as "rights," although something like this idea would lie behind the Spanish debates of the sixteenth century over the slaughter of the Indians. Could they be regarded as infidels and so be enslaved or killed if they had never had a chance to accept or reject Christianity?[3] But here rights are rather basic: reduced to the right to remain alive. What Christianity was thought to confer, according to at least a segment of medieval opinion, was a certain minimal human dignity and, related to that, a certain minimal human freedom.

Before examining the implications of Christianity for the humanity of the peasant, I want first to look at some other responses to the dominant images of peasants as stupid, envious, and disorderly.

Clever Peasants

The peasant could be credited with a degree of cleverness, not that of literate erudition but a certain practical shrewdness. While the dominant image of the peasant was that he was stupid, it was also possible to regard him as cunning, a trait shading more than challenging his supposed ignorance. At times the fool and trickster are the same person, and a subordinated person attempting to deploy his cleverness must appear stupid, to convince his complacent betters that he is simple and innocent. To be sure, stories of trickery in which the weak turn the tables on more powerful (but thereby less agile) opponents are among the most versatile and prolific forms celebrating indirect resistance.[4] The Brer Rabbit folktales of the American slaves are well-known examples of ingenuity triumphing over strength, stories in which the wily rabbit outwits the fox and the wolf. The tales could serve as oblique denunciations of oppression, a "hidden transcript," in James Scott's formulation. Yet this defiance did not always have to be completely hidden. The wealthy are not quite so unobservant as to be utterly unaware of the opinions of their servants. There have always been acceptable forms of at least slightly subversive texts not only permitted but enjoyed by the dominant groups. The sanitized but not completely innocuous version of the Brer Rabbit cycle, the Uncle Remus stories, is not wholly divorced from its original inspiration.[5] Those regarded as inferior are often simultaneously credited with a certain practical cunning. The trickster may lose his dissident status and move from inspiration for the oppressed group to amusing rogue whose very need to be so clever serves to reassure a complacent observer.

It is difficult to recover authentic peasant tales from the Middle Ages, as opposed to discourse *about* peasants, and the study of medieval texts is replete with examples of those erroneously regarded as pure expressions of the common folk. But our interest is actually more in the cunning attributed to peasants by those above them in society than in the peasants' own estimation of their acuity. As early as the eleventh-century Latin poem *Unibos* (composed probably in the Low Countries before the Gregorian Reform), the peasant appears as resourceful and shrewd. The comically named Unus Bos (i.e., "one ox"), a poor peasant, becomes rich despite the hatred of the three village tyrants—the priest, the steward, and the village mayor—whom he outsmarts.[6]

More often than as major actor in a story, the *vilain* figured as a generalized repository of folk-wisdom. Chrétien's *Eric et Enide*, for example, opens by citing a saying "among the *vilains*" that many things are held in contempt that are better than commonly thought.[7] Lancelot, bemoaning his imprisonment by the treacherous Maleagant, cites the supposed rustic commonplace "it's hard to find a friend."[8] In the *Romance of Thebes*, the peasants are the putative authors of the saying that he who makes a sword will find it turned against him, a slight modification of Matthew 26:52.[9]

Most observations attributed to the wisdom of the lowly describe an imperfect world, regarded not with indulgence but with a grim sense of the power of misfortune.[10] Marie de France, in *Eliduc*, cites a saying of the *vilains* that it is foolish to count on the affection or constancy of one's lord.[11] Slightly more positive, but still in the nature of advice on surviving in a hostile world, is a rustic teaching found in Wace's *Brut*: it is sometimes necessary to accept a modicum of evil in order to prevent greater harm.[12] The virtues of compromise and flexibility are exemplified as well, in the Anglo-Norman allegorical treatise on the reckoning of time, Philip de Thaon's *Comput* (written 1113 or 1119).[13]

Such attributions of common sense and worldly wisdom to the rustics are, of course, hardly incompatible with an attitude of quite ordinary contempt. Thus in Wace's *Brut* and the *Roman de Thèbes*, the *vilain* is both source of folk sagacity and emblem of unsuitability for war.[14] The thirteenth-century German author Der Stricker wrote short moral tales such as "Der Kluge Knecht," in which the peasant is an adroit trickster, and other works in which peasants are typically stupid and violent.[15]

Among the *fabliaux*, which tend to depict rustics as gross, hapless, and foolish, one finds certain stories in which the *vilains* outsmart their superiors, reversing relations of power by cunning. A high-stakes contest of weak against strong is the subject of "Le vilain qui conquist Paradis par Plait."[16] A nameless peasant dies and his soul sneaks into heaven behind Saint Michael, who is guiding an authorized soul. Saint Peter discovers the trespasser and is about to expel him, for *vilains* are not allowed in paradise (a comical reworking of the commonplace of heavenly egalitarianism, that there will be no serfs in heaven).[17] The stubborn soul argues not only with Peter but with Saint Paul and Saint Thomas as well. What has he done to be barred from heaven? Has he denied Christ as Peter did? Has he doubted the resurrection as did Saint Thomas, or persecuted Christians in the manner of Paul before his conversion? They may be saints, but what gives them the right to deny him admittance? God Himself appears, and the lowly soul presents Him, in effect, with a contractual obligation: in life the rustic had been charitable, and he died having confessed and received the sacraments; now God should live up to His word. The rustic soul is finally let into paradise.

The sharp peasant is not always so virtuous. In "Le vilain mire," a wife victimized by her brutal husband plots vengeance by informing the king's messengers, who are desperately searching for a learned doctor, that her husband is the wisest of all healers but requires being beaten to admit it.[18] He is beaten and then dragged before the king to cure the princess, who has a fish bone caught in her throat. The quick-witted peasant thinks to dislodge the bone by making the princess laugh, which he manages to do by taking his clothes off and pretending to grill himself in the hearth. His next challenge is to cure several dozen people suffering from a variety of ailments. Figuring that the one thing all surely suffer from is the fear of death (for not even those most gravely ill truly long for death), he offers a sinister cure that can be fabricated if the sickest of the patients agrees to give up his life and be burned. The ashes are the medicine's vital ingredient, but of course the sickest patient refuses to sacrifice himself. The rustic has offered a credible solution that cannot be put to the test, hence his skill remains unquestioned. Here we are invited to admire the ingenuity of the peasant without placing him on especially high moral ground. Peasants are able to outwit their superiors; in an amoral and exploitative world, they can win at least small victories by cunning.

The German peasant character Markolf, popular from the thirteenth century but particularly toward the end of the Middle Ages, embodies and combines various strands of attributed cleverness. Markolf is presented as the author of proverbial sayings, as a player of pranks in the Eulenspiegel mode, and as interlocutor of King Solomon. Markolf is the antithesis of the lordly Solomon, who embodies measure and courtesy. Markolf seems at first to represent a crude foolishness but ultimately typifies practical folk knowledge of the real world as against the grave, somewhat distant wisdom of the king.[19]

The peasant's wisdom is not the cheerful, life-affirming earthiness of what might be called the Zorba-the-Greek model. If we look at the collection of poems entitled *Li proverbe au vilain*, containing observations on the world and its ways, we find a grim, occasionally sardonic opinion of a world set up to reward those who are already powerful.[20] Each of the 280 poems, written between 1174 and 1191, consists of six lines followed by a moral. They all conclude with the words "so says the *vilain*." They contain cynically resigned advice on how to survive. A few describe the cruelty of oppressive lords, the rare joy of having a good lord, the foolishness of hoping for something from the wealthy. A basic instruction is that to be poor is unfortunate while to be rich is to be happy:

> A poor man labors all the time,
> He thinks, works, and weeps,
> He never laughs heartily;
> The rich man laughs and sings,
> He boasts of many things,
> He is not troubled by anything,
> Everyone is made glad if they already have something,
> So says the *vilain*.[21]

Whatever their momentary success, the weak merely survive while the powerful enjoy their existence. This is not an ethnographic transcription of what peasants said in the privacy of their own gatherings but rather an artful composition that presents what purports to be a distillation of popular wisdom.

Virtuous Peasants

Fiction and legend present certain instances in which the peasant and princely worlds intersect. In some peculiar distress, the members of the ruling dynasty are forced to seek the aid of their erstwhile subjects. It is a sign of desperation or of outcast status that nobles, such as Tristan and Yseult or Yvain, take refuge in the wild and live like rustics. The *Gregorius*, by Hartmann von Aue (written ca. 1187–89), depicts an extreme case of giving up power and wealth: the hero, upon discovering his incestuous marriage to his mother, chains himself to a desolate rock for seventeen years.[22] But in these renunciations there is no connection with any human community: solitude is itself an aspect of the radical distancing from civilization.

The best-known example of a royal personage taking refuge with peasants occurs in connection with King Alfred and the cakes, a legend first found in the late-tenth-century *Vita Sancti Neoti*.[23] During the battles against the Danish invaders, Alfred was said to have spent a few days incognito with a herdsman and his wife. On one occasion he was berated by the wife for failing to notice that the bread baking in the oven was burning, an insulting reproach he bore meekly rather than revealing his true rank. In this brief encounter the rustics are not especially virtuous but serve rather as an occasion to demonstrate the king's exemplary kindness and wisdom.

More prolonged and emotionally charged contact between worlds takes place in Hartmann's *Der arme Heinrich*, written about 1195. The Swabian noble Heinrich contracts leprosy and learns from the physicians of Salerno that the only cure for the disease is the heart's blood of a maiden willing to die for him (an example of medication by self-sacrifice more serious than that in "Le Vilain Mire").[24] Abandoning hope, Heinrich goes to live in a forest clearing, taking refuge with a free peasant tenant (whom Heinrich, in his happier days, had the goodness and foresight to treat well). The peasant, a model of industry and humble contentment, has an eight-year-old daughter. She is of noble bearing and extremely fond of Heinrich, and he of her. In three years, as his sufferings grow, Heinrich yields to the family's questions about his condition and tells them of the impossible cure. Overcoming the resistance of both her parents and the unhappy Heinrich, the girl demands to be brought to Salerno. Heinrich complies, but as the doctor sharpens his knife, Heinrich is so overcome by the cruelty of the sacrifice and by the girl's beauty that he forbids the doctor to continue. By God's mercy he is miraculously cured and marries the heroic maiden. Here the girl is so exceptional as hardly to be considered a peasant, but her parents act within the plausible order of peasant virtues: they are hard-working and extremely deferential to their lord (acquiescing, out of loyalty to him, to their daughter's determined self-sacrifice).

A Pomeranian legend of the late fifteenth century tells another tale of nobles taking refuge with peasants.[25] The family of Duke Erik was sent to a remote area during a time of danger. His son, the future Duke Bogeslav, lived as a commoner and received little favor from his mother, so that he was essentially abandoned. A peasant named Hans Lange adopted him, and his mother was happy to consent to the arrangement. The peasant was sufficiently well-off to clothe the prince and give him a horse and sword. When Duke Erik died, the stout-hearted Hans Lange convinced the nobles to recognize Bogeslav, even against his wicked mother's wishes. Bogeslav rewarded his faithful guardian by giving him a free lease and exemption from taxes and services.

A more dramatic transformation of fortune appears in the legendary origin of the Přemyslid rulers of Bohemia.[26] The founder, Přemysl, was said to have been a plowman who became the first duke of the Bohemians in a fashion slightly reminiscent of the story of Cincinnatus.[27] According to the *Chronicae Bohemorum*, written by Cosmas of Prague (who died in 1125), the eponymous founder Boemus settled an empty land with a group of followers.[28] In these happy early years, peace reigned and the Bohemians seem to have paid deference to wise persons who resolved disputes rather than having formal rulers. A certain Krak (Latinized in the *Chronicle* as Croccus) "arose among them" sometime after Boemus. He left three daughters, all of them with supernatural powers. The youngest, Libuse (Lubossa) is described as seer or prophetess (*phitonissa*) and, like her father, was recognized as a wise conciliator. A dispute between two notables over a field boundary, however, erupted into denunciations of female rule when the loser refused to accept Libuse's judgment. Bowing to the imputation of female weakness, Libuse consented to marry and told messengers that her consort would be a man whom they would find at a certain village and know by the markings of his oxen. They followed her horse, which led them to Stadice (Ztadici), where they found a peasant, Přemysl, who (along with his oxen) answered Libuse's description. Called thus to rule, Přemysl abandoned the plow, released the oxen, and stuck into the ground the hazelnut stick used to guide the animals, which later turned into two fruitful trees. Cosmas does not describe Přemysl as taking office in accordance with any ceremony, but dwells on the divestiture of his peasant clothes and the putting on of raiment appropriate to a prince. Subsequent dukes of Bohemia were enthroned rather than crowned. In Cosmas's time this ceremony took place at Vyšehrad (across the river from Prague Castle), where, according to Cosmas, Přemysl's pouch and peasant shoes made of bark were kept.[29] The peasant garb and the transformation of a peasant into a ruler thus symbolized the distinct, semi-magical origin of the dynasty.

A briefer version of these events that may antedate Cosmas's rendition was written by the monk Christian, author of a *vita* of the holy king of Bohemia, Saint Wenceslas.[30] According to Christian the ancient Bohemians were decimated by a plague and sought the advice of a wise woman. She had them establish the city of Prague and elect Přemysl, "who was very skilled at agriculture." The wise woman married the talented farmer, a union with overtones of fertility and prophecy.

During the high and late Middle Ages Přemysl was rivaled and ultimately eclipsed by Saint Wenceslas, duke of Bohemia, who had been murdered in 929 or 935 by his brother Boleslav. Wenceslas became a royal saint on the model of Stephen of Hungary, and the protector of a people (like Saint James of Compostela). His lance became part of the Přemyslids' regalia. He was the protector and embodiment of the Bohemians, who were "servants of Saint Wenceslas" according to an ecclesiastical source. His likeness appeared on ducal/royal seals and two-sided pennies from the early eleventh to early thirteenth centuries.[31]

The kings who followed the extinction of the Přemyslid Dynasty in 1306 continued and even amplified royal devotion to Wenceslas. The Luxembourg ruler Charles IV conferred on his newly founded university of Prague a seal with the likeness of Saint Wenceslas and also named his son after the royal saint, signifying the continuity of dynastic sanctity.[32] But neither was the memory of Přemysl by any means obliterated. The shoes of Přemyslid kept at Vyšehrad were ceremonially paraded before Charles IV and King Wenceslas IV on the mornings before their coronations.[33]

The legend of Přemysl may have influenced the elaboration of stories concerning Wenceslas (although it is hard to date the confection of the legends). Like Přemysl, Wenceslas was reputed to have been a farmer (*cui tantum agricultore officium erat*). According to the *vita*, he was accustomed to work at night, secretly preparing from scratch, as it were, the elements of the communion. While others slept, Wenceslas reaped, threshed, and milled wheat, and also tended vineyards.[34]

Wenceslas was sufficiently identified with rustic occupations to serve as a convenient vehicle for anti-Czech sentiment. A German guildsman of Prague was punished in 1338 for refusing to mark the feast day "of that rustic," as he called the holy prince.[35] When the Přemyslid line came to an end in 1306, and with the death of Rudolf of Hapsburg imminent, the leader of the Hapsburg party, Tobias of Bechyně, derisively suggested that those who feared electing a foreigner to rule Bohemia go back to Stadice and find themselves another peasant to elect, a remark that, according to Beneš of Weitmühl, got him killed.[36] Such flippant observations were taken seriously, evidence of the sensitivity of the fourteenth-century Bohemians to the aura of rusticity surrounding their royal cults.[37]

There are other legends (in Poland, for example) of the sudden elevation of a rustic to rulership, or of coronation rituals (in Poland and Carinthia) incorporating gestures identifying the ruler with the peasantry.[38] Another example of the association of a peasant with a polity lies in the symbolism of the city of Cologne. The Latin name of the city, *Colonia*, was thought to derive from "rustic" (*colonus*) and was given an allegorical meaning in the Middle Ages. Cologne was one of four cities of the Reich identified with peasants in Peter von Andlau's *Quaternion der deutschen Reichverfassung* (1422), the others being Constance, Regensburg, and Salzburg.[39] Here the peasant symbolized steadfastness and (interestingly enough) cleverness and resourcefulness. A heraldic symbol of late-medieval Cologne was a peasant with a scythe and flail. This appears in the frontispiece of a chronicle of the city printed in 1499, in which the peasant is superimposed on an imperial eagle.[40] The *Chronik van der hilligen stat van Coellen* interprets the peasant as an emblem of the city's holiness and God's solicitude. Far from being a strange or lowly symbol, the heraldic peasant figures Cologne as the "holy peasant of the Reich." Indeed the spiritual work of God that nourishes the soul is likened to the labor of the noble plowman who feeds all, laity and clergy.[41]

Such images of the holy labor of the peasant were characteristic of the late fifteenth and early sixteenth centuries, as we shall see, but the peasant symbol of Cologne was well known in an earlier era. In the late thirteenth century it was sufficiently embarrassing to cause Godefrit Hagen, author of a rhymed urban chronicle, to devote some lines to denying the connection. The name of the town has nothing to do with peasants, who are gross, ambitious, and unworthy, he insists.[42]

The most famous historical example of the virtuous peasant, and indeed the single most renowned medieval peasant, was Joan of Arc, the rustic visionary of Lorraine who instilled confidence in the dauphin and his armies and rescued the city of Orléans from the English siege.[43] That a female and a peasant should receive heavenly communications from Saint Michael the Archangel touching the salvation of France is a dramatic example of the inversion of power, the unlooked-for triumph of the meek. It was also a triumph not of rebellion but of the literal legitimation of the monarch. Yet it is Joan as woman, or really as young woman, a virgin, that forms the essential paradox, not her social rank. True, it is of key importance that she was well below the social status of plausible political actors.[44] In later years attempts were made to deny that she was of rustic origin, and even to claim she was of royal birth (an illegitimate child of Isabella of Bavaria and Louis of Orléans, for example).[45] But it is as "La Pucelle," "the Maid of Orléans," that she was celebrated and remembered. Status was behind sex and age in her paradoxical image. What impressed her contemporaries was that she was a girl of more or less humble birth and not that she a was peasant. Her divine inspiration conferred a paradoxical heroism of military vocation and extraordinary fortitude. These also could be considered to contradict peasant character: that a peasant should prove brave or adept at warfare was in the nature of things unlikely and, if it occurred, deeply disturbing. Nevertheless, in her own self-fashioning it was as "The Maid" that she warned the duke of Bedford that God had shown her that Charles was the true king of France and as "The Blessed Maid" that she won the praise of Christine de Pisan.[46]

Noble Peasants: Productive, Simple, Pious

Beginning in the late fourteenth century, particularly in Germany, praise for the peasant poured out. Poems, plays, and exhortations lauded their diligence and selfless toil. Much of this *Bauernlob* amounted to a rediscovery of the dependence of all of society on peasant labor, a theme we have examined in the context of the Three Orders and mutuality. Labor could, it is true, be regarded with contempt or considered a penitential duty incumbent on a cursed segment of the population. From quite early on, however, the idea that such necessary work was in some (not merely negative) sense spiritually beneficial received at least grudging assent.

Texts that most bitterly satirized or denounced the late-medieval peasant denied that he performed any useful labor. The Neidhart tradition depended on an image of lazy, pretentious, and, above all, useless villagers for its more dehumanizing forms of satire. In contrast, literature in praise of peasants, *Bauernlob*, extolled the "noble peasant" whose work nourishes the world. What this literature expresses is thus not merely a neutral awareness of the peasant's social role but a stylized form of gratitude. His labor and its fruits confer on the peasant a certain nobility that is accentuated in the *Bauernlob* genre.

In about 1350 the poet Heinrich "Der Teichner" wrote:

> Thus I praise the peasant,
> Who can feed all the world.
> He labors with his plow,
> Who can compare with him?
>
> . . .
>
> Thus the poor peasant is better than you rich people.[47]

Contemporary with Der Teichner is the well-known image of the pious "friend of God" in the work of the mystic Johannes Tauler (died 1361). Here what the peasant wins by his labors is his own bread rather than food for the entire world, but the work itself is of sufficient merit to obviate the need to go to church.[48]

Hans Rosenplüt of Nuremberg, composer of satiric Carnival plays that mocked the stupidity and boorishness of peasants, also wrote of the "noble plowman" in a song-poem, "Der Bauern Lob" (ca. 1450). In all God's creation, none is so truly noble as the plowman. The author has no better friend, for the peasant has fed him and his parents. He praises "the noble, pious peasant" (*den edlen frumen Paur*) because "it is often hard labor for him when he goes with his plow, with which he feeds all the world, lords, townsmen, and artisans. If there were no peasant, things would be in a sad condition."[49] The peasant is praiseworthy because his difficult labor feeds all and makes him close to God.

The true nobility of the peasant is even more strongly emphasized in the late-fifteenth-century anonymous Franconian "Poem on the First Nobleman." There is no prince so worthy of praise as the peasant who is truly noble, for all the world lives off his labor.[50] The poem concludes by warning peasants against trying to better their circumstances, for their way of life shields them from temptations of excess and idleness by which God is forgotten. The spiritual benefit accrues not only through labor but through simplicity: "Peasants seldom go to church, but this does not disturb God. He rewards them for their work with a healthy body and an eternal crown."[51]

In this instance the virtue or nobility of the peasant consists of work, imputed piety (through work), and austerity. It is often hard to separate exaltation of the peasant for his piety from the antique theme of exaltation of the simple life. Godliness is more than mere sobriety or the mere absence of temptation, far from the corrupt world of city, court, and civilization. Texts such as the "Poem on the First Nobleman" differ from the Arcadian dream of the pastorale, for the former evoke an image of healthful and productive toil rather than happy idleness, the labor-intensive world of the *Georgics* rather than the world of the carefree *Eclogues* or their Theocritan predecessors.

From the examples above, all of which share a recognition of the importance of the peasant's productivity, two conceptions of the nobility of the peasant's labor emerge, conceptions that may at times overlap. On the one hand, work ennobles the peasant both because it is of such great service to society and because it is intrinsically improving for the laborer himself, both physically and morally (if only negatively on the moral side, in that it keeps him from the wickedness of wealth). On the other hand, work ennobles the peasant through the suffering it causes him; its merit lies in its pain more than its productivity. His work is unremunerated; it entails arbitrary mistreatment; it earns God's mercy and the inversion of worldly power and comfort only in the next life. Productivity was praiseworthy within a secular set of values, but it was through suffering that the peasant approached a condition of sanctity.

SIMPLICITY

The basic text in praise of the simple but industrious life of rural labor is book 2 of Virgil's *Georgics*, beginning with line 458:

O happy husbandmen! too happy should they come to know their blessings! for

whom, far from the clash of arms, most righteous Earth, unbidden pours forth
from her soil an easy sustenance. What though no stately mansion with proud
portals disgorges at dawn from all its halls a tide of visitors, though they never
gaze at doors inlaid with lovely tortoise-shell or at raiment tricked with gold or
at bronzes of Ephyra, though their white wool be not stained with Assyrian dye,
or their clear oil's service spoiled by cassia? Yet theirs is repose without care, and
a life that knows no fraud, but is rich in treasures manifold. Yea, the ease of
broad domains, caverns, and living lakes, and cool vales, the lowing of the kine,
and soft slumbers beneath the trees—all are theirs. They have woodland glades
and the haunts of game; a youth hardened to toil and inured to scanty fare;
worship of gods and reverence for age; among them, as she quitted the earth,
Justice planted her latest steps.[52]

Those whom Virgil addresses are not at leisure and are not carefree. The
earth, while yielding her riches willingly, still requires toil. The virtues of the
simple life are in large measure negative: freedom from the trauma of great
affairs, especially war, and removal from the debilitating allure of luxury. Yet
rural simplicity does have certain tangible rewards: health, repose, and an
austere harmony.

Horace's *Epode* 2 is another eloquent, though not completely serious, evocation of rural simplicity.[53] The poem begins: "Happy the man who, far away
from business cares, like the pristine race of mortals, works his ancestral acres
with his steers." Again the farm's virtue is partially its distance from the tribu-
lations of war and the intrigue of the Forum. This particular epode includes
the same images of productive labor that Virgil employs throughout the
Georgics: lowing cattle, pruning and grafting, straining honey, and other useful and innocent tasks. The modest wife milks or prepares "unbought repasts"
from the farm's own produce. In place of exotic delicacies (Lucrine oysters or
Ionian pheasant), there is sorrel gathered from the meadow, or the odd sacrificial lamb. The recital of simple joys is put in the mouth of the moneylender
Alfius as he is on the point of renouncing the city, but the debts he calls in
upon the Ides of this month, he lends out again by the Kalends of the next,
changing his mind and reinvesting his shady gains.

In other instances, of course, Horace quite sincerely praises the simple life
of his farm in the Sabine countryside, but in Horace as well as Virgil, the
farmer is a landowner or a tenant of substantial means and independence.
Horace's "Beatus ille" imagines the labor of faithful slaves as one of the pleasant aspects for the farm owner to contemplate, along with the dutiful oxen.

Influential and always well known, images of rural rectitude nevertheless
had only a limited resonance in the Middle Ages, in part because of the relative absence of small independent proprietors, or at least the absence of such

a class in the literary imagination. Simplicity carried great advantages. Ambrose remarked, in a passage later cited by the Cistercian Odo of Cheriton, "the poor man in his hut, wealthy in conscience, sleeps safer upon the earth than the rich man in his gold and purple."[54] Petrarch quotes Virgil, acknowledging that Justice did indeed leave her last traces among the rustics, but that was long ago. Now they are thoroughly wicked and less likely than anyone to return to the good example of the past.[55] Chaucer, in his version of the story of the patient Griselda, describes the idyllic situation of her small village, whose poor folk live off their own labor, by which the earth yields its abundance.[56] As Henrik Specht has pointed out, however, the image of quiet, honorable contentment is Chaucer's addition to sources (Petrarch and the *Livre Griseldis*) that merely state that Griselda lived in a sparsely inhabited village.[57] The fifteenth-century humanist Maffeo Vegio, author of bitter antipeasant satires, expressed amazement that Virgil (who was in all other respects his model) should admire rural life.[58]

In the Christian tradition, the austere benefits of the hardships of rustic life greatly outweighed any notion of the simple joys of farming. In part this emphasis stemmed from the Christian teachings of the moral superiority of the poor and helpless. To some extent it repeated the classical commonplace that the absence of inducements to vice was in itself beneficial. Lactantius praised the poor whose faith is stronger on the metaphorical march toward heaven because they are not weighed down with the baggage of worldly ambitions and temptations.[59] The issue was not rural versus urban but poor versus rich, and the poor meant those below the modest landowner.

An additional reason for the early-medieval lack of interest in the health-giving and pleasant ways of the country was that labor was more closely joined to pain in the Christian tradition. God's curse upon Adam was that he should feed himself only with great effort, no longer with the ease and natural bounty of Eden. The Middle Ages could certainly praise simple rustic joys, but more intensely imagined a painful productivity and a hard simplicity. Psalm 127, it is true, speaks of the happiness of those who eat the labor of their own hands (more unbought meals), and was cited often in medieval didactic and exegetical works. Honorius Augustodunensis invoked this psalm in praising the simplicity of the rustics' existence, but the spiritual benefit of labor is also derived from the sweat required of the rustics to support the people of God.[60] The Franconian poem concerning "the first nobleman" (cited above) does claim that among the rewards of the peasant's life is a healthy body by virtue of avoiding the vices of the wealthy, but this is unusual.

The advantages of simplicity are more typically conveyed by a popular story of a poor man who arrived in Chartres without so much as a penny to obtain lodging. After an unpleasant night outdoors, he blessed his indigent condition upon learning that the inn where he would have stayed had he had the money had burned to the ground in the night.[61] The negative virtues of simplicity stem not from a deliberate decision to leave the city and its vices, in the Roman manner, but from unwilling but beneficial deprivation; poverty rather than renunciation. As such, the advantages of simplicity resemble a gentler version of the Isidorian formulation that servitude was instituted as a result of the Fall to restrain those of weak character from the vices they would sink into without some external coercion.[62]

Astuteness was invidiously contrasted with pious simplicity in the New Testament, most pertinently in 2 Corinthians 11:3: "But I fear lest, as the serpent beguiled Eve by his subtlety, so your minds should be corrupted, and fall from the simplicity that is in Christ" (*astutia* as opposed to *simplicitas*). Lack of education was the clearest evidence of a simple nature. In a famous passage of his *Confessions*, Augustine recalls his chagrin at learning about the ascetic heroism of the uneducated monks who "storm the gates of heaven" while he and his friends seemed incapable of action.[63] Saint Jerome was the paramount source for a notion of holy simplicity conceived in terms of "rusticity." In a passage from Letter 52, which would become a *locus classicus*, Jerome states that "holy rusticity" is preferable to sinful eloquence. The context is a comparison of those brothers who confuse sanctity with ignorance and better educated brothers who confuse holiness with adroit use of words. By *rusticitas* Jerome means rough inarticulateness, a characteristic not limited to rural folk. But the passage would later be understood to express a preference for simple piety, especially that of literal rustics.[64] *Rusticitas* in later centuries could simply mean boorishness, especially lack of proper religious reverence, as in Caesarius of Arles; this deficiency was not necessarily limited to rural laborers but was more closely identified with them than with others.[65] Martin of Braga (fl. 556–72), in his "De correctione rusticorum," contributed significantly to the identification of countrymen as essentially pagan.[66] By *rustici* Martin clearly meant rural folk whose crude ways exemplify credulity and deliberate paganism, not simple Christian piety.

During the Middle Ages, holy simplicity was not the tranquil pleasure of the small proprietor but a result of labor, poverty, and suffering. This is especially, although not exclusively, a Franciscan teaching. The German Minorite known as Brother Ludovicus stated that peasants (*agricolae*) were beloved of God by reason of their endless labor and unjust treatment at the hands of their secular masters.[67] Misery on earth gives the peasants a claim to spiritual merit, and this misery consists of both toil and oppression. Heinrich von Burgus, a Tyrolese poet writing in the early fourteenth century under the influence of the Franciscans, described poverty as the hell of the peasants, but added that through this pain they become worthy in God's sight. They suffer and their labor is hard, but their pain is a sign of God's particular care.[68] Hugo von Trimberg relates misery on earth to wealth in God's Kingdom, and deems misery not as something "natural" but as the result of human injustice.[69]

Spiritual benefit rather than secular simplicity was what interested those who extolled the rustic in the Middle Ages. Such benefit derived from three things chiefly, none of which produced any special reward here on earth: labor that feeds the world, poverty (rather than comfortable simplicity), and oppression. Suffering is what gives the peasantry a spiritual advantage, and with this suffering is included the labor of Adam's children, the indigence of peasant life, and exploitation by those above them.

SPIRITUAL BENEFIT

What was the nature of this spiritual advantage? Not the intrinsic satisfaction of an austere life of virtue but the promise of heaven. The Epistle of James (2:5) asks rhetorically, "Hath not God chosen the poor in this world, rich in faith, and heirs of the kingdom which God hath promised to them that love him?" From this it appears that simplicity (poverty) has more than the negative benefit of shielding one from temptation but is in itself a blessed condition. The words of the epistle would be repeated in medieval sermons and didactic literature, by the English Dominican John of Bromyard and by Michael of Northgate's *Ayenbite of Inwyt*, for example.[70]

A passage from Honorius's *Elucidarium* (ca. 1100), noted earlier, encapsulates quite succinctly the spiritual advantages not just of the poor but of rustic laborers specifically. In the dialogue the disciple asks the master about what the prospects in the next life are for peasants. Most of them will be saved, he is informed, because of the simplicity of their lives and because of their toil (literally "sweat", which recalls the destiny of Adam), which feeds all.[71] Addressing the rustics in his *Speculum Ecclesie*, Honorius offers a vision of what they will earn by their honest labors and obedience to their priests: a heaven of flowers, with splendid odors and thousands of joyful inhabitants.[72] Yet in the *Imago mundi*, in connection with human history and genealogy, Honorius repeats the commonplace of Noah's curse and the descent of the unfree (*servi*) from Ham.[73] It was quite possible to maintain both opinions: that peasants are cursed through their ancestor Ham, and yet objects of God's solicitude.

The contradiction between the peasants as cursed and peasants as blessed is more apparent than real, for there were several avenues of resolution. Their misery and what we have called the failure of mutuality (unrewarded labor) could be derived from both hereditarily transmitted misdeeds and expiatory toil. Their labor is a penance containing both a positive or forward-looking component (the hope of heaven) and a negative origin in sin (Noah's curse). In fact this is generally true of humankind: all are lost with Adam but redeemed with Christ, cursed but saved.[74]

Another way of encompassing both positions was to acknowledge the peasants' theoretical moral advantage while bemoaning their greed, envy, or other manifestations of essential baseness that prevent them from utilizing that advantage. We saw this dialectic in Stephen of Fougères's *Livre de manières*, written in the 1170s.[75] After complaining that the peasant receives little though he maintains the other estates, Stephen observes that the greater his impoverishment, the greater is his merit if he bears his misfortunes with fortitude. But in real life the peasants complain constantly and show ingratitude toward God, so that they fail to profit from what would otherwise be to their advantage.

The spiritual privileges of poverty and the failure to realize them concerned several thirteenth-century observers of the social order in relation to God's purpose. A sermon directed at peasants, supposedly by Berthold von Regensburg but probably by a later Franciscan author, states that they are given lowly status here on earth but would be exalted in heaven.[76] Another sermon attributed to Berthold speaks of Christ plowing the "field" of Christianity Himself, not wanting anyone else to carry out this labor. The wood and iron of the plow recall the wood and nails of the cross.[77] Other sermons note, however, that although the rustics receive spiritual benefit from their hard lives, there have been few peasants who were saints. Moreover, they are given to cursing, jealousy, and dishonesty.[78] Brother Ludovicus pointed to the special merit of the peasants in God's eyes but regretted their propensity to theft, mendacity, drunkenness, and blasphemy.[79] The poor are beloved by God, and woe to those who oppress them, for they are the apple of His eye (Zechariah 2:8). But alas, so many of them are ungrateful and dishonest, forgetting God. They are the targets of Jeremiah 5:4: "Perhaps these are poor and foolish, that know not the way of the Lord, the judgment of their God."[80]

A survey of estates by Guillaume Le Clerc entitled *Besant de Dieu* denounces the poor for their envy, arrogance, and rebelliousness, which waste the advantages they have over the rich in entering the kingdom of heaven.[81] The same sentiments appear in the Spanish prince Don Juan Manuel's *Libro de los estados* except that here the characteristic sins of the *labradores* are laziness and stupidity.[82]

All these instances imply or assert that the peasants' invincibly wicked character causes them to depreciate their substantial spiritual capital. Some observers, however, represented the spiritual advantage of the peasants as a realizable potential rather than an irrecoverably squandered resource: if they did not seek to alter their status, complain, or act wickedly, they would receive the benefit of their closeness to God. According to a Spanish "Dance of Death" poem of the mid- or late fourteenth century, for example, the peasants will win eternal glory if they perform their work honestly, not seeking to encroach on their neighbor's land (by plowing an extra furrow across the boundary, for example).[83] Or again, in the *Buch der Rügen*, peasants are blessed by reason of their labors but must remain obedient, not rising above themselves.[84] In the passages mentioned earlier, however, the peasants have demonstrated that they are inclined not to fulfill the conditions for salvation. In such cases the consequences of their low nature, or of Noah's curse, are not really affected by divine care for the humble.

Other writers, however, were less grudging, less preoccupied with the shortcomings of the subjugated, and more impressed with the contrasting fortunes of the rich and an undifferentiated "poor" that included peasants. According to Peter of Blois (died 1204), it is "the weakest of men, who will inherit the kingdom of God and the Holy Land: the two Jerusalems, terrestrial and celestial."[85] This evokes the accounts of the discovery of the Holy Lance during the siege of Antioch on the First Crusade. Raymond of Aguilers, chaplain of Count Raymond of Toulouse, described how Saint Andrew appeared before the "rustic pauper" Peter Bartholomew, revealing where the lance was hidden. Peter asked if someone else might be chosen since his poverty made him ashamed to present the lance before the army. Saint Andrew replied that he was elected by God not in spite of his lowly condition but because of it. The poor surpass in merit and grace those who precede them on earth, just as gold comes before silver.[86] More graphically, away from the context of the crusade, Jacques de Vitry, in an *exemplum*, describes the sufferings of a peasant shivering in the cold, who comforts himself with the thought that in heaven he will be able to warm his feet whenever he wishes by extending them a little over the pit of hell, where the rich will be burning.[87]

In these instances it is not labor or even seigneurial oppression but poverty that confers spiritual superiority. What is most impressive is the reversal of fortunes that occurs in moving from one world to the next. Rustics are here joined to the condition of the destitute poor rather than constituting a separate class of productive if subjugated laborers. Mark 10:31, "But many that are first, shall be last: and the last, first" is a biblical maxim that warns the rich and powerful and exalts the impoverished. In 1 Corinthians 1:26–29,

Saint Paul says that not many are called, and that God has chosen the foolish and weak of the world for His Kingdom.[88]

Some authors, such as Francesc Eiximenis, would exclude the peasants from the category of the blessed poor by reason of their greed and impiety, while others considered them part of the general social category of the poor. In the early-medieval period the image of reversal would dominate. Recounting the life of Saint Portianus, Gregory of Tours remarks that God has arranged for the poverty of this world to serve as the way toward heaven, "so that the poor rustic [*rusticus*] can go there when he that is dressed in the purple cannot."[89] The "just pauper" will reach heaven, whereas the unjust powerful in this life will be lost, according to Hrabanus Maurus.[90] Another Carolingian poet contrasted this world, where the rich rejoice in acquiring wealth while beggars suffer from hunger, with the world to come, where the wealthy who "consumed the tears of orphans" will lie in Tartarus while the paupers will find bliss.[91]

Another influential biblical image appears in Matthew 19:24, likening the difficulty of the rich entering heaven to that of a camel passing through the eye of a needle. In a sermon on human misery, Gautier de Coincy (writing in the thirteenth century) likens the time of the rich on earth to a pleasant summer, to be followed by a long winter in hell, while the poor dwell in heaven. The rich are like the camel, too plump to enter the realm of felicity, but the thin, ill-nourished poor will have no difficulty.[92] A French treatise written in about 1500 concerning the vices of the different estates was inspired, the anonymous author says, by his meditation on the "very hard and weighty words" of Matthew 19:24.[93] The peasants (*laboureurs*) receive the promise of eternal life and enjoy God's favor over the rich.[94]

Subordination, earthly misery, and dishonor are shared by peasant and destitute alike and confer a certain merit by themselves. How then can one explain why very few peasants are numbered among the many saints the Church recognizes?[95] André Vauchez writes of a medieval "hagiocracy," an aristocratically dominated order of saints. Of those canonized between 1198 and 1431, 60 percent were nobles while only 8 percent came from the lower classes.[96] A sociological study of 1,280 Catholic saints of identifiable social origin for the entire history of the Church showed similar results: 7 percent (a total of 92 individuals) were peasants while about 70 percent were nobles.[97] The proportion of peasant saints who lived in the fifteenth century is noticeably greater, according to the ambitious study undertaken by Donald Weinstein and Rudolph Bell: 13.3 percent, as opposed to 4.7 percent for the fourteenth century and 6.9 percent for the sixteenth.[98] This corresponds to what appears to be the apogee of both the hatred of peasants and their reputation for intrinsic piety.

Throughout the Middle Ages, however, noble saints dominated, especially north of the Mediterranean, while royal saints, although found all over Europe, were especially visible in the East.[99] The figures changed somewhat after 1150, when movements advocating poverty, asceticism, and the apostolic life gained strength, but the almost magical quality of high birth, and the better renunciatory narrative that such rank created, meant that the peasantry made no significant dent in the noble domination of the beatified. If the peasant's way of life removed him from temptation, it also allowed him little opportunity for heroic abstinence.

Here one must distinguish between striking individual examples of renunciation and the basic spiritual condition of an entire class. The peasantry was widely considered to hold certain privileges with respect to salvation, but not with respect to individual spiritual distinction meriting sainthood.[100] The individual heroic piety requisite to sainthood was manifest and dramatic when there was more to renounce. The aristocratic saint could on the one hand counter the prevailing violence and pride of his class and on the other hand gain saintly stature from attributed aristocratic virtues (noble bearing, restraint, or sternness), especially the high medieval saint, who was seldom the holy fool, hermit, or simpleton so prominent in desert monasticism and the Orthodox world.

But some peasants did achieve sainthood, albeit proportionally few, as noted above. A Saint Wulfstan of the tenth or eleventh century (not either of the two sainted bishops of that name) died while cutting hay and so served as the patron of haymakers. Saint Guy of Anderlecht and Saint Engelmar of Bavaria were patrons of the peasants.[101] Saint Gaudry, a peasant who dwelt near Toulouse sometime before 900, was invoked in Languedoc, Rousillon, and the Pyrenees against destructive rain.[102] The most widely diffused cult of a peasant saint was that of Saint Isidore, supposedly a Spanish tenant farmer who died in 1130.[103] Isidore's qualities, according to a life written in the thirteenth century, were diligence, modesty, and piety rather than any heroic or miraculous virtues. Isidore served the same master faithfully over the course of his life. He and his wife abstained from sexual relations after the death of their son. Isidore the Farmer is the patron saint of Madrid, and his feast day remains a grand civic and folkloric occasion. Festive plays about him were composed by Calderón and Lope de Vega. Isidore enjoyed a certain reputation in Iberia and perhaps Germany during the Middle Ages, but his real popularity came after he was formally canonized in 1622 (in the company of Ignatius Loyola, Phillip Neri, Theresa of Avila, and Francis Xavier). After his canonization, the cult spread to the rest of Europe and survives with some vigor in Mexico, Paraguay, and Peru. In seventeenth- and eighteenth-century Poland, Isidore served as the model of peasant obedience and acceptance. Reviving medieval instructions to the peasantry, Andrzej Goldonowski's *Short Lessons on the Duties of Christian Farmers* (1629) exhorted serfs to obey their masters in order to win a heavenly reward. Their suffering cleanses them of sin and preserves them from the excesses that afflict the gentry.[104]

Christ and the Pious Plowman

In previous chapters I touched on the fairly complex image of the plowman, an emblem of productivity but also of the wickedness of Cain, the first man to till the earth. That all of society was fed by the peasant's labor was, of course, a commonplace, but the symbolism of the plow in this connection was particularly popular in German and English literature. The father in *Helmbrecht* summarizes his paean to agricultural labor by the statement that many a king owes his crown to the toil of the plowman. The peasant's plow relieves humanity of hunger, according to Hans Rosenplüt, Der Teichner, and an anonymous sung dialogue between a knight and peasant.[105]

The plow was a token of secular productivity but also of spiritual nourishment. A song in the Colmar Collection of the fifteenth century joins the peasant and the priest, both of whom nourish, the former with the plow.[106] The metaphor of preaching as plowing can be traced back to Eucherius of Lyon in the fifth century, and it was popularized in Gregory the Great's *Moralia*.[107] But such similarities do not necessarily imply anything about the people who actually engage in nonmetaphorical plowing. Indeed, the plowman was often invidiously represented in terms of degraded sublapsarian labor. The fratricide Cain was associated with the plow in *Der Renner*, and shown furiously and foolishly plowing with a mixed team in the Holkham Bible (put together between 1315 and 1321).[108] Yet the Bible itself mentions the plow and plowing in the context of virtuous labor contrasted with idleness (Proverbs 12:11 and 20:4), peaceful productivity (Isaiah 28:24–29), and spiritual over literal interpretation of Scripture (1 Corinthians 9:10).

The plowman thus functioned as a symbol of both virtue and wickedness.[109] Adam, although more often shown as delving than as plowing, combined both these worthy and unworthy qualities: punished by this hard labor for his disobedience (a curse transmitted to his posterity), he was also a symbol of earthly labor in anticipation of the spiritual labor of Christ.

The plowman could be conceived in even more exalted terms, as an emblem not only of the preacher's labor but of Christ Himself. John 15:1, "I am the true vine; and my Father is the husbandman" (*agricola* in the Vulgate), suggested images of humility, labor, and preaching that were applied to the second person of the Trinity. Carrying the cross was likened to laboring at the plow.[110] The wooden cross with its iron nails was linked to the plow in the remarks (noted above) attributed to Berthold von Regensburg but also as early as Bede.[111] A Byzantine hymn translated into Latin in the ninth century described Mary as the "nourisher of the loving plowman," the first instance of the metaphor of Christ as plowman.[112] This becomes a popular theme in German texts. In *Der arme Heinrich*, when the young maiden argues with her parents over her decision to sacrifice herself, she contrasts marriage to a rich peasant (their desire but something she would hate and lament) to embracing God, the "free peasant" (*vrîer bûman*) who seeks her hand. His "plow moves steadily," and He will be her protector.[113] Christ "the faithful peasant" restored the blighted fields according to a fourteenth-century Swiss life of Mary.[114] Christ is both plow and plowman according to the Franconian poet Muskatblut (fl. 1415–38). The plowshare is the cross that Christ dragged to His death for our redemption, but Christ Himself is the true plowman who has restored us after the fall of Adam, the first plowman.[115] In praising the noble peasant, Peter Frey, also in the fifteenth century, cites images of Christ as the good shepherd (John 10:34) as well as God the "husbandman" (John 15:1), which Frey gives as *ackermann* (plowman), adding that Christians should not doubt that God compared Himself to a peasant.[116]

Christ was also likened to a gardener, following John 20:15, in which Mary Magdalen mistook the resurrected Christ for the gardener who tended the graveyard. Christ planted the seeds of virtue in her breast according to Gregory the Great, an image well known throughout the Middle Ages.[117] Christ is shown with a spade in an alabaster sculpture now in the Victoria and Albert Museum (Fig. 11).[118]

None of this necessarily exalts earthly plowmen. The ambiguous attitude toward work could accommodate metaphorical use of images of plowing and agricultural labor applied to a spiritually superior form of work such as preaching. The selfless daughter in *Der arme Heinrich* might liken Christ to a plowman, but the whole point of her speech is that she rejects marriage to an earthly plowman. The most famous example of the plowman who not only is likened to Christ but is an emblem of piety in himself is the protagonist of Langland's *Piers Plowman*. This complex masterpiece can be approached as a social satire, as an allegorical vision, and as a proposal for religious and moral reform. The figure of Piers sanctifies agricultural work, although the book also extols a rather different Franciscan ethic of renunciation by which charity, wandering, and "kindness" are preferred to labor in the world.[119]

11. Christ with a spade. English alabaster
sculpture, fifteenth century, now in the Victoria
and Albert Museum. Reproduced by permission
of the Victoria and Albert Museum, London.

Piers is a free peasant, but if his land really amounts to only a half acre (VI.106), he must depend almost entirely on hiring himself out for wages.[120] The plowmen, who appear first in the Dreamer's vision of estates of society, labor strenuously to obtain what the rich "wastours with glotonye destruyeth" (Prol. vv. 20–22). By means of their natural intelligence ("Kynde Wit"), the Commons established plowmen to till and to labor honestly for the benefit of all (Prol. vv. 118–20).[121] Earthly necessity confers, or at least corresponds to, a high spiritual status. Plowmen are the first to receive pardon from Truth, who instructs Piers to stay at home and plow (VII.1–8). Piers himself is equated with Peter and Christ when the Dreamer asks where and how he might find Charity. Neither by words nor by work, responds the Soul (Anima), but through will alone, "and that knoweth no clerk ne creature on erthe / But Piers the Plowman—*Petrus id est christus*" (XV.211–12).[122] Toward the end of the work, Christ is seen dressed in Piers's armor and riding on an ass (as on Palm Sunday), preparing to joust with the Devil (the Crucifixion) (XVIII.10–36). The Dreamer falls asleep in church and has a vision of Piers stained with blood, carrying a cross and bearing the likeness of Jesus:

> I fel eftsoones aslepe—and sodeynly me mette
> That Piers the Plowman was peynted al blody,
> And com in with a cros bifore the comune peple,
> And right lik in alle lymes to Oure Lord Jesu.
> (XIX.5–8)

Langland's poem would make the image of the pious and virtuous plowman familiar from Wales to Bohemia. John Ball's sermon at Blackheath in 1381 and the letters circulated by the organizers of the English Rising appropriate from *Piers Plowman* the language of complaint against the clergy, the fundamental equality of humanity, and the figure (and name) of the virtuous plowman. The modifications embodied in the C Version seem to reflect Langland's response to the unpleasantness of 1381 and the unwanted use of his vision.[123]

Langland was not mounting a direct challenge to the existing order of society. He affirmed the Three Orders model while lamenting its overthrow by a money-driven economy and by an ethic in which everything was for sale, labor included, and loyalty and mutuality yielded before self-interest and greed.[124] Langland offered a quite traditional counsel of obedience, especially to the hated Statute and Ordinance of Laborers of 1349 and 1351, which froze wages to combat what otherwise would have been the economic negotiating advantage of a smaller labor pool after the demographic collapse caused by the Black Death. Langland was not especially opposed to serfdom, though recommending to lords that they treat their serfs (*bondemen*) decently (VI.45). In fact, as David Aers has noted, the villeins were not really central to the poem.[125]

Landless but free laborers occupied considerably more of Langland's concern, for they embodied his distress over idleness and greed. Once they were diligent, but now they formed an undisciplined class given to loitering in taverns. In fact they *do* work, but they profit from their labor in a way that violates the Statute and undermines the fabric of society.

On the one hand, Langland has a "hard" attitude toward work whereby those who do not labor and produce will starve. According to Hunger, he who feeds himself with his faithful labors is blessed in body and soul, an assertion followed by the first words of Psalm 127:2 (VI.250–52). The worthy (especially crippled) poor are to be distinguished from the healthy idle class, who ask for consideration merely for their insolent convenience (VI.115–98).[126] On the other hand, beginning with Passus VII, Piers rejects the stern exaltation of work in favor of voluntary poverty, a Franciscan ideal of charity and rootlessness. Rather than preoccupying oneself with labor in the world, one should hold it in contempt. "Si quis amat Christum mundum non diligit istum" (If a man cares for Christ he will not cleave to this world) (XIV.59). In the same Passus, Patience states that Christians should hold all in common, none desiring his own gain (XIV.201). It follows that the beggar is to be embraced not because he is "genuinely needy" but out of fraternal love and in Christ's name. Poverty is in itself beneficial to the soul and advances its admission to heaven.[127] Langland was in certain respects quite reactionary, rejecting the dominion of "Mede" that reduces everything to a monetary transaction, as exemplified both in the demands of the laborers over wages and in the cold calculations and applied ethics of the newly rich and their apologists.[128]

It does not in any way detract from the power and originality of Langland's poem to locate it among medieval images of the plowman, piety, and Christ. Piers is much more active and individual than his predecessors, so that the key step mentioned above is certainly more vividly exemplified with him than previously, namely the change from a general religious symbolism of the plow to attributing virtue to actual plowmen in the world. But it is not quite true, Elizabeth Kirk's statement to the contrary notwithstanding, that previously the plowman had been exclusively identified with wickedness (Cain), nor is it true that Langland was the first to offer the revolutionary image of the virtuous plowman.[129] Edward Wheatley has pointed to the fable "De Duello militis et aratoris" in the widely diffused compilation of Latin school texts put together (probably in England) during the twelfth century, the *Liber Catonianus*.[130] The story was not part of the Aesopian collections that go back to Phaedrus but appears to have been added by the probable compiler of the *Liber Catonianus*, Walter, chaplain to Henry II. A wicked soldier accuses a wealthy citizen of robbing the public treasury and proposes to fight a duel to back up his assertion. Not only is the elderly man not capable of fighting, but only his loyal tenant, a plowman, is willing to fight on his behalf. The plowman defeats the soldier by striking him on the elbow as the solider prepares to dispatch him. Explanations of the moral and allegorical significance of the tale appeared in the *Esopus moralizatus* and the *Auctores octo* commentaries. They explained the citizen as essentially the well-intentioned ordinary Christian, the soldier as the devil, and the plowman as simple liberating faith. A fifteenth-century interpretation says that the plowman is Christ, the enemy of the devil. Christ arrayed in Piers's armor (XVIII.10−26) may represent a borrowing from the fable.

The use of the plowman as a figure for Christ or of the plow for the cross was common before Langland, as was the notion that peasant labor provided not only material benefit for others but spiritual benefit for those who toiled. It cannot be denied, however, that Piers ennobles the image of the actual plowmen. Allegorical and shifting in his symbolic meaning though he may be, Piers does incorporate the dignity of labor and its symbolic association with religious duties and with Christ. The late Middle Ages would produce a number of other examples of the pious plowman.

A late-fourteenth-century Welsh poem, "The Plowman," by Iolo Goch, praises the work of this "plodder of the fields," whose labor is comparable to King Arthur's destruction of a fortified tower. The author cites the *Elucidarium* of Honorius Augustodunensis to the effect that those who plow are singled out for blessing by God.[131]

Johannes von Tepl's *Der Ackermann aus Böhmen* is a short prose dialogue between Death and the author, a "plaintiff" who excoriates Death for taking his wife.[132] As with *Piers Plowman*, there are problems in dating this work, the closest approximation being 1404−10. It has an extremely complicated textual history, and its relation to the Czech *Tkadlecek* (in which a weaver complains of the unfaithfulness of his beloved, Adliczka) remains unclear. Both the *Ackermann* and *Tkadlecek* may be descended from an earlier "Ur-Ackermann."[133] The plowman is a sympathetic figure of grief and anger closer to Everyman than an allegory of Christ.[134] In fact he is only allegorically a plowman, for his "plow" is made from a bird's feather: he is a writer, his plow is a pen. The dialogue is a moving lament and rather bitter consolation. The plowman as a figure has a metaphorical significance, but a rather distant one.

The plowman described in the prologue to the *Canterbury Tales* is more clearly a worthy rustic whose piety exemplifies Christian rectitude:[135]

> With hym [*i.e., the Parson*] ther was a plowman, was his brother
> That hadde ylad of dong ful many a fother.
> A trewe swynkere and a good was he,
> Lyvynge in pees and parfit charitee.
> God loved he best with al his hoole herte
> At alle tymes, thogh him gamed or smerte,
> And thanne his neighebor right as hymselve.
> He wolde threshe, and therto dyke and delve,
> For Christes sake, for every poure wight,
> Withouten hire, if it lay in his myght.
> His tithes payde he ful faire and wel,
> Bothe of his propre swynk and his catel.

Chaucer's plowman is not directly credited with feeding all of society, but his labor is beneficial to his neighbors (whom he aids for Christ's sake) and to the Church, whose tithes he pays obediently. He is not influenced by the desire for remuneration; thus he is immune to Langland's allegorical destroyer, "Mede." Rustic labor is hard and even unpleasant—the association with dung, a canonical negative topos, is the first to be mentioned, but he lives in peace with the world. The Parson and his brother are two on the very short list of good pilgrims, a symbolic pair representing conservative ideals of clerical and peasant life.

So far we have seen three grounds for attributing to rustics a certain closeness to God—what we may call three types of peasant virtue: first, their labor is valuable because all of society depends on it; second, their suffering confers a spiritual merit that will be rewarded; and third, their labor is virtuous in itself and emblematic of divine labor and sacrifice. These are not mutually exclusive, but have different implications and connections with other themes we have followed. The first is related to the theory of the Three Orders and in the hands of clerical writers was an aspect of hierarchy and mutuality. When joined to the third peasant virtue, the exaltation of work, however, it could have a sharper, antihierarchical edge. A late-medieval folksong in which a peasant and a knight debate has the peasant point out that were it not for his plow, the knight would not long survive. The verse explicitly denies mutuality by mocking the knight's useless dancing and jousting ("was hilft dein stechen und dein tanz?").[136] As discussed earlier, fifteenth- and early-sixteenth-century peasant movements condemned idleness and praised work in religious terms.[137]

The second peasant virtue ameliorates the failure of mutuality but also extols the redeeming effects of suffering and the inversion of wealth and poverty in the life to come. Franciscan writers in particular employed this argument to console the peasant and offer hope in return for acceptance and obedience. Here too, however, the discourse can take a less complacent turn in which suffering is not ennobling in God's eyes but a violation of divine law that degrades people to the level of animals. Christ's sacrifice for fundamental human equality could ennoble suffering in a way that led to action in the world to combat it.

Recognition of the third ground for peasant sanctity, that peasant labor is virtuous "in itself," is more characteristic of the late Middle Ages, with fewer ties to earlier forms of discourse than exist for the first two peasant virtues. Even here, however, we find a reworking of older themes, such as Jerome's *sancta rusticitas*, rather than the coining of a new lexicon. The key change reflected in images of the third type of virtue was a move from purely symbolic evocations of peasant life (Christ as bread or as plowman) to ascriptions of spiritual virtue to ordinary peasants on the basis of their manner of life and supposed piety.

What we are chiefly concerned to explain is the exaltation of the pious peasant in the late Middle Ages and early Reformation. An older language could be given not so much a completely new meaning as a more pointed implication. It is one thing, for example, to describe the Eucharist and the Real Presence in terms of the image of milling: the "mill of the host," figuring Christ as spiritual sustenance ground up like wheat for our salvation, a metaphor based on John 6:35, "I am the bread of life." Such imagery appeared as early as the twelfth century.[138] It may have certain implications concerning rustic labor but hardly says anything directly about those who mill real grain for everyday consumption. It is quite another thing to portray such ordinary laborers as God's army. A Swiss pamphlet of 1521 uses the traditional "mill of the host" imagery in a depiction of Luther and Erasmus distributing the Bible, which is baked from the flour of a mill in which the Word is being ground. Erasmus is the miller and Luther is the baker. The pope and his minions try to oppose this action, but they are held at bay by a peasant named Karsthans (Hans-the-Hoe), who in this instance wields another emblematic peasant tool, a flail.[139]

It would be too simple, however, to oppose an earlier passive, symbolic vocabulary of rustic virtue to a later more literal one. The themes we have identified were in fact combined routinely. One of the most important writers on the peasantry at the end of the Middle Ages, the Carthusian Werner Rolevinck, exemplifies this complexity. In his *De regimine rusticorum*, written in 1472, Rolevinck states that God revealed the secrets of salvation to uneducated rustics rather than to princes or the learned.[140] The peasant is the "partner [*cooperator*] of God, the angels, and Nature," he asserts, citing Jerome's praise of holy rusticity to support the claim. So far, Werner is reworking old themes, but he differs significantly from Honorius Augustodunensis, for whom it is the labor of rustics and their negative advantages (simplicity, removal from temptation) that pave the path for their entry into heaven. Here the peasant is credited with a theological insight given directly by God.

In quite traditional fashion Rolevinck simultaneously draws back from the implications of this formulation, requiring that peasants obey their masters (citing Romans 13:1) and resign themselves to servitude. They should accept even an unjust lord since he keeps them from opportunities to sin and unwittingly draws them toward a heavenly crown. The peasants' suffering and lack of freedom is not a punishment for sin but evidence of God's love.[141] Also in traditional fashion, Rolevinck berates peasants for their inclination to disobey and blames their ignorance and weak moral control for their debased condition.[142]

The notion that God reveals His secrets to rustics could also have more active consequences. This is what distinguishes the third category of peasant virtue: peasants are divinely elected not by reason of suffering or productivity but by reason of their innate character and way of life. This could easily mean that rustics should preach, dispute, or in other respects forward the work of God on earth. This is precisely what happened in the early sixteenth century in Germany. It does not minimize the Reformation to point to the background of the image of the pious peasant that could be transformed by the upheavals after 1517.

The peasant in the aforementioned Swiss image of the sacred mill not only is pious but actively defends the Gospel with a symbol of his labor, one that could be used as a weapon. Previously comical images of "typical" peasants showed them with two-pronged hoes or with flails, thus "Karsthans" or "Flegelhans" (Hans-the-Flail). These images were appropriated in the years leading up to 1525, as in the Swiss pamphlet of 1521 or in Hans Kolb's undated denunciation of clerical corruption (composed between 1520 and 1525) in which Karsthans and Flegelhans menace priests who waste tithes and keep concubines. Nine pamphlets denouncing the cruelty and greed of landlords, dating to 1523–24 and written by James Locher, a former Franciscan, were addressed to "Karsthans."[143] A pamphlet entitled *New Karsthans*, attributed to the distinguished reformer Martin Bucer, called for an alliance between peasants and lesser nobles to reform the Church.[144] Bucer presents righteous fighters for the Gospel with the same iconographic accompaniments (rustic tools) as those possessed by the boorish villagers of the Neidhart illustrators. In the text of the *Divine Mill* pamphlet we are told that Karsthans still has his flail but now also understands the Bible. He remains a simple man but for that very reason stands ready to defend the Gospel should any rise against it to restore deception.[145]

Those opposed to such tendencies saw disputatious or literate peasants as an inversion of order. An illustration accompanying the prophetic text by Joseph Gruenbeck shows a peasant officiating at the altar of an upside-down church while outside a monk is plowing (Fig. 12).[146] It is as if the nightmare of Adalbero of Laon had come true. Illustrations to Thomas Murner's tract *On the Great Lutheran Fool* ridicule the notion of the evangelical peasant. In one picture the peasant is mounted on a snail and carries a rake, not so much a threat as simply a representation of the peasant's lack of military skill and equipment. Another woodcut, however, shows the peasant dressed as a mercenary soldier carrying a banner labeled "Freedom."[147] That peasants should be the equal of priests in interpreting the Bible must lead to violence and the overturning of the social order as well, warned Catholic opponents of Luther, and of course they were in some sense correct.[148]

For the early reformers, however, the peasant was credited with a degree of ingrained skill at religious disputation, an ability to cut through the sophistries of the learned with his simple piety. The concept of simple piety is obviously not new, and even the idea of actually mobilizing it goes back at least to Langland. It is put into effect rather dramatically, however, particularly as a result of Luther's early teaching concerning the primacy of the Bible and the priesthood of all believers.[149] The view that the Bible rather than a learned theological tradition contained religious truth, together with Luther's notion of the dignity of the common man, encouraged a more pointed version of the traditional theme of pious simplicity, a version capable of defending faith against learned impiety. The peasant, embodying this faith, was close to God not merely for negative reasons (lack of sophistication) but in his everyday existence; through work rather than renunciation. Luther remained firmly within the tradition that regarded rustic labor as most truly "real" work. By deprecating ascetic practice and traditional penance, he gave an even more positive valuation to rustic labor. In Flugschriften of the years before the Peasants' War of 1525, work in the fields was exalted as a duty incumbent on all estates, clergy and nobility included.[150]

Luther did not himself devote considerable attention to the peasants before the events of 1525, although he did make use of traditional images of la-

Das erste Capitel von der vrrend

rung aller ftende der Chriftenheyt/die mag bewert
werden auß den fichtbarn zeychen des himels.

¶ Nach dem die menfchlich fchwach eyt mag von der dick
en wolcken wegen der fleyfchlichen begirligkeyten/vnd des
tieffen werfels der lafter/die verborgen maieftet gottes nit er
kennen / noch die heymlichen/vnd von der fundligkeyt abge
fcheyden/werck der natur begriffen / dem nach will ich den

12. The world turned upside down: a peasant at the altar and a priest plowing. Woodcut engraving from Joseph Gruenbeck, *Spiegel der naturlichen, himelischen und prophetischen sehungen* (Leipzig, 1522), fol. [5r]. Reprinted by permission of the British Library, London.

bor, piety, sweat, and the plow.[151] His influence on the cult of the pious peasant was more indirect. Attacking those with claims to spiritual superiority, he encouraged the already strong tendency to see the common man as the exemplar of piety.

In the years following 1517, ending cataclysmically in 1525, the "evangelical peasant" appears as wise and as able to read and cite Scripture, dispute with schoolmen, and see through their hypocritical rationalizations for abuse.[152] Andreas Bodenstein von Karlstadt, who was sufficiently enthusiastic about rustics to affect peasant dress, argued in 1520 that the poor pray with more fervor than regular clergy, that craftsmen are more knowledgeable about Scripture than bishops, and that neither the pope nor a general council should be ashamed to heed the words of a Christian plowman.[153] The weapons of the peasant were at this point thought to be words rather than flails and pitchforks (which were more emblems or attributes). Peasants appear in an immense number of *Flugschriften*, particularly in the guise of "the disputatious peasant" in dialogues with opponents of reform.

The peasants depicted themselves as exemplars of piety in Dithmarschen in 1500 and in the Bundshuh uprisings of the late fifteenth and early sixteenth centuries, in which flags, for example, show peasants kneeling in prayer before a crucifix. Another flag is simply a plowshare.[154] In keeping with Luther's teaching but also in accord with traditional arguments, labor was depicted as ennobling, as in a dialogue of 1525 in which the parasitic existence of the clergy is contrasted to the life of Christ, who labored, and the pious toil of the peasant: "Man was born to work as the bird to fly."[155] But the peasant was saved by his piety, his labor being its exemplification, not merely a potential source of negative advantage. The curious case of the "Peasant of Wöhrd" illustrates how far the attribution of rustic inspiration had progressed. A former Benedictine monk named Diepold Peringer preached a popular sermon (printed nine times in the period 1524–25) that attracted attention because he was supposedly an unlettered rustic miraculously blessed by God with the ability to preach. In this example of life imitating art, a literate cleric pretended to be an ignorant peasant.[156]

The pious peasant was not an invention of the Reformation, although the image of peasants as actively reading the Bible, disputing theological points, or engaging in struggle to protect the reform movement were new. We have seen that certain ideas of peasant piety grew out of the functional identification of the peasant with work. To the extent that such work was regarded positively, as nourishing society, the peasant was at least worthy of esteem. To the extent that work was regarded as degrading or penitential, the peasant was credited with a spiritual benefit in God's eyes. The particular conception that becomes stronger in the late Middle Ages is what we have identified as the third peasant virtue, the third tendency in the attribution of spiritual advantage: the sanctification of the peasant by his pious character and by the simplicity of his manner of life. In part this reflects a shift toward considering lay people in general as capable of exemplifying piety, not so much by heroic sainthood as by observation of God's law in everyday life. In surveys of the estates of society, and in particular in discussions of their different sins, clerical writers of the twelfth to fourteenth centuries either limited their praise of peasant labor to its penitential quality (stemming from its difficulty and lack of fair remuneration) or made spiritual benefit conditional on good behavior (docility).

The growth of *Bauernlob* and the image of the pious plowman of the late Middle Ages do not so much break from clerical precedent as make the attribution of spiritual virtue less dependent on meekness and suffering. In Hugo von Trimberg's convenient formulation: "He who desires wealth in heaven should live wretchedly on earth, and not take account of his mistreatment if he hopes to approach eternal joy."[157]

Piers or the "noble peasant" of the fifteenth-century poets is ennobled by labor and self sacrifice but not by uncomplaining acceptance of oppression. The conception of justice changes in relation to Christianity. Unjust suffering, rather than indicating divine favor, comes to be regarded as irreconcilable with the teachings of Christianity. The particular emblem of unjust oppression incompatible with the status of the peasant as Christian is serfdom. In one set of teachings, servitude is to be borne because it shields weak minds from temptation and promises a reversal of fortunes in the world to come. According to another set of ideas that emphasize the peasants' status as Christians, servitude is an intolerable contradiction of that liberty bought by Christ's blood and promised to all the faithful. On the one hand we have the spiritual benefit of suffering: what is spiritually ennobling are poverty and oppression. On the other hand we have the spiritual benefit of what might be considered the normal difficulty of agricultural toil: what is spiritually ennobling is work, simplicity, and simple piety. In one case servitude is merely an aspect of difficult testing and purifying circumstances; in the other it becomes more disturbing, a direct contradiction of humanity defined in terms of one's status as Christian. In the following chapter, we will look at the question of serfdom in connection with piety, Christian teaching, and human dignity.

Part 5

The Revolt Against Servitude

Chapter 10

The Problem of Servitude

Arbitrary Mistreatment, Symbolic Degradation

In discussing theories of human equality and inequality we saw that the problem for those defending the order of things was not to explain differences of birth or wealth. That some were rich and others poor was no more bothersome to the articulate classes than it is now. What did present difficulties was the failure of mutuality demonstrated by the deprivation of freedom, the legally enforced subordination of one person to another. The shared ancestry of humanity and more particularly adhesion to the Christian faith seemed to confer upon all believers, regardless of their momentary fortunes for good or ill, an irreducible dignity that precluded domination by fellow believers.

Slavery had been explained in several ways. The Aristotelian tradition taught that some people were simply fit to be slaves. Roman law contrasted the law of nature, which forbids slavery, with the law of nations, which permits it. Such a distinction could fit a Christian world in which slavery was excused by reference either to an underlying equality to be realized in heaven (St. Paul), to overall human sinfulness and weak character (Augustine, Isidore), or to an original moment dividing society (Noah's curse against Ham).

It was, nevertheless, tricky to explain why Christians should be held in subjugation by other Christians. Non-Christians presented considerably less of a problem since their infidelity made it appropriate to subjugate them. Only those with the most tender consciences were troubled by the enslavement of aliens and infidels, terms that could be defined generously so as to include rebels, heretics, even mere foreigners. The medieval Mediterranean enjoyed a brisk traffic in Saracen slaves but also in Christian peoples from the Balkans and Caucasus.

Explaining serfdom among Western European Christians was a greater challenge because the serfs were neither heretics nor foreigners. One could theorize that their ancestors had committed some hereditary crime (as in Catalonia or Hungary), or that they were not fit for anything better (the import of satirical literature), but it required ingenuity to represent them as sufficiently different from the free population to justify their subjugated status. That they were Christian made it difficult to regard them as subhuman or alien unless they could be typified as only nominal Christians who were in fact pagans or heretics. As we have found, however, the accusation that peasants were irreligious was not among the most frequent reproaches made against them. The very qualities that provoked derision from a worldly point of view (poverty, simplicity, lack of status) were at the same time spiritually beneficial.

Christianity did not confer what would now be understood as "rights." Rather, according to at least a segment of medieval opinion, it implied a certain minimal human dignity and, related to that, a certain minimal human freedom or immunity from arbitrary domination by others. The twelfth-century codification of Catalan customary law governing the relations between the king and his nobles, the *Usatges of Barcelona*, discusses compensation for killing rustics and others "who have no other dignity than that of being Christians."[1] They were neither members of the aristocracy nor privileged townsmen nor a special group with a defined status (such as Jews), but at the same time they were not serfs.[2] Unprivileged, they were nevertheless free, a status manifested or proven by the minimal but significant dignity conferred by membership in the Christian community.

Freedom was not a "natural" or inherent human condition but a privilege. Freedom was understood not as a release from all bonds to others but as immunity from the arbitrary will of another. The infringement of freedom was not lordship as such but bad lordship; being routinely and lawfully subjected to arbitrary treatment or, more pertinently, mistreatment without recourse to a higher authority.[3]

To be able to exact payment or to impose punishment without answering either to effective local resistance or to any higher jurisdiction was the essence of lordship over the unfree or those whom one wanted to present as unfree. In 1202 the Catalan nobility wrested from King Peter I recognition of exemption from royal intervention if they "mistreated" (*maletractaverint*) their rustics. This right, later known as the *ius maletractandi*, would be among the key indications of servile status, denoting as it did removal from the legal protections normally afforded by the public law of the principality. This was not merely a theoretical right but one that was tested in litigation, shaped for local customary codifications such as the fourteenth-century *Customs of the Diocese of Girona*, and brought up by lords in their negotiations with the monarchy during the Catalan Civil War in about 1475.[4]

One finds similar practices elsewhere. In the Vaud, the customary law allowed a lord to chastise his serf moderately, with or without cause, although he could not torment him.[5] Beaumanoir posited the existence of such a seigneurial right in his collection of the customary laws of Beauvaisis: "Some serfs are so subjected to their lord that he can take all they have, when they die or when they are still alive, and he can keep them in prison any time he wants, rightly or wrongly, for he is answerable for them only to God."[6] Here the right affects only the lowest category of serfs, although they are not otherwise very clearly defined. As in Catalonia, here the particular mistreatment envisaged is imprisonment and seizure of goods, and it is not merely a right of judgment or jurisdiction but a prerogative to be exercised irrespective of any justification. The canons of Notre Dame in Paris claimed the right to imprison or even kill their serfs during a quarrel with their tenants at Orly. The serfs had appealed to the queen (who was acting as regent for the absent Louis IX), whereupon they were cast into the chapter's prison. They were exercising a putative right of jurisdiction, but one that had an arbitrary character similar to that in the examples previously mentioned. According to the *Grandes chroniques*, the canons asserted their right to distrain and imprison their serfs "as they wished."[7]

In some customary law traditions, manifestly unjust conduct was not expressly permitted, but lords could mete out punishment that approached an essentially arbitrary control over life and death. The symbolic importance of shedding blood or of execution might be reserved to the prince, but this did not prevent extreme treatment. In Aragon, according to the thirteenth-century jurist and bishop Vidal de Canellas, a lord could kill a man who murdered another of his dependents, but only by such means as avoided the shedding of blood (death in prison from starvation, thirst, or cold was suggested).[8]

According to Exodus 21:20–21, a master who killed his slave was to be punished unless the slave lingered a day or two before dying. This inspired a number of law codes such as that of King Alfred in 892–93 and Ruprecht von Freising's *Freisinger Rechtsbuch* (compiled in 1328). According to the latter, a man who killed his serf by flogging was guilty of a crime unless the serf lived for more than a day after the punishment. In that case, the master was considered not to have deliberately killed him and so was guiltless.[9] In these instances the lords were presumed to be acting for some reason, not out of cruel caprice, but obviously they could exert a nearly uncontrolled level of coercion.

Pierre Bonnassie has reminded us of the importance of the symbolism of violence that demonstrated with graphic and exemplary clarity the degree to which lords held their unfree subordinates in thrall. Marc Bloch has written of the "essence profonde" of servitude, a condition broader than the specific economic obligations of bondage to a lord.[10] Bloch cites examples of mutilation, torture, and burning.[11] Lords who wanted to punish in a fashion that would cow others tempted to poach or otherwise violate his monopolies might inflict cruel reminders of their power. Ordericus Vitalis recounts that Count Galceran of Meulan in 1124 cut the feet off of peasants who illegally cut wood.[12] Lords who wanted to undermine what had previously been free communities would resort to beatings, threats of mutilation, and holding peasants for ransom, as, for example, in twelfth-century Catalonia in the decades before the right of seigneurial mistreatment was finally officially recognized.[13]

Lords could not, of course, consistently act in this fashion toward their tenants without finding their wealth threatened by demoralization and desertion—the "Giles de Rais model" of pathologically wicked lordship was not viable economically. And in fact the serfs led their lives largely outside of the shadow of immediate seigneurial supervision, a circumstance that differentiated them from slaves. "Seigneurial piracy" (the expression is Bonnassie's) had to be engaged in judiciously, to encourage obedience.[14] I have mentioned Felix Hemmerli's recommendation that peasant farms be burned every 50 years to teach respect. Arson was also envisaged as an official measure of coercion further east, in Carinthia. According to Johann von Viktring, writing in 1336, the Carinthian dukes appointed a *Landesbrandschatzamt* ("territorial incendiary") to set fires in order to create and maintain fear of the ruler. This official is attested in documents from 1302 until the seventeenth century, but his duties were probably to regulate and suppress feuds (which often involved the punitive or threatened burning of houses and farms) rather than to terrorize the rural populace.[15]

It remains difficult to determine to what degree peasants lived in vivid fear of their lords, but it is unlikely that they were completely cowed, given their control of the immediate circumstances of cultivation.[16] There is no doubt, however, that the selective demonstration of savagery was useful if not vital to the maintenance of lordship. Extrajudicial violence was not so much an everyday form of control as a symbolic statement of arbitrary power, and consequently of subjugation to that power.

It is important to underscore the significance of symbolic acts of oppression and violence that marked the borders between freedom and servitude. Servile status did not inevitably mean economic or even social degradation. In England, for example, extensive holdings of land and substantial local status might coexist with villeinage.[17] Nevertheless, servile status was felt to be onerous, unjust, and worth sacrifice to cast off or resist even in places where there was little if any short-term gain in moving out of villeinage. The litigation or payments to induce lords to accept an improvement in their tenants' condition were expenses borne by villeins in many parts of thirteenth- and early-fourteenth-century England.[18] Studies of servitude in Catalonia, southeastern Germany, and the region around Sens similarly demonstrate that servile status was perceived as an extra-economic indignity that peasants attempted to evade, buy out, or resist.[19]

The next chapter, which deals with the peasant wars of the late Middle Ages, will examine more closely how important questions of freedom and legal status actually were to peasant rebels. Here I am concerned to show the symbolic representation of servitude, which centered on capricious domination. Even if in the everyday economic sense the servile regime was a carefully administered structure of obligation, it depended on certain dramatic images and proofs of subordination for its effectiveness.

Acts of seigneurial domination were not necessarily as violent as the aforementioned burning, maiming, and killing. The lowliness of the peasant was portrayed by a comical helplessness that symbolically reinforced his inferiority. In a judicial proceeding over proof of unfree status in 1387, a witness recalled the harsh treatment meted out by the lords of Rocourt (in the bishopric of Basel, now the canton of Jura). Ferry de Rocourt on one occasion had answered complaints of the village mayor by observing that the mayor knew very well he was a serf (*homme de morte main*) and that if Ferry wished, "he could take him by the foot and sell him in the market."[20] It was imagined that in earlier times, lords had exercised tyrannical rights over their rustic dependents, compared to which mere taxation (by way of commutation of these rights) was an amelioration. There was a mythical periodization of unfreedom, an invented tradition memorializing a primitive but still influential servitude. In mid-thirteenth-century Liège it was claimed that the saintly bishop Adalbero had, over a century earlier, abolished the practice of routinely cutting off one of the hands of a peasant, a brutal token of controlling his inheritance, in favor of the relatively mild *mainmorte* (literally, "dead hand").[21]

The phantom "droit de seigneur" or "droit de cuissage"—the supposed right of a lord to deflower peasant brides—is a curious example of arbitrariness and its supposed commutation. In the eighteenth century it served as an the emblem of aristocratic caprice and corruption, made famous especially by Beaumarchais's *Marriage of Figaro*. This "custom" was in fact almost exclusively mythical. Over a century ago, Karl Schmidt laboriously and conclusively demonstrated that the historical basis for this right was either completely fabricated or resulted from a confusion of seigneurial control over marriage off the estate (the right known in France as *formariage*).[22] Such confusion is to some degree understandable in that lords could enforce marriage exactions in peculiar ways. Ferry de Rocourt claimed the right to decide where a newly married couple should spend the first night after their wedding. The brides were not originally from his jurisdiction, so the ceremony was designed to show that the new couple belonged to the lord of Rocourt. A similar right is found in the fourteenth-century *Coutumier bourgignon*.[23]

Recently Alain Boureau, in a masterful treatment already cited in a number of contexts, showed how the mythical *droit de cuissage* made its varied appearances, from its use by lords eager to inflate the estimated value of their fiefs in sixteenth-century Béarn to the rhetoric of liberal and anticlerical opposition in the era of Napoleon III. Boureau agrees with Schmidt that there never was a legal claim to exact this "right," but the legend does have a medieval context, thus it amounts to more than an antifeudal invention of the Enlightenment. The earliest instance in Boureau's dossier is the *cullage* mentioned in a peculiar poem of 1247 concerning the *vilains* of Verson in Normandy.[24] Boureau also describes a small number of "troubling [i.e., perhaps valid] cases" that, although forming an infinitesimal proportion of the seigneurial records of the period, suggest the geographical and chronological range of this myth.

Much of its imaginative power came from the graphic demonstration of lordship and the symbolic sexual humiliation of dependents. The supposed *droit de cuissage* is thus a version of the same image of sexual helplessness seen in the *fabliaux* (peasant males as easily cuckolded) or the *pastourelles* (chivalric predation directed against peasant girls).[25]

The *droit de seigneur* was, among other things, an extralegal "proof" of servitude, a more vivid demonstration of control than such indices as *mainmorte* (death duties), *taille* (a head tax or taxation at will), or *formariage* (a fine for marriage off the estate). In Catalonia, where the equivalent of formariage was simply integrated into the system of manumission payments for servile tenants, a peculiar indication of servile status was *cugucia*, a fine paid by a servile husband if his wife was adulterous. This was one among a group of so-called "bad customs" (*mals usos*) that coalesced by the late twelfth or early thirteenth centuries into the legal and symbolic characteristics of servitude.[26] Late fifteenth-century Catalonia also furnishes the most striking example of the *droit de seigneur*, not quite as a genuine right but as a symbol and perhaps reality of seigneurial mistreatment that figures in the complaints of the peasants themselves. In 1462, on the eve of the rebellion that would eventually result in the abolition of serfdom in Catalonia, negotiators for both sides met at Vic to discuss the grievances of the *remences* (as Catalan serfs were called). The peasants demanded an end to the practice of lords spending the night with peasant brides or, as a symbol of lordship, claiming a right to "pass over" the newly married woman while she lay in bed. This was regarded by the peasants not only as evil but as a degrading symbol of unjust subjugation. At Vic the lords responded that they never heard of such a right and renounced it willingly if it existed.[27] That lords did, in fact, occasionally demand such privileges receives support from an account by the Silesian traveler Nicholas von Popplau, who described its exercise in 1486, on the eve of its abolition.[28]

The issue would be raised upon the conclusion of the civil war and peasant rebellion. The document that officially ended serfdom in 1486, the royal Sentence of Guadalupe, referred to this abusive custom, which it abolished.[29]

The Catalan peasants also complained of other degrading obligations, such as the lords' practice of requisitioning wet nurses for their infants from among their tenants, or the *ius maletractandi* itself.[30] The Catalan example shows a spectrum of signs of harsh lordship: the economically important "bad customs" (whose acknowledged "badness" and degrading overtones shade into such demeaning obligations as wet-nurse service), arbitrary levies, a right of mistreatment, and at least the echo of the *droit de seigneur*. In Galicia, where an antiseigneurial rebellion erupted in 1467, complaints of arbitrary treatment included references to various forms of real and symbolic sexual exploitation.[31] At Fuenteovejuna in 1476, the murdered commander of the Order of Calatrava was accused of having robbed and violated female villagers, but the causes of the rebellion (jurisdictional and fiscal) appear to have been more prosaic.[32]

Arbitrary lordship symbolized and proved servile status in such realms as Catalonia, where serfdom was a legally recognized and economically important form of land tenure. In other regions, where servitude was either waning or unknown, or where lords attempted to revive it, arbitrary lordship was interpreted by peasants themselves as the key to a degradation of their condition.

In Upper Swabia the abbey of Kempten was master of an extensive principality of its own that included serfs (*Leibeigenen* or *Eigenleute*), but also nonservile tenants who paid a *census* or head tax in acknowledgment of lordship (*Freizinser*), and tenants completely free of seigneurial incidents other than rent (*Muntleute*). During the fifteenth century, the prince-abbots of Kempten tried to degrade free tenants to the level of *Freizinser* and the latter to the level of servitude. In 1423 the peasants managed to take their case to the imperial court at Ulm, where the abbot produced a forged charter of Charlemagne that gave the same rights over *Freizinser* as those held over serfs. The *Freizinser* of the town of Kempten itself were able to appeal to Pope Martin V, who upheld their argument. Another struggle took place in 1460, when the abbot required death taxes, labor services, and other servile obligations from *Freizinser*. He also implemented marriage regulations that had the effect of degrading men who married below them. Beginning in 1481, the monastery began confiscating one half of a peasant's estate upon his death, requiring in addition the payment of death duties from the remaining half. A rebellion in 1491 (when taxes were raised during a famine) resulted in the defeat of the peasants by the Swabian League and the degradation of 1,200 *Freizinser* to servitude.[33]

Shortly before the outbreak of the German Peasants' War, in January 1525, the Kempten peasants renewed their complaints. The response of the abbot was that he had indeed made serfs out of *Freizinser* who married serfs, but that in no case had he acted differently from what was customary among neighboring lords.[34] On this occasion, a register of 335 complaints (representing 1,220 individuals) was drawn up by members of each category of tenants, the so-called *Kemptener Leibeigenschaftsrodel*. The complaints centered around degradation by reason of marriage, the prohibitions on leaving the abbey's jurisdiction, and arbitrary fines and imprisonment.[35] In September 1525, during the general rebellion of the south German peasants, the Kempten tenants summarized their grievances by stating that their forefathers had been free, in possession of "Libertet und Freiheit," but that they had been forced to relinquish this liberty and to submit to oppressive obligations and arbitrary punishment at the hands of the abbots.[36]

Similar pressures on free and semifree peasants were exerted by the monastery of Saint Gall during the fifteenth century. The monastery attempted to level its tenants (*Gotteshausleute*) to a single level, that of serfs (*leibeigene Gotteshausleute*).[37] In south Germany, as in England, Catalonia, and elsewhere, serfdom and complaints about servitude were not simply masks for economic or communal issues. Personal unfreedom had a substantial effect and was deeply resented. In addition to the examples of Kempten and Saint Gall, there were localized revolts over servitude against a number of German secular and clerical lords.[38] I have tried to argue similarly that the Catalan peasant revolt of 1462–86 was essentially about serfdom.[39] In general, as Yves-Marie Bercé has observed for early modern France, the instigation to revolt resulted from a sense of injustice, along with a certain calculation of opportunity, rather than an absolute level of economic misery.[40]

Servitude represented the most telling encapsulation of injustice, not necessarily or exclusively because of its economic impact but because the serf was rendered subhuman. Ill treatment, or the idea that coercion is justified and necessary to compel work, placed the serf in a conceptual setting resembling that of a domestic animal. We have seen a tendency to speak of peasants as if they were either a subordinate form of humanity or at least partially bestial. While such depiction was often comical ("the peasant resembles an ox except that he lacks horns"), the reiteration of the peasants' essentially nonhuman nature excused inhuman treatment, although peculiar distinctions might be made among degrees of degradation. Judges on the London eyre of 1244 stated that servile tenants might be put in stocks but not in irons. Their owners might sell such serfs "like oxen and cows" but were not to kill or maim them since their bodies belonged to the king.[41] Serfs could thus be likened to domesticated animals and subjected to arbitrary but not unlimited mistreatment.

In peasant remonstrances, especially those written during the German Peasants' War of 1525 (these, of course, have been much better preserved than remonstrances from any other revolt), unjust subjugation was described with the same animal metaphors, but now in order to emphasize a gross injustice, not to characterize peasant nature. Tenants of the abbey of Ochsenhausen in Upper Swabia stated in a manifesto that they should not be "sold like cattle and sheds, for we all have one lord, that is God in heaven."[42] In 1525, serfs of the prince-archbishop of Salzburg complained that servitude violated the Gospels, amounting to a right to compel men to submit to seigneurial greed and brutality, to be led around by the nose. They were treated like cattle, "only even more tyrannically."[43] At Kempten in 1525, after listing the oppressive practices of the abbey, the protesting peasants complained that they were treated more harshly than serfs and dogs.[44] Inhumane treatment violated not so much an abstract notion of human rights but a particular dispensation accorded by Christ's sacrifice to those who believed in Him. To be Christian, in this sense, was to be fully human, or at least possessed of a basic humanity that was violated by servitude.

I will examine the issue of servitude in the great peasant revolts up to 1525 in the next chapter and try to see what connections there might have been between how peasants framed their demands and earlier ideas of equality, Christianity and natural law. Here I want to delineate what those ideas were (an effort to some extent anticipated in Chapter 6), paying particular attention to serfdom, which seemed not only to symbolize the violation of human dignity by arbitrary treatment but to go against the Christian idea of an ultimate shared human nature.

Servitude, Force, and Christ's Sacrifice

In discussing medieval ideas of equality, I argued that the crux was not a leveling of social condition but a recognition of a basic status shared by all humanity. God's creation of Adam and Eve and descent from a common ancestor conferred an ultimate likeness. Various arguments could be put forward to explain why this original equality no longer held, and why some people were justly or at least appropriately subordinated.

Another strategy was to deny that servitude, the most obvious violation of minimal equality, affected anything more than the material body, the life in the temporal world. St. Paul instructed servants (*servi* in the Vulgate) to obey and honor their masters (Ephesians 6:5; 1 Timothy 6:1; Colossians 4:1), and his counsel that God does not distinguish between free and unfree (1 Corinthians 7:21–23) was followed by Church fathers such as Ambrosiaster and Lactantius, who stated that God did not recognize slavery. Precisely because of this, there was no reason to overthrow the secular practices that deprived certain individuals of freedom. The same argument would appear again in Luther's *The Freedom of a Christian* and his later refutation of peasant claims to a literal, worldly liberty as a carnal understanding of spiritual freedom.[45] Luther's doctrine of acceptance of the social order actually contains two arguments: the contention that Christians are not harmed in the sight of God by servile condition (a view unexceptionable and fully supported by the New Testament), and the more tendentious position that the Bible actually sanctions servitude, so that rebellion against it is therefore seditious and heretical.[46]

In order to deny that servitude among Christians was licit, two assertions were necessary: first, that there was no basis for a differentiated penalty for general human sinfulness that imposed servitude on some but not on others, and second, that servitude violated not only original equality but a continuing intention of God to uphold it. That sin entered the world through Adam did not necessarily excuse subordination. The result of sin might be that the powerful illegitimately dominated the weak, not that the weak were appropriately restrained by force.

Augustine had treated servitude as a consequence of sin but distinguished between adverse circumstance and human iniquity as its direct cause.[47] Later authors who condemned slavery and serfdom made use of this distinction, arguing that subordination proceeded not as a natural result of the fallen condition of man, nor as part of a hidden divine purpose, but from specific wicked intent and action. The contrast in approaches to servitude was sometimes subtle. Smaragdus, Agobard of Lyons, Jonas of Orléans, and Atto of Vercelli, for example, all asserted the ultimate equality of humanity.[48] Agobard and Jonas followed Gregory the Great, distinguishing original equality, whereby all were created in His image, from a just if mysterious divine decree by which some were, at least externally, subordinated into servitude. Smaragdus, however, attributed domination to wicked acts, not to nature; Atto stated that servitude came not from the natural order of things but from iniquity, not from Ham but from human injustice.[49] Iniquity here was not in keeping with God's purpose but purely human.

Naturally, such attitudes by no means dominated within the medieval Church, which continued to regard servitude as not only licit but praiseworthy in many instances. The monastery of Marmoutier kept records of its servile dependents and the acts, dramatically represented, by which they placed themselves in pious subjection to the monastery as serfs.[50] Andrew of Fleury's contribution to the *Miracles of Saint Benedict* includes the story of Stabilis, a serf who escaped and prospered in Burgundy. Brought finally to justice by the monks, Stabilis attempted to prove his free status, but a coin in his sleeve (symbolic of his servile head tax) grew suddenly and miraculously weighty and immense as he appeared before a tribunal. He was forced to acknowledge his servitude to Fleury.[51]

Nevertheless, a number of voices both clerical and nonclerical questioned the assumptions by which serfdom was presented as natural and routine. Deliberate injustice, rather than circumstance against a background of universal sinfulness, would be emphasized in one of the best-known medieval denunciations of servitude, Eike von Repgow's *Sachsenspiegel*, a vernacular law code composed between 1221 and 1224. This passage was cited above in connection with the denial that Noah's curse could be used to justify serfdom. Eike ends his refutation of biblical justifications by stating that servitude comes from coercion unjustly imposed by men, not from any kind of divine purpose or dispensation. Servitude is an evil custom imposed by power, which now seeks acceptance as if it were law.[52] The same formulation appears in the south-German legal collection the *Schwabenspiegel*, and it would figure in other German law books of the later Middle Ages.[53]

That servitude violated natural law was, of course, an idea as old as the Greek philosophers and the Roman lawyers. Christian theologians such as Augustine, Agobard, and Aquinas could countenance modification to natural law because of sin and the need to restrain the wicked in a radically imperfect world. This relative natural law was opposed by Eike von Repgow but also by John Ball, the author of the *Reformatio Sigismundi*, and a number of peasant spokesmen in 1525. They insisted, in effect, on an absolute natural law that could not licitly be modified or set aside.[54] It is here that we arrive at the second argument identified above: that God's original creation of humanity in His image and with a fundamental equality of condition was still valid. The Fall had not so debased humanity that servitude became either licit or necessary. The Incarnation broke the bonds of servitude that had placed man in the devil's power.

Concretely, it was argued that Christ's sacrifice had freed humanity from bondage to sin, rendering servitude thereafter a violation of Christian liberty. Slavery (and later serfdom) were imposed by human wickedness—by force—not by a hidden dispensation of God to a fallen humanity. The fallibility of human intentions and institutions did not excuse the imposition of a servitude that violated a still-valid divine and natural law.

By nature we are all equal, Gregory the Great argued. Borrowing from Augustine, he contrasted God's command to Noah and his offspring to increase and multiply and to subdue the denizens of the earth with human domination of other humans. Man was commanded to inspire fear in animals, not in other men.[55] Gregory acknowledged that some should rule and others be ruled, and that equality was not, under the circumstances, possible.[56] Nevertheless, the contrast between domination over animals and domination over humans would continue to be a fundamental way of both attacking and justifying the oppression and particularly the servitude of rustics. On the one hand, Alcuin, Jonas of Orléans, Hrabanus Maurus, Rather of Verona, Honorius Augustodunensis, and Stephen Langton condemned the oppression of men by their fellows because God had given man dominion only over animals. Similar reasoning appears in the grievances of south-German peasants.[57] Gregory's contrast between divinely ordained domination over animals and illicit control over humans figured in the sermons of the head of the Hungarian Franciscans, Oswald of Lasko. Denouncing lords who impose servitude and oppression on their servile tenants, Oswald, writing at the end of the fifteenth century, invoked Gregory as well as our common origin in Adam.[58] On the other hand, apologists for seigneurial mistreatment regarded peasants as animals and thus as meriting subhuman conditions. Peasant advocates of course condemned their treatment as animals in violation of their created nature. In both instances an unstable border between human and nonhuman was evoked by serfdom.

Arguments over servitude were not generally framed in terms of abstract human right, at least not before the controversies of the sixteenth century over the enslavement of the inhabitants of the New World. What held more rhetorical and moral sway was the image of Christ as the breaker of human bondage to Satan and to sin.[59] Christ's sacrifice could be interpreted as conferring a presumption of liberty on His people, a more than merely internal spiritual liberty, implying that servitude of Christians not otherwise conquered or legitimately held captive violated divine law.

In a passage that would be frequently cited in later centuries, Gregory the Great, upon freeing two dependents of the Church of Syracuse, described the effect of Christ's assuming human flesh as the restoration of our earlier liberty and release from the chain of servitude.[60] For Gregory, it was a good deed to free slaves, men born by nature free but subjugated by the law of nations. On the other hand, this was hardly a call to abolition. Gregory's manumission appears in Gratian's *Decretum* in connection with the freeing of Church dependents notwithstanding the prohibition against alienation of ecclesiastical property.[61] A twelfth-century manumission from Chartres refers to the example of Christ, the liberator of humanity.[62]

Christ's sacrifice was extended beyond the narrow question of emancipating dependents to the upholding of a doctrine of essential equality and dignity. It conferred a similitude on all humanity, or at least on all Christians. In denouncing the Forest Laws of Henry II, Adam of Eynsham joins together the two themes we have been tracing: the distinction between the treatment of animals and the treatment of humans, and the equality of humanity in Christ's sacrifice. The punitive laws against hunting in the forest meant a reversal of divine order—animals were protected while human beings, beneficiaries of Christ's sacrifice, were destroyed or mutilated: "In revenge for irrational wild animals, which ought by natural law to be available to all in common, he had either punished by death or cruelly mutilated in their limbs human beings, who employ reason, were saved by the same blood of Christ and share the same nature in equality."[63]

The *Sachsenspiegel* also reflects the influence of the passage from Gregory, beginning the discussion of servitude with the statement: "God formed all human beings after His image and suffered agony for all. The poor are in His keeping as much as are the rich."[64] In the *Schwabenspiegel* the wording is changed slightly to emphasize the salvation brought by Christ, while human equality is less explicitly emphasized: "God has created man after Himself, for which men should honor Him. He has also saved mankind from hell with His suffering."[65] It is probably through the influence of the German law books that the sacrifice of Christ was placed in a number of later texts in opposition to servitude and servile incidents. In a denunciation of seigneurial exactions (especially inheritance taxes), the archbishop of Prague, Johann von Jenštejn (Jenzenstein) wrote in the late fourteenth century that Christian princes must fulfill their duties toward the populace whom Christ's blood redeemed. The archbishop considered the practice of confiscating peasant holdings in the event of death without children as no better than a "pagan custom."[66] Princes and priests must use their power in accord with Christ's teachings of peace and liberty, and the death duties are in this sense a defiance of natural and divine law, neither of which can be derogated.[67] Here, as in the *Sachsenspiegel*, Christ's sufferings and the unalterable nature of natural law are marshaled against servitude. More radical Bohemian observers also invoked Christ's sacrifice against servitude. The Hussite Peter Chelčický rejected the Three Orders model on the grounds that nobles' privileges were based on illegitimate violence, not on function or divine ordinance. Servitude was sinful, for had not Christ redeemed all with His blood, rendering traffic in human beings immoral?[68]

Better known is the *Reformatio Sigismundi*, in which a Turk argues before the emperor's court in Basel that Christians violate their own doctrine in the treatment of serfs. Acknowledging the power of what the Bible and the Church teach, the Turk contrasts the liberation of Christians for eternal life purchased with Christ's sacrifice with the actual fact that Christians are held by their fellows in bondage.[69]

At the end of the fifteenth century, Alexander Seitz of Württemberg stated that God had created us all as nobles and that Christ had paid the same price for all.[70] Here the idea of equality is joined to that of freedom, but it is an equality of dignity that is the product not so much of natural law as of Christian dispensation. Similarly, Erasmus argued in the *Institutio principis christiani* that human beings had been created free, a condition violated by servitude. Christ had freed all from servitude. How shameful, therefore, that servitude should be imposed on those whom Christ, by His blood, had made free. This would be translated into German and, along with the law books, exert a significant influence on the framing of peasant demands in 1525.[71]

Equality and liberty in Christ's blood would be marshaled by the German peasant movements in 1525. The *Twelve Articles of the Peasants of Swabia*, the most widely disseminated peasant manifesto of that fateful year, argued for the end of serfdom on the basis of Christ's blood, which was shed for all, "the shepherd just as the highest, no one excepted."[72] The peasants denied that they wanted freedom at the expense of authority, so that neither an absolute freedom nor an absolute equality was demanded, but rather an irreducible likeness and liberty in Christ as promised by Scripture. Article 3 concludes: "We have no doubt that as true and genuine Christians, you will gladly release us from serfdom, or else show us from the Gospel that we are serfs."

Peter Bierbrauer and Walter Müller have shown the connections between peasant demands in 1525 and the *Sachsenspiegel* and *Schwabenspiegel* (the latter being the more influential lawbook in south Germany, where the rebellion was centered). Specifically, assertions that servitude contradicts the Bible, that Christ saved all with His suffering, and that servitude is therefore a violation of Christian liberty are all found in grievances and demands of peasants in 1525 from communities such as Memmingen, Salzburg, Äpfingen, Bitsch, and Hanau as well as in the *Twelve Articles*.[73]

In one case, the idea of Christ's sacrifice and human freedom was joined to the myths of heroic freedom examined in Chapter 9. The late-fifteenth-century laws of Schwyz claimed that the Swiss came originally from Sweden and that upon settling the new land they agreed to recognize no earthly lord other than Christ Jesus, whose suffering, blood, and death had saved them.[74]

Outside of German-speaking lands, away from the influence of the *Sachsenspiegel*, however, one finds a more extended joining of liberty, historical manipulation, and Christ's sacrifice. In Catalonia, where servitude would eventually be abolished after a long civil war in 1486, an earlier attempt by peasants to buy out seigneurial rights failed but not without producing local syndicates organized both to agitate for the end of serfdom and to raise money to achieve it. The formation of these local groups is recorded in a document, preserved in the municipal archive of Girona, whose prologue attempted to justify the ending of a long-standing custom.[75] The prologue begins with the words of Gregory's letter to the bishop of Syracuse and then attempts to prove by a historical argument that the Catalan peasants were unjustly held in unchristian servitude. Answering the legend of the cowardly peasants (i.e., that Charlemagne had punished with perpetual servitude those who failed to aid his liberating armies), the prologue claims that the inhabitants of Catalonia at the time the Christian armies arrived were in fact Muslims ("pagans"). Harsh treatment was meted out to them not to punish any betrayal of their faith as Christians but to encourage them to become Christians. Servitude could not be considered compatible with Christian liberty. As an inducement to convert, the Christian conquerers promised that those who became Christians would be freed of the "bad customs" and servile status that properly should affect only infidels. Conversion had not led to liberty, however. Christians were kept in servitude, even after the entire population had converted, in violation of divine and natural law. When Christ took on human flesh, His passion broke the bonds of servitude and (again evoking Gregory) restored to us our pristine liberty. Thus this document combines several themes: Christ's sacrifice and human liberty, a refutation of a historical explanation for servitude applied to a particular nation, and denial that servitude is an inevitable and licit consequence of sublapsarian conditions.

The prologue to the document describing the formation of the Catalan syndicates should probably not be taken as an example of the peasants' voice in quite the same manner as the German *Flugschriften* published 75 years later. The document was written in Latin, and moreover, although tracing the peasants' ancestry to Saracens rather than timid Christians was an ingenious answer to seigneurial justifications for serfdom, it is unlikely that the peasants themselves would have accepted the idea of Muslim ancestry with much enthusiasm. We are concerned, however, to show not so much the specific producers and consumers of the image of Christ's sacrifice and human equality as its range.

Thus even earlier than the assembly of the peasants, the illicit nature of servitude was raised within the circle of the royal court. Maria de Luna, queen of Aragon-Catalonia at the opening of the fifteenth century, attempted to have serfdom (which affected only certain parts of Catalonia) abolished on Church lands by appealing to her kinsman, Pope Benedict XIII, the pope of the Avignonese party, who would ultimately be supported solely by the Kingdom of Aragon. Among her arguments was the example of Christ (*ad exemplum Crucifixi*), who had liberated us from servitude and whom the pope should follow in releasing the servile population from bondage.[76] This followed unsuccessful attempts by King Joan I, first in 1388 and again shortly before his death in 1395, to procure the abolition of the "bad customs" affecting the Catalan serfs.[77] On the first occasion, King Joan also asked for evidence to be produced from the royal archives confirming his understanding that "the time of servitude . . . according to the chronicles has already passed."[78] The king seems to be referring to a version of the legend that attributed serfdom to the curse of Charlemagne, whose validity he does not deny but which he believed was a punishment with a limited term (500 years?). Maria, daughter-in-law of King Joan I by her marriage to his son King Martin I, argued from a less historical point of view. Describing the "bad customs" and the *ius maletractandi* with adjectives such as "depraved and detestable," "pestiferous and reprobate," Maria asserted that they violate divine and natural law. Maria detailed the specific exactions and arbitrary power of the lords that placed the wretched *remences* in a worse and more vile status than that afflicting any other people in the world oppressed by the yoke of servitude. Such a "singular, detestable, and execrable monstrosity" stained the honor and reputation of Catalonia as well as contravening natural justice and human liberty given by God at the beginning of time.

The pope, besieged in Avignon (from which he would escape in March of 1403), in need of friends as one presumes he was, nevertheless declined to give in on this (or for that matter any other) issue, despite the queen's repeated entreaties and various arguments and inducements.[79] Throughout the fifteenth century, despite various turns of policy and opportunism, the court of the kings of Aragon (and certain jurists) could at least imagine and portray servitude as unjust. On several occasions the king agreed to accept peasant demands to compel a buyout of seigneurial claims, but reneged. An explanation for the peculiar success of the peasants in Catalonia at obtaining the abolition of serfdom must incorporate the willingness of powerful elements of society to accept the justice of peasant claims, to acknowledge that they merited a degree of liberty consequent on a certain basic human equality.[80]

~~~

I stated above that in order for servitude to be effectively denounced, the claim that it was a natural consequence of human sinfulness had to be refuted. One strategy was to show that there was no basis for servitude to affect only part of society. This is the purport of the *Sachsenspiegel* and the prologue to the assembly of Catalan peasants in 1448–49, both of which take issue with attempts to justify such partial servitude by reference to Noah's curse and the historical myth of the cowardly peasants. But other arguments justifying serfdom or relegating it to minor importance tended to posit a universal human sinfulness that led to the subordination of some people for reasons unconnected to a specific transgression. This is the position taken by Ambrosiaster, Augustine, Isidore, and Agobard: sin had introduced what Gregory the Great referred to as "diversity" into the world, by which some dominated over others, either because they had a superior character (Isidore) or because they had a hidden dispensation from God (Gregory).

To refute this idea required asserting that the Fall had not obscured the original equality of Creation, nor had it diminished the force of natural or divine law. Christ's sacrifice had restored original liberty so that all who embraced His teachings (Christians) should be free. That they were not was the result of specific unjust coercion, not of a general sublapsarian order; a wicked usurpation, not a circumstantial adaptation. The key step was to argue that this freedom could not be merely otherworldly or exist only in the eyes of God as Paul had said;[81] it had to be realized in this world.

Human law had to coincide with divine law. This form of what Gerald Strauss has called "legal primitivism" characterized much of the thought of the early Reformation and clearly stands behind the peasants' assertion of Godly Law on the occasion of the Bundshuh uprisings and the great war of 1525.[82] This law of the Gospels could not be modified by positive law or by arguments of circumstance or custom. As Peter Bierbrauer has observed, some of the late-medieval thinkers dissented from the scholastic and canonistic consensus that posited a relative natural law permitting modification of the dictates of Christianity because of sin. To this the *Sachsenspiegel*, Wyclif, the Taborites, and peasant leaders from 1381 to 1525 opposed an unmodified, absolute Godly law that serfdom violated.[83] Custom and positive law contrary to divine and natural law could not be allowed to persist, according to this view, which had many less radical adherents. The *Schwabenspiegel* first argued that lords who did not protect their dependents did not merit obedience, then repeated the *Sachsenspiegel*'s formulation that servitude comes not from law but from force dressed up as law. Such force, however long its history and however deep its acceptance as custom, remains contradictory to God's law, hence invalid.[84]

The ability of positive law to impose practices contrary to divine law was also disputed, as in a commentary on Catalan parliamentary legislation drawn up in 1438 by Tomàs Mieres. Arguing against the *ius maletractandi*, Mieres stated that even though it had been enacted by the king and parliament, it could not invalidate divine law.[85]

We should hardly imagine peasants rallying to a cry of "down with modified natural law." More vividly, they formulated their demands in terms of a divine ordinance of equality through Christ, one that could not be abrogated by custom, historical explanations, Old Testament reasons, or positive law.

The image of the peasant as naturally meant for servile work, or as cursed by circumstance, or as forming a lower, semibestial level of humanity justified servitude. Against this the assertion of liberty reiterated the humanity of those, however lowly, who professed Christianity. To be Christian was to merit treatment as a human being, a right that the incidents and reality of servitude violated. This outlook is hardly an assertion of universal equality. The emphasis on the sufferings of Christ fed into the growth of anti-Jewish sentiment, sentiment against those supposed to be responsible for Christ's torment.[86] Equating human dignity with Christian status encouraged an attitude toward the Jews that dehumanized and demonized them. Accusations of ritual murder and cannibalism were linked to the cult of Christ's wounds, and anxiety over the eucharistic real presence. The peasants' assertion of their humanity as defined by adherence to the Christian religion certainly excused in their minds, if it did not cause, the association of anti-Semitic violence with antiseigneurial rebellions.[87]

The peasants' agitation against serfdom in the late Middle Ages is therefore hardly to be represented as the origin or exemplar of human fraternity. It was, however, aided by a certain appropriation of common ideas equating liberty, humanity, and Christianity. The idea of Christian-as-human as opposed to unchristian-as-unhuman reminds one of Carlo Levi's report on the peasants of Lucania, who told him, "We're not Christian, we're not human beings; we're not thought of as men but simply as beasts."[88] This fundamental complaint would also underlie the peasant rebellions of the late Middle Ages.

Chapter II

Peasant Rebellions of the Late Middle Ages

This chapter looks at a few of the more notable peasant insurrections that arose beginning in the fourteenth century. Most, although not all, were unsuccessful and present us with the problem of ascertaining an effaced set of ideas. It would radically oversimplify to claim that these conflicts shared ideological presuppositions, spread as they were over centuries and across geographical boundaries. Renouncing, therefore, any notion of a single and authentic peasant "voice" consistent from 1320 to 1525, we nevertheless can trace ideas discussed in previous chapters mobilized in favor of the peasants. Among these ideas are the fundamental equality of humanity as ongoing rather than as permanently abrogated by a biblical or historical event; the failure of the nobility to live up to its duties of protection and the consequent calling into question of their right to rule; the piety of the rustics, a population not only ennobled by unjust suffering but close to God by reason of their work and manner of life.

It is worth examining both the response of elite writers to the threat and reality of peasant rebellion and peasants' justifications of their own conduct, some of which can be apprehended through the distorting glass of hostile accounts of contemporaries. Both kinds of discourse, attacking and justifying resistance to authority, employ images and ideas delineated in previous chapters.

Some examples of the "peasants' answer" to a seigneurial and urban discourse of contempt were described earlier in connection with the Swiss and other free communities. Although what survives in the way of songs, plays, and chronicles cannot be considered unmediated peasant opinion, in celebrating their victories and justifying their claims to liberty, peasants (or their spokesmen) accepted and made use of aristocratic commonplaces concerning bravery, freedom, and piety. For the Swiss and the men of Dithmarschen, liberty was to be gained by military courage and a steadfast faith allowing them to vanquish an overconfident and impious enemy. Texts produced during the large-scale revolts of the later Middle Ages are less celebratory (after all, most peasant revolts *were* defeated), more on the order of collections of grievances. Their complaints employ images that should by now be familiar: assertions of peasant humanity and protests against treatment as animals; denunciations of arbitrary lordship as contravening divine law; refutations of claims of domination based on social function (the Three Orders) or historical precedent (myths of freedom and subjugation).[1]

Beyond protests against injustice, some texts offer more radical alternatives. Well-known schemes, notably those of the Bohemian Taborites, Thomas Müntzer's plan for Franconia, and Michael Gaismair's for the Tyrol, presented utopian blueprints for a remodeled society. These celebrated instances have prompted a tendency to think of all peasant movements of this period as proclaiming an egalitarian and apocalyptic ideal, the avenging hand of the Lord in Chelčický's vision.[2] Even in a less fervid setting, some scholars expect peasant rebellions to depict a remade social order. In a recent account of the Flemish revolt of 1323–28, William TeBrake titles his chapters with such phrases as "For a World Without Corruption" and "For a World Without Privilege," but offers no evidence that such ideologies were actually put forward.[3]

It is necessary to separate radical means (insurrection) from ends that might be described as extreme only if the Middle Ages had a completely solid, hegemonic discourse of hierarchy and subordination. If the latter were the case, *any* criticism or subversion of the social order would either have been unthinkable or have caused hysteria. But what we find in the texts of hostile contemporaries of peasant rebellion is consternation more often than hysteria; and the former attitude did not necessarily prevent chroniclers or other elite observers from imagining what peasant grievances were, or lead them to entirely ignore such grievances in their reports of events.

This is especially true if elite discourse was not completely unified and occasionally expressed dissent from the prevailing order. I have tried to show that such dissent existed, my aim being not to argue that elites favored peasant rebellions (although in Catalonia this seems to be a close approximation), but to demonstrate that the moral and religious dubiousness of the existing order was not altogether lost on the upper echelons and that the theoretical texts and topoi they produced against the status quo could be put to practical use, turned against fatalistic assumptions that the righting of wrongs must await the next world. Hence the literalism of the peasants, the "carnal" reading of Luther and of Scripture according to his remonstrance (and later violent condemnation) in 1525, and the assertion of human equality and the illicit nature of servitude in John Ball's sermon during the 1381 uprising. That the peasants or their spokesmen might indeed take as literal what had been conceived as theoretical argument or even stylized lament is the point of this chapter. In discussing Duby's approach to laments over exploitation in the twelfth and thirteenth centuries, I argued that such complaints, mere vent-ings or rationales though they might have been, carried the possibility of a more pointed questioning of society. What had perhaps been harmless and academic ruminations when they were written could be regarded, by the era of the rebellions, as ideas whose currency invited appropriation.

Here we confront the problems put forward by recent critical approaches to subordination, specifically the problem of how to interpret popular move-ments when surviving materials are for the most part hostile accounts of those who put them down. I will defer until the conclusion my discussion of the implications of hegemony and counterdiscourse. On the specific question of medieval peasant uprisings I agree with Paul Strohm and Steven Justice, who have recently thought about this problem in examining peasant de-mands in England in 1381. Rather than attempt to piece together an authentic voice from hostile texts by means of a sort of ventriloquism, they argue, one can examine in a useful and not entirely naive way both chroniclers and what seem to be peasant texts as reported by chroniclers.[4] One looks not so much for a hidden, separate peasant discourse as for a manner of contestation. De-mands based on issues of justice, piety, and liberty were new with respect to who was putting them forward and with what degree of immediacy, but their content was traditional, hence comprehensible, and they were frightening not because they were alien or "other" but because they were familiar.

Medieval Peasant Rebellions

Marc Bloch has remarked that peasant uprisings were as routine within the medieval agrarian economy as strikes would be within the world of industrial capitalism.[5] This holds more for local, small-scale events than for the large re-gional insurrections that characterized the late Middle Ages, from the Flemish revolt of 1323–28 to the German Peasants' War of 1525. Sustained revolts did of course occur in earlier centuries, and they did express ideas that would be familiar to later advocates of equality. The *Capuciati* in late twelfth-century France invoked claims of original equality and shared human dignity.[6] Peas-ants also were involved in the world of politics before the fourteenth century.[7] Most of the conflicts before 1300, however, were local and centered around particular grievances. Insofar as they involved claims for liberty, such claims were based more on privileges for certain well-defined communities than on sweeping arguments regarding natural or divine law.[8]

After 1300 a large number of both local and larger regional peasant uprisings occurred. For the German Empire alone Peter Bierbrauer has counted 59 peasant insurrections between 1336 and 1525.[9] The distinction between "local" and large-scale movements is somewhat misleading, but the rebellions that left at least indirect evidence of motivations tend to be those that attracted more than glancing attention from chroniclers. I have therefore limited the following discussion to the better-known conflicts of the fourteenth to sixteenth centuries, although setting them in the context of a climate of frequent smaller revolts.

The best documented is of course the German uprising of 1525. From this conflict innumerable printed pamphlets listing grievances and demands (*Flugschriften*) have survived, providing a record of arguments intended for the consumption of other peasants (witness the use made of the model *Twelve Articles of the Peasants of Swabia*) and as a remonstrance. For the other conflicts—in England, Catalonia, and Hungary—one is forced to rely on a thin dossier, which nevertheless contains material evocative of themes we have traced before.

The English Rising of 1381

The immediate cause of the English rebellion was the imposition of a poll tax by the royal government. Resistance to the tax began in May 1381. Rebels from Kent and Essex marched on London in June, congregating at Blackheath and Mile End. The most dramatic phase of the rebellion—the execution of Archbishop Simon Sudbury, the burning of John of Gaunt's palace, the invasion of the Tower of London, and the death of Wat Tyler at Smithfield—took place on and around the Feast of Corpus Christi. The festive inversion of social power and propriety that took place during the rebels' brief hold on the capital has been linked, both by contemporaries and by recent observers, to the traditional celebrations of Corpus Christi.[10] The significance of the date might also have affected the planning of the convergence on London, which was more a planned, coordinated movement than a spontaneous mob activity.[11]

What were the demands of those who revolted? On the one hand they seem to have involved a radical political restructuring that would, in effect, have abolished the nobility. Rodney Hilton describes the rebels' goal as that of imposing a state ruled by a king with a very circumscribed church and altogether without nobles, thus essentially the king and common people with few intermediaries.[12] On the other hand, the agenda of the local rebels (those who did not flock to London to confront the king) was not so different from that of previous movements that had aimed at restoring a supposed earlier just relation between lords and men without eliminating lordship altogether.[13] Recent scholarship has tended to emphasize not only the coherence of peasant aims but also their connections to older ideas of justice, especially with regard to complaints of arbitrary lordship. Whether the rebels were or were not inspired by Wyclif or Langland's *Piers Plowman* is now again debated after a long period when theories of such influence were dismissed as overly imaginative.[14] There do seem to be connections between the peasant movement and literate high culture. We can reconstruct some idea of peasant ideology even from the works of hostile chroniclers who were intent on portraying the peasants as unreasoning savages.

While the peasants in London demanded the abolition of lordship, local movements made more moderate challenges to onerous and arbitrary incidents and rights of lordship, calling for rights to use common woods and meadows, rights to hunt game, and an end to monopolies and death duties.[15]

Even seemingly moderate demands, such as the right of tenants of St. Albans to use hand-mills, had radical symbolic significance and imagery. In an earlier rebellion the abbot of St. Albans had confiscated hand-mills that had allowed tenants to thwart his efforts to compel them to bring their grain to his mill for a fee. The abbot used the stone hand-mills as paving for the floor of his parlor. In 1381, they were dug up and split into fragments to be given out as proof that the rebels (townsmen and peasants) had accomplished their goal and as a symbol of their solidarity, a token of communion.[16]

Although chroniclers such as Thomas Walsingham described the rebels as rustics, or more pointedly as "most vile rustics," "barefoot ribald men," or "abject peasants," it has long been recognized that among the rebels were members of village officialdom, artisans, and others from London and its environs.[17] The fact that many of those involved in the revolt were leaders of rural communities, and that Kent in particular did not have villeinage but rather a custom known as *gavelkind* by which tenants were legally free, has led some observers to doubt that the event can accurately be described as a peasant revolt or that the rebels' demands for the abolition of servitude should be taken seriously.[18] I would argue that a central part of this movement was indeed a peasant revolt. Studies of the rebels who did not march on London show that their demands concerned seigneurial and manorial jurisdiction and administration, in particular serfdom and claims to levy exactions by reason of lordship over villeins.[19] As in other great rebellions of the period, in the English Rising opportunities afforded by the weakness of government or alliances with other groups did not obscure the issues of status and rural lordship that most concerned peasants. Those who came to London and held the young King Richard II hostage went beyond the expression of grievances against taxation and the corruption of royal officials to demand the abolition of servitude and a radical alteration of lordship.[20] The revolt resulted from a combination of what might be called "political" circumstances, involving both grievances against governmental administration and tensions in the relationship between landlords and tenants.

The Black Death of 1348 and 1349 and the consequent radical diminution of population had altered rural economic and social relationships. Squeezed by rising wages and falling prices for agricultural products, landlords attempted to control more closely those tenants who remained by limiting wage increases, restricting freedom of movement, and levying exactions that could be claimed from servile tenants. Not only were peasants' expectations of improvement thus frustrated, but in many instances their social condition was lowered as lords either imposed servitude on those previously considered free or coerced those who had been allowed to escape supervision. Between 1350 and 1381, marriage fines increased in frequency and amount, those who departed from tenancies illegally were more vigorously pursued, prohibitions on serfs' acquiring of free land were enforced, and court perquisites and other jurisdictional privileges were increased. Lords also attempted to restrain upward pressure on wages (the result of the diminished supply of labor) by enlisting the aid of the state. The Ordinance of Laborers (1349) and the Statute of Laborers (1351) required the able-bodied to accept work and prohibited wages from surpassing their pre-plague levels. While this legislation was often evaded, it was also vigorously enforced and widely resented.[21]

The seigneurial reaction was motivated by economic considerations rather than a desire for social control, but its effect was to sharpen the resentment of tenants against servitude. Those who were legally of villein status now saw a disparity between their opportunities and obligations and those of their free neighbors, who were more able to take advantage of a favorable labor and rental market.[22] Christopher Dyer, a careful observer of the entire sweep of medieval English social and economic history, writes of a "second serfdom" imposed by lords in the years leading up to the great rebellion.[23] The primary motive for revolt was the conflict between peasants' expectations of improved negotiating positions and their masters' attempts to preserve or reimpose servile dues and arbitrary lordship.

Questions of freedom and servitude were not exclusively focused on matters of legal status, but neither were they mere rhetorical masks for other demands. What was at issue both before and after 1381 was the ability of lords to constrain their tenants by overturning or undermining traditions and practices favorable to peasants. This background lends to many of the revolts, in

England and elsewhere, a seemingly conservative character, with the peasants defending the "good old law" against attempts to consolidate holdings or to regularize obligations. Radical means (violent insurrection) were deployed for conservative ends, to restore what was perceived as an earlier just order. Peasants did not need a paradigm shift or a revolutionary religious sentiment to desire the overthrow of at least certain aspects of the seigneurial regime. Peasant grievances made use of commonly agreed-upon definitions of liberty, servitude, human equality, and Christ's sacrifice.

Long before 1381, persistent lawsuits and local revolts had been sparked by changes in manorial custom imposed by landlords.[24] In the thirteenth and early fourteenth centuries, before the economic consequences of the disaster of 1348–49 had unfolded, lords attempted to rationalize their holdings and to define their tenants as villeins. In the mid–thirteenth century, Robert de Mares and then his widow, Sibyl, attempted to reduce the status of the villagers of Peatling Magna in Northamptonshire to villeinage, asserting the right to tallage at will and the collection of a marriage fine (*merchet*).[25] The inhabitants of Peatling Magna won their case in 1261. Not so fortunate were their neighbors in Stoughton, who lost their claims to freedom to Leicester Abbey in 1276.[26] A poem written at the abbey on that occasion asked, "What can a serf do unless serve, and his son?" It answered: "He shall be a pure serf deprived of freedom. / The law's judgment and the king's court prove this."

Beginning around 1277, the men of the villages of Darnell and Over in Cheshire quarreled with their lord, the abbot of Vale Royal, over his claims that they owed huge death duties, *leyrwithe* upon marriage of a daughter, and various annoying services (feeding the abbot's puppies, keeping his wild horses and bees).[27] The villages had formerly belonged to the crown, and the conditions under their new master were perceived as dramatically inferior. The Darnell villagers had complained to King Edward I shortly after the gift was made. The king is supposed to have told a throng of men carrying plowshares, "As villeins you have come, and as villeins you shall return." There ensued a long series of suits and acts of violence. The villagers rose up against the abbey in 1336, complaining that they were free and that the abbot had imposed on them the obligations of villeins. They petitioned Sir Hugh de Fren (justice of Chester), King Edward III, Parliament, and Queen Phillippa. The queen ordered the abbot to restore what he had despoiled, but after the abbot appeared before the rulers, they once again declared the villagers villeins. They ambushed the abbot in Rutland on his way back from the court, managing to kill his groom before being captured. They threw themselves upon the abbot's mercy and were compelled to perform repeated ceremonies demonstrating their unfree status. One is struck not only by the persistence of these unfortunate tenants of Vale Royal but by their touching faith in the judicial process of the realm, a faith similar to that exhibited by the tenants of Kempten in southern Germany over a century later.

Peasant movements seeking legal redress were organized before 1381. Opposition to arbitrary treatment in the fourteenth century is evident in the petition of the villagers of Albury in Hertsfordshire to Parliament in 1321–22 over seizures and imprisonment perpetrated by their lord. Numerous complaints were registered in various localities by tenants attempting to prove their free status against lords' claims to hold them as serfs, as for example at Elmham in Suffolk (1360) and Great Leighs in Essex (1378).[28] No fewer than 40 villages in the south of England in 1377 were swept by what a contemporary called the "Great Rumor": a movement employing Domesday Book to assert personal liberty and oppose labor-service demands.[29] By purchasing certified copies of extracts from Domesday (exemplifications) referring to their tenancies, the villagers attempted to prove that they formed part of the ancient demesne of former crown lands whose tenants should be protected by the royal courts. The peasants who submitted Domesday exemplifications considered them proof of freedom from villein status altogether. Parliament and the Royal Council rejected attempts to use Domesday in this fashion, but the effort shows the peasants' knowledge of law, belief in its efficacy, and a continuity between actions at law and local organized opposition, as among the tenants of Vale Royal and St. Albans, which brought pressure by extralegal means.

Many of the locales involved in the 1381 revolt had experienced earlier suits or acts of insubordination, and a sample of individuals identified as rebels in 1381 shows that many of them already had confronted their lords over fines or servile status.[30] At issue in 1381 and before were questions of rent, service, and other obligations of tenants that lords had attempted either to impose, reimpose, or preserve in an environment of what can fairly be termed rising expectations. Questions of status were inextricably linked with these quarrels over revenues because if lords could show that those who complained were villeins, they could prevent them from appealing to the public courts.[31] The petitions for freedom from servitude in 1381 were not a cover for more practical, economic conflicts but the point at issue.

Such demands were couched according to a traditional vocabulary, although the conclusions and programs that followed might be more radical. According to Thomas Walsingham's report on John Ball's famous sermon to the peasants assembled at Blackheath on the day of Corpus Christi itself, Ball argued on the basis of the proverb about Adam and Eve that all were created equal by nature. Servitude had been introduced contrary to God's will, by the wickedness of men (thus not by some primordial, divinely punished trespass).

Had God wished to create serfs, He would have established right at the beginning who was a serf and who was a lord.[32]

Ball's sermon is known through Walsingham and Froissart. According to
their reports, Ball did not explicitly invoke Christ's sacrifice and the freedom
His blood purchased for all humanity, a traditional theme in Corpus Christi
sermons. One of the letters attributed to Ball in which the rebellion is promoted, however, says that John the Miller has ground "smal smal smal" and
that "the kynges sone of hevene shalle pay for alle." The theme of Christ as
the wheat, ground in the divine mill for human salvation, is joined to that of
Christ ransoming humanity from its servitude to the devil.[33]

Steven Justice has shown how Ball's sermon and letter fit with five other
English letters preserved in Henry Knighton's chronicle rallying peasants to
the cause. They were probably not all written by John Ball, as used to be believed, but by other rebel spokesmen. Justice argues that the very act of fomenting rebellion by means of circular letters and broadsides is a defiant gesture against those who regarded peasants as little better than animals, an act
announcing "the documentary competence of the insurgent population, a determination not to be excluded from documentary rule."[34] One may not
completely accept this assessment of literacy as the crux of rebellion. Nevertheless, Justice allows us to appreciate not only that the chroniclers' view of
the peasants as unreasoning savages was false, but also that much of what they
report in the way of the burning of documents was not the act of frenzied
mobs intent on destroying education along with lordship.[35] Not only were the
rebels rather selective in what they destroyed (Walsingham and the author of
the *Westminster Chronicle* acknowledged that the burning of the Savoy Palace
was carefully policed and that looting was strictly forbidden), they also did
not assume that all written records were tools of their subjugation.[36]

An exaggerated reverence for charters and ancient documents that had inspired earlier movements is apparent again in 1381. Townsmen at St. Albans
burned charters and rolls listing obligations but demanded possession of an
older parchment issued by King Offa with azure and gold capital letters,
which they believed had established their freedom from villeinage. At a safe
distance one can smile at the belief that the Mercian ruler wrote such a charter, and at the abbot's bewildered promise to search even though he had never
seen or heard of it. In fact, however, the rebels were echoing (or rather turning to their advantage) the official monastic account of a foundation in 793. A
supposed charter of King Offa's was repeatedly confirmed by English rulers
from the thirteenth to sixteenth centuries.[37] Similarly we can be confident
that Bury St. Edmunds did not, in fact, possess a charter of liberties issued by
the monastery's founder King Cnut, as the rebels there claimed.[38] The rebels

manifested the same reverence before writing when they insisted that the king, whom they had in their power, write a charter freeing them from service to their lords and pardoning them. Dissatisfied with the document they obtained, they supposedly then ordered that men of law and others familiar with legal documents be executed.[39]

The peasants displayed an understanding of law and legal procedure both during and before the rebellion of 1381. They also appear to have been capable of using to their own purposes arguments constructed by Wyclif and Langland for a different purpose and for a different audience. This appropriation consisted in a deliberate shaping, not an ill-digested misunderstanding. Thus Wyclif himself carefully joined his denunciations of excessive Church property-holding with provisions for the orderly transfer of such property to secular rulers, while the peasants enunciated his program in terms of a more literal understanding of the canon-law phrase (which Wyclif frequently invoked) that the goods of the Church belong to the poor (*bona ecclesiae sunt bona pauperum*). Wyclif may have meant his words to inspire the king and the great men of his realm to action, but his address to the laity was, as Steven Justice put it, "overheard" by the peasants.[40] Similarly, peasants took the figure of Piers Plowman from Langland to serve as a vivid emblem of the virtuous countryman and adapted Langland's allegory of "Truth" to the more activist idea of imposing a new and just social order.[41]

Protection of traditional local rights and an end to servile status were the substance of the revolt. Despite the radical means by which the rebels' demands were put forward, one observes the same faith in written documents and legal concepts that informed earlier movements such as the "Great Rumor" of 1377. Thomas Walsingham claims that the rebels wanted to kill lawyers and justices and to burn all records they could find "so that the memory of ancient things would vanish," but he also says they hoped thereby to procure their "original liberty" (*ingenua libertas*).[42]

In discerning (if not actually reconstituting) a peasant "voice" from the hostile texts that have survived, scholars often want to see an authentic alternative ideology, what Justice calls the "idiom of rural politics" and Strohm refers to as "rebel ideology."[43] Such ideas were sufficiently antithetical to the dominant ways of thought for contemporary observers to regard them with fear and ridicule. For Strohm, the chroniclers deliberately manipulated their accounts to show the peasants in the worst possible light. For Justice, they had no need to do so because they did not see the peasants as having any legitimacy that would require distortion in the first place. The one interpretation finds a deliberate distortion, the other an inability to see that the peasants might have some idea of what they were doing.[44]

Naturally it would be hard to argue that Walsingham, Knighton, or Froissart displayed any sympathy for the rebels, but they did put into their mouths arguments that were neither novel nor incomprehensible. Froissart says that the people of Kent, Essex, Sussex, and Bedford stirred because they were kept in servitude and declared that no one should be a bondsman unless he betrayed his lord, as Lucifer betrayed God. They were not of treacherous nature, for they were men, formed in the same fashion as their masters, and so should not be kept like beasts.[45] That bondage violates divine law, that it was instituted by force, that it amounts to treating humans as animals— these were by no means new ideas, and they were comprehensible to peasant and lord alike.

It was possible for the chroniclers to imagine the terms in which peasant insurrection would be justified and expressed. To say so does not minimize their scorn, their occasional hysteria, or their portrayal of the rustics as vermin or as domestic animals who have gone wild. Of course the chroniclers were aghast at the danger to order and hierarchy, but they did not live in a world completely deaf to the plaintive voice of those under them. Their reports depict this voice in stylized terms, yet authentic details are revealed through chinks in what might otherwise seem an effective hegemonic discourse.

It has been argued that the English chroniclers were more objective in their opinions than the historians of the French *Jacquerie* of 1358, who described this peasant uprising as an act of unmitigated savagery.[46] Yet even chroniclers of the *Jacquerie* varied in their attributions of rational motives to the rebelling peasants and of blame to the nobility for causing the uprising in the first place.[47] Walsingham, Knighton, Froissart, and the *Anonimalle Chronicle* did not have to acknowledge the legitimacy of peasant demands to reproduce them in a way that is legible not only to the modern critic or historian inclined to be sympathetic to the rebels' cause but to contemporary members of the literate elite who were not.

The Catalan Civil War, 1462–1486

I have written elsewhere about the ideological background to this protracted conflict, the only successful large-scale peasant revolt in late-medieval Europe, and so will not linger over it here. Instead I will simply attempt to point out a process of appropriation, contestation, and comprehensibility in peasant demands, which in this case quite clearly centered on the abolition of servitude.

The servile peasants of northern Catalonia ("Old Catalonia" as distinguished from the territories to the south and west wrested from Islam in the twelfth century) were known in the late Middle Ages as *remences*, a Catalanized version of the Latin *redimencia* (redemption). These tenants made up about one half of the rural population of Old Catalonia and had been subordinated in several stages, beginning perhaps as early as the eleventh century but culminating in the decades around 1200, when restrictions on their freedom were first effectively defined and enforced.[48] They were subject to a group of customary levies that included a "redemption," or manumission payment, which gave the name to their condition. The exactions were collectively known as the "bad customs" (*mals usos*), even in official documents (a circumstance revealing something of the limits of euphemism in the Middle Ages). The bad customs included the right to require heavy death payments in cases where there was no adult male heir (*exorquia*) or in the event of intestate death (*intestia*). In addition, lords could confiscate as much as one third of the property of a peasant whose wife committed adultery and left him (a right with the humiliating name of *cugucia*, i.e., cuckoldry). The Catalan lords also held a legal right to "mistreat" their servile tenants, who could not appeal to the public courts for relief.

The actual success of the sustained peasant revolt is due to the complicated circumstances of the Catalan Civil War that pitted an alliance of urban, noble, and parliamentary groups against an unpopular ruler whose political and military survival depended in significant measure on the support of peasant armies.[49] The political context of the struggle does not obscure the consistent purpose of the peasant demands to put an end to servitude. Indeed, the king owed much of his unpopularity to a policy instituted by his predecessors that favored the peasants and that opportunistically, inconsistently, but nevertheless dangerously (from the nobles' point of view) raised the possibility of their liberation.

What we lack from this war (as from every peasant movement before 1525) is substantial evidence of how peasants might have framed their objections to their subjugation. We do have the curious document from shortly before 1450 regarding the organizing of peasant syndicates, as discussed in the previous chapter. It begins by invoking the letter of Gregory the Great, according to whom Christ assumed human flesh in order to restore to us that original liberty taken from us by the bond of servitude.[50] The document then denies that serfdom is the legacy of cowardly Christian peasants who failed to aid Charlemagne, refuting this notion by the counterclaim that the ancestors of the *remences* had not been Christians at all but in fact Muslims.

As an argument against serfdom, the prologue follows the pattern of much of the rest of Europe in pointing to Christ's sacrifice (especially as interpreted through the letter of Pope Gregory) as the basis for a Christian liberty that servitude violated. Catalonia as a whole demonstrates the possibility of constructing a moral argument against servitude in the absence of a religious reform movement. Unlike Germany in 1525 or England in 1381 (if one accepts the connection between the Rising and Wyclif), fifteenth-century Catalonia witnessed no religious revolutionary sentiment. The Church, to be sure, owned a large number of unfree peasants, but the revolt neither targeted churches nor expressed any particular anticlericalism. The Catalan peasant movement shows the possibilities for achieving a radical agenda within a traditional vocabulary.

Catalonia also demonstrates more clearly than other nations the fissures that undermined the unity of the powerful classes. The crown did not consistently side with the peasants, but its grudging support and dependence on peasant armies led to the abolition of servitude in 1486 after the resolution of the civil war. Even aside from the opportunistic alliance, however, members of the royal court and jurists harbored serious doubts about whether servitude could be justified, and suspicion that it violated religious, natural, and national law was widespread.[51]

The Hungarian Revolt of 1514

The Hungarian peasantry launched a short-lived but powerful revolt from April to July of 1514.[52] What had begun as a crusade against the Turks rapidly evolved into a holy war against the nobility, who stood accused by the peasants of betraying the crusade by exploiting their tenants rather than defending the realm. Hungarian royal and ecclesiastical authorities attempted to cancel the crusade, but the result was a full-scale uprising. The now-rebellious crusaders were led by a frontier captain referred to in the sources as George Zeckel, or György Székely (with other variations), known later as György Dózsa. He was victorious against a baronial army in Eastern Hungary at Nagylak on May 24 and continued to operate with some success in the east until the failed siege of Temesvár (now Rumanian Timisoara) in July.

János Zápolya, *voivod* of Transylvania, led the army that put down the rebellion, defeating Dózsa outside of Temesvár and executing him in a barbarous manner that astounded contemporaries. While musicians played and (according to one report) sung a Te Deum, Dózsa was placed on an iron throne which was then heated while he was "crowned" with an iron circlet. Partially roasted in this manner but still alive, Dózsa was offered to his followers, who had been starved and were now forced to eat his flesh. Those who refused were immediately dispatched to encourage the others.[53]

Even in an era accustomed to horrifying public executions, this made an impression. Dózsa's terrifying punishment would serve as the quintessence of

13. The execution of György Dózsa. Woodcut illustration from Stephanus Taurinus, *Stauromachia* (Vienna, 1519).

cowardice and cruelty for Montaigne seventy years later.[54] The most famous contemporary illustration of Dózsa's death, a woodcut dating to 1519, evokes the crucifixion of Christ, with a mocking crown being placed upon Dózsa's head as tormentors surround him (Fig. 13). A very early report of the rebellion, printed in Nuremberg in 1514, appeared in a revised edition that included a report of Dózsa's end and an engraving that shows a more peaceful martyrdom, the rebel leader crowned by thorns (Fig. 14). As Marianna Birnbaum notes, without the two musicians and the man biting the calm figure, the scene would be readily identifiable as a depiction of Christ, the Man of Sorrows.[55]

Legislation enacted as the result of the war was also harshly if less spec-

Die auffrur so geschehen ist im Vngerlandt/mit den Creützern/Vnnd auch darbey wie man der Creützer Haubtman hat gefangen vnnd getödt Zeckel Jorg.

1512

14. The execution of György Dózsa. Woodcut illustration from the pamphlet *Die auffrur so geschehen ist im Ungelandt mit den Creutzern* (Nuremberg, 1514). Wolfenbüttel, Herzog August Bibliothek: 198.13 Hist. (2). Reprinted by permission of the Herzog August Bibliothek, Wolfenbüttel, Germany.

tacularly repressive. It confirmed and strengthened the servile status of the Hungarian peasantry, restricting movement from one lord to another and declaring perpetual servitude as the consequence of the insurrection.[56]

The wars against the Turks had given the Hungarian peasants more military skill and experience than peasants had elsewhere in fifteenth- and sixteenth-century Europe. The appeal of a crusade was unusually strong and easily turned into a denunciation of the failure of the nobility to live up to its putative role as the protector of society. Rather than defending the land, it was argued, the aristocracy preferred to oppress their peasants in an even more barbarous fashion than the Turks.[57] The perceived breakdown of the functional mutuality of orders was hardly unique to Hungary, but was felt there with more immediate anger. Nobles' dereliction was all the more obvious and reprehensible in the face of a nearby infidel enemy.

Like Poland and Bohemia, Hungary experienced a serious erosion of peasant liberty at the end of the Middle Ages. The overwhelming majority of the Hungarian population were dependent tenants referred to in documents as *jobagiones* (Latinized from the Hungarian *jobbágy*). The more prosperous elements had acquired certain economic liberties in the fifteenth century, producing for the market, even settling in new towns (*oppida*) without thereby loosening the legal ties to their lords. The establishment of seigneurial market-towns for a time benefited both landlord and tenant, but toward the end of the fifteenth century, attempts were made to reinforce the dependent status of all peasants. As agrarian prices rose, landlords imposed heavier labor-service obligations to replace fixed monetary rents. They enforced this shift and maintained their supply of peasant labor by limiting the ability of remaining manorial tenants to leave the land. They also dramatically increased customary exactions in money and kind. The status of the peasant tended to be universally degraded to that of serf, a process codified by the laws of 1514 and 1521 but already under way in the fifteenth century.[58]

Although in Catalonia a revolt against serfdom accomplished its aims and in England rebellious incidents and erosion of servile status persisted despite repression of the peasants, in Hungary, as in much of east-central Europe, serfdom would effectively be maintained until at least the end of the eighteenth century, legally until 1848.[59]

The Hungarian war touches on a number of points already raised in discussing the transmission of ideas of justice and subordination. As described previously, Hungary, like Catalonia, borrowed from France the theory of a dual descent of the populace from a courageous and a cowardly population. The Hungarian peasants were thought to be descended from those who in (mythical) Hunnic times had failed to answer the call to arms. During the period in which France and Catalonia were transforming this literary theme into the basis for a legal justification for servitude, first Simon of Kéza and then János Thuróczy explained the differences in status among Hungarians by reference to crucial acts of bravery and cowardice at the founding of the nation and its institutions.

In Hungary, as in Catalonia, social myths that might at first seem mere learned fantasies were popularized by lords eager to convert an occasional, by no means universal form of unfree tenure to the basic rule of tenancy. In Hungary this ambition was fulfilled in the aftermath of 1514: the Hungarian peasantry was legally degraded to serfdom. István Werbőczy, author of the authoritative legal collection the *Tripartitum* (published in 1517), justified this treatment as punishment for the rebellion but also derived arguments for a retrospective servitude—for a primordial separation of free and unfree Hungarians—from thirteenth-century Hungarian adaptations of French legends of Charlemagne.[60] Serfdom, which gradually weakened in France and was thrown off in Catalonia, would be imposed and nearly universalized in early-modern Hungary.

Social images and ideas concerning the moral basis for serfdom became practical justifications in Hungary. What had been derivative and antiquarian came to structure legal beliefs, not merely as a hortatory rationale but as an effective discourse of repression. Similar transformation of ideas and mentalities can be traced in the *peasants'* program. Jenő Szűcs has shown how traditional themes of Franciscan preaching were used by the peasant leaders of 1514 to explain their attack on the nobility.[61] Although the antinoble revolt has often been related to the nearly simultaneous Protestant Reformation, or to the earlier impress of the Hussite movement, Szűcs demonstrated that the ideological roots of the 1514 revolutionaries were Catholic and conservative, not proto-Protestant, apocalyptic, or even particularly anticlerical.

A similar interplay of action and ideas appears in the peasants' accusations of deceit, treachery, and cowardice on the part of the nobility for abandoning the crusade. Here the peasants leveled against the nobility the very charge of cowardice in the face of military threat that had been associated with serfdom for centuries. Finally, the very idea of the crusade itself and the identification with the cross, sacrifice, suffering, and human equality mingle what might easily be dismissed as elements of archaic thinking (a crusade in the sixteenth century) with a revolutionary program (abolition of the nobility, abolition of servitude, and reduction of the number of bishops to one).

The end of serfdom and the throwing off of noble control were obvious goals of the peasant crusade and were reported by chroniclers and participants. In most accounts Dózsa appears as the evil instigator of the rebellion. King Vladislav wrote with evident satisfaction to the imperial legate, describing the execution with equanimity, even joy.[62] Among other things this grisly text reflects a tendency to blame the entire matter on Dózsa. A widely circulated poetic account of the rebellion first published in 1519, the *Stauromachia*, by Taurinus, presents Dózsa as militarily skillful and courageous, facing his death unrepentant. In language derived from Sallust's accounts of Marius and Cataline, Taurinus has Dózsa inveigh against the "tyrants" who rule Hungary. Although Dózsa anticipates a heavenly apotheosis as the "prince of peasants" (*regulus agricolum*), he is in fact received in a thoroughly classical underworld according to Taurinus's vivid and labored imagery.[63] Another contemporary chronicler, Ludovicus Tubero, blamed the rebellion at least partly on the oppressive conduct of the nobility toward their tenants, but still depicted Dózsa as the evil manipulator of this resentment.[64]

Dózsa and other prominent rebels could be accused of leading otherwise passive peasants into violent insurrection. Dózsa is portrayed with more imagination than accuracy by sixteenth-century historians as haranguing his followers and stirring them to bloodthirsty action.[65] But according to more immediate observers, it was not only Dózsa's supposed eloquence but the rustics' innate weakness, timidity, and ignorance that led them into treason. In a letter remitting the taxes of the loyal city of Kassa in Upper Hungary (modern Košice, Slovakia), King Vladislav remarked that in many parts of Hungary, "people led either by fear or by treachery wandered from the proper observance of loyalty."[66] In a charter pardoning the chamberlain John Szokoly for surrendering a castle to the rebels, the king singled out Dózsa for "seducing the rustics and servile populace with guile and with wicked persuasions."[67] In the same document, however, Vladislav II also referred generally to "evil and heretical men" who had incited rebellion by taking advantage of the religious fervor of the populace and their natural desire to aid (as they wrongly thought) the defense of the kingdom.[68]

The peasants could thus be depicted as credulous and easily misled. After all, they thought they were embarked on a crusade (and the sources continued to refer to the rebels as "crusaders," as did even the *voivod* Zápolya in pardoning the town of Dés).[69] A certain rhetoric of leniency appears even in the text of the punitive laws reducing the peasants to permanent servitude.[70] Here the king and parliament explained that although those who rebel against their "natural lords" deserve capital punishment as traitors, the peasants were to be spared the death sentence unless guilty of murder or rape. Recalling by implication the juridical association of treason with reduction to slavery, the ordinances of November 1514 present subjugation to "perpetual rusticity" as a merciful alternative to a merited execution. The law explained the practical impossibility of shedding so much blood, even if deserved, lest "the entire peasantry, without which the nobility would not fare very well, be wiped out."[71] The peasant leaders were to be executed, but the rest, having paid reparations, were to be spared and degraded to servitude. It might be tempting to do away with the peasantry, but the other orders of society depend on them—a peculiarly grudging example of the commonplace that rustic labor supports the privileged.

That the bulk of the peasantry acted out of ignorance might be a convenient fiction when levying fines from the hapless survivors, but during the rebellion itself this was not the preferred way of thinking about what motivated the rebels. The rebellion was most often described as a deliberate insurrection, the crusade being a mere pretext. In a letter written during the uprising to the nobles of the county of Valkó, the king lamented the "temerity and insolence displayed by the peasants and commoners under the name of a crusade."[72] Violent disobedience under the guise of a holy war would become a formulaic description of the rebellion in retrospective accounts.[73]

The crusade was viewed either as a cover for the wicked machinations of leaders or simply as a vehicle for the natural turbulence and subversion of the peasants. The relatively indulgent assumption that the peasants could easily be swayed from their natural loyalty was accompanied by fear that they were always dangerous, barely tamed beasts held in check only by severe coercion. Their "natural" condition was not loyalty but evildoing; the insurrection was not the work of a few conspirators playing off rustic credulity but the result of underlying rustic wickedness.

The *comites* of Nógrád, Hont, Pest, and Heves, writing at the height of the disturbances to their colleague in charge of the province of Abaúj,[74] open their frantic communication with a denunciation of the murder, rape, and destruction perpetrated by the peasants calling themselves crusaders. They label the rebels *crucifixores* (crucifiers) who call themselves *cruciferos* (crusaders, those bearing the cross), persecutors rather than defenders of Christ and the Cross.[75] Their aim is to exterminate the nobility, and the letter calls on the count of Abaúj to help repress their "rage" and "furor" lest not only the nobles but their wives and children suffer the peasants' barbarity. Dózsa is mentioned as the leader of the insurrection, but it is the rustics' innate savagery that is said to have "boiled over" (*efferbuit*).

The sources frequently refer to the "tumult" of the peasantry as if it were a form of natural disaster, the instinct of an undisciplined mass that, given an opportunity, is always ready to follow its evil nature and explode. The Italian chronicler Giovanni Vitale, writing in November 1514, acknowledged that some of the peasants might have assembled initially at Pest out of religious devotion, but those who were sincere dispersed quickly when so ordered. Those who persisted in rebellion Vitale excoriates as "impudent cattle" eager to foment what might be considered "classic" atrocities such as impaling nobles before the eyes of their wives and children, or raping the wives while their husbands were forced to watch. The rebellion is presented as an occasion for realizing an always potential lawlessness, lust, and rage.[76] The emblem of the terrifying wildness of the peasants is rape. As in other peasant rebellions, here chroniclers returned with obsessive horror to stories of rape as graphic demonstrations of rustic savagery.[77]

Occasionally the desire of the peasants to end servitude figured in contemporary descriptions of the rebellion. Writing to Pope Leo X in early July 1514, King Vladislav describes (in what might be said to be conventional terms) the murders and sexual violations perpetrated by these rustics, worse than Turks or Tartars, whose savagery is of unheard-of intensity, surpassing that reported in histories and even tragedies.[78] Interestingly enough, Zeckel/Dózsa is not mentioned. The peasants, "always eager for new things," have struggled to throw off servitude.[79] This explains their insurrection against the nobility and serves as prologue to the lurid accounts of their barbarity. What we would consider rational or plausible explanations for rebellion are seamlessly joined to conceptions of an underlying savagery.

Any attempt to understand what the motivations of the peasants of 1514 might really have been runs up against the usual problems of the poverty of sources and the prejudices of such accounts as do survive. There was neither *Flugschrift* literature nor lists of grievances as there would be in Germany shortly thereafter.

The closest thing to a program of the rebellion is a brief manifesto issued by Dózsa supposedly from the town of Cegléd in June 1514, at the point at which the crusade had turned from the Turks to attack the nobles as the enemy.[80] Here Dózsa calls himself the prince of the "blessed people who bear the cross," a fixation on the symbolism of the cross reflecting Franciscan apocalyptic tendencies.[81] Against this army of the elect the "infidel" nobles have risen up to "violate" the crusade. It is the *nobles* therefore who are the rebels, having thwarted the campaign against the Turks, for which they merit excommunication and eternal damnation.[82]

This document has received considerable attention because it fits with the notion that Dózsa was responsible for formulating an ideological program out of an otherwise inchoate body of peasant resentments. Dózsa is pictured by sixteenth-century historians as giving a speech at Cegléd to his followers. The most plausible version is that given by Tubero, in which Dózsa rehearses a number of familiar arguments denouncing the nobles' oppression of the peasantry: that servitude stems from human violence and greed, not nature; that those who labor in the fields and support all others are robbed and enslaved; and that God, "the author of your liberty," will protect the army of His righteous servants.[83]

Unfortunately, even this relatively restrained and well-reasoned address reported by Tubero has no basis in fact, although it may represent fairly enough Dózsa's program and is another instance of chroniclers having some idea of how peasant claims might be justified. Careful reconstruction of the chronology and geography of the rebellion shows that Dózsa was not at Cegléd when the proclamation was issued (it was sent by Dózsa to his brother Gregory in Cegléd). He and his army were already in the field, far from where the peasants were gathering in May and June. While the Cegléd Proclamation reflects Dózsa's justifications, he should not be thought of as haranguing peasants from the proverbial balcony. In any event, they appear to have been capable of forming their own justifications for rebellion.[84]

The Cegléd Proclamation itself reflects earlier formulations of the crusaders' goals. A document purporting to be a summary of the original crusading bull of Pope Leo X was composed in mid-May by Tamás Kecskés and Lörinc Mészáros, who, like Dózsa, described themselves as *principes cruciferorum* and who were recruiting in the county of Abaúj (at some distance from Dózsa's army). Their version of the crusade bull confers authority on the *principes cruciferorum*, whereas the original reserved ultimate authority to the pope, king, and archbishop. The poor are given more prominence, but most importantly, the sanctions against those impeding the crusade (a previously routine condemnation) are now specifically directed against lords who continue to exact unjust tribute from their tenants. They are to be excommunicated *tanquam membrum dyaboli* (a locution found earlier in Hungarian Hussite documents), and the community (*tota conventus*) is exhorted to rise up against those attempting to extort from them.[85] The Turkish threat not only preserved the appeal of the crusade longer in Hungary than elsewhere but gave a particular edge of outrage to complaints against the greed of the nobles. It had long been a common rhetorical strategy throughout Europe to lament the mistreatment of peasants as worse than that meted out by Muslims and "pagans."[86] The atmosphere of the Hungarian frontier (as well as that of eastern and southern Austria) made comparison between noble and Turkish greed and savagery more than a rhetorical device.

Peasant rebels accepted the aristocratic syllogism whereby military skill and force conferred the rightful enjoyment of liberty. As if in answer to the widely diffused myth of peasant cowardice, Dózsa mustered his followers by sending around to sympathetic villages a bloody sword and impaling pole, symbols of the grim realities of war and the penalties for cowardice. The bloody sword, at least, accompanied the summons to the frontier soldiers, the *Székely*, according to the Transylvanian military regulations of 1463.[87] The grim symbols also recall the alleged customs of the Huns in mustering the populace, a test of bravery that explained the separation between nobles and serfs.[88] Against this mytho-historical background the sixteenth-century peasants could all the more pointedly present themselves as courageous warriors while disparaging the nobles' failure to obey the military summons to the crusade. The constitutional fiction of Simon of Kéza was reversed: peasants obeyed the call to battle that nobles shirked.

The Hungarian rebellion can be understood as a crusade in which a sense of election galvanized long-standing resentments against the nobles. The rapid spread of the rebellion argues for the preexistence of a nexus of ideas encouraging and justifying revolt.[89] Behind the crusade and the practical concerns over land tenure can be discerned a sense of the breakdown of mutuality of orders that extends to those not immediately involved in the circles of rebellion.

The most elaborate and pointed criticisms of the nobility at the end of the fifteenth and beginning of the sixteenth century were offered by friars of the Observant wing of the Franciscan order. In 1509 there were some 70 Franciscan houses in the kingdom; there had been only 25 in 1448. This efflorescence responded to the need for anti-Turkish preachers but also reflected a rediscovery of apostolic poverty experienced in the fifteenth-century vicariate of Bosnia-Hungary.[90] Without doubt, much of the tone of the 1514 rebellion—the sense of election visible in the Cegléd Proclamation, for example—is traceable to Franciscan preaching.

The mendicant orders had been given the task of preaching the Crusade to the populace by Gregory IX.[91] History offered precedents for the deviation of both spontaneous crusade movements and popular crusades from the original intentions of those who instigated them. The Shepherds' Crusade (Pastoureaux) of 1250, the Childrens' Crusade of 1212, and even the host summoned by the preaching of Peter the Hermit at the time of the First Crusade—all these movements combined belief in direct revelation with a conviction that the knights were unable or unwilling to do what was necessary to win God's favor for the success of the armed pilgrimage.

The Hungarian Crusade, however, amounted to something more than a movement that escaped its (Franciscan) organizers. Certain Franciscans were themselves instrumental in changing or expanding the target of popular wrath. Through their preaching, members of the order inspired and even directed the turn from anti-Turkish to antinoble movement. The centers of peasant agitation in the late spring of 1514 correspond to the location of Observant houses, and three or four of the captains of the army were Franciscans.[92] The degree to which the order was split by the events of 1514 can be deduced from a manuscript discovered by Szűcs in the Széchényi National Library of Budapest.[93] This manuscript is a collection of 188 documents (those that are datable are almost all from between 1509 and 1517) that deal with "apostate" friars guilty of preaching rebellion to the peasants. The documents from after the war, which take the form of disciplinary inquiries to purge apostates, reveal divisions extant before 1514 within the Observant Franciscan order over preaching and social doctrines.

The influence of the Observant Friars was visible in terms of apocalyptic reformism (as might be expected), but also in more conventional teachings of human equality and denunciations of the oppression of the poor. Within a traditional discourse concerning fundamental human equality, it was possible to construct a compelling set of potentially revolutionary ideas. This is most evident in the sermons of Oswald of Lasko (ca. 1450–1511), provincial vicar of the Franciscans in Hungary, a figure of what might be considered the Franciscan establishment. Oswald embraced the conservative ideal of a mutuality of orders, but his awareness that reality diverged severely from the organic model led him to vivid and apparently influential denunciations of the powerful.[94] He elaborated on Augustine's statement from *The City of God* that rulership without justice amounts to little more than robbery, and he denounced princes who inflict unjust exactions and "devour" their serfs with taxes and oppressive customs.[95] They do not merit obedience, and it is licit to defend oneself against an abusive superior.[96] Oswald also defends those who act out of righteous anger to chastise those who defy God. Although this pronouncement is not specifically joined to the denunciations of servitude, the condemnation of injustice and defense of the right to oppose it with force could be read as more than laments over seigneurial violence, indeed as something approaching a right of insurrection.[97]

Oswald's desire to restore a lost order led him to combine "Old-Law" with divine-law arguments. Moreover, he rejected the fatalistic assumption that wicked conduct results from a world fallen into universal sin and decay. What provides a conceptual link between complaints about oppression and the theory of righteous anger is Oswald's conviction that although the coming of Antichrist will bring suffering, an elect of those who follow the Cross will emerge. This army will not comprise magnates and knights but the ignoble, the weak, and the unlearned, who will impose the rule of God.[98] The fierce identification of the 1514 crusaders with the Cross and their conviction of election in an antinoble crusade can be traced to Oswald of Lasko, whose sermons were specifically directed, he informs the reader, to the poor and to unlearned rustics.[99] Beginning in 1510 the Franciscan authorities denounced those who expounded dangerously on texts affording occasion for disobedience and sin. The undisciplined wanderings of renegade friars and their subversive preaching were also the objects of censure before and after the 1514 revolt.[100]

It should be emphasized that Oswald of Lasko's sermons display little originality, scarcely deviating from common discursive themes. Oswald went further than others in justifying action and anger, but he worked with a popular theological vocabulary culled from the Church Fathers, Franciscan tradition, and earlier sermons rather than a radical or visionary reformism. The influence of Franciscans in Hungary can be demonstrated not only in the geography and leadership of the crusade, but in the way in which peasant demands turned on denunciations of the nobles for destroying the mutual service that justified their privileges. The threat of the Turks underscored the unwillingness of the nobility to abandon their exactions and defend their subjects, giving force to ideas that crystallized around the breakdown of mutuality, the violation of human equality, and the question of how a just order might be restored. Oswald himself seems to have given up such social criticism after 1507, and it is clear that he did not see himself as excusing a large-scale armed revolt, but in Hungary conventional attacks on oppression were applied to particular circumstances not only to justify retrospectively but to institute a popular movement.

The German Peasants' War of 1525

Even more than the English and Catalan revolts, the German Peasants' War has been viewed as something greater than a mere peasant insurrection. Several factors underlie this perspective, among them an assumption that peasants were unlikely to have acted on their own initiative and a concentration on the two dramatic and lasting aspects of sixteenth-century German history: the Reformation and the inability of the emperor (or anyone else) to achieve a unified rule over German-speaking lands. Regarded as a crucial event in the overall history of the German nation, the 1525 uprising was until recently annexed to the perennial question of the origins of German disunity and early-modern backwardness.

Scholars' rediscovery of peasant agency has tended to restore to our understanding of this war the actual demands of those who revolted. Nevertheless, it is still often maintained that the revolt of 1525 was not really about agrarian grievances, or that it was touched off by the more progressive and articulate forces of society. The historiography of the former East Germany, following the formulations of Friedrich Engels, considered 1525 an "early bourgeois revolution," the assumption being that the real vanguard and significant element in the movement came from the towns.[101] The importance of the cities in the Reformation has also led non-Marxist historians to trace the origin of unrest to the cities, with the concomitant assumption that the countryside was acted on rather than enacting its own program.[102]

The peasants might also be regarded as unwitting participants in the unsuccessful struggle for German unity, their defeat marking the definitive triumph of German particularism.[103] But the event that inevitably colors any interpretation is of course the Reformation. The teachings of Luther, Bucer, Karlstadt, and Zwingli emphasized the dignity of the laity, the ability of ordinary people to interpret Scripture, the right to question authority and tradition, and a more favorable view of the common man. The Reformation is thought to have inflamed peasant resentment, a sentiment already inspired by the long habit of anticlericalism.[104]

The charged climate of religious ferment that prevailed just before and during 1517 is supposed to have produced a crucial change in the nature of peasant demands. No longer defending what they perceived as traditional relations with their lords, relations that protected communal rights, the peasants now took up arms for a universal idea of social-religious justice. Instead of fighting for local privileges or custom, they now demanded a reordering of society in accord with divine justice. Günther Franz gave this distinction its classic formulation as that between a conservative "Old Law," a circumscribed defense of custom, and a radical "Godly Law," a more sweeping application of religious doctrine to social conditions.[105] Beginning in the mid–fifteenth century with the so-called Bundshuh movements, but gaining substantial momentum with the reception of Luther's teachings, peasants of the fragmented German seigneurial jurisdictions could unite in a cause that transcended mere quarrels over local grazing rights. According to Franz, a struggle on the scale of the 1525 war required belief in a widely applicable divine law that questioned all forms of seigneurial oppression, and this belief really began with the Reformation.

The German historiographic distinction between conservative (Old Law) and radical (Godly Law) movements resembles that invoked by comparative historians of peasant movements to account for the difference between purely localized insurrections in the name of a supposedly better past and uprisings of wider appeal focused on building a new form of society.[106] Long before the sixteenth century, however, justifications for revolt combined particular grievances against exactions, servitude, and arbitrary lordship with a general assertion of human liberty and divine law. Servitude was among the most important issues in 1525, and the complaints about it were neither new nor completely dependent on the radical energies and vocabulary generated by the Reformation.

Servitude and seigneurial rights attendant on serfdom were major issues in German revolts that antedated 1525. What might seem to have been purely economic struggles over taxes or levies were enmeshed in questions of status. Thus, for example, lords attempted to increase revenues by reimposing large succession fines, but doing so required depriving peasants of the right to inherit freely, which in turn meant placing them in servitude. The extension of territorial lordship, the demands of lords in the face of declining revenues, and questions of servile status were intermingled.

The previous chapter touched on the struggle between the abbot of Kempten and his tenants over their status. A large number of similar revolts boiled up in small south-German territories where feudal dues were the principal source of revenues for petty secular and ecclesiastical landlords: Weingarten (1432), Schlussenried (1438), Weissenau (1448), Staufen (1466), Salem (1468), St. Peter (1500), Habsburg lands of Triberg (1500), Ochsenhausen (1501–2), Berchtesgaden (1506), Rufach (1514), and Solothurn (1513–15).[107] Regional conflicts between 1442 and 1517 (the Bundshuh uprisings) also concerned servitude.[108] Restriction of movement, inheritance taxes, and the seigneurial right to impose new levies figured in the revolt of Appenzell against the monastery of Saint Gall at the opening of the fifteenth century. This revolt exemplifies a successful radical result stemming from what was perceived as a defense of Old Law, for the peasants rose up to prevent the monastery from making its exactions more onerous and arbitrary.[109] Seigneurial economic pressure on tenants increased during the fifteenth century, especially in Swabia and the Upper Rhine, a development aggravated by the reimposition of servile status, which the peasants resisted in many cases, albeit with limited effect.[110]

In 1525 these same quarrels reappeared. Many sorts of grievances came together in that fateful year, from objections to war levies to protests against violation of fixed rents, but the issue of serfdom covered the widest territory. In an analysis of 54 grievance lists from Upper Swabia (consisting of 550 individual grievances), Peter Blickle found that 90 percent of the complaints denounced servitude and that serfdom was the single most important grievance.[111] Moreover, this was not merely a negotiating strategy but a crucial demand. Of 20 such texts concerning ecclesiastical jurisdictions in Upper Swabia, 15 (comprising 18 articles) call for the abolition of serfdom. Only one envisions its mere diminution.[112] While the greatest number of complaints about servitude come from southwestern Germany, serfdom was also at issue in revolts in the diocese of Augsburg, Alsace, and the archiepiscopal principality of Salzburg.[113]

The peasants of Stühlingen (in the Black Forest), where the first revolts began, described their opposition to servitude in these terms:

> We are by right born free, and it is no fault of ours or of our forefathers that we have been subjected to serfdom, yet our lords wish to have and to keep us as their own property, and consider that we should perform everything that they ask, as though we were born serfs; and it may come in time to pass that they will also sell us. It is our plea that you adjudge that we should be released from serfdom, and no one else be forced into it, in which case we will perform for our lords what we are obliged to perform of old, excepting this burden.[114]

Here servitude as punishment for some past or present transgression is rejected. The other articles of the grievance list deal with specific exactions, but they follow from the ability of the lords to treat servile tenants with ever-greater harshness and arbitrariness.

The peasants of Stühlingen were not attacking servitude as such but rather denying their particular liability. They had not been born in servile condition; therefore their lord could not impose it. Elsewhere, broader complaints were voiced against the very nature of servitude. At Embrach (near Zurich) and in rural lands subject to the imperial city of Rothenburg, for example, it was argued that to hold another in subjugation violates Scripture and the unity of all in Christ.[115]

Peasants asserted claims of human freedom against servitude without specifically invoking Christian doctrine at Altbirlingen (part of the Baltringen alliance), Wiedergeltingen, Rheinfelden, and Mühlhausen (in Hegau).[116] Other grievances against serfdom were expressed in more religious language: only God can licitly own a person; He alone is really Lord. Peasants of the *Gemeinde* (local community) of Attenweiler (Baltringen) protested to the abbey of Weingarten that they were "burdened with servitude, for they wish to have no other lord but Almighty God alone who has created us. For we believe Holy Scripture, which is not to be obscured, that no lord should possess others [*kain Aigenmensch haben soll*], for God is the true Lord."[117] In the region of Schaffhausen, villagers complained that Scripture prohibited anyone other than God Himself from possessing *Aigenleute* (serfs).[118]

To what extent did religious discontent and the Reformation stimulate the revolt of 1525? Grievances were everywhere informed by an idea of scriptural authority and the right of resistance based on a higher law. The *Twelve Articles of the Peasants of Swabia* (March 1525) describes not only serfdom but restrictions on fishing and hunting as contrary to the word of God and supports its very specific and material claims with references to Scripture.[119] Such manifestos grew out of Lutheran resistance theory, according to Martin Brecht, and the demands reflect a religious-social program based on Lutheran biblicism: the right of a community to elect a pastor, rejection of serfdom as contrary to Christian equality of salvation, the love of one's neighbor, and the protection of the weak (the latter was the basis for opposition to death duties, for example, which fell on widows and orphans).[120]

Günther Franz argued that the Reformation did not create an entirely new justification but that Lutheranism made possible a rebellion on a much greater scale than had been reached previously.[121] Luther brought a new awareness of equality and a vivid language and symbolism, providing, in Oberman's words, "a means to read the timetable of God."[122]

Luther himself hardly mentioned peasants or oppressive lordship before 1525. His warnings, fury, and later unapologetic defense of his "harsh" views all reflect an immediate response to what he saw as a gross misunderstanding of his views on Christian freedom, a carnal, worldly literalism at odds with the spiritual freedom he advocated.[123] The opinion that the peasants were inspired by an opportunistic misreading of Luther has had some modern defenders,[124] but scholars have shown more interest in learning what aspects of Luther's teaching or of the political situation resulting from the Reformation provided openings for constructing a large-scale movement.

Luther's pamphlet *The Freedom of a Christian*, published in 1520, clearly dealt with spiritual freedom and spiritual equality, but such ideas could be used to apply to earthly liberty as well. The widely circulated pamphlet *Dialogue Between a Priest and a Bailiff* (ca. 1521, attributed to Martin Bucer) cites Luther in advocating human freedom against servitude.[125] The Memmingen *Bundesordnung* of March 7, 1525, containing peasant demands, ends with a list of learned authorities who have demonstrated and defended Godly Law, including Luther, Melanchthon, Osiander, and Zwingli.[126] Thus even if Luther and other reformers were "misunderstood," their ideas certainly lent themselves to appropriation. The Reformation for a time destabilized imperial and princely control, showed how authority could be successfully challenged, and furthered (if it did not create) a language of scriptural authority, Christian liberty, and action in the world. Arguments over servitude and oppressive lordship became increasingly general—focusing on whether such practices were in harmony with God's purpose—rather than oriented around custom and precedent.[127]

On the other hand, the justifications for revolt and the self-awareness of the peasants were not completely dependent on the Reformation. The scale of the Peasants' War of 1525 may be due as much to the advances in inexpensive printing and the proliferation of pamphlets (*Flugschriften*) as to the Reformation, although the stimulus to reading and disputation can hardly be separated from the impetus given by the religious upheaval itself.[128] The language of revolt and the context of its demands remained oriented toward the *Gemeinde* even as insurrection became generalized throughout territories beyond individual lordships.[129]

Above all, there is a theological, moral, and legal background to the peasants' demands in 1525 that antedates the Reformation. Peter Bierbrauer has argued that the Reformation did not by itself inspire a Godly Law peasant argument in contrast to earlier Old Law local challenges.[130] The real distinction was between two types of Christian natural law: the relative variety, modifiable and hence capable of legitimating servitude, and the absolute variety, unchangeable and thus permanently prohibitive of arbitrary lordship and the holding of Christians as serfs. Controversies over how much divine and natural law might be modified by circumstance, the Fall, human necessity, and sin antedated the Reformation, appearing, as mentioned previously, in the German law books of the thirteenth century (notably, *Sachsenspiegel* and *Schwabenspiegel*), Wyclif, the *Reformatio Sigismundi,* Taborite doctrines, the pamphlet by the so-called Upper Rhine Revolutionary, and Erasmus.

The third of the *Twelve Articles of the Swabian Peasants* denounces serfdom in similar terms:

> Third, it has until now been the custom for the lords to own us as their property. This is deplorable, for Christ redeemed us and bought us all with his precious blood, the lowliest shepherd as well as the greatest lord, with no exceptions. Thus the Bible proves that we are free and want to be free.[131]

The text is accompanied by marginal citations to the Bible (Isaiah 53:1; 1 Peter 1; 1 Corinthians 7; Romans 13; Wisdom 6; 1 Peter 2). But as Walter Müller has suggested, the language invoking Christ's sufferings that purchased human freedom is more closely derived from the German law books, along with the *Reformatio Sigismundi* and Erasmus.[132] Bierbrauer points to the *Schwabenspiegel* as especially influential, not only because it was more widely circulated and accessible in south Germany than the *Sachsenspiegel, Reformatio Sigismundi* or Erasmus, but because of its specific formulations. Comparing the south-German lawbook to the articles of the peasants of Äpfingen (part of the Baltringen group, dating from February of 1525) and the *Twelve Articles,* Bierbrauer notes two key reworked *Schwabenspiegel* passages: first, nowhere in Scripture does it say that one man can own another; second, God created man after His image and saved him with His sufferings. In addition, the Äpfingen demands repeat the context for the passages in the

Schwabenspiegel (and its source, the *Sachsenspiegel*): render to Caesar the things that are Caesar's, and to God the things that are God's (Mark 12:17).[133]

In the *Twelve Articles* and the complaints of the Äpfingen *Gemeinde* we see the reappearance of venerable themes in discourse about equality in servitude, but now in a more urgent key. Without in any way minimizing specific socioeconomic pressures or the ideological impact of the Reformation, it can be argued that medieval concepts of justice played a role in the German Peasants' War, as in those large-scale insurrections that preceded it. Such notions as the ultimate equality of humanity, Christ's sacrifice to release humanity from bondage, the obligation placed upon all humanity to labor, and the mutuality of social orders could be brought from the realm of speculation and made to serve revolutionary aims that did not depend entirely on a radically new way of looking at the world. In this sense Luther was correct, not that the peasants ignorantly mistook his teachings concerning Christian liberty, but that they applied them in a more immediate way, along with the disquisitions of others who commented on the breakdown of mutuality and the difficulty of explaining the servitude of Christians.

Conclusion

In his study of injustice, Barrington Moore devotes a chapter to "the rejection of suffering and oppression," asking at what point ideas of mutuality and dignified suffering break down and become transformed into direct challenges to authority.[134] Rebellion springs not only from specific economic pressures but from a cultural change: a change in which a social environment is no longer taken for granted but rather perceived as intolerable. This change is related to delegitimation, the point at which authority is no longer perceived as sanctioned by some higher or impersonal law. We have found this to be implicit in the *Sachsenspiegel*'s dismissal of rationales for serfdom on the basis of biblical authority in favor of a stark, demystified statement that serfdom comes about from willful human wickedness. This argument, denouncing as human invention what had previously been regarded as divinely ordained injustice, appears repeatedly in peasant justifications for revolt.

I do not of course mean to suggest that mutuality among the orders was suddenly discovered no longer to work in the fourteenth century. One can assume that peasants themselves realized this rather early on, and certainly the failure of the Three Orders model elicited theological lament almost from the moment of the model's post-Carolingian invention. The change in the fourteenth century did not, therefore, consist in the sudden collapse of a universally accepted justification but in the confluence of long-term developments—perceived oppression, opportunity, and the conceptual means of resistance.

Perceived oppression in the late Middle Ages had much to do with the demographic collapse and consequent labor shortage following the Black Death of the mid–fourteenth century. While one cannot ultimately cite the Black Death as a cause for everything that took place as late as 1525, the crisis of the landlords and their efforts to recoup by tightening the conditions of tenure, including the reimposition of servitude, form the background to a perception of injustice. Even without an ideology of supply and demand, peasants could expect better bargains for their labor but instead saw the power of the aristocracy and the state mobilized to extract more from them to make up for the decline of prices, the devaluation of land, and the shortage of labor.

The fourteenth to early sixteenth centuries afforded a number of opportunities for rebellion. In all the cases examined above, internal crises within the governing order opened practical as well as ideological doors to peasants. The unpopularity of the poll tax and parliamentary investigations of the corrupt administration of John of Gaunt affected the development of events in England in 1381, just as dynastic and factional disputes would alter the course of events in Catalonia a century later. The Reformation not only divided German authorities internally but provided powerful images of peasant righteousness and exaltation of divine law that encouraged a powerful peasant movement.

The conceptual means of resistance developed not only from the undermining of authority but also from what Moore refers to as "the creation of standards of condemnation for explaining and judging current sufferings," and "a new diagnosis and remedy for existing forms of suffering."[135] That the diagnosis did not need to be completely new is essentially what I have been arguing. In classic models of peasant insurrection, including Moore's, there is little that stands between meek acceptance of a dominant ideology and revolutionary activity born of a sudden collapse of that ideology's inevitability and legitimacy. Uprisings need not be viewed as the spasmodic frenzy of an essentially subjugated population, or as an outburst of apocalyptic irrationality. They can be seen instead as more planned, opportunistic, and even optimistic (if in most instances wrongly so) events. Peasant revolts were accompanied by a traditional discourse of indignation and resentment; they did not require the external stimulus of a new ideology, be it Godly Law, a secular new order, or chiliastic expectation.

The origins of rebellion therefore do not lie in a sudden shift from acceptance of hierarchical legitimacy to revolutionary sentiment. Rather, the roots of revolt may be found in a more continuous change from everyday evasion to public challenge. The standards of condemnation are key aspects of the construction of a revolt, but those standards develop not from religious upheaval, nor from the export of subversive ideologies from the towns, nor even from an internal collapse of the state, but from a process of ideological appropriation and reorientation toward immediate practical application.

Not every peasant war involved the same set of justifications for rebellion. In England the premise of original equality provided a way to attack the servile condition of peasants and what was regarded as the unjust lordship that it made possible. In Catalonia propeasant figures argued that servitude violated divine and natural law, in at least one case using the words of Gregory the Great's well-known passage on Christ's universally liberating sacrifice. In Hungary the justification for revolt was linked to the nobles' betrayal of mutuality and functional orders. In Germany both equality at Creation and the meaning of Christ's sacrifice were deployed.

In all these wars, as well as in smaller conflicts, servile status was either among the direct causes in the eyes of chroniclers and the peasants themselves, or provided the point of argumentation against more concrete conditions of lordship perceived as unjust: restrictions on common lands, the imposition of taxes, and attempts to reimpose obligations that had fallen into disuse, such as residence requirements or death duties. Servitude was the focus of material and symbolic conflict over human dignity.

In attacking servitude, peasants made use of a vocabulary comprehensible to their masters. What they said was not unthinkable across the divide of class or order and did not derive entirely from an idiosyncratic, peasant way of reasoning about the world.

Conclusion

Harmony and Dissonance

Favorable and unfavorable depictions of the peasant coexisted and interlaced in the period between the eleventh century and the German Peasants' War of 1525. Although contempt was the dominant position of elite observers with regard to rural labor, the dependence of knights and clerics on the peasantry for survival was usually at least grudgingly acknowledged. Beyond such practical realization, the elite expressed an uneasy awareness that by the very fact of their despised lowliness, peasants were advantageously placed in the sight of God.

Some of the apparent contrast among images comes from the differing predispositions of genres (satire versus sermon, for example), but imagery varies *within* genres as well. Thus while *fabliaux* conventionally depicted peasants as stupid, filthy, and gullible, within the *fabliau's* structure and in accord with its purpose as entertainment, it was possible to conceive of a clever and resourceful peasant, one who still fit into an overall image of lowliness that made such nimble inventiveness necessary.

Sermons also simultaneously lauded and blamed rustics. Sermons intended for rural audiences preached acceptance of oppression and praised those who endured their lot patiently while condemning those who questioned the will of God. Here positive and negative images were compatible, differentiated according to whether or not peasants recognized their situation as a spiritual test with deferred benefits. Thus within a particular genre, multiple notions of peasant humanity, savagery, abjectness, and sanctity intersected.

The corpus of peasant representations cannot be reduced to a general statement about "the medieval peasant in the eyes of elite observers." Texts about rustics harbor an indeterminacy.[1] Rather than aiming for a synthesis that obscures the polyphony of this discourse, we should regard these medieval voices as intelligible but not united. Literary texts and others not purporting to be sociologically descriptive have to be related to a social context without being squeezed into a banal center. Texts that in themselves frustrate interpretation or offer apparent contradictions become more coherent when examined along with other works, even those from different genres. That such an approach is appropriate and feasible can be seen in a post-medieval case of comparably various figuration: images of the nineteenth-century Russian peasant included the simple pious representative of the nation's soul, the debased ignorant rustic, and the grasping *kulak*. These were different but not incompatible responses to emancipation and a rediscovery of rural life.[2]

Even within the same author or work, a range of opinions can be seen to fit together, not harmoniously or even dialectically but crudely, inadvertently, allowing spaces for dissent, appropriation, contestation. The didactic poet Hugo von Trimberg is an example of a medieval writer who incorporated a number of different ideas about the nature of peasants without either blatantly contradicting himself or resolving them oversimply. His *Der Renner* stands as a prolix summation of conventional ideas of human sinfulness in relation to the estates of society around 1300, shortly before the conflicts of the fourteenth century moved favorable and unfavorable representations of peasants further apart.

Throughout the poem Hugo laments the mistreatment of rustics, whose meager resources are extorted from them by violence. Their tyrannical masters boast openly of various evil deeds yet are acclaimed as men of honor. Lords who coerce the poor are worse than the devil, for Satan, after all, does not enlist the unwilling in his service as they do.[3] In a passage connecting Christian/pagan and human/animal distinctions, Hugo remarks that even a "wild heathen" would pity a dog so mistreated as are the peasants. Anticipating the *Reformatio Sigismundi*, he recommends that preachers target wicked nobles rather than non-Christians for conversion. The Jews were chastised in Leviticus for mere minor transgressions, yet the greater iniquity of Christians goes unpunished, at least here on earth.[4] Hugo is confident, however, that wickedness will receive its just retribution in the next life, where the nobles will assuredly burn. The poor will find it easier to enter heaven, but they must be patient in this life. He who wishes for heavenly riches must endure earthly misery.[5]

Hugo's protests of nobles' depredations are offset by a more succinct passage in which he moves between images of debasement and piety. As discussed above in connection with Noah's curse, Hugo describes a (probably) imaginary encounter with boorish, idle rustics.[6] He introduces the story of his conversation with the villagers with a flat declaration that peasants are often stubborn and resistant. Were it not that their lords treat them firmly, many would gladly serve the devil.[7]

He rides through the benighted village, where peasants are lying about idly on their stomachs, doing nothing much, "as is their custom." The women are picking lice out of the hair of their men, "searching like animals."[8] Hugo engages in a discussion with the drunken and ignorant villagers in response to their challenge, "How docs it come about that you lords are so much better off than us poor peasants? Are some people bondsmen while others are free?" The story of Ham's transgression convinces the rustics that their lack of freedom has a reason, that they are deservedly cursed. Hugo then has himself assuring his audience that freedom is not so very advantageous and that they are nearest to God's care. Earthly freedom does not last very long, and "you poor people" will enter heaven more easily than those who oversee their labor.[9]

Not only are the peasants unfree by divine decree, but their essential nature has been debased nearly to the level of brute animals. Nevertheless, they are beloved of God, if only they accept their place. Hugo now makes it clear that he is chiefly anxious over the possibility of a blurring of boundaries between peasants and knights. In a series of Aesopian animal stories, Hugo demonstrates the folly of peasants seeking to rise above their station.[10]

The poem thus touches many of the topics we have discussed: the laziness and comical ignorance of peasants, their childish or animal nature, their merited subordination, but also their unjust oppression, their closeness to God. These positions come together in a historical understanding of human sinfulness that explains both the wickedness of lords, which is the legacy of Adam's fall, and the debased lot of the peasants, resulting from Ham's misdeeds. Sin, nevertheless, has a limited dominion and is absorbed into the economy of salvation. Suffering is not in vain, nor will the oppressors escape punishment. With regard to the peasants, the variety of their portrayal is explicable by the movement of sacred history. They were to be understood as accursed in the past, oppressed in the present, and blessed in the future.

Hugo's was neither an unusually comprehensive nor an original view. He harks back to Honorius Augustodunensis, who also made Ham responsible for the debased condition of peasants but nevertheless considered them more likely to be rewarded in the next life.[11] We can paraphrase the argument in terms of themes traced in the preceding chapters: peasants are of a lower order of humanity, base and uncouth in their character and behavior. All humanity derives from Adam and Eve, but peasants are subordinated to their betters by reason of Noah's curse. Only strict control by their lords prevents their base nature from leading them into further mischief. Yet even if their oppression is part of God's will, it is not in itself just. The nobles live off their the rustics' labor and rob them, treating them disgracefully. The peasants are ennobled through their suffering, which, if accepted meekly, will earn them a heavenly crown, for simple and unlearned as they are, they merit God's particular care.

As Hugo and other didactic writers would emphasize and bewail, the fact that peasants have built-in spiritual advantages does not mean that they realize this potentiality. Unfortunately, peasants tend to be ungrateful and disobedient, defying the order of the world rather than obeying God and fulfilling His ordinances. Their singular favor in God's eyes tends to remain theoretical.

Certain arguments are missing from Hugo. He evinces little concern for mutuality among the orders of society, for example. But a harmonious (if multifaceted) image of peasant subordination is still assumed in this poem. The villagers accept with pathetic credulity what Hugo tells them. Later in the fourteenth century and throughout the fifteenth, the image of the pious rustic would be completely separate from that of the savage or ludicrous subhuman, but here in Hugo von Trimberg they are still compatible.

Changes After 1348

The Black Death of 1348 and 1349 was an event of such obvious magnitude that historians tend to ascribe everything that happened for over a century afterward to its influence. One should not simply assume that because traumatic events occurred after the Black Death, they were necessarily caused by it (*post hoc ergo propter hoc*). This is especially the case with the peasant rebellions examined in the last chapter. Whatever degree of significance we ascribe to the epidemic or its repeated visitations, the years between 1350 and 1525 witnessed not only a spate of uprisings but also a new sharpness and urgency in discourse about the peasantry. The Black Death may not have "caused" the insurrections directly, but it did usher in an age of heightened social conflict.

Holding the range of attitudes described above became less feasible. After 1350 the peasants tended to be depicted *either* as sanctified *or* as bestial; as unjustly oppressed *or* as amenable only to coercion (or even as useless). It is as if the links among a variety of conventional views of the peasantry had been broken and the pieces reconstituted separately. We have seen the evolution of Neidhart from comical victim to the vengeful enemy of increasingly boorish peasants, culminating in the Neidhart Fuchs cycle of the fifteenth century. Attitudes of total hostility toward rustics were common in fifteenth-century Germany, such as are expressed in the poem "Edelmannslehre," which recommends that knights pillage and rob peasants, and when they have no money left, slit their throats.[12] Peasants are either no longer useful at all, or useful only if toil can be extracted from them through harsh supervision. They must be "bled" or "trimmed like a willow tree" in order to produce anything.[13]

Felix Hemmerli's *De nobilitate et rusticitate dialogus*, written in the mid–fifteenth century, presents a conversation with peasants that contrasts usefully with that imagined by Hugo von Trimberg. Hemmerli may also have invented this considerably more hostile dialogue, but it has a certain verisimilitude. Interrupting the tirade of a knight against the rustics, Hemmerli suddenly addresses the reader with "here is a true story."[14] While traveling in Baden, Hemmerli dined at an inn where he was forced to listen to a group of peasants "behaving in their usual demented fashion" and roundly denouncing clerical immorality. Prudently waiting until he finished his meal, Hemmerli addressed the hostile audience. The previous day during his travels up the Rhine, he stated, he had seen 24 corpses of thieves who had been broken on the wheel. Not one was a noble or cleric. They were all rustics (and, moreover, from the same village), but if even one had been a member of another estate, his listeners would never cease to attack the wickedness of the upper classes. The few lecherous clerics that the rustics had been castigating were merely following natural human instincts, but the thievery of peasants is both routine and a flagrant violation of nature. At this point, with the peasants increasingly furious, Hemmerli advised his curate that perhaps it was time to depart.[15]

At the same time, denunciations of seigneurial oppression become both more strident and less likely to be offset by counsels to rustic passivity. In this period peasant grievances themselves became at least dimly visible, and not surprisingly, they were less focused on the afterlife than on more immediate justice. Elite denunciations of servitude, such as those found in the *Reformatio Sigismundi* or Erasmus's *Institutio principis Christiani*, pointed to an unalterable natural law that servitude violated, a transgression not to be excused by appeals to either mutuality or a heavenly reward.[16] Also in the late fifteenth and early sixteenth centuries the image of the peasant as pious exemplar gained particular prominence in Germany.[17] At the same time that the Carnival plays, Neidhart poems, and denunciations of peasant wickedness reached the height of their popularity, images such as those of the pious Karsthans or of the Christ-like plowman also took hold. There were certain curious crossovers: Karsthans began as an antipeasant caricature but became an evangelical emblem.[18] Certain authors, such as Hans Rosenplüt, wrote both in praise and in mockery of peasants.[19]

What seems to have fallen into abeyance or at least obscurity in the fifteenth century were the forms that mediated apparently contradictory themes referring to the peasantry. These include the idea of mutuality, the distinction between injustice in this life and a better afterlife, the contrast between peasants' supposed base behavior and God's special care for them, and in general a less optimistic notion of God's immediate governance of the temporal world.

Ideas of mutuality did not drop completely from view. The Three Orders would enjoy a long career and a notable revival in the seventeenth century.[20] What seems to have diminished in the late Middle Ages is confidence in hierarchical stability and the sense of orderly historical change according to divine plan. As long as one could maintain that peasants received something in return for their labor, or that their subordination was in their own interest, even bondage could be excused. Insofar as the theory of mutuality was undermined almost from its inception by a manifestly exploitative reality, a promise of eternal and underlying justice rendered its shortcomings transitory, hence explicable. Mutuality and the justice of the afterlife were thus related sequentially as explanations of contrasting worldly fortunes. Mutuality served as an initial response to inequality, offering a system that was certainly hierarchical but that benefited the lowly whose labor services were recompensed by prayer and protection. To the degree that this exchange did not work fairly (and I have argued that its flaws were always apparent—that the Three Orders was never a hypnotically compelling fantasy), the recompense (and punishment) would take place in eternity. Mutuality was a contract between the peasants and God more than between the orders themselves. Fulfilling their duty of work, even though their masters failed to live up to *their* obligations, the peasants would receive eternal rewards for their labor.

Such explanations for lowliness and oppression served to justify the social order while admitting its defects. They were less confidently asserted after 1350 not only because of the long-recognized shortcomings of the theory of mutuality but because of a change in the timing of the putative recompense. Peasant grievances demand conformity with divine and natural law in the present, temporal world. In the *Reformatio Sigismundi*, as in the doubts expressed by Queen Maria de Luna of Aragon, the moral danger of unjust servitude was not ameliorated by positing a heavenly future when it was to be made right.

The emphasis in both elite and popular discourse on work and the spiritual capital it produces is worth noting in connection with the structuring of peasant demands. It is not so much that work became prized in the Weberian sense, where before it had been despised. Labor had long been credited, if grudgingly, with a certain merit, as expiation and as sacrifice for others, conforming to God's purpose and assured of heavenly recompense; but it would also retain a stigma of punishment, continuing to symbolize the Fall by reason of its physical difficulty and lack of dignity. In the late Middle Ages the merit of work took on an added luster and urgency. The peasants in England in 1381 and in Germany in 1525 used the rhetoric of mutuality not only to protest its ineffectiveness but to assert the spiritual value of labor. The moral superiority of the peasants to their masters was to be recognized, not in a heavenly future but immediately. This was not a chiliastic expectation of God's justice appearing as an end to history, but a reordering of lordship and tenancy to end the arbitrary extraction of wealth from the rural laborers and to restore some relationship between labor and reward. Spiritual rewards were not rejected; this was not a dispute over the consolations of religion. Rather, in a pattern of appropriation typical for the period, the widely acknowledged spiritual merit of the toiling peasantry was turned to justify rebellion.

As argued previously, the late-medieval peasant movements did not so much invent a new political or moral vocabulary as use already existing, commonplace ideas, such as the dignity of labor or the closeness of rustics to God, in a more immediate fashion. Ideas of difference, justice, and recompense were medieval representations of a dynamic social world, not merely after-the-fact rationales or hegemonic constructs. They were, in Roger Chartier's words, "constituents of social reality"; not external ideologies but part of the elaboration of social reality itself.[21]

Hegemony or Appropriation

The belief that different representations of peasants constitute social meaning justifies the forgoing elaboration of images separately as parts of a large vocabulary. I am nowhere near arguing that texts are in themselves the only form of socially intelligible action. They do influence historical events and the mentalities of historical actors, however. More than that, as opposed merely to affecting social status, opinions, images, and rhetorical formulations in some sense *produce* it through law, justifications, confidence in the way things are organized, or resistance to unfavorable change.[22]

The historian Helmut Smith has pointed to a strong and a weak manner of maintaining what he calls "the productive quality of discourse." I would adhere to the weak side of this particular estimate of the significance of language; that is, I believe that texts do have some influence on social reality beyond the influence that they exert simply as evidence or documentation. A strong version would see the text as the only reality, as completely self-referential, with no world "out there" to which it pertains.[23]

One could maintain the strong opinion were one convinced that reality revealed itself only through hopelessly distorted texts, or that any apparent intelligibility was imposed on it by the interests of the powerful for whom most of these texts were elaborated. However contingent our understanding of the past, its material remains (documentary and archaeological) are valid within limits. Modesty and tentativeness are preferable to wholesale rejection of the factual basis of historical records, of their reliability for reconstructing a vanished world external to its textual remains.

I have tried, in Michel de Certeau's words, to "circulate around acquired rationalizations"—to examine medieval explanations for subordination and difference across the grain of likeness (especially religious likeness) and ultimate equality.[24] I have done so with a belief that these images can be understood but also that they fit together to form an idea system, one whose very complexity and even awkwardness gave it malleability.

To what degree could medieval peasants contest the terms that described who they were and that justified their subordination? This question comes up against two tendencies of contemporary thought about peasants and other subaltern groups, one emphasizing their agency, the other insisting on the power of hegemonic discourses.

At one time the peasant was regarded as helpless, passive, and outside the movement of modernity (whether that modernity was represented in Marxist or capitalist terms).[25] This pessimistic assessment has been superseded by a positive evaluation of peasant culture and peasant agency. Rather than being seen as affected by but not creative of history, peasants now tend to be regarded by both historians and anthropologists as possessing a coherent, well-articulated worldview, as having rational goals and even a certain confidence in their abilities to influence their circumstances. This perspective has been especially noteworthy in consideration of the ability of peasants to resist landlords and state powers that, from the official records, seem to dominate them. Everyday forms of peasant resistance provide a less visible but, it is thought, more effective means of assertion and contestation than insurrections. Evasion, foot-dragging, and subversion of plans dictated from above resourcefully deflect the plans of those supposedly in charge, postponing or going around the forces of enterprise, "rationalization," or technological change that would displace or further subordinate them.[26] For the Middle Ages, the fact that peasants were effectively in charge of specific pieces of land—that the lords' supervision could not be consistent or close, given the fragmented nature of lordship and communication—has led some observers to consider peasants sufficiently powerful to render the seigneurial system of their exploitation marginal or irrelevant.

Attention to agency also includes a more favorable estimation of the peasants' ability to understand their situation and to create a specifically peasant discourse and action.[27] This ability can take the form of resistance, direct or indirect, but is more a somewhat hidden form of knowledge than a strategy. In his study of Tanganyika/Tanzania in the last decades of British rule, Steven Feierman points out that the myth of the intellectually underdeveloped peasant survives because of the failure of most peasant movements, but these failures are due more to circumstance than to some innate weakness of conception or structure.[28]

Such views conflict with the opinion that the subordinate classes in general have been slow to act by reason of the power of the dominant discourse, a conceptual and intellectual construct in certain respects backed up by physical force, but so successful as to have created a form of false consciousness whereby notions of hierarchy, deference, and legitimacy of exploitation are accepted by their victims even without visible coercion. Antonio Gramsci's concept of hegemony has been adopted and modified by observers of modern state and class power. Here too, however, "strong" and "weak" versions have been enunciated (James Scott refers to them respectively as "thick" and "thin"). In the strong conception of hegemony and false consciousness, the elite has a grip of such strength (through institutions such as educational and religious systems) that the subordinate fully, even enthusiastically accept the way things are. In the weak conception, subordinate people take a fatalistic or "realistic" view of the situation as somehow natural. In this sense, according to Bourdieu, "every established order tends to produce . . . the naturalization of its own arbitrariness."[29]

James Scott has shown, to my mind convincingly, the flaws of both the strong and weak versions of hegemony and false consciousness by emphasizing the need of dominant elites to devise a rationale for the social order, their vulnerability to having these rationales used against them, and the sheer quantity and frequency of resistance. With regard to this last point, Scott remarks that it is the exaggeration of their own power by subordinate groups that needs explaining—their tendency to overestimate their opportunities—not their passivity or a perceived irresistibility of power.[30]

Our perception of hegemony, in Scott's opinion, stems in large measure from the nature of our sources, which obviously foreground what he calls "the official transcript" rather than what the mass of people really thought. It also comes from the desire to find "real revolutionaries" with an ideology that breaks completely from that of the dominant classes rather than the cautious, even reactionary formulations of those who remonstrate in the name of established values ("traditionalist" or "primitive" rebels). Scott takes issue with scholars, such as Barrington Moore, who consider grievances over failure to abide by a social contract inferior to those relatively rare contestations of the right of an elite class to exist.[31] The version of false consciousness expressed in this view is also disputed by Scott on the grounds that protests based on agreed-upon principles of rule are more plausible and compelling than inventing entirely new concepts of society. The public presentation of claims may not conform to the deepest preferences of the rebels, but one should not mistake prudence for ethical submission. Seemingly naive beliefs, such as the Russian peasants' expressed faith in a tsar who would deliver them from oppression, have been shown to be effective, adaptable ways of legitimating resistance to authority as it was actually constituted by referring to a seemingly conservative ideal.[32] In the Middle Ages, attacks on Jews or lepers and the often related phenomenon of popular crusades, such as the Pastoureaux of 1320, functioned as disguised attacks on the crown. Far from being spontaneous outbreaks manifesting a growing irrationality, the Shepherds' Crusade and similar movements deployed an exaggerated and violent piety to further specific political and fiscal rebellion.[33]

Claims by rulers that the idea system justifying their position serves the interests of all can ultimately legitimate resistance when the elites fail to live up to those claims.[34] In the context of medieval and early-modern insurrections, an "Old Law" argument could serve to inspire thoroughly radical forms of protest. As Scott remarks, "Whether he believes the rules or not, only a fool would fail to appreciate the possible benefits of deploying such readily available ideological resources."[35] Peasants need not have bought into the dominant rationales in order to make use of them. As argued in the previous chapter, medieval peasant rebellions did make use of the "ideological resources" at hand. The available discourse in this case afforded opportunities for both internal justifications by peasants themselves and plausible external structuring of grievances.

Of course not all opposition leads to defiance. Such low-key expressions of dissatisfaction as gossip, grumbling, and satire can perfectly well accord with deference and even bolster the terms of the dominant discourse.[36] More explicitly supportive of that discourse are what Christine Pelzer White refers to as "everyday forms of peasant collaboration."[37] One should not depict all forms of uncooperative or antisocial behavior as "resistance," or romanticize resistance, or minimize the internal dissensions within communities.[38] Peasants did not form a unified force nor define themselves in terms of a binary opposition between themselves and their lords.

Neither, on the other hand, is there an obvious line between complicitous and subversive behavior: one can easily lead to the other as, for example, in forms of local gossip.[39] Similarly, there is no fixed boundary between traditionalist and radical peasant movements. Irwin Scheiner identified some 2,809 peasant rebellions that occurred during the Tokugawa period of Japanese history (along with about 1,000 "riots"), ranging from petitions, to small-scale symbolic violence, to "world renewal rebellions." Although the differences of scale, anger, and ambition among these rebellious activities are obvious, Scheiner found no line between traditional versus "truly radical" uprisings.[40]

If medieval peasants (and peasants generally) were less passive and accepting than once thought, neither was the elite so tenacious or confident at all times in defense of a supposedly hegemonic vision. This is not to argue that they were somehow "tolerant" or progressive, but to assert that their discourse about peasants contains fissures, doubts, and points that could be appropriated by their subordinates. Elite and popular worlds were not closed off from each other. Ideas could be regarded differentially—for example, opinions differed on whether the original equality of humanity remained valid in the present—but the dialogue about such issues was mutually comprehensible. No clear frontier between learned and popular culture existed, if only because there were intermediate levels of discourse (vernacular sermons, for example). Moreover, positing such a frontier accepts too readily the statements (such as those of the clergy) of the debased condition of rural piety and practice.

Roger Chartier has effectively criticized the overall notion of a completely separate popular culture, emphasizing the ability of popular movements to shape according to different goals and strategies the ideas and justifications of the elite.[41] For the Middle Ages, such interchange has been accepted by Le Goff and rather more enthusiastically defended by Gurevich.[42] In a study of late-medieval Soria in Old Castile, John Edwards concludes that opinions and ideas flowed between learned and uneducated, and did so in both directions.[43] In Metz, by the year 1200, pious lay men and women had French translations of numerous books, including Gregory's *Moralia in Job*.[44] It was possible for information about ideas and texts to be widespread without individual knowledge or practice or reading.[45]

Peasants were therefore neither cowed nor entirely unaware of their situation. It remains questionable, however, to what extent their agenda can be recovered, especially for the distant past. My primary interest in this study has been to look at how peasants were regarded by the articulate classes above them. Nevertheless, I have also tried to show connections between the images applied to them and their own conceptions and movements, thus bringing up the question of how the opinions and voice of such people can be recovered without gross distortion, sentimentality, or false claim to speak for the silenced.[46]

A goal of this book has been to show that there was a certain structure of elite thought about the peasant. This amounted to a discourse across genre, a "register" in Zumthor's terms, a "polyhedron of intelligibility" in Foucault's locution, something with many facets but with an internal consistency.[47] At the same time, such consistency was achieved at the cost of recognizing certain tensions: between the peasant as subhuman and the peasant as God's special concern; between original equality and present difference; between mutuality as an ideal and its failure in practice. These tensions amounted to something more than occasional or involuntary admissions that an otherwise hegemonic representation might be flawed. Medieval observers saw that there were problems with regarding the peasants as removed from common humanity, and with reconciling the New Testament to the reality of social hierarchy. They traced out paradoxes of equality and subordination, of punishment and divine favor. Internal tensions increased in the late Middle Ages, eventually provoking a division between the peasant regarded as licitly subjugated and the peasant as spiritually elevated by suffering. But at no time were elites completely unified, confident, or single-minded in asserting the naturalness or unquestionable moral validity of those aspects of the social structure, especially servitude, that seemed to contradict minimal notions of Christian equality.

I have also suggested, without minimizing the autonomous thought patterns of medieval peasants, that they and their spokesmen could appropriate to their own ends commonplace statements and shared assumptions about God in relation to society, statements and assumptions that in the dominant discourse were used to justify domination based on a supposed mutuality.

The Peasant as "Other"

Ultimately the existence of a complex system of representation may be said to degrade the peasants, if for no other reason than that they did not occupy the subject position in such discourse: peasants were perceived as objects of their masters' discourses, as "other" in relation to the powerful, not as autonomous actors. But I would question the reach and utility of the term "Other" in this context. The Middle Ages is hardly known for its tolerance, and indeed a considerable amount of recent research has rediscovered just how many groups— Jews, lepers, homosexuals, Muslims, "monstrous races"—were demonized.[48] In keeping with a change in how the modern era is viewed (with less confidence in its supposed inclusiveness and in the march of progress), the medieval is now often seen as the origin of a "bad modern," including European expansionism, repression of difference, and a colonial or enslaving mentality.[49]

Occasionally, an open, pluralist "good" Middle Ages (with the twelfth century as its high point) is contrasted with a rigid, authoritarian, intolerant scholastic and late-medieval era.[50]

The concept of the Other has been used in the context of sudden discoveries of new and troubling worlds.[51] It has had an even more extensive run as a process ("Othering") by which more or less familiar strangers, the exotic, or those standing in the way of progress are represented as inferior, primitive, degenerate, or even alluring. Their otherness is "invented" by being structured as radically different from an unexamined but anxiously defended "normalcy."[52] The concept has also been applied to representations of sexuality, race, and gender within cultures and nations.[53] Alterity itself and how it is presented and shaped are the subjects of a theoretical literature and are especially prominent in critiques of anthropological objectivity.[54]

Several problems stem from too sweeping (or inclusive) an application of the concept of "the Other" to medieval society. In the first place it becomes a reified concept in itself, the "fetishization of alterity" that imposes a convenient name on a more complex reality.[55] It also tends to reinforce the dominant culture's self-image by referring everything to it by way of comparison. This monolithic system of reference obscures the relation between different marginal groups, such as Jews and Muslims under Christian rule in Iberia, reducing them to mere categories within the exercise of state power.[56]

A totalizing notion of the Other also fails to discriminate among groups regarded or constructed as different. This is especially the case in the context of the Middle Ages, with its panoply of othering discourses. One must distinguish those "others" completely outside the orbit of everyday medieval European life: the monstrous races or the dimly perceived inhabitants of India, Ethiopia, or sub-Saharan Africa. The "monsters" were most obviously an invented other in the purest sense, resulting from acts of the imagination. Peoples more proximate but religiously alien—Jews and Muslims—were regarded along different axes depending on whether they lived across a frontier, appeared powerful and threatening, or were considered subordinated tributaries. Lepers were both more radically different and yet, by virtue of their origin, similar to those who segregated them.

All of these people could be represented as troubling, subhuman, dangerous, if at some level part of a divine plan. Imagined races were related to the apocalyptic prophecies of the Book of Revelation, or their possible salvation was taken as evidence of the reach of the Gospel (as in the famous depiction of the Pentecost on the sculpted tympanum of Vézelay, which shows the apostles preaching to pygmies, big-eared people, and dog-headed people). Lepers, too, were objects of both fear and redemptive ambitions. The Jews figured in the divine plan retrospectively but also prospectively, for their conversion would herald the arrival of the millennium.

When considering European peasants and women, however, we are dealing with groups so obviously numerous that they could not be literally marginal. Language used to describe other despised peoples could be applied to them (as in the crossover use of Noah's curse, for example), but clearly they constitute an "Other" very different from distant or religiously different peoples. Women and peasants counted at most as "proximate others," not only because of their physical closeness to those who dominated society but because of their secular necessity.[57] While they were, like Jews and lepers, vaguely part of some divine unfolding, peasants and women also underpinned society in the temporal world in a unique and indispensable way.

Discourse about peasants and women therefore oscillated violently among three poles: unfavorable alterity, similarity, and favorable dissimilarity. The terms of this constant shifting differed for the two groups: for women, beauty and defilement, misogyny and adoration, sexuality and virginity; for peasants (peasant women being subject to all vocabularies), bestiality and childlike simplicity, stupidity and cleverness, intractability and pliant patience. The dominant discourse figured both women and peasants, however, in terms of embodiment and earthiness, as divinely favored, as requiring coercive control, and as paradoxically equal yet subordinate.

The dominant culture of any society, including the medieval, does not simply classify with confidence or consistency those whom it regards as different. There are some "differences" that it must deal with. It can do this by a compulsive proliferation of negative stereotypes.[58] In that very proliferation, however, the internal consistency of vision and purpose is strained, and its complexity contains within it its own contestation.

~~~~

Although the peasant has not disappeared from the rural world in the way that both Marxist and capitalist theories predicted, in Western Europe the peasantry has become vestigial or nonexistent. This is a relatively recent phenomenon in France, Spain, and Italy. The impact of mechanization, consumer culture, consolidation of holdings, and the decline of protective tariffs has decimated the rural agricultural population in recent decades. This process has been felt with a sense of loss, especially in France, where the emptying of the productive countryside, though well under way by the end of the nineteenth century, accelerated in the 1950s.[59] Fernand Braudel, at the end of his final great work, *The Identity of France*, observed: "To my mind the spectacle that overshadows all others, in the France of the past and even today, is the collapse of a peasant society. . . . An ancient peasant France, a France of bourgs, villages, hamlets, and scattered houses survived more or less unchanged until at least 1914 and some would say 1945."[60] The very identity of France and its regions is at issue, a nation of 120 cheeses, in De Gaulle's famous words. The disappearance of the peasantry is set off against the threat of Americanization or globalization. It has been lamented in the popular press, in songs, and throughout the earnest debate that characterizes French public culture.[61]

In a world that by and large celebrates technological progress and what are perceived as improved living standards, the disappearance of the class that undergirded European society for its medieval and modern centuries should provoke ambivalence. The peasant, even in eclipse, represents the human, the natural, the organic nation.

Reference Matter

Notes

Introduction

1. La Bruyère, *Les caractères*, no. 128 (4) (p. 339): "Certains animaux farouches, des mâles et des femelles, répandues par la campagne, noirs, livides et tout brûlés du soleil, attachés à la terre qu'ils fouillent et qu'ils remuent avec une opiniâtré invincible; ils ont comme une voix articulée, et quand ils se lèvent sur leurs pieds, ils montrent une face humaine, et en effet ils sont des hommes."

2. Levi, *Christ Stopped at Eboli*, p. 3.

3. General treatments of the social and economic position of the medieval peasantry include Duby, *Rural Economy*; Rösener, *Peasants in the Middle Ages*; Genicot, *Rural Communities*; and Fossier, *Peasant Life*.

4. Blankenburg, *Der Vilain*; Reich, *Beiträge zur Kenntnis*.

5. Galpin, *Cortois and Vilain*.

6. Gudde, *Social Conflicts*.

7. Coulton, *Medieval Village*.

8. Hügli, *Der deutsche Bauer im Mittelalter*; Martini, *Das Bauerntum*.

9. Heald, "Peasant in Medieval German Literature"; Schüppert, "Der Bauer in der deutschen Literatur des Spätmittelalters"; Ebner, "Der Bauer." These writers were primarily concerned with the degree to which literary or historical works give an accurate or "realistic" account of peasant life and material culture.

10. For this, see Jonin, "La révision d'un topos."

11. Louis Althusser's definition, as cited in Vovelle, *Ideologies and Mentalities*, p. 2.

12. Zumthor, *Le masque et la lumière*, p. 51.

13. Vovelle, *Ideologies and Mentalities*, p. 11.

14. Freedman, *Origins of Peasant Servitude*.

15. I owe this observation to Professor Ihor Ševčenko, of Harvard University, whose help I gratefully acknowledge.

16. Le Goff, "Les paysans et le monde rural," translated as "Peasants and the

Rural World," in Le Goff, *Time, Work, and Culture*, quotation from p. 88 of the English version.

17. Greenblatt, "Murdering Peasants," especially pp. 11, 21.

18. A curious and rather extensive journal by a Tuscan peasant of the fifteenth century has survived, but it deals for the most part with financial accounts: *La zappa e la retorica*. For this information I am grateful to Paolo Squattriti, of the University of Michigan, who is preparing an English translation of this work.

19. Schmitt, *Holy Greyhound*, p. 171.

20. Le Goff, "Le vocabulaire des catégories sociales"; Lavilla Martín, *La imagen del siervo en el pensamiento de San Francisco*.

21. Definitions of the contemporary peasantry may be found in Eric Wolf, *Peasants*, pp. 1–7; and *Peasants and Peasant Societies*, pp. 14–17 (Shanin's introduction). A multifaceted meditation on the subject is Shanin, *Defining Peasants*.

22. On slavery in relation to unfree peasantries, see the collection *Serfdom and Slavery*.

23. Maddicott, *English Peasantry*, p. 68.

24. M. Bloch, *Feudal Society*, pp. 255–74; Fourquin, *Lordship and Feudalism*, pp. 173–83; Freedman, *Origins of Peasant Servitude*, pp. 4–18; and Hilton, *Decline of Serfdom*.

25. On the Latin terms used in the early Middle Ages, see Köbler, "'Bauer' (*agricola, colonus, rusticus*)."

26. Conte, *Servi medievali*.

27. Stackmann, "Bezeichnungen für 'Bauer,'" especially p. 160.

28. Wenskus, "'Bauer'—Begriff und historische Wirklichkeit."

29. Hilton, *Decline of Serfdom*, pp. 15–19. On Anglo-Saxon slavery, see Pelteret, *Slavery in Early Mediaeval England*.

30. Batany, "Les pauvres et la pauvreté."

31. Le Goff, *Time, Work, and Culture*, p. 94.

32. Bosl, "Potens und Pauper."

33. Ibid., p. 123.

34. Le Goff, "Le vocabulaire des catégories sociales," p. 104.

35. Mollat, *Poor in the Middle Ages*, pp. 193–293; Geremek, *Margins of Society*.

36. On the distinction between *laboratores*, those with no land or less than a full holding, and *masoverii*, who could support themselves from their tenements, see Bois, *Crisis of Feudalism*, pp. 179–87; Hilton, "Reasons for Inequality"; and Rösener, *Peasants in the Middle Ages*, pp. 191–207.

Chapter 1

1. "Der Bauernlob" ("Das Gedicht vom ersten Edelmann"), published in two versions, one in Tettau, "Über einige bis jetzt unbekannte Erfurter Drucke," pp. 319–25; and one in Weller, "Gedicht vom ersten Edelmann," pp. 231–38. The passage below is from Tettau's edition, p. 322:

Wer uns der Pauer nit geborn,
wer pawet uns den weitz und das korn,
Und auch dartzu den guten wein,
darbey wir offt gar frölich sein?

2. Ordericus Vitalis, *Ecclesiastical History* 2: 52, cited in Constable, *Three Studies*, p. 316.

3. Thomas of Wimbledon, cited in Aers, *Community, Gender, and Individual Identity*, p. 33.

4. Caggese, "La Repubblica di Siena," p. 84: "Ad hoc ut status civium per comitatum et comitatinos utilius conserventur, quorum comitatus comitationorum conservatio est augmentatio civitatis cum exinde et victualia proveniat et fertilitas oportuna."

5. Abbo of Fleury, *Liber apologeticus*, in *PL* 139: 464: "Primo de virorum ordine, id est de laicis, dicendum est, quod alii sunt agricolae, alii agonistae, et agricolae quidem insudant agricultorae et diversis artibus in opere rustico, unde sustentatur totius Ecclesiae multitudo; agonistae vero, contenti stipendis militiae . . . omni sagacite expugnant adversarios sanctae Dei Ecclesiae."

6. Mostert, *Political Theology of Abbo of Fleury*, pp. 93, 103; Duby, *Three Orders*, p. 90.

7. Duby, *Three Orders*, p. 108.

8. Aelfric, *Colloquy*, p. 39: "Agricultura, quia arator nos omnes pascit." A discussion of Aelfric's scheme of society is provided in Ruffing, "Labor Structure of Aelfric's *Colloquy*," but Ruffing deals more with the monastic understanding of useful occupations than with relations among social orders.

9. Wulfstan, *Die "Institutes of Polity, Civil and Ecclesiastical,"* pp. 55–56.

10. Aelfric, *Colloquy*, p. 21. On this passage see Pelteret, *Slavery in Early Mediaeval England*, pp. 64–66.

11. Aelfric, *Letter to Sigeward* and *Passio Machabeorum*, as described in E. Anderson, "Social Idealism in Aelfric's *Colloquy*," p. 157.

12. On the date of the *Gesta*, see Oexle, "Die 'Wirklichkeit' und das 'Wissen,'" pp. 74–76.

13. Adalbero of Laon, *Poème au roi Robert.* The *Carmen* may date from as early as 1010 and probably dates from no later than 1031. See Constable, *Three Studies*, p. 283 n. 130; and Oexle, "Adalbero von Laon," p. 635.

14. As noted by Oexle, "Le travail au XIe siècle," pp. 53–55. In fact, according to Jacques Le Goff, the term *laboratores* at the time of Adalbero meant not just agricultural workers but those at the higher levels of the peasantry who farm a property that produces a surplus and who are thus productive from the vantage of those who receive revenues from their profitable labor: Le Goff, *Time, Work and Culture*, p. 57; idem, "Le travail dans les systèmes de valeur," pp. 16–17.

15. Adalbero of Laon, *Poème au roi Robert*, vv. 290–93 (p. 22):

Nam valet ingenuus sine seruis uiuere nullus.
Cum labor occurit sumptus et habere peroptant,

Rex et pontifices seruus seruire uidentur.
Pascitur a seruo dominus quem pascere sperat.

16. Augustine, *De civitate Dei* 19.14, cited in Oexle, "Le travail au XIe siècle,"
p. 54.

17. Adalbero of Laon, *Poème au roi Robert*, vv. 286–88 (p. 22).

18. Wernher de Gartenaere, *Helmbrecht*, vv. 543–60 (pp. 36–38).

19. *Buch der Rügen*, vv. 1457–62 (p. 86):

Liebiu kint, sît staete vrô:
mit iuwerr reinen arbeit
spist ir alle kristenheit.
dar an belîbet staet:
swer iu iht ander raet,
der wil iuch vêrkeren,

(Dear children, you are
of fortunate rank. With
your pure work you feed
all of Christendom; thus
yours is a beloved estate.
Whoever tells you other-
wise wishes to deceive
you.)

20. Hans Rosenplüt, "Der Baurn Lob," in *Der Bauer im deutschen Liede*, pp.
109–12; also in *Quellen zur Geschichte des deutschen Bauernstandes*, no. 217, pp. 549–
52. Although primarily concerned with Rosenplüt's epigrammatic poetry, Reichel's
Der Spruchdichter Hans Rosenplüt is the only recently published general work on this
writer.

21. *Quellen zur Geschichte des deutschen Bauernstandes*, no. 219, p. 555.

22. Ibid., no. 177, p. 465.

23. *Meisterlieder der Kolmarer Handschrift*, song no. 71, vv. 8–10 (BLVS 68, p.
378): "den frumen bûman ich dem priester allezît gelîche, / Wan er uns neret vor des
hungers freisen / mit sînem pfluog sîn arbeit ûz der erde guot."

24. *Historical Poems of the XIVth and XVth Centuries*, no. 35, pp. 97–98.

25. *Drei deutsche Minoritenprediger*, pp. 88, 90.

26. Étienne de Fougères, *Le livre des manières*, vv. 693–704 (pp. 84–85).

27. Enguerrard de Monstrelet, *Chronique*, chap. 273 (p. 387):

Hélas! hélas! hélas! hélas!
Prélats, princes, et bons seigneurs,
Bourgeois, marchans et advocats,
Gens de mestiers grans et mineurs,
Gens d'armes, et les trois estats,

> Qui vivez sur nous laboureurs,
> Confortez nous d'aucun bon ayde:
> Vivre nous fault, c'est le remède.

28. Gower, *Vox clamantis*, bk. 1, vv. 2093–96 (p. 79):

> Sic cum rusticitas fuerat religata cathenis
> Et paciens nostro subiacet illa pede,
> Ad iuga bos rediit, que sub aruis semen aratis
> Creuit, et a bello rusticus ipse silet.

The translation is Stockton's, in Gower, *Major Latin Works*, p. 94.

29. Oswald von Wolkenstein, *Die Lieder*, no. 112, vv. 172–74 (p. 276); no. 39, v. 34 (p. 130); no. 44, vv. 45–48 (p. 145), cited in Classen, "Peasant Life and Peasant Reality," pp. 86–87.

30. This account is by the fourteenth-century jurist Bertran de Ceva, as repeated by Joan de Socarrats in 1476, edited in Freedman, "Catalan Lawyers," apps. 3 and 4 (pp. 313–14); also in Freedman, *Church, Law and Society*, no. 14. See below, Chapter 5, pp. 116–17.

31. *Monumenta rusticorum in Hungaria rebellium*, no. 202, p. 260: "Item quamquam omnes rustici, qui adversus dominos eorum naturales insurrexerunt, tanquam proditores capitali pena sint plectendi, ne tamen tot sanguinis efusio adhuc sequatur et omnis rusticitas, sine qua nobilitas parum valet, deleatur."

32. Duby, *Three Orders*; Oexle, "Die funktionale Dreiteilung"; idem, "Deutungsschemata"; and Constable, "Orders of Society," in his *Three Studies*, pp. 251–350. Also significant is Niccoli, *I sacerdoti, i guerrieri, i contadini*.

33. Peter the Chanter, *De oratione et speciebus illius,*, pp. 224–26, cited in Constable, *Three Studies*, p. 319.

34. These lifestyles and roles are described and related to the three functional social orders in Constable, "Orders of Society," in his *Three Studies*, pp. 251–350.

35. Dumézil, *Mythe et épopée*; idem, *Les Dieux souverains des Indo-Européens*; Dubuisson, "Le roi indo-européen"; Le Goff, "Les trois fonctions indo-européennes"; and Rouche, "De l'Orient à l'Occident."

36. In Germany, for example, it is found in the German didactic poets Freidank and Hugo von Trimberg and the sermons attributed to Berthold von Regensburg; see Hügli, *Der deutsche Bauer im Mittelalter*, pp. 64–65. For the use of the Three Orders by the laity, especially in the early-modern era, see Niccoli, *I sacerdoti, i guerrieri, i contadini*, pp. 35–124.

37. Iogna-Prat, "Le 'baptême' du schéma"; Ortigues, "Haymon d'Auxerre." Duby, *Three Orders*, p. 109, did mention Haimo of Auxerre, but only as a figure anticipating the "revelation" of the fully developed theory in Adalbero of Laon and Gerard of Cambrai.

38. Oexle, "Deutungsschemata," pp. 94–95.

39. Duby, *Three Orders*, p. 177. A similarly reductionist view is found in the

works of Carozzi, Rouche, and others writing on this subject at the time Duby's *Three Orders* appeared (see Oexle, "Deutungsschemata," pp. 76–77).

40. Gurevich, "Medieval Culture and *Mentalité*," pp. 37–40. Also see Oexle, "Die 'Wirklichkeit' und das 'Wissen,'" pp. 81–84.

41. Oexle, "Deutungsschemata," pp. 76–83; idem, "Le travail au XIe siècle," pp. 57–58; idem, "Die 'Wirklichkeit' und das 'Wissen,'" pp. 80–84.

42. Oexle, "Le travail au XIe siècle," p. 58: "Autrement dit, on ne peut pas exclure que les *bellatores* et même les *laboratores* aient partagé une telle interprétation des structures sociales et de leur rôle à l'intérieur de la société."

43. Oexle, "Deutungsschemata," pp. 90–105.

44. Adalbero of Laon, *Poème au roi Robert*, vv. 286–88, 294 (p. 22). See below, Chapter 2, note 6.

45. Duby, *Three Orders*, pp. 274–85, 319–21.

46. These laments are discussed below in Chapter 2.

47. The ancient world did not have a completely negative opinion of agriculture. The Stoics, for example, conceived of agricultural labor in positive terms, but their intention was more to praise the simple life than to extol productive labor in itself. See van den Hoven, *Work in Ancient and Medieval Thought*, pp. 38–49. For the "Carolingian Renaissance of labor," see Le Goff, *Time, Work, and Culture*, pp. 83–86.

48. Le Goff, "Pour une étude de travail," p. 22.

49. Holdsworth, "Blessings of Work," p. 63, also see p. 72 in connection with Guerric of Igny's statement "labor in actione, fructus seu merces in contemplatione."

50. Issac of Stella, "Sermo L in Nativitate Petri et Pauli," in his *Sermones* (*PL* 194: 1858), cited in Holdsworth, "Blessings of Work," p. 62.

51. Bernard of Clairvaux, "Sermo in Feria IV Hebdomadae Sanctae."

52. Aelred of Rievaulx, *Speculum caritatis* 2.15 (CC Continuatio medievalis 1, p. 83), cited in Holdsworth, "Blessings of Work," p. 63.

53. On the lay brethren, see Lekai, *Cistercians*, pp. 334–46; and Newman, *Boundaries of Charity*, pp. 101–6.

54. Although not to the degree often assumed. See Alfonso, "Cistercians and Feudalism." The difficulties experienced by educated monks engaging in field work is illustrated by William of St. Thierry's account of Saint Bernard weeping because he didn't know how to cut wheat; cited in Holdsworth, "Blessings of Work," p. 63.

55. Conrad of Eberbach, *Exordium magnum*, dist. 4, chap. 18 (*PL* 185, pt. 2, 1106–10). Also in Herbert, *De miraculis*, bk. 1, chap. 15 (*PL* 185, pt. 2, 1291–92).

56. As is pointed out by Martha G. Newman in "Crucified by the Virtues." I am very grateful to Professor Newman for her advice concerning the Cistercian miracle stories. On the lay brothers, see Hallinger, "Woher kommen die Laienbrüder?"; and Lescher, "Lay Brothers."

57. Goswin of Villers, *Vita Arnulfi*, bk. 1, chap. 4 (especially pp. 563–64).

58. Herbert, *De miraculis*, bk. 1, chap. 29 (*PL* 185, pt. 2, 1301–3), cited in Lekai, *Cistercians*, p. 338; Newman, "Crucified by the Virtues."

59. Conrad of Eberbach, *Exordium magnum* 5.10 (*PL* 185, pt. 2, 1140–44), cited in Newman, "Crucified by the Virtues."

60. Le Goff, "Le travail dans les systèmes de valeur," pp. 15–20.

61. Ibid., p. 21.

62. Ibid., pp. 7–8; Le Goff, *Time, Work, and Culture*, pp. 77–79, 87–97.

63. Van den Hoven, *Work in Ancient and Medieval Thought*, pp. 233–37.

64. Le Goff, "Le travail dans les systèmes de valeur," pp. 4–13; idem, *Time, Work, and Culture*, pp. 73–79.

65. Camille, "When Adam Delved," pp. 270–72.

66. Ovitt, "Cultural Context of Western Technology," pp. 79–80.

67. Constable, "Interpretation of Martha and Mary," in his *Three Studies*, pp. 1–141.

68. Elias, *Civilizing Process*, pp. 206–12.

69. J. Alexander, "*Labeur* and *Paresse*." For the combination of lowliness and productivity in the Berry Book of Hours see below, Chapter 6, p. 144.

70. As correctives to this tendency, see Holzapfel, *Die sittliche Wertung*; and Ovitt, "Cultural Context of Western Technology," pp. 71–94.

71. Le Goff, "Le travail dans les systèmes de valeur," pp. 7–8.

72. Honorius Augustodunensis, *Elucidarium* 2.61 (p. 429). On this passage see below, Chapter 9, note 71. On Honorius and his extensive output, see editor Lefèvre's introductory remarks, especially pp. 191–230 and 259–329. See also the articles by Flint now collected in her *Ideas in the Medieval West* and her recent *Honorius Augustodunensis of Regensburg*. See also Gottschall, *Das "Elucidarium" des Honorius Augustodunensis*.

73. Honorius Augustodunensis, *Imago mundi* 3.1 (p. 125).

74. Berthold von Regensburg, *Vollständige Ausgabe seiner Predigten* 2: 14: "Sô woltest dû gerne ein ritter sîn, sô muost dû ein gebûre sîn unde muost uns bûwen korn und wîn. Wer solte uns den acker bûwen, ob ir alle herren waeret?" That the vernacular sermons attributed to Berthold were probably written by later writers seems to be widely acknowledged. See the long note and bibliography in Fössel, *Die Ortlieber*, pp. 24–25. I am grateful to Professor Robert Lerner, of Northwestern University, for this information.

75. *Drei deutsche Minoritenprediger*, p. 88: "Quintum genus per quintum filium figuratur, ut sunt agricole, qui tam dilecti filii Dei sunt tam propter laborem continuum, qui Deo placet, tam propter oppresionem, qua a dominus opprimuntur iniuste. . . . Sed lamentabile nimis est, quod multi inter eos damnantur." p. 90: "Rustici, qui frumenta laborant, estu uruntur, gelu frigent, de quorum laboribus uiuit omnis populus; [si] cauerent isti sibi de furto, mendacio, periurio et his similibus, sancti fierent."

76. *Buch der Rügen*, vv. 1479–82 (p. 87):

> sô hât iu unser herre bereit
> nâch iuwer grôzer arbeit
> in sînem himelrîche ruo:
> dâ bring uns got alle zuo.

(So has our Lord a place
prepared for you after your
great work, in His heav-
enly peace, when God
brings us all to Him.)

77. *Die poetische Bearbeitung des Buches Daniel,* vv. 1777–1830 (pp. 28–29). See also Martini, *Das Bauerntum,* p. 225.

78. Jacques de Vitry, "Sermo ad agricolas et vinitores et alios operarios," *Sermones vulgares,* in Welter, *L'exemplum,* p. 458. The translation is from Wunderli, *Peasant Fires,* p. 35.

79. Barney, "Plowshare of the Tongue,"p. 269. On the plow and the pious peasant, see also Burdach, *Der Dichter des Ackermann aus Böhmen* 1: 61–68, 109–14.

80. Proverbs 20:4: "Because of the cold the sluggard would not plough: he shall beg therefore in the summer, and it shall not be given him." Proverbs 12:11: "He that tilleth his land shall be satisfied with bread, but he that pursueth idleness is very foolish."

81. Barney, "Plowshare of the Tongue," pp. 268–69.

82. Ibid.

83. Kirk, "Langland's Plowman," especially pp. 3, 11.

84. Reiss, "Symbolic Plow and Plowman," pp. 3–14.

85. J. Alexander, "*Labeur* and *Paresse*," p. 444.

86. Reiss, "Symbolic Plow and Plowman," pp. 11.

87. J. Alexander, "*Labeur* and *Paresse*," p. 440. Here Alexander takes issue with Panofsky's interpretation of the *Très Riches Heures* of the Duc de Berri.

88. On the depiction of rustics in the *Très Riches Heures* see below, Chapter 6, p. 144.

89. R. Williams, *The Country and the City,* pp. 27–34. On images of rural productivity and labor in early-modern Europe, see Vardi, "Imagining the Harvest."

90. Camille, "When Adam Delved," pp. 247–76.

91. R. Baldwin, "Peasant Imagery," p. 101; Kavaler, "Peter Bruegel and the Common Man," pp. 114–35. On different literary and artistic images of plowmen, see also O. Hill, *The Manor, the Plowman, and the Shepherd.*

92. Landes, "La vie apostolique en Aquitaine," 582–85.

93. Duby, *Three Orders,* pp. 132–33.

94. Le Roy Ladurie, *Montaillou,* pp. 571–73.

95. Leguai, "Les révoltes rurales," pp. 65–66.

96. Chelčický, "O torjím lidu (On the Three Peoples)," pp. 137–67, especially p. 165. See also Iwanczak, "Between Pacifism and Anarchy."

97. On Wyclif and the Three Orders see Gilchrist, "Social Doctrine of John Wyclif," pp. 157–69.

98. Regarding the nickname bestowed by Sebastian Brant in 1494 as an indication of both Hans's station and his foolishness, see *Niklashausen 1476,* p. 85. A subjective and informal survey of this affair is given by Wunderli, *Peasant Fires.*

99. *Niklashausen 1476,* pp. 283–86; also excerpted in *Quellen zur Geschichte des Bauernkrieges,* ed. Franz, no. 14a, p. 63.

100. *Niklashausen 1476,* pp. 191–96, 215, 262, 281.

101. Ibid., pp. 195–96; also in *Quellen zur Geschichte des Bauernkrieges,* ed. Franz, no. 14b, pp. 66–67.

102. Sider, *Andreas Bodenstein von Karlstadt,* pp. 177–78.

103. Cited in Packull, "Image of the 'Common Man,'" pp. 262–63. The saying could also serve as a lament for the lot of fallen humanity, as in, for example, Lotario dei Segni, *De miseria condicionis humane* 1.10 (p. 109).

104. Uhrig, "Der Bauer in der Publizistik," pp. 176–77.

105. Examples of these sentiments are provided in Uhrig, "Der Bauer in der Publizistik," pp. 177–79.

106. Hemmerli, *De nobilitate et rusticitate,* cap. 32, fol. 124r.

107. Ibid., cap. 33, fol. 127v.

108. *Quellen zur Geschichte des deutschen Bauernstandes,* no. 218, vv. 19–25 (p. 553):

> Derwüsch in bi dem Kragen,
> erfreuw das Herze din,
> nim im, was er habe,
> span uss di Pferdelin sin!
> bis frisch und darzu unverzagt,
> wann er nummen Pfennig hat
> so riss im dGurgel ab!

109. See below, Chapter 6.

Chapter 2

1. Further examples of such literature are available in Falk, *Étude sociale,* p. 113.

2. Cited in Niccoli, *I sacerdoti, i guerrieri, i contadini,* p. 24.

3. Szűcs, "Die oppositionelle Strömung," pp. 502–3.

4. Hemmerli, *De nobilitate et rusticitate,* cap. 3, fols. 11v–12v; cap. 31, fols. 117r–121r.

5. Gower, *Vox clamantis,* bk. 5, chap. 9 (pp. 216–18); idem, *Mirour de l'omme,* vv. 26425–484 (p. 293).

6. Adalbero of Laon, *Poème au roi Robert,* vv. 286–94 (p. 22), corrected by Oexle, "Die funktionale Dreiteilung," p. 30:

> Hoc genus afflictum nil possidet absque labore.
> Quis abaco poterit numerando retexere uerbis
> Seruorum studium, cursus, tantosque labores?
> Tesaurus, uestis, cunctis sunt pascua serui;
> Nam ualet ingenuus sine seruis uiuere nullus.
> Cum labor occurrit, sumptus et habere perobtant,

Rex et pontifices seruis seruire uidentur.
Pascitur a seruo dominus quem pascere sperat.
Seruorum lacrimae gemitus non terminus ullus.

7. Duby, *Three Orders*, pp. 160–61.

8. Ibid., p. 160: "His point was to emphasize this humiliation." p. 161: "An attempt was made to convince them [the *servi*] that there was in fact a mutual exchange of services."

9. Adalbero of Laon, *Poème au roi Robert*, vv. 37–41 (p. 4).

10. Oexle, "Deutungsschemata," pp. 103–4.

11. Duby, *Le moyen âge*, p. 98, a view effectively challenged by Bisson, "Feudal Revolution," pp. 30–31.

12. Buc, *L'ambiguïté du livre*, pp. 40–49.

13. Benedict de Sainte-Maure, *Chronique*, vv. 13269–74 (1: 384); the translation is Goldhammer's, in Duby, *Three Orders*, pp. 274–75.

14. Benedict de Sainte-Maure, *Chronique*, vv. 13279–317 (1: 384–85).

15. Ibid., vv. 28853–76 (2: 197–98). On the rebellion of 997, see Köhn, "Freiheit als Forderung."

16. Benedict de Sainte-Maure, *Chronique*, vv. 28877–958 (2: 198–200). For Wace, see below, note 90 for this chapter.

17. Étienne de Fougères, *Le livre des manières*, vv. 689–92, 697–700 (pp. 84–85).

18. Duby, *Three Orders*, p. 284.

19. Étienne de Fougères, *Le livre des manières*, vv. 705–20 (p. 85).

20. Duby, *Three Orders*, p. 285.

21. Ibid., p. 320.

22. Friedrich Stegmüller, *Repertorium Biblicum medii acvi*, vol. 5 (Madrid, 1955), nos. 7704–7939.

23. Lacombe and Smalley, *Studies on the Commentaries of Cardinal Stephen Langton*, especially pp. 64–85, 145–51.

24. Vaux Saint Cyr, "Les deux commentaires d'Étienne Langton sur Isaïe."

25. Ibid., pp. 233–34; Friedrich Stegmüller, *Repertorium Biblicum medii acvi*, vol. 5 (Madrid, 1955), nos. 7817, 7824. The versions of Langton's moral commentaries on Isaiah in turn differ from one another substantially. Some fourteen manuscripts have the incipit "Audite celi et auribus. . . . Ideo invocat celum et terram." From this group I have examined the following:

London, Lambeth Palace Library, MS 441

Cambridge, University Library, MS Peterhouse 119

Cambridge, Corpus Christi College, MS 55

Paris, Bibliothèque de l'Arsenal, MSS 87 and 87A

Paris, Bibliothèque Mazarine, MS 177

Paris, Bibliothèque Nationale, MSS lat. 393 and 492.

An important Isaiah commentary that Vaux Saint Cyr did not see—London, Lambeth Palace Library, MS 71, fols. 123r–150v—was placed in a class by itself by Friedrich Stegmüller (*Repertorium Biblicum medii acvi*, vol. 5, no. 7824). It also begins with Isaiah's words "Audite celi" but contains yet another type of moral gloss on Isaiah and ends abruptly at 34:15. Still another recension of the moralized commentary on Isaiah begins "Audite celi auribus. . . . Ecce in ultionem inimicorum elementa invocantur." In this category I have looked at Troyes, Bibliothèque Municipale, MS 893, and the manuscript cited in Duby's *Three Orders* (pp. 319, 374), Vienna, Österreichische Nationalbibliothck, MS 1395, rendered erroneously in the English translation as being in "Vienne." The Vienna manuscript was not available to Vaux Saint Cyr but is classified on the basis of its incipit in accord with his categories.

26. I have relied on the following manuscripts of Langton's Minor Prophets commentaries:

Cambridge, Corpus Christi College, MS 31

Cambridge, University Library, Peterhouse, MS 119

London, Lambeth Palace Library, MS 441

Paris, Bibliothèque Nationale, MS lat. 505

Vatican City, Biblioteca Apostolica, MS Borghese 374

The commentaries in these manuscripts resemble each other, but not closely. The Hosea commentary in Corpus Christi MS 31, for example, is considerably longer (fols. 25r–78r) than the Lambeth Palace version (fols. 37v–49v).

27. Paris, Bibliothèque National, MS lat. 505, fols. 23r–23v, to Hosea 8:5, *Proiectus est vitulus tuus, Samaria*. Samaria signifies *custodia*, the duty of prelates to care for others. Clerics who rejoice in luxury neglect their sheep and anger God (Hosea 8:5 continues, *iratus est furor meus in eos*), and will suffer in the world to come more than even the sinner among those placed under them (fol. 23v): "et notatur que sicut longe maius est ululare quam clamare, sic maior erit pena prelatorum quam subditorum."

28. Isaiah 13:20–21: *Nec pastores requiescent ibi, sed requiescent ibi bestiae*. Langton remarks: "Prelatus enim qui in amore mundi delectatur non debet dici pastor sed bestia, quia oves suas devorat" (Paris, Bibliothèque Mazarine, MS 177, fol. 134v). Other versions: London, Lambeth Palace Library, MS 441, fol. 120v, "non est pastor sed bestia"; Paris, Bibliothèque de l'Arsenal, MS 87, fol. 165r, "et non est dicendus pastor sed bestia"; Cambridge, Corpus ChristiCollege, MS 55, fol. 250v, "non est pastor sed bestia qui oves suas devorat"; Paris, Bibliothèque Nationale, MS lat. 492, fol. 24v, "non debet dici [i.e., *prelatus*] sed bestia."

29. Vienna, Österreichische Nationalbibliothek, MS 1395, fols. 3v and 8v; Troyes, Bibliothèque municipale, MS 893, fols. 59r–59v and 79v.

30. Vienna, Österreichische Nationalbibliothek, MS 1395, fol. 8v; Troyes, Bibliothèque municipale, MS 893, fol. 80r: "Ale principum et prelatorum debent esse potentia ad defendendum subditos et abundantia ad subueniendum, sed contra hiis alis

opprimunt eos . . . quod in alis ipsorum inuenitur sanguis animarum pauperum nec inueniuntur in fossis et non occulte sed manifeste opprimuntur."

31. Troyes, Bibliothèque municipale, MS 893, fol. 80r: "*Dentes eius* precisores sunt maiores prelati qui sententiam fecerunt, sed *molares* totum commouentes iusticiarii sunt sub eis constituti qui totum depascunt" (Vienna, Österreichische Nationalbibliothek, MS 1395, fol. 8v: "*Dentes eius* precissim [*sic*] sunt maiores prelati qui sententiam fecerunt, sed *molares* totum commouentes sunt minores iusticiarii sub eis constituti qui totum depascunt"). The influence of this interpretation is visible in a sermon by Jacques de Vitry that describes the *dentes* as the greater prelates and the *molares* as lesser prelates; see Longère, "Un sermon de Jacques de Vitry," p. 55.

Compare Cambridge, Corpus Christi College, MS 31, fol. 92v, commenting on Amos 7:1, where the *dentes* signify *both* prelates and nobles of the greater sort while *molares* are the lesser figures. Here all are guilty of a more general pride and greed.

In directly commenting on Joel 1:6, Langton has the teeth and molars refer to the evils of *secular* princes only, major and minor (Cambridge, Corpus Christi College, MS 31, fol. 70v).

32. London, Lambeth Palace Library, MS 441, fol. 112v: "*Quare populum meum atteritis* et cetera. Officiales prelati pauperes commoliunt. Quod prelati non rapiunt hoc officiales obiecta calumpnis extorquent. Isti sunt quasi catuli parua rapientes, prelati leones."

33. London, Lambeth Palace Library, MS 71, fol. 125v: "*Ve vobis qui depasti estis uineam meam et rapina pauperum in domibus* [f. 126r] *vestris. Populum meum* et cetera. Istud prelatos modernos qui bona subditorum rapiunt tangit. . . . Isti spoliunt populum et cetera. Hoc dicit dominus ad prophetas. *Qui seducunt populum dentibus mordent et pacem predicant* (Micah 3:5)." Cf. Peter the Chanter, discussing Psalms 13:4 (Paris, Bibliothèque Nationale, MS Lat. 12011, fol. 98r): "*Qui devorant plebam meam*, vel sua ei auferenda sicut faciunt tyranni, uel cotidiano ministerio marsupia pauperum hauriendo sicut faciunt sacerdotes, isti bibunt iniquitatem sicut aquam, et ita hoc potest dici ad populum et ad clerum."

34. Commenting on Isaiah 7:8, *sed caput Syrie Damasus, et caput Damascus Rasin*, the Cambridge, Corpus Christi College, MS 55, fol. 247r, states: "Caput igitur Syrie est superbia qui per Damascum significantur sunt qui sanguinem bibunt, qui *facies pauperum conmoliuntur* [Isaiah 3:15], qui de sudore pauperum ornant equos Phaleris." Cambridge, University Library, MS Peterhouse 119, pt. 4, fol. 3r, states: "Caput Syrie est superbia, sunt hii qui significantur per Damascenam sunt qui sanguinem bibunt, qui *facies pauperum conmoliuntur*, qui de sudore pauperum ornant equos Phaleris." The words "ornant equos Phaleris" mean "they adorn their horses with noble trinkets made from the sweat of the poor."

35. London, Lambeth Palace Library, MS 441, fol. 38v: "Damascus interpretatur potus sanguinis. Galaad translatio testimonium et significat pauperes. Per Damascum intelliguntur hic diuites et potentes qui sanguinem pauperum bibunt spoliando eos et opprimendo."

36. In similar language, and with citations of Amos and Micah, Jacques de Vitry

likens the prelates who despoil and extort from those subject to them to leeches who suck the blood of the poor; see Longère, "Un sermon de Jacques de Vitry," p. 55, "De sanguisegis prelatorum et spoliatoribus subditorum."

37. Cited and excerpted in Buc, *L'ambiguïté du livre*, pp. 219–20. Langton uses this same horrific image from Micah in commenting on Amos 1:9 (Cambridge, Corpus Christi College, MS 31, fol. 79v) and on Isaiah 7:8 (Cambridge, Corpus Christi College, MS 55, fol. 247r; Cambridge, University Library, MS Peterhouse 119, pt. 4, fol. 3r). Langton's comments on Micah 3:3 itself are on fol. 108v of Corpus Christi 31.

38. Buc, *L'ambiguïté du livre*, p. 220.

39. Ibid., pp. 206–31. See also Aurell, "Le roi mangeur."

40. Gregory I, *Moralia in Job* 21.15.22–23 (CC 143A, p. 1082).

41. Buc, *L'ambiguïté du livre*, pp. 82–83, 97–100.

42. Ibid., pp. 206–17.

43. Map, *De nugis curialium*, dist. 1, chap. 9 (p. 10). The metaphor appears in the context of an anecdote with a pun on "keepers" and "kept out" (*forestarii, foris stare*). Seeing a group of foresters shouting abuse in front of the royal chamber of Henry II, from which they had been excluded, the prior asked them who they were. They replied they were the forest keepers, whereupon Hugh remarked, "Keepers, keep out" (*forestarii foris stent*). Henry II laughed at this witticism, but the words applied to the king as well, Hugh told him, for he too would be kept out when the poor, tormented in this life by the royal keepers, were admitted to heaven (*pauperibus quos hii torquent paradisum ingressis, cum forestariis foris stabitis*).

44. Buc, *L'ambiguïté du livre*, pp. 219–20. Commenting on Psalms 3:7 (*Dentes peccatorum contrivisti*, Paris, Bibliothèque Nationale, MS Lat. 12011, fol. 7r), Peter distinguishes *dentes* from *molares*: the former are the *raptores*, while the latter are those who consume what the raptors have appropriated, thereby consenting to or profiting from the acts of the actual pillagers. At the same time, however, *dentes* denotes the expositors of Scripture.

45. Lotario dei Segni, *De miseria condicionis humane* 1.15 (p. 117).

46. Cambridge, Corpus Christi College, MS 31, fol. 78v (to Amos, 1:3): "Quia miseria pauperum in diuites transferetur. Pauperes enim oppressi et repulsam pacientes testimonium ferunt quod miseria sit ab eis transferenda in eorum oppresores. *Et mittam ignem* pene eterne *in domum Azael* id est diuitum." London, Lambeth Palace Library, MS 441, fol. 38v: "Quia miseria pauperum transferetur in diuites. Pauperes enim oppressi et repulsam pacientes testimonium ferunt quod miseria ab eis sit transferenda in eorum oppressores. *Et mittam ignem*, pene eterne, *in domum Azahel* scilicet in domum diuitum."

47. Cambridge, Corpus Christi College, MS 31, fol. 79v, and London, Lambeth Palace Library, MS 441, fol. 39v. Langton directly glosses Malachi 2:10 in Lambeth Palace 441, fol. 108r, and in Corpus Christi 31, fols. 107v–108r.

48. Cambridge, Corpus Christi College, MS 31, fol. 28r: "Diuites et potentes de regno suo temporali pauperes eiciunt et igitur non mirentur si pauperes eos eiciant de regno suo. Beati enim pauperes quam ipsorum est regnum celorum. Faciamus ig-

itur eos nobis amicos ut recipiant nos in eterna tabernacula." London, Lambeth Palace Library, MS 441, fol. 3v, is the same except that it gives "ne igitur mirentur" rather than "et igitur non mirentur."

49. London, Lambeth Palace Library, MS 441, fol. 16r.

50. Buc, *L'ambiguïté du livre*, pp. 222–23.

51. Jacques de Vitry, *Historia occidentalis*, p. 81, cited in Buc, *L'ambiguïté du livre*, p. 224: "Exinanite, exinanite usque ad fundamentum, crucifige, crucifige, macta et manduca."

52. Buc, *L'ambiguïté du livre*, p. 221.

53. Le Roy Ladurie, *Montaillou*, p. 559.

54. Cited in Owst, *Literature and Pulpit*, p. 305: "And covetise maketh, also, that rich men eat the poore, as beastes done their lesous [pasture], holding them lowe."

55. Cited in Iwanczak, "Between Pacifism and Anarchy," p. 280.

56. Benedict de Sainte-Maure, *Chronique*, vv. 42792–977 (2: 593–98), cited in Buc, *L'ambiguïté du livre*, pp. 226–27.

57. Gerald of Wales, *De principis instructione liber*, dist. 3, chap. 30 (pp. 322–24); Map, *De nugis curialium*, dist. 5, chap. 6 (pp. 464–68).

58. John of Worcester, *Chronicle*, p. 32. See also Constable, *Three Studies*, pp. 315–16.

59. *Miraculi S. Bertini Sithiensia*, MGH Scriptores 15, pt. 1, p. 513: "Quoque imbelle vulgus gemitum mugitus ad caelum mittebat, brachiis indefatigabiliter tensis palmisque pansis finem certaminis Dei miserationi commendantes! . . . dicamus, karissimi . . . quod in huius certaminis anxietate oratores et imbelles pulsatibus et inprobitatibus orationum aures Dei ad clementiam inclinabant."

60. Lambert of Ardres, *Historia comitum Ghisnensium*, chap. 18 (MGH Scriptores 24, pp. 570–71).

61. "Et clamor oppressorum ascendit in caelum, vindictam petens contra crudeles dominos," cited in Martini, *Das Bauerntum*, p. 236.

62. Der Stricker, "Beispiel von den Gäuhühnern," in his *Märe von den Gäuhühnern*, p. 72.

63. *Alte hoch- und niederdeutsche Volkslieder*, no. 143, st. 7 (1: 235). See below, Chapter 8, note 36.

64. Roquetaillade (Rupescissa), "Vade mecum in tribulatione," p. 499: "Consurget enim infra illos V. annos justitia popularis, et tyrannos proditores nobiles in ore bis-acuti gladii devorabit, et cadent multi principum et nobilium et potentium a dignitatibus suis et a gloria divitarum suarum; et fiat afflictio in nobilibus ultra quam credi possit, et rapientur majores, qui cum proditionibus depraedari facerant populum tam afflictum." On Rupescissa in general, see Bignami-Odier, *Études sur Jean de Roquetaillade*; and the more recent work by Lerner, "Popular Justice," especially pp. 41–43; and Lerner's introduction to *Johannes de Rupescissa*.

65. Lerner, "Popular Justice," pp. 48–50.

66. "Vom Rechte," vv. 217–66 (pp. 121–22).

67. Bromyard, cited in Owst, *Literature and Pulpit*, pp. 299–303, especially p. 301.

68. Hugo von Trimberg, *Der Renner*, vv. 6930–47 (BLVS 247, 1: 289–90).
69. Ibid., vv. 3405–36 (pp. 140–41).
70. Ibid., vv. 2221–24 (p. 92):

> Daz in wehset ûf der erden.
> Swer uber reht arme liute twinget
> Und si ze grôzem schaden bringet
> Mit bete, mit ungelte und mit stiure,
> Des sêle gâhet ze dem hellischen fiure.
>
> (Those that rule the earth certainly
> weigh on the poor people and bring
> great harm to them with exactions,
> monopolies, and taxes. Their souls go
> to the fires of hell.)

71. Ibid., vv. 7300–7314 (pp. 304–5):

> Und wêrz ein hunt,
> Ez möhte einen wilden heiden erbarmen,
> Sô man die unschuldigen armen
> Vindet sô jêmerlich gevangen,
>
> . . .
>
> Uf dem sölte man daz kriuze vil mêr
> Predigen denne dort über mer
> An tatan, valwen und an heiden,
> Der geloube von uns ist gescheiden!
> Wöllen dise kristen bî uns sîn
> Und wöllen als unmenschliche pîn
> Legen an unsern ebenkristen,
> Wer sölte ir leben denne fristen?
>
> (And were he a dog, a wild heathen
> would pity him, so are the innocent
> poor so miserably imprisoned. . . .
> The cross should be preached to
> those [the oppressors] much more
> than to those overseas, to Tartars,
> Waldensians [?], and pagans. If these
> Christians here with us wish to lay
> inhuman burdens on our fellow
> Christians, who will save *their* souls?)

72. *Reformation Kaiser Siegmunds*, MGH Staatsschriften des späteren Mittelalters 6, p. 278: "Darumb wyss yderman, wer der ist, der da getar sprechen: 'Du bist mein eygen!' der ist nit cristen; stet einer nit ab un geit got dye ere, so sol man in ab-

nemen als ein heyden, wan er ist Christo widerig und seind dye gebot gotz ann im verloren." (Thus we know, whoever says to his neighbor "you are my property," he is not a Christian. Whoever does not refrain from doing that and fails to give honor to God should be considered a heathen, since he is repulsive to Christ and since God's commandments are lost on him.)

73. Ibid., pp. 86, 88: "Der hertzog antwort und sprach, 'Ich merck dich woll, es ist war, was sagestu nach der gschriefft laüterung . . . aber ich bekenne, das yr sein nit begerent noch ym lebent; ir verswerent in; einer nympt dem anndernn sein ere und sein gut ab; einer spricht den andernn an fur eygen. . . . Wann yr unns erschlagen mogent, so meynet yr, das ewig leben dadurch zu haben; do betriegent yr euch sel-ber; blibent yr doheym und fechtent mit den falschen cristen und weysset dye zümm rechtenn, das wer ein gute merfart.'" (The duke answered, "mark you well, it is true what you say according to the textual passage [Scripture], but I know you do not de-sire to follow it in life. You forswear each other; one takes another's honor and goods. One speaks to another as if he were his property. You would like to strike us down and think to gain from that eternal life, but you deceive yourselves. Stay at home and settle that account with false Christians. That would be a good crusade.)

74. See below, Chapter 11, pp. 272–78.

75. Brutus János Mihály, *Magyar Históriája* 1: 261–62.

76. See below, Chapter 8, note 115.

77. Froissart, *Chronique, Livre I* 3: 139; Jean de Venette, *Chronique*, excerpted in Medeiros, *Jacques et chroniqueurs*, p. 192, discussed pp. 75–78.

78. Étienne de Fougères, *Le livre des manières*, vv. 581–84 (p. 81):

> Choiles! ja sunt il crestïen,
> ne sunt paien ne Sulïen,
> S'a grant sorfet nes prenïen,
> nes devrion mestre en lïen.
>
> (Now then! As they are
> Christians, neither pagans
> nor Syrians, thus let us not
> put excessive demands on
> them; we must not put
> them in bondage.)

79. Barcelona, Arxín de la Corona d'Aragó, MS Salva de Infançonia 69. I owe this reference to Elena Lourie via David Nirenberg.

80. On contemptuous typification of peasants as animals, see below, Chapter 6, pp. 139–50.

81. Thomasin von Zerclaere, *Der Welsche Gast*, vv. 8513–21 (GAG 425, vol. 1, p. 293):

> daz du dir einen vrien man
> woldest machen undertan,

als ob er ein vihe were:
swerz tut, der is got unmere.

82. J. Baldwin, *Masters, Princes and Merchants* 1: 237–38 and 2: 172–73.

83. Ebner, "Der Bauer," p. 96.

84. *Quellen zur Geschichte des Bauernkrieges*, ed. Franz, no. 94, p. 301: "Das allain Got mit Aigentumb zuegehört, und die Menschen fur aigen under sich wellen biegen und schmuckhen und bei der Nesen in ir Geltnetz wellen zichen . . . wo ain armer Man zu ainer Khirchen oder Altar zinsper ist, so wellen si mit armen Leudten Gwalt haben als ainer uber sein Vieh und noch vil tiransicher."

85. As given in Buszello, *Der deutsche Bauernkrieg*, p. 17: "nit wie die kye und kölber verkouft werden, dieweil wir alle nur ain herren, das ist got den herrn im hymel, haben."

86. *Quellen zur Geschichte des Bauernkrieges*, ed. Franz, no. 27, p. 129: "damit sich die Prelaten understanden haben und das auch geton . . . davon genötigt, getrangt und vergwaltigt, unsern Bestant herter und erger gemacht, dann die Knecht und Hund seien."

87. Tomàs Mieres, gloss to *Institutiones* 7.2 ("De hiis qui sui vel alieni iuris sunt"), Vatican City, Biblioteca Apostolica, MS Borghese 374, fol. 5V: "Nota quod dicit supra modum quia humanitas seruis debetur. Homines enim sunt, castigari tamen possunt pro modo culpe citra mortem et membra mutilationem. Nulli enim est licitum aliud maletractare uel iniuste opprimere aut inhumaniter seuire." The manuscript is briefly described in A. Maier, "Un manuscrito de Tomás Mieres." For the right of mistreatment, see my essay "Catalan *ius maletractandi*," in Freedman, *Church, Law and Society*. Mieres specifically denied the validity of this law sanctioning seigneurial mistreatment in his *Apparatus* (completed in 1439, printed in 1621), 2: 513–14.

88. Chelčický, "*O torjtm lidu* (On the Three Peoples)," pp. 158–59.

89. Froissart, *Oeuvres* 9: 387. See Patterson, *Chaucer and the Subject of History*, p. 264.

90. Wace, *Roman de Rou*, vv. 867–70 (1: 193):

> Nus sumes humes cum il sunt,
> tels membres avum cum il unt
> e autresi granz cors avum
> et autretan suffrir poum.
>
> (We are men as they are, with
> the same members as they have
> and hearts as large, equally ca-
> pable of suffering pain.)

91. I thus disagree with the opinion of Johan Huizinga in his *Waning of the Middle Ages*, p. 60, that no one in the late Middle Ages understood that the wealth of the nobles came from the lower orders.

Chapter 3

1. Walther von der Vogelweide, *Die Gedichte*, no. 22, vv. 12–15 (p. 28):

> wer kan den hêrren von dem knehte scheiden,
> swa er ir gebeine blôzez fünde,
> het er ir joch lebender künde,
> sô gewürme dez fleisch verzert?

2. Radbruch and Radbruch, *Der deutsche Bauernstand*, pp. 30–37.

3. Huizinga, *Waning of the Middle Ages*, pp. 64–65.

4. Beaumanoir, *Coutumes de Beauvaisis*, chap. 45, par. 1453 (2: 235–36).

5. London, Lambeth Palace Library, MS 441, fol. 108r: "*Numquid non pater unus omnium nostrum. Numquid non dominus unus creauit nos.* Quare igitur despicit un-usquisque fratrem suum. Istud est contra auaros qui elemosinas facere nolunt, fratrem enim despicit qui indigentem contempsit."

6. Walsingham, *Historia Anglicana* 2: 32, and idem, *Chronicon Angliae*, p. 321. See A. Friedman, "When Adam Delved," pp. 213–14. On the implications and context of Ball's sermon, see Justice, *Writing and Rebellion*, pp. 14–23, 102–19, 233–37; and Burdach, *Der Dichter des Ackermann aus Böhmen* 1: 167–203.

7. Cited in Owst, *Literature and Pulpit*, p. 291.

8. Walsingham, *Historia Anglicana* 2: 33, and idem, *Chronicon Angliae*, p. 321: "Continuansque sermonem inceptum, nitebatur, per verba proverbii quod pro themate sumpserat, introducere et probare, ab initio omnes pares creatos a natura, servitutem per injustam oppressionem nequam hominum introductam, contra voluntatem Dei; quia, si Deo placuisset servos creasse, utique in principio mundi constituisset quis servus, quisve dominus futurus fuisset." For a discussion of this passage, see Justice, *Writing and Rebellion*, pp. 108–9.

9. A. Friedman "When Adam Delved," pp. 214–19.

10. See below, note 127 for this chapter.

11. Adalbero of Laon, *Poème au roi Robert*, vv. 41–42 (p. 4): "Nudi pontifices sine fine sequantur aratrum, / Carmina cum stimulo primi cantando parentis." This passage is discussed in Carozzi's introduction to the *Poème*, p. lxxxi.

12. Resnikow, "History," pp. 391–405.

13. Ibid., p. 394. The poem is also cited in Tettau, "Über einige bis jetzt unbekannte Erfurter Drucke," p. 320:

> Nu wolt ich wissen also geren:
> wann die Edelleut herkumen weren;
> Seintmal das die pösen und die frumen,
> nit mer dan von Adam und Eva sin kumen.
> Da Adam reutet und Eva span,
> wer was die zeit da ein Edelman?

14. Cited in Resnikow, "Cultural History," p. 395.

15. Cited ibid., p. 396.

16. Ibid., pp. 397, 405.

17. A. Friedman, "When Adam Delved," pp. 213–20. Huizinga, *Waning of the Middle Ages*, p. 64, remarks that at first "one is inclined to fancy that the nobles must have trembled on hearing it [the couplet]. But, in fact, it was the nobility themselves who for a long time had been repeating this ancient theme."

18. Boethius, *De consolatione philosophiae* 3.6 (lyric):

> Omne humanum genus in terris simili surgit ab ortu.
> Unus enim rerum pater est, unus cuncta ministrat.
> Ille dedit Phoebo radios dedit et cornua lunae,
> Ille homines etiam terris dedit ut sidera caelo,
> Hic clausit membris animos celsa sede petitos.
> Mortales igitur cunctos edit nobile germen.

19. Thus Boethius in *Consolatio* 3.6 (prose) observes that the title of nobility is foolish and worthless ("Iam uero quam sit inane quam futile nobilitatis nomen, quis non uideat?"). For a general discussion, see Curtius, *European Literature*, p. 179.

20. Resnikow, "Cultural History," p. 396: "Ich bin ein man wie ein ander man, / Allein das mir Gott die ehr vergahn."

21. Boockmann, "Zu den geistigen," p. 15.

22. In Gower's *Mirour de l'omme* and *Confessio Amantis*, cited in A. Friedman, "When Adam Delved," p. 223.

23. The original is cited in Resnikow, "Cultural History," p. 395:

> Do adam sich mit frass vergifft
> Da hiess jn got sein prot gewynnen
> Mit hacken rewten vnd eua mit spynnen
> In sweiss jres antlitzes auf der erden.

24. Andreas Capellanus, *On Love* 1.6 (p. 44).

25. Froissart, *Oeuvres* 9: 387.

26. Hugo von Trimberg, *Der Renner*, vv. 1328–86 (BLVS 247, 1: 55–57) (the peasant argument here is that "we are all descended from the same mother"); Hemmerli, *De nobilitate et rusticitate*, cap. 6, fols. 19r–19v; Wittenwiler, *Der Ring*, vv. 7235–44 (pp. 308–10).

27. *Boke of Seynt Albans*, pt. 3, sig. a 1 recto. See below, Chapter 4, p. 102.

28. Niccolò Machiavelli, *Istorie fiorentine* 1 terzo, 13, cited in Guglielmi, "Reflexiones," p. 328.

29. Suard, "Hugues Capet," pp. 220–22; Ribémont and Salvat, "De Francion à Hugues Capet."

30. Rigg, "Legend of Hugh Capet."

31. *Hugues Capet*, ed. la Grange, p. 126, cited in Falk, *Étude sociale*, p. 115. I have

also used the edition of Larry S. Crist and François Suard (vv. 3297–99), under preparation for the Anciens Textes Français series: "il est biaulz et bons, et s'il n'est de haut lin, / Au vrai considerer, et tout povre meschin, / Sont tout estrait d'Adam, et Vilart et Justin."

32. *Li Romans de Bauduin de Sebourc* 1: 80, cited in Falk, *Étude sociale*, p. 116. An edition of this by Crist and Suard has also been completed and is forthcoming in the Anciens Textes Français series, vv. 2653–54 (p. 107): "Car il n'est nulz gentis, s'il n'est a bien pensans, / Car trestout venons d'Eve, nos peres fu Adans."

33. Paris, Bibliothèque Nationale, MS lat. 16793, fol. 145r: "*Quoniam Adam* humani generis princeps *exemplum meum est* ut agricola comedam panem meum in sudore vultus mei." I am indebted to Philippe Buc, of Stanford University, for this reference.

34. Cited in DuBruck, *Aspects of Fifteenth-Century Society*, p. 18.

35. Caviness, *Early Stained Glass*, p. 113 and plate 6; Camille, "When Adam Delved," pp. 247–65, 272. Note that at Sigena, Adam is digging while Eve is spinning.

36. Martini, *Das Bauerntum*, pp. 229–30.

37. Östling, "The Ploughing Adam," pp. 13–19. I thank Michael Camille, of the University of Chicago, for this reference.

38. On Christ as a plowman and the associated symbolism, see below, Chapter 9.

39. Camille, "Labouring for the Lord," pp. 430–32.

40. On the value of labor see above, Chapter 1.

41. Several German examples are given in Heald, "Peasant in Mediaeval German Literature," pp. 139–50.

42. This view appears most clearly in the pamphlet literature of the early Reformation through such themes as the dereliction of the clergy and nobility, their former willingness to work in the fields, their refusal to undertake the labor of Adam owed by all his progeny, and the righteousness of those who earn their bread by their physical efforts, who alone can be said to fulfill His commandments. See the examples cited in Uhrig, "Der Bauer in der Publizistik," pp. 176–78.

43. Petrarch, *Von der Artzney*. On the date of the illustrations, see Raupp, *Bauernsatiren*, p. 9. For the portrayal of peasants in early sixteenth-century Germany, see Raupp, *Bauernsatiren*, pp. 12–18; Scribner, "Images of the Peasant"; and Packull, "Image of the 'Common Man.'" The identity of the artist has not been definitively established. In the early twentieth century the woodcuts were ascribed to Hans Weiditz; see Röttinger, *Hans Weiditz*. This was accepted by the Radbruchs, *Der deutsche Bauernstand*, pp. 60–61. Raupp, *Bauernsatiren*, p. 9, regards it as likely that Weiditz was the Petrarch Master, but Manfred Lemmer rejects this identification in his discussion accompanying the reprinted edition of *Von der Artzney*, p. 198.

44. Petrarch, *De remediis*, bk. 1, no. 57 (1: 53–54), "De fertilitate terrae." This is repeated in the remedies for misfortune, bk. 2, no. 59, "De villico malo ac superbo" (1: 153).

45. Petrarch, *De remediis*, bk. 1, no. 85 (1: 72–73), "De bono domino"; Petrarch, *Von der Artzney*, bk. 1, fol. 101r, "Von einem guten herrn."

46. Petrarch, *De remediis*, bk. 2, no. 7 (1: 112–13), "De servitute"; idem, *Von der Artzney*, bk. 2, fol. 8v, "Von Dienstparkeyt."

47. Petrarch, *De remediis*, bk. 2, no. 29 (1: 134), "De servis malis"; idem, *Von der Artzney*, bk. 2, fol. 38r, "Von den bösen knechten."

48. Cicero, *Ein Buch, so Marcus Tullis Cicero der Römer zu seynem Sune Marco . . .* (Augsburg, 1531), illustration reprinted in Jäckel, *Kaiser, Gott und Bauer*, p. 31.

49. Petrarch, *De remediis*, bk. 1, no. 16 (1: 13–14), "De origine generosa"; idem, *Von der Artzney*, bk. 1, fols. 17r–18v, "Von adelichem Ursprung."

50. There are several classical precedents for the observation that since all people come from the same origin, nobility is conferred by character, not birth. They include Sallust, *Bellum Iugurthinum* 85.15; Juvenal, *Satirae* 8.20; and Seneca, *De beneficiis* 3.28.

51. Vanderjagt, *Qui sa vertu anoblist*.

52. Scheidig, *Die Holzschnitte des Petrarca-Meisters*, p. 60.

53. Ibid., pp. 60–61; Zschelletzschky, "Ihr Herz war auf der Seite der Bauern," p. 340.

54. Mohl, *Three Estates*, pp. 268–69.

55. Radbruch and Radbruch, *Der deutsche Bauernstand*, pp. 57–61.

56. Ibid., pp. 61–71.

57. Raupp, *Bauernsatiren*, pp. 13–19.

58. Martini, *Das Bauerntum*, pp. 230–31.

59. On bagpipes, see Nordstrom, *Virtues and Vices*; and Jones, "Wittenweiler's Becki." I thank John B. Friedman for pointing these articles out to me.

60. Oexle, "Deutungsschemata," pp. 76–80; idem, "Le travail au XIe siècle," p. 55.

61. On medieval ideas of freedom in relation to the common origin of humanity, see Graus, "'Freiheit' als soziale Forderung."

62. Aristotle, *Politics* 1254a–1255b, 1258b.

63. Aristotle, *Politics*, 1255a–b.

64. Carlyle and Carlyle, *Mediaeval Political Theory* 5: 7–8; Voltelini, "Der Gedanke der allgemeinen Freiheit," p. 192.

65. Cicero, *Paradoxa Stoicorum*, no. 5: only the wise man is free, and every foolish man is a slave.

66. Seneca, *De beneficiis* 3.20: "Errat, si quis existimat servitutem in totum hominem descendere. Pars melior eius excepta est. Corpora obnoxia sunt et adscripta dominis; mens quidem sui iuris, quae adeo libera et vega est."

67. Cicero, *De officiis* 1.13; Seneca, *De beneficiis* 3.20; Carlyle and Carlyle, *Mediaeval Political Theory* 1: 23 and 5: 5; Voltelini, "Der Gedanke der allgemeinen Freiheit," pp. 192–93.

68. *Digest* (*Codex Justinianus*) 1.5.4, giving Florentinus's derivation of *servus* from the term for those spared (*servare*) from being killed as war captives.

69. Ibid. 1.17.32: "Quod attinet ad ius civile, servi pro nullis habentur: non tamen et iure naturali, quia, quod ad ius naturale attinet, omnes homines aequales sunt." *Digest* 1.1.4: "Quae res a iure gentium originem sumpsit, utpote cum iure naturali

omnes liberi nascerentur nec esset nota manumissio, cum servitus esset incognita: sed postquam iure gentium servitus invasit, secutum est beneficium manumissionis."

70. Cortese, *La norma giuridica* 1: 74–86, 118–21.

71. Bierbrauer, "Das Göttliche Recht," pp. 217–22.

72. An important recent work on the relation between sin and coercive power is Stürner, *Peccatum und potestas.*

73. Bonnassie, "The Survival and Extinction of the Slave System in the Early Medieval West," in his *From Slavery to Feudalism,* pp. 16–32; de Ste. Croix, "Early Christian Attitudes."

74. Discussed in Carlyle and Carlyle, *Mediaeval Political Theory* 1: 113–14; Stürner, *Peccatum und Potestas,* pp. 57–60.

75. Lactantius, *Divinae institutiones* 5.15–16 (Sources Chrétiennes 204, pp. 204–12).

76. Ambrose, *Exhortatio virginitatis* 1.3 (*PL* 16: 352): "Nullum ergo ad commendationem hominis condicio affert impedimentum; nec dignitas prosapiae meritum, sed fides affert. Sive servus, sive liber, omnes in Christo unum sumus." See also selections from Ambrose cited in Carlyle and Carlyle, *Mediaeval Political Theory* 1: 115, 118.

77. Augustine, *De civitate Dei* 19.15. Behind this passage in Genesis stands Genesis 1:26, where God decided to create man in His own image and gave him dominion over the earth's creatures.

78. Above, Chapter 2; below, Chapter 10.

79. *Cambridge History of Medieval Political Thought,* Robert Markus's discussion on pp. 108–13. See also Stürner, *Peccatum und Potestas,* pp. 67–85.

80. Augustine, *Quaestionum in Heptateuchum* 1.153 (*PL* 34: 589–90).

81. Misfortune would become a standard explanation for servitude (as in Petrarch), one that combined lament with resignation. See, e.g., the contrast between natural equality and the ravages of fortune in Lotario dei Segni, *De miseria condicionis humane* 1.15 (p. 117): "O extrema condicio servitutis! Natura liberos genuit, set fortuna servos constituit."

82. Augustine, *Lettres 1–29,* letter 10.2 (pp. 168–70); letter 24 (pp. 382–86).

83. Gregory I, *Moralia in Job* 21.15 (CC 143A, p. 1082).

84. Markus, *End of Ancient Christianity,* esp. pp. 1–17, 213–28.

85. Stürner, *Peccatum und Potestas,* pp. 89–94, 100–102.

86. Gregory I, *Regula pastoralis* 2.6 (*PL* 77: 34–35): "Nam sicut in libris Moralibus dixisse me memini, liquet quod omnes homines natura aequales genuit, sed variante meritorum ordine alio aliis culpa postponit."

87. See, e.g., Gerard of Cambrai's discourse at the Council of Arras (1025), in his *Acta synodi Attrebatensis in Manicheos,* in *PL* 142: 1308: "Liquit, inquit beatus Gregorius, quod omnes homines natura aequales genuit; sed variante meritorum ordine alios aliis culpa postponit. Ipsa autem diversitas quae accessit ex vitio, divino judicio dispensatur, ut, quia omnis homo aeque stare non valet, alter rogatur ab altero." See also Duby, *Three Orders,* p. 35.

88. *Cambridge History of Medieval Political Thought*, Markus's statement on p. 121: "There is a strong streak of egalitarianism in Gregory's *omnes natura aequales sumus*: whereas Augustine pushed this equality back into primordial origins to explain its evident absence from our present world, Gregory made it a moral demand here and now." See also Recchia, *Gregorio Magno*, especially pp. 118–20. Recchia sees Gregory as unusually sympathetic toward the lower orders but draws a sharper distinction than Markus between Gregory's sense of original natural equality and the present arrangement of society (*ordo dispensationis*). Stürner, *Peccatum und Potestas*, pp. 85–94, argues that while Gregory sees rulership and subordination as necessary consequences of sin, he also believes that control must be exercised constructively, mercifully, and in accord with God's will. Human sinfulness is not an excuse for untrammeled domination.

89. Gregory I, *Registrum epistolarum* 9.27 (CC 140A, p. 588).

90. Buc, *L'ambiguïté du livre*, pp. 98–104.

91. The passage is edited in Dahan, "L'exégèse de *Genèse* I, 26," p. 152.

92. Gregory I, *Registrum epistolarum* 6.12 (CC 140, p. 380): "Cum redemptor noster totius conditor creaturae ad hoc propitiatus humanam uoluit carnem assumere ut diuinitatis suae gratia, disrupto quo tenebamur capti uinculo seruitutis, pristinae nos restitueret libertati, salubriter agitur, si homines, quos ab initio natura liberos protulit et ius gentium iugo substituit seruitutis, in ea qua nati fuerant manumittentis beneficio libertate reddantur."

93. Aelfric, *Catholic Homilies*, cited in Pelteret, *Slavery in Early Mediaeval England*, pp. 61–64. Even more explicit is Archbishop Wulfstan of York, who quoted Aelfric, adding that Christ bought the emperor and the poor man with His blood for the same price (Wulfstan, *Die "Institutes of Polity, Civil and Ecclesiastical,"* p. 90).

94. See below, Chapter 10, pp. 250–251.

95. E.g., Oexle, "Die funktionale Dreiteilung," pp. 27–28.

96. Isidore of Seville, *Sententiarum libri tres* 3.47 (*PL* 83: 717): God has placed some men under the domination of others so that "licentia male agendi servorum potestate dominantium restringatur."

97. Oexle, "Die funktionale Dreiteilung," p. 28, citing the Council of Aachen (816), Rather of Verona, Burchard of Worms, and Ivo of Chartres. Carlyle and Carlyle, in *Mediaeval Political Theory* 2: 119–20, note Isidore's influence on the Decretists Paucapalea and Rufinus.

98. Stürner, *Peccatum und Potestas*, pp. 95–102.

99. On the question of changes in slavery from the late Roman Empire to 1000, see Martino, *Uomini e terre in occidente*, pp. 65–206; Goetz, "Serfdom and the Beginnings of a 'Seigneurial System'"; and H. Hoffmann, "Kirche und Sklaverei."

100. Alcuin, *Interrogationes et responsiones*, no. 273 (*PL* 100: 557). For the Roman definition of *servi*, see below, Chapter 5, note 55. For the discussion of Carolingian writers I am indebted to Milani, *La schiavitù*, pp. 356–57, and Ignor, *Über das allgemeine Rechtsdenken*, pp. 234–37.

101. Hrabanus Maurus, *Commentaria in Genesim* 4.9 (*PL* 107: 646–47).

102. Agobard of Lyon, *Contra praeceptum impium*, CC, Continuatio medievalis 52, p. 187.

103. Haimo of Auxerre, *Expositio in epistolas S. Pauli*, chap. 3 (*PL* 117: 762–63): "Servi non sunt per naturam, sed per culpam et propter peccatum, sicut Chanaan, filius Cham. Propter peccatum enim venit captivitas et per captivitatem servitus." *Expositio in epistolas S. Pauli* is wrongly attributed to Haimo of Halberstadt. On Haimo's authorship see Iogna-Prat, "L'oeuvre d'Haymon d'Auxerre," esp. 161–62.

104. Jonas of Orléans, *De institutione laicali* 2.22 (*PL* 106: 213).

105. Rather of Verona, *Praeloquia* 1.22 (CC, Continuatio medievalis 46A, pp. 22–23); the translation is Reid's in Rather of Verona, *Complete Works*, p. 40.

106. Ibid. 1.29 (pp. 30–31), translated in Reid, pp. 47–48.

107. Smaragdus, *Via Regia* 30 (*PL* 102: 967–69). Voltelini, "Der Gedanke der allgemeinen Freiheit," p. 207, notes that the Carlyles exaggerate Smaragdus's position as calling for the abolition of slavery (Carlyle and Carlyle, *Medieval Political Theory* 1: 208–9).

108. Atto of Vercelli, *Expositio in Epistolas Pauli*, chap. 6 (*PL* 134: 583).

109. H. Hoffmann, "Kirche und Sklaverei," pp. 1–6; Pelteret, *Slavery in Early Mediaeval England*, p. 78; *Councils and Synods with Other Documents* 1: 678.

110. Paris, Bibliothèque Nationale, MS 355, fol. 5r, passage edited in Dahan, "L'exégèse de *Genèse* 1, 26," p. 151: "*Et presit piscibus*. Non est dictum quod presit hominibus. Quare? Forte dices: quia nondum homines erant. Certe eodem modo dictum post diluvium: *Terror noster erit super omnia animalia* (*Gen.* 9, 2). Non dicit 'super homines,' et assignat Gregorius rationem in *Moralibus*, quia, etsi presit homo aliis, potius debet attendere conditionem equalitatemque conditionis quam potestatem ordinis, et esse in illis quasi unus ex illis."

111. Verlinden, *L'esclavage dans l'Europe médiévale*; Bresc, "L'esclave dans le monde méditerranéen"; Stuard, "Ancillary Evidence for the Decline of Medieval Slavery."

112. Vincke, "Königtum und Sklaverei"; Bensch, "From Prizes of War to Domestic Merchandise"; Meyerson, "Slavery and the Social Order."

113. Krekić, "L'abolition de l'esclavage à Dubrovnik."

114. Burchard of Worms, *Decretum*, bk. 9, chap. 18 (*PL* 140: 818); repeated by Ivo of Chartres, *Decretum*, pt. 8, chap. 156 (*PL* 161: 618); Ivo of Chartres, *Panormia* 4, chap. 38 (*PL* 161: 1254); and Gratian, *Decretum*, C.29 q.2 c.1.

115. Landau, "Hadrians IV. Dekretale 'Dignum est,'" especially pp. 517–21.

116. On the Roman and canon law regarding serfdom, see Gilchrist, "Medieval Canon Law on Unfree Persons," pp. 278–81; idem, "Saint Raymond of Penyafort," pp. 302–7; Conte, *Servi medievali*; and Sahaydachny Bocarius, "The Marriage of Unfree Persons."

117. Carlyle and Carlyle, *Medieval Political Theory* 5: 11–12, 21–23. On tensions and contradictions within Aquinas's consideration of slavery, see Killoran, "Aquinas and Vitoria," pp. 87–92.

118. Aquinas, *Commentarium in VIII*, bk. 1, lects. 3 and 4 (pp. 377, 379); *Summa theologica* 2, 2, q. 57, art. 3 (p. 212). These passages are cited in Feo, "Dal *pius agricola*," p. 118.

119. Aquinas, *In X. libros Ethicorum ad Nicomachum*, bk. 8, lect. 11 (p. 286). Correspondingly, a tool is an inanimate slave.

120. Carlyle and Carlyle, *Mediaeval Political Theory* 5: 23–24; Nicholas of Oresme, *Le livre des politiques d'Aristote*, p. 322.

121. Hugo von Trimberg, *Der Renner*; Wittenwiler, *Der Ring*; see above, note 26 for this chapter. Chaucer, "The Parson's Tale," *Canterbury Tales*, vv. 762–68; Konrad von Ammenhausen, *Schachzabelbuch*, col. 411, vv. 10764–71.

122. Szűcs, "Theoretical Elements," pp. 268–69; Freedman, "Catalan Lawyers," pp. 291–98, 314.

123. Southern, *Making of the Middle Ages*, pp. 103–7.

124. *Quellen zur Geschichte des Bauernkrieges*, ed. Wopfner, pp. 46, 61, 134–35.

125. Southern, *Making of the Middle Ages*, pp. 107–8.

126. Wace, *Le Roman du Rou*, vv. 867–70 (1: 193). See above, Chapter 2, pp. 44, 55.

127. *Historia episcopum Autissiodorensium*, p. 729: "Diabolicum profecto et perniciosum inventum! Nam de hoc sequebatur, quod nullus timor, nulla reverentia superioribus potestatibus haberetur; sed in eam libertatem sese omnes asserere conabantur, quam ab initio conditae creaturae a primis parentibus se contraxisse dicebant, ignorantes peccati fuisse meritum servitutem." Discussed in Duby, *Three Orders*, pp. 331–32; Köhn, "Freiheit als Forderung," pp. 360–64; and Bouchard, *Spirituality and Administration*, pp. 101–4.

128. Simeoni, "La liberazione dei servi," pp. 24–25.

129. M. Bloch, *Rois et serfs*, p. 151 n. 2: "Natura omnes homines sunt liberi; set jus gencium aliquos servos fecit; et quia res ad suam naturam de facili revertitur."

130. M. Bloch, *Rois et serfs*, p. 150.

131. Bierbrauer, "Das Göttliche Recht," p. 224.

132. Regarding Catalonia, for example, see Freedman, "Catalan Lawyers."

133. Aristotle's teachings on slavery would become of key importance again in the sixteenth century with the conquest of the New World. In justifying enslavement of non-Christians, one could posit a debased nature that did not seem to violate Christian equality immediately, but this strategy usually required additional support from an argument concerning punishment of sin rather than mere Aristotelian inferiority. Ginés de Sepúlveda, the best-known defender of the enslavement of the Indies, referred to Aristotle in his 1550 work, the *Apology*, where, against Melchior Cano, he adduced an argument concerning sin. Indians might not quite be natural slaves, but their conduct (especially cannibalism) merited enslavement. In his debate with Bartolomé de las Casas in 1550–51, Sepúlveda stated that the Indians were inferior and needed supervision, but also that their "crimes" deprived them of any claim to self-governance. This is discussed in Pagden, *Fall of Natural Man*, p. 112.

Chapter 4

1. T. Hill, *"Rígsthula"*; J. Friedman, *Monstrous Races*, pp. 99–105; idem, "Nicholas's 'Angelus ad Virginem.'"

2. The best consideration of early Jewish commentary on Genesis 9 is Aaron, "Early Rabbinic Exegesis." I am grateful to Benjamin Braude, Steven Benin, and Alexandra Cuffel for their help with the talmudic and midrashic material.

3. Aaron, "Early Rabbinic Exegesis," pp. 722–29, citing the *Oxford Companion to the Hebrew Bible* and a number of other texts, including the scurrilous assertions of Tony Martin, *The Jewish Onslaught: Dispatches from the Wellesley Battlefront* (Dover, Mass., 1993), pp. 32–33.

4. As correctives, in addition to Aaron's work, see Isaac, "Genesis, Judaism and the 'Sons of Ham'"; and Davis, *Slavery and Human Progress*, p. 337 n. 144.

5. *Babylonian Talmud*, Sanhedrin 70a (pp. 477–78): Rab opting for sodomy, R. Samuel for castration, 'Ubr the Galilean for both.

6. Ibid., Sanhedrin 108b (p. 745). On this passage see Aaron, "Early Rabbinic Exegesis," p. 740. Noah's curse on the raven also figures in Hugo von Trimberg, *Der Renner*, vv. 2515–20 (BLVS 247, 1: 104).

7. *Midrash Rabbah*, Bereshith Rabbah 36.7 (1: 293). See also *Pirke de Rabbi Eliezer*, p. 170; Gero, "Legend of the Fourth Son of Noah," pp. 321–22.

8. On the context and implications of these statements, see Aaron, "Early Rabbinic Exegesis," pp. 740–41.

9. For the context and moral implications of the story of Ham and other seemingly harsh biblical legislation, see Goodman, "Biblical Laws of Diet and Sex."

10. Benjamin of Tudela, *Itinerary*, p. 127. See Aaron, "Early Rabbinic Exegesis," pp. 725–27. Earlier in his *Itinerary*, Benjamin calls the inhabitants of Khulam (Quilon) on the Malabar coast "sons of Cush," describing them as black, honest, prosperous traders with a passion for stargazing. Among them dwell Jews who are also black (pp. 120–21).

11. Philo, *De Ebrietate*, chap. 2 (LCL 227, pp. 319–23); idem, *Quaestiones et solutiones in Genesim* 2.65 (LCL 380, pp. 165–67); Justin Martyr, *Dialogus cum Tryphone*, cap. 139, p. 488; Origen, *In Genesim*, in *PG* 12: 108 (to Genesis 9:25).

12. J. Friedman, "Nicholas's 'Angelus ad Virginem,'" pp. 176–77.

13. Funkenstein, "Basic Types of Christian Anti-Jewish Polemics."

14. Justin Martyr, *Dialogus cum Tryphone*, cap. 139, p. 488; Ambrose, *Epistolae* 7.37.6–7 (CSEL 82, pt. 1, pp. 45–46); idem, *De Noe et Arca*, chap. 30–32 (*PL* 14: 432–35); Ambrosiaster, *Commentarius in epistolam ad Colossenses* 4.1 (CSEL 81, pt. 3, p. 202); Claudius Marius Victorinus, *Alethia* 3.76 (CC 128, p. 169); Sulpicius Severus, *Chronica* 1.4 (CSEL 1, p. 6). Ham's laughter also appears in a ninth-century riddling dialogue and an eleventh-century Anglo-Saxon prose miscellany attributing slavery to Ham's mockery of Noah: see T. Hill, *"Rígsthula,"* pp. 82–83.

15. Such a connection does appear in a text attributed to Ephraim of Syria (died 373), which adds to the supposition that Canaan first saw Noah's inebriated condi-

tion the statement that Noah cursed both Canaan and Ham by turning them black. The passage is in *Materialien zur Kritik und Geschichte des Pentateuchs* 2: 86–87, and is mentioned in Lewis, *Race and Slavery*, p. 124. The passage is known only from an Arabic text of centuries later, and it is doubtful that Ephraim wrote it. In his Syriac commentary on Genesis, the connections among blackness, servitude, and the curse are not made; *Sancti Ephraem Syri*, Corpus Scriptorum Christianorum Orientalium 152, pp. 63–64 (Latin trans., Corpus Scriptorum Christianorum Orientalium 153, p. 51). I thank Father Columba Stewart for his help with these texts and Professor Sebastian Brock for his advice on the question of authenticity.

16. In general, see Lewis, *Race and Color in Islam*; idem, *Race and Slavery*; Davis, *Slavery and Human Progress*, pp. 32–51; and Evans, "From the Land of Canaan."

17. Lewis, *Race and Color in Islam*, pp. 124–25. Other early examples are given in Devisse, *Image of the Black in Western Art* 2: 221 n. 179.

18. Al-Tabari, *History* [215] 2: 14.

19. J. Friedman, *Monstrous Races*, p. 101.

20. This was an opinion, it should be pointed out, that Ibn Khaldun sought to refute, in his *Muqaddimah* 1: 169–70. On the other hand, he was confident that black Africans were unique in that they accepted enslavement because they were of a lower order of humanity, more like animals capable of domestication; see Lewis, *Race and Color in Islam*, p. 38.

21. Evans, "From the Land of Canaan," pp. 27–34.

22. These people were associated as much with Asia as with Africa. For medieval scholars, Ham was not as exclusively connected with Africa as he would be in the modern era. Moreover, Africa, understood in its ancient sense as largely Mediterranean Africa, was not necessarily thought of as inhabited by blacks. I am grateful to Benjamin Braude for pointing this out to me. See also Fischer, *Oriens—Occidens—Europa*, pp. 10–19.

23. Isidore of Seville, *Etymologiae*, bk. 9, chap. 2, nos. 2, 10, 13, 25, 39, 59 (pp. 127–35).

24. J. Friedman, *Monstrous Races*, pp. 99–103. Benjamin Braude is working on disentangling the manuscript tradition of Mandeville, especially with regard to his treatment of the medieval concepts of race, genealogy, and Noah's offspring.

25. Southern, *Western Views of Islam*, pp. 16–17; Zacour, *Jews and Saracens*, pp. 17–22.

26. *Das frühmittelhochdeutsche Wiener Genesis*, vv. 655–56 (p. 135): "Sumelich flurn begarewe ir scônen varwe: / si wurten swarz unt egelîch den ist nehein liut gelîch." (They completely lost their beautiful appearance. They became black and terrible; there are no people like them.) On Cain's descendants see Ruth Mellinkoff, *Mark of Cain*; J. Friedman, *Monstrous Races*, pp. 93–106; Emerson, "Legends of Cain."

27. Emerson, "Legends of Cain," pp. 925–26. That Cain (rather than Ham) was the progenitor of black Africans was still a common assumption in eighteenth-century Portugal, as evidenced by a dialogue between a miner and a lawyer concerning Brazilian slavery (published 1764), cited in Davis, *Problem of Slavery*, pp. 459–60.

The Mormon church held that the offspring of Cain were black, that their descendants were Egyptian, and that Canaan married an Egyptian with the result that Africans were doubly cursed (as noted by Mellinkoff, *Mark of Cain*, pp. 78–80). A special revelation allowed blacks full membership in the Mormon Church in 1978 without explicitly renouncing the Cain-Ham theory of their origin.

28. In general, see J. Friedman, *Monstrous Races*; Mellinkoff, *Mark of Cain*; and Dahan, "L'exégèse de l'histoire de Cain et Abel."

29. Tübingen, Universitätsbibliothek MS Mc 295; a glossed manuscript of the codex, fol. 153r, accompanies Codex 6, 1 "De fugitivis servis." I am grateful to Professor Michael Camille for pointing this illustration out to me. Compare it with the Cambridge, St. John's College, MSK. 26, fol. 6v, showing Cain with horns and kinky hair, illustration 7.

30. This picture is also described in Mellinkoff, *Outcasts* 1: 134, and vol. 2, plate 6.50.

31. Prudentius, *Hamartigenia*, vv. 1–35 (LCL 387, pp. 200–202).

32. Heald, "Peasant in Mediaeval German Literature," pp. 119–20.

33. Hugo von Trimberg, *Der Renner*, v. 15636 (BLVS 248 2: 261).

34. Petrarch, *De remediis*, bk. 2, no. 59 (1: 154), "De villico malo ac superbo": "Profecto autem et si Poeta rusticos ultimos a iustitia derelictos faciat, ut bis dixi, apud uos tamen hominem primum humano semine genitum, et agricolam fuisse constat et parricidam, ut fuisse semper pessimi videantur." A poem attributed to Cecco d'Ascoli, edited in Merlini, *Satira contro il villano*, p. 185, slightly corrected by Feo, "Dal *pius agricola*," pp. 125–26:

> el to ricolto invola
> et impe il suo granaro,
> e po cerca comperare,
> e cosí rico doventa,
> perché l'è della somenta
> del traditor Cain.
>
> (He [the rustic] steals
> your harvest and fills
> his granary and then
> tries to buy [more?].
> And so he becomes
> rich, for he is of the
> seed of the traitor
> Cain.)

A sixteenth-century Italian "Alphabet Against the Villeins" states (under the letter "D") that the rustic "nation" derived from Cain. It is printed in Merlini, *Satira contro il villano*, app. 6, pp. 225–28, in two versions: "Da Cain derivò questa natione" (p. 225) and "Deriva da Cain questa natione" (p. 227).

35. Konrad von Ammenhausen, *Schachzabelbuch*, cols. 379–380, vv. 9744–70 (Cain); cols. 411–12, vv. 10758–77 (Ham). Also see cols. 427–28 for the editor's discussion of the relationship between Konrad von Ammenhausen and Jacobo de Cessolis with regard to Ham. In William Caxton's English version of the chess allegory (the first book printed in England), Cain was the first to work the land, and those who now do so expiate Adam's transgression; but nothing is said about Ham or servitude: "And we rede in the bible that the first labourer that euer was cayn the first sone of adam . . . it behoueth for necessyte that some shold laboure the erthe, after the synne of adam" (Caxton, *Game of the Chesse*, pp. 76–77).

36. Gower, *Vox clamantis*, bk. 1, chap. 10, vv. 747–82 (pp. 42–43). The rubric to the chapter reads: "Hic dicit se per sompnium vidisse progenies Chaym maledictas una cum multitudine seruorum nuper regis Vluxis, quos Circes in bestias mutauit, furiis supradictis associari." Verses 757–58 (p. 43) refer to the "Septem progenies, quas ipse Chaÿm generauit, / Cum furiis socii connumerantur ibi."

37. See above, Chapter 1, pp. 28, 34.

38. Snowden, *Before Color Prejudice*, especially pp. 99–108.

39. Davis, *Slavery and Human Progress*, pp. 46–50.

40. Baudet, *Paradise on Earth*, p. 17.

41. Mark, *Africans in European Eyes*, pp. 19–53.

42. Gliozzi, *Adamo e il nuovo mondo*, pp. 111–46.

43. Azurara, *Crónica dos feitos notáveis* 2: 103–4. I am grateful to Professor Kenneth Wolf, of Pomona College, for this reference.

44. Winthrop Jordan, *White over Black*, pp. 40–41.

45. I owe this information to Professor Jorge Cañizares, of Illinois State University. His paper "New World, New Stars: Patriotic Astrology and the Invention of Indian and Creole Bodies in Colonial Spanish America, 1600–1650," delivered at the John Carter Brown Library of Brown University, explores how explanations of racial subordination fit with patriotic efforts to dispute theories that the climate and astrological configurations of the New World were pernicious. The native inhabitants were inferior not because of the physical condition of the colonies but because of their own debased nature. I am grateful to Professor Cañizares for permission to cite his work.

46. Braude, "Sons of Noah," pp. 134–38; Hannemann, *Curiosum scrutinium*, cited in Perbal, "La race nègre," pp. 158–59. Hannemann was less concerned with the origins of slavery than were his Spanish and English colleagues. His main concern was to construct an ethnography based on classical authorities that could be reconciled with the curse of Noah.

47. Blakely, *Blacks in the Dutch World*, pp. 207–9, 218–19.

48. Fredrickson, *White Supremacy*, pp. 170–71.

49. C. Brown, "Foundations of British Abolitionism," pp. 228–36; Tise, *Proslavery*, pp. 41–96.

50. A number of such arguments are described by Peterson, *Ham and Japheth*. For scriptural arguments justifying slavery, including Noah's curse upon Ham, see Tise, *Proslavery*, pp. 116–25, especially the table on p. 117.

51. A notable example is the physician Samuel A. Cartwright, who supposed that the physiological deficiencies of blacks and their consequent indolence and misery showed that the account of Noah's curse in Genesis was assuredly true, "as if the revelations of anatomy, physiology and history, were a mere re-writing of what Moses wrote" (cited in Peterson, *Ham and Japheth*, pp. 72–73). But Cartwright later gave up Noah's curse in favor of a theory of the separate origins of the races; see Fredrickson, *Black Image*, pp. 87–88. Cartwright had a pre-Adamic black population intermarrying with Cain, thus moving the origins of a cursed race from Ham back to Adam's son.

52. An unsigned article entitled "The Black Race in North America: Why Was Their Introduction Permitted?" contains a fanciful dialogue (pp. 657–58) in which the sons of Ham accept their "long and fearful penance." They acknowledge, "we also, fallen as we are, have a duty to perform," the duty, namely, of providing the labor to fulfill the mission of the sons of Japheth to tame the land. The article was probably written by George Tucker, a congressman and professor of moral philosophy at the University of Virginia, according to Peterson, *Ham and Japheth*, pp. 92–95, 106.

53. As in, for example, Stringfellow's "A Brief Examination of Scripture Testimony." See also Ron Bartour, "Cursed Be Canaan"; and Peterson, *Ham and Japheth*, pp. 42–44.

54. Peterson, *Ham and Japheth*, pp. 45–46; Fredrickson, *Black Image*, pp. 63–64. Proslavery arguments could be connected with various theories of government affecting the free: evocation of a seigneurial order (Genovese, *World the Slaveholders Made*); egalitarian racism condemning the exploitation of white labor in Britain and the industrial North (Fredrickson, *Black Image*, pp. 58–70); and a defense of a generalized inequality joined to order, enterprise, and moral reform—what has been called "conservative Republicanism" (Tise, *Proslavery*, pp. 347–62).

55. Burnett and Dalché, "Attitudes Towards the Mongols," pp. 160–61.

56. J. Friedman, *Monstrous Races*, pp. 102–3.

57. *Das frühmittelhochdeutsche Wiener Genesis*, vv. 766–67 (p. 145): "Vone Chames sculde wurde allêrlist scalche. / ê wâren si alle eben vrî unde edele." (From Ham's guilt there were from then on serfs. Once all had been equally free and noble.)

58. Anton Chekhov, "V Ssylke" ("In Exile"), *Sochineniya* (Moscow) 8 (1977), p. 43: "Ya, bratusha, ne muzhik prostoi, ne iz Khamskovo zvaniya a d'yakovski sin." (English translations normally leave out the reference to Ham.) I am grateful to Vladimir Mazhuga, of Saint Petersburg University, for this reference.

59. Matuszewski, *Geneza Polskiego Chama*. I thank Professor Wacław Uruszczak, of the Jagiellonian University, Cracow, for this reference.

60. Milani, *La schiavitù*, pp. 288–339; Teja, "San Basilio y la esclavitud."

61. Basil, *De Spiritu Sancto* 20.51 (*PG* 32: 162); Ambrose, *Epistolae* 2.7 (CSEL 82, pt. 1, pp. 44–47).

62. Ambrose, *De Noe et Arca*, chaps. 30–32 (*PL* 14: 432–35).

63. Ambrose, *De Helia et Ieiunio* 5.10 (CSEL 32, pt. 2, p. 419); Gratian, *Decretum*, D.35 C.8, 3. See Weigand, *Die Naturrechtslehre*, pp. 133–36, 144–48, 195–214, 262–63.

64. Ambrosiaster, *Commentarius in epistolam ad Colossenses* 4.1 (CSEL 81, pt. 3, p. 202): "Denique peccati causa Cam servus audivit. Cui sententiae veteres adsensere, ita ut definirent omnes prudentes esse liberos, stultos autem omnes esse servos, quia prudens abstinet a peccatis, ut hic ingenuus sit, qui recta sequitur, servus autem qui per stultitiae inprudentiam subicit se peccato. Unde et Cam propter stultitiam, quia risit nuditatem patris stulte, servus est appellatus."

65. John Chrysostom, *Homiliae de Lazaro*, concio 6, 7 (*PG* 48: 1037–38).

66. John Chrysostom, *Sermones in Genesim*, no. 4, 2 (*PG* 54: 595).

67. Ibid., no. 5, 1 (*PG* 54: 599).

68. John Chrysostom, *Homiliae in Genesim* 29.6–7 (*PG* 53: 269–73).

69. Augustine, *De civitate Dei* 16.1–2, 19.15.

70. Augustine, *Quaestionum in Heptateuchum* 1.153 (*PL* 34: 589–90). This formulation is repeated in Alcuin, *Interrogationes et responsiones*, no. 273 (*PL* 100: 557); Haimo of Auxerre, *Expositio in epistolas S. Pauli* (incorrectly attributed to Haimo of Halberstadt), chap. 3 (*PL* 117: 762–63); and Hrabanus Maurus, *Commentaria in Genesim* 4.9 (*PL* 107: 646–47).

71. Stürner, *Peccatum und Potestas*, pp. 106, 112.

72. Gregory I, *Moralia in Job* 21.14–15 (CC 143A, pp. 1081–82). See also Gregory's *Regula pastoralis* 2.6 (*PL* 77: 34).

73. Isidore of Seville, *Sententiarum libri tres* 3.47 (*PL* 83: 717).

74. Oexle, "Die funktionale Dreiteilung," p. 28. For the *Capuciati*, see above, Chapter 3, p. 84.

75. J. Friedman, *Monstrous Races*, pp. 101–3; T. Hill, "*Rígsthula*," pp. 82–83.

76. Honorius Augustodunensis, *Imago mundi* 3.1 (p. 125). In the German *Lucidarius*, an amalgam of several works of Honorius and William of Conches, written in the latter half of the twelfth century, this passage appears with *servi* rendered as *eigenleute* (bondsmen), indicating serfs rather than slaves: "In dez kúnegez ziten wurde die lúte indrú geteilet: von Sem kamen die frigen, von Jafet camen die ritere, von Kam camen die eigin lúte." *Lucidarius aus der Berliner Handschrift*, p. 8. On *eigenleute* in connection with other German terms for peasants in the period 1060–1180, see Stackmann, "Bezeichnungen für 'Bauer,'" p. 172. On *servi* as serfs rather than slaves, see Barthélemy, "Qu'est-ce que le servage," especially pp. 271–72.

77. Alexander of Hales, *Summa theologica* 5: 708, cited in Milani, *La schiavitù*, p. 376.

78. Antoninus, *Summa theologica*, bk. 2, tit. 3, chap. 6, cited in Milani, *La schiavitù*, p. 377.

79. *Mirror of Justices*, p. 76.

80. W. Müller, "Wurzeln und Bedeutung," p. 30; M. Bloch, *Rois et serfs*, p. 140 n. 2.

81. J. Friedman, "Nicholas's 'Angelus ad Virginem,'" pp. 175–80.

82. *Southern Version of "Cursor Mundi,"* vv. 2133–36 (1: 102–3). The Northern Version is excerpted in T. Hill, "*Rígsthula*," p. 84.

83. *Dives and Pauper*, precept 4, chap. 1 (Early English Text Society 275, p. 305):

"And thus for scornynge & vnworchepe that the sone dede to his fadir began first bondage & thraldom & was confermyd of God."

84. Chaucer, "The Parson's Tale," *Canterbury Tales*, vv. 762–68. For Gower, see above, note 36 for this chapter.

85. Patterson, *Chaucer and the Subject of History*, pp. 262–70. On Ham as astrologer, see also J. Friedman, "Nicholas's 'Angelus ad Virginem,'" pp. 177–78.

86. Hugo von Trimberg, *Der Renner*, vv. 15634–37 (BLVS 248, 2: 261) (Cain), and vv. 1315–1406 (BLVS 247, 1: 55–58) (Ham); Konrad von Ammenhausen, *Schachzabelbuch* (see above, note 35 for this chapter). Konrad follows his discussion of Noah's curse with a denunciation of drunkenness (cols. 411–16, vv. 10766–958). He cites Saint Ambrose on drunkenness and subordination but changes the consequence of the invention of wine from slavery to serfdom (*dienstes von eigenschaft*), col. 411, vv. 10768–10771.

87. Enikel, *Weltchronik*, vv. 2917–44 (MGH Deutsche Chronikon 3, pt. 1, pp. 56–58); Gengenbach, "Der Bundtschu," vv. 67–72, 93–96 (pp. 24–25); Hemmerli, *De nobilitate et rusticitate*, cap. 6, fol. 19r; cap. 7, fol. 28r.

88. The French example is the fifteenth-century *Le mistére du Viel Testament*, vv. 6472–78 (1: 252).

89. Hemmerli, *De nobilitate et rusticitate*, cap. 6, fol. 19r; cap. 7, fols. 28r–28v.

90. Hugo von Trimberg, *Der Renner*, vv. 1323–29 (BLVS 247, 1: 55):

> "Vil lieber herre, wie gefüeget sich daz,
> Daz iu herren is vil baz
> Denne uns armen gebûren sî?
> Sint ein liute eigen, die andern frî?"
> "Ja," sprach ich. Das war im zorn.
> Und sprach: "Nu sî wir doch geborn
> Von einer muoter alle!"

> (Very dear lord, how does it come
> about that you lords are so much bet-
> ter off than us poor peasants? Are
> some people bondsmen while others
> are free? "Yes," I said. That made him
> angry, and he said "But we are all born
> of one mother.")

91. Ibid., vv. 1376–79 (p. 57):

> Und sprach: "Verfluocht sî Chanaân
> Und allez sîn geslehte
> Sol diener und eigen knehte
> Mîner zweier süne sîn!"

92. Ibid., vv. 1387–93 (pp. 57–58):

Dô sprach der gebûr einer sâ zehant:
"Nu alerêst mir bekant
Daz wir immer müezen wesen
Vernoyert volc, sît ir gelesen
Habt daz er Noyer hiez,
Der uns disen segen liez
Daz uns immer sol wesen wê."

(Then one of the peasants spoke suddenly, saying "Only now I understand that we must always be an apostate people, because you have read that he was called Noah who left us this blessing, for which we all must suffer.")

93. Ibid., vv. 1394–1459 (pp. 58–60).

94. Wittenwiler, *Der Ring*, vv. 7207–44 (pp. 308–10).

95. Ibid., vv. 7242–44 (p. 310): "Also sein wir nicht geleich: / Einr ist arm, der ander reich, / Einr ein gpaur, der ander edel." The translation is from *Wittenwiler's "Ring" and the Anonymous Scots Poem "Colkelbie Sow,"* p. 97.

96. *Boke of Seynt Albans*, pt. 3, sig. a 1 recto: "A bonde man or a churle wyll say, 'All we be cummyn of Adam.' So Lucifer with his cumpany may say, 'All we be cummyn of heuyn.'"

97. Jonas of Orléans, *De institutione laicali* 2.21 (*PL* 106: 213), citing Gregory I, *Moralia in Job* 21.10 and 21.15, which restates Augustine's statement in *De civitate Dei* 19.15 that God conferred dominion over animals, not over other men.

98. Atto of Vercelli, *Expositio in Epistolas Pauli*, chap. 6 (*PL* 134: 582–83).

99. *Sachsenspiegel Landrecht* 3.42.3 (pp. 223–26). On this section of the *Sachsenspiegel*, see W. Müller, "Wurzeln und Bedeutung," pp. 25–29; Kisch, *Sachsenspiegel and Bible*, pp. 133–40; and Voltelini, "Der Gedanke der allgemeinen Freiheit," pp. 182–86.

100. *Sachsenspiegel Landrecht* 3.42.3 (pp. 224–25): "Ok seggen sumleke lude, it queme egenscap van Cam, Noes sone; Noe segende twene sine sone, an deme dridden ne gewuch he nener egenscap; Cam besatte Affricam mit sime geslechte, Sem blef in Asia, Japhet, unse vordere, besatte Europam; sus ne blef er nen des anderen." (There are some who say that servitude began with Ham, Noah's son. Noah blessed two of his sons; nothing is said about servitude as regards the third. Ham settled Africa with his progeny. Shem remained in Asia. Japhet, our ancestor, settled Europe. Thus neither can be said to belong to the other.)

Cf. Petrus Comestor, *Historia scholastica*, Genesis, chap. 36 (*PL* 198, col. 1087): "Maledixit autem non filio, sed filio filii, quia sciebat in spiritu filium non serviturum fratribus, sed semen eius, nec omnes de semine sed eos, qui de Chanaan descenderant. . . . Sem Asiam, Cham Africam, Japhet Europam sortitus est." Kisch,

Sachsenspiegel and Bible, p. 138, points out that by making Ham settle Africa *with his progeny,* so that all of Ham's offspring are independent of their cousins and hence free, Eike von Repgow changes the implication of Petrus Comestor, who believed Canaan's descendants were subjugated.

101. The author of the *Book of St. Albans* claimed that Ham settled not in Africa but in the cold northern regions that would be called Europe, "that is to say the contre of churlys" (*Boke of Seynt Albans,* pt. 3, sig. a 2 recto). This eccentric theory had at least the virtue of accounting for the ubiquity of European serfs or churls, but it had few if any imitators.

Eike von Repgow, however, was himself unusual in placing Ham exclusively in Africa. Although this is consistent with the passage from Petrus Comestor cited in the previous note, in other works Petrus located Ham's progeny in both Africa and Asia (I thank Benjamin Braude for this information).

A refutation somewhat similar to Eike's argument that the offspring of one biblical figure do not serve the descendants of the other was offered by the Islamic jurist Ahmad Baba (died 1627), an African writing in Timbuktu. Ahmad Baba agreed with the common opinion that heathens could be licitly enslaved but he denied that Muslims could be, no matter what their color. He rejected the notion that Ham's descendants were cursed with enslavement, since God in his mercy could not inflict such a punishment on so many in retribution for one man's sin (Lewis, *Race and Slavery,* pp. 57–58).

102. Wyclif, "De servitute civili et dominio seculari," p. 146.

103. Ibid., p. 147.

104. Luther, *Lectures on Genesis* (to 9:26 and 10:7), pp. 174–78 and 193–95.

Chapter 5

1. "Nation" in this chapter is used to denote both political entities (for the most part kingdoms) and peoples who identified themselves as forming a linguistic or cultural unity. Although the modern terms "nation-state" and "nationalism" make the use of "nation" in connection with the Middle Ages tricky if not dangerous (as noted by Reynolds, *Kingdoms and Communities,* pp. 252–53), its use to describe political or linguistic collectivities is not anachronistic, for "nation" was a medieval concept and word. See also Szűcs, "'Nationalität' und 'Nationalbewusstsein' im Mittelalter," in his *Nation und Geschichte,* pp. 163–243.

2. In theory the state might simply deny internal differences of status and treat the nation as an egalitarian community. In the sixteenth century all Basques were recognized by the Spanish crown as having a legitimate claim to noble status. (Monreal, "Annotations Regarding Basque Traditional Political Thought," pp. 33–34). But this approach would hardly suffice for larger regions with servile populations.

3. Goldberg, "Popular Revolt," p. 471; Bartlett, *Making of Europe,* pp. 214–17; Setton, *Catalan Domination of Athens,* pp. 248–57.

4. Bartlett, *Making of Europe,* pp. 197–242. Bartlett describes what he considers

to be problems of medieval European "race relations." On the dangers of the concept of race applied to conquests within Europe, see Reynolds, *Kingdoms and Communities*, p. 255.

5. Patterson, *Chaucer and the Subject of History*, pp. 266–70.

6. C. Hill, "Norman Yoke"; Faith, "'Great Rumour' of 1377."

7. Grafton, "Higher Criticism Ancient and Modern"; Borchardt, *German Antiquity in Renaissance Myth*.

8. B. Anderson, *Imagined Communities*.

9. *Invention of Tradition*, ed. Hobsbawm and Ranger (1983).

10. Reynolds, "Medieval *Origines Gentium*," pp. 375–90.

11. Coll i Alentorn, "La llegenda d'Otger Cataló"; idem, *Guifré el Pilós*; Bisson, "Rise of Catalonia."

12. Linehan, *History and the Historians*.

13. Klaniczay, "Paradoxes of Royal Sainthood."

14. Beaune, *Birth of an Ideology*; Spiegel, *Romancing the Past*.

15. Tate, "Mythology in Spanish Historiography." The idea of Tubal as the founder of Iberia was adopted from Josephus via Saint Ambrose and Isidore of Seville and put into peninsular circulation by Ximénez de Rada in the thirteenth century.

16. Mannyng, *Chronicle*, pt. 1, vv. 261–428 (pp. 97–101).

17. Coll i Alentorn, "La llegenda d'Otger Cataló," pp. 39–40.

18. Spiegel, *Romancing the Past*, pp. 55–151.

19. On the importance of vigor and controlled savagery, see Bartlett, *Making of Europe*, pp. 85–105.

20. Of course, when exalting the ruler's authority, mythography could combine heroism and constitutionalism, as in the account of the origins of the Catalan heraldic symbol, consisting of four red bars on a yellow ground. This symbol supposedly originated when the emperor Louis the Pious traced it in blood as a symbol of heroism *and* legitimacy, having dipped his fingers in a wound that Count Guifré had suffered while in the emperor's service. See Udina i Martorell, "En torno a la leyenda de las 'Barras' catalanes"; Fluvià, *Els quatre pals*.

21. See below, Chapter 8.

22. Combarieu, "Image et représentation du *vilain*," p. 16. In Germany the existence of peasant soldiers and servile knights gave rise to propaganda against rustics becoming knights, not necessarily because they were physically incapable or cowardly but because they lacked chivalric character.

23. The *Pseudo-Turpin* formed part of the *Liber Sancti Jacobi*, the best-known version of which is the *Codex Calixtinus* at Santiago de Compostela. The *Codex* also contains the pilgrims' guide to Santiago along with liturgical and miracle texts connected with the relics of Saint James. As a separate work, the *Pseudo-Turpin Chronicle* would enjoy great popularity in Latin and in vernacular languages, and consequently it survives in several hundred manuscripts. In general, see Spiegel, *Romancing the Past*, pp. 55–98.

24. The Latin *Descriptio*, probably written at Saint-Denis between 1080 and

1095, is discussed in Rauschen, *Die Legende Karls des Grossen*, pp. 97–102, and edited on pp. 103–25. The passage concerning the penalties for failure to accompany Charlemagne is on p. 108.

25. *Old French Johannes*; Walpole, "Charlemagne's Journey to the East." See Spiegel, *Romancing the Past*, p. 71.

26. *Old French Johannes*, p. 143, especially lines 5–8: "Il manda et commenda par tote France que tuit cil qui serf erent de lor chars par les mauveses costums des seignors, fussent franc permenablement, et il et lor ligniee, cele qui ert presente et a venir." (Spiegel, *Romancing the Past*, p. 86, renders this as follows: "He directed and commanded throughout all France that all those who were serfs in their persons on account of the evil customs of lords should be free in perpetuity, they and their line, both in the present and to come.") A similar passage appears in other versions of Pseudo-Turpin: *Anglo-Norman Pseudo-Turpin Chronicle of William de Briane* ll.372–81; *Anonymous Old French Translation of the Pseudo-Turpin Chronicle* 9.3–9 (p. 49); *Le Turpin français, dit le Turpin I* ll.4–11 (pp. 13–14).

27. Walpole, "Charlemagne's Journey," p. 446: "Cil qui porroient armes porter et avec lui n'iroient, devroient .iiii. deniers de lor chief a toz jors mais, et il et lor ligniee, celle qui ert presente et a venir." (Spiegel, *Romancing the Past*, p. 85, translates as follows: "those who were able to bear arms and would not go with him owed four pennies a head henceforth, they and their line, both in the present and to come.")

28. *Old French Johannes*, p. 132, lines 11–12: "qui n'i iroit, il seroit sers, et il et si oir, a toz jorz." (Spiegel, *Romancing the Past*, p. 86, translates as follows: "he who will not go shall be a serf, both he and his heirs forever.")

29. Discussed by Lemaître, "Le refus de service d'ost," pp. 231–32.

30. *Gui de Bourgogne*, vv. 177–80 (p. 6):

> Mais une chose voil que sachent de verté
> Par la foi que doi sainte crestienté
> Il et touz ses linages sera sers racheté
> Touz les jors de sa vie sera il sers clamé.

31. Ibid., vv. 181–84 (pp. 6–7).

32. Lemaître, "Le refus de service d'ost," pp. 232–35.

33. *Le Roman de Renart le Contrefait*, Redaction A, fol. 140 (1: 353):

> Et plusseur qui le contredirent,
> Que il n'i vostrent pas aler,
> Iceulz fist il cers apeller,
> Eus et leur anfans ansugant.
> Encor l'ot l'en maintenant,
> A Paris en a un millier.

34. *Le Roman de Renart le Contrefait*, sixième branche, vv. 37430–521 (2: 155–56).

35. Ibid., vv. 37545–47 (p. 156): "Dist le roy: 'Cilz ont bien ouvré, / Et par Dieu bien s'i sont prouvé.' / Et pour cest mot, Prouvins ot nom."

36. Beaumanoir, *Coutumes de Beauvaisis*, chap. 45, par. 1438 (2: 226–27); par. 1453 (2: 235–36).

37. Quoted in M. Bloch, *Rois et serfs*, p. 132: "Comme selonc le droit de nature chascun doie nestre franc et par aucuns usages ou coustumes qui de grant ancienneté ont esté encredités et gardees jusques ci en nostre reaume, et par aventure par le mesfait de leurs predecesseurs moult de personnes de nostre commun peuple soient encheues en lyans de servitutes et de diverses condicions, qui moult nous desplet, nous, considerans que nostre reaume est dit et nommé le royaume des Frans."

38. *Digest* (*Codex Justinianus*) 4.2.22, 37.1.13, 48.1.2, 48.13.6. See the discussion of this in Szűcs, "Theoretical Elements," pp. 268–69.

39. On *heribannum*, see the Capitulary of Boulogne (811), in MGH Legum, sec. 2, Regum Francorum, 1 p. 166. On *lantweri*, see Contamine, *War in the Middle Ages*, p. 24; and Ganshof, *Frankish Institutions*, pp. 60, 153.

40. Ganshof, *Frankish Institutions*, p. 68.

41. M. Bloch, *Rois et serfs*, p. 144.

42. For King Joan I's request that the pope abolish the "bad customs" characteristic of servitude, see Barcelona, Arxiu de la Corona d'Aragó, Cancelleria, Registre 1968, fol. 11r; the inquiry concerning the end of servitude ("haiam entes qual temps de la servitut. . . . segons les Chroniques, es ja passat") is in Barcelona, Arxiu de la Corona d'Aragó, Cancelleria, Registre 1955, fols. 105v–106r.

43. On French emancipation, see M. Bloch, *Rois et serfs*, pp. 40–70, 94–172; and William Jordan, *From Servitude to Freedom*.

44. Kelley, "Clio and the Lawyers."

45. Freedman, "Catalan Lawyers," especially pp. 304–14; idem, "Cowardice, Heroism." These articles are reprinted in Freedman, *Church, Law and Society*.

46. Barcelona, Arxiu de la Corona d'Aragó, MS Ripoll 99. See Hämel, "Arnaldus de Monte und der Liber S. Jacobi," pp. 147–59.

47. *Gesta comitum Barcinonensium*, pp. 3–6. On parallels with Frankish legends see Aurell, *Les noces du comte*, pp. 507–13.

48. Zimmermann, "La prise de Barcelone."

49. Paris, Bibliothèque National, MS Espagnol 13, fols. 76v–77r.

50. However, it was possible elsewhere to depreciate Charlemagne's efforts in Spain. Rodrigo Ximénes de Rada, archbishop of Toledo, in his *Historia de rebus Hispanie* (written in the mid-thirteenth century), bk. 4, chap. 10 (CC 72, pp. 126–28), minimized the extent of Charlemagne's conquests. Radulphus Niger, in his *Moralia Regum* 19.14, accused Charlemagne of making an unfavorable treaty with the Moors; for this see Buc, "Exégèse et pensée politique," p. 150.

51. El Escorial, Real Biblioteca de San Lorenzo, MS d.II.18, fols. 94r–93v (the foliation is backwards), edited in Freedman, *Origins of Peasant Servitude*, p. 226.

52. El Escorial, Real Biblioteca de San Lorenzo, MS d.II.18, fol. 93v: "Ex post venerunt Christiani et conquistabant istam terram et, cum continue preliabant contra Saracenos, petierunt secrete adiutorium ab istis Christianis captiuis, qui timore Saracenorum nullum sufragium voluerunt dare Christianis."

53. Ibid., fol. 93v: "Et Christiani per gratiam Iesu Christi totam terram conquistarunt et aplicarunt fidey Christiane, et multi fuerunt in oppinione quod interficerent Christianos istos sic captiuos ex eo quare tempore conquiste nullum sufragium voluerunt prestare Christianis. Alii tenuerunt quod illesi remanerent et sub Christianis sicuti erant tempore Saracenorum, et quod redimerent se et cultiuarent et alia seruicia facerent Christianis sicuti facere solebant Saracenis et sic fuerunt a morte liberati."

54. *Digest (Codex Justinianus)* 41.5.7, attributed to Gaius.

55. Ibid., 1.5.4 (Florentius): "Servi ex eo appellati sunt, quod imperatores captivos vendere ac per hoc servare nec occidere solent."

56. Bresc, "L'esclave dans le monde méditerranéen," pp. 89–91; Verlinden, *L'esclavage dans l'Europe médiévale* 1: 249–545.

57. El Escorial, Real Biblioteca de San Lorenzo d.II.18, fols. 121v–114r (the foliation is backwards), especially fols. 118r–117v.

58. Ibid., fol. 118r (edited in Freedman, *Origins of Peasant Servitude*): "Christiani captiui, dubitantes quis eorum obtineret triumphum, noluerunt prebere auxilium regi Karolo nec Christianis. Deo duce Christiani deuincerunt Saracenos [fol. 117v] et hanc terram subdiderunt fidey Catholice. Et facta subieccione huius patrie, dixerunt Christiani regi ut interficeret Christianos captiuos eo quia cum eo noluerunt debellare pro fide. Rex deliberauit habito consilio, cum ipse tenuit gentes armigeras et non poterant cultiuare, ut sinerent illos captiuos Christianos uiuere et ut captiui, sicut antea faciebant apud infideles, uiuerent et nunch et in perpetuum apud Christianos."

59. Freedman, "Cowardice, Heroism," pp. 10–11.

60. Tomich, *Historias e conquestas*, fol. 18v.

61. Joan de Socarrats, *Ioannis de Socarratis*, p. 501.

62. Coll i Alentorn, "La llegenda d'Otger Cataló."

63. Tomich, *Historias e conquestas*, fols. 11r–18v.

64. Cited in Coll i Alentorn, "La llegenda d'Otger Cataló," p. 27: "E aquest és lo principi de les llibertats de Cathalunya, car no principia en hòmens rústichs ni aplegadiços, sinó en alts e valerosos."

65. Simon of Kéza, *Gesta Hungarorum*, pp. 147–48.

66. Macartney, *Studies on the Earliest Hungarian Historical Sources*.

67. I have relied on Szűcs, "Theoretical Elements," and R. Hoffmann, "Outsiders by Birth and Blood."

68. *Das Nibelungenlied*, from chap. 21 ("Wie Kriemhilt zuo den Hiunen fuor"), on pp. 208ff.

69. Szűcs, "Die Nation in historischer Sicht und der nationale Aspekt der Geschichte," in his *Nation und Geschichte*, pp. 85–86.

70. Simon of Kéza, *Gesta Hungarorum*, chap. 4, p. 144.

71. Szűcs, "Theoretical Elements," pp. 258–59.

72. Simon of Kéza, *Gesta Hungarorum*, chap. 7, pp. 147–48: "Quicunque ergo edictum contempsisset praetendere non valens rationem, lex Scitica per medium cultro huius detruncabat, vel exponi in causas desperatas, aut detrudi in communium

servitutem." On the meaning of "exponi in causas desperatas," a Roman-law formulation, see Szűcs, "Theoretical Elements," pp. 268–69.

73. Simon of Kéza, *Gesta Hungarorum*, chap. 7, p. 148: "Vitia itaque et excessus huius unum Hungarum ab alio separavit, alias cum unus pater et una mater omnes Hungaros procreaverit, quorum unus nobilis, alter innobilis diceretur, nisi victus per tales casus criminis haberetur." I reproduce the translation given by R. Hoffmann, "Outsiders by Birth and Blood," p. 15.

74. Szűcs, "Theoretical Elements," pp. 251–52.

75. Ibid., pp. 268–69.

76. Ibid., pp. 278–80.

77. *Hungarian Illuminated Chronicle*, facsimile fol. 4v.

78. Thuróczy, *Chronica Hungarorum*, vol. 1, chap. 12, pp. 33–34.

79. Ibid., p. 33: "Edictum etiam fuit, quod, cum res communitatem equa sorte tangentes occurrerent, aut generalis expeditio exercitus incumberet, ut mucro sanguinis aspergine tinctus media Hunorum per habitacula castraque deferretur."

80. Ibid., p. 34: "Hec consuetudo inter Hunos sive Hungaros usque ad tempora Geyse ducis filii ducis Toxon filii Arpad inviolabiliter extitit observata, et multos generatione de hac perpetuam redegit in rusticitatem."

81. Ibid, p. 34: "Nam cum una et eadem fuerint generatio, et a quondam Hunor et Magor unanimiter processerint, aliter fieri nequivisset, ut alter dominus, alter servus vel rusticus effici potuisset." The translation is from R. Hoffmann, "Outsiders by Birth and Blood," p. 17.

82. Bak, *Königtum und Stände*, pp. 62–79. For the historiography of the Doctrine and its polemical uses in the modern era, see Várdy, *Modern Hungarian Historiography*, pp. 179–89.

83. For the capitulation of Vladislav II (1490), see in Bak, *Königtum und Stände*, pp. 152–54.

84. On the Hungarian uprising see below, Chapter 11, pp. 269–80.

85. The 1152 peace ordinance (*Reichslandfrieden*) of Frederick I included provisions against rustics' carrying lances, swords, or "weapons" (*arma*) generally; see *Quellen zur Geschichte des deutschen Bauernstandes*, no. 83, p. 222. Also see below, Chapter 8.

86. *Monumenta rusticorum in Hungaria rebellium*, no. 202, Prologue, p. 148: "considerassemusque pericula omnia, que hucusque huic Hungarie regno nostro ab infidelibus hostibus illata sunt, ruinas quoque et desolaciones castrorum finitimorum atque eciam tumultum illum nefandissimum, quem plebs rustica . . . crudelitate concitaverat."

87. Ibid., Article 14, p. 260: "Item quamquam omnes rustici, qui adversus dominos eorum naturales insurrexerunt, tanquam proditores capitali pena sint plectendi."

88. Ibid., p. 260: "per hanc infidelitatis ipsorum notam amissa libertate eorum, qua de loco in locum recedendi habebant facultatem, dominis ipsorum terrestribus mera et perpetua rusticitate sint subiecti"; cited in R. Hoffmann, "Outsiders by Birth and Blood," p. 33 n. 64.

89. Ibid., Article 47, pp. 270–71: "ut nunquam de cetero de illorum progenie iudex aut iuratus civis vel villicus in medio aliorum rusticorum aliquis eligatur nemoque in curia principis vel dominorum ac nobilium ex eis famulari unquam possit et nullus eorum ad aliquem honorem promoveatur, sed tanquam maledicte generacionis iugo perpetue servitutis et rusticitate subiecti reatus ipsorum penam lugeant sine fine."

90. *Werbőczy István Hármaskönyve* pt. 1, tit. 3, pp. 56, 58.

91. Ibid., pt. 3, tit. 25, p. 406: "hujusmodi tamen ipsorum libertatem superiore hac aestate, propter seditionem, et tumultuarium eorum adversus universam nobilitatem, sub nomine cruciatae, ductu cujusdam sceleratissimi latronis Georgii Zekel appellati insurrectionem ex eoque notam perpetuae infidelitatis eorum incursionem, penitus amiserunt. Dominisque ipsorum terrestribus, mera et perpetua jam rusticitate subjecti sunt."

92. Ibid., pt. 1, tit. 3, p. 58: "Haec sanctio plurimos Hungarorum (ut praefertur) plebae perhibetur effecisse conditionis. Nam cum una et eadem de generatione a quondam scilicet Hunnor et Magor unanimiter processerint, aliter fieri nequivisset, ut hic dominus, ille servus, hic nobilis, ille ignobilis, et rusticus efficeretur."

93. Szűcs, *Nation und Geschichte*, p. 89.

94. Bak, *Königtum und Stände*, pp. 74–79.

95. *Werbőczy István Hármaskönyve*, pt. 1, tit. 4, p. 228: "Nomine autem, et appellatione populi, hoc in loco intellige: solummodo dominos praelatos, barones, et alios magnates, atque quoslibet nobiles; sed non ignobiles."

96. Székely, "Le passage à l'économie."

97. Roger of Wendover, *Flowers of History*, p. 66: "et quod nullus remaneat, qui arma portare possit, sub nomina culvertagii et perpetuae servitutis."

98. *Two of the Saxon Chronicles Parallel*, p. 200.

99. Henry of Huntingdon, *History of the English*, p. 8.

100. Hanning, *Vision of History in Early Britain*, pp. 44–62, 77–83.

101. Turville-Petre, "Politics and Poetry"; Moffat, "Sin, Conquest, Servitude"; Summerfield, "*Bondage & Destres*." I am grateful to Drs. Moffat and Summerfield for sharing their work with me and helping me with this section.

102. *Metrical Chronicle of Robert of Gloucester*, vv. 7498–7501 (2: 541).

103. Ibid., vv. 7503–13 (pp. 541–42).

104. Castleford, *Chronicle*, vol. 2, bk. 10 pt. 3, vv. 31,931–38 (p. 863).

105. *Chronicle of Pierre de Langtoft* 1: 288–90.

106. Mannyng, *Chronicle*, pt. 2, vv. 139–41 (p. 490): "Sithen he & his haf had the lond in heritage / that the Inglis haf so lad that thei lyue in seruage. / He sette the Inglis to the thralle, that or was so fre." See also pt. 2, vv. 6317–18 (pp. 644–45), where Edward I is quoted as saying: "For alle this thraldam that now on Inglond es. / Thorgh Normans it cam, bondage & destres."

107. As pointed out by Summerfield, "*Bondage & Destres*."

108. Mannyng, *Chronicle*, pt. 2, vv. 617–21 (p. 529):

> this vision is yit to drede, think & gif gode kepe.
> I trowe it is ouergone thorgh William conqueroure.
> He com & slouh ilkone tho wikked men in stoure
> & sette vs in seruage, of fredom felle the floure;
> The Inglis borgh taliage lyue yit in sorow fulle soure.

> (This vision is still to be dreaded, think on it well. I
> say it happened through William the Conqueror.
> He came and slew the wicked men in battle and re-
> duced us to servitude, the flower of freedom fell.
> The English still live in great sorrow because of tax-
> ation.)

Ibid., vv. 1760–63 (p. 533):

> that bondage, that brouht was ouer the se;
> now ere thei in seruage, fulle fele that or was fre.
> Our fredom that day for euer toke the leue;
> for Harald it went away, his falshed did vs greue.

> (. . . that bondage that was brought from over
> the sea. Now they who formerly were free fell
> into servitude. Our freedom departed that day
> forever. Through Harold it went away; his false-
> ness hurt us.)

109. Turville-Petre, "Politics and Poetry." Moffat takes issue with this view in "Sin, Conquest, Servitude."

110. *Matthaei Parisiensis, Monachi Sancti Albani, Historia Anglorum* 1: 28–29.

111. See above, note 108 for this chapter. Tallage was levied on villeins, but Mannyng here is complaining about taxes paid by higher orders of society ("us"), likening them all to servile (oppressive) obligations.

112. Dyer, "Memories of Freedom."

113. Faith, "'Great Rumour' of 1377," pp. 43–48.

114. Ibid., pp. 56–57.

115. Walsingham, *Gesta Abbatum Monasterii Sancti Albani*, pp. 157–63. See Faith, "Class Struggle in Fourteenth Century England."

Chapter 6

1. Among the many studies of the harsh treatment of peasants in medieval texts are Martini, *Das Bauerntum*, pp. 41–102, 135–213; Hügli, *Der deutsche Bauer im Mittelalter*; Wunder, "Der dumme und der schlaue Bauer"; Merlini, *Satira contro il villano*; Feo, "Dal *pius agricola*," pp. 89–136, 206–23; Coulton, *Medieval Village*,

pp. 231–52; Galpin, *Cortois and Vilain*; Algazi, *Herrengewalt*; and Jonin, "La revision d'un topos."

2. Cited in Galpin, *Cortois and Vilain* pp. 8–9. See also Ribard, *Un ménestral du XIVe siècle, Jean de Condé*, p. 117.

3. "Des vilains ou des XXII manieries de vilains," especially pp. 249–55.

4. This "Peasant Catechism" is in a Munich manuscript signed by Georg Prenperger, a graduate of the University of Vienna, edited in *Parodistische Texte*, no. 7, pp. 21–22.

5. Cited in Le Goff, *Medieval Civilization*, p. 300; and Specht, *Poetry and the Iconogrphy of the Peasant*, p. 49. There is also a late-medieval version from northern Italy (in *Carmina medii aevi*, p. 28), and another "declension" in the Prenperger satire that emphasizes the blackness and bestial nature of the rustic (in *Parodistische Texte*, p. 22).

6. Nykrog, *Les fabliaux*, especially pp. 105–7.

7. Galpin, *Cortois and Vilain*; Gravdal, *Vilain and Courtois*. Gravdal (pp. 13 and 100) singles out Galpin as an example of over-literal social interpretation, which is not completely fair since Galpin acknowledges (pp. 10–11) that *villanie* is a quality opposed to courtesy more than an attribute of peasants, who tend to be peripheral in the literature he considers.

8. Gravdal, *Vilain and Courtois*, pp. 6–14. See also Zumthor, "Intertextualité et mouvance." The game-versus-lesson simile is from Nabakov as cited by Gravdal, p. 6.

9. Bonnassie, "Marc Bloch, Historian of Servitude," in his *From Slavery to Feudalism*, p. 330.

10. Gravdal, *Vilain and Courtois*, pp. 81–112, especially 97–100.

11. The best-known edition is *Die Lieder Neidharts*, edited by Edmund Weissner, 2nd ed., which embodies a restrictive definition of what poems are to be included within the genuine Neidhart corpus. This edition is supplemented by *Die Berliner Neidhart-Handschrift c*. I am indebted to Dr. Elizabeth I. Traverse for her advice and help with the poems of Neidhart. I have profited greatly from her book *Peasants, Seasons and Werltsüeze*. Also of fundamental importance are Simon, *Neidhart von Reuental*; and Schweikle, *Neidhart*.

12. On the complicated questions about the manuscripts of Neidhart and about which of the poems attributed to him are genuine, see Traverse, *Peasants, Seasons and Werltsüeze*, pp. 50–121; H. Becker, *Die Neidharte*; Bennewitz-Behr, *Original und Rezeption*; and Beyschlag, "Neidhart von Reuental in neuer Sicht." On the violence of the peasants, see Traverse, "Hie saget Neidhart."

13. *Neidhartspiele* and *Die Historien des Neithart Fuchs*.

14. On Neidhart's reputation as the opponent of the peasantry, see Jöst, *Bauernfeindlichkeit*, pp. 46–55. See also Margetts, "Das Bauerntum in der Literatur"; Heald, "Peasant in Mediaeval German Literature," p. 195; and Simon, "Neidharte and Neidhartianer," especially pp. 183–84.

15. *Scorn for the World*, bk. 2, vv. 257–59 (p. 90).

16. "Alphabeto disposto contra i villani" (dating from ca. 1500), cited in *Carmina*

medii aevi, p. 27: "Christo fo da villan crucificò, / e stagom sempre in pioza, in vento
e in neve, / perchè havom fato così gran peccò." (Three other Italian examples of this
theme are given in Merlini, *Satira contro il villano,* p. 3 n. 1.) "De natura rusticorum,"
a fourteenth-century Italian poem, also in *Carmina medii aevi,* vv. 86–90 (p. 37):

> Hi non curant de doctrina,
> tegunt se pelle asinina:
> intus vero sunt lupina,
> verba latrant ut canina,
> infelices rustici.

17. Chrétien de Troyes, *Le chevalier au lion (Yvain),*v. 286 (p. 9): "Uns vileins, qui
resanbloit Mor."

18. Mellinkoff, *Outcasts* 1: 26, 149, 202, 231.

19. *Thesaurus lingue latinae,* vol. 10, pt. 1 (Leipzig, 1982), pp. 81–84.

20. Martin of Braga, "De correctione rusticorum."

21. P. Brown, *Cult of the Saints,* pp. 119–20; idem, "Relics and Social Status in the
Age of Gregory of Tours," pp. 230–33; Köbler, "'Bauer' (*agricola, colonus, rusticus*)."

22. Grundmann, *Religious Movements in the Middle Ages,* p. 14.

23. Le Goff, *Time, Work, and Culture,* pp. 92–93.

24. Köbler, "'Bauer' (*agricola, colonus, rusticus*)," pp. 239–40.

25. Burchard of Worms, *Decretum,* bk. 10 (*PL* 140: 831–54).

26. Schmitt, *Holy Greyhound*; Ginzburg, *Night Battles*; idem, *Ecstasies.*

27. Cited in Coulton, *Medieval Village,* pp. 265–66.

28. Galpin, *Cortois and Vilain,* p. 84.

29. *Nouveau Recueil complet des fabliaux,* no. 39 (5: 34).

30. *Liber miraculorum Sancte Fidis* 1.7 (pp. 99–100): "Nec tamen mirum, si
quidam rusticus, ab omni scientia alienus prorsusque totius divine virtutis inexper-
tus, quodque deterius est, sinistre mentis pravitate falsus, tam grave erroris periculum
incurrit." The translation is Sheingorn's in *Book of Sainte Foy,* p. 64.

31. Cited in Medeiros, *Jacques et chroniqueurs,* p. 51.

32. *L'Archivo Capitolare della Cattedral di Mantova,* p. 63. I thank Duane Osheim
of the University of Virginia for this reference.

33. Camille, "Labouring for the Lord," and his forthcoming book, *A Mirror in
Parchment?*

34. *Li romans de Claris et Laris,* vv. 8371–84 (BLVS 169, pp. 226–27):

> Li vilain sont de laide forme,
> Ainc si tres laide ne vit home;
> Chaucuns a .xv. pies de granz,
> En auques resemblent jaianz,
> Mes trop sont de laide maniere;
> Boçu sont devant et derriere,
> Les cheveus noirs comme arremenz,

Les ongles grandes con serpenz,
Les mentons demi pie de grant,
Lors euls resemblent feu ardant,
Denz de senglier et nes de chat,
Hure de lou, qui se combat,
Trop resembloient bien deable,
Tant sont fier et espoantable.

(The *vilains* are ugly in form,
more ugly than anyone has ever
seen. Each one is fifteen feet tall
and in some ways they resemble
giants, but of a very ugly sort.
A paunch in front, and hump-
backed, hair black like ink, with
nails long as serpents, their chins
half a foot wide, their eyes resemble burning fire, teeth of wild
boar, nose like a cat's, snout like
a ravening wolf. They are very
much like devils, ferocious and
frightening.)

35. Chrétien de Troyes, *Le chevalier au lion (Yvain)*, vv. 286–305 (pp. 9–10):

Uns vileins, qui resanbloit Mor,
leiz et hideus a demesure,
einsi tres leide criature
qu'an ne porroit dire de boche,
assis s'estoit sor une çoche,
une grant maçue en sa main.
Je m'aprochai vers le vilain,
si vi qu'il ot grosse la teste
plus que roncins ne autre beste,
chevox mechiez et front pelé,
s'ot pres de deus espanz de lé,
oroilles mossues et granz
autiex com a uns olifanz,
les sorcix granz et le vis plat,
ialz de çuete, et nes de chat,
boche fandue come lous,
danz de sengler aguz et rous,
barbe rosse, grenons tortiz,
et la manton aers au piz,
longe eschine torte et boçue

(. . . a lowborn creature, black as a
Moor [literally "resembled a
Moor"], huge and hideously ugly—
indeed, so incredibly awful that
there are no words to describe
him—and holding a great club in
his hand. And riding toward this
fellow I saw that his head was bigger than a packhorse's, or any other
beast's. His hair was tufted, and his
forehead bald and wide as two out-
spread hands, his ears all mossy and
immense, exactly like an elephant's,
his eyebrows huge, his face as if
flattened. He had eyes like an owl,
a nose like a cat, and jaws split like
a wolf's, with a boar's wild teeth, all
yellowed, and his beard was black,
his moustache crooked. His chin
met his chest, his backbone long
and twisted. [*Yvain, the Knight of
the Lion*, pp. 11–12])

36. *Aucassin et Nicolette*, chap. 24, p. 114: "Grans estoit et mervellex et lais et hidex. Il avoit une grande hure plus noire qu'une carbouclee et avoit plus de planne paume entre deus ex, et avoit unes grandes joes et un grandisme nés plat et unes grans narines lees et unes grosses levres plus rouges d'une carbounee et uns grans dens gaunes et lais." (He was tall and weird and alarmingly ugly. He had a great mop of a head as black as smut with eyes set a palm's width apart, broad cheeks, an enormous flat nose with cavernous nostrils, thick lips redder than underdone meat and great, ugly yellow teeth. [*"Aucassin and Nicolette" and Other Tales*, p. 45.])

37. *Historia Gaufredi*, p. 184. See Bisson, "Feudal Revolution," pp. 34–35.

38. Rigord, *Gesta Phillippi* 1.3 (1: 10–11). Owen, "The Prince and the Churl," pp. 141–44, argues that this story is probably derived from *Yvain*.

39. Hemmerli, *De nobilitate et rusticitate*, cap. 1, fol. 1r: "Qui quidem homo vix et indignanter eleuato dorso montoso. Recuruoque gipposo, vultuque swalido tortuoso necnon aspectu stolido, pariter et asinino, fronte rugosa sulcuta, barba hyspida, capito pilos nodosis et cannis cirrosis comato, lippis oculis." The rustic notes (fol. 1v) that the apostles and prophets, too, were untaught; that Barlaam's ass could talk; and that a bull warned the city of Rome (according to Valerius Maximus). On Hemmerli and this text, see Hieronymous, "Felix Hemmerli und Sebastian Brant."

40. Le Goff, "Le désert-forêt dans l'Occident médiéval"; and idem, "Lévi-Strauss en Brocéliande." English versions of these essays appear in Le Goff, *Medieval Imagination*, pp. 47–59 and 107–31.

41. Chrétien de Troyes, *Le chevalier au lion (Yvain)*, vv. 326–30 (p. 11):

> je li dis: "Va, car me di
> se tu es boene chose ou non."
> Et il me dist qu'il ert uns hom.
> "Quiez hom ies tu?—Tex con tu voiz;
> si ne sui autres nul foiz.

On this exchange see the cogent remarks of Peter Haidu in his essay "Romance.".

42. *Historia Gaufredi*, p. 184: "Quam videns liberalis Gaufredus, non ut pauperem dives contempsit, sed, ut homo hominem recognoscens, in unius miseria communem hominum calamitatem deplorat, elogium illud primi hominis remeniscens: 'In sudore,' inquit, 'vultus tui vesceris pane tuo.'"

43. Hemmerli, *De nobilitate et rusticitate*, cap. 1, fol. 1r.

44. Ibid., cap. 34, fol. 141v.

45. *La chanson de Roland*, vv. 1631–40 (1: 175); vv. 1913–34 (1: 188–89).

46. Ibid., vv. 24–61 (1: 94–95).

47. Ibid., vv. 894–99 (1: 138):

> Uns amurafles i ad de Balaguez,
> Cors ad mult gent et le vis fier e cler.
> Puis quë il est sur sun cheval muntét,
> Mult se fait fiers de des armes porter;
> De vasselage est il ben alosez:
> Fust chrestïens, asez oüst barnét.
>
> (An emir is there from Balaguer.
> His body is very handsome and his face fierce and fair.
> When he is mounted on his horse,
> He bears his arms with great ferocity.
> He is well known for his courage;
> Had he been a Christian, he would have been a worthy baron.
> *[Song of Roland, p. 57])*

48. On Vézelay, see Mâle, *L'art religieux*, pp. 326–32. On the Plinian races and the problem of their humanity see J. Friedman, *Monstrous Races*.

49. See Bhabha, "Difference, Discrimination and the Discourse of Colonialism," pp. 202–4, and, for his critique of Edward Said's "Orientalist" idea of alterity, pp. 199–201.

50. "Du prestre et du chevalier," cited in Falk, *Étude sociale*, p. 83; and edited in *Recueil général et complete des fabliaux* 2: 34: "Maleureus de toute part / Hideus comme leu ou lupart / Qui ne savent entre gens estre."

51. Cited in Feo, "Dal *pius agricola*," pp. 105–6.

52. *Quellen zur Geschichte des deutschen Bauernstandes*, no. 117, p. 312: "et ferino more, feris bestiis crudelius sevientes."

53. As translated in Coulton, *Medieval Village*, p. 134.

54. Bonjour et al., *Short History of Switzerland*, p. 106.

55. Hemmerli, *De nobilitate et rusticitate*, cap. 33, fol. 131v.

56. Gower, *Vox clamantis*, bk. 1, pp. 20–81.

57. Ibid., bk. 1, vv. 2093–96 (p. 79).

58. *Eupolemius*, trans. Ziolkowski, p. 32.

59. For works concerning wild men, see below, Chapter 7, note 5.

60. Combarieu, "Image et représentation du *vilain*," p. 11; Hemmerli, *De nobilitate et rusticitate*, cap. 1, fol. 1r.

61. *Li Romans de Garin le Loherain* 2: 152–53, cited in Le Goff, *Medieval Civilization*, p. 300:

> Gros out les bras et les membres fornis,
> Entre deus iaus plaine paume accompli;
> Larges épaules et si out gros le pis;
> Hireciés fu, s'ot charbonné le vis,
> Ne fu lavés de six mois accomplis,
> Né n'i ot aive sé du ciel ne chaï.

62. Alvarus Pelagius, *De planctu ecclesiae*, fol. 147r, as translated in Coulton, *Medieval Village*, p. 244.

63. Sánchez de Arévalo, *Speculum vitae humanae* 1.21, as translated in Coulton, *Medieval Village*, app. 31, pp. 517–19.

64. "Le despit au vilain," vv. 39–42 (in *Jongleurs et trouvères*, p. 108), cited in Braet, "A Thing Most Brutish," p. 196.

65. Panofsky, *Early Netherlandish Painting* 1: 66.

66. J. Alexander, "*Labeur* and *Paresse*," pp. 438–39.

67. Ibid., pp. 439–45.

68. Specht, *Poetry and the Iconography of the Peasant*, pp. 51–54. Specht considers the possibility that the artist sympathized with the plight of the peasantry, but thinks the bent posture more likely to be the result of a limitation of the artist's technical skill. The illustration of Virgo shows two young women picking flowers, a scene in which coercion is "unthinkable," but their posture is contrasted with the graceful attitude of three differently clothed young women and a man who looks on. The issue is not just coercion but nature; the posture is awkward because the people are inured to exhausting and lowly tasks.

69. "Le conte des vilains de Verson," pp. 668–73. The poem has also been edited by Léchaudé d'Anisy, "Recherches historiques," pp. 105–12; and by Hunger, *Histoire de Verson*, pp. 28–35. I am grateful to Cassandra Potts, of Middlebury College, and Larry Crist, of Vanderbilt University, for help with this document. It has recently been discussed briefly in Arnoux, "Classe agricole," pp. 35–37, and in a more detailed and nuanced way in Boureau, *Le droit de cuissage*, pp. 216–26.

70. "Le conte des vilains de Verson," v. 10 (p. 668): "Eus sunt plus cuverz que

mastins"; vv. 230–32 (p. 673): "Sire, sachez quel firmament / Je ne sai plus cuverte gent / Que sunt les vileins de Verson."

71. Boureau, *Le droit de cuissage*, p. 221.

72. Ibid., pp. 218–19.

73. Ibid., p. 219, with regard to the arbitrary calculation of the proportions of harvest due to the lord: "Peut-on imaginer un tel cynisme d'exposition, s'il s'agit d'une description de la réalité de l'exploitation monastique?"

74. "Le conte des vilains de Verson," vv. 159–74 (pp. 671–72):

> Beim me conta Rogier Adé,
> Qué honte ait vilein eschapé:
> Se vilain sa fille marie
> Pars de dehors la seignorie
> Le seignor en a le culage:
> iii sols en a del mariage;
> iii sols en a reison por quei,
> Sire, je l'vos di par ma fei:
> Jadis avint que le vilein
> Ballout sa fille par la mein
> Et la livrout à son seignor,
> Jà ne fust de si grant valor
> A faire idonc sa volonté,
> Ancies qu'il eust el doné
> Rente, chatel ou héritage
> Por consentir le mariage.

75. Ibid., v. 200 (p. 672): "Itant au vilenage apent."

76. Arnoux, "Classe agricole," pp. 35–60; Musset, "Réflexions autour du problème de l'esclavage."

77. Meyer, "Dit sur les vilains," pp. 14–28 (the original is given on pp. 20–24).

78. Ibid., vv. 75–128 (pp. 21–22), esp. vv. 80–88:

> Como fo l'istoria
> De soa natevita,
> Voyo che mi intenda.
> La zoxo, in uno hostero,
> Si era un somero:
> De dre si fe un sono
> Si grande como un tono.
> De quel malvaxio vento
> Nasce el vilan puzolento.
>
> (Thus was the history of his
> nativity, you who under-
> stand what I mean. Down

there, in an inn, there was an
ass. From behind he made a
sound, as loud as thunder.
From that evil wind, was
born the stinking peasant.)

79. Ibid., vv. 145–285 (pp. 22–24).

80. Alberti, *Family in Renaissance Florence*, pp. 189–90.

81. *Proverbia sententiaeque*, no. 27026 (4: 641): "Rusticus est quasi bos, nisi quod sua cornua desunt." A German rhyming version is cited in Ebner, "Der Bauer," p. 95: "Der Bauer ist an Ochsen statt, nur dass er keine Hörner hat." The proverb is also cited as a late-medieval folksong by Ranke, "Agrarische und bäuerliche Denk—und Verhaltensweisen im Mittelalter," p. 212.

82. *Proverbia sententiaeque*, no. 27016 (4: 640): "Rusticus ac asinus, nux, hec tria connumerata, / Non faciunt fructum, fuerint nisi combaculata."

83. Ibid., no. 26997 (4: 637): "Rusticus gens est optima flens et pessima ridens." Hemmerli, *De nobilitate et rusticitate*, cap. 32, fol. 124r, gives the proverb as "rustica gens, optima flens, pessima gaudens." On this and similar proverbs, see Algazi, *Herrengewalt*, pp. 199–210.

84. "Oignez vilain, il vous poindra; poignez vilain il vous oindra," cited in Coulton, *Medieval Village*, p. 234. Hemmerli, *De nobilitate et rusticitate*, cap. 32, fol. 124r, gives the same proverb in Latin. A version is also given by Rabelais in *Gargantua*, chap. 22.

85. Francesc Eiximenis, *Lo Crèstia*, bk. 12, excerpted in *Francesc Eiximenis, la societat catalana*, p. 59: "e del hòmens servills qui jamés no es poden res inclinar, sinó ab força e ab mal. Per tal, diu que aquests no són apellats hòmens mas bèsties. E, per raó d'açò, los deu hom tractar així com à bèsties feres e cruels, que doma hom ab batiments, e ab fam, e ab clausures forts e terribles."

86. Ruprecht von Freising, *Freisinger Rechtsbuch*, chap. 46, p. 52: "und di maister di ëhalten in vorcht haben muezzen oder si worchten nimmer nicht." This edition by Claussen, based on MS A (Munich, Stadtarchiv, Codex urbis Monacensis 1), represents the original text better than the edition of Georg Ludwig von Maurer (*Das Stadt- und das Landrechtbuch Ruprechts von Freising*). Maurer used five manuscripts in order to show the influence of the *Schwabenspiegel* on later versions of the lawbook. This is significant because the reworked *Freisinger Rechtsbuch* took from the *Schwabenspiegel* its condemnation of servitude (c. 197, pp. 213–14 in Maurer's edition), and left out, among other things, the passage about the master's right to flog his serf.

87. Hügli, *Der deutsche Bauer im Mittelalter*, p. 3.

88. *Reimchronik des Appenzellerkrieges*, vv. 1496–98 (p. 47): "doch muoss mans ettwen stucken / das mans dester bas mug bucken, / so muossentz dester füro buwen." (But one must silence him in order better to force him to farm.)

89. "Zwei Flugschriften aus der Zeit Maximilians I," vv. 373–77 (p. 178):

Also solt man dich all iar straffen
   wie ain felber mit den waffen
All iar wirt gestimlet, blut und gar
   zeiar wirt er nun dester fruchtbar;
Sein wachsen wurd hinren das holtz.

(Thus you should be punished
every year, like a willow tree,
trimmed with knives, bleeding, and
in a while it will be fruitful, the
wood will grow sufficiently.)

90. Hemmerli, *De nobilitate et rusticitate*, cap. 32, fol. 124r: "Ex quibus quidem experientia doctissimi congruenter arguunt immo arbitrati fuerunt reipublice fore salutiferum salutare ac salutis humane et insuper rusticitatis et ruralitatis et ruris saluberrimum ritissimum et congruissimum vitale remedium dum rusticorum habitacula lares et ordea magalia per gule predia caule domos et tuguria per singulos annos iubileos deuastantur aut igne consumuntur, denudantur, spoliantur, et exuuntur."

91. Mollat and Wolff, *Popular Revolutions*, p. 89.

92. Gower, *Mirour de l'omme*, vv. 26425–80 (p. 293).

93. Frederic C. Tubach, *Index exemplorum: A Handbook of Medieval Religious Tales* (Helsinki, 1969), no. 3652, pp. 282–83 (six citations).

94. Traverse, *Peasants, Seasons and Werltsüeze*, pp. 59–60.

95. Vandenbroeck, "Verbeeck's Peasant Weddings," p. 98; Braet, "A Thing Most Brutish," p. 192.

96. Jones, "Function of Food"; Guerrau-Jalabert, "Aliments symboliques"; Adams, "Egregious Feasts." Although agreeing with the association of the *vilain* with ravenous and indiscriminate appetite, Susan E. Farrier calls attention to some cases in which aristocratic characters in *chansons de geste* act in the fashion of *vilains*, fighting with non-noble weapons and eating voraciously. See her "Hungry Heroes in Medieval Literature."

97. Examples are given in Jonin, "La revision d'un topos," p. 179.

98. *Nouveau Recueil complet des fabliaux*, no. 40, 5: 46–48.

99. Discussed by Simon, *Neidhart von Reuental*, pp. 164–80; Jöst, *Bauernfeindlichkeit*.

100. Eiximenis, *Lo Crestià*, bk. 3, from his *Contes i faules*, pp. 38–40.

101. *Materialien zur Neidhart-Überlieferung*, pp. 153–59; Simon, "Origin of Neidhart Plays"; Jöst, *Bauernfeindlichkeit*, pp. 117–35.

102. Examples are collected in *Erzählungen des späten Mittelalters* 2: 353–91, 497–503.

103. Simon, "Rustic Muse."

104. Ibid., pp. 246–47, 249–51.

105. Perger, Höhle, and Pauch, *Neidhart Frescoes ca. 1400*.

106. *Nouveau Recueil complet des fabliaux*, no. 55, 5: 368–70. Very similar is a Latin poem, "The Rustic and Pluto," cited in Merlini, *Satira contro il villano*, pp. 80–81.

107. R. H. Bloch, *Scandal*, pp. 22–100, especially p. 51.

108. *Nouveau Recueil complet des fabliaux*, no. 92, 8: 213–14, cited in Jonin, "La revision d'un topos," p. 180. The same story appears in an exemplum by Jacques de Vitry, in his *Exempla or Illustrative Stories*, no. 191, p. 80. More than ten versions are cited in Frederic C. Tubach, *Index exemplorum: A Handbook of Medieval Religious Tales*, no. 3645, p. 282.

109. *Nouveau Recueil complet des fabliaux*, no. 57, 6: 31–32, cited in R. H. Bloch, *Scandal*, pp. 52–53.

110. *Nouveau Recueil complet des fabliaux*, no. 10, 2: 204–14. Cited in R. H. Bloch, *Scandal*, pp. 50–51.

111. "*Audigier* et la chanson de geste," pp. 511–26. See also Gravdal, *Vilain and Courtois*, pp. 51–80.

112. *Fastnachtspiele aus dem 15. Jahrhundert*, BLVS 28–30. The enumeration of peasant plays is given in Lefèbvre, *Les fols et la folie*, p. 51. On fools and peasants, see Ragotzky, "Der Bauer in der Narrenrolle."

113. DuBruck, "Conspectus of the Peasant," p. 40.

114. Wunder, "Der dumme und der schlaue Bauer," p 35. In Vienna and Strasbourg in the late fifteenth century, "dressing up as a peasant" meant the general practice of donning costumes for Carnival (Vandenbroeck, "Verbeeck's Peasant Weddings," p. 85).

115. Merlini, *Satira contro il villano*, app. 1, pp. 175–77.

116. Ibid., vv. 6–15 (p. 175):

> Dentro del uostro bursello
> Non habetis numeros,
> Inter dumos
> Cum li piedi discalçi,
> E cum li falzi
> Inciditis herbas
> Inter merdas
> De le uostre uache
> Cum chali e rache
> In corpore toto.
>
> (In your purse you have no
> money, you go among the
> thorns with bare feet, and with
> the sickle you attack the grass.
> Among the turds of your cat-
> tle, with callouses and sores [?]
> all over your body.)

117. Ibid., vv. 18–19 (p. 175); vv. 45–47 (p. 176).

118. Ibid., vv. 34–57 (p. 176).

119. Ibid., vv. 84–87 (p. 177): "Homines rident / Quando vident / Li uostri dañi." (Men laugh when they see the harm you cause.) Vv. 104–19 (p. 177):

> Perchè in vuy regna
> Ogni maliçia
> E ogni tristitia
> E siti ignoranti
> Tuti quanti,
> Mendatori
> Robatori,
> Li uostri errori
> Si purgano cusì
> Como vedeti
> Che siti tractati,
> Perchè non vi leuati
> Troppo in alteça
> La uostra aspreça
> Ve fa stentare
> El dì e la nocte.
>
> (For in you reigns
> every sort of malice
> and grief. You are
> all thoroughly igno-
> rant, liars, robbers.
> Thus are your er-
> rors purged; you are
> treated in such a
> way that you can-
> not rise too high.
> Your bitterness
> makes you miser-
> able day and night.)

120. Ibid., vv. 122–28 (p. 177):

> Serui seruorum
> Asini asinorum
> Maledicat uos deus,
> In secula seculorum
> Amen. Ab insidiis diaboli et
> signoria de villano et a furore
> rusticorum libera nos domine.

121. There are two versions, both in Merlini, *Satira contro il villano*, app. 6, pp. 225–28. One begins: "A lavorar è sempre destinato / Il perfido villan, malvagio, ingrato." (He is destined always to labor, the perfidious, evil, ungrateful peasant.) The other begins: "A lavorare sempre è destinato / Il villano maligno et ostinato." (He is destined always to labor, the wicked and obstinate peasant.)

122. Aristotle, *Politics* 1254a–1255b.

Chapter 7

1. Mellinkoff, *Outcasts* 1: 137–40.

2. Fredrickson, *Black Image*; Winthrop Jordan, *White over Black*, pp. 150–63.

3. Bahktin, *Rabelais and His World*, pp. 196–277, 303–67.

4. See above, Chapter 4.

5. Bernheimer, *Wild Men in the Middle Ages*; Sprunger, "Wildfolk and Lunatics in Medieval Romance"; Bartra, *Wildmen in the Looking Glass*; and idem, *Artificial Savage*. The wild man avoided civilization but, unlike the peasant, did present something of a sexual threat (specifically a propensity for abducting women).

6. As noted by Zink, "La suffisance du paysan," p. 37.

7. E.g., poem no. 117, sts. 10–13, in *Die Berliner Neidhart-Handschrift c*, pp. 292–93.

8. "Berengier au lonc Cul," in *Nouveau Recueil complet des fabliaux*, no. 34, vv. 14–23 (4: 270).

9. *Medieval Pastourelle*, no. 24 (1: 184); no. 78 (1: 218); no. 112 (1: 288); No. 146 (2: 386–88) is similar, but involves a *vilain* who lives in Paris.

10. Boccaccio, *Decameron*, third day, novella 1 (1: 198).

11. Bullough, "Medieval Medical and Scientific Views of Women"; Bynum, "Female Body and Religious Practice."

12. Margetts, "Die Darstellung der weiblichen Sexualität"; R. H. Bloch, *Medieval Misogyny*, pp. 65–91.

13. Cadden, *Meanings of Sex Difference*, pp. 134–65.

14. Juan del Encina, "Representación . . . ante el muy esclarecido muy ilustre principe don Juan, nuestro soberano señor . . . " (written 1497), in his *Obras completas* 4: 118–34, especially pp. 128–29. One finds similar surprise at the ability of rustics to feel the pangs of love in Boccaccio (see above, note 10 for this chapter) and Maffeo Vegio da Lodi (cited in Merlini, *Satira contro il villano*, pp. 48–49).

15. Andreas Capellanus, *On Love* 1.11 (p. 222).

16. From a treatise on love edited by Arthur Langfors, "Deux traités sur l'amour tirés du manuscrit 2200 de la Bibliothèque Saint-Geneviève," p. 367: "Volentei d'amer ki en vilain se met et ki estruer le fait ausi comme une beste salvage, ne (ne) poet son corage aploiier a nule cortoisie ne a nule bonté, ains aime folement et sans coverture. Et che n'est mie amours, ains est ensi comme rage, quant vilains s'entremet d'amer." (The desire of love that puts itself in the *vilain* causes him to go about it in the fashion of a savage beast. He can't bend his art to any courtesy or goodness;

rather he loves foolishly, out in the open. It is not love but rather wildness when *vilains* set themselves to love.)

17. Kavaler, "Pieter Bruegel and the Common Man," pp. 13–14.

18. Hemmerli, *De nobilitate et rusticitate*, cap. 33, fol. 129v.

19. J. Baldwin, *Language of Sex*, pp. 66–68.

20. "Le Vilain de Bailleul," pp. 110–17, cited in Boureau, *Le droit de cuissage*, p. 178.

21. "Le Prestre qui abvete," cited in Boureau, *Le droit de cuissage*, p. 178.

22. Wack, *Lovesickness*. On the context of the *Viaticum* and medieval lovesickness, see Lowes, "Loveres Maladye of Hereos," especially pp. 23–27. I thank Eugene Lyman, of Rowan University, for this reference.

23. Wack, "*Liber de heros morbo* of Johannes Afflacius."

24. Wack, *Lovesickness*, pp. 17–20.

25. Guillaume de Lorris and Jean de Meun, *Le Roman de la Rose*, vv. 522–628 (1: 17–20).

26. Andreas Capellanus, *On Love* 1.11 (p. 222).

27. J. Baldwin, *Language of Sex*, p. 60. See also Boureau, *Le droit de cuissage*, pp. 176–86; Leupin, *Barbarolexis*, pp. 106–18.

28. Cited in Niccoli, *I sacerdoti, i guerrieri, i contadini*, p. 57. The three are also typified as descendants of Shem, Japheth, and Ham. This is also found, according to Niccoli, in a chronicle by Johann Nauclerus of Tübingen, printed in 1504.

29. There are some German literary instances of malformed rustics, in *Ruodlieb* and *Parzifal*, for example, as noted in Heald, "Peasant in Mediaeval German Literature," pp. 33–38.

30. Traverse, "Peasants, Seasons and *Werltsüeze*" (Ph.D. diss.), p. 57, refers to "prancing peasants with astounding amounts of free time to entertain themselves."

31. Traverse, *Peasants, Seasons and Werltsüeze*, pp. 63–68, 141–42; idem, "Hie saget Neidhart," pp. 9–12.

32. *Die Lieder Neidharts*, Winter Song no. 34, st. 5, vv. 3–9 (p. 128):

> nu ist in allen landen niht wan trûren unde klagen,
> sît der ungevüege dörper Engelmâr
> vil der lieben Vriderûne ir spiegel nam.
> dô begrunde trûren vreude ûz al den landen jagen,
> daz si gar verswant
> mit der vreude wart versant
> zuht und êre; disiu driu sît leider neimen vant.

> (Now in all the world there is only lamentation
> since the wicked boor Engelmâr took the mirror
> from the beloved Vriderûne. Thereafter true joy
> was withdrawn from the land so that it completely disappeared along with breeding and
> honor. These three are unfortunately nowhere to
> be found.)

33. *Die Berliner Neidhart-Handschrift c*, no. 11, st. 8 (pp. 33–34); no. 33 (32), st. 5 (p. 91).

34. Andreas Capellanus, *On Love* 1.11 (p. 222).

35. Ruiz, *Libro del Arcipreste*, st. 431, lines 3–4 (p. 48): "si podieres non quieras amar muger villana, / que de amor non sabe, es como bausana." (If you can, avoid loving a peasant girl, for she knows nothing and is a fool where love is concerned.)

36. *Parodistische Texte*, no. 7, p. 22: "Deus, qui perpetuam discordiam inter leccatores et rusticos seminasti, da nobis de eorum uxoribus et filiabus uti et de eorum morte gaudere." Cf. a British Library MS cited in Niccoli, *I sacerdoti, i guerrieri, i contadini*, p. 39.

37. Chaucer, "The Miller's Tale," in *Canterbury Tales*, vv. 82–84: "She was a prymerole, a piggesnye / For any lord to leggen in his bedde, / Or yet for any good yeman to wedde." I thank John B. Friedman for pointing this out to me.

38. For two version of this poem and a discussion, see U. Müller, "Gaude mihi!"

39. On the genre of the pastourelle, see Zink, *La pastourelle*.

40. This is the term used by Gilbert and Gubar, *Madwoman in the Attic*, p. 506.

41. Paris, *Mélanges de littérature française*, p. 566; Jackson, "Medieval Pastourelle as a Satirical Genre."

42. Paden, "Rape in the Pastourelle," p. 344.

43. Gravdal, *Ravishing Maidens*, p. 111.

44. Ibid., pp. 104–21. Paden, "Rape in the Pastourelle," pp. 331–49, denies that the poems are essentially about rape. Rather, in Paden's opinion, they exemplify a cultivated and lyrical sensuality, with the actual assault being something of an extraneous fantasy or Freudian dirty joke.

45. *Medieval Pastourelle*, no. 30 (1: 98–101).

46. Ibid., no. 35 (1: 110–15).

47. Ibid., no. 109, (1: 278–83).

48. Compare Gaunt's interpretation of certain troubadour poems as contests between men, in his "Poetry of Exclusion."

49. Dozer-Rabedeau, "*Rusticus.*"

50. "L'autrier jost'una sebissa," in *Medieval Pastourelle*, no. 8 (1: 36–41).

51. "Quant li dous estés define," ibid., no. 42 (1: 132–33).

52. J. Baldwin, *Language of Sex*, p. 205.

53. Ferrante, "Male Fantasy and Female Reality," p. 70.

54. Zink, "La suffisance du paysan," pp. 42–46, elaborates a view opposite that of Baldwin and Ferrante: that the shepherdess exists in a world completely closed off from the chivalric and that the dialogue is one of mutual incomprehensibility. This seems to me to exaggerate the social distance and does not account for the sophistication of the female character in the poems, her responsiveness to love, or her bantering knowledge of the knight's desires.

55. *Medieval Pastourelle*, no. 31 (1: 102–3).

56. Ibid., no. 44 (1: 136–37).

57. Trans. Gravdal, *Ravishing Maidens*, p. 116.

58. *Medieval Pastourelle*, no. 43 (1: 132–33); no. 115 (1: 296–97); no. 13 (1: 50–51).

59. Burns, *Bodytalk*.

60. *Medieval Pastourelle*, no. 172 (2: 434–39).

61. See Ziolkowski, "Avatars of Ugliness"; and Brewer, "Ideal of Feminine Beauty."

62. Deyermond, "Some Aspects of Parody"; Marino, *La serranilla española*, pp. 48–64; Tate, "Adventures in the Sierra."

63. Ruiz, *Libro del Arcipreste*, sts. 950–71 (pp. 97–100).

64. Ibid., sts. 972–92 (pp. 100–103).

65. Ibid., sts. 993–1021 (pp. 103–6).

66. Deyermond, "El hombre salvaje"; Mazur, *Wild Man in the Spanish Renaissance*, pp. 8–10.

67. Deyermond, "Some Aspects of Parody," p. 77.

68. *Medieval Pastourelle*, nos. 202–5 (2: 514–23); Marino, *La serranilla española*, pp. 116–19.

69. Santillana, *Poesías completas*, pp. 63–71, 77–80; Lapesa, *La obra literaria del Marqués de Santillana*, pp. 53–63; Marino, *La serranilla española*, pp. 65–107.

70. Traverse, "Hie saget Neidhart," pp. 16–17.

71. *Die Lieder Neidharts*, no. 14, pp. 79–81.

72. *Die Berliner Neidhart-Handschrift c*, no. 117, pp. 289–95.

73. Ibid., no. 17 (16), pp. 55–57; *Materialien zur Neidhart-Überlieferung*, pp. 153–59.

74. Jöst, *Bauernfeindlichkeit*, p. 105 n. 28.

75. Wittenwiler, *Der Ring*. For the little that is known about Wittenwiler, see Sowinski's discussion on pp. 499–501.

76. *Der Bauernhochzeitsschwank*. See Wittenwiler, *Der Ring*, pp. 505–14, for Sowinski's discussion of the peasant wedding and Neidhart background to Wittenwiler's poem.

77. Wittenwiler, *Der Ring*, vv. 61–94 (pp. 4–6).

78. Vandenbroeck, "Verbeeck's Peasant Weddings"; Moxey, "Social Function of Secular Woodcuts," especially pp. 63–68; idem, "Festive Peasants and Social Order."

79. Vandenbroeck, "Verbeeck's Peasant Weddings," p. 82.

80. Ibid., pp. 109–16. *Grobian* refers to the anonymous work *Grobianus* (1538) and especially the widely read *Grobianus: Von groben Sitten und unhöflichen Geberden* of Caspar Scheidt (1551). *Grobian* appears as a synonym for *rusticus* as early as 1482.

81. Stewart, "Paper Festivals and Popular Entertainment," for example, rejects the view that these prints depicting peasant holidays are satires, regarding them instead as celebrations of revelry with certain moralizing overtones. Given the considerable medieval background for what these woodcuts present, I do not find her argument very convincing. Because Nuremberg was a typically dirty and disorderly early-modern city with crude tastes and habits, Stewart (p. 304) reasons that the engravings merely represent good times. This seems to me to perpetuate unexamined clichés about the past in the guise of combating anachronism. On the background of con-

troversy over realistic or favorable interpretation of art involving peasants, see Alpers, "Bruegel's Festive Peasants"; Miedema, "Realism and Comic Mode"; and Alpers, "Taking Pictures Seriously." Vandenbroeck, "Verbeeck's Peasant Weddings," pp. 79–81, faults both Alpers and Miedema for reductionist simplification but takes particular issue with Alpers, demonstrating (especially by reference to inscriptions) just how negatively the artists intended to present the peasants' behavior. See also Raupp, *Bauernsatiren;* and Carroll, "Peasant Festivity and Political Identity," pp. 289–95.

82. R. Baldwin, "Peasant Imagery"; Kavaler, "Pieter Bruegel and the Common Man," pp. 114–44.

Chapter 8

1. Duby, *Three Orders,* p. 187.

2. Falk, *Étude sociale,* pp. 77–78; Bessmertny, "Le paysan vu par le seigneur," especially pp. 601–2; Bertran de Born, "Be.m plai lo gais temps de pascor," in his *Poems,* no. 30, p. 339.

3. From the *Oustillement au Vilain,* cited in Braet, "A Thing Most Brutish," p. 194.

4. B. Arnold, *German Knighthood,* pp. 53–75; idem, "Instruments of Power."

5. Kaiser, *Textauslegung und gesellschaftliche Selbstdeutung,* pp. 21–69.

6. Ibid., pp. 34–35, citing *Chronicon Eberheimense,* MGH Scriptores 23, p. 432: "[Julius Caesar] . . . cum Romam redire disponeret, conventum in Germania celebravit omnibusque valedicens, minores milites principibus commendavit, ut non quasi servis ac famulis uterentur, sed quasi domini ac defensores ministeria ipsorum reciperent. Inde accidit, quod preter nationes ceteras Germani milites fiscales regni et ministeriales principum nuncupantur."

7. Hugo von Trimberg, *Der Renner,* vv. 1565–2280 (BLVS 247, 1: 65–95).

8. Excerpted in *Quellen zur Geschichte des deutschen Bauernstandes,* no. 146, pp. 374–79.

9. Ottokar von Steiermark, *Österreichische Reimchronik,* lines 26176–98 (MGH Deutsche Chronikon 5, pt. 1, p. 346).

10. Carmen Carlé, *Del concejo medieval Castellano Leones;* Pescador del Hoyo, "La caballería popular en León y Castilla"; Powers, *Society Organized for War.*

11. Wickham, *Early Medieval Italy,* pp. 144–45.

12. Rather of Verona, *Praeloquia* 1.23 (CC, Continuatio medievalis 46A, p. 24), cited in Wickham, *Early Medieval Italy,* p. 145.

13. Wernher de Gartenaere, *Helmbrecht,* vv. 289–91 (pp. 36–38).

14. For Audigier, see Gravdal, *Vilain and Courtois,* pp. 51–80; and *Li Romans de Garin le Loherain* 2: 152–53, cited in Le Goff, *Medieval Civilization,* p. 300.

15. *Ottonis et Raheweni gesta Friderici I. imperatoris* 2.23 (MGH Scriptores rerum Germanicarum, pp. 126–27). See Fleckenstein, "Zur Frage der Abgrenzung von Bauer und Ritter," p. 247.

16. *Quellen zur Geschichte des deutschen Bauernstandes,* no. 83, p. 222.

17. Ibid., no. 122, pp. 326–28.

18. *Buch der Rügen*, pp. 86–88.

19. Cited in Sokol, "Das Grundproblem der Gesellschaft," p. 155.

20. Berthold von Regensburg, *Vollständige Ausgabe seiner Predigten* 1: 14.

21. *Die poetische Bearbeitung des Buches Daniel*, vv. 2716–20 (p. 43):

> O buman, wider wiche
> vrolichen zu dem pluge,
> so wirt dir rechte vuge
> gegeben und ein crone
> von Gote dort zu lone!

22. Szűcs, "Die Ideologie des Bauernkrieges," in his *Nation und Geschichte*, pp. 333–34.

23. *Schwabenspiegel Kurzform*, Landrecht 308 (p. 387): "Wir sullen den hernn dar umb dienen day sy vns schirmen, vnd als sy die lant nit schirment so sind si nicht diensts schuldig." (We should therefore serve the lords that protect us, and if they do not protect the land, then they are not owed service.)

24. *Quellen zur Geschichte des deutschen Bauernstandes*, no. 121, p. 326: "Gens quidem est libera extra gentem suam, alterius domino non subjecta. Morti se opponunt gratia libertatis et potius mortem eligunt quam jugo opprimi servitutis."

25. Bartlett, *Making of Europe*, p. 77.

26. Landes, "La vie apostolique en Aquitaine"; idem, "Between Aristocracy and Heresy."

27. Bonnassie, "From One Servitude to Another," in his *From Slavery to Feudalism*, pp. 288–313, especially pp. 305–13.

28. Jacob, "La meurtre du seigneur dans la société féodale."

29. Ibid., p. 252, citing a report from Galbert de Marchienne's *Miracula Sanctae Rictrudis*.

30. Cabrera and Moros, *Fuenteovejuna*, pp. 139–84.

31. Barros, "Violencia y muerte del señor en Galicia."

32. *Eupolemius*, p. 11.

33. *Eupolemius*, bk. 2, vv. 123–24, trans. Ziolkowski (p. 33).

34. Der Stricker, "Beispiel von den Gäuhühnern," in his *Märe von den Gäuhühnern*, p. 72:

> Ir zorn machet bürge val:
> swie groze veste ein burc habe,
> si brennents oder stozents abe,
> alss Kirchelinge taten.

See Hügli, *Der deutsche Bauer im Mittelalter*, pp. 71–73; and Baier, *Der Bauer in der Dichtung des Strickers*, pp. 93–103. Otfrid Ehrismann ("Tradition und Innovation," pp. 185–87) believes that the above-quoted passage refers not to a peasant insurrection but rather to the official mobilization of forces assembled by the *Landesherr*, among which are peasants.

35. Ferrer i Mallol, "El sagramental," especially pp. 66–70.

36. An anonymous poem in *Alte hoch- und niederdeutsche Volkslieder*, no. 143, st. 7 (1: 375–76):

> Die armen sölt der adel
> beschützen auss ir pflicht,
> so hat er selbs ain tadel
> und ist zum tail entwicht;
> das wirt gott nit vertragen,
> die bösen schwärlich plagen,
> si werden noch erschlagen
> von dem gemain pauersman,
> cs facht icz darzu an.

The translation is from Gudde, *Social Conflicts*, pp. 116–17.

37. On the medieval history of Andorra, see Baudon de Mony, *Relations politiques*; Font i Rius, "Els origens del co-senyoriu andorrà"; Viader, "Pouvoirs et communautés en Andorre"; *Andorra romànica*, pp. 19–60; and Baraut, "L'evolució política de la senyoria d'Andorra."

38. The original parishes are Andorra, Lòria, La Maçana, Encamp, Canillo, and Ordino. The parish of Escaldes-Engordany was formed later. The importance of the parishes remains evident in the nature of the National Archive of Andorra, whose oldest component is the "Archive of the Seven Keys," so-called because opening it requires the consent of each parish that guards one of the keys.

39. Ourliac, "De la féodalité méridionale."

40. The ability of the Andorrans to preserve their local rights against secular lords and the bishop of Urgell is described by Viader, "La irracional possessió." On the erosion of rural rights and the imposition of exactions in this region, see Bonnassie and Guichard, "Les communautés rurales en Catalogne"; Freedman, *Origins of Peasant Servitude*, pp. 79–88; and Bonnassie, *La Catalogne*, esp. 2: 575–610, 781–829.

41. Vela i Palomares, "Andorra a la baixa edat mitjana."

42. These privileges are recorded in vol. 3 of *Privilegis i ordinacions de les valls pyrenenques*. Particularly important are those from the fifteenth century (especially nos. 26 and 27, from 1419), which are not recorded in the more recent collections edited by Baraut and by Baiges and Fages, cited below and in the bibliography.

43. *Cartulari de la Vall d'Andorra, segles IX–XIII*, no. 76 (1: 220–26).

44. Ibid., nos. 129 and 135 (1: 307–15, 323–34).

45. Font i Rius, "Els origens del co-senyoriu d'Andorra," p. 749. Ourliac, "De la féodalité méridionale," pp. 64–66, describes the use of *pariages* by French kings in extending their rule over new territories.

46. See, for example, the documents collected in *Privilegis i ordinacions de les valls pyrenenques*, the third volume of which concerns Andorra.

47. La Seu d'Urgell, Arxiu Capitular, Liber Dotaliorum I, fol. 265v (1085), in "Els documents, dels anys 1076–1092, de l'Arxiu Capitular de La Seu d'Urgell," no. 1014, p. 134; Arxiu Capitular de La Seu d'Urgell, Liber Dotaliorum I, fols. 265r–265v (1095) (not in Baraut's collection); Liber Dotaliorum I, fol. 265v (1097), in "Els documents, dels anys 1093–1100, de l'Arxiu Capitular de La Seu d'Urgell," no. 1154, p. 84.

48. *Diplomatari de la Vall d'Andorra, segle XIV*, no. 40 (1: 98–110) (from the year 1347).

49. Ibid., nos. 94–98, 102, 104 (pp. 216–23, 235–38); Vela i Palomares, "Andorra a la baixa edat mitjana," pp. 264–66.

50. *Diplomatari de la Vall d'Andorra, segle XIV*, nos. 21, 25, 57 (1: 51–52, 62–65, 151–59).

51. Fiter i Rossell, *Manual digest* (written 1748), prologue to book 6, p. 487.

52. Bélinguer, *La condition juridique*, pp. 170–73.

53. Ibid., p. 170. The French government has intervened, but as co-prince (the king of France and president of the Republic having succeeded the count of Foix).

54. *Cartulari de la Vall d'Andorra, segles IX–XIII*, no. 1 (1: 89–90). That Charlemagne founded Andorra was still accepted in the nineteenth century; see, e.g., Roussillon, *De l'Andorre*; Chevalier, *La République d'Andorre*, p. 5; Boucoiran, *Ariège, Andorre et Catalogne*, p. 171.

55. Fiter i Rossell, *Manual digest*, pp. 84–86.

56. Riberaygna Argelich, *Los Valles de Andorra*, p. 30:

> El gran Carlemany mon Pare,
> Dels Alarbs me deslliurà
>
> . . .
>
> Sols resto l'única filla
> Del Imperi Carlemany
> Creient i lliure onse segles
> Creient i lliure vull ser.

57. Psalm 82:11, "Who perished at Endor: and became as dung for the earth." Fiter i Rossell, *Manual digest*, pp. 25–29, accepts this as a possibility, noting that Saint Jerome said Endor was the site of a castle built in preparation for war, and that others have said it was a redoubt for a refuge from infidel attacks. Charlemagne, Fiter notes, was well acquainted with Scripture.

58. "Ha seguit la Seca, la Mecca, i la Vall d'Andorra." First found in the *Spill* by Jaume Roig (written between 1455 and 1462), cited in *Gran geografia comarcal de Catalunya* 16: 288.

59. Sahlins, *Boundaries*, pp. 16–17.

60. Wickham, *The Mountains and the City*, pp. 360–65.

61. Miret i Sans, *Investigación histórica*, pp. 203–18; Tragó, *Spill manifest*.

62. Le Roy Ladurie, *Montaillou*, pp. 34–50; Boureau, *Le droit de cuissage*, pp. 124–35.

63. Boureau, *Le droit de cuissage*, p. 140.

64. Fiter i Rossell, *Manual digest*, maxima 26, p. 504. Merchants were also to be favored.

65. Ibid., maxima 49: "No demostrar may riquesas, ni propalar poder, y forsas, sinos predicar miserias, y flaquessas delas Valls; pues es aixi."

66. Ibid., p. 7: "pues yo Escrich tansolament per los naturals delas Valls . . . â mes que esta Obra deu quedar manuscrita, en una dos ô tres Copias en sos archius . . . no es bo, que la Ciencia del govern, politica, Economia, y regimen deles Valls, se fasia Comuna, y Vulgar als forasters." (For I write solely for the natives of the Valleys . . . moreover this work must remain in manuscript, in one, two, or three copies in its [Andorra's] archives . . . it would not be a good thing for the science of government, political organization, economy, and the rulership of the Valleys to be common and public knowledge among foreigners.) These instructions were followed until 1987. The publication of the *Manuel digest* in that year, its distribution to every Andorran household, and its availability to foreigners marked a step toward changing the constitution and international status of Andorra.

67. *Constitució del Principat d'Andorra* (Andorra, 1993). Before this, Andorra was held to be incapable of diplomatic representation and could not of its own accord make legislation or conclude treaties (Bélinguer, *La condition juridique*, pp. 221–28).

68. Frisch, *Andorra*.

69. McPhee, *La Place de la Concorde Suisse*.

70. Dettwiler, *William Tell*, pp. 54–55.

71. Bergier, *Guillaume Tell*, p. 9. On the Tell legend see also the recent article by Head, "William Tell and His Comrades," which concerns the absence of images of fraternity (as opposed to images of comradeship) in the early Swiss self-conception.

72. Hughes, *Switzerland*, p. 20.

73. See P. Blickle, "Das Gesetz der Eidgenossen."

74. "Zwei Flugschriften aus der Zeit Maximilians I," v. 86 (p. 169): "Denn sy wolten herschafft frey leben." Vv. 100–101 (p. 170): "Dann sy wolten sein gar niemands knecht, / Selber herr wolten sy bleiben."

75. Martini, *Das Bauerntum*, pp. 302–10.

76. This point is made by Weishaupt in his *Bauern, Hirten und "frume edle puren,"* pp. 150–65.

77. What follows is largely based on Bergier, *Guillaume Tell*, pp. 15–22, 57–79.

78. *Das Weisse Buch von Sarnen*, pp. 14–19.

79. *Das Lied von der Entstehung*, pp. 34–50; *Das Urner Tellspiel*, pp. 70–99. Other sources before 1580 are listed in Head, "William Tell and His Comrades," p. 528 n. 2.

80. Aegidius Tschudi, *Chronicon Helveticum* 1: 451–55 (for the year 1307).

81. *Das Urner Tellspiel*, p. 82:

> Nüt, nüt, Thell, du must dran
> Dann kein gnad solt an mir han!
> Ich wil mich an üch buren rechen
> Vnd solt üch das herz im lyb zerbrechen.

Translated in Head, "William Tell and His Comrades," p. 542.

82. This story appears in *The White Book of Sarnen*, the *Urner Tellspiel*, and elsewhere (see Head, "William Tell and His Comrades," pp. 534–36).

83. An insult to a woman by a lecherous officer was also the legendary cause of the Sicilian Vespers of 1282 (Fentress and Wickham, *Social Memory*, pp. 176–79).

84. See above, Chapter 5, pp. 114–15.

85. Rothkrug, "Icon and Ideology," pp. 43–45.

86. E.g., *Die historischen Volkslieder*, vol. 1, nos. 34, 80, 83; vol. 2, nos. 130, 197.

87. Marchal, "Die Antwort der Bauern," pp. 759–60.

88. Hemmerli, *De nobilitate et rusticitate*, cap. 33, fol. 131v: "Est plebs que non plebs, gens que non gens, qui / Non homines dici sed fera monstra queunt."

89. Ibid., cap. 33, fols. 130r–130v.

90. Ibid., fol. 129v–130r, where the men are like women and the women like men: "quemadmodum in hermafrodita mysterium perturbent." The men are possibly also given to intercourse with their animals.

91. "Zwei Flugschriften aus der Zeit Maximilians I," vv. 100–112 (p. 170), vv. 459–71 (pp. 180–81).

92. Ibid., vv. 175–76 (p. 172): "Die sweitzer hab ich dem türcken gleicht, / wyt von seiner art der schweitzer weicht."

93. Marchal, "Die Antwort der Bauern," p. 757; Brady, *Turning Swiss*, p. 58. On the Swabian War see Brady, pp. 57–72.

94. Brady, *Turning Swiss*, especially pp. 34–42.

95. From Jacob Unrest, *Österreichische Chronik*, in *Quellen zur Geschichte des Bauernkrieges*, ed. Franz, no. 3, p. 21. Discussed by Algazi, *Herrengewalt*, pp. 74–78.

96. "Zwei Flugschriften aus der Zeit Maximilians I," vv. 225–26 (p. 174): "Den buntschuh auff allen erden, / Das wir auch all frey möchten werden."

97. Quoted in Brady, *Turning Swiss*, p. 35.

98. Quoted and translated in Head, "William Tell and His Comrades," p. 540:

> edellüt sind buren worden
> vnnd die buren edellüt
>
> . . .
>
> Aber die Schwizer sind die rëchten edellüt:
> ir tugent inen den adel voruss gitt.

99. Ibid.:

> weger wers, frisch erschlagen
> weder allso ein grosses ioch tragen.
> darumb sind ir die glückhafftigsten lüt

die hie lëbent in disem zytt
so ir kein herren wend han
lugend nun, vnnd land nit darvon.

100. *An die Versammlung gemeiner Bauernschaft*, p. 118.
101. Ibid., p. 87.
102. Brady, *Turning Swiss*, pp. 34–42.
103. *Die historischen Volkslieder*, no. 81 (1: 393). See also no. 79 (1: 386), another pro-Austrian song from the same era in which the Swiss are "heathen" (*haiden*), and no. 231 (2: 491), a song of 1503 against the Swiss campaigns in Bellinzona (Ticino) (the Swiss as *verleugneten Christen*).
104. *Die historischen Volkslieder*, no. 80 (1: 389–91).
105. P. Blickle, "Das gesetz der Eidgenossen," p. 584.
106. Examples in Marchal, "Die Antwort der Bauern," pp. 768–69 n. 37.
107. *Die historischen Volkslieder*, no. 144 (2: 102).
108. Ibid., no. 34 (1: 134):

> Herzog Lupolt von Oesterrich
> was gar ein freidig man
> keins guten rats belud er sich,
> wolt mit den puren schlan,
> he gar fürstlich wolt ers wagen:
> do er an die buren kam,
> hands in zetod erschlagen.

109. Ibid., no. 34 (1: 125): "die Schwitzer wend wir zwingen / und inen ein herren geben." (We will master the Swiss and give them a lord.)
110. For example, *Die historischen Volkslieder*, no. 210 (2: 422), a song from 1499, written during the Swabian War:

> Es lit ein tiefer grab bi Hard,
> dar in vil Schwaben getöufet ward,
> des kamend si in truren!
> der bär der touft si nach siner art,
> menger Schwizer da ir göti ward,
> si schrüwend: "was böser puren!"

111. Ibid., no. 93 (1: 284–88, 433), from 1450, a song about the Markgrafenkrieg:

> und schrein: "heut mussens unser eigen sein!"
>
> . . .
>
> Tauss ess kan niemants abgeweisen,
> so nemen die Sweizer niemant gefangen,
> darumb last uns von hinnen wenden,
> der grimmig zorn hat sie durchgangen,
> sie werden den adel hie morden und schenden.

English translation from Brady, *Turning Swiss*, p. 36.

112. *Die historischen Volkslieder*, no. 93 (1: 429).

113. Examples are cited in Marchal, "Die Antwort der Bauern," pp. 772–73.

114. Ibid., pp. 766–75.

115. *Die historischen Volkslieder*, no. 197 (2: 373):

> Schand schand si allen fürsten
> von got und der welt geseit,
> dass sie nit wil dirsten,
> zu beschirmen die cristenheit,
> und nit weren die schande,
> die der Türk alltag tut
> so vil in tutschem lande
> und an dem cristen blut!
>
> (Shame, shame upon all princes
> who go against [?] God and the
> world, that they refuse to bestir
> themselves to protect Christen-
> dom, doing nothing to oppose
> the many shameful acts com-
> mitted every day by the Turks in
> German lands and against the
> blood of Christians.)

116. Martini, *Das Bauerntum*, pp. 319–21.

117. See above, note 24 for this chapter. On this region and its culture see Lammers, "Nordelbische Mentalitätsstudien."

118. On the Stedingen Revolt, see Köhn, "Freiheit als Forderung," pp. 325–34.

119. Lammers, *Die Schlacht bei Hemmingstedt*, pp. 46–56; Urban, *Dithmarschen*, pp. 26–28; Franz, *Geschichte des deutschen Bauernstandes*, pp. 92–95.

120. The documents are collected in *Urkundenbuch zur Geschichte des Landes Dithmarschen*, especially nos. 26, 28–30, 32–33, 46–47 (pp. 31–85).

121. *Die historischen Volkslieder*, no. 45 (1: 216); also in *Quellen zur Geschichte des deutschen Bauernstandes*, no. 197 (p. 502):

> Do sprack sick Roleffs Bojeken söne,
> de beste in unsem lande:
>
> "Tredet herto, gi stolten Ditmarschen!
> unsen kummer wille wi wreken,
> wat hendeken gebuwet haen,
> dat können wol hendken tobreken."
>
> De Ditmarschen repen averlut:
> "Dat lide wi nu und nummermere,

wi willen darumme wagen hals und gut
und willen dat gar ummekeren.

Wi willen darumme wagen goet und bloet
und willen dar alle umme sterven,
er dat der Holsten er avermoet
so scholde unse schone lant vorderven."

(Then spoke Roleffs Bojeken's son,
the best in our land: come hither you
proud Dithmarschers! We shall cast
off our grief, for what hands have
built, hands can destroy. The Dithmarschers respond loudly, "We will
suffer now and nevermore, for this we
will risk life and possessions and will
not turn back. We would rather sacrifice goods and blood and all die than
that the Holsteiners' arrogance should
ruin our beautiful land.")

122. *Quellen zur Geschichte des deutschen Bauernstandes,* no. 213, p. 542.

123. On this event, see Lammers, *Die Schlacht bei Hemmingstedt.*

124. Fontane, "Der Tag von Hemmingsted," in his *Gedichte* 1: 179–85; Bartels, *Die Dithmarscher.*

125. *Die historischen Volkslieder,* no. 219 (2: 454) (also in Neocorus, *Chronik des Landes Dithmarschen* 1: 522):

De sik jegen Ditmerschen setten will,
  de stelle sik wol tor were:
Ditmerschen dat schölen buren sin,
  it mögen wol wesen heren!

126. *Die historischen Volkslieder,* no. 215 (2: 446): "Dar hest so manich stolt edel-man / syn levent umb vorlaren."

127. Ibid., no. 216 (2: 447) (also in Neocorus, *Chronik des Landes Dithmarschen* 2: 561):

se [the Danish army] repen: "wolan, gi ditmarschen buren
gi moten (noch alle) van avende sterven!"

. . .

"nu help, Maria du maged rein,
wi laven di mit gantser truwen:
beholden wi nu de averhand,
ein kloster willen wi di buwen!"

. . .

Ein crucifix hadden se all mit gebracht,
dar sik de garde so ser verschrak:
an einer korten ure
der garde blef söven dusent dod
dat dede god dorch Ditmarsche buren!

(The Danish army says: "Beware, you
Dithmarscher peasants. You will all be
dead by evening." . . . "Now help, Maria,
pure maid, we adore you with all our
faith. Give to us the victory and we will
build you a church." . . . They had
brought with them a crucifix before
which the Danish troops were so frightened; in a brief hour the Danes left seven
thousand dead. This is what God did
through the Dithmarschen peasants!)

128. Neocorus, *Chronik des Landes Dithmarschen* 1: 503:

In unsen Dagen dit Wunder is geboert,
Dat in velen Olderen nicht is gehört
Dat Heren unde Knechte, in velen Striden vorfaren,
So wunderliken hebben den Sege vorlaren.
Nu iss dit gescheen dorch Gadess Raedt,
All were wi denne noch so quaet,
Ein Iderman schal sick sulven tuchten,
So dorve wi des Dodes nicht fruchten.

Cf. the twelfth-century poem *Eupolemius* (cited above in note 32 for this chapter), in which Seon mocks his peasant enemies as half-men who once were afraid of the knights. Sother responds, "let our deeds astound you," and kills Seon with a dart through the throat.

In Serbia, the early-nineteenth-century uprising against the Turks was regarded as a marvel made possible by peasants who shed blood for the Cross (Halpern, *Serbian Village*, pp. 28–29).

129. Neocorus, *Chronik des Landes Dithmarschen* 1: 515.

130. Ibid., p. 516:

Sie fruchteden ock weinig den allmechtigen Gott,
So heelden ein Deel der Hilligen vor Spott,
Se reepen: "o Buer, amechtiger Wicht
Vorlath di nu up de Hilligen nicht,
De Kele schall di aff in dusser Stundt,
Ick wil di morden alss einen Hundt"

. . .

Vele Fursten hir nu enjegen doet
Vorgeten ahne Nodt Christen-Bloet
Se scholden up de Unchristen schlaen,
So sprikt nun de gemeine Man.

(They also had little fear of Almighty
God, and thus held many saints up to
mockery. They taunted, "O peasant,
powerless little dwarf, don't entrust yourself now to the saints. I will slay you like
a dog. . . . Many princes then hunted
them down thus, needlessly forgetting
the blood of Christ. They ought to strike
down the infidels, so says now the common man!)

See also Lammers, *Die Schlacht bei Hemmingstedt,* pp. 67–68.

131. Neocorus, *Chronik des Landes Dithmarschen* 1: 465. Translation from Urban, *Dithmarschen,* p. 112.

Chapter 9

1. London, Lambeth Palace Library, MS 441, fol. 3v (to Hosea 1:4).

2. Ibid., fol. 41v (to Amos 4:9).

3. This question is explored in Pagden, *Fall of Natural Man.* For the medieval background to this debate, see Muldoon, *Popes, Lawyers and Infidels.*

4. See James C. Scott, *Domination,* pp. 162–66. For the figure of the trickster in Africa and among African Americans, see Gates, *Signifying Monkey,* pp. 3–88; and Levine, *Black Culture,* pp. 111–16.

5. Harris, *Complete Tales of Uncle Remus.* For James Scott's discussion of the "hidden transcript," see his *Domination and the Arts of Resistance.*

6. "Versus de Uniboue." See also Martini, *Das Bauerntum,* pp. 6–10.

7. Chrétien de Troyes, *Eric et Enide,* vv. 1–3 (p. 1): "Li vilains dit a son respit / que tel chose a l'an an despit / qui mult valt mialz l'an ne cuide."

8. Chrétien de Troyes, *Le chevalier de la charrete,* vv. 6502–3 (p. 198): "Li vilains dit bien voir qu'a poinne / puet an mes un ami trover."

9. *Le Roman de Thèbes,* vv. 8579–80 (2: 79): "Li vilains dit: 'Qui glaive fet / sanz dotance a glaive revet.'" See also the editor's note to this passage (2: 156).

10. Darnton, "Peasants Tell Tales."

11. Marie de France, *Les lais,* p. 157.

12. Wace, *Le Roman de Brut,* vv. 4409–14 (p. 236):

Mal faire pur pis remaneir,
Ço tient li vilains a saveir;
E un mal deit l'on bien suffrir

Pur sun cors de peior guarir;
E pur sun enemi plaissier
Se deit l'on alques damagier.

(To do evil to prevent
something worse, thus the
vilain teaches us; one
must suffer pain in order
to cure the body of some-
thing worse; to hurt an
enemy one must accept
some damage to oneself.)

13. Philippe de Thaon, *Comput*, vv. 131–38 (p. 6):

Çoe dit en repruver
Li vilain al buver:
La pirre reuëlette
Criet de la charette;
Mult est la pume dure
Qui unques ne maüre;
La verge est a preiser
Qui se lest pleier.

(Thus says the *vilain*
to the cowherd by way
of reproach: the worst
wheel of the cart is the
noisiest; it is the hard
apple that never
ripens; the stick that
lets itself be bent is to
be praised.)

14. Wace, *Le Roman de Brut*, vv. 6101–2 (1: 325): "N'aveit fors la vilanaille, / Ki n'aveit cure de bataille." (There were none save the mob of *vilains*, who were not in-terested in battle.) Shortly after this passage the *vilains* are said to be like mad dogs, turbulent and pointlessly violent, in contrast to the virtuous rustics, the "povre gent" and "païsanz," vv. 6131–38 (1: 326).

Le Roman de Thèbes, vv. 3045–46 (1: 95): "Malÿagés, mout ies vilains, / N'ies pas de hardement certeins. / Malement veus toi foi menti." (Meleager, you're like a *vi-lain*; you're not very bold, that's for certain. You wickedly go back on your word.)

15. As noted by Margetts, "Das Bauerntum in der Literatur," pp. 155–57.

16. *Nouveau Recueil complet des fabliaux*, no. 39 (5: 8–38). Discussed in Jonin, "La revision d'un topos," p. 183.

17. An example of this commonplace, for which I am indebted to Philippe Buc,

of Stanford University, is a commentary on the Psalms in Vatican City, Biblioteca Apostolica, MS Ottobbon. 228, fol. 160r, to Psalm 104:11: "*Dicens, Tibi dabo terram Canaan.* . . . Similiter in futuro Chanaan, mali et viles eicientur a regno celorum, secundum illud, *Maledictus Chanaan, servus sit fratrum suorum.* In celis non erit aliquis servus, secundum illud, in regno autem omnes erunt filii, nullus servus."

18. *Nouveau Recueil complet des fabliaux*, no. 13 (2: 311–47). Described in Jonin, "La révision d'un topos," pp. 182–83.

19. Hügli, *Der deutsche Bauer im Mittelalter*, pp. 113–15; Martini, *Das Bauerntum*, pp. 169–78.

20. *Li proverbe au vilain. Die Sprichwörter.* On this and related collections see Rattunde, *Li proverbes au vilain: Untersuchungen.*

21. *Li proverbe au vilain. Die Sprichwörter*, no. 52, pp. 23–24:

> Povres touz tens laboure,
> Pense et travaille et ploure,
> Onques de cuer ne rit;
> Li riches rit et chante,
> De grant chose se vante,
> De prou il est petit
> *Touz se fait lié, qui auques a,*
> ce dit li vilains.

22. Hartmann von Aue, *Gregorius, der "gute Sünder."*

23. On this story see the resume by Simon Keynes and Michael Lapidge in their translation of primary materials about Alfred: *Alfred the Great*, pp. 197–206.

24. Hartmann von Aue, *Der arme Heinrich.*

25. The story is given in Theodore Kantzow, *Chronik von Pommern* (written ca. 1536), excerpted in *Quellen zur Geschichte des deutschen Bauernstandes*, no. 243, pp. 602–4.

26. For what follows concerning Bohemia I am very grateful for the help given to me by Lisa Wolverton, of Harvard University.

27. The story of Přemysl is even more similar to Plutarch's account of the deposition of Paphos, king of Cyprus, by Alexander the Great. The new ruler chosen by Alexander was a market-gardener, sole survivor of the legitimate dynasty. The parallel is noted in Krappe, "La légende de Libuse," p. 87.

28. Cosmas, *Chronicae Bohemorum* 1.3–7 (MGH Scriptores rerum germanicarum, n.s. 2, pp. 5–17).

29. On this legend see Graus, "Kirchliche und heidnische Komponenten"; and idem, *Lebendige Vergangenheit*, pp. 89–109.

30. *Legenda Christiani.* See also Ludvíkovský, "La légende du prince-laboureur Přemysl." Material on Wenceslas has been translated from Slavonic and Latin sources in Kantor, *Origins of Christianity in Bohemia.*

31. Graus, "Kirchliche und heidnische Komponenten," pp. 157–60.

32. Graus, *Lebendige Vergangenheit*, pp. 173–76.

33. Burdach, *Der Dichter des Ackermann aus Böhmen* 3: 109–11.

34. Klaniczay, "Paradoxes of Royal Sainthood," p. 366.

35. Graus, "Kirchliche und heidnische Komponenten," p. 160.

36. Ibid., p. 157.

37. Other recollections of the origin of the dynasty during the succession crisis of 1306–10 are cited in Burdach, *Der Dichter der Ackermann aus Böhmen* 1: 38–46.

38. On peasant ancestors see Krappe, "La légende de Libuse," pp. 86–89; and Banaszkiewicz, "Königliche Karrieren." On coronation rituals, see Gieysztor, "Gesture in the Coronation Ceremonies," p. 157; and Ranke, "Agrarische und bäuerliche Denk- und Verhaltensweisen," pp. 210–11. None of this association with rusticity was at all incompatible with images of royal sanctity; see Klaniczay, "Paradoxes of Royal Sainthood."

39. Werminghoff, "Die Quaternionen der deutschen Reichsverfassung," p. 293, cited in Martini, *Das Bauerntum*, p. 229. On German "holy cities" in general, see Haverkamp, "'Heilige Städte' im hohen Mittelalter."

40. Epperlein, *Der Bauer im Bild des Mittelalters*, p. 139; Radbruch and Radbruch, *Der deutsche Bauernstand*, pp. 59–60 and plate 12.

41. Cited in Martini, *Das Bauerntum*, p. 229: "Want gelijch als van dem Edelen ackerman alle staede geystlich ind ouch wertlich gevoit und gespijset werden, so doet ouch got der vader, der allit dat levende is in hemel und in erde spijset." (For since all estates, temporal and spiritual, are fed and nourished by the noble plowman, so also God the Father nourishes all the living in heaven and on earth.)

42. Hagen, *Reimchronik der Stadt Cöln*, vv. 1291–94 (p. 44):

> so wist dar weder, dat neyt so suyr
> in is, as van arde ein gebuyr,
> wan e dat hie up stigende is,
> hie is gijr ind valsch, des sijt gewijs.

> (You should know that there is
> nothing so unpleasant ["sour"] as is
> the nature of a peasant, for when
> he attempts to rise to a higher sta-
> tion he is greedy and false, be sure
> of that.)

I am grateful to Geert Claassens, of the Katholieke Universiteit Leuven, for his generous help in interpreting these lines.

43. On Joan and her image, see Warner, *Joan of Arc*; and Wood, *Joan of Arc*, pp. 125–51.

44. Although commonly imagined as tending sheep in Domremy, Joan was quite concerned to emphasize at her trial that she never herded animals of any sort (Wood, *Joan of Arc*, p. 132).

45. Grandeau, *Jeanne insultée*.

46. Ibid., pp. 127, 142.

47. *Quellen zur Geschichte des deutschen Bauernstandes*, no. 177, p. 465: "Dâ vür lob ich den Bûman, der alle Werlt nern kan. Er lât sîn Pfluoc umb strîchen, wer mac sich im gelîchen? . . . Alsô der Bûren Armuot ist bezzer dan ir Rîchen."

48. *Quellen zur Geschichte des deutschen Bauernstandes*, no. 178, pp. 465–66: "Ich weis einen den aller höchsten Frúnt Gotz, der ist alle sine Tage ein Ackerman gewesen, me denne vierzig Jor und noch ist. Und er fragte einest unsern Herren, ob er wolte, das er das begebe und in die Kilchen gienge sitzen. Do sprach er: nein, er ensolt es nút tün; er solte sin Brot mit sinem Sweisse gewinnen sinem edelen túren Blüte ze eren." (I know a most honorable friend of God, who has been a plowman all his days, forty years and more, and still is such. And he once asked Our Lord if He wished that he should betake himself to attend the church. He [Christ] replied that he should not do so. Rather should he earn his bread with his sweat and in this fashion honor His [Christ's] precious blood.)

49. Hans Rosenplüt, "Der Bauern Lob," in *Der Bauer im deutschen Liede*, pp. 109–12; also in *Quellen zur Geschichte des deutschen Bauernstandes*, no. 217, pp. 549–52.

50. "Der Bauernlob" ("Das Gedicht vom ersten Edelman"), in Tettau, "Über einige bis jetzt unbekannte Erfurter Drucke," p. 321:

> So ist denn och kein Fürst so lobeleich,
> der sich dem Paurn mag gleich
> Der Paur ist wol ein Edelman,
> wer das rechtlich erkennen kann.
> Wann alles, das in der werlt lebt,
> alles nach des Paurn arbeit strebt.

51. Ibid., p. 325:

> Es wer gut das mancher ein Paur blib,
> vil grosser sünd er vermid,
> Die sunst all werden volpracht,
> bey tag und auch bey nacht,
> Mit müssig geen, trincken und mit essen;
> darmit wirt got des Herren vergessen.
> Die Paurn kumen gen kirchen selten,
> doch lest sichs got nit entgelten;
> Für ir arbeit gibt er yn lon,
> gesunden leib und die ewige kron.

52. Virgil, *Georgics*, no. 2, vv. 458–74, trans. Fairclough (LCL 63, p. 149).

53. Horace, *Odes and Epodes*, no. 2, trans. Bennett (LCL 33, p. 365).

54. Cited in Owst, *Literature and Pulpit*, p. 571.

55. Petrarch, *De remediis*, bk. 1, no. 57 (1: 53), "De fertilitate terrae." The Virgilian

reference to justice and the rustics appears again in the remedies for misfortune and is immediately followed by the statement that the first man born of human seed (Cain) was a farmer and a parricide (see above, Chapter 4, note 34).

56. Chaucer, *Canterbury Tales*, "The Clerk's Tale," vv. 199–203:

> Ther stood a throp [*hamlet*], of site delitable,
> In which that povre folk of that village
> Hadden hir bestes and hir herbergage,
> And of hir labour took hir sustenance
> After that th'erthe yaf hem habundance.

57. Specht, *Poetry and the Iconography of the Peasant*, p. 58.

58. Merlini, *Satira contro il villano*, pp. 46–47.

59. Lactantius, *Divinae institutiones* 7.1.19, cited in Schreiner, "Zur biblischen Legitimation des Adels," p. 322.

60. Honorius Augustodunensis, *Elucidarium* 2.61, (p. 429).

61. Owst, *Literature and Pulpit*, p. 574.

62. See above, Chapter 3, p. 78.

63. Augustine, *Confessiones* 8.8.

64. Jerome, Epistola 52, chap. 9 (CSEL 54, p. 431): "Nec rusticus et tantum simplex frater ideo se sanctum putet, si nihil nouerit, nec peritus et eloquens in lingua aestimet sanctitatem. Multoque melius est e duobus inperfectis rusticitatem sanctam habere quam eloquentiam peccatricem." Medieval examples of *sancta rusticitas* applied literally to the peasantry include lines from the twelfth-century poem "De diversis ordinibus hominum," formerly attributed to Walter Map: "Ruralis conditio merito laudatur; / nam sancta rusticitas jure veneratur" (Map, *Latin Poems Commonly Attributed to Walter Mapes*, p. 235).

Felix Hemmerli denied that Jerome or Augustine meant anything favorable about the rustics of their time. Answering the peasant's citations, the knight exclaims: "O sancta rusticitas per te fraudulenter allegata" (Hemmerli, *De nobilitate et rusticitate*, cap. 2, fol. 7v).

For the use of Jerome's formulation by the fifteenth-century Carthusian Werner Rolevinck, see below, note 140 for this chapter.

65. P. Brown, "Relics and Social Status," pp. 230–33; idem, *Cult of the Saints*, pp. 119–20; Köbler, "'Bauer' (*agricola, colunus, rusticus*) im Frühmittelalter," especially p. 240. But Gregory of Tours also referred to the individual *rusticus* with favor; see below, note 89 for this chapter.

66. Martin of Braga, "De correctione rusticorum."

67. *Drei deutsche Minoritenprediger*, p. 88: "Quintum genus per quintum filium figuratur, ut sunt agricole, qui tam dilecti filii dei sunt tum propter laborem continuum, qui deo placet, tum propter oppressionem, qua a dominis opprimuntur iniuste." See also Martini, *Das Bauerntum*, p. 113.

68. Heinrich von Burgus, *Der Seele Rat*, vv. 2791–828 (pp. 53–54), esp. vv. 2791–801:

Leident sy es gedultlichleiche
Die armuet ist ir vech fewer,
Es were in schade, wer sy in tewer.
Es ist ein zaichen das sy sint
Die aus erwelten Gotes chint
Dew Got im selwen haben wil;
Durch das muessen sy vil
Hie chumer leiden und arbait.
Der Gotes sun auch durch sy leit
Angst und not ein miechel tail.
Armuet ist der selen hail.

(They must suffer patiently,
poverty is their hell, but through
this pain they become worthy. It
is a sign that they are God's chosen children, whom God himself
wants to have. Through this they
must suffer many hurts and work.
God's Son also suffered, because
of them, fear and need in great
measure. Poverty is the salvation
of the soul.)

69. Hugo von Trimberg, *Der Renner*, vv. 3807–10 (BLVS 247, 1: 157):

Swer rîch wil werden in himelrîche,
Der lebe ûf erden jêmerlîche
Und ahte niht vil ob man in smêhe,
Wil er sich êwiger fröude nêhe.

(He who desires wealth in heaven
should live wretchedly on earth,
and not take account of his mistreatment if he hopes to approach
eternal joy.)

70. Owst, *Literature and Pulpit*, p. 574.

71. Honorius Augustodunensis, *Elucidarium* 2.61 (p. 429): "D.—Quid de agrico-
lis? M.—Ex magna parte salvantur, quia simpliciter vivunt et populum Dei suo sudore
pascant, ut dicitur: 'Labores manuum suarum qui manducant beati sunt' [Psalm 127,
2]." Shortly before this passage, Honorius has the Master observe that the vast majority of knights, however, are damned since they live off of plundering and destruction.
The wrath of God will fall upon them (*Psalm 72:30*), he says at 2.54 (p. 427).

72. Honorius Augustodunensis, *Speculum Ecclesie-Sermo Generalis* in *PL* 172:
866–67.

73. Honorius Augustodunensis, *Imago mundi* 3.1 (p. 125).

74. A similar belief that peasants are more likely than other laymen to be redeemed, but with the simultaneous evaluation of labor as suffering in expiation of Adam's sin, is found in sermons of Humbert of Romans, discussed in van den Hoven, *Work in Ancient and Medieval Thought*, pp. 235–37.

75. Etienne de Fougères, *Le Livre des manières*, vv. 705–12 (p. 85). See above, Chapter 4.

76. Berthold von Regensburg, *Vollständige Ausgabe seiner Predigten* 1: 14: "Sît er dir nû ein niderez hât gegeben, sô soltû dich ouch nideren unde dêmüeten durch got mit dînem amte, sô wil er dir oben ûf dem himel ein vil hôhez amt geben." (Since he has given you now a low place, you should also lower and humble yourself before God in your station, so will he give you a much higher place in heaven.)

77. Ibid., p. 358: "Dâ was im der acker alse liep, diu heilige kirstenheit, daz er in nieman wolte lâzen bûwen, und er hât den pfluoc selber gehabt aller engele herre. Ein pfluoc muoz von îsin und von holz sîn; alsô was daz heilige kriuze von holze, unde von îsin die nagele, die im dâ giengen durch hende unde durch füeze, und alsô habte er den pfluoc, unze er den tôt dar an nam." (So dear to Him was the field, O Holy Christianity, that he did not wish for anyone else to work it. He put His own hand to the plow, the Lord of all the angels. A plow must be made of iron and wood; thus also was the holy cross made of wood while the nails, that went through His hands and feet, were of iron. Thus He took up the plow until He assumed death.)

78. Schönbach, *Studien zur Geschichte*, Sitzungsberichte 155, pp. 53, 89; Sitzungsberichte 154, p. 122.

79. *Drei deutsche Minoritenprediger*, p. 90: "[rustici] qui frumenta laborant, estu uruntur, gelu frigent, de quorum laboribus uiuit omnis populus; [si] cauerent isti de furto, mendacio, periurio et his similibus, sancti fierent." P. 92: "Quantum ue sit eis in laboribus! Utinam non peccarent in ebrietate, periurio, mendacio et turpitudine uerborum. Vere beati fierent."

80. Ibid., p. 89.

81. Cited in Batany, "Les pauvres et la pauvreté," pp. 478–79.

82. Juan Manuel, *Libro de los estados* 1.98 (pp. 204–5).

83. *Poesía crítica y satírica del siglo XV*, p. 59:

> Si vuestro trabajo fue siempre sin arte,
> non faziendo surco en la tierra ajena
> en la gloria eternal habredes gran parte,
> e por el contrario sufriredes pena.
>
> (If your labor is always performed
> without deception, not plowing fur-
> rows in another's land, you will have a
> great share in the eternal glory, but if
> not [i.e., if you do not act well], you
> will suffer pain.)

84. *Buch der Rügen*, vv. 1439–1603 (pp. 86–88).

85. Peter of Blois, *De Hierosolymitana peregrinatione acceleranda*, in *PL* 207: 1069, cited in Mollat, *Poor in the Middle Ages*, pp. 73–74.

86. Raymond de Aguylhers, *Historia Francorum*, pp. 253–55.

87. Jacques de Vitry, *Exempla or Illustrative Stories*, no. 108, p. 50.

88. On the implications and use of this passage, see Schreiner, "Zur biblischen Legitimation des Adels."

89. Gregory of Tours, *Vitae patrum* 5 (MGH Scriptores rerum Merovingicarum 1, p. 667): "Praefecit enim de hac mundane aegrestate in caelo, quo scandere non potuit terrenum imperium, ut accedit illuc rusticus, quo accedere non meruit purpuratus." While Gregory often uses *rusticitas* to mean lack of reverence, here the *rusticus* is clearly a humble country-dweller if not a person of very precise status; cf. Martin of Braga, "De correctione rusticorum."

90. Hrabanus Maurus, carmina 11, vv. 37–40; carmina 14, vv. 13–14 (MGH Poetae Latini aevi Carolini 2, pp. 174, 177), cited in Bosl, "Potens und Pauper," p. 121.

91. MGH Poetae Latini aevi Carolini, vol. 4, fascicle 2, p. 536, cited in Bosl, "Potens und Pauper," p. 127:

> Gaudent potentes dum adquirunt munera,
> Mendici dolent prae famis inopia,
> Post finem vero divites in tartara,
> Qui consumserunt orfanorum lacrimas,
> Pauperi autem pergant ad sublimia.

92. Gautier de Coincy, "De la misère d'homme et de femme," cited in Batany, "Les pauvres et la pauvreté," pp. 479–80.

93. Paris, Bibliothèque National, MS Français 1148, fols. 1r–1v.

94. Ibid., fols. 33v–34r: "Et pourtant mes biaux laboureurs et mes biaux amys, je vous prye et vous conseille que continuellement labourez . . . car vous estes en la voye pour saillir le plustost et le plus ligerement de ce miserable monde au royaulme des cieulx." (However, my good laborers and friends, I pray and counsel you that you labor unceasingly . . . for you are on the way to leave earliest and most easily this miserable world for the kingdom of heaven.)

95. Schönbach, *Studien zur Geschichte*, Sitzungsberichte 155, p. 53.

96. Vauchez, *La sainteté en occident*, pp. 324–26. See also Coulton, *Medieval Village*, pp. 239, 241, 253, 526–27; Gurevich, *Medieval Popular Culture*, pp. 39–77.

97. Tazbir, "Cult of St. Isidore," p. 99, citing Sorokin's *Altruistic Love.*

98. Weinstein and Bell, *Saints and Society*, table on p. 197.

99. Vauchez, *La sainteté en occident*, pp. 209–10; Klaniczay, "Paradoxes of Royal Sainthood."

100. A somewhat parallel situation of spiritual privilege without sainthood existed in Iberia, where no saints at all were canonized between 1198 and 1431, a time when the Reconquest was in progress and the Spanish kings enjoyed exceptional prestige and power over their churches, which a grateful papacy did not choose to

contest. Vauchez attributes this lack of saints to the hostilities between Aragon-Catalonia and the papacy during the Albigensian Crusade, but this would hardly explain the entire period, nor would it hold much significance for Castile. (Vauchez, *La sainteté en occident*, pp. 318–24.) It was possible for an entire nation to enjoy high spiritual status without producing saints.

101. Tazbir, "Cult of St. Isidore," pp. 100–101.

102. Cahier, *Characteristiques des saints*, p. 690; Acta Sanctorum, Oct., 7: 1107, 1117, 1119.

103. Tazbir, "Cult of Saint Isidore," pp. 99–103.

104. Ibid., pp. 107–11.

105. See above, Chapter 1, notes 20–22.

106. See above, Chapter 1, note 23.

107. Barney, "Plowshare of the Tongue," p. 268. John Cassian (died 435), in his *Collationes*, likened the disciplined life of religious contemplation to the endurance of the plowman in his veritable "frenzy of work," but this analogy appears along with references to other callings that evoke effort and persistence, those of the soldier and the merchant. See Kirk, "Langland's Plowman," pp. 10–11.

108. See above, Chapter 1, note 86. According to a humerous English monastic text, it was Ham who invented the plow. See Dean, *The World Grown Old*, p. 133.

109. Camille, "Labouring for the Lord"; Reiss, "Symbolic Plow and Plowman."

110. Reiss, "Symbolic Plow and Plowman," p. 16.

111. Berthold von Regensburg, *Vollständige Ausgabe seiner Predigten* 1: 358; Bede, *In Lucae Evangelium expositio* 3.9 (CC 120, p. 213), cited in Reiss, "Symbolic Plow and Plowman," p. 17.

112. Mann, *Chaucer and Medieval Estates Satire*, p. 239 n. 61. Reiss, "Symbolic Plow and Plowman," p. 16, points out that as early as Clement of Alexandria in the third century (and frequently thereafter) "the plow" was one of the names or titles given to Christ.

113. Hartmann von Aue, *Der arme Heinrich*, vv. 775–93 (pp. 45–46), cited in Reiss, "Symbolic Plow and Plowman," pp. 16–17.

114. *Das Marienleben des Schweizers Wernher*, vv. 12647–59 (p. 208):

> Maria die gedacht och vil dar an
> War umb ir sun uf erde kam:
> Allain umb úns vil armen.
> Die wurdent si erbarmen,
> So das seines todes burde
> Uns allen núcze wurde
> Und das erstorben weisen korn,
> Sam hin geworfen und verlorn,
> Mit aller frucht uf gienge,
> Sin mengelich nucz enphienge,
> Und der getrúwe buman

Och vollen kasten moechte han
Nach sinem willen voelleklich.

(Maria often reflected on why her
Son came into this world, alone
among us so poor, so that the
weight of His death would benefit
all of us. And the withered white
corn, lost and thrown away, would
grow and bear fruit, bestowing
good on us all. And the faithful
peasant thus would provide rich
fields according to His perfect
will.)

115. Muskatblut, *Lieder*, song no. 28, st. 3 (p. 79).

116. Peter Frey, "Vom Edlen Bawman," in *Das Ambraser Liederbuch vom Jahre 1582*, song no. 133, vv. 39–45 (BLVS 12, p. 160):

Der keyser solt sich gen dem bawman neigen
als ich im evangelio wil zeigen,
wie denn Christus selbs gesprochen hat,
ich bin ein guter hirt secht an,
mein vater ist ein ackerman,
wir christen sollen kein zweiffel han,
Gott selber sich dem bawman gleichen thete.

(The emperor should bow before the peasant;
and I shall prove by the Gospels that Christ
himself has spoken: Behold, I am a good shepherd, my father is a plowman; we Christians
should not doubt it, God likened himself to a
peasant. [Gudde, *Social Conflicts*, p. 108])

117. Reiss, "Symbolic Plow and Plowman," p. 16.

118. See Cheetham, *English Medieval Alabasters*, illus. 212, p. 285.

119. This contradiction or shift is explored by Aers, "*Piers Plowman*," in his *Community, Gender, and Individual Identity*, pp. 35–72.

120. References are to A. V. C. Schmidt's edition of the B Text: Langland, *The Vision of "Piers Plowman."*

121. Cited in A. Baldwin, "Historical Context," p. 68.

122. Kirk, "Langland's Plowman," pp. 1–3.

123. Langland, "*Piers Plowman*": *The C Text*, pp. 108–9; Hudson, "Epilogue"; Justice, *Writing and Rebellion*, pp. 102–39, 231–51. See below, Chapter 11, p. 266.

124. Aers, *Chaucer, Langland and the Creative Imagination*, pp. 1–37.

125. Aers, "Justice and Wage-Labor," pp. 171–73.

126. Aers, *Community, Gender, and Individual Identity*, pp. 36–48.

127. Langland, *Piers Plowman*, B, VII.100–105; C, XII.194–209; C, XIII.79–92, all cited in A. Baldwin, "Historical Context," p. 72.

128. Aers, *Community, Gender, and Individual Identity*, pp. 54–68.

129. Kirk, "Langland's Plowman," p. 11.

130. Wheatley, "A Selfless Ploughman."

131. Translated in G. Williams, *Burning Tree*, pp. 106–11, cited in Kirk, "Langland's Plowman," p. 12, and in Holdsworth, "Blessings of Work," pp. 72–73.

132. Johannes von Saaz, *Der Ackermann aus Böhmen*; Johannes von Tepl, *Der Ackermann*; and most recently Johannes de Tepla, *Epistola cum Libello Ackerman*. The author was from Tepl (modern Tepla) but served for many years as town clerk of Saaz, hence the two names. A useful summary of the various points in question concerning this work is provided by Hahn, *Der Ackermann*.

133. This is the thesis of Hruby, *Der "Ackermann" und seine Vorlage*. On the text see Bertau, *Die Handschrift Stuttgart*; Walshe, "Der Ackermann aus Böhmen"; and idem, "Some Notes on *Der Ackermann aus Böhmen*."

134. Martini, *Das Bauerntum*, pp. 214–19.

135. Chaucer, *Canterbury Tales*, General Prologue, vv. 529–40. See Horrell, "Chaucer's Symbolic Plowman."

136. Quoted in Uhrig, "Der Bauer in der Publizistik," p. 90.

137. See above, Chapter 1, pp. 36–37.

138. See the examples of a capital at Vézelay and stained glass from St. Denis in Aston, "Corpus Christi and Corpus Regni," pp. 27–31.

139. Described and illustrated in Scribner, "Images of the Peasant," pp. 32–33.

140. Rolevinck, *De regimine rusticorum*, pp. 86–90, 144. That peasants have knowledge denied by God to the wise is also the theme of a sermon delivered in 1419 by John Želivský, a radical Hussite preacher and political leader in Prague. According to Želivský, the learned Pharisees did not know why Christ consorted with publicans and sinners (Mark 2:16), but the *vilani* understood: "Ecce magistri autem ignoraverunt quare sedit in mensa cum peccatoribus, sed vilani non ignoraverunt"; cited in Kaminsky, *History of the Hussite Revolution*, pp. 275–76 n. 45. On Rolevinck, see Henn, "Der Bauernspiegel des Werner Rolevinck"; and Martini, *Das Bauerntum*, pp. 233–37.

141. Rolevinck, *De regimine rusticorum*, pp. 144–45; Martini, *Das Bauerntum*, p. 234.

142. Rolevinck, *De regimine rusticorum*, p. 107.

143. Packull, "Image of the 'Common Man,'" pp. 258–60, 267–72.

144. Ibid., p. 259.

145. Ibid., p. 260.

146. Gruenbeck, *Spiegel*, fol. [5r]. This does not appear in the Nuremberg 1508 edition.

147. Scribner, "Images of the Peasant," illus. 2 and 3, pp. 31, 34–37.

148. Uhrig, "Der Bauer in der Publizistik," pp. 184–88.

149. On Luther and the image of the pious peasant, see ibid., pp. 95–106, 165–76.

150. Ibid., pp. 176–77.

151. Ibid., p. 97.

152. Ibid., pp. 117–25; Scribner, "Images of the Peasant," p. 30; Brackert, *Bauernkrieg und Literatur*, pp. 30–35.

153. Sider, *Andreas von Bodenstein von Karlstadt*, p. 137.

154. Scribner, "Images of the Peasant," pp. 36–37; Radbruch and Radbruch, *Der deutsche Bauernstand*, pp. 67–71.

155. Packull, "Image of the 'Common Man,'" pp. 262–63.

156. Ibid., pp. 264–67; Scribner, "Images of the Peasant," p. 31.

157. See above, note 69 for this chapter.

Chapter 10

1. *Usatges de Barcelona*, cap. 11 (us. 3), p. 60: "Rusticus interfectus seu alius homo qui nullam habet dignitatem, preter quod christianus est, emendetur per .VI. uncias."

2. Freedman, *Origins of Peasant Servitude*, pp. 86–88.

3. On this subject in general, see Bisson, "Medieval Lordship."

4. Legislation of the Corts (parliament) of Cervera, 1202, in *Les constitucions de pau i treva de Catalunya*, p. 127: "Ibidem, eciam inviolabiliter constituit quod si domini suos rusticos maletractaverint, vel sua eis abstulerint . . . nullo modo teneantur domino regi in aliquo, nisi sint de feudo domini regis vel religiosorum locorum." On this right of mistreatment and its exercise, see my essay "Catalan *Ius Maletractandi*," in Freedman, *Church, Law, and Society*; Martínez, "Violencia señorial.".

5. *Li Livre de Justice et de Plet*, cited in Anex, *Le servage au Pays de Vaud*, p. 105.

6. Beaumanoir, *Coutumes de Beauvaisis*, chap. 45, par. 1452, trans. Akehurst, p. 518.

7. M. Bloch, "Blanche de Castile."

8. *Vidal Mayor*, p. 510.

9. Ruprecht von Freising, *Freisinger Rechtsbuch*, chap. 46, p. 52. On the laws of Alfred, see Pelteret, *Slavery in Early Mediaeval England*, p. 84.

10. See the discussion by Bonnassie, "Marc Bloch, Historian of Servitude," in Bonnassie, *From Slavery to Feudalism*, pp. 330–34.

11. Ibid., p. 333.

12. Ordericus Vitalis, *Ecclesiastical History* 6: 348.

13. Bisson, "Crisis of the Catalonian Franchises"; Garí, "Las *querimoniae* feudales."

14. Bonnassie, *La Catalogne* 2: 590.

15. Hemmerli, *De nobilitate et rusticitate*, cap. 32, fol. 124r; Brunner, *Land and Lordship*, cited in Buc, *L'ambiguïté du livre*, p. 200.

16. Sivéry, "Le Moyen Âge a-t-il connu des communautés rurales silencieuses et soumises?"

17. Dyer, *Lords and Peasants*, pp. 103–6; Hatcher, "English Serfdom and Villeinage," pp. 22–26.

18. Examples in Dyer, "Memories of Freedom," pp. 280–83.

19. Freedman, *Origins of Peasant Servitude*; P. Blickle, "Peasant Revolts"; William Jordan, *From Servitude to Freedom.*

20. *Monuments de l'histoire de l'ancien évêché de Bâle* 5: 886: "et s'il me plaisait je te pourroye prendre par le pied et te mener vendre au marché."

21. Boureau, *Le droit de cuissage*, pp. 224–25.

22. Schmidt, *Ius Primae Noctis.*

23. *Monuments de l'histoire de l'ancien évêché de Bâle* 5: 887–88; Boureau, *Le droit de cuissage*, p. 164.

24. Boureau, *Le droit de cuissage*, pp. 216–26.

25. Ibid., pp. 118–35. Boureau points out, however, that the *droit de cuissage* never appears in the *fabliaux* (pp. 179–80).

26. Freedman, *Origins of Peasant Servitude*, pp. 79–83, 103–10.

27. El Escorial, Real Biblioteca de San Lorenzo d.II.15, fols. 27r–31v, edited in Hinojosa, *El régimen señorial*, p. 318: "Item, pretenen alguns senyors, que com lo pages pren muller lo senyor ha de dormir la primera nit ab ella, e en senyal de senyoria, lo vespre que lo pages deu fer noces esser la mullel colgada, ve lo senyor e munte en lo lit pessant de sobre la dit adona, e com aço sia infructuos al senyor e gran subiugatio al pages mal eximpli e occasio de mal demanen suppliquen totalament esser lavat." (Item, certain lords claim that when the peasant takes a woman, the lord has to sleep the first night with her, and [or?] as a symbol of lordship, the eve of the wedding, when the woman is lying in bed, climb into the bed and pass over the said woman. And as this is of no profit to the lord and a great subjugation of the peasant, a bad example and occasion for wickedness, they [the peasants] demand and supplicate its complete removal.)

28. See Wettlaufer, "Jus primae noctis," pp. 246–50.

29. The Sentence of Guadalupe, edited in Vives, *Historia de los remensas*, p. 342, employs the same wording (this time in Castilian) as the 1462 negotiations: "Ni tampoco puedan [i.e., *los seniores*] la primera noche quel pages prende mujer dormir con ella o en señal de senyoria la noche de las bodas de que la muger sera echada en la cama pasar encima de aquella sobre la dicha muger." (Neither have they the right, when a peasant takes a wife, to sleep the first night with her, nor, as a sign of lordship, to pass over her on her wedding night as she lies in bed.)

30. Hinojosa, *El régimen señorial*, app. II, pp. 313–23, especially chap. 6 and chap. 7 (pp. 317–18).

31. Barros, "Rito y violación," considers these incidents and complaints evidence of a *ius primae noctis*, but see Boureau's response, *Le droit de cuissage*, pp. 264–67.

32. Cabrera and Moros, *Fuenteovejuna.*

33. Franz, *Der deutsche Bauernkrieg*, 7th ed., pp. 11–13.

34. *German Peasants' War: A History in Documents*, pp. 73–78.

35. *Die Kemptener Leibeigenschaftsrodel.*

36. *Quellen zur Geschichte des Bauernkrieges,* ed. Franz, no. 27, pp. 128–29.

37. W. Müller, "Wurzeln und Bedeutung," pp. 3–4.

38. P. Blickle, "Peasant Revolts," p. 232.

39. Freedman, *Origins of Peasant Servitude,* pp. 179–202.

40. Bercé, "Offene Fragen der französischen Bauernrevolten."

41. Cited in Carpenter, "English Peasants in Politics" p. 344.

42. Cited in Buszello, *Der deutsche Bauernkrieg,* p. 17: "nit wie die kye und kölber verkoufft werden, dieweil wir alle nur ein herren, das ist got den herrn im hymel, habe."

43. *Quellen zur Geschichte des Bauernkrieges,* ed. Franz, no. 94, p. 301: "Zu den 8. [i.e., the eighth article of their grievance list] haben sich Geistlich und Weltlich frävenlich wider Got aufgeworfen, und sich trotzt gesetzt wider das Ewangeliumb, und haben sich des Aigentumb angezogen, das allain Got mit Aigentumb zuegehört, und die Menschen fur aigen under sich wellen biegen und schmuckhen und bei der Nesen in ir Geltnetz wellen ziehen . . . so wellen si mit armen Leudten Gwalt haben als ainer uber sein Vieh und noch vil tiranischer."

44. Ibid., no. 27, p. 129.

45. Luther, *Freedom of a Christian,* pp. 277–316; idem, *Admonition to Peace,* pp. 17–43 (especially the response to the peasants' third article against serfdom, p. 39); and idem, *Against the Robbing and Murdering Hordes of Peasants,* pp. 49–55.

46. As pointed out by Kirchner, *Luther and the Peasants' War,* p. 26.

47. Augustine, *Quaestiones in Heptateuchum* 1.153 (*PL* 34: 589–90).

48. Smaragdus, *Via Regia* 30 (*PL* 102: 967–68); Agobard of Lyons, *Epistola ad proceres palatii,* in *PL* 104: 177; Jonas of Orleans, *De institutione laicali* 2.22 (*PL* 106: 213); Atto of Vercelli, *Expositio in Epistolas Pauli,* chap. 6 (*PL* 134: 583).

49. Smaragdus, *Via regia* 30 (*PL* 102: 968): "Vere obedire debet homo Deo, et ejus praeceptis, in quantum ille possibilitatem dederit, obedire. Et inter alia praecepta salutaria, et opera recta, propter nimiam illius charitatem unusquisque liberos debet dimittere servos, considerans quia non illi eos natura subegit, sed culpa; conditione enim aequaliter creati sumus, sed aliis alii culpa subacti." Atto of Vercelli, *Expositio in Epistolas Pauli,* chap. 6 (*PL* 134: 583): "non natura, sed iniquitas fecit. Servi enim non a Cham, cujus maledictio in Chananaeis impleta est, ex quo reges orti sunt, sed ab injustitia, et mundi iniquitate facti sunt."

50. *Le livre des serfs de Marmoutier.* For a recent discussion of what sorts of persons actually gave themselves to the monastery and for what purposes, see Barthélemy, "Les auto-déditions en servage."

51. Rollason, "Miracles of St. Benedict," pp. 78–79.

52. *Sachsenspiegel Landrecht* 3.42.6 (p. 228): "Na rechter warheit so hevet egenscap begin van dwange unde van venknisse under van unrechter gewalt, de men van aldere in unrechte gewonheit getogen hevet unde nu vor recht hebben wel." (In actual truth serfdom has its origin in coercion and captivity and in unjust force, which in former times were regarded as unjust custom, but now are taken as lawful.)

53. *Schwabenspiegel Kurzform,* Landrecht 308 (p. 387).

54. On this distinction between relative and absolute natural law, see Bierbrauer, "Das Göttliche Recht," pp. 222–26.

55. Gregory I, *Moralia in Job* 21.15.22 (CC 143A, p. 1082): "Omnes namque homines natura aequales sumus. . . . Et cum Noe Dominus filiisque eius diceret: *Crescite et multiplicamini et implete terram,* subdidit: *Et terror uester ac tremor sit super cuncta animalia terrae.* Non enim ait: Sit super homines, qui futuri sunt; sed: *Sit super cuncta animalia terrae.*" Cf. Augustine, *De civitate Dei* 19.15.

56. See above, Chapter 3, note 88.

57. Stürner, *Peccatum und Potestas,* pp. 106, 112, 151.

58. Oswald of Lasko, *Sermones de sanctis,* unfoliated, sermon no. 50 (for Saint Ladislas): "O stulticia humana. O fatuitas maxima appetere dominari quam naturalis conditio nostra suadet fugiendam. Nam natura omnes homines equales fecit quam non preposuit hominem homini nisi per rationis abusum peccando se faciat brutum . . . unde Greg. in Moral. *Non est data homini prelatio ut dominetur hominibus sed ut presit bestiis terre piscibus maris et volatibus celi.*" Sermon no. 61 (On Saint James the Apostle), to Matthew 20:21–22, concerning the dangers of ambition: "natura omnes homines equalis conditionis fecit, non ei fecit unum Adam de auro, alium de argento, tercium de luto, sed omnes de luto ne aliquis alteri preferret . . . Hinc Greg. in Moral. *Non est data homine prelatio ut dominetur hominibus sed ut presit bestiis terre.*" Sermon no. 32 (for Gregory the Great): "quod est contra illos qui rusticos etiam bonos reputant quasi bruta."

59. This association was manifested in many forms, such as the Middle English "Charters of Christ," wherein Christ's sacrifice is allegorized as a charter granting salvation and liberty to humanity. See Spalding, *Middle English Charters of Christ.* Many of the manuscripts of the so-called "Short Charter" of Christ bear titles of colophons such as *Carta Redempcionis humanae* or, in one instance (London, British Library, MS Sloane 3292, fol. 2), *Magna Carta de libertatibus Mundi.* I thank Emily Steiner, of Yale University, for this reference.

60. Gregory I, *Registrum epistolarum* 6.12 (CC 140, p. 380): "Cum redemptor noster totius conditor creaturae ad hoc propitiatus humanam uoluit carnem assumere, ut diuinitatis suae gratia, disrupto quo tenebamur capti uinculo seruitutis, pristinac nos restiueret libertati, salubriter agitur, si homines, quos ab initio natura liberos protulit et ius gentium iugo substituit seruitutis, in ea qua nati fuerant manumittentis beneficio libertate reddantur."

61. Gratian, *Decretum,* C.12 q.2 c.68.

62. M. Bloch, *Rois et serfs,* p. 140.

63. Adam of Eynsham, "Vision of the Monk of Eynsham," chap. 41, p. 348: "Seuientes enim carnifices hec ei improperabant, insultantes preterea uehementissime quia in ulcionem ferarum irracionabilium, que de iure naturali communiter omnibus cedere deberant, homines racione utentes & eodem sanguine Christi redemptos & nature indifferentis parilitate consortes aut multasset leto aut membris

diuersis crudeliter mutilasset." I thank Robert Bartlett, of the University of Saint Andrews, for this reference.

64. *Sachsenspiegel Landrecht* 3.42.1 (p. 223): "Got hevet den man na eme selven gebildet unde hevet ene mit siner martere geledeget, den enen alse den anderen; eme is de arme alse beswas alse de rike."

65. *Schwabenspiegel Kurzform*, Landrecht 308 (pp. 383–84): "Got hat den menschen nach im selber gepildet. des sol im der mensch genade sagen. er hat auch den menschen mit seiner marter von der helle erlost."

66. Graus, "'Freiheit' als soziale Forderung," p. 420.

67. Cited in Burdach, *Der Dichter des Ackermann aus Böhmen* 3: 63 n. 1: "ad omnes principes saeculi christianos pertineat cunctum populum Christi sanguine praetioso redemptum suis temporibus videre pacatum et debitis libertatibus, quas jus et natura concessit, facere consolatum . . . eo quod pasturam tenemus ab eo qui libertatis et pacis est princeps . . . hujusmodi consuetudinem utpote . . . superstitiosam, legibus et canonibus et rationi naturali et juri divino, cui per consuetudinem derogari non potest, contrariam."

68. Brock, *Political and Social Doctrines*, pp. 63–64; Chelčický, "O torjím lidu (On the Three Peoples)," pp. 137–67, especially p. 157.

69. *Reformation Kaiser Siegmunds*, MGH Staatsschriften des späteren Mittelalters 6, p. 86: "so hat euch Cristus mit seinem tode gekaufft und gefreyet zü dem ewigen leben."

70. Michael Seidlmayer, "Weltbild und Kultur Deutschlands im Mittelalter," in *Handbuch der Deutschen Geschichte*, vol. 1 (Constance, 1957), p. 66.

71. W. Müller, "Wurzeln und Bedeutung," p. 25.

72. *German Peasants' War: A History in Documents*, no. 125, pp. 254–55.

73. W. Müller, "Wurzeln und Bedeutung," pp. 16–29; Bierbrauer, "Das Göttliche Recht," pp. 226–28. See also P. Blickle, "Freiheit und Gerechtigkeit," pp. 98–102.

74. Cited in P. Blickle, "Freiheit und Gerechtigkeit," p. 100.

75. Girona, Arxiu Històric de l'Ajuntament, Secció 25.2, Llibres manuscrits de tema divers, lligall 1, MS 8, fols. 1r–2v, discussed and edited in Freedman, *Origins of Peasant Servitude*, pp. 190–92, 224–26.

76. Riera i Melis, "El bisbat de Girona," app. 4, p. 200: "Dignemi itaque, pater clemens, ad exemplum Crucifixi, qui quos tenebat servitus antiquata a servitutis nexibus liberavit, vestro generali edicto seu bulla sufficienti, statuere et rite etiam ordinare ut quicumque ex dictis oppressis se redimere a nexibus dicte servitutis voluerit et abinde penitus liberare, servando ac cum effectu complendo formam et modum redempcionis et liberacionis superius et inferius posite, possunt se redimere et totaliter liberare."

77. Barcelona, Arxiu de la Corona d'Aragó, Cancelleria, Registre 1955, fol. 103v; Registre 1968, fol. 12v, edited in Riera i Melis, "El bisbat de Girona," apps. 2 and 3, pp. 197–98.

78. Barcelona, Arxiu de la Corona d'Aragó, Cancelleria, Registre 1955, fols. 105v–106r, edited in Riera i Melis, "El bisbat de Girona," app. 2, p. 198: "E com hajam entès que.l temps de la servitut en qual foren estrets e obligats tots los habitands e habitadors de Cathalunya la Veyla, ço és, dellà Lobregat . . . segons les cròniques, és ja passat e açò deja ésser en lo nostro arxiu, manam-vos que de continent ho façats cerquar e certifficats-nos, per vostres letres, de ço que.n trobarets." (And since we have understood that the time of servitude that binds and obligates the inhabitants of Old Catalonia, i.e., this side of the Llobregat River, . . . has passed according to the chronicles, and this should be in our archive, we order you to search this out and certify to us by your letters what you have found.)

79. Correspondence edited in Fita, "Lo Papa Benet XIII."

80. Freedman, *Origins of Peasant Servitude*, pp. 179–202.

81. 1 Corinthians 7:22: "For he that is called in the Lord being a bondman, is the freeman of the Lord. Likewise he that is called, being free, is the bondman of Christ."

82. Strauss, *Law, Resistance and the State*, pp. 38–55.

83. Bierbrauer, "Das Göttliche Recht," pp. 210–34.

84. *Schwabenspiegel Kurzform*, Landrecht 308 (p. 387): "wir sullen den hern dar umb dienen das sy vns schirmen. vnd als sy die lant mit schirment so sind si nicht diensts schuldig. nach rechter barhait so hat sich aigenschaft erhaben uon getwange vnd uon fangknuss vnd uon manigen vnrechten gewalt den die hernn her uon alter in vnrecht gewonhait habent gezogen vnd die hernn habent das nu fur recht." (We should therefore serve lords who protect us, and if they do not protect the land, they are not worthy of service. In truth servitude was established by coercion and captivity and by much unjust power that the lords have been accustomed to impose as unjust customs and that they now wish to be accepted as law.) Algazi, *Herrengewalt*, pp. 86–91, disputes the view that this indicates that lords must defend their tenants. Algazi attaches the passage to what comes before, regarding the emperor's authority, rather than to what comes after, the power of lords over serfs. While I agree with Algazi that there was no expectation in late-medieval Germany that lords would offer real benefits of defense to tenants, I regard the *Schwabenspiegel* as offering justification for defying oppressive lords, especially those who impose servitude.

85. Mieres, *Apparatus* 2: 513: "Rex etiam cum tota curia non potuit, neque potest facere legem iniquam contra legem Dei, quae si facta foret, non valeret; nec esset lex, quia oportet, quod lex sit iusta et rationabilis."

86. Chazan, "Deteriorating Image of the Jews," pp. 226–28; Langmuir, "Tortures of the Body of Christ."

87. Peasant revolts linked to anti-Semitism include the Franconian Armleder movement of 1336–39 (see K. Arnold, "Die Armlederbewegung in Franken 1336"), the pogroms that took place in Catalonia in 1391 (Freedman, *Origins of Peasant Servitude*, p. 182), and those that occurred during the Hungarian revolt in 1514 (*Monumenta rusticorum*, no. 80, p. 122). On popular insurrection and violence against lepers and Jews, see Nirenberg, *Communities of Violence*, pp. 43–124.

88. Levi, *Christ Stopped at Eboli*, p. 3.

Chapter 11

1. A useful and wide-ranging essay on late-medieval peasant movements and their ideological background is Graus, "'Freiheit' als soziale Forderung."

2. In general, see N. Cohn, *Pursuit of the Millennium*, pp. 191–280.

3. TeBrake, *Plague of Insurrection*, pp. 45–107. To judge from TeBrake's own description, the rebellion seems to have been a protest against taxation and a reproach to the governing classes for their cowardice in paying a tribute to the French—more an example of the failure of mutuality than a movement for a remade world.

4. Strohm, *Hochon's Arrow*; Justice, *Writing and Rebellion*.

5. M. Bloch, *French Rural History*, p. 170.

6. See above, Chapter 3, p. 84.

7. For peasant political involvement apart from revolt, see Carpenter, "English Peasants in Politics"; and Goheen, "Peasant Politics?"

8. This point is emphasized in the study of peasant revolts of the High Middle Ages by Köhn, "Freiheit als Forderung."

9. Bierbrauer, "Bäuerliche Revolten," pp. 26, 62–65.

10. Strohm, *Hochon's Arrow*, pp. 45–56; Aston, "Corpus Christi and Corpus Regni"; Justice, *Writing and Rebellion*, pp. 156–76.

11. Brooks, "Organization and Achievements."

12. Hilton, *English Peasantry*, p. 15.

13. Especially important in this regard is Faith, "Great Rumour."

14. Notably Hudson, "*Piers Plowman* and the Peasants' Revolt"; and Justice, *Writing and Rebellion*, pp. 67–139 (two chapters, "Wyclif in the Rising" and "*Piers Plowman* in the Rising"). See also Aston, "Corpus Christi and Corpus Regni," pp. 33–47. Christina van Nolcken acknowledges possible connections between Wyclif and the Rising but not between Langland and Wyclif nor between Langland and the Rising; see her "*Piers Plowman*," pp. 73–78.

15. Faith, "Great Rumour," pp. 62–70.

16. Justice, *Writing and Rebellion*, pp. 168–76; Faith, "Great Rumour," p. 66 (translating from Walsingham's *Gesta Abbatum Monasterii Sancti Albani*): "They took the stones outside and handed them over to the commons, breaking them into little pieces and giving a piece to each person, just as the consecrated bread is customarily broken and distributed in the parish churches on Sundays, so that the people, seeing these pieces, would know themselves to be avenged against the abbey in that cause."

17. Dyer, "Social and Economic Background"; Strohm, *Hochon's Arrow*, pp. 35–39.

18. E.g., Davies, "Die bäuerliche Gemeinde," pp. 41–44.

19. See, e.g., the case of Essex in Poos, *Rural Society After the Black Death*, pp. 231–52.

20. On the English Rising and its causes, see Dyer, "Social and Economic Background," pp. 9–42; Fryde and Fryde, "Peasant Rebellion"; Hilton, *Bondmen Made Free*; and Hatcher, "England in the Aftermath of the Black Death."

21. Massive documentation is contained in Putnam, *Enforcement of the Statutes*.

22. Tillotson, "Peasant Unrest," p. 14.

23. Dyer, "Social and Economic Background," p. 25.

24. Hilton, "Peasant Movements in England Before 1381," in his *Class Conflict*, pp. 122–38; Hanawalt, "Peasant Resistance," pp. 30–40.

25. Carpenter, "English Peasants in Politics," pp. 325–26.

26. Ibid., p. 342; Hilton, "A Thirteenth-Century Poem on Disputed Villein Services," in his *Class Conflict*, pp. 108–13.

27. On these disputes and the uprising of 1336, see *Ledger-Book of Vale Royal Abbey*, pp. 37–42. This passage is reprinted in several sources: Coulton, *Medieval Village*, pp. 132–35; *Peasants' Revolt of 1381*, pp. 80–83; Hallam, "Life of the People," pp. 846–49.

28. Examples cited in Dyer, "Social and Economic Background," p. 31.

29. Faith, "Great Rumour"; Tillotson, "Peasant Unrest."

30. Dyer, "Social and Economic Background," pp. 34–35; Nichols, "Early Fourteenth Century Petition." Tillotson, "Peasant Unrest," pp. 7–8, notes the importance of Wiltshire in the 1377 disturbances, a region that was relatively quiet in 1381.

31. Hilton, *Class Conflict*, pp. 127–38. On the centrality of the demand for the end to serfdom, see also Hilton's essays "Social Concepts of the English Rising of 1381" and "Popular Movements in England at the End of the Fourteenth Century," both in his *Class Conflict*, pp. 216–26 and 152–64.

32. Walsingham, *Historia Anglicana* 2: 33, and idem, *Chronicon Angliae*, p. 321.

33. Aston, "Corpus Christi and Corpus Regni," pp. 19–21, 26–33.

34. Justice, *Writing and Rebellion*, p. 36.

35. A point argued strongly in Justice, *Writing and Rebellion*, pp. 43–51.

36. Strohm, *Hochon's Arrow*, p. 44.

37. Walsingham, *Gesta abbatum monasterii Snacti Albani* 1: 147–52, 3: 70–74.

38. Justice, *Writing and Rebellion*, p. 47.

39. Ibid., pp. 49–50.

40. Ibid., pp. 82–90.

41. Ibid., pp. 118–39.

42. Walsingham, *Chronicon Angliae*, p. 287.

43. Justice, *Writing and Rebellion*, pp. 140–92; Strohm, *Hochon's Arrow*, pp. 51–56.

44. The different approaches are summarized in Justice, *Writing and Rebellion*, pp. 258–61.

45. Froissart, *Chroniques* 10.97–107, trans. John Bourchier, Lord Berners, reproduced in *Peasants' Revolt of 1381*, pp. 369–72.

46. Bulst, "'Jacquerie' und 'Peasants' Revolt.'"

47. As shown in Medeiros, *Jacques et chroniqueurs*.

48. Freedman, *Origins of Peasant Servitude*, pp. 56–118.

49. On the war, see Vives, *Historia de los remensas*; and Sobrequés i Vidal and Sobrequés i Callicó, *La guerra civil catalana*.

50. Girona, Arxiu Històric de l'Ajuntament, Secció XXV.2, Llibres manuscrits

de tema divers, lligall 1, MS 8, fols. 1r–2v, edited in Freedman, *Origins of Peasant Servitude*, pp. 224–26.

51. See above, Chapter 10, pp. 253–55.

52. The course of this war and its aftermath are laid out in the documents assembled in *Monumenta rusticorum*. There is very little on the war in languages other than Hungarian, but see Barta, "Der ungarische Bauernkrieg"; Gunst, "Der ungarische Bauernaufstand von 1514"; and Housely, "Crusading as Social Revolt." On the Hungarian peasants' war, I have been helped immeasurably by János Bak and Gábor Klaniczay, of the Central European University in Budapest.

53. On the execution and its later iconography, see Birnbaum, "Mock Calvary in 1514?"

54. Báti, "Montaignes Aufzeichnung." Montaigne thought the incident had occurred in Poland.

55. Birnbaum, "Mock Calvary in 1514?"

56. *Monumenta rusticorum*, no. 202, p. 260.

57. This argument had been made earlier, on the occasion of the Belgrade Crusade of 1456, in which a successful peasant army denounced the absence of the nobility. The events of this crusade were observed by Giovanni de Tagliacozzo, who reported the anger against the nobility in his "Victoriae mirabilis," 793.

58. On rural conditions before 1514, see Székely, "Le passage à l'économie basée"; Barta, "Der ungarische Bauernkrieg," pp. 63–69; and Pach, "Die Stellung des ungarischen Bauernkrieges."

59. Király, "Neo-Serfdom in Hungary"; Bak, *Königtum und Stände*, p. 119 n. 47.

60. *Werbőczy István Hármaskönyve*, pt. 1, tit. 3, pp. 56, 58; and pt. 3, tit. 25, p. 406. The material from part 1 on the supposed Hunnic origins of servitude is excerpted in Bak, *Königtum und Stände*, p. 164, and in R. Hoffmann, "Outsiders by Birth and Blood," p. 27.

61. Szűcs, *Nation und Geschichte*, pp. 331–38; idem, "Die oppositionelle Strömung."

62. *Monumenta rusticorum*, no. 142, pp. 175–76.

63. Taurinus Olomucensis, *Stauromachia*, bk. 5, vv. 123–49 (p. 41), 199–267 (pp. 42–44).

64. Tubero, *Commentariorum de rebus*, bk. 4, pp. 330–31.

65. Taurinus Olomucensis, *Stauromachia*, bk. 1, vv. 381–423 (p. 13); Brutus János Mihály, *Magyar históriája* 1: 350–58.

66. *Monumenta rusticorum*, no. 222, p. 302: "tempore, quo plura huius regni loca sive timore sive perfidia ducti a recti fidelitatis tenore aberrarunt."

67. Ibid., no. 126, p. 166: "Inter quos unus feritate et crudelitate in genere humano nulli secundus Georgius Zekel rusticitati proximior quam nobilitati rusticos et populum servilem arte et persuasionibus sinistris seducens."

68. Ibid., p. 165: "nonnulli ex Christiano populo zelo sancte religionis atque defensionis huius regni ducti cruces sibi applicari iuxta ritum huius modi iubilei fecissent quumque mali et perversi—ut plerumque fieri assolet—bonis immixti nacta

hac effundendi latens virus eorum occasione sedicionem et tumultum in hoc regno excitassent."

69. Ibid., no. 221, p. 300.

70. Ibid., no. 202, p. 260.

71. Ibid.: "Item quamquam omnes rustici, qui adversus dominos eorum naturales insurrexerunt, tanquam proditores capitali pena sint plectendi, ne tamen tot sanguinis effusio adhuc sequatur et omnis rusticitas, sine qua nobilitas parum valet, deleatur, statutum est, quod universi capitanei et centuriones et decuriones concitatoresque aliorum rusticorum ac manifesti homicide nobilium, preterea violatores virginum ac mulierum omni gracia remota occidantur et ubilibet extirpentur."

72. Ibid., no. 41, p. 88: "ad quantam temeritatem et insolencias rustici et populares . . . sub nomine cruciate progressi sunt." Similar language appears in letters designed to rouse the nobility of other parts of Hungary, ibid., nos. 53, 56, 68 (pp. 97, 99, 110).

73. Ibid., pp. 234, 238, 294, 302, 335, 370, 418, 443, 468, 473, 523, 537, 540, 542.

74. The Hungarian *comites* were royal provincial administrators, and the title was official rather than patrimonial. The English word "count" in this context conveys a misleading sense of independent noble status apart from office. The *comes* more closely resembled the English sheriff.

75. *Monumenta rusticorum*, no. 73, p. 116: "Quot homicidia, quot stupra et adulteria quotque cedes et incendia per maledictos sceleratissimosque crucifixores illos, qui se se cruciferos appellabant, sed crucis pocius Christi persecutores fuerant."

76. Ibid., no. 200, p. 244: "Evocati interdum quotquot nobilium vi apprehendere possunt, eorum corpora acutissimis sudibus transfodiunt ante uxorum et liberorum oculos; neque hoc satis videtur vindictae, sed coram maritis miseras uxores stupro violant omnisque exercitus. . . . O facinus et diis et hominibus invisum! O impudentes belluas! O immensam ultionem!"

77. E.g., Taurinus Olomucensis, *Stauromachia*, bk. 2, vv. 151–60 (p. 19).

78. *Monumenta rusticorum*, no. 104, pp. 142–44.

79. Ibid., p. 142: "ut est plebs novarum rerum semper studiosa, ideo ea moliri, ut a servitute in libertatem se se vendicarent."

80. Ibid., no. 79, pp. 121–22. Here too, the stirring but unreliable version of the "speech" reported by Tubero (*Commentariorum de rebus*, bk. 4, pp. 331–32) and Taurinus Olomucensis (*Stauromachia*, bk. 1, vv. 381–423 [p. 13]) has influenced even recent historians, such as Székely, in his "Les révoltes paysannes."

81. Szűcs, "Die oppositionelle Strömung," pp. 499–500. Townsmen of Košice (Kassa) referred to the peasant soldiers as the "faithful slaves of the Holy Cross," while an anonymous crusader promised that God and the Holy Cross worn by the soldiers would avenge the murder of prisoners held by their enemies (*Monumenta rusticorum*, no. 45, p. 92; no. 50, p. 96).

82. *Monumenta rusticorum*, no. 79, p. 122: "Noveritis, quod infideles nobiles adversus et contra nos et omnem comitivam cruciferorum ad presentem expedicionem

sancte congregacionis violenta manu insurrexerunt {ut} sic persequi, molestare et turbare volentes."

83. Tubero, *Commentariorum de rebus*, bk. 4, pp. 331–32.

84. Szűcs, *Nation und Geschichte*, pp. 341–43.

85. *Monumenta rusticorum*, no. 49, p. 95. See Szűcs, *Nation und Geschichte*, pp. 350–53.

86. E.g., Étienne de Fougères, writing between 1174 and 1178, in his *Le livre des manières*, vv. 705–12 (p. 85); *Reformation Kaiser Siegmunds*, MGH Staatsschriften des späteren Mittelalters 6, pp. 86, 88.

87. Mályusz, "Hungarian Nobles of Medieval Transylvania," p. 46 (the article is a translation of a part of *Az erdélyi magyar társadalom a középkorban*, written 1947 and published in Budapest in 1988).

88. The bloody sword is mentioned in a Transylvanian customary collection of 1463, according to Mályusz and Kristó's commentary in Thuróczy, *Chronica Hungarorum* 2: 89. See above, Chapter 5, p. 122, for the bloody sword in connection with the supposed mustering of the Huns. For the use of the symbols in 1514, see Taurinus Olomucensis, *Stauromachia*, bk. 1, vv. 480–83 (p. 15); *Monumenta rusticorum*, no. 108, p. 147; no. 178, p. 207; and Szűcs, *Nation und Geschichte*, pp. 362–67.

89. Szűcs, *Nation und Geschichte*, p. 339.

90. Szűcs, "Die oppositionelle Strömung," pp. 483–84.

91. See C. Maier, *Preaching the Crusades*.

92. Szűcs, *Nation und Geschichte*, pp. 345–46.

93. Szűcs, "A Ferences Obszervancia." Six documents from the codex discussed by Szűcs are edited in an appendix to this article, pp. 257–60.

94. Szűcs, "Die oppositionelle Strömung," pp. 503–4.

95. Oswald of Lasko, *Sermones de sanctis* (unfoliated), sermon no. 77 to '*Ecce constitui te super gentes . . .*' (Jeremiah 1:10): "Ve principi qui suos subditos grauat iniustis exactionibus. Ve inquam principi qui contra consuetudinem illegitime vexat suos propinatione sui vini et ceruisce. Ve illis omnibus qui iobagiones suas deuorant inordinate dica et angaria." It is noteworthy that here, as elsewhere in the sermons, Oswald uses the Latinized Hungarian term for serfs, *iobagiones*.

96. Ibid., sermon no. 50: "quia talis fur est et latro et continue est in peccato . . . nec tali domino subditi tenentur obedire et solvere tributum." Sermon no. 49: "Et etiam adversus suum superiorem posset quis se defendere, dummodo superior iniuriose vult ipsum ledere." Discussed in Szűcs, "Die oppositionelle Stromung," p. 508.

97. See especially Oswald of Lasko, *Sermones dominicales*, sermon no. 85.

98. Ibid., sermons nos. 2, 123, 124; idem, *Sermones de sanctis*, sermon no. 41. See Szűcs, "Die Oppositionelle Strömung," pp. 511–12.

99. Szűcs, "Die Oppositionelle Strömung," p. 506.

100. Ibid., pp. 493–99; Szűcs, *Nation und Geschichte*, p. 348.

101. E.g., Laube, Steinmetz, and Vogler, *Illustrierte Geschichte; Die frühbürgerliche Revolution in Deutschland*; and Vogler, *Nürnberg 1524/25*.

102. Moeller, *Imperial Cities and the Reformation*; Ozment, *Reformation in the Cities*; Dickens, *German Nation and Martin Luther*; Oberman, "Tumultus rusticorum." See also Hsia, "Myth of the Commune."

103. In the words of Franz, *Der deutsche Bauernkrieg*, 12th ed., p. 288: "Der Bauernkrieg ist ein Glied in dem Kampf der Deutschen um das Reich." This theme occurs even more strongly in the first (1933) edition. See also Waas, *Die Bauern im Kampf um Gerechtigkeit*, pp. 5–25. Critiques of this view are given by Buszello, *Der deutsche Bauernkrieg*, pp. 12–15; and Stalnaker, "Towards a Social Interpretation."

104. H. Cohn, "Anti-Clericalism"; Oberman, "Tumultus rusticorum"; Goertz, *Pfaffenhass und gross Geschrei*.

105. Franz, *Der deutsche Bauernkrieg*, 12th ed., pp. 1–91. Bierbrauer, "Bäuerliche Revolten," pp. 38–39, points out that Old Law and Godly Law were ways of legitimating revolt and not categories of the actual goals of the peasants, which tended to be political, economic, or related to social or legal standing.

106. E.g., Burke, *Popular Culture*, pp. 173–78.

107. P. Blickle, "Peasant Revolts," p. 232.

108. Their demands are in *Quellen zur Geschichte des Bauernkrieges*, ed. Franz, no. 12, pp. 59–61 (Schliengen, diocese of Constance); no. 13, pp. 61–62 (Hegau); no. 15, pp. 67–70 (Schlettstadt/Sélestat, Alsace); no. 16, pp. 70–76 (Untergrombach, diocese of Speyer); no. 17, pp. 76–79 (Freiburg im Breisgau); no. 18, pp. 79–81 (Upper Rhine).

109. P. Blickle, "Peasant Revolts," pp. 230–31; Schläpfer, "Die Appenzeller Freiheitskriege."

110. Ulbrich, *Leibherrschaft am Oberrhein*; W. Müller, *Entwicklung und Spätformen*; P. Blickle, "Agrarkrise und Leibeigenschaft"; Rösener, "Zur Sozialökonomischen Lage"; R. Blickle, "Leibeigenschaft."

111. P. Blickle, *Revolution of 1525*, pp. 26–27, 202–5.

112. Holenstein, "Äbte und Bauern," p. 264.

113. *Quellen zur Geschichte des Bauernkrieges*, ed. Franz, no. 70, p. 239; no. 94, pp. 305–9; no. 112, p. 343; *Quellen zur Geschichte des Bauernkrieges*, ed. Wopfner, pp. 46, 61, 134–35; Hollaender, "Die vierundzwanzig Artikel," especially p. 83.

114. *Quellen zur Geschichte des Bauernkrieges*, ed. Franz, no. 25, pp. 121–22; translation from *German Peasants' War: A History in Documents*, no. 1, p. 72.

115. Regarding Embrach, see W. Müller, "Wurzeln und Bedeutung," p. 12; regarding Rothenburg, see *Quellen zur Geschichte des Bauernkrieges*, ed. Franz, no. 101, p. 329.

116. *Quellen zur Geschichte des Bauernkrieges*, ed. Franz, no. 23, pp. 97–98; Franz, *Der deutsche Bauernkrieg*, vol. 2 Aktenband, no. 26c (p. 149), no. 30 (p. 164), no. 44 (p. 180).

117. *Quellen zur Geschichte des Bauernkrieges*, ed. Franz, no. 34b, p. 153: "Die seint beschwert mit der Lübaigenschaft, wann sie wellent kain andern Her haben, dann anlain Gott den Allmechtigen, wann der hat uns erschaffen. Wann mir vermeinden auch, das die gotlich Geschrift, das nit auswisse, das kain Hern kain Aigenmensch haben soll, wann Gott ist der recht Her."

118. *Quellen zur Geschichte des Bauernkrieges*, ed. Franz, no. 87, p. 263.

119. Text in P. Blickle, *Revolution of 1525*, pp. 195–201.

120. Brecht, "Der theologische Hintergrund."

121. See the summary and reworking of Franz's views by Wunder, "'Old Law' and 'Divine Law.'"

122. The phrase appears in the English version of Oberman's "Tumultus rusticorum" ("The Gospel of Social Unrest"), p. 43.

123. Kirchner, *Luther and the Peasants' War*.

124. Notably W. Becker, "Göttliches Wort." Against this view, see Oberman, "Tumultus Rusticorum," pp. 160–65.

125. This point is made by H. Cohn, "Anti-Clericalism." See "Ain schoener dialogus und gesprech zwischen aim Pfarrer and aim Schulthayss" (in *Martin Bucers Deutsche Schriften*, vol. 1) especially p. 486 (Pfarrer): "meer muoss ich eüch sagen: wohaer kommend die aigen leüt? ich maint, wir soelttendt alle frey von got sein, wie dan eür Luther auch schriebt in der freyhait des menschen." ([The priest:] moreover I must tell you, whence come serfs? I believe we should all be free by God's ordinance, as your Luther writes in "the freedom of men" [i.e., *The Freedom of a Christian*].)

126. *Urkunden zur Geschichte des Bauernkrieges und der Wiedertäufer*, p. 24.

127. P. Blickle, "Freiheit und Gerechtigkeit."

128. A recent study of the complicated problem of literacy and the Reformation is Scribner, "Heterodoxy, Literacy and Print."

129. The importance of strong local communities in furthering the revolt has been emphasized by P. Blickle, *Communal Reformation*.

130. Bierbrauer, "Das Göttliche Recht." Also important in noting the precedents to the Peasants' War antedating the Reformation are Brecht, "Der theologische Hintergrund," pp. 174–208; W. Müller, "Wurzeln und Bedeutung"; Grundmann, "Freiheit als religiöses," pp. 49–53; and Boockmann, "Zu den geistigen."

131. *Quellen zur Geschichte des Bauernkrieges*, ed. Franz, no. 43, p. 176: "Züm dritten ist der Brauch bisher gewesen, das man für ir aigen Leüt gehalten haben, wölchs zu erbarmen ist, angesehen das uns Christus all mit seinem kostparlichen Plutvergüssen erlösst und erkauft hat, den Hirten gleich als wol als den Höchsten, kain ausgenommen. Darumb erfindt sich mit der Geschrift, das wir frei seien un wöllen sein." The translation is from P. Blickle, *Revolution of 1525*, p. 197.

132. See the table on p. 29 of W. Müller, "Wurzeln und Bedeutung."

133. Bierbrauer, "Das Göttliche Recht," table on p. 226.

134. B. Moore, *Injustice*, pp. 81–89.135. Ibid., p. 87.

Conclusion

1. In thinking about text and context I am especially influenced by the approach of LaCapra, *History, Politics and the Novel*.

2. Frierson, *Peasant Icons*; Donskov, *Changing Image of the Peasant*.

3. Hugo von Trimberg, *Der Renner*, BLVS 247, vv. 6930–47 (1: 289–90). On

Hugo's complaints concerning the oppression of rustic laborers, see above, Chapter 2, p. 52.

4. Ibid., vv. 3405–23 (pp. 140–41).

5. Ibid., vv. 843–45 (p. 34); vv. 1453–59 (p. 60); vv. 2220–28 (pp. 92–93); vv. 3807–10 (p. 157).

6. See above, Chapter 4.

7. Hugo von Trimberg, *Der Renner*, vv. 1309–14 (BLVS 247, 1: 54–55):

> Noch sint einer leie liute,
> Die man gebûrvolc heizet hiute,
> Der maniger vil trazmüetic wêre:
> Wêren in die herren niht ze swêre,
> Sô möhte man ir vil manigen vinde
> Bî der hôchferte ingesinde.

8. Ibid., vv. 1315–20 (p. 55):

> In ein dorf kam ich geriten,
> Dâ lâgen gebûr nâch iren siten
> An irm gemache ûf irn wammen.
> Zuo irn houbten sâzen ir ammen,
> Die mit flîze tierlich suochten
> Der si lützel hin nâch geruochten.

9. Ibid., vv. 1453–56 (p. 60):

> Nieman ist schoene, edel und rîch
> Denne der dâ kumt ze himelrîch:
> Dar kumt vil lîhte ir armen ê
> Denne iuwer vögte, die in tuont wê.

10. Ibid., vv. 1565–4000 (pp. 65–164).

11. See above, Chapter 9, notes 71–73.

12. *Quellen zur Geschichte des deutschen Bauernstandes*, no. 218, p. 553.

13. As in the *Reimchronik des Appenzellerkrieges*, vv. 1495–98 (p. 47); and "Heintz von Bechwinden" (actually Heinrich Bebel), in "Zwei Flugschriften aus der Zeit Maximilians I," vv. 373–77 (p. 178). These passages are discussed above in Chapter 6, p. 149. Hemmerli repeats the supposed truism about peasants needing to be bled and trimmed, and additionally recommends burning rustic properties every 50 years, but more to restrain them than to get anything out of them; see Hemmerli, *De nobilitate et rusticitate*, cap. 32, fol. 124r. "Trimming" and other images of harsh late-medieval lordship are discussed by Algazi, *Herrengewalt*, pp. 188–214.

14. Hemmerli, *De nobilitate et rusticitate*, cap. 33, fol. 127v.

15. Ibid.: "et dixi clerico meo, 'nunc vadamus' prout fecimus."

16. Bierbrauer, "Das Göttliche Recht," pp. 222–28.

17. Scribner, "Images of the Peasant"; Packull, "Image of the 'Common Man'"; Uhrig, "Der Bauer in der Publizistik," pp. 95–106, 165–76.

18. Packull, "Image of the 'Common Man,'" pp. 258–60.

19. Hans Rosenplüt was primarily a writer of antipeasant Carnival plays, and his praise of peasants is a separate apology showing his conformity to this tendency of public opinion. See the contrasting excerpts from his work in *Quellen zur Geschichte des deutschen Bauernstandes*, nos. 216–17, pp. 548–52.

20. Duby, *Three Orders*, pp. 1–4.

21. Chartier, "Intellectual History or Sociocultural History?," p. 30.

22. On the thesis that language constitutes experience rather than simply reflecting it, see Joan W. Scott, "Experience," p. 34.

23. Smith, "Geschichte zwischen den Fronten," p. 600 (in this German version of an originally English composition, the terms are rendered somewhat neutrally as "eine mehr und eine weniger Radikale Einsicht").

24. Certeau, *Writing of History*, p. 79.

25. Kroeber, *Anthropology, Race*, p. 284; Robert Redfield, "Social Organization of Tradition," in *Peasant Society*, ed. Potter; George F. Foster, introduction to *Peasant Society*, pp. 10–14.

26. James C. Scott, *Weapons of the Weak*; *Everyday Forms of Peasant Resistance*, ed. Colborn; *Contesting Power*.

27. E.g., Feierman, *Peasant Intellectuals*; Stern, "New Approaches to the Study of Peasant Rebellion."

28. Feierman, *Peasant Intellectuals*, pp. 39–45.

29. Bourdieu, *Outline of a Theory of Practice*, p. 164, cited in James C. Scott, *Domination*, p. 75.

30. James C. Scott, *Domination*, p. 79.

31. Ibid., pp. 92–94, citing B. Moore, *Injustice*, p. 84.

32. Field, *Rebels in the Name of the Tsar*.

33. Nirenberg, *Communities of Violence*, especially pp. 43–68.

34. James C. Scott, *Domination*, pp. 90–96.

35. Ibid., p. 95.

36. Of particular relevance to the Middle Ages is Wickham, "Gossip and Resistance."

37. White, "Everyday Resistance," p. 56.

38. See especially Ortner, "Resistance and the Problem of Ethnographic Refusal."

39. Wickham, "Gossip and Resistance," pp. 20–22.

40. Scheiner, "Benevolent Lords and Honorable Peasants."

41. Chartier, "Culture as Appropriation"; idem, "Intellectual History and the History of *Mentalités*."

42. Le Goff, "Learned and Popular Dimensions"; Gurevich, "Medieval Culture and *Mentalité*," p. 39; idem, "Oral and Written Culture"; idem, "Bachtin und der Karneval," p. 425; and idem, "Popular Culture and Medieval Latin Literature," in his *Medieval Popular Culture*, pp. 37–38.

43. Edwards, "Religious Faith and Doubt," especially p. 24.

44. Bolton, "Poverty as Protest," p. 5.

45. Stock, *Implications of Literacy*.

46. On the question of how the voice of the oppressed is silenced, manifested, or ventriloquized, see Spivak, "Can the Subaltern Speak?"; Prakash, "Subaltern Studies as Postcolonial Criticism"; and idem, "Can the 'Subaltern' Ride?" For the Middle Ages, see Biddick, "Decolonizing the English Past."

47. As cited by R. H. Bloch, *Medieval Misogyny*, p. 7; and Bordo, *Intolerable Weight*, p. 32.

48. The large bibliography on these subjects includes N. Cohn, *Europe's Inner Demons*; Chazan, "Deteriorating Image of the Jews"; Langmuir, *Toward a Definition of Antisemitism*; Cohen, *The Friars and the Jews*; Daniel, *Islam and the West*; Southern, *Western Views of Islam*; R. I. Moore, "Concept of Heresy as Disease"; Barber, "Lepers, Jews and Moslems"; and Boswell, "Jews, Bicycle Riders, and Gay People."

49. Bartlett, *Making of Europe*; Mellinkoff, *Outcasts*; Fernández-Armesto, *Before Columbus*; R. I. Moore, *Formation of a Persecuting Society*; Richards, *Sex, Dissidence and Damnation*.

50. Heer, *Medieval World*, distinguishes between the "open" society of the twelfth century and the "closed" society that succeeded it after the early thirteenth century. Boswell, *Christianity, Homosexuality and Social Tolerance*, pp. 269–332, applies a similar paradigm to the history of toleration, regarding natural law, Aristotelianism, and scholastic doctrine as leading to a break with an earlier acceptance. Richards, *Sex, Dissidence and Damnation*, pp. 1–13, regards the twelfth century as an open though threatened society and the thirteenth as seeing the triumph of intolerance. In the field of Spanish history, an earlier era of intercommunal coexistence (*convivencia*) among Muslims, Christians, and Jews is contrasted with the inquisitorial climate of the later medieval centuries; see especially Castro, *España en su historia*.

51. Todorov, *Conquest of America*; Boucher, *Cannibal Encounters*; Pagden, *European Encounters with the New World*; *Implicit Understandings*.

52. Of fundamental importance is Said, *Orientalism*. Specific applications include Bassin, "Inventing Siberia"; Batteau, *Invention of Appalachia*; L. Wolf, *Inventing Eastern Europe*; *American Indian and the Problem of History*.

53. Irigaray, *This Sex Which Is Not One*; Gilman, *Difference and Pathology*; *Out There*; Trinh, *Woman, Native, Other*; *Race, Writing and Difference*.

54. Certeau, *Heterologies*; *Writing Culture*; Said, "Representing the Colonized."

55. The term "fetishization of alterity" appears in N. Thomas, *Colonialism's Culture*, p. 159.

56. A successful and intriguing attempt to get away from the limitations of the paradigm of "the Other" and examine Jewish-Muslim relations is Nirenberg, *Communities of Violence*, pp. 166–99.

57. "Proximate other" is used by Dollimore, *Sexual Dissidence*, p. 135, in reference to Augustine's view of the Manicheans.

58. Bhabha, "Difference, Discrimination and the Discourse of Colonialism," es-

pecially pp. 204-5. See also Bhabha's articles "The Other Question," "Of Mimicry and Man," and "Signs Taken for Wonders." The three last are reprinted in Bhabha, *Location of Culture.*

59. Weber, *Peasants into Frenchmen*; Sokoloff, "Rural Change and Farming Politics"; *La fin de la France.* Similar observations are made for contemporary Catalonia in Duran, *Adéu, els pagesos.*

60. Braudel, *Identity of France*, pp. 674-75.

61. Bess, "Ecology and Artifice."

Bibliography

Unpublished Sources

Barcelona, Arxiu de la Corona d'Aragó, Cancelleria, Registre 1955 and Registre 1968.

Barcelona, Arxiu de la Corona d'Aragó, MS Ripoll 99.

Barcelona, Arxiu de la Corona d'Aragó, MS Salva de Infançonia 69.

Cambridge, Corpus Christi College, MSS 31, 55.

Cambridge, St. John's College, MS K. 26.

Cambridge, University Library, MS Peterhouse 119.

El Escorial, Real Biblioteca de San Lorenzo, MSS d.II.15 and d.II.18.

Girona, Arxiu Històric de l'Ajuntament, Secció XXV.2, Llibres manuscrits de tema divers, lligall 1, MS 8.

London, British Library, MS Sloane 3292.

London, Lambeth Palace Library, MSS 71 and 441.

Paris, Bibliothèque de l'Arsenal, MSS 87 and 87A.

Paris, Bibliothèque Mazarine, MS 177.

Paris, Bibliothèque National, MS Espagnol 13; MS Français 1148; MSS lat. 393, 492, 505, 12011, and 16793.

Troyes, Bibliothèque Municipale, MS 893.

Tübingen, Universitätsbibliothek, MS Mc 295.

Vatican City, Biblioteca Apostolica, MS Borghese 374 and MS Ottobbon. 228.

Vienna, Österreichische Nationalbibliothek, MS 1395.

Published Primary Sources

Abbo of Fleury. *Liber apologeticus.* In *PL* 139: 462–72.

Adalbero of Laon. *Poème au roi Robert.* Edited by Claude Carozzi. Les Classiques de l'histoire de France au Moyen Âge 32. Paris, 1979.

Adam of Eynsham, "Vision of the Monk of Eynsham." In *Eynsham Cartulary,* edited by H. E. Salter, 2: 284–371. Oxford Historical Society 51. Oxford, 1908.

Aelfric. *Aelfric's "Colloquy."* Edited by G. N. Garmonsway. 2d edition. London, 1947.

Aelred of Rievaulx. *Speculum caritatis.* CC, Continuatio medievalis 1.

Agobard of Lyon. *Contra praeceptum impium de baptismo Iudaiorum manciporum.* CC, Continuatio medievalis 52.

————. *Epistola ad proceres palatii.* In *PL* 104: 173–78.

Alberti, Leon Battista. *The Family in Renaissance Florence: A Translation of I Libri della Famiglia.* Translated by Renée Neu Watkins. Columbia, S.C., 1969.

Alcuin. *Interrogationes et responsiones in Genesim.* In *PL* 100: 516–66.

Alexander of Hales. *Summa theologica.* Vol. 5. Quaracchi, Italy, 1948.

Alte hoch- und niederdeutsche Volkslieder. Edited by Ludwig Uhland. Stuttgart, 1891.

Alvarus Pelagius. *De planctu ecclesiae.* Lyons, 1517.

Das Ambraser Liederbuch vom Jahre 1582. Edited by Joseph Bergmann. BLVS 12. Stuttgart, 1845.

Ambrose. *De Helia et Ieiunio.* CSEL 32, pt. 1, pp. 409–65.

————. *De Noe et Arca.* In *PL* 14: 379–436.

————. *Epistolae.* CSEL 82.

————. *Exhortatio virginitatis.* In *PL* 16: 351–80.

Ambrosiaster. *Commentarius in epistolam ad Colossenses.* CSEL 81, pt. 3, pp. 165–207.

An die Versammlung gemeiner Bauernschaft: Eine revolutionäre Flugschrift aus dem Deutschen Bauernkrieg (1525). Edited by Siegfried Hoyer and Bernd Rüdiger. Leipzig, 1975.

Andreas Capellanus. *On Love.* Edited and translated by P. G. Walsh. London, 1982.

The Anglo-Norman Pseudo-Turpin Chronicle of William de Briane. Edited by Ian Short. Anglo-Norman Text Society 25. Oxford, 1973.

An Anonymous Old French Translation of the Pseudo-Turpin Chronicle. Edited by Roland N. Walpole. Cambridge, Mass., 1979.

Aquinas, Thomas. *Commentarium in VIII. libros Politicorum.* In Thomas Aquinas, *Opera omnia* 21: 364–716. New York, 1949.

————. *In X. libros Ethicorum ad Nicomachum.* In Thomas Aquinas, *Opera omnia* 21: 1–363. New York, 1949.

————. *Summa theologica.* Vols. 1–4 of Thomas Aquinas, *Opera omnia.* New York, 1948.

L'Archivo Capitolare della Cattedral di Mantova fino alla caduta dei Bonacolsi. Edited by Pietro Torelli. Verona, 1924.

Atto of Vercelli. *Expositio in Epistolas Pauli—In epistolam ad Ephesios.* In *PL* 134: 545–86.

"Aucassin and Nicolette" and Other Tales. Translated by Pauline Matarasso. Harmondsworth, Eng., 1971.

Aucassin et Nicolette. Edited by Jean Dufournet. Paris, 1973.

"Audigier et la chanson de geste, avec une édition nouvelle du poème."* Edited by Omer Jodogne. *Le Moyen Âge* 66 (1960): 511–26.

Augustine of Hippo. *De civitate Dei.* CC 47–48.

————. *Lettres 1–29.* Edited by Johannes Divjak. Oeuvres de Saint Augustin 46B. Paris, 1987.

————. *Quaestionum in Heptateuchum.* In *PL* 34: 547–824.

Azurara, Gomes Eannes de [Gomes Eanes de Zurara]. *Crónica dos feitos notáveis que se passaram no conquista de Guiné por mandado do Infante D. Henrique.* Edited by Torquato de Sousa Soares. Vol. 2. Lisbon, 1978.

The Babylonian Talmud. Edited by I. Epstein. Translated by Jacob Schachter and H. Freeman. London, 1935.

Basil. *De Spiritu Sancto.* In *PG* 32: 67–218.

Der Bauer im deutschen Liede. Edited by J. Bolte. Berlin, 1980.

Der Bauernhochzeitsschwank: Meier Betz und Metzen hochzit. Edited by Edmund Weissner. Altdeutsche Textbibliothek 48. Tübingen, 1956.

Beaumanoir, Philippe de. *Coutumes de Beauvaisis.* Edited by Amédée Salmon. Vol. 2. Paris, 1900. Reprint, Paris, 1970.

————. *The "Coutumes de Beauvaisis" of Philippe de Beaumanoir.* Translated by F. R. P. Akehurst. Philadelphia, 1992.

Bede. *In Lucae Evangelium expositio.* CC 120.

Benedict de Sainte-Maure. *Chronique des ducs de Normandie par Benoît.* Edited by Carin Fahlin. 2 vols. Uppsala, 1951–54.

Benjamin of Tudela. *The Itinerary of Benjamin of Tudela: Travels in the Middle Ages.* Translated by Marcus Nathan Adler. Malibu, Calif., 1987.

Die Berliner Neidhart-Handschrift c (mgf 779): Transkription der Texte und Melodien. Edited by Ingrid Bennewitz-Behr. GAG 356. Göppingen, 1981.

Bernard of Clairvaux. "Sermo in feria IV hebdomadae sanctae." Edited by J. Leclerq and H. Rochais. In *Sancti Bernardi opera* 5: 64–65. Rome, 1968.

Berthold von Regensburg. *Vollständige Ausgabe seiner Predigten mit Anmerkungen und Wörterbuch.* Edited by Franz Pfeiffer. 2 vols. Vienna, 1862. Reprint, Berlin, 1965.

Bertran de Born. *The Poems of the Troubadour Bertran de Born.* Edited by William Paden, Jr.; Tilde Sankovitch; and Patricia H. Stoablein. Berkeley, Calif., 1986.

Boccaccio. *Decameron.* Translated by John Payne. Revised Charles Singleton. Vol. 1. Berkeley, Calif., 1982.

The Boke of Seynt Albans. Saint Albans, 1486. Reprint, London, 1901.

The Book of Sainte Foy. Translated by Pamela Sheingorn. Philadelphia, 1995.

Brutus János Mihály [Gian Michele Bruto]. *Magyar Históriája 1490–1552 (Ungaricarum rerum).* Edited by Ferencz Toldy. Monumenta Hungariae Historica XII. Pest, 1863.

Buch der Rügen. Edited by Theodor von Karajan. *Zeitschrift für deutsches Altertum* 2 (1842): 15–92.

Burchard of Worms. *Decretum.* In *PL* 140: 506–1058.

Carmina medii aevi. Edited by Francesco Novati. Florence, 1883.

Cartulari de la Vall d'Andorra, segles IX–XIII. Edited by Cebrià Baraut. Vol. 1. Andorra, 1988.

Castleford, Thomas. *Castelford's "Chronicle" or "The Boke of Brut."* Edited by Caroline D. Eckhardt. Early English Text Society 305–6. Oxford, 1996.

Caxton, William. *The Game of the Chesse.* Westminster, 1476. Reprint, London, 1860.

La chanson de Roland. Edited by Cesare Segre. 2 vols. Geneva, 1989.

Chelčický, Peter. "O torjím lidu (On the Three Peoples)." Edited by Howard Kaminsky. In "Peter Chelčický: Treatises on Christianity and the Social Order," *Studies in Medieval and Renaissance History* 1 (1964): 104–79.

Chrétien de Troyes. *Le chevalier au lion (Yvain).* Edited by Mario Roques. Paris, 1967.

———. *Le chevalier de la charrete.* Edited by Mario Roques. Paris, 1967.

———. *Eric et Enide.* Edited by Mario Roques. Paris, 1966.

———. *Yvain, the Knight of the Lion.* Translated by Burton Raffel. New Haven, Conn., 1987.

The Chronicle of Pierre de Langtoft in French Verse from the Earliest Period to the Death of King Edward I. Edited and translated by Thomas Wright. Vol. 1. Rolls Series 47. London, 1866.

Chronicon Eberheimense. MGH Scriptores 23, pp. 431–53.

Claudius Marius Victorinus. *Alethia.* CC 128, pp. 117–93.

Conrad of Eberbach. *Exordium magnum.* In *PL* 185, pt. 2, cols. 995–1198.

———. *Les constitucions de pau i treva de Catalunya (segles XI–XIII).* Edited by Gener Gonzalvo i Bou. Barcelona, 1994.

"Le conte des vilains de Verson." In *Études sur la condition de la classe agricole et l'état de l'agriculture en Normandie au moyen âge,* by Léopold Delisle, appendix 8. Evreux, 1851. Reprint, Brionne, 1978.

Cosmas of Prague. *Chronicae Bohemorum.* MGH Scriptores rerum Germanicarum, n.s., 2. Berlin, 1923.

Councils and Synods with Other Documents Relating to the English Church. Edited by Dorothy Whitelock. Vol. 1. Oxford, 1981.

"Deux traités sur l'amour tirés du manuscrit 2200 de la Bibliothèque Saint-Geneviève." Edited by Arthur Langfors. *Romania* 56 (1930): 361–88.

Diplomatari de la Vall d'Andorra, segle XIV. Edited by Ignasi J. Baiges and Mariona Fages. Vol. 1. Andorra, 1993.

Dives and Pauper. Edited by Priscilla Heath Barnum. Early English Text Society 275. 1976.

"Els documents, dels anys 1076–1092, de l'Arxiu Capitular de La Seu d'Urgell." Edited by Cebrià Baraut. *Urgellia* 7 (1984–85): 7–218.

"Els documents, dels anys 1093–1100, de l'Arxiu Capitular de La Seu d'Urgell." Edited by Cebrià Baraut. *Urgellia* 8 (1986–87): 7–149.

Drei deutsche Minoritenprediger aus dem XIII. und XIV. Jahrhundert. Edited by Adolph Franz. Freiburg im Breisgau, 1907.

Eiximenis, Francesc. *Contes i faules.* Edited by Marçal Olivar. Barcelona, 1925.

Enguerrard de Monstrelet. *Chronique.* Vol. 4 of *Collection des chroniques nationales françaises,* edited by J. A. Buchon. Paris, 1826. Reprint, Paris, 1975.

Enikel, Jansen. *Weltchronik.* MGH Deutsche Chronikon 3, pt. 1.

Erzählungen des späten Mittelalters und ihr Weiterleben in Literatur und Volksdichtung bis zur Gegenwart. Edited by Lutz Röhrich, vol. 2. Bern and Munich, 1967.

Étienne de Fougères. *Le livre des manières.* Edited by R. Anthony Lodge. Textes littéraires français, vol. 275. Geneva, 1979.

Eupolemius. Translated by Jan M. Ziolkowski. *Journal of Medieval Latin* 1 (1991): 1–45.

Fastnachtspiele aus dem 15. Jahrhundert. Edited by Adelbert von Keller. 3 vols. BLVS 28–30. Stuttgart, 1853–58. Reprint, Darmstadt, 1965–66.

Fiter i Rossell, Antoni. *Manual digest de les valls neutras de Andorra.* Andorra, 1987.

Fontane, Theodor. *Gedichte.* Vol. 1. Berlin and Weimar, 1989.

Francesc Eiximenis, la societat catalana al segle XIV. Edited by Jill Webster. Barcelona, 1967.

Froissart, Jean. *Chronique, Livre I. Le manuscrit d'Amiens Bibliothèque Municipale.* Edited by George T. Diller. Vol. 3. Geneva, 1992.

———. *Oeuvres de Froissart.* Edited by Kervyn de Letternhove. 25 vols. Brussels, 1867–77.

Das frühmittelhochdeutsche Wiener Genesis: Kritische Ausgabe mit eimem einleitenden Kommentar zur Überlieferung. Edited by Kathryn Smits. Philologische Studien und Quellen 59. Berlin, 1972.

Gengenbach, Pamphilus. "Der Bundtschu." Edited by Karl Goedecke. In *Sämtliche Werke,* by Pamphilus Gengenbach, pp. 24–25. Hanover, 1856. Reprint, Amsterdam, 1966.

Gerard of Cambrai. *Acta synodi Attrebatensis in Manicheos.* In *PL* 142: 1267–1312.

Gerald of Wales. *De principis instructione liber.* Edited by George F. Warner. Roll Series 21, vol. 8. London, 1891.

The German Peasants' War: A History in Documents. Edited and translated by Tom Scott and Bob Scribner. Atlantic Highlands, N.J., 1991.

Gesta comitum Barcinonensium. Edited by Louis Barrau Dihigo and Jaume Massó Torrents. Barcelona, 1925.

Giovanni de Tagliacozzo. "Victoriae mirabilis divinitus de Turcis habitae," in *Annales Minorum seu trium ordinum a S. Francisco institutorum.* Edited by Luke Wadding. Vol. 12, pt. 3, 753–96. Quaracchi, 1932.

Goswin of Villers. *Vita Arnulfi.* Acta Sanctorum, June, 7: 558–79.

Gower, John. *The Major Latin Works of John Gower: "The Voice of One Crying," and "The Tripartite Chronicle."* Edited by Eric W. Stockton. Seattle, 1962.

———. *Mirour de l'omme.* Edited by G. C. Macaulay. Vol. 1 of *The Complete Works of John Gower.* Oxford, 1899.

———. *Vox clamantis.* Edited by G. C. Macaulay. Vol. 4 of *The Complete Works of John Gower.* Oxford, 1902.

Gregory I. *Moralia in Job.* CC 143A.

———. *Registrum epistolarum.* CC 140 and 140A.

———. *Regula pastoralis.* In *PL* 77: 12–128.

Gregory of Tours. *Vitae patrum*. MGH Scriptores rerum Merovingicarum 1, pt. 2, pp. 211–94.

Gruenbeck, Joseph. *Spiegel der naturlichen, himelischen und prophetischen sehungen . . .* Leipzig, 1522.

Gui de Bourgogne. Edited by F. Guessard and H. Michelant. Paris, 1859.

Guillaume de Lorris and Jean de Meun. *Le Roman de la Rose*. Edited by Félix Lecoy. Paris, 1965.

Hagen, Godefrit. *Reimchronik der Stadt Cöln aus dem dreizehnten Jahrhundert*. Edited by Eberhard von Groote. Cologne, 1834. Reprint, Wiesbaden, 1972.

Haimo of Auxerre. *Expositio in epistolas S. Pauli—In epistolam ad Colossenses*. In *PL* 117: 753–78.

Hannemann, Johann Ludwig. *Curiosum scrutinium nigredinis posterorum Cham, i.e. Aethiopum*. Kiel, 1677.

Harris, Joel Chandler. *The Complete Tales of Uncle Remus*. Boston, 1955.

Hartmann von Aue. *Der arme Heinrich: Mittelhochdeutsche Text und Übertragung*. Edited by Hermann Henne. Frankfurt, 1985.

———. *Gregorius, der "gute Sünder"*. Edited by Friedrich Neumann. 4th edition. Wiesbaden, 1972.

Heinrich von Burgus. *Der Seele Rat*. Edited by Hans-Friedrich Rosenfeld. Deutsche Texte des Mittelalters 37. Berlin, 1932.

Hemmerli, Felix. *De nobilitate et rusticitate dialogus*. Strasbourg [c. 1497].

Henry of Huntingdon, *The History of the English*. Edited by Thomas Arnold. Rolls Series 74. London, 1879.

Herbert. *De miraculis*. In *PL* 185, pt. 2, cols. 1273–1384.

Historia episcopum Autissiodorensium. Recueil des historiens des Gaules et de la France 18. Paris, 1879.

Historia Gaufredi, Ducis Normannorum et Comitis Andegavorum. In *Chroniques des comtes d'Anjou et des seigneurs d'Amboise*, edited by Louis Halphen and René Poupardin, pp. 172–231. Paris, 1913.

Historical Poems of the XIVth and XVth Centuries. Edited by Rossell Hope Robbins. New York, 1959.

Die Historien des Neithart Fuchs nach dem Frankfurter Druck von 1566. Edited by Erhard Jöst. Litterae: Göppinger Beiträge zur Textgeschichte 49. Göppingen, 1980.

Die historischen Volkslieder der Deutschen. Edited by Rochus von Liliencron. 4 vols. Leipzig, 1865–69. Reprint, Hildesheim, 1966.

Honorius Augustodunensis. *L'Elucidarium et les Lucidaires*. Edited by Yves Lefèvre. Bibliothèque des Écoles Françaises d'Athènes et de Rome 180. Rome, 1954.

———. *Imago mundi*. Edited by V. I. J. Flint. *Archives d'histoire doctrinale et littéraire du Moyen Âge* 49 (1982): 7–153.

———. *Speculum Ecclesie-Sermo Generalis*. In *PL* 172: 807–1100.

Horace. *Odes and Epodes*. Translated by C. E. Bennett. LCL 33.

Hrabanus Maurus. *Commentaria in Genesim*. In *PL* 107: 439–670.

Hugo von Trimberg. *Der Renner*. Edited by Gustav Ehrismann. BLVS 247, 248, 252, 256. Tübingen, 1908–11.

Hugues Capet. Edited by Marquis de la Grange, 1864.

The Hungarian Illuminated Chronicle (Chronica de Gestis Hungarorum). Edited by Dezsö Dercsényi. New York, 1969.

Ibn Khaldun. *The Muqaddimah: An Introduction to History.* Translated by Frank Rosenthal. 3 vols. New York, 1958.

Isaac of Stella. *Sermones.* In *PL* 194: 1689–1876.

Isidore of Seville. *Etymologiae.* Edited by W. M. Lindsay. 2 vols. Oxford, 1911.

———. *Sententiarum libri tres.* In *PL* 83: 537–738.

Ivo of Chartres. *Decretum.* In *PL* 161: 47–1036.

———. *Panormia.* In *PL* 161: 1045–1344.

Jacques de Vitry. *The Exempla or Illustrative Stories from the "Sermones vulgares" of Jacques de Vitry.* Edited by Thomas F. Crane. London, 1890. Reprint, Nendeln, 1967.

———. *The "Historia occidentalis" of Jacques de Vitry.* Edited by John Frederick Hinnesbuch. Freiburg, 1972.

Joan de Socarrats. *Ioannis de Socarratis iurisconsulti Cathalani in tractatum Petri Alberti.* Barcelona and Lyons, 1551.

Johannes de Tepla. *Epistola cum libello Ackermann und des büchlein ackermann.* Edited by Karl Bertau. 2 vols. Berlin and New York, 1994.

Johannes von Saaz. *Der Ackermann aus Böhmen.* Edited by Günther Jungbluth. Heidelberg, 1969.

Johannes von Tepl [Johannes von Saaz]. *Der Ackermann.* Edited by Willy Krogmann. Deutsche Klassiker des Mitelalters, n.s. 1. Wiesbaden, 1954.

John Chrysostom. *Homiliae de Lazaro.* In *PG* 48: 963–1054.

———. *Homiliae in Genesim.* In *PG* 53: 21–54: 580.

———. *Sermones in Genesim.* In *PG* 54: 581–628.

John of Worcester. *Chronicle of John of Worcester, 1118–1140.* Edited by J. R. H. Weaver. Anecdota Oxoniensia 13. Oxford, 1908.

Jonas of Orléans. *De institutione laicali.* In *PL* 106: 121–278.

Jongleurs et trouvères. Edited by Achille Jubinal. Paris, 1835. Reprint, Geneva, 1977.

Juan del Encina. *Obras completas.* Vol. 4. Madrid, 1983.

Juan Manuel, Don. *Libro de los estados.* Edited by R. B. Tate and I. R. Macpherson. Oxford, 1974.

Justin Martyr. *Dialogus cum Tryphone.* Edited by Karl Otto. In *Iustini philosophi et martyris opera quae feruntur omnia,* vol. 1, pt. 2, 2d edition, pp. 1–499. Jena, 1877. Reprint, Wiesbaden, 1969.

Juvenal. *Satirae.* LCL 91.

Die Kemptener Leibeigenschaftsrodel. Edited by Peter Blickle and Heribert Besch. *Zeitschrift für bayerische Landesgeschichte* 42 (1979): 567–629.

Konrad von Ammenhausen. *Das Schachzabelbuch Kunrats von Ammenhausen, Mönchs und Leutpriesters zu Stein am Rheim.* Edited by Ferdinand Vetter. Frauenfeld, 1892.

La Bruyère, Jean de. *Les caractères de Theophraste, traduits du grec, avec les caractères ou les moeurs de ce siècle.* Edited by Robert Garapon. Classiques Garnier. Paris, 1962.

Lactantius. *Divinae institutiones.* Sources Chrétiennes 204. Paris, 1973.

Lambert of Ardres. *Historia comitum Ghisnensium.* MGH Scriptores 24, pp. 550–642.

Langland, William. *"Piers Plowman": The C Text and Its Poet.* Edited by E. Talbot Donaldson. New Haven, Conn., 1949.

———. *The Vision of "Piers Plowman": A Critical Edition of the B-Text Based on Trinity College Cambridge MS b.15.17.* Edited by A. V. C. Schmidt. Vol. 1. London, 1995.

The Ledger-Book of Vale Royal Abbey. Edited by John Brownbill. Lancashire and Cheshire Record Society 68. 1914.

Legenda Christiani: Vita et passio Sancti Wenceslai et Sancte Ludmile ave eius. Edited by Jaroslav Ludvíkovský. Prague, 1978.

Liber miraculorum Sancte Fidis. Edited by Luca Robertini. Biblioteca di medioevo latino 10. Spoleto, 1994.

Das Lied von der Entstehung der Eidgenossenschaft. Edited by Max Wehrli. In *Quellenwerk zur Entstehung der Schweizerischen Eidgenossenschaft,* Abt. 3, vol. 2, pt. 1, pp. 34–50. Aarau, 1952.

Le livre des serfs de Marmoutier. Edited by Amédée Salmon. Tours, 1864.

Lotario dei Segni [Pope Innocent III]. *De miseria condicionis humane.* Edited and translated by Robert E. Lewis. Athens, Ga., 1978.

Lucidarius aus der Berliner Handschrift. Edited by Felix Heidlauf. Deutsche Texte des Mittelalters 28. Berlin, 1915. Reprint, Berlin, 1970.

Luther, Martin. *Admonition to Peace: A Reply to the Twelve Articles of the Peasants of Swabia.* In *Luther's Works,* vol. 46, edited by Robert C. Schultz, pp. 17–43. Philadelphia, 1967.

———. *Against the Robbing and Murdering Hordes of Peasants.* In *Luther's Works,* vol. 46, edited by Robert C. Schultz, pp. 45–55. Philadelphia, 1967.

———. *The Freedom of a Christian.* In *Three Treatises,* by Martin Luther, translated by W. A. Lambert, pp. 261–316. Philadelphia, 1979.

———. *Lectures on Genesis.* In *Luther's Works,* edited by Jaroslav Pelikan, vols. 1–8. Saint Louis, 1958–66.

Mannyng, Robert. *Robert Mannyng of Brunne: The Chronicle.* Edited by Idelle Sullens. Binghamton, N.Y., 1996.

Map, Walter. *De nugis curialium.* Edited by M. R. James, C. N. L. Brooke, and R. A. B. Mynors. Revised edition. Oxford, 1983.

———. *The Latin Poems Commonly Attributed to Walter Mapes.* Edited by Thomas Wright. London, 1841. Reprint, Hildesheim, 1968.

Marie de France. *Les lais de Marie de France.* Edited by Jean Rychner. Paris, 1973.

Das Marienleben des Schweizers Wernher aus der Heidelberger Handschrift. Edited by Max Päpke. Deutsche Texte des Mittelalters 27. Berlin, 1920.

Martin of Braga. "De correctione rusticorum." In *Martini episcopi Bracarensis opera omnia,* edited by C. W. Barlow, pp. 183–203. Papers of the American Academy in Rome 12. New Haven, Conn., 1950.

Materialien zur Neidhart-Überlieferung. Edited by Dietrich Boueke. Münchener

Texte und Untersuchungen zur Deutschen Literatur des Mittelalters 16. Munich, 1967.

Matthaei Parisiensis, Monachi Sancti Albani, Historia Anglorum. Edited by Frederic Madden. Rolls Series 44, vol. 1. London, 1866.

The Medieval Pastourelle. Edited and translated by William D. Paden. 2 vols. New York and London, 1987.

Meisterlieder der Kolmarer Hansdchrift. Edited by Karl Bartsch. BLVS 68. Stuttgart, 1862.

The Metrical Chronicle of Robert of Gloucester. Edited by William Aldis Wright. Rolls Series 86, vol. 2. London, 1887.

Midrash Rabbah. Translated by H. Freeman. Vol. 1, Genesis. London, 1938.

Mieres, Tomás. *Apparatus super constitutionibus curiarum generalium Cathaloniae.* 2d edition. Vol. 2. Barcelona, 1621.

Miraculi S. Bertini Sithiensia. MGH Scriptores 15, pt. 1, pp. 509–22.

The Mirror of Justices. Edited by William Joseph Whittaker. Selden Society, vol. 7. London, 1895.

Le mistére du Viel Testament. Edited by James de Rothschild. Vol. 1. Paris, 1878.

Monumenta rusticorum in Hungaria rebellium anno MDXIV. Edited by Antal Fekete Nagy, Victor Kenez, and Laszlo Solymosi. Publicationes Archivi Nationalis Hungarici 2, Fontes 12. Budapest, 1979.

Monuments de l'histoire de l'ancien évêché de Bâle. Edited by Joseph Trouillat. Vol. 5. Porrentruy, 1867.

Muskatblut. *Lieder Muskatblut's.* Edited by Eberhard von Groote. Cologne, 1852.

Neidhart [Neidhart von Reuental]. *Die Lieder Neidharts.* Edited by Edmund Weissner. 2d edition. Altdeutsche Textbibliothek 44. Tübingen, 1984.

Neidhartspiele. Edited by John Margetts. Wiener Neudrucke 7. Graz, 1982.

Das Nibelungenlied. Edited by Karl Bartsch, revised by Helmut de Boor. 22d edition. Mannheim, 1988.

Nicholas of Oresme. *Maistre Nicole Oresme: Le livre des politiques d'Aristote.* Edited by Albert Douglas. Transactions of the American Philosophical Society, n.s., 60. Philadelphia, 1970.

Niklashausen 1476: Quellen und Untersuchungen zur sozialreligiosen Bewegung des Hans Behem und zur Agrarstruktur einer spatmittelalterlichen Dorfes. Edited by Klaus Arnold. Saecula spiritualia 3. Baden-Baden, 1980.

Nouveau Recueil complet des fabliaux. Edited by Willem Noomen and Nico van den Googard. 9 vols. Assen, 1983–96.

The Old French Johannes Translation of the Pseudo-Turpin Chronicle. Edited by Ronald N. Walpole. Berkeley, Calif., 1976.

Ordericus Vitalis. *The Ecclesiastical History of Orderic Vitalis.* Edited and translated by Marjorie Chibnall. 6 vols. Oxford, 1969–80.

Origen. *In Genesim.* In *PG* 12: 45–146.

Oswald of Lasko. *Sermones de sanctis perutiles a quodam fratre Hungaro Ordinis Minorum de Obseruantia comportati Biga Salutis intitulati.* Hagenau, 1497.

———. *Sermones dominicales perutiles a quodam fratre Hungaro Ordinis Minorum de Obseruantia compartati Biga Salutis intitulati.* Hagenau, 1498.

Oswald von Wolkenstein. *Die Lieder Oswalds von Wolkenstein.* Edited by Karl Kurt Klein and Hans Moser. 3d edition. Altdeutsche Textbibliothek 55. Tubingen, 1987.

Ottokar von Steiermark. *Österreichische Reimchronik.* MGH Deutsche Chronikon 5, pts. 1–2.

Ottonis et Raheweni gesta Friderici I. imperatoris. MGH Scriptores rerum Germanicarum.

Parodistische Texte: Beispiele zur lateinischen Parodie im Mittelalter. Edited by Paul Lehmann. Munich, 1923.

The Peasants' Revolt of 1381. Edited by R. B. Dobson. London, 1970.

Peter of Blois. *De Hierosolymitana peregrinatione acceleranda.* In *PL* 207: 1057–79.

Peter the Chanter. *De oratione et speciebus illius.* Edited and translated by Richard C. Trexler as *The Christian at Prayer: An Illustrated Prayer Manual Attributed to Peter the Chanter (d. 1197).* Medieval and Renaissance Texts and Studies 44. Binghamton, N.Y., 1987.

Petrarch. *De remediis utriusque fortunae.* In Petrarch, *Opera quae extant omnia,* 2d edition, 1: 1–225. Basel, 1581.

———. *Von der Artzney bayder Glück des guten und widerwertigen.* Augsburg, 1532. Reprint, Hamburg, 1984.

Petrus Comestor. *Historia scholastica.* In *PL* 198, cols. 1053–1722.

Philippe de Thaon. *Comput (MS BL Cotton Nero A.V.).* Edited by Ian Short. Anglo-Norman Text Society Plain Text Series 2. London, 1984.

Philo. *De Ebrietate.* LCL 227. Cambridge, Mass., 1930.

———. *Quaestiones et solutiones in Genesim.* LCL 380. Cambridge, Mass., 1953.

Pirke de Rabbi Eliezer. Translated by Gerald Friedlander. New York, 1965.

Poesía crítica y satírica del siglo XV. Edited by Julio Rodríguez Puértolas. Madrid, 1981.

Die poetische Bearbeitung des Buches Daniel aus der Stuttgarter Handschrift. Edited by Arthur Hübner. Deutsche Texte des Mittelalters 19. Berlin, 1911.

"Le Prestre qui abvete." In *Fabliaux érotiques: Textes de jongleurs des XIIe et XIIIe siècles,* edited by Luciano Rossi, pp. 156–63. Paris, 1992.

Privilegis i ordinacions de les valls pyrenenques. Edited by Ferran Valls i Taberner. 3 vols. Barcelona, 1915–20. Reprint of vol. 3, Saragossa, 1990.

Li proverbe au vilain. Die Sprichwörter des geminen Mannes. Altfranzösische Dichtung. Edited by Adolf Tobler. Leipzig, 1895.

Proverbia sententiaeque latinitatis medii aevi. Edited by Hans Walther. Vol 4. Göttingen, 1966.

Prudentius. "Hamartigenia." LCL 387, pp. 200–272.

Quellen zur Geschichte des Bauernkrieges. Edited by Günther Franz. Darmstadt, 1963.

Quellen zur Geschichte des Bauernkrieges in Deutschtirol 1525. Edited by Hermann Wopfner. Innsbruck, 1908.

Quellen zur Geschichte des deutschen Bauernstandes im Mittelalter. Edited by Günther Franz. Darmstadt, 1974.

Rather of Verona. *The Complete Works of Rather of Verona.* Translated by Peter L. D. Reid. Binghamton, N.Y., 1991.

―――. *Praeloquia.* CC, Continuatio medievalis 46A.

Rauschen, Gerhard. *Die Legende Karls des Grossen im 11. und 12. Jahrhundert.* Leipzig, 1890.

Raymond de Aguylhers. *Historia Francorum.* Recueil des historiens des croisades 3. Paris, 1866.

Recueil général et complete des fabliaux des XIII et XIVe siècles. Edited by Anatole de Montaignon and Gaston Reynaud. 6 vols. Paris, 1872–90.

Reformation Kaiser Siegmunds. MGH Staatsschriften des späteren Mittelalters 6.

Reimchronik des Appenzellerkrieges (1400–1404). Edited by Traugott Schiess. Mitteilungen zur vaterländischen Geschichte 35. Saint Gall, 1913.

Rigord, *Gesta Phillippi.* In *Oeuvres de Rigord et de Guillaume le Breton, historiens de Philippe-Auguste,* edited by H. François Delaborde, 1: 1–167. Paris, 1882.

Rodrigo Ximenes de Rada. *Historia de rebus Hispanie.* CC 72.

Roger of Wendover. *The Flowers of History.* Edited by Henry G. Hewlett. Rolls Series 84, vol. 2. London, 1887.

Rolevinck, Werner. *De regimine rusticorum.* Edited by Egidius Holzapfel. Freiburg, 1959.

Le Roman de Renart le Contrefait. Edited by Gaston Raynaud and Henri Lemaître. 2 vols. Paris, 1914.

Le Roman de Thèbes. Edited by Guy Raynaud de Lage. 2 vols. Paris, 1966–67.

Li Romans de Bauduin de Sebourc, IIIe roy de Jhérusalem. 2 vols. Valenciennes, 1841.

Li Romans de Claris et Laris. Edited by Johann Alton. BLVS 169. Tübingen, 1884.

Li Romans de Garin le Loherain. Edited by Paulin Paris. 2 vols. Paris, 1833–35. Reprint, Geneva, 1969.

Roquetaillade, Jean de [Johannes de Rupescissa]. "Vade mecum in tribulatione." In *Appendix ad fasciculum rerum expetendarum et fugiendarum,* edited by Gratius Ortuinus, 496–508. London, 1690.

Ruiz, Juan. *Libro del Arcipreste (también llamado "Libro de Buen Amor"): Edición sinóptica.* Edited by Anthony N. Zahareas and Thomas McCallum. Hispanic Seminary of Medieval Studies, Spanish Series no. 44. Madison, Wis., 1989.

Ruprecht von Freising. *Freisinger Rechtsbuch.* Edited by Hans-Kurt Claussen. Weimar, 1941.

Sachsenspiegel Landrecht. MGH Fontes iuris Germanici antiqui, n.s., 1, pt. 1, 3d edition.

Sánchez de Arévalo, Rodrigo. *Speculum vitae humanae.* Venice, 1513.

Sancti Ephraem Syri in Genesim et in Exodum commentarii. Edited by R.-M. Tonneau. Corpus Scriptorum Christianorum Orientalium 152, Scriptores Syri 71. Latin translation Corpus Scriptorum Christianorum Orientalium 153, Scriptores Syri 72.

Santillana, Marqués de. *Poesías completas*. Edited by Miquel Angel Pérez Priego. Madrid, 1983.

Schwabenspiegel Kurzform. MGH Fontes iuris Germanici antiqui, n.s., vol. 4, 2d edition.

Scorn for the World: Bernard of Cluny's "De Contemptu Mundi." Edited and translated by Ronald E. Pepin. Medieval Texts and Studies 8. East Lansing, Mich., 1991.

Simon of Kéza. *Gesta Hungarorum*. Edited by Alexander Domanovszky. In *Scriptores rerum Hungaricarum* 1: 141–94. Budapest, 1937.

Smaragdus. *Via Regia*. In *PL* 102: 233–970.

The Song of Roland. Translated by Glyn Burgess. London, 1990.

The Southern Version of "Cursor Mundi." Edited by Sarah M. Horrall. Vol. 1. Ottawa, 1978.

Der Stricker. *Märe von den Gäuhühnern*. Edited by Franz Pfeiffer. Vienna, 1859.

Sulpicius Severus. *Chronica*. CSEL 1, pp. 3–105.

al-Tabari. *The History of al-Tabari*. Translated by William M. Brinner. Vol. 2. Albany, N.Y., 1987.

Taurinus Olomucensis, Stephanus. *Stauromachia, id est cruciatorum servile bellum (servilis belli Pannonici libri V)*. Edited by Ladislaus Juhász. Biblioteca Scriptorum Medii Recentisque Aevorum. Budapest, 1944.

Thomasin von Zerclaere. *Der Welsche Gast*. Edited by F. W. von Kreis. 4 vols. GAG 425. Göppingen, 1984–85.

Thuróczy, János. *Chronica Hungarorum*. Edited by Elisabeth Galántai and Julius Kristó. 2 vols. Budapest, 1985.

Tomich, Pere. *Historias e conquestas dels excellentissims e Catholics Reys de Arago e de lurs anteçessors los Comtes de Barçelona*. Barcelona, 1534. Reprint, Valencia, 1970.

Tragó, Pere. *Spill manifest de totes les coses del vescomdat de Castellbò*. Edited by Cebrià Baraut. La Seu d'Urgell, 1982.

Tschudi, Aegidius. *Chronicon Helveticum*. Vol. 1. Supplemental vol. (1200–1315). Edited by Bernhard Stettler. Quellen zur Schweizer Geschichte neue Folge, Abt. 1, vol. 7, pt. 1a. Bern, 1970.

Tubero, Ludovicus. *Commentariorum de rebus suo tempore*. In *Scriptores rerum Hungaricum*, edited by Georg Schwandtner. 2: 112–381. Vienna, 1746.

Le Turpin français, dit le Turpin I. Edited by Roland N. Walpole. Toronto, 1985.

Two of the Saxon Chronicles Parallel. Edited by John Earle. Revised by Charles Plummer. Oxford, 1892. Reprint, Oxford 1972.

Urkundenbuch zur Geschichte des Landes Dithmarschen. Edited by Andreas Ludwig Jacob Michelson. Altona, 1834.

Urkunden zur Geschichte des Bauernkrieges und der Wiedertäufer. Edited by Heinrich Böhmer. Berlin, 1933.

Das Urner Tellspiel. Edited by Max Wehrli. In *Quellenwerk zur Entstehung der Schweizerischen Eidgenossenschaft*, Abt. 3, vol. 2, pt. 1, pp. 70–99. Aarau, 1952.

Usatges de Barcelona: El Codi a mitjan segle XII. Edited by Joan Bastardas. Barcelona, 1984.

"'Versus de Uniboue': Neuedition mit kritischem Kommentar." Edited by Thomas A.-P. Klein. *Studi medievali*, 3d ser., 32 (1991): 843–86.

Vidal Mayor: Traducción aragonesa de la obra In Excelsis Dei Thesauris de Vidal de Canellas. Edited by Gunar Tilander. Vol. 2. Lund, 1956.

"Le Vilain de Bailleul." In *Fabliaux érotiques: Textes de jongleurs des XIIe et XIIIe siècles*, edited by Luciano Rossi, pp. 110–17. Paris, 1992.

"Des vilains ou des XXII manieries de vilains." Edited by Edmond Faral. *Romania* 48 (1922): 243–64.

Virgil. *Eclogues, Georgics, Aeneid 1–6*. Translated by H. Rushton Fairclough. LCL 63.

"Vom Rechte." In *Kleinere deutsche Gedichte des 11. und 12. Jahrhunderts*, edited by Albert Waag and Werner Schröder, pp. 112–31. Altdeutsche Textbibliothek 71/72. Tübingen, 1972.

Wace. *Le Roman de Brut de Wace*. Edited by Ivor Arnold. Paris, 1938.

———. *Le Roman du Rou de Wace*. Edited by A. J. Holden. 2 vols. Paris, 1970.

Walsingham, Thomas. *Chronicon Angliae*. Edited by Edward Maunde Thompson. Rolls Series 64. London, 1874.

———. [Thomas of Walsingham]. *Gesta Abbatum Monasterii Sancti Albani*. 3 vols. Edited by Henry Thomas Riley. Rolls Series 28, pt. 4. London, 1867–69.

———. *Historia Anglicana*. Edited by Henry Thomas Riley. Rolls Series 28, pt. 1, vol. 2. London, 1864.

Walther von der Vogelweide. *Die Gedichte Walthers von der Vogelweide*. Edited by Karl Lachmann and Carl von Kraus. 12th edition. Berlin, 1959.

Das Weisse Buch von Sarnen. Edited by Hans Georg Wirz. In *Quellenwerk zur Entstehung der Schweizerischen Eidgenossenschaft*, Abt. 3, Chroniken 1: 13–19. Aarau, 1947.

Werbőczy István Hármaskönyve [Istvan Werbőczy, *Tripartitum*]. Edited by Sándor Kolosvári and Kelemen Ovári. Budapest, 1897.

Wernher de Gartenaere. *Helmbrecht*. Edited by Ulrich Seelbach. Translated by Linda B. Parshall. New York, 1987.

Williams, Gwyn, trans. *The Burning Tree: Poems from the First Thousand Years of Welsh Verse*. London, 1956.

Wittenwiler, Heinrich. *Der Ring*. Edited by Bernhard Sowinski. Stuttgart, 1988.

Wittenwiler's "Ring" and the Anonymous Scots Poem "Colkelbie Sow": Two Comic-Didactic Works from the Fifteenth Century. Edited by George Fenwick Jones. Chapel Hill, N.C., 1956.

Wulfstan. *Die "Institutes of Polity, Civil and Ecclesiastical." Ein Werk Erzbischof Wulfstans von York*. Edited by Karl Jost. Schweizer Anglistische Arbeiten 47. Bern, 1959.

Wyclif, John. "De servitute civili et dominio seculari." Edited by Johann Loserth. In *Opera minora*, by John Wyclif, pp. 145–64. Wyclif's Latin Works, vol. 21. London, 1913. Reprint, New York, 1966.

La zappa e la retorica: Memorie familiari di un contadino toscano del Quattrocento. Edited by Duccio Balestracci. Quaderni di storia urbana e rurale 4. Florence, 1984.

"Zwei Flugschriften aus der Zeit Maximilians I." Edited by Theodor Lorentzen. *Neue Heidelberger Jahrbücher* 17 (1913): 139–218.

Secondary Sources

Aaron, David H. "Early Rabbinic Exegesis on Noah's Son Ham and the So-Called 'Hamitic Myth.'" *Journal of the American Academy of Religion* 63 (1995): 721–59.

Adams, Robert. "The Egregious Feasts of the Chester and Towneley Shepherds." *Chaucer Review* 21 (1986): 96–107.

Adolfi, Johann. See Neocorus.

Aers, David. *Chaucer, Langland and the Creative Imagination.* London, 1980.

———. *Community, Gender, and Individual Identity: English Writing, 1360–1430.* London, 1988.

———. "Justice and Wage-Labor After the Black Death: Some Perplexities for William Langland." In *The Work of Work*, pp. 169–90.

Agriculture in the Middle Ages: Technology, Practice and Representation. Edited by Del Sweeney. Philadelphia, 1995.

Alexander, Jonathan. "*Labeur* and *Paresse*: Ideological Representations of Medieval Peasant Labor." *Art Bulletin* 72, no. 3 (1990): 436–52.

Alfonso, Isabel. "Cistercians and Feudalism." *Past and Present* 133 (1991): 3–30.

Algazi, Gadi. *Herrengewalt und Gewalt der Herren im späten Mittelalter: Herrschaft, Gegenseitigkeit und Sprachgebrauch.* Frankfurt and New York, 1996.

Alpers, Svetlana. "Bruegel's Festive Peasants." *Simiolus* 6 (1972–73): 163–76.

———. "Taking Pictures Seriously: A Reply to Hessel Miedema." *Simiolus* 10 (1978–79): 46–50.

The American Indian and the Problem of History. Edited by Calvin Martin. New York, 1987.

Anderson, Benedict. *Imagined Communities: Reflections on the Origin and Spread of Nationalism.* London, 1983.

Anderson, Earl R. "Social Idealism in Aelfric's *Colloquy.*" *Anglo-Saxon England* 3 (1974): 153–62.

Andorra romànica. Andorra and Barcelona, 1989.

Anex, Danielle. *Le servage au Pays de Vaud (XIIIe–XVIe siècle).* Lausanne, 1973.

Arnold, Benjamin. *German Knighthood, 1050–1300.* Oxford, 1985.

———. "Instruments of Power: The Profile and Profession of *Ministeriales* Within German Aristocratic Society, 1050–1225." In *Cultures of Power: Lordship, Status, and Process in Twelfth-Century Europe*, edited by Thomas N. Bisson, pp. 36–55. Philadelphia, 1995.

Arnold, Klaus. "Die Armlederbewegung in Franken 1336." *Mainfränkisches Jahrbuch für Geschichte und Kunst* 26 (1974): 35–62.

Arnoux, Mathieu. "Classe agricole, pouvoir seigneurial et autorité ducale: L'évolution de la Normandie féodale d'après le témoignage des chroniquers (Xe–XIIe siècles." *Le Moyen Âge* 98 (1992): 35–62.

Aston, Margaret. "Corpus Christi and Corpus Regni: Heresy and the Peasants' Revolt." *Past and Present* 143 (May 1994): 3–47.

Aurell, Martin. *Les noces du comte: Mariage et pouvoir en Catalogne (785–1213)*. Paris, 1995.

———. "Le roi mangeur et les élites à table." In *La sociabilité à table: Commensalité et convivialité à travers les âges*, pp. 119–29. Rouen, 1993.

Aus der Geschichte der ostmitteleuropäischen Bauernbewegungen im 16.–17. Jahrhundert. Edited by Gusztáv Heckenast. Budapest, 1977.

Bahktin, Mikhail. *Rabelais and His World*. Translated by Helene Iswolski. Cambridge, Mass., 1968.

Baier, Clair. *Der Bauer in der Dichtung des Strickers: Eine literar-historische Untersuchung*. Tübingen, 1938.

Bak, János M. *Königtum und Stände in Ungarn im 14.–16. Jahrhundert*. Wiesbaden, 1973.

Baldwin, Anna P. "The Historical Context." In *A Companion to Piers Plowman*, edited by John A. Alford, pp. 67–86. Berkeley, Calif., 1988.

Baldwin, John W. *The Language of Sex: Five Voices from Northern France around 1200*. Chicago, 1994.

———. *Masters, Princes and Merchants: The Social Views of Peter the Chanter and His Circle*. 2 vols. Princeton, N.J., 1970.

Baldwin, Robert. "Peasant Imagery and Bruegel's *Fall of Icarus*." *Konsthistorisk Tidskrift* 55 (1986): 101–14.

Banaszkiewicz, Jacek. "Königliche Karrieren von Hirten, Gärtnern und Pflüger. Zu einem mittelalterlichen Erzählschema vom Erwerb der Königsherrschaft." *Saeculum* 3–4 (1982): 265–86.

Baraut, Cebrià. "L'evolució política de la senyoria d'Andorra des dels orígens fins als pariatges (segles IX–XIII)." *Urgellia* 11 (1992–93): 225–99.

Barber, Malcolm. "Lepers, Jews and Moslems: The Plot to Overthrow Christendom in 1321." *History* 66 (1981): 1–17.

Barney, Stephen A. "The Plowshare of the Tongue: The Progress of a Symbol from the Bible to *Piers Plowman*." *Mediaeval Studies* 35 (1973): 261–93.

Barros, Carlos. "Rito y violación: Derecho de pernada en la Baja Edad Media." *Historia social* 16 (1993): 3–17.

———. "Violencia y muerte del señor en Galicia a finales de la edad media." *Studia Historica. Historia medieval* 9 (1991): 111–57.

Barta, Gábor. "Der ungarische Bauernkrieg vom Jahre 1514." In *Aus der Geschichte der ostmitteleuropäische Bauernbewegungen*, pp. 63–69.

Barta, Roger. *The Artificial Savage: Modern Myths of the Wildman*. Translated by Christopher John Follett. Ann Arbor, Mich., 1996.

———. *Wildmen in the Looking Glass: The Mythic Origins of European Otherness*. Translated by Carl T. Berrisford. Ann Arbor, Mich., 1994.

Bartels, Adolf. *Die Dithmarscher*. Kiel, 1898.

Barthélemy, Dominique. "Les auto-déditions en servage à Marmoutier (Touraine) au

XIe siècle." In *Commerce, Finances et Société (XIe–XVIe siècles): Recueil de travaux d'histoire médiévale offert à M. le Professeur Henri Dubois*, edited by Philippe Contamine, Thierry Dutour, and Bernard Schnerb, pp. 397–415. Paris, 1993.

————. "Qu'est-ce que le servage, en France au XIe siècle." *Revue historique* 287 (1992): 233–84.

Bartlett, Robert. *The Making of Europe: Conquest, Colonization and Cultural Change, 950–1350*. Princeton, N.J., 1993.

Bartour, Ron. "'Cursed Be Canaan, a Servant of Servants Shall He Be unto His Brethren': American Views on 'Biblical Slavery' 1835–1865. A Comparative Study." *Slavery and Abolition* 4 (1983): 41–55.

Bassin, Mark. "Inventing Siberia: Visions of the Russian East in the Early Nineteenth Century." *American Historical Review* 96 (1991): 763–94.

Batany, Jean. "Les pauvres et la pauvreté dans les revues des 'estats du monde.'" In *Études sur l'histoire de la pauvreté (Moyen Âge–XVIe siècle)*, edited by Michel Mollat, 2: 469–85. Paris, 1974.

Báti, László. "Montaignes Aufzeichnung über György Dózsas Tod." In *Aus der Geschichte der ostmitteleuropäische Bauernbewegungen*, pp. 457–60.

Batteau, Allen W. *The Invention of Appalachia*. Tuscon, 1990.

Baudet, Henri. *Paradise on Earth: Some Thoughts on European Images of Non-European Man*. Translated by Elizabeth Wentholt. New Haven, Conn., 1965.

Baudon de Mony, Charles. *Relations politiques des comtes de Foix avec la Catalogne jusqu'au commencement du XIVe siècle*. 2 vols. Paris, 1896.

Beaune, Colette. *The Birth of an Ideology: Myths and Symbols of Nation in Late-Medieval France*. Translated by Susan Ross Huston. Berkeley, Calif., 1991.

Becker, Hans. *Die Neidharte. Studien zur Überlieferung, Binnentypisierung und Geschichte der Neidharte der Berliner Handschrift germ. fol. 779 (c)*. GAG 255. Göppingen, 1978.

Becker, Winifried. "'Göttliches Wort,' 'göttliches Recht,' 'göttliche Gerechtigkeit': Die Politisierung theologischer Begriffe?" In *Revolte und Revolution in Europa*, edited by Peter Blickle. *Historische Zeitschrift*, Beiheft, 4 (1975): 232–63.

Bélinguer, Bertran. *La condition juridique des Vallées d'Andorre*. Paris, 1970.

Bennewitz-Behr, Ingrid. *Original und Rezeption: Funktions- und überlieferungsgeschichtliche Studien zur Neidhart-Sammlung R*. GAG 437. Göppingen, 1987.

Bensch, Stephen P. "From Prizes of War to Domestic Merchandise: The Changing Face of Slavery in Catalonia and Aragon, 1000–1300." *Viator* 25 (1994): 63–91.

Bercé, Yves-Marie. "Offene Fragen der französischen Bauernrevolten vom 16.–18. Jahrhundert." In *Aufstände, Revolten, Prozesse: Beiträge zu bäuerlichen Widerstandsbewegungen im frühneuzeitlichen Europa*, edited by Winfried Schulze, pp. 60–75. Stuttgart, 1983.

Bergier, Jean-François. *Guillaume Tell*. Paris, 1988.

Bernheimer, Richard. *Wild Men in the Middle Ages: A Study in Art, Sentiment and Demonology*. Cambridge, Mass., 1952.

Bertau, Karl. *Die Handschrift Stuttgart HB X 23 als Grundlage einer neuen 'Acker-mann'-Ausgabe.* Bayerische Akademie der Wissenschaften, Philosophisch-His-torische Klasse, Sitzungsberichte 1991, Heft 4. Munich, 1991.

Bess, Michael. "Ecology and Artifice: Shifting Perceptions of Nature and High Tech-nology in Postwar France." *Technology and Culture* 36 (1995): 830–62.

Bessmertny, Youri. "Le paysan vu par le seigneur: La France des XIe et XIIe siècles." In *Campagnes médiévales: L'homme et son espace. Études offertes à Robert Fossier,* edited by Elisabeth Mornet, pp. 601–11. Paris, 1995.

Beyschlag, Siegfried. "Neidhart von Reuental in neuer Sicht." In *Akten des V. Inter-nationalen Germanisten-Kongresses, Cambridge, 1975* 2: 369–75. Frankfurt, 1976.

Bhabha, Homi K. "Difference, Discrimination and the Discourse of Colonialism." In *The Politics of Theory: Proceedings of the Essex Conference on the Sociology of Lit-erature, July 1982,* edited by Francis Barker, Peter Hulme, Margaret Iverson, and Diana Loxley, pp. 194–211. Colchester, Eng., 1988.

———. *The Location of Culture.* London and New York, 1994.

———. "Of Mimicry and Man: The Ambivalence of Colonial Discourse." *October* 28 (1984): 317–25.

———. "The Other Question—The Stereotype and Colonial Discourse." *Screen* 24 (Nov.–Dec. 1983): 18–36.

———. "Signs Taken for Wonders: Questions of Ambivalence and Authority Under a Tree Outside Delhi, May 1817." *Critical Inquiry* 12 (Autumn 1985): 144–65.

Biddick, Kathleen. "Decolonizing the English Past: Readings in Medieval Archaeol-ogy and History." *Journal of British Studies* 32 (1993): 1–23.

Bierbrauer, Peter. "Bäuerliche Revolten im alten Reich. Ein Forschungsbericht." In *Aufruhr und Empörung? Studien zum bäuerlichen Widerstand im Alten Reich,* edited by Peter Blickle, Peter Bierbrauer, Renate Blickle, and Claudia Ulbrich, pp. 1–68. Munich, 1980.

———. "Das Göttliche Recht und die naturrecthliche Tradition." In *Bauer, Reich und Reformation: Festschrift für Günther Franz zum 80. Geburtstag am 23. Mai 1982,* edited by Peter Blickle, pp. 210–34. Stuttgart, 1982.

Bignami-Odier, Jeanne. *Études sur Jean de Roquetaillade (Johannes de Rupescissa).* Paris, 1952.

Birnbaum, Marianna D. "A Mock Calvary in 1514? The Dózsa-Passion." In *European Iconography East and West: Selected Papers of the Szeged International Conference, June 9–12, 1993,* edited by György E. Szőnyi, pp. 91–108. Leiden, 1996.

Bisson, Thomas N. "The Crisis of the Catalonian Franchises (1150–1200)." In *La for-mació i expansió del feudalisme català,* edited by Jaume Portella i Comas, pp. 153–72. Girona, 1986.

———. "The 'Feudal Revolution.'" *Past and Present* 142 (1994): 6–42.

———. "Medieval Lordship." *Speculum* 70 (1995): 743–59.

———. "The Rise of Catalonia: Identity, Power, and Ideology in a Twelfth-Century Society." In *Medieval France and Her Pyrenean Neighbours,* by Thomas N. Bisson, pp. 125–52. London and Ronceverte, W. Va., 1989.

"The Black Race in North America: Why Was Their Introduction Permitted?" *Southern Literary Messenger* 21 (Nov. 1855): 641–84.

Blakely, Allison. *Blacks in the Dutch World: The Evolution of Racial Imagery in a Modern Society*. Bloomington, Ind., 1993.

Blankenburg, Wilhelm. *Der Vilain in der Schilderung der altfranzösischen Fabliaux*. Greifswald, 1902.

Blickle, Peter. "Agrarkrise und Leibeigenschaft im spätmittelalterlichen deutschen Südwesten." In *Studien zur geschichtlichen Bedeutung des deutschen Bauernstandes*, edited by Peter Blickle, pp. 19–35. Stuttgart, 1989.

———. *Communal Reformation: The Quest for Salvation in Sixteenth-Century Germany*. Translated by Thomas Dunlap. Atlantic Highlands, N. J., 1992.

———. "Freiheit und Gerechtigkeit: Ethische Fragen der Deutschen an die Theologen der Reformation." *Lutherjahrbuch* 62 (1995): 83–103.

———. "Das Gesetz der Eidgenossen: Überlegungen zur Entstehung der Schweiz 1200–1400." *Historische Zeitschrift* 225 (1992): 561–86.

———. "Peasant Revolts in the German Empire in the Late Middle Ages." *Social History* 4 (1979): 223–39.

———. *The Revolution of 1525: The German Peasants' War from a New Perspective*. Translated by Thomas A. Brady, Jr., and H. C. Erik Midelfort. Baltimore, 1981.

Blickle, Renate. "Leibeigenschaft: Versuch über Zeitgenossenschaft im Wissenschaft und Wirklichkeit, durchgeführt am Beispiel Altbayerns." In *Gutsherrschaft als soziales Modell: Vergleichende Betrachtungen zur Funktionsweise frühneuzeitlicher Agrargesellschaften*, edited by Jan Peters, pp. 53–79. Munich, 1995.

Bloch, Marc. "Blanche de Castile and the Serfs of the Chapter of Paris." In *Slavery and Serfdom in the Middle Ages: Selected Essays by Marc Bloch*, translated by William R. Beer, pp. 163–77. Berkeley, Calif., 1975.

———. *Feudal Society*. Translated by L. A. Manyon. Reprint, Chicago, 1961. (Originally published in Paris, 1949.)

———. *French Rural History: An Essay on Its Basic Characteristics*. Translated by Janet Sondheimer. Berkeley, Calif., 1966.

———. *Rois et serfs: Un chapitre d'histoire capétienne*. Paris, 1920. Reprint, Geneva, 1976.

Bloch, R. Howard. *Medieval Misogyny and the Invention of Western Romantic Love*. Chicago, 1991.

———. *The Scandal of the Fabliaux*. Chicago, 1986.

Bois, Guy. *The Crisis of Feudalism: Economy and Society in Eastern Normandy c.1300–1550*. Cambridge, Eng., 1984.

Bolton, Brenda. "Poverty as Protest: Some Inspirational Groups at the Turn of the Twelfth Century." In *Innocent III: Studies on Papal Authority and Pastoral Care*, by Brenda Bolton, no. 13. Aldershot, 1995. (Originally published in *The Church in a Changing Society: Conflict, Reconciliation or Adjustment?* pp. 1–11. Uppsala, 1978.)

Bonjour, Edgar; H. S. Offler; and G. R. Potter. *A Short History of Switzerland*. Oxford, 1952.

Bonnassie, Pierre. *La Catalogne du milieu du Xe à la fin du XIe siècle: Croissance et mutations d'une société.* 2 vols. Toulouse, 1975–76.

———. *From Slavery to Feudalism in South-Western Europe.* Translated by Jean Birrell. Cambridge, Eng., 1991.

Bonnassie, Pierre, and Pierre Guichard. "Les communautés rurales en Catalogne et dans le Pays Valencien (IXe-milieu XIVe siècle)." *Flaran* 4 (1982): 79–115.

Boockmann, Hartmut. "Zu den geistigen und religiösen Voraussetzungen des Bauernkrieges." In *Bauernkriegs-Studien*, edited by Bernd Moeller, pp. 9–27. Gütersloh, 1975.

Borchardt, Frank L. *German Antiquity in Renaissance Myth.* Baltimore, 1971.

Bordo, Susan. *Intolerable Weight: Feminism, Western Culture and the Body.* Berkeley, Calif., 1993.

Bosl, Karl. "Potens und Pauper." In *Frühformen der Gesellschaft im mittelalterlichen Europa: Ausgewahlte Beiträge zu einer Strukturanalyse der mittelalterlichen Welt*, pp. 106–34. Munich, 1964.

Boswell, John. *Christianity, Homosexuality and Social Tolerance: Gay People in Western Europe from the Beginning of the Christian Era to the Fourteenth Century.* Chicago, 1980.

———. "Jews, Bicycle Riders, and Gay People: The Determination of Social Consensus and Its Impact on Minorities." *Yale Journal of Law and the Humanities* 1 (1989): 205–28.

Bouchard, Constance Brittain. *Spirituality and Administration: The Role of the Bishop in Twelfth-Century Auxerre.* Cambridge, Mass., 1979.

Boucher, Philip P. *Cannibal Encounters: Europeans and Island Caribs, 1492–1763.* Baltimore, 1992.

Boucoiran, Louis. *Ariège, Andorre et Catalogne.* Paris, 1854.

Bourdieu, Pierre. *Outline of a Theory of Practice.* Translated by Richard Nice. Cambridge, Eng., 1977.

Boureau, Alain. *Le droit de cuissage: La fabrication d'un mythe, XIIIe–XXe siècle.* Paris, 1995.

Brackert, Helmut. *Bauernkrieg und Literatur.* Frankfurt, 1975.

Brady, Thomas A., Jr. *Turning Swiss: Cities and Empire, 1450–1550.* Cambridge, Eng., 1985.

Braet, Herman. "'A Thing Most Brutish': The Image of the Rustic in Old French Literature." In *Agriculture in the Middle Ages*, pp. 191–204.

Braude, Benjamin. "The Sons of Noah and the Construction of Racial Identity in the Medieval and Early Modern Periods." *William and Mary Quarterly*, 3d ser., 54 (1997): 103–42.

Braudel, Fernand. *The Identity of France.* Translated by Siân Reynolds. Vol. 2. Glasgow, 1990.

Brecht, Martin. "Der theologische Hintergrund der Zwölf Artikel der Bauernschaft in Schwaben von 1525: Christoph Schappelers und Sebastian Lotzers Beitrag zum Bauernkrieg." *Zeitschrift für Kirchengeschichte* 85 (1974): 30–64.

Bresc, Henri. "L'esclave dans le monde méditerranéen des XIVe et XVe siècles: Problèmes politiques, religieux et moraux." In *XIII Congrès d'història de la Corona d'Aragó (Palma de Mallorca, 27 Septembre–1 Octobre 1987)* 1: 89–102. Palma de Mallorca, 1990.

Brewer, D. S. "The Ideal of Feminine Beauty in Medieval Literature, Especially 'Harley Lyrics,' Chaucer, and Some Elizabethans." *Modern Language Review* 50 (1955): 257–69.

Brock, Peter. *The Political and Social Doctrines of the Unity of Czech Brethren in the Fifteenth and Early Sixteenth Centuries.* The Hague, 1957.

Brooks, Nicholas. "The Organization and Achievements of the Peasants of Kent and Essex in 1381." In *Studies in Medieval History Presented to R. H. C. Davis*, edited by Henry Mayr-Harting and R. I. Moore, pp. 247–70. London, 1985.

Brown, Christopher L. "Foundations of British Abolitionism, Beginnings to 1789." Doctoral dissertation, Oxford University, 1994.

Brown, Peter. *The Cult of the Saints: Its Rise and Function in Latin Christianity.* Chicago, 1981.

———. "Relics and Social Status in the Age of Gregory of Tours." In *Society and the Holy in Late Antiquity*, by Peter Brown, pp. 222–50. Berkeley, Calif., 1982.

Brunner, Otto. *Land and Lordship: Structures of Governance in Medieval Austria.* Translated by Howard Kaminsky and James Van Horn Melton. Philadelphia, 1992.

Buc, Philippe. *L'ambiguïté du livre: Prince, pouvoir, et peuple dans les commentaires de la Bible au moyen âge.* Théologie historique 95. Paris, 1994.

———. "Exégèse et pensée politique: Radulphus Niger (vers 1190) et Nicolas de Lyre (vers 1330)." In *Représentation, pouvoir et royauté à la fin du moyen âge*, edited by Joel Blanchard, pp. 145–64. Paris, 1995.

Bullough, Vern L. "Medieval Medical and Scientific Views of Women." *Viator* 4 (1973): 485–501.

Bulst, Neithard. "'Jacquerie' und 'Peasants' Revolt' in der französischen und englischen Chronistik." In *Geschichtsschreibung und Geschichtsbewusstsein im Spätmittelalter*, edited by Hans Patze, pp. 791–817. Vorträge und Forschungen 31. Sigmaringen, 1987.

Burdach, Konrad. *Die Dichter des Ackermann aus Bohmen und seine Zeit.* 3 vols. Vom Mittelalter zur Reformation, Forschungen zur Geschichte der deutschen Bildung. Berlin, 1926.

Burke, Peter. *Popular Culture in Early Modern Europe.* New York, 1978.

Burnett, Charles, and Patrick Gautier Dalché. "Attitudes Towards the Mongols in Medeival Literature: The XXII Kings of Gog and Magog from the Court of Frederick II to Jean de Mandeville." *Viator* 22 (1991): 153–67.

Burns, E. Jane. *Bodytalk: When Women Speak in Old French Literature.* Philadelphia, 1993.

Buszello, Horst. *Der deutsche Bauernkrieg von 1525 als politische Bewegung.* Berlin, 1969.

Bynum, Caroline Walker. "The Female Body and Religious Practice in the Later Middle Ages." *Zone* 3 (1989): 174–88.

Cabrera, Emilio, and Andrés Moros. *Fuenteovejuna: La violencia antiseñorial en el siglo XV.* Barcelona, 1991.

Cadden, Joan. *Meanings of Sex Difference in the Middle Ages: Medicine, Science, and Culture.* Cambridge, Eng., 1993.

Caggese, Romolo. "La Repubblica di Siena e il suo contado nel secolo decimoterzo." *Bullettino Senese di storia patria* 13 (1906): 3–120.

Cahier, Charles. *Characteristiques des saints dans l'art populaire.* Vol. 2. Paris, 1867.

The Cambridge History of Medieval Political Thought c.350–1450. Edited by J. H. Burns. Cambridge, Eng., 1988.

Camille, Michael. "Labouring for the Lord: The Ploughman and the Social Order in the Luttrell Psalter." *Art History* 10 (1987): 423–54.

———. *A Mirror in Parchment? The Luttrell Psalter and the Making of Medieval England.* Forthcoming.

———. "'When Adam Delved': Laboring on the Land in English Medieval Art." In *Agriculture in the Middle Ages,* pp. 247–76.

Carlyle, R. W., and A. J. Carlyle. *A History of Mediaeval Political Theory in the West.* Edinburgh and London, 1928.

Carmen Carlé, María del. *Del concejo medieval Castellano Leones.* Buenos Aires, 1968.

Carpenter, D. A. "English Peasants in Politics, 1258–1267." In *The Reign of Henry III,* by D. A. Carpenter, pp. 309–48. London and Rio Grande, Ohio, 1996. (Originally published in *Past and Present* 136 [1992]: 3–42.)

Carroll, Margaret D. "Peasant Festivity and Political Identity in the Sixteenth Century." *Art History* 10 (1987): 289–314.

Castro, Americo. *España en su historia: Cristianos, moros, y judíos,* 2d edition. Barcelona, 1983.

Caviness, Madeline Harrison. *The Early Stained Glass of Canterbury Cathedral, circa 1175–1220.* Princeton, N.J., 1977.

Certeau, Michel de. *Heterologies: Discourse on the Other.* Translated by Brian Massumi. Minneapolis, 1986.

———. *The Writing of History.* Translated by Tom Conley. New York, 1988.

Chartier, Roger. "Culture as Appropriation: Popular Cultural Uses in Early Modern France." In *Understanding Popular Culture: Europe from the Middle Ages to the Nineteenth Century,* edited by Steven L. Kaplan, pp. 229–53. Berlin, 1984.

———. "Intellectual History and the History of *Mentalités*: A Dual Re-Evaluation." In *Cultural History: Between Practices and Representations,* by Roger Chartier, translated by Lydia G. Cochrane, pp. 19–52. Cambridge, Eng., 1988.

———. "Intellectual History or Sociocultural History? The French Trajectories." In *Modern European Intellectual History: Reappraisals and New Perspectives,* edited by Dominick LaCapra and Steven L. Kaplan. Ithaca, N.Y., 1982.

Chazan, Robert. "The Deteriorating Image of the Jews—Twelfth and Thirteenth Centuries." In *Christendom and Its Discontents: Exclusion, Persecution, and Rebel-*

lion, 1000–1500, edited by Scott L. Waugh and Peter D. Diehl, pp. 220–33. Cambridge, Eng., 1996.

Cheetham, Francis. *English Medieval Alabasters*. Oxford, 1984.

Chevalier, Michel. *La République d'Andorre ou une république séculaire, heureuse et stable depuis Charlemagne jusqu'à nos jours (790.–1848.)* Paris, 1848.

Classen, Albrecht. "Peasant Life and Peasant Reality in the Lyric Poetry of Oswald von Wolkenstein." *Medieval Perspectives* 3, no. 2 (1988): 83–111.

Cohen, Jeremy. *The Friars and the Jews: The Evolution of Medieval Anti-Judaism*. Ithaca, N.Y., 1982.

Cohn, Henry J. "Anti-Clericalism in the German Peasants' War, 1525." *Past and Present* 83 (1979): 3–31.

Cohn, Norman. *Europe's Inner Demons: An Enquiry Inspired by the Great Witch-Hunt*. New York, 1975.

———. *The Pursuit of the Millennium: Revolutionary Millennarians and Mystical Anarchists of the Middle Ages*. 2d edition. New York, 1970.

Coll i Alentorn, Miquel. *Guifré el Pilós en la historiografia i en la llegenda*. Barcelona, 1990.

———. "La llegenda d'Otger Cataló i els nou barons." *Estudis Romànics* 1 (1947–48): 1–47.

Combaricu, Micheline de. "Image et représentation du *vilain* dans les chansons de geste (et dans quelques autres textes médiévaux)." In *Exclus et systèmes d'exclusion dans la littérature et la civilisation médiévales. Senefiance* 5 (1978): 9–26.

Constable, Giles. *Three Studies in Medieval Religious and Social Thought*. Cambridge, Eng., 1995.

Contamine, Philippe. *War in the Middle Ages*. Translated by Michael Jones. Oxford, 1984.

Conte, Emanuele. *Servi medievali: Dinamiche del diritto comune*. Ius nostrum 21. Rome, 1997.

Contesting Power: Resistance and Everyday Social Relations in South Asia. Edited by Douglas Haynes and Gyan Prakash. Berkeley, Calif., 1992.

Cortese, Ennio. *La norma giuridica: Spunti teorici del diritto comune classico*. Vol. 1. Milan, 1962.

Coulton, G. G. *The Medieval Village*. Cambridge, Eng., 1925. Reprint, New York: Dover, 1989.

Curtius, Ernst Robert. *European Literature and the Latin Middle Ages*. Translated by Willard R. Trask. New York, 1953.

Dahan, Gilbert. "L'exégèse de *Genèse* I, 26 dans les commentaires du XII siècle." *Revue des études Augustiniennes* 38 (1992): 124–53.

———. "L'exégèse de l'histoire de Cain et Abel du XIIe au XIVe siècle en Occident." *Recherches de théologie ancienne et médiévale* 49 (1982): 21–89; and 50 (1983): 5–68.

Daniel, Norman. *Islam and the West: The Making of an Image*. Edinburgh, 1960.

Darnton, Robert. "Peasants Tell Tales: The Meaning of Mother Goose." In *The Great Cat Massacre and Other Episodes in French Cultural History*, by Robert Darnton, pp. 53–65. New York, 1984.

Davies, Clifford S. L. "Die bäuerliche Gemeinde in England (1400–1800)." In *Aufstände, Revolten, Prozesse: Beiträge zu bäuerlichen Widersbewegungen im frühneuzeitlichen Europa*, edited by Winifried Schulze. Stuttgart, 1983.

Davis, David Brion. *The Problem of Slavery in Western Culture.* Ithaca, N.Y., 1966.

———. *Slavery and Human Progress.* New York and Oxford, 1984.

Dean, James. *The World Grown Old in Later Medieval Literature.* Cambridge, Mass., 1997.

Dettwiler, Walter. *William Tell: Portrait of a Legend.* Zurich, 1991.

Devisse, Jean. *The Image of the Black in Western Art.* Translated by William Granger Ryan. Vol. 2. Cambridge, Mass., 1979.

Deyermond, Alan. "El hombre salvaje en la novela sentimental." *Filología* 10 (1964): 98–100.

———. "Some Aspects of Parody in the *Libro de Buen Amor.*" In *Libro de Buen Amor Studies*, edited by G. B. Gybbon-Moneypenny, pp. 53–78. London, 1970.

Dickens, A. G. *The German Nation and Martin Luther.* New York, 1974.

Dollimore, Jonathan. *Sexual Dissidence: Augustine to Wilde, Freud to Foucault.* Oxford, 1991.

Donskov, Andrew. *The Changing Image of the Peasant in Nineteenth-Century Russian Drama.* Annales Academiae Scientiarum Fennicae, Ser. B, 177. Helsinki, 1972.

Dozer-Rabedeau, Jane. "*Rusticus*: Folk-Hero of Thirteenth-Century Picard Drama." In *Agriculture in the Middle Ages*, pp. 217–20.

DuBruck, Edelgard E. *Aspects of Fifteenth-Century Society in the German Carnival Comedies: Speculum Hominis.* Lewiston, N.Y., 1993.

———. "A Conspectus of the Peasant on the Late-Medieval German Carnival Stage." *Fifteenth-Century Studies* 14 (1988): 39–53.

Dubuisson, Daniel. "Le roi indo-européen et la synthèse des trois fonctions." *Annales E.-S.-C.* 33 (1978): 21–34.

Duby, Georges. *Le moyen âge: De Hugues Capet à Jeanne d'Arc, 987–1460.* Paris, 1987.

———. *Rural Economy and Country Life in the Medieval West.* Translated by Cynthia Postan. Columbia, S.C., 1968.

———. *The Three Orders: Feudal Society Imagined.* Translated by Arthur Goldhammer. Chicago, 1980.

Dumézil, Georges. *Les dieux souverains des Indo-Européens.* Bibliothèque des sciences humaines. Paris, 1977.

———. *Mythe et épopée.* 3 vols. Bibliothèque des sciences humaines. Paris, 1968–73.

Duran, Maurici. *Adéu, els pagesos.* Barcelona, 1996.

Dyer, Christopher. *Lords and Peasants in a Changing Society: The Estates of the Bishopric of Worcester, 680–1540.* Cambridge, Eng., 1980.

———. "Memories of Freedom: Attitudes Towards Serfdom in England, 1200–1350." In *Serfdom and Slavery: Studies in Legal Bondage*, edited by M. L. Bush, pp. 291–94. Haworth, Essex, 1996.

———. "The Social and Economic Background to the Rural Revolt of 1381." In *The English Rising*, edited by in R. H. Hilton and T. H. Aston, pp. 9–42. Cambridge, Eng., 1984.

Ebner, Herwig. "Der Bauer in der mittelalterlichen Historiographie." In *Bäuerliche Sachkultur des Spätmittelalters: Internationaler Kongress Krems an der Donau 21. bis 24. September 1982*, pp. 93–122. Veroffentlichungen des Instituts für Mittelalterliche Realienkunde Österreichs 7. Österreichische Akademie der Wissenschaften, Philosophisch-Historische Klasse, Sitzungsberichte 439. Vienna, 1984.

Edwards, John. "Religious Faith and Doubt in Late Medieval Spain: Soria, circa 1450–1500." *Past and Present* 120 (1988): 3–25. (Reprinted in *Religion and Society in Spain, c. 1492*, by John Edwards. Aldershot, 1996.)

Ehrismann, Otfrid. "Tradition und Innovation. Zu einigen Novellen des Stricker." In *Deutsche Literatur des Spätmittelalters: Ergebnisse, Probleme und Perspectiven der Forschung*, pp. 179–92. Greifswald, 1986.

Elias, Norbert. *The Civilizing Process.* Translated by Edmund Jephcott. New York, 1978.

Emerson, Oliver F. "Legends of Cain, Especially in Old and Middle English." *Proceedings of the Modern Language Association* 21 (1906): 831–929.

Epperlein, Siegfried. *Der Bauer im Bild des Mittelalters.* Leipzig, 1975.

Evans, William McKee. "From the Land of Canaan to the Land of Guinea: The Strange Odyssey of the 'Sons of Ham.'" *American Historical Review* 85 (1980): 25–33.

Everyday Forms of Peasant Resistance. Edited by Forrest D. Colborn. Armonk, N.Y., 1989.

Faith, Rosamond. "The Class Struggle in Fourteenth Century Englannd." In *People's History and Socialist Theory*, edited by Raphael Samuel, pp. 50–80. London, 1981.

———. "The 'Great Rumour' of 1377 and Peasant Ideology." In *The English Rising of 1381*, edited by in R. H. Hilton and T. H. Aston, pp. 43–73. Cambridge, Eng., 1984.

Falk, Josef. *Étude sociale sur les chansons de geste.* Nyköping, 1899.

Farrier, Susan E. "Hungry Heroes in Medieval Literature." In *Food in the Middle Ages: A Book of Essays*, edited by Melitta Weiss Adamson, pp. 145–59. New York and London, 1995.

Feierman, Steven. *Peasant Intellectuals: Anthropology and History in Tanzania.* Madison, Wis., 1990.

Fentress, James, and Chris Wickham. *Social Memory.* Oxford, 1992.

Feo, Michele. "Dal *pius agricola* al villano empio e bestiale (a proposito di una infedeltà virgiliana de Caro)." *Maia*, n.s., 20 (1968): 89–223.

Fernández-Armesto, Felipe. *Before Columbus: Exploration and Colonization from the Mediterranean to the Atlantic, 1229–1492.* Philadelphia, 1987.

Ferrante, Joan M. "Male Fantasy and Female Reality in Courtly Literature." *Women's Studies* 11 (1984): 67–97.

Ferrer i Mallol, Maria Teresa. "El sagramental: Una milícia camperola dirigida per Barcelona." *Barcelona, quaderns d'història* 1 (1995): 61–70.

Field, Daniel. *Rebels in the Name of the Tsar.* Boston, 1976.

La fin de la France paysanne de 1914 à nos jours. Edited by Michel Gervais. Histoire de la France rurale, vol. 4. Paris, 1976.

Fischer, Jürgen. *Oriens—Occidens—Europa: Begriff und Gedanke "Europa" in der späten Antike und im frühen Mittelalter.* Wiesbaden, 1957.

Fita, Fidel. "Lo Papa Benet XIII y los pagesos de remensa." *La Renaxensa* 5 (1875): 122–30.

Fleckenstein, Josef. "Zur Frage der Abgrenzung von Bauer und Ritter." In *Wort und Begriff,* pp. 246–53.

Flint, Valerie I. J. *Honorius Augustodunensis of Regensburg.* Aldershot, 1995.

———. *Ideas in the Medieval West: Texts and Their Contexts.* London, 1988.

Fluvià, Armand de. *Els Quatre pals: L'Escut dels comtes de Barcelona.* Barcelona, 1994.

Font i Rius, Josep Maria. "Els origens del co-senyoriu andorrà." In *Estudis sobre els drets i institucions locals en la Catalunya medieval,* by Josep Maria Font i Rius, pp. 737–57. Barcelona, 1985.

Fössel, Amalie, *Die Ortlieber: Eine spiritualische Ketzergruppe im 13. Jahrhundert.* Hanover, 1993.

Fossier, Robert. *Peasant Life in the Medieval West.* Translated by Juliet Vale. Oxford, 1988.

Fourquin, Guy. *Lordship and Feudalism in the Middle Ages.* Translated by Iris Lytton Sells and A. L. Lytton Sells. London, 1976.

Franz, Günther. *Der deutsche Bauernkrieg.* 7th edition. Bad Homburg, 1965.

———. *Der deutsche Bauernkrieg.* 12th edition. Darmstadt, 1984.

———. *Der deutsche Bauernkrieg.* Vol. 2 Aktenband. Munich and Berlin, 1935. Reprint, Darmstadt, 1968.

———. *Geschichte des deutschen Bauernstandes: Vom frühen Mittelalter bis zum 19. Jahrhundert.* 2nd ed. Stuttgart, 1976.

Fredrickson, George M. *The Black Image in the White Mind: The Debate on Afro-American Character and Destiny, 1817–1914.* New York, 1971.

———. *White Supremacy: A Comparative Study in American and South African History.* Oxford, 1981.

Freedman, Paul. "Catalan Lawyers and the Origins of Serfdom." *Mediaeval Studies* 48 (1986): 288–314.

———. *Church, Law and Society in Catalonia, 900–1500.* Aldershot, Eng., 1994.

———. "Cowardice, Heroism and the Legendary Origins of Catalonia." *Past and Present* 121 (1988): 3–29.

———. *The Origins of Peasant Servitude in Medieval Catalonia.* Cambridge, Eng., 1991.

Friedman, Albert B. "'When Adam Delved . . .': Contexts of an Historic Proverb." In *The Learned and the Lewed: Studies in Chaucer and Medieval Literature,* edited by Larry D. Benson, pp. 213–30. Cambridge, Mass., 1974.

Friedman, John Block. *The Monstrous Races in Medieval Art and Thought.* Cambridge, Mass., 1981.

———. "Nicholas's 'Angelus ad Virginem' and the Mocking of Noah." *Yearbook of English Studies* 22 (1992): 162–80.

Frierson, Cathy A. *Peasant Icons: Representations of Rural People in Late Nineteenth-Century Russia.* New York and Oxford, 1993.

Frisch, Max. *Andorra*. Frankfurt, 1961.

Die frühbürgerliche Revolution in Deutschland: Referat und Diskussion zum Thema Probleme der frühbürgerlichen Revolution in Deutschland 1476–1535. Edited by Gerhardt Brendler. Berlin, 1961.

Fryde, E. B., and Natalie Fryde. "Peasant Rebellion and Peasant Discontents." In *The Agrarian History of England and Wales*, edited by Edward Miller, 3: 744–819. Cambridge, Eng., 1991.

Funkenstein, Amos. "Basic Types of Christian Anti-Jewish Polemics in the Later Middle Ages." *Viator* 2 (1971): 373–82.

Galpin, Stanley Leman. *Cortois and Vilain: A Study of the Distinctions Made Between Them by the French and Provençal Poets of the Twelfth, Thirteenth, and Fourteenth Centuries*. New Haven, Conn., 1905.

Ganshof, F. L. *Frankish Institutions Under Charlemagne*. Translated by Bryce and Mary Lyon. Providence, 1968.

Garí, Blanca. "Las *querimoniae* feudales en la documentación catalana del siglo XII (1131–1178)." *Medievalia* 5 (1985): 7–49.

Gates, Henry Louis, Jr. *The Signifying Monkey: A Theory of Afro-American Literary Criticism*. New York and Oxford, 1988.

Gaunt, Simon. "Poetry of Exclusion: A Feminist Reading of Some Troubadour Lyrics." *Modern Language Review* 85 (1990): 310–29.

Genicot, Léopold. *Rural Communities in the Medieval West*. Baltimore, 1990.

Genovese, Eugene D. *The World the Slaveholders Made: Two Essays in Interpretation*. New York, 1969.

Geremek, Bronislaw. *The Margins of Society in Late Medieval Paris*. Translated by Jean Birrell. Cambridge, Eng., and Paris, 1987.

Gero, Stephen. "The Legend of the Fourth Son of Noah." *Harvard Theological Review* 73 (1980): 321–30.

Gieysztor, Aleksander. "Gesture in the Coronation Ceremonies of Medieval Poland." In *Coronations: Medieval and Early Modern Monarchic Ritual*, edited by János M. Bak, pp. 152–64. Berkeley, Calif., 1990.

Gilbert, Sandra M., and Susan Gubar. *The Madwoman in the Attic: The Woman Writer and the Nineteenth-Century Literary Imagination*. New Haven, Conn., 1979.

Gilchrist, John. "The Medieval Canon Law on Unfree Persons: Gratian and the Decretist Doctrines, c. 1141–1234." *Studia Gratiana* 19 (1976): 273–361.

———. "Saint Raymond of Penyafort and the Decretalist Doctrines on Serfdom." *Escritos del Vedat* 7 (1977): 299–327.

———. "The Social Doctrine of John Wyclif." *Canadian Historical Association: Historical Papers* 1969: 157–69.

Gilman, Sander. *Difference and Pathology: Stereotypes of Sexuality, Race and Madness*. Ithaca, N.Y., 1985.

Ginzburg, Carlo. *Ecstasies: Deciphering the Witches' Sabbath*. Translated by Raymond Rosenthal. New York, 1991.

—. *The Night Battles: Witchcraft and Agrarian Cults in the Sixteenth and Seventeenth Centuries.* Translated by John Tedeschi and Anne Tedeschi. Baltimore, 1983.

Gliozzi, Giuliano. *Adamo e il nuovo mondo. La nascita dell'antropologia come ideologia coloniale: Dalle genealogie bibliche alle teorie razziali (1500–1700).* Florence, 1977.

Goertz, Hans-Jürgen. *Pfaffenhass und gross Geschrei: Die reformatorischen Bewegungen in Deutschland, 1517–1529.* Munich, 1987.

Goetz, Hans-Werner. "Serfdom and the Beginnings of a 'Seigneurial System' in the Carolingian Period: A Survey of the Evidence." *Early Medieval Europe* 2 (1993): 29–51.

Goheen, R. B. "Peasant Politics? Village Community and the Crown in Fifteenth-Century England." *American Historical Review* 96 (1991): 42–62.

Goldberg, Eric J. "Popular Revolt, Dynastic Politics and Aristocratic Factionalism in the Early Middle Ages: The Saxon *Stellinga* Reconsidered." *Speculum* 70 (1995): 467–501.

Goodman, L. E. "The Biblical Laws of Diet and Sex." In *Jewish Law Association Studies*, edited by B. S. Jackson, 2: 17–57. Atlanta, 1986.

Gottschall, Dagmar. *Das "Elucidarium" des Honorius Augustodunensis: Untersuchungen zu seiner Überlieferungs- und Rezeptionsgeschichte im deutschsprachigen Raum mit Ausgabe der niederdeutschen Übersetzung.* Texte und Textgeschichte 33. Tübingen, 1992.

Grafton, Anthony. "Higher Criticism Ancient and Modern: The Lamentable Deaths of Hermes and the Sibyls." In *The Uses of Greek and Latin: Historical Essays*, edited by A. C. Dionisotti et al., pp. 156–70. Warburg Institute Surveys and Texts 16. London, 1988.

Grandeau, Yann. *Jeanne insultée: Procès en diffamation.* Paris, 1973.

Graus, František. "'Freiheit' als soziale Forderung: Die Bauernbewegungen im Spätmittelalter." In *Die abendländische Freiheit vom 10. zum 14. Jarhhundert: Die Wirkungszussamenhang von Idee und Wirklichkeit im europäischen Vergleich*, edited by Johannes Fried, pp. 409–33. Vorträge und Forschungen 39. Sigmaringen, 1991.

—. "Kirchliche und heidnische (magische) Komponenten der Stellung der Přemysliden: Přemyslidensage und St. Wenzelsideologie." In *Siedlung und Verfassung Böhmens in der Frühzeit*, edited by František Graus and Herbert Ludat, pp. 148–61. Wiesbaden, 1967.

—. *Lebendige Vergangenheit: Überlieferung im Mittelalter und in den Vorstellungen vom Mittelalter.* Cologne and Vienna, 1975.

Gravdal, Kathryn. *Ravishing Maidens: Writing Rape in Medieval French Literature and Law.* Philadelphia, 1991.

—. *Vilain and Courtois: Transgressive Parody in French Literature of the Twelfth and Thirteenth Centuries.* Lincoln, 1989.

Greenblatt, Stephen. "Murdering Peasants: Status, Genre, and the Representation of Rebellion." *Representations* 1 (1983): 1–29.

Grundmann, Herbert. "Freiheit als religiöses, politisches und persönliches Postulat im Mittelalter." *Historische Zeitschrift* 183 (1957): 23–53.

———. *Religious Movements in the Middle Ages.* Translated by Steven Rowan. Notre Dame, Ind., 1995.

Gudde, Erwin Gustav. *Social Conflicts in Medieval German Poetry.* University of California Publications in Modern Philology, vol. 18, no. 1. Berkeley, Calif., 1934.

Guerrau-Jalabert, Anita. "Aliments symboliques et symbolique de la table dans les romans arthuriens (XIIe–XIIIe siècles)." *Annales E.-S.-C.* 47 (1992): 561–94.

Guglielmi, Nilda. "Reflexiones sobre la marginalidad." *Anuario de estudios medievales* 20 (1990): 317–48.

Gunst, Peter. "Der ungarische Bauernaufstand von 1514." In *Revolte und Revolution in Europa,* edited by Peter Blickle, pp. 62–83. Munich, 1975.

Gurevich, Aaron. "Bachtin und der Karneval: Zu Dietz-Rüdiger Moser: 'Lachkultur des Mittelalters? Michael Bachtin und die Folgen seiner Theorie.'" *Euphorion* 85 (1991): 423–29.

———. "Medieval Culture and *Mentalité* According to the New French Historiography." In *Historical Anthropology of the Middle Ages,* by Aaron Gurevich, edited by Jana Howlett, pp. 21–49. Chicago, 1992.

———. *Medieval Popular Culture: Problems of Belief and Perception.* Translated by János M. Bak and Paul A. Hollingsworth. Cambridge, Eng., 1988.

———. "Oral and Written Culture of the Middle Ages: Two 'Peasant Visions' of the Late Twelfth to Early Thirteenth Centuries." In *Historical Anthropology of the Middle Ages,* by Aaron Gurevich, edited by Jana Howlett, pp. 50–64. Chicago, 1992.

Hahn, Gerhard. *Der Ackermann aus Böhmen des Johannes von Tepl.* Darmstadt, 1984.

Haidu, Peter. "Romance: Idealistic Genre or Historical Text?" In *The Craft of Fiction: Essays in Medieval Poetics,* edited by Leigh A. Arrathoon, pp. 1–46. Rochester, Mich., 1984.

Hallam, H. E. "The Life of the People." In *The Agrarian History of England and Wales,* edited by Hallam, 2: 815–57. Cambridge, Eng., 1988.

Hallinger, Kassius. "Woher kommen die Laienbrüder." *Analecta sacri ordinis cisterciensis* 12 (1956): 1–104.

Halpern, Joel Martin. *A Serbian Village.* New York, 1958.

Hämel, Adalbert. "Arnaldus de Monte und der Liber S. Jacobi." *Estudis universitaris catalans* 21 (1936): 147–59.

Hanawalt, Barbara A. "Peasant Resistance to Royal and Seigniorial Impositions." In *Social Unrest in the Late Middle Ages: Papers of the Fifteenth Annual Conference of the Center for Medieval and Early Renaissance Studies,* edited by Francis X. Newman, pp. 23–47. Binghamtom, N.Y., 1986.

Hanning, Robert. *The Vision of History in Early Britain from Gildas to Geoffrey of Monmouth.* New York, 1966.

Hatcher, John. "England in the Aftermath of the Black Death." *Past and Present* 144 (1994): 3–35.

———. "English Serfdom and Villeinage: Towards a Reassessment." *Past and Present* 90 (1981): 3–39.

Haverkamp, Alfred. "'Heilige Städte' im hohen Mittelalter." In *Mentalitäten im Mit-*

telalter: Methodische und inhaltliche Probleme, edited by František Graus, pp. 119–56. Vorträge und Forschungen 35. Sigmaringen, 1987.

Head, Randolph C. "William Tell and His Comrades: Association and Fraternity in the Propaganda of Fifteenth- and Sixteenth-Century Switzerland." *Journal of Modern History* 67 (1995): 527–57.

Heald, David Ronald Lacey. "The Peasant in Medieval German Literature: Realism and Literary Traditionalism, c. 1150–1400." Doctoral dissertation, University of London, 1970.

Heer, Friedrich. *The Medieval World: Europe 1100–1300*. Translated by Janet Sondheimer. New York, 1961.

Henn, Volker. "Der Bauernspiegel des Werner Rolevinck 'De regimine rusticorum' und die soziale Lage westfälischer Bauern im späten Mittelalter." *Westfälische Zeitschrift* 128 (1978): 289–313.

Hieronymous, Frank. "Felix Hemmerli und Sebastian Brant, oder: Zürich und die Eidgenossen—Basel, die Eidgenossen und das Reich. Engagierte Literatur und Politik im 15. Jahrhundert." In *Für Christoph Vischer, Direktor der Basler Universitätsbibliothek*, pp. 21–57. Basel, 1973.

Hill, Christopher. "The Norman Yoke." *Puritanism and Revolution: Studies in Interpretation of the English Revolution of the 17th Century*, by Christopher Hill, 50–122. London, 1958.

Hill, Ordelle G. *The Manor, the Plowman, and the Shepherd: Agrarian Themes and Imagery in Late Medieval and Early Renaissance English Literature*. Selinsgrove, Pa., 1993.

Hill, Thomas D. "*Rígsthula*: Some Medieval Christian Analogues." *Speculum* 61 (1986): 79–89.

Hilton, Rodney H. *Bondmen Made Free: Medieval Peasant Movements and the English Rising of 1381*. New York, 1973.

———. *Class Conflict and the Crisis of Feudalism: Essays in Medieval Social History*. London, 1985.

———. *The Decline of Serfdom in Medieval England*. 2d edition. London, 1983.

———. *The English Peasantry of the Later Middle Ages*. Oxford. 1975.

———. "Reasons for Inequality Among Medieval Peasants." *Journal of Peasant Studies* 5 (1978): 271–84.

Hinojosa, Eduardo de. *El régimen señorial y la cuestión agraria en Cataluña durante la Edad Media* [1905]. In Eduardo de Hinojosa, *Obras*, vol. 2, app. 11. Madrid, 1955.

Hoffmann, Hartmut. "Kirche und Sklaverei im frühen Mittelalter." *Deutsches Archiv für Erforschung des Mittelalters* 42 (1986): 1–24.

Hoffmann, Richard C. "Outsiders by Birth and Blood: Racist Ideologies and Realities Around the Periphery of Medieval European Culture." *Studies in Medieval and Renaissance History*, n.s., 6 (1983): 14–21.

Holdsworth, Christopher J. "The Blessings of Work: The Cistercian View." In *Sanctity and Secularity: The Church and the World*, edited by Derek Baker, pp. 59–76. Studies in Church History 11. Oxford, 1973.

Holenstein, André. "Äbte und Bauern: Vom Regiment der Klöster im Spätmittelalter." In *Politische Kultur in Oberschwaben*, Edited by Peter Blickle, pp. 243–68. Tübingen, 1993.

Hollaender, Albert. "Die vierundzwanzig Artikel gemeiner Landschaft Salzburg. 1525." *Mitteilungen der Gesellschaft für Salzburger Landeskunde* 71 (1931): 65–88.

Holzapfel, Helmut. *Die sittliche Wertung der körperlichen Arbeit im christlichen Altertum*. Würzburg, 1941.

Horrell, Joseph. "Chaucer's Symbolic Plowman." In *Chaucer Criticism*, vol. 1, *The Canterbury Tales*, edited by Richard J. Schoeck and Jerome Taylor, 84–97. Notre Dame, Ind., 1960. (Originally published in *Speculum* 14 [1939]: 82–92.)

Housely, Norman. "Crusading as Social Revolt: The Hungarian Peasant Uprising of 1514." *Journal of Ecclesiatical History* 49 (1998): 1–28.

Hruby, Antonín. *Der "Ackermann" und seine Vorlage*. Münchener Texte und Untersuchungen zur deutschen Literatur des Mittelalters 35. Munich, 1971.

Hsia, R. Po-Chia. "The Myth of the Commune: Recent Historiography on City and Reformation in Germany." *Central European History* 20 (1987): 203–15.

Hudson, Anne. "Epilogue: The Legacy of *Piers Plowman*." In *A Companion to Piers Plowman*, edited by John A. Alford, pp. 251–66. Berkeley, Calif., 1988.

———. "*Piers Plowman* and the Peasants' Revolt: A Problem Revisited." *Yearbook of Langland Studies* 8 (1994): 85–106.

Hughes, Christopher. *Switzerland*. New York, 1975.

Hügli, Hilde. *Der deutsche Bauer im Mittelalter dargestellt nach den deutschen literarischen Quellen vom 11.–15. Jahrhundert*. Bern, 1929. Reprint, Nendeln, 1970.

Huizinga, Johan. *The Waning of the Middle Ages*. Translated by F. Hopman. New York, 1954.

Hunger, Victor. *Histoire de Verson*. Caen, 1908. Reprint, Paris, 1992.

Ignor, Alexander. *Über das allgemeine Rechtsdenken Eikes von Repgow*. Paderborn, 1984.

Implicit Understandings: Observing, Reporting, and Reflecting on the Encounters Between Europeans and Other Peoples in the Early Modern Era. Edited by Stuart B. Schwartz. Cambridge, Eng., 1994.

The Invention of Tradition. Edited by Eric Hobsbawm and Terence Ranger. Cambridge, Eng., 1983.

Iogna-Prat, Dominique. "Le 'baptême' du schéma des trois ordres fonctionnels: L'apport de l'école d'Auxerre dans la seconde moitié du IXe siècle." *Annales E.-S.-C.* 41 (1986): 101–26.

———. "L'oeuvre d'Haymon d'Auxerre: État de la question." In *L'école carolingienne d'Auxerre de Murethach à Remi, 830–908*, edited by Dominique Iogna-Prat, Colette Jeudy, and Guy Lobrichon, pp. 157–79. Paris, 1991.

Irigaray, Luce. *This Sex Which Is Not One*. Translated by Catherine Porter and Carolyn Burke. Ithaca, N.Y., 1985.

Isaac, Ephraim. "Genesis, Judaism and the 'Sons of Ham.'" *Slavery and Abolition* 1 (1980): 3–17.

Iwanczak, Wojciech. "Between Pacifism and Anarchy: Peter Chelčický's Teaching About Society." *Journal of Medieval History* 23 (1997): 271–83.

Jäckel, Günter. *Kaiser, Gott und Bauer: Reformation und deutscher Bauernkrieg.* 2d edition. Berlin, 1983.

Jackson, William T. H. "The Medieval Pastourelle as a Satirical Genre." *Philological Quarterly* 31 (1952): 156–70.

Jacob, Robert. "La meurtre du seigneur dans la société féodale. La mémoire, le rite, la fonction." *Annales E.-S.-C.* 45 (1990): 247–63.

Jones, George Fenwick. "The Function of Food in Medieval German Literature." *Speculum* 35 (1960): 78–86.

———. "Wittenweiler's Becki and the Medieval Bagpipe." *Journal of English and Germanic Philology* 48 (1949): 209–28.

Jonin, P. "La révision d'un topos ou la noblesse du vilain." In *Mélanges Jean Larmat: Regards sur le Moyen Âge et la Renaissance (histoire, langue et littérature),* pp. 177–94. Annales de la Faculté des Lettres et Sciences Humaines de Nice 39. Nice, 1982.

Jordan, William Chester. *From Servitude to Freedom: Manumission in the Sénonais in the Thirteenth Century.* Philadelphia, 1986.

Jordan, Winthrop D. *White over Black: American Attitudes Toward the Negro, 1550–1812.* New York, 1977.

Jöst, Erhard. *Bauernfeindlichkeit: Die Historien des Ritters Neithart Fuchs.* GAG 192. Göppingen, 1976.

Justice, Steven. *Writing and Rebellion: England in 1381.* Berkeley, Calif., 1994.

Kaiser, Gert. *Textauslegung und gesellschaftliche Selbstdeutung: Aspekte einer sozialgeschichtlichen Interpretation von Hartmanns Artusepen.* Frankfurt, 1973.

Kaminsky, Howard. *A History of the Hussite Revolution.* Berkeley, Calif., 1967.

Kantor, Marvin. *The Origins of Christianity in Bohemia: Sources and Commentary.* Evanston, Ill., 1990.

Kavaler, Ethan Matt. "Peter Bruegel and the Common Man: Art and Ideology in Sixteenth-Century Antwerp." Doctoral dissertation, New York University, 1994.

Kelley, Donald R. "Clio and the Lawyers: Forms of Historical Consciousness in Medieval Jurisprudence." *Medievalia et humanistica,* n.s., 5 (1974): 25–49.

Killoran, John B. "Aquinas and Vitoria: Two Perspectives on Slavery." In *The Medieval Tradition of Natural Law,* edited by Harold J. Johnson, pp. 87–101. Studies in Medieval Culture 22. Kalamazoo, Mich., 1987.

Király, Béla K. "Neo-Serfdom in Hungary." *Slavic Review* 34 (1975): 269–78.

Kirchner, Hubert. *Luther and the Peasants' War.* Translated by Darrell Jodock. Philadelphia, 1972.

Kirk, Elizabeth D. "Langland's Plowman and the Recreation of Fourteenth-Century Religious Metaphor." *The Yearbook of Langland Studies* 2 (1988): 1–21.

Kisch, Guido. *Sachsenspiegel and Bible.* Notre Dame, Ind., 1941. Reprint, Notre Dame, Ind., 1990.

Klaniczay, Gábor. "The Paradoxes of Royal Sainthood as Illustrated by Central European Examples." In *Kings and Kingship in Medieval Europe*, edited by Anne J. Duggan, pp. 351–74. London, 1993.

Köbler, Gerhard. "'Bauer' (*agricola, colonus, rusticus*) im Frühmittelalter." In *Wort und Begriff*, pp. 230–45.

Köhn, Rolf. "Freiheit als Forderung und Ziel bäuerlichen Widerstandes (Mittel- und Westeuropa, 11.–13. Jahrhundert)." In *Die abenländische Freiheit vom 10. zum 14. Jahrhundert: Der Wirkungszusammenhang von Idee und Wirklichkeit im europäischen Vergleich*, edited by Johannes Fried, pp. 325–87. Vorträge und Forschungen 39. Sigmaringen, 1991.

Krappe, Alexander H. "La légende de Libuse et de Přemysl." *Revue des études slaves* 3 (1923): 86–89.

Krekić, Barisa. "L'abolition de l'esclavage à Dubrovnik (Raguse) au XVe siècle— mythe ou réalité?" *Byzantinische Forschungen* 12 (1987): 309–17.

Kroeber, A. L. *Anthropology, Race, Language, Culture, Psychology, Prehistory*. New York, 1948.

LaCapra, Dominick. *History, Politics and the Novel*. Ithaca, N.Y., 1987.

Lacombe, Gilbert, and Beryl Smalley. *Studies on the Commentaries of Cardinal Stephen Langton. Archives d'histoire doctrinale et littéraire du moyen âge* 5 (1930): 5–266.

Lammers, Walther. "Nordelbische Mentalitätsstudien." In *Mentalitäten in Mittelalter: Methodische und inhaltliche Probleme*, edited by Františck Graus, pp. 47–63. Vorträge und Forschungen 35. Sigmaringen, 1987.

———. *Die Schlacht bei Hemmingstedt: Freies Bauerntum und Fürstenmacht im Nordseeraum*, 3d edition. Heide in Holstein, 1982.

Landau, Peter. "Hadrians IV. Dekretale 'Dignum est' (X.4.9.1) und die Eheschliessung Unfreier in der Diskussion von Kanonisten und Theologen des 12. und 13. Jahrhunderts." *Studia Gratiana* 19 (1967): 514–54.

Landes, Richard. "Between Aristocracy and Heresy: Popular Participation in the Limousin Peace of God, 994–1033." In *The Peace of God: Social Violence and Religious Response in France Around the Year 1000*, edited by Richard Landes and Thomas Head, pp. 184–218. Ithaca, N.Y., 1992.

———. "La vie apostolique en Aquitaine en l'an mil: Paix de Dieu, culte des reliques, et communautés hérétiques." *Annales E.-S.-C.* 46, no. 3 (1991): 573–93.

Langmuir, Gavin I. "The Tortures of the Body of Christ." In *Christendom and Its Discontents: Exclusion, Persecution, and Rebellion, 1000–1500*, edited by Scott L. Waugh and Peter D. Diehl, pp. 287–309. Cambridge, Eng., 1996.

———. *Toward a Definition of Antisemitism*. Berkeley, Calif., 1990.

Lapesa, Rafael. *La obra literaria del Marqués de Santillana*. Madrid, 1957.

Laube, Adolf; Max Steinmetz; and Günter Vogler. *Illustrierte Geschichte der deutschen frühbürgerlichen Revolution*. Berlin, 1974.

Lavilla Martín, Miguel Angel. *La imagen del siervo en el pensamiento de San Francisco de Asís según sus escritos*. Valencia, 1995.

Léchaudé d'Anisy, M. "Recherches historiques sur quelques paroisses de l'arrondissement de Caen." *Mémoires de la Société des Antiquaires de Normandie*, 2d ser., 2 (1840–41): 105–12.

Lefèbvre, Joel. *Les fols et la folie: Étude sur les genres du comique et la création littéraire en Allemagne pendant la Renaissance*. Paris, 1968.

Le Goff, Jacques. "Le désert-forêt dans l'Occident médiéval." In *L'imaginaire médiéval*, by Jacques Le Goff, pp. 59–75. Paris, 1985.

———. "The Learned and Popular Dimensions of Journeys to the Otherworld in the Middle Ages." In *Understanding Popular Culture*, edited by Steven L. Kaplan, pp. 19–37.

———. "Lévi-Strauss en Brocéliande: Esquisse pour une analyse d'un roman courtois." In *L'imaginaire médiéval*, by Jacques Le Goff, pp. 151–87. Paris, 1985.

———. *Medieval Civilization, 400–1500*. Translated by Julia Barrow. London, 1988.

———. *The Medieval Imagination*. Translated by Arthur Goldhammer. Chicago, 1988.

———. "Les paysans et le monde rural dans la littérature du Haut Moyen Âge (Ve–VIe siècles)." In *Agricoltura e mondo rurale in occidente nell'alto medioevo*, pp. 723–41. Settimane di Studio del Centro Italiano di Studi sull'Alto Medioevo 13. Spoleto, 1965.

———. "Pour une étude de travail dans les idéologies et les mentalités du Moyen Âge." In *Lavorare nel Medio Evo: Rappresentazioni ed esempi dall'Italia dei sec. X–XVI*, pp. 9–23. Convegni del Centro di studi sulla spiritualita medievale, vol. 2. Todi, 1983.

———. *Time, Work, and Culture in the Middle Ages*. Translated by Arthur Goldhammer. Chicago, 1980.

———. "Le travail dans les systèmes de valeur de l'Occident médiéval." In *Le travail au moyen âge: Une approche interdisciplinaire: Actes du colloque international de Louvain-la-Neuve, 21–23 mai 1987*, edited by Jacqueline Hamesse and Colette Muraille-Samaran, pp. 7–21. Publications de l'Institut d'Études Médiévales. Textes, études, congrès, vol. 10. Louvain-la-Neuve, 1990.

———. "Les trois fonctions indo-européennes, l'historien et l'Europe féodale." *Annales E.-S.-C.* 34 (1979): 1187–1215.

———. "Le vocabulaire des catégories sociales chez saint François d'Assise et ses biographes du XIIIe siècle." In *Ordres et classes: Colloque d'histoire sociale, Saint-Cloud, 24–25 mai 1967*, edited by Daniel Roche and Ernest Labrousse, pp. 93–123. Congrès et colloques 12. Paris and The Hague, 1973.

Leguai, André. "Les révoltes rurales dans le royaume de France du milieu du XIVe siècle à la fin du XVe." *Le Moyen Âge* 88 (1982): 49–76.

Lekai, Louis Julius. *The Cistercians: Ideals and Reality*. Kent, Ohio, 1977.

Lemaître, Henri. "Le refus de service d'ost et l'origine du servage." *Bibliothèque de l'Ecole des Chartes* 75 (1914): 231–38.

Lerner, Robert E. Introduction. In *Johannes de Rupescissa, Liber secretorum*, edited by Robert E. Lerner and Christine Morerod-Fattebert, pp. 13–85. Fribourg, 1994.

———. "Popular Justice: Rupescissa in Hussite Bohemia." In *Eschatologie und Hus-*

sitismus, edited by Alexander Patschovsky and František Šmahel, pp. 39–54. Prague, 1996.

Le Roy Ladurie, Emmanuel. *Montaillou, village occitan de 1294 à 1324.* Paris, 1975.

Lescher, Bruce. "Lay Brothers: Questions Then, Questions Now." *Cistercian Studies Quarterly* 23 (1988): 63–85.

Leupin, Alexandre. *Barbarolexis: Medieval Writing and Sexuality.* Translated by Kate M. Cooper. Cambridge, Mass., 1989.

Levi, Carlo. *Christ Stopped at Eboli: The Story of a Year.* Translated by Frances Frenaye. 2d edition. New York, 1963.

Levine, Lawrence W. *Black Culture and Black Consciousness.* New York, 1977.

Lewis, Bernard. *Race and Color in Islam.* New York, 1979.

———. *Race and Slavery in the Middle East: An Historical Inquiry.* New York and Oxford, 1990.

Linehan, Peter. *History and the Historians of Medieval Spain.* Oxford, 1993.

Longère, Jean. "Un sermon de Jacques de Vitry (+1240) 'Ad praelatos et sacerdotes.'" In *L'écrit dans la société médiévale, divers aspects de sa pratique du XIe au XVe siècles: Textes en hommage à Lucie Fossier,* edited by Caroline Bourlet and Annie Dufour, pp. 47–60. Paris, 1991.

Lowes, John Livingston. "The Loveres Maladye of Heroes." *Modern Philology* 11 (1913–14): 1–56.

Ludvíkovský, Jaroslav. "La légende du prince-laboureur Přemysl et sa version primitive chez le moine Christian." In *Charisteria Thaddaeo Sinko/Księga pamiątkowa Tadeuszowi Since,* pp. 152–68. Warsaw and Wroclaw, 1951.

Macartney, C. A. *Studies on the Earliest Hungarian Historical Sources.* Parts 6–7. Oxford, 1951.

Maddicott, J. R. *The English Peasantry and the Demands of the Crown, 1294–1341.* Past and Present, Supplement no. 1. Oxford, 1975.

Maier, Annaliese. "Un manuscrito de Tomás Mieres, con notas autógrafas, en la Biblioteca Vaticana." *Anales del Instituto de Estudios Gerundenses* 7 (1952): 351–54.

Maier, Christoph T. *Preaching the Crusades: Mendicant Friars and the Cross in the Thirteenth Century.* Cambridge, Eng., 1994.

Mâle, Émile. *L'art religieux du XIIe siècle en France: Étude sur les origines de l'iconographie du moyen âge.* Paris, 1947.

Mályusz, Elemér. "Hungarian Nobles of Medieval Transylvania." *History and Society in Central Europe* 2 (1994): 25–53.

Mann, Jill. *Chaucer and Medieval Estates Satire.* Cambridge, Eng., 1973.

Marchal, Guy P. "Die Antwort der Bauern: Elemente und Schichtungen des eidgenössischen Geschichtsbewusstseins am Ausgang des Mittelalters." In *Geschichtsschreibung und Geschichtsbewusstsein im Spätmittelalter,* edited by Hans Patze, pp. 757–90. Vorträge und Forschungen 31. Sigmaringen, 1987.

Margetts, John. "Das Bauerntum in der Literatur und in der Wirklichkeit bei Neidhart und in den Neidhart-Spielen." In *Deutsche Literatur des späten Mittelalters:*

Hamburger Colloquium 1973, edited by Wolfgang Harms and L. Peter Johnson, pp. 153–63. Berlin, 1975.

———. "Die Darstellung der weiblichen Sexualität in deutschen Kurzerzählungen des Spätmittelalters: Weibliche Potenz und männliche Versagensangst." In *Psychologie in der Mediävistik: Gesammelte Beiträge des Steinheimer Symposions*, edited by Jürgen Kühnel, Hans-Dieter Mück, Ursula Müller, and Ulrich Müller, pp. 259–76. GAG 431. Göppingen, 1985.

Marino, Nancy F. *La serranilla española: Notas para su historia e interpretación.* Potomac, Md., 1987.

Mark, Peter. *Africans in European Eyes: The Portrayal of Black Africans in Fourteenth and Fifteenth Century Europe.* Syracuse, N.Y., 1974.

Markus, Robert. *The End of Ancient Christianity.* Cambridge, Eng., 1990.

Martínez, Manuel Sánchez. "Violencia señorial en la Cataluña Vieja: La posible práctica del 'ius maletractandi' en el término de Castellfollit (primer tercio del siglo XIV)." *Miscellània de textos medievales* 8 (1996): 199–229.

Martini, Fritz. *Das Bauerntum in deutschen Schrifttum von den Anfängen bis zum 16. Jahrhundert.* Halle [Saale], 1944.

Martino, Francesco de. *Uomini e terre in occidente tra tardo antico e medioevo.* Naples, 1988.

Materialien zur Kritik und Geschichte des Pentateuchs. 2 vols. Edited by Paul de Lagarde. Osnabrück, 1867. Reprint, Wiesbaden, 1967.

Matuszewski, Józef. *Geneza Polskiego Chama (Studium semazjologiczne)* (The origins of the Polish "Cham": A semiological study). Acta Universitatis Lodziensis, Folia Juridica 11. Lodz, 1982.

Maurer, Georg Ludwig von. *Das Stadt- und das Landrechtsbuch Ruprechts von Freising nach fünf Münchener Handschriften: Ein Beitrag zur Geschichte des Schwabenspiegels.* Stuttgart and Tübingen, 1839.

Mazur, Oleh. *The Wild Man in the Spanish Renaissance and Golden Age Theater.* Ann Arbor, Mich., 1980.

McPhee, John. *La Place de la Concorde Suisse.* New York, 1984.

Medeiros, Marie-Thérèse de. *Jacques et chroniqueurs: Une étude comparée de récits contemporains relatant la Jacquerie de 1358.* Paris, 1979.

Mellinkoff, Ruth. *The Mark of Cain.* Berkeley, Calif., 1981.

———. *Outcasts: Signs of Otherness in Northern European Art of the Late Middle Ages.* 2 vols. Berkeley, Calif., 1993.

Merlini, Domenico. *Saggio di ricerche sulla satira contro il villano.* Turin, 1894.

Mews, C. J., and Valerie I. J. Flint. *Peter Abelard.* Authors of the Middle Ages. Aldershot, 1995.

Meyer, Paul. "Dit sur les vilains par Matazone de Calignano." *Romania* 12 (1883): 14–28.

Meyerson, Mark D. "Slavery and the Social Order: Mudejars and Christians in the Kingdom of Valencia." *Medieval Encounters* 1 (1995): 144–73.

Miedema, Hessel. "Realism and Comic Mode: The Peasant." *Simiolus* 9 (1977): 205–19.

Milani, Piero A. *La schiavitù nel pensiero politico dai Greci al basso medio evo.* Milan, 1972.

Miret i Sans, Joaquin. *Investigación histórica sobre el vizcondado de Castellbò.* Barcelona, 1900.

Moeller, Bernd. *Imperial Cities and the Reformation: Three Essays.* Translated by H. C. Erik Midelfort and Mark U. Edwards, Jr. Philadelphia, 1972.

Moffat, Douglas. "Sin, Conquest, Servitude: English Self-Image in the Chronicles of the Early Fourteenth Century." In *The Work of Work,* pp. 146–68.

Mohl, Ruth. *The Three Estates in Medieval and Renaissance Literature.* New York, 1933.

Mollat, Michel. *The Poor in the Middle Ages: An Essay in Social History.* Translated by Arthur Goldhammer. New Haven, Conn., 1986.

Mollat, Michel, and Philippe Wolff. *The Popular Revolutions of the Late Middle Ages.* Translated by A. L. Lytton-Sells. London, 1973.

Monreal, Gregorio. "Annotations Regarding Basque Traditional Political Thought in the Sixteenth Century." In *Basque Politics: A Case Study in Ethnic Nationalism,* edited by William A. Douglas, pp. 19–49. Reno, 1985.

Moore, Barrington, Jr. *Injustice: The Social Bases of Obedience and Revolt.* White Plains, N.Y., 1987.

Moore, R. I. "The Concept of Heresy as Disease." In *The Concept of Heresy in the Middle Ages (11–13 C.),* edited by W. Lourdaux and D. Verhelst, pp. 1–11. Mediaevalia Lovaniensia. Leuven and The Hague, 1976.

———. *The Formation of a Persecuting Society: Power and Deviance in Western Europe, 950–1250.* Oxford, 1987.

Mostert, Marco. *The Political Theology of Abbo of Fleury: A Study of the Ideas About Society and Law of the Tenth-Century Monastic Reform Movement.* Middeleeuwse studies en bronnen, vol. 2. Hilversum, 1987.

Moxey, Keith. "Festive Peasants and Social Order." In *Peasants, Warriors, and Wives: Popular Imagery in the Reformation,* by Keith Moxey, pp. 35–66. Chicago, 1989.

———. "The Social Function of Secular Woodcuts in Sixteenth-Century Nuremberg." in *New Perspectives on the Art of Renaissance Nuremberg: Five Essays,* edited by Jeffrey Chipps Smith, pp. 63–81. Austin, 1985.

Muldoon, James. *Popes, Lawyers and Infidels: The Church and the Non-Christian World, 1250–1550.* Philadelphia, 1979.

Müller, Ulrich. "Gaude mihi! oder Das Neidhart-Lied vom 'Wengling' (Lied c. 7, f. 12)." In *Deutsche Literatur des Spätmittelalters: Ergebnisse, Probleme und Perspectiven der Forschung,* pp. 123–42. Deutsche Literatur des Mittelalters 3. Greifswald, 1986.

Müller, Walther. *Entwicklung und Spätformen der Leibeigenschaft am Beispiel der Heiratsbeschränkungen: Die Ehegenosssame im alemannisch-schweizerischen Raum.* Sigmaringen, 1974.

———. "Wurzeln und Bedeutung des grundsätzlichen Widerstandes gegen die

Leibeigenschaft im Bauernkrieg 1525." *Schriften des Vereins für Geschichte des Bodensees und seiner Umgebung* 93 (1975): 1–41.

Musset, Lucien. "Réflexions autour du problème de l'esclavage et du servage en Normandie ducale (Xe–XIIe siècles)." In *Aspects de la société et de l'économie dans la Normandie médiévale (Xe–XIIIe siècles)*, Cahier des Annales de Normandie, vol. 22, pp. 5–24. Caen, 1988.

Neocorus [Johann Adolfi]. *Chronik des Landes Dithmarschen.* Edited by Friedrich Dahlmann. 2 vols. Kiel, 1827.

Newman, Martha G. *The Boundaries of Charity: Cistercian Culture and Ecclesiastical Reform, 1098–1180.* Stanford, Calif., 1996.

———. "Crucified by the Virtues: The Creation of a Laybrother Spirituality." Paper given at the American Historical Association, Atlanta, 1996.

Niccoli, Ottavia. *I sacerdoti, i guerrieri, i contadini: Storia di un'immagine della società.* Turin, 1979.

Nichols, John F. "An Early Fourteenth Century Petition from the Tenants of Bocking to Their Manorial Lord." *Economic History Review* 2 (1929–30): 300–307.

Nirenberg, David. *Communities of Violence: Persecution of Minorities in the Middle Ages.* Princeton, N.J., 1996.

Nordstrom, Folke. *Virtues and Vices on the Fourteenth-Century Corbels in the Choir of Uppsala Cathedral.* Uppsala, 1956.

Nykrog, Per. *Les fabliaux.* Geneva, 1973.

Oberman, Heiko A. "The Gospel of Social Unrest." In *The German Peasant War of 1525—New Viewpoints*, edited by Robert W. Scribner and Gerhard Benecke, pp. 23–38. London, 1979.

———. "Tumultus rusticorum: Von 'Klosterkrieg' zum Fürstensieg." *Zeitschrift für Kirchengeschichte* 85 (1974): 157–72.

Occident et Orient au Xe siècle: Actes du IXe congrès de la Société des Historiens Médiévistes de l'Enseignement Supérieur Public, Dijon, 2–4 juin 1978. Publications de l'Université de Dijon, n.s., 57. Paris, 1979.

Oexle, Otto Gerhard. "Adalbero von Laon und sein 'Carmen ad Rotbertum Regem': Bemerkungen zu einer neuen Edition." *Francia* 8 (1980): 629–38.

———. "Deutungsschemata der sozialen Wirklichkeit im frühen und hohen Mittelalter. Ein Beitrag zur Geschichte des Wissens." In *Mentalitäten im Mittelalter. Methodische und inhaltliche Probleme*, edited by František Graus, pp. 65–117. Vorträge und Forschungen 35. Sigmaringen, 1987.

———. "Die funktionale Dreiteilung der 'Gesellschaft' bei Adalbero von Laon. Deutungsschemata des sozialen Wirklichkeit im früheren Mittelalter." *Frühmittelalterliche Studien* 12 (1978): 1–54.

———. "Le travail au XIe siècle: Réalités et mentalités." In *Le travail au moyen âge: Une approche interdisciplinaire. Actes du colloque international de Louvain-la-Neuve, 21–23 mai 1987*, edited by Jacqueline Hamesse and Colette Muraille-Samaran, pp. 49–60. Publications de l'Institut d'Études Médiévales. Textes, études, congrès, vol. 10. Louvain-la-Neuve, 1990.

———. "Die 'Wirklichkeit' und das 'Wissen': Ein Blick auf das sozialgeschichtliche Oeuvre von Georges Duby." *Historische Zeitschrift* 232 (1981): 61–91.

Ortigues, Edmond. "Haymon d'Auxerre, théoricien des trois ordres." In *L'école carolingienne d'Auxerre de Murethach à Remi, 830–908,* edited by Dominique Iogna-Prat, Colette Jeudy, and Guy Lobrichon, pp. 183–215. L'histoire dans l'actualité. Paris, 1991.

Ortner, Sherry B. "Resistance and the Problem of Ethnographic Refusal." In *The Historic Turn in the Human Sciences,* edited by Terrence J. McDonald, pp. 281–304. Ann Arbor, Mich., 1996. (Originally published in *Comparative Studies in Society and History* 37 [1995]: 173–93.)

Östling, Christine. "The Ploughing Adam in Medieval Church Paintings." In *Man and Picture: Papers from the First International Symposium for Ethnological Picture Research in Lund, 1984,* edited by Nils-Arvid Bringués, pp. 13–19. Stockholm, 1986.

Ourliac, Paul. "De la féodalité méridionale au pariage d'Andorre." In *Annals de la primera Universitat d'Estiu, Andorra 82: El segle XIII,* pp. 56–61. Andorra, 1983.

Out There: Marginalization and Contemporary Cultures. Edited by Russell Ferguson, Martha Gever, Trinh T. Min-ha, and Cornel West. New York and Cambridge, Mass., 1990.

Ovitt, George, Jr. "The Cultural Context of Western Technology: Early Christian Attitudes Toward Manual Labor." In *The Work of Work,* pp. 71–94.

Owen, D. D. R. "The Prince and the Churl: The Traumatic Experience of Philip Augustus." *Journal of Medieval History* 18 (1992): 141–44.

Owst, G. R. *Literature and Pulpit in Medieval England: A Neglected Chapter in the History of English Letters and of the English People.* 2d edition. Oxford, 1961.

Ozment, Steven. *The Reformation in the Cities: The Appeal of Protestantism to Sixteenth-Century Germany and Switzerland.* New Haven, Conn., 1975.

Pach, Zsigmond Pál. "Die Stellung des ungarischen Bauernkrieges von 1514 in der Agrargeschichte." In *Wirtschaftliche und soziale Strukturen im saekularen Wandel: Festschrift für Wilhelm Abel zum 70. Geburtstag,* edited by Ingomar Bog et al., 1: 199–211. Hanover, 1974.

Packull, Werner. "The Image of the 'Common Man' in the Early Pamphlets of the Reformation (1520–1525)." *Historical Reflections* 12 (1985): 253–77.

Paden, William D. "Rape in the Pastourelle." *Romanic Review* 80 (1989): 331–49.

Pagden, Anthony. *European Encounters with the New World from Renaissance to Romanticism.* New Haven, Conn., 1993.

———. *The Fall of Natural Man: The American Indian and the Origins of Comparative Ethnology.* Cambridge, Eng., 1982.

Panofsky, Erwin. *Early Netherlandish Painting, Its Origins and Character.* Vol. 1. Princeton, N.J., 1953.

Paris, Gaston. *Mélanges de littérature française du moyen âge.* Edited by Mario Roques. Paris, 1912.

Patterson, Lee. *Chaucer and the Subject of History.* Madison, Wis., 1991.

Peasant Society: A Reader. Edited by Jack M. Potter, May N. Diaz, and George M. Foster. New York, 1967.

Peasants and Peasant Societies: Selected Readings. Edited by Teodor Shanin. New York, 1971.

Pelteret, David Anthony Edgell. *Slavery in Early Mediaeval England: From the Reign of Alfred Until the Twelfth Century.* Studies in Anglo-Saxon History 7. Woodbridge, Suffolk, and Rochester, N.Y., 1995.

Perbal, Albert. "La race nègre et la malédiction de Cham." *Revue de l'Université d'Ottawa* 10 (1940): 156–77.

Perger, Richard; Eva-Maria Höhle; and Oskar Pauch. *The Niedhart Frescoes ca. 1400: The Oldest Secular Mural Paintings in Vienna.* Vienna, n.d.

Pescador del Hoyo, Carmela. "La caballería popular en León y Castilla." Parts 1–8. *Cuadernos de historia de España,* 33–34 (1961): 101–238; 35–36 (1962): 56–201; 37–38 (1963): 88–198; 39–40 (1964): 169–260.

Peterson, Thomas Virgil. *Ham and Japheth: The Mythic World of Whites in the Antebellum South.* Metuchen, N.J., 1978.

Poos, L. R. *A Rural Society After the Black Death: Essex 1350–1525.* Cambridge, Eng., 1991.

Powers, James F. *A Society Organized for War: The Iberian Municipal Militias in the Central Middle Ages, 1000–1284.* Berkeley, Calif., 1988.

Prakash, Gyan. "Can the 'Subaltern' Ride? A Reply to O'Hanlon and Washbrook." *Comparative Studies in History and Society* 34 (1992): 168–84.

———. "Subaltern Studies as Postcolonial Criticism." *American Historical Review* 99 (1994): 1475–90.

Putnam, Bertha Haven. *The Enforcement of the Statutes of Labourers During the First Decade After the Black Death, 1349–1359.* New York, 1908.

Race, Writing and Difference. Edited by Henry Louis Gates, Jr. Chicago, 1986.

Radbruch, Renate Maria, and Gustav Radbruch. *Der deutsche Bauernstand zwischen Mittelalter und Neuzeit.* 2d edition. Göttingen, 1961.

Ragotzky, Helga. "Der Bauer in der Narrenrolle. Zur Funktion 'Verkehrter Welt' im frühen Nürnberger Fastnachtspiel." In *Typus und Individualität im Mittelalter,* edited by H. Wenzel, pp. 77–101. Munich, 1983.

Ranke, Kurt. "Agrarische und bäuerliche Denk- und Verhaltensweisen im Mittelalter." In *Wort und Begriff,* pp. 207–21.

Rattunde, Eckhard. *Li proverbes au vilain: Untersuchungen zur romanischen Spruchdichtung des Mittelalters.* Studia Romanica no. 11. Heidelberg, 1966.

Raupp, Hans-Joachim. *Bauernsatiren: Entstehung und Entwicklung des bäuerlichen Genres in der deutschen und niederländischen Kunst, ca. 1470–1570.* Niederzier, 1986.

Recchia, Vincenzo. *Gregorio Magno e la società agricola.* Rome, 1978.

Reich, Oskar. *Beiträge zur Kenntnis des Bauernlebens im alten Frankreich auf Grund der zeitgenössischen Literatur.* Göttingen, 1909.

Reichel, Jörn. *Der Spruchdichter Hans Rosenplüt: Literatur und Leben im spätmittelal- terlichen Nürnburg.* Stuttgart, 1985.

Reiss, Edmund. "The Symbolic Plow and Plowman and the Wakefield *Mactacio Abel.*" *Studies in Iconography* 5 (1979): 3–30.

Resnikow, Sylvia. "The Cultural History of a Democratic Proverb." *Journal of English and Germanic Philology* 36 (1937): 391–405.

Reynolds, Susan. *Kingdoms and Communities in Western Europe, 900–1300.* Oxford, 1984.

———. "Medieval *Origines Gentium* and the Community of the Realm." *History* 68 (1983): 375–90

Ribard, Jacques. *Un ménestral du XIVe siècle, Jean de Condé.* Geneva, 1969.

Ribémont, Bernard, and Michel Salvat. "De Francion à Hugues Capet, descendant d'un boucher. Légende des origines et encyclopédisme." *Le Moyen Âge* 99 (1993): 249–62.

Riberaygna Argelich, Buenaventura. *Los Valles de Andorra. Recopilación histórica.* Barcelona, 1949.

Richards, Jeffrey. *Sex, Dissidence and Damnation: Minority Groups in the Middle Ages.* London, 1991.

Riera i Melis, Antoni. "El bisbat de Girona al primer terç del segle XV. Aproximació al context socio-econòmic de la sèrie sísmica olotina (1427–1428)." *Anuario de es- tudios medievales* 22 (1992): 163–204.

Rigg, A. G. "The Legend of Hugh Capet: The English Tradition." In *The Centre and Its Compass: Studies in Medieval Literature in Honor of Professor John Leyerle,* edited by Robert A. Taylor et al., pp. 389–406. Studies in Medieval Culture 33. Kalamazoo, Mich., 1993.

Rollason, D. W. "The Miracles of St. Benedict: A Window on Early Medieval France." In *Studies in Medieval History Presented to R. H. C. Davis,* edited Henry Mayr-Harting and R. I. Moore, pp. 73–90. London and Ronceverte, W. Va., 1985.

Rösener, Werner. *Peasants in the Middle Ages.* Translated by Alexander Stürzer. Ur- bana, Ill., 1992.

———. "Zur Sozialökonomischen Lage der bäuerlichen Bevölkerung im Spätmitte- lalter." In *Bäuerliche Sachkultur des Spätmittelalters,* pp. 9–47. Österreichische Akademie der Wissenschaften, Philosophisch-Historische Klasse, Sitzungsberichte 439. Vienna, 1984.

Rothkrug, Lionel. "Icon and Ideology in Religion and Rebellion, 1300–1600: *Bauernfreiheit* and *religion royale.*" In *Religion and Rural Revolt: Papers Presented to the Fourth Interdisciplinary Workshop on Peasant Studies, University of British Co- lumbia, 1982,* edited by János Bak and Gerhard Benecke, pp. 31–61. Manchester, 1984.

Röttinger, Heinrich. *Hans Weiditz der Petrarkameister.* Strasbourg, 1904. Reprint, Nendeln, 1979.

Rouche, Michel. "De l'Orient à l'Occident: Les origines de la tripartition fonctionelle et les causes de son adoption par l'Europe chrétienne à la fin du Xe siècle." In *Occident et Orient au Xe siècle*, pp. 31–49. Paris, 1979.

Ruffing, John. "The Labor Structure of Aelfric's *Colloquy*." In *The Work of Work*, pp. 55–70.

Roussillon, Chevalier de. *De l'Andorre*. Toulouse, 1823.

Sahaydachny Bocarius, Antonia. "The Marriage of Unfree Persons: Twelfth-Century Decretals and Letters." *Studia Gratiana* 29 (1996) (Festschrift R. Weigand): 483–506.

Sahlins, Peter. *Boundaries: The Making of France and Spain in the Pyrenees*. Berkeley, Calif., 1989.

Said, Edward W. *Orientalism*. New York, 1979.

———. "Representing the Colonized: Anthropology's Interlocutors." *Critical Inquiry* 15 (1989): 205–25.

Scheidig, Walter. *Die Holzschnitte des Petrarca-Meisters zu Petrarcas Werk Von der Artzney bayer Glück des guten und widerwärtigen Augsburg 1532*. Berlin, 1955.

Scheidt, Caspar. *Grobianus: Von groben Sitten und unhöflichen Geberden*. N.p., 1551.

Scheiner, Irwin. "Benevolent Lords and Honorable Peasants: Rebellion and Peasant Consciousness in Tokugawa Japan." In *Japanese Thought in the Tokugawa Period, 1600–1868: Methods and Metaphors*, edited by Tetsuo Najita and Irwin Scheiner, pp. 39 62. Chicago, 1978.

Schläpfer, Walter. "Die Appenzeller Freiheitskriege." In *Appenzeller Geschichte* 1: 123–225. Appenzell, 1964. Reprint, Appenzell, 1976.

Schmidt, Karl. *Ius Primae Noctis. Eine geschichtliche Untersuchung*. Freiburg-im-Breisgau, 1881.

Schmitt, Jean-Claude. *The Holy Greyhound: Guinefort, Healer of Children Since the Thirteenth Century*. Translated by Martin Thom. Cambridge Studies in Oral and Literate Culture 6. Cambridge, Eng., 1983. (Originally published in Paris, 1979.)

Schönbach, Anton E. *Studien zur Geschichte der altdeutschen Predigt*. Kaiserlichen Akademie der Wissenschaften, Philosophisch-Historische Klasse, Sitzungsberichte 154 and 155. Vienna, 1906 and 1908.

Schreiner, Klaus. "Zur biblischen Legitimation des Adels: Auslegungsgeschichtliche Studien zu I. Kor. 1, 26–29." *Zeitschrift für Kirchengeschichte* 85 (1974): 317–57.

Schüppert, Helga. "Der Bauer in der deutschen Literatur des Spätmittelalters— Topik und Realitätsbezug." In *Bäuerliche Sachkultur des Spätmittelalters: internationaler Kongress Krems an der Donau 21. bis 24. September 1982*, pp. 126–44. Veroffentlichungen des Instituts fur Mittelalterliche Realienkunde Österreichs 7; Österreichische Akademie der Wissenschaften, Philosophisch-Historische Klasse, Sitzungsberichte 439 . Vienna, 1984.

Schweikle, Günther. *Neidhart*. Sammlung Metzler 253. Stuttgart, 1990.

Scott, James C. *Domination and the Arts of Resistance: Hidden Transcripts*. New Haven, Conn., 1990.

———. *Weapons of the Weak: Everyday Forms of Peasant Resistance*. New Haven, Conn., 1985.

Scott, Joan W. "Experience." In *Feminists Theorize the Political*, edited by Judith Butler and Joan W. Scott, pp. 22–40. New York, 1992.

Scribner, Robert (Bob) W. "Heterodoxy, Literacy and Print in the Early German Reformation." In *Heresy and Literacy, 1000–1530*, edited by Peter Biller and Anne Hudson, pp. 255–78. Cambridge, Eng., 1994.

———. "Images of the Peasant, 1514–1525." In *The German Peasant War of 1525*, edited by János Bak, pp. 29–47. London, 1976.

Serfdom and Slavery: Studies in Legal Bondage. Edited by M. L. Bush. Harlow, Essex, 1996.

Setton, Kenneth. *Catalan Domination of Athens 1311–1388*. Cambridge, Mass., 1948.

Shanin, Teodor. *Defining Peasants: Essays Concerning Rural Societies, Expolary Economies, and Learning from Them in the Contemporary World*. Oxford, 1990.

Sider, Ronald J. *Andreas Bodenstein von Karlstadt: The Development of His Thought, 1517–1525*. Studies in Medieval and Reformation Thought, vol. 11. Leiden, 1974.

Simeoni, Luigi. "La liberazione dei servi a Bologna nel 1256–57." *Archivo storico italiano* 109 (1951): 3–26.

Simon, Eckehard. "Neidharte and Neidhartianer: Notes on the History of a Song Corpus." *Beiträge zur Geschichte der deutschen Sprache und Literatur* 94 (1972): 153–97.

———. *Neidhart von Reuental*. Twayne's World Authors Series 364. Boston, 1975.

———. "The Origin of Neidhart Plays: A Reappraisal." *Journal of English and Germanic Philology* 67 (1968): 458–74.

———. "The Rustic Muse: *Neidhartschwänke* in Murals, Stone Carvings, and Woodcuts." *The Germanic Review* 46 (1971): 243–57.

Sivéry, Gérard. "Le Moyen Âge a-t-il connu des communautés rurales silencieuses et soumises?" *Revue du Nord* 72 (1990): 621–29.

Smith, Helmut Walser. "Geschichte zwischen den Fronten: Meisterwerke der neuesten Geschichtsschreibung und postmoderne Kritik." *Geschichte und Gesellschaft* 22 (1996): 592–608.

Snowden, Frank M., Jr. *Before Color Prejudice: The Ancient View of Blacks*. Cambridge, Mass., 1983.

Sobrequés i Vidal, Santiago, and Jaume Sobrequés i Callicó. *La guerra civil catalana del segle XV: Estudis sobre la crisi social i econòmica de la Baixa Edat Mitjana*. 2 vols. Barcelona, 1973.

Sokol, A. E. "Das Grundproblem der Gesellschaft im Spiegel Bertholds von Regensburg." *Germanic Review* 11 (1936): 147–63.

Sokoloff, Sally. "Rural Change and Farming Politics: A Terminal Peasantry." In *French Politics and Public Policy*, edited by Philip G. Cerny and Martin A. Schain, pp. 218–42. New York, 1980.

Sorokin, Pitirim A. *Altruistic Love: A Study of American "Good Neighbors" and Christian Saints*. Boston, 1950.

Southern, Richard W. *The Making of the Middle Ages*. New Haven, Conn., 1953.

———. *Western Views of Islam in the Middle Ages*. Cambridge, Mass., 1962.

Spalding, Mary Caroline. *The Middle English Charters of Christ.* Bryn Mawr, Pa., 1914.

Specht, Henrik. *Poetry and the Iconography of the Peasant: The Attitude to the Peasant in Late Medieval English Literature and in Contemporary Calendar Illustration.* Anglica et Americana 19. Copenhagen, 1983.

Spiegel, Gabrielle M. *Romancing the Past: The Rise of Vernacular Prose Historiography in Thirteenth-Century France.* Berkeley, Calif., 1993.

Spivak, Gayatri Chakravorty. "Can the Subaltern Speak?" In *Marxism and the Interpretation of Culture,* edited by Cary Nelson and Lawrence Grossberg, pp. 271–313. Urbana, Ill., 1988.

Sprunger, David A. "Wildfolk and Lunatics in Medieval Romance." In *The Medieval World of Nature: A Book of Essays,* edited by Joyce E. Salisbury, pp. 145–63. New York, 1994.

Stackmann, Karl. "Bezeichnungen für 'Bauer' in frühmittelhochdeutschen Quellen." In *Wort und Begriff,* pp. 153–79.

Stalnaker, John C. "Towards a Social Interpretation of the German Peasant War." In *The German Peasant War of 1525—New Viewpoints,* edited by Robert W. Scribner and Gerhard Benecke, pp. 23–38. London, 1979.

Ste. Croix, G. E. M. de. "Early Christian Attitudes to Property and Slavery." In *Church, Society and Politics.* edited by Derek Baker, pp. 1–38. Studies in Church History 12. Oxford, 1975.

Stern, Steve J. "New Approaches to the Study of Peasant Rebellion and Consciousness: Implications of the Andean Experience." In *Resistance, Rebellion, and Consciousness in the Andean Peasant World, Eighteenth to Twentieth Centuries,* edited by Steve J. Stern, pp. 3–25. Madison, Wis., 1987.

Stewart, Alison. "Paper Festivals and Popular Entertainment: The Kermis Woodcuts of Sebald Beham in Reformation Nuremberg." *Sixteenth Century Journal* 24 (1993): 301–50.

Stock, Brian. *The Implications of Literacy: Written Language and Models of Interpretation in the Eleventh and Twelfth Centuries.* Princeton, N.J., 1983.

Strauss, Gerald. *Law, Resistance and the State: The Opposition to Roman Law in Reformation Germany.* Princeton, N.J., 1986.

Stringfellow, Thornton. "A Brief Examination of Scripture Testimony on the Institution of Slavery." In *The Ideology of Slavery: Proslavery Thought in the Antebellum South, 1830–1860,* edited by Drew Gilpin Faust, pp. 136–67. Baton Rouge, La., 1981.

Strohm, Paul. *Hochon's Arrow: The Social Imagination of Fourteenth-Century Texts.* Princeton, N.J., 1992.

Stuard, Susan Mosher. "Ancillary Evidence for the Decline of Medieval Slavery." *Past and Present* 149 (1995): 3–28.

Stürner, Wolfgang. *Peccatum und Potestas: Der Sündenfall und die Entstehung der herrscherlichen Gewalt im Mittelalterlichen Staatsdenken.* Beiträge zur Geschichte und Quellenkunde des Mittelalters 11. Sigmaringen, 1987.

Suard, François. "Hugues Capet dans la chanson de geste au XIVe siècle." In *Religion et culture autour de l'an mil: Royaume capétien et Lotharingie*, edited by Dominique Iogna-Prat and Jean-Charles Picard, pp. 215–25. Paris, 1990.

Summerfield, Thea. "'*Bondage & Destres*': Popular Complaints in Vernacular Verse Chronicles." Paper delivered at Goldsmiths' College, London.

———. *The Matter of Kings' Lives: The Design of Past and Present in the Early Fourteenth-Century Verse Chronicles by Pierre de Langtoft and Robert Mannyng*. Amsterdam and Atlanta, 1998.

Székely, György. "Le passage à l'économie basée sur la corvée en Europe centrale et orientale et l'année 1514." In *Études historiques hongroises 1975* 1: 311–25. Budapest, 1975.

———. "Les révoltes paysannes et la noblesse hongroise au début du XVIe siècle." In *Noblesse française, noblesse hongroise, XVIe–XIXe siècles*, edited by Béla Köpeczi and Eva H. Balázs, pp. 137–54. Budapest and Paris, 1981.

Szűcs, Jenő. "A Ferences Obszervancia és az 1514 évi parasztháború. Egy kódex tanúsága" [The observant Franciscans and the Peasant War of 1514: Evidence of a codex]. *Levéltári Közlemények* 43 (1972): 216–61.

———. *Nation und Geschichte: Studien*. Translated by Johanna Kerekes. Cologne, 1981.

———. "Die oppositionelle Strömung der Franziskaner im Hintergrund des Bauernkrieges und der Reformation in Ungarn." In *Études historiques hongroises 1985* 2: 483–513. Budapest, 1985.

———. "Theoretical Elements in Master Simon of Kéza's *Gesta Hungarorum* (1282–1285 A. D.)." In *Études historiques hongroises 1975* 1: 241–81. Budapest, 1975.

Tate, R. B. "Adventures in the Sierra." In *Libro de Buen Amor Studies*, edited by G. B. Gybbon-Moneypenny, pp. 219–29. London, 1970.

———. "Mythology in Spanish Historiography of the Middle Ages and Renaissance." *Hispanic Review* 22 (1954): 1–18.

Tazbir, Janusz. "The Cult of St. Isidore the Farmer in Europe." In *Poland at the 14th International Congress of Historical Sciences in San Francisco: Studies in Comparative History*, pp. 99–111. Wroclaw, 1975.

TeBrake, William H. *A Plague of Insurrection: Popular Politics and Peasant Revolt in Flanders, 1323–1328*. Philadelphia, 1993.

Teja, Ramón. "San Basilio y la esclavitud: Teoría y praxis." In *Basil of Caesarea: Christian, Humanist, Ascetic: A Sixteen-Hundredth Anniversary Symposium*, edited by Paul Jonathan Fedwick, 1: 393–403. Toronto, 1981.

Tettau, Wilhelm Freiherr von. "Über einige bis jetzt unbekannte Erfurter Drucke aus dem 15. Jarhrhundert." *Jahrbücher der Königlichen Akademie gemeinütziger Wissenschaften zu Erfurt*, n.s., 6 (1870): 319–25.

Thomas, Nicholas. *Colonialism's Culture: Anthropology, Travel and Government*. Princeton, N.J., 1994.

Tillotson, J. H. "Peasant Unrest in the England of Richard II: Some Evidence from Royal Records." *Historical Studies* (Melbourne) 16 (1974): 1–16.

Tise, Larry E. *Proslavery: A History of the Defense of Slavery in America, 1701–1840.* Athens, Ga., 1987.

Todorov, Tzvetan. *The Conquest of America: The Question of the Other.* Translated by Richard Howard. New York, 1984.

Le travail au moyen âge: Une approche interdisciplinaire: Actes du colloque international de Louvain-la-Neuve, 21–23 mai 1987. Edited by Jacqueline Hamesse and Colette Muraille-Samaran. Publications de l'Institut d'Études Médiévales. Textes, études, congrès, vol. 10. Louvain-la-Neuve, 1990.

Traverse, Elizabeth I. "'Hie saget Neidhart wie die Bawren einander schlugen': Peasant Violence in the Neidhart Tradition." Paper presented at Princeton University, 1994.

————. "Peasants, Seasons and *Werltsüeze*: Cyclicity in Neidhart's Songs Reexamined." Doctoral dissertation, Pennsylvania State University, 1995.

————. *Peasants, Seasons and Werltsüeze: Cyclicity in Neidhart's Songs Reexamined.* GAG 637. Göppingen, 1997.

Trinh, T. Minh-Ha. *Woman, Native, Other: Writing Post-Coloniality and Feminism.* Bloomington, Ind., 1989.

Turville-Petre, Thorlac. "Politics and Poetry in the Early Fourteenth Century: The Case of Robert Manning's *Chronicle*." *Review of English Studies*, n.s., 39 (1988): 1–29.

Udina i Martorell, Frederic. "En torno a la leyenda de las 'Barras' catalanes." *Hispania* 9 (1949): 531–65.

Uhrig, Kurt. "Der Bauer in der Publizistik der Reformation bis zum Ausgang des Bauernkrieges." *Archiv für Reformationsgeschichte* 33 (1936): 70–125; 165–225.

Ulbrich, Claudia. *Leibherrschaft am Oberrhein im Spätmittelalter.* Göttingen, 1979.

Urban, William L. *Dithmarschen: A Medieval Peasant Republic.* Lewiston, N.Y., 1991.

Vandenbroeck, Paul. "Verbeeck's Peasant Weddings: A Study of Iconography and Social Function." *Simiolus* 14 (1984): 79–124.

van den Hoven, Birgit. *Work in Ancient and Medieval Thought: Ancient Philosophers, Medieval Monks and Theologians and Their Concept of Work, Occupations and Technology.* Dutch Monographs on Ancient History and Archaeology 14. Amsterdam, 1996.

Vanderjagt, Arjo. *Qui sa vertu anoblist: The concepts of "Noblesse" and "Chose Publique" in Burgundian Political Thought.* Groningen, 1981.

van Nolcken, Christina. "*Piers Plowman*, the Wycliffites, and *Pierce the Plowman's Creed*." *Yearbook of Langland Studies* 2 (1988): 71–102.

Vardi, Liana. "Imagining the Harvest in Early Modern Europe." *American Historical Review* 101 (1996): 1356–97.

Várdy, Steven Belá. *Modern Hungarian Historiography.* New York, 1976.

Vauchez, André. *La sainteté en occident aux derniers siècles du moyen âge.* 2nd edition. Rome, 1988.

Vaux Saint Cyr, M.-B. de. "Les deux commentaires d'Étienne Langton sur Isaïe." *Revue des sciences philosophiques et théologiques* 39 (1955): 228–36.

Vela i Palomares, Sussanna. "Andorra a la baixa edat mitjana (segles XIV–XV). L'estat de la qüestió." *Annals de l'Institut d'Estudis Andorrans* [2](1991): 261–83.

Verlinden, Charles. *L'esclavage dans l'Europe médiévale.* 2 vols. Bruges, 1955–77.

Viader, Roland. "La irracional possessió de les esglésies d'Andorra (segles XI–XII)." *Annals de l'Institut d'Estudis Andorrans* 4 (1993): 109–25.

———. "Pouvoirs et communautés en Andorre (Xe–XIIIe siècle)." Mémoire de D.E.A., Université de Toulouse-Le Mirail, n.d. [ca. 1992].

Vincke, Johannes. "Königtum und Sklaverei im aragonischen Staatenbund während des 14. Jahrhunderts." *Gesammelte Aufsätze zur Kulturgeschichte Spaniens* 25 (1970): 19–40.

Vives, Jaime Vicens. *Historia de los remensas (en el siglo XV)* [1945]. Barcelona, 1978.

Vogler, Günther. *Nürnberg 1524/25.* Berlin, 1982.

Voltelini, Hans von. "Der Gedanke der allgemeinen Freiheit in den deutschen Rechtsbüchern." *Zeitschrift der Savigny-Stiftung für Rechtsgeschichte: Germanistische Abteilung* 57 (1937): 182–209.

Vovelle, Michel. *Ideologies and Mentalities.* Translated by Eamon O'Flaherty. Chicago, 1990.

Waas, Adolf. *Die Bauern im Kampf um Gerechtigkeit, 1300–1525.* 2d edition. Munich, 1976.

Wack, Mary Frances. "The *Liber de heros morbo* of Johannes Afflacius and Its Implications for Medieval Love Conventions." *Speculum* 62 (1987): 324–44.

———. *Lovesickness in the Middle Ages: The Viaticum and Its Commentaries.* Philadelphia, 1990.

Walpole, Ronald N. "Charlemagne's Journey to the East: The French Translation of the Legend by Pierre de Beauvais." *University of California Publications in Semitic Philology* 11 (1951): 445–52.

Walshe, Maurice O'C. "'Der Ackermann aus Böhmen': Quellenfrage und Textgestaltung." In *Deutsche Literatur des späten Mittelalters, Hamburger Colloquium 1973,* edited by Wolfgang Harms and L. Peter Johnson, pp. 282–92. Berlin, 1975.

———. "Some Notes on *Der Ackermann aus Böhmen.*" In *Deutung und Bedeutung: Studies in German and Comparative Literature Presented to Karl-Werner Maurer,* pp. 70–76. The Hague and Paris, 1973.

Warner, Marina. *Joan of Arc: The Image of Female Heroism.* New York, 1981.

Weber, Eugen. *Peasants into Frenchmen: The Modernization of Rural France, 1870–1914.* Stanford, Calif., 1976.

Weigand, Rudolf. *Die Naturrechtslehre der Legisten und Dekretisten von Irnerius bis Accursius und von Gratian bis Johannes Teutonicus.* Munich, 1967.

Weinstein, Donald, and Rudolph M. Bell. *Saints and Society: The Two Worlds of Western Christendom, 1000–1700.* Chicago, 1982.

Weishaupt, Matthias. *Bauern, Hirten und "frume edle puren": Bauern- und Bauernstaatsideologie in der spätmittelalterlichen Eidgenossenschaft und der nationalen Geschichtsschreibung der Schweiz.* Basel and Frankfurt, 1992.

Weller, Emil, ed. "Gedicht vom ersten Edelman." *Serapeum: Zeitschrift für Biblio-thekwissenschaft, Handschriftenkunde und ältere Literatur* 24 (1863): 231–38.

Welter, J.-Th. *L'exemplum dans la littérature religieuse et didactique du Moyen Âge.* Paris, 1927.

Wenskus, Reinhard. "'Bauer'—Begriff und historische Wirklichkeit." In *Wort und Begriff,* pp. 11–28.

Werminghoff, Albert. "Die Quaternionen der deutschen Reichsverfassung." *Archiv für Kulturgeschichte* 3 (1905): 288–300.

Wettlaufer, Jörg. "Jus primae noctis: Historisch-anthropologische Überlegungen zum Verständnis eines 'Mittelalterlichen Feudalrechts.'" *Francia* 21 (1994): 245–62.

Wheatley, Edward. "A Selfless Ploughman and the Christ/Piers Conjunction in Langland's *Piers Plowman.*" *Notes and Queries,* n.s., 40 (1993): 135–42.

White, Christine Pelzer. "Everyday Resistance, Socialist Revolution, and Rural Development: The Vietnamese Case." *Journal of Peasant Studies* 13, no. 2 (1986): 49–63.

Wickham, Chris J. *Early Medieval Italy: Central Power and Local Society 400–1000.* Totowa, N.J., 1981.

———. "Gossip and Resistance Among the Medieval Peasantry." Inaugural Lecture, University of Birmingham, School of History (printed separately). Birmingham, Eng., 1995.

———. *The Mountains and the City: The Tuscan Appenines in the Early Middle Ages.* Oxford, 1988.

Williams, Raymond. *The Country and the City.* New York, 1973.

Wolf, Eric R. *Peasants.* Engelwood Cliffs, N.J., 1966.

Wolf, Larry. *Inventing Eastern Europe: The Map of Civilization in the Mind of the Enlightenment.* Stanford, Calif., 1994.

Wood, Charles T. *Joan of Arc and Richard III: Sex, Saints, and Government in the Middle Ages.* New York and Oxford, 1988.

The Work of Work: Servitude, Slavery, and Labor in Medieval England. Edited by Allen J. Frantzen and Douglas Moffat. Glasgow, 1994.

Wort und Begriff "Bauer": Zusammenfassender Bericht über die Kolloquium der Komission für die Altertumskunde Mittel-und Nordeuropas. Edited by Reinhard Wenskus et al. Akademie der Wissenschaften zu Göttingen, Philosophisch-Historische Klasse, series 3, Abhandlungen 89. Göttingen, 1975.

Writing Culture: The Poetics and Politics of Ethnography. Edited by James Clifford and George E. Marcus. Berkeley, Calif., 1986.

Wunder, Heide. "Der dumme und der schlaue Bauer." In *Mentalität und Alltag im Spätmittelalter,* edited by Cord Meckseper, pp. 34–51. Göttingen, 1985.

———. "'Old Law' and 'Divine Law' in the German Peasant War." In *The German Peasant War of 1525,* edited by János Bak, pp. 54–62. London, 1976.

Wunderli, Richard M. *Peasant Fires: The Drummer of Niklashausen.* Bloomington, Ind., 1992.

Zacour, Norman. *Jews and Saracens in the Consilia of Oldradus de Ponte.* Toronto, 1990.

Zimmermann, Michel. "La prise de Barcelone par al-Mansur et la naissance de l'historiographie catalane." *Annales de Bretagne et des Pays de l'Ouest* 87 (1980): 191–218.

Zink, Michel. *La pastourelle. Poésie et folklore au moyen âge.* Paris, 1972.

———. "La suffisance du paysan dans la littérature française du moyen âge." In *Der Bauer im Wandel der Zeit,* edited by Willi Hirdt, pp. 35–48. Bonn, 1986.

Ziolkowski, Jan. "Avatars of Ugliness in Medieval Literature." *Modern Language Review* 79 (1984): 1–20.

Zschelletzschky, Herbert. "'Ihr Herz war auf der Seite der Bauern.' Kunstlerschaffen zur Bauernkriegszeit." In *Der Bauer in Klassenkampf,* edited by Gerhard Heitz, Adolf Laube, Max Steinmetz, and Günther Vogler, pp. 333–75. Berlin, 1975.

Zumthor, Paul. "Intertextualité et mouvance." *Littérature* 41 (1981): 8–16.

———. *Le masque et la lumière: La poétique des grands rhétoriqueurs.* Paris, 1978.

Index

In this index an "f" after a number indicates a separate reference on the next page, and an "ff" indicates separate references on the next two pages. A continuous discussion over two or more pages is indicated by a span of page numbers, e.g., "57–59." *Passim* is used for a cluster of references in close but not consecutive sequence.

Aaron, David, 87
Abbo of Fleury, 17
Adalbero of Laon, 17–18, 23–28 *passim*, 41–42, 61, 182, 309n13
Adam and Eve, 59–66
Adam de la Halle, 166
Adam of Eynsham, 78, 251
Adolphi, Johann, 200–201
Adrian IV, Pope, 82
Aelfric, abbot of Eynsham, 17, 22, 78
Aelred of Rievaulx, 25
Aers, David, 227
Agobard of Lyons, 80, 248f, 255
Africans, origin of, 89–96
Ahmad Baba, 340n101
Alberti, Leon Battista, 148
Alcuin, 79, 98, 250
Alexander of Hales, 99
Algazi, Gadi, 390n84
"Alphabet Against the *Villani*," 154
Alphonse of Poitiers, 85
Alvaro Pelayo, bishop of Silves, 143–44
Ambrose, 74–75, 76, 97, 216
Ambrosiaster, 74, 97, 248, 255
Andorra, 185–90, 365n38
Andreas Capellanus, 63, 160–64 *passim*
Andrew of Fleury, 178f, 182, 249

Anglo–Saxon Chronicle, 127
Anonimalle Chronicle, 267
Anti Semitism, 256, 390n87
Antoninus, Saint, 99
Aquinas, Thomas, 73, 82–83, 85, 249
Aristotle, 62, 72–73, 75f, 82–85 *passim*, 155, 239, 331n133
Arme Heinrich, Der, 208–9, 224
Arnoul III of Ardres, 183
Arnulf of Villers, 26
Ascoli, Cecco d', 91
Atto of Vercelli, 81, 102f, 248–49
Aucassin et Nicolette, 140, 143, 157
Audigier, 180
Augustine, 18, 72, 102, 137, 217, 279; on sin and slavery, 75–79, 98, 239, 248ff, 255
Aurora, 88
Auxerre, 84, 98
Azurara, Gomes Eannes de, 94

Bagpipes, 69ff
Bakhtin, Mikhail, 157
Baldwin, John, 160, 162
Ball, John, 60f, 226, 249, 258, 264–65
Barney, Stephen, 34
Barros, Carlos, 183
Bartels, Adolf, 200

Bartholomaeus Anglicus, 182, 199
Basil, Saint, 97
Baudouin de Sebourc, 64, 326n32
Bauer, use of, 10
Bauernlob, 213–14, 235
Beaumanoir, Philippe de, 59–60, 85, 112, 114, 241
Beaune, Colette, 108
Bebel, Heinrich, 149, 191
Bechwinden, Heintz von, 149
Bede, 89, 127, 224
Behem, Hans, 37
Bell, Rudolph, 221
Benedict of Sainte-Maure, 24, 43–44, 50
Benedict, St., 25, 28, 31
Benedict XIII, Pope, 254
Benes of Weitmühl, 211
Benjamin of Tudela, 88, 332n10
Beowulf, 89
Bercé, Yves-Marie, 246
Bernard of Angers, 138–39
Bernard of Clairvaux, 25, 26
Bernard of Cluny, 136
Berthold von Regensburg, 19, 32, 53, 181, 219, 224, 313n74
Bertran de Born, 178
Bertran de Ceva, 116–17, 311n30
Best, George, 94
Bierbrauer, Peter, 85, 252, 255, 260, 285
Birnbaum, Marianna, 270
Bisson, Thomas, 108
Black Death, effects of, 262, 287, 292
Blankenburg, Wilhelm, 3
Blickle, Peter, 282
Bloch, Marc, 85, 113, 148, 241–42, 259
Boccaccio, Giovanni, 159
Bodel, Jean, 150–51, 160–61
Bodenstein von Karlstadt, Andreas, 37, 234
Boethius, 62
Bohemia, legendary origins of, 210
Bonaventura, Saint, 151
Bonet, Honoré, 69
Bonnassie, Pierre, 135, 241f
Book of St. Albans, 63, 102, 340n101
Book of Sainte Foy, 138–39
Borrell, Count of Barcelona, 115
Bourdieu, Pierre, 297

Boureau, Alain, 146, 244
Bozon, Nicholas, 51
Brachylogus, 85
Bracton, 84
Braudel, Fernand, 302–3
Brecht, Martin, 284
Bruegel, Pieter, 35, 173
Bruto, Gian Michele, 52
Buc, Philippe, 43, 48
Bucer, Martin, 231–32, 281, 284
Buch der Rügen, 18, 32, 181, 220
Bulgarus, 85
Burchard of Worms, 82, 98, 138

Caboet family, 186
Caesarius of Arles, 217
Cain, as first peasant, 91–93
Camille, Michael, 28
Canaan, *see* Noah's curse
Cañizares, Jorge, 335n45
Capitein, Jacobus, 95
Capuciati, 61, 84, 98, 259
Carmina Burana, 171
Carozzi, Claude, 17
Cartwright, Samuel A., 336n51
Carvajales, 171
Castellbò, viscounts of, 186
Castleford, Thomas, 128
Catalonia: legendary origins of, 108–9, 114–18, 244–45, 253–55; civil war in, 267–69
Caxton, William, 335n35
Cegléd Proclamation, 276–77, 278
Certeau, Michel de, 296
Cessolis, Jacobo de, 62, 91, 100
Charlemagne, legends of, 20, 106, 108–12, 115–18, 120, 188–89, 195, 254
Charles IV of Bohemia, 211
Charles of Anjou, 121
Charles the Good, Count of Flanders, 183
Chartier, Roger, 295, 299
Chaucer, Geoffrey, 35, 83, 100, 150, 162ff, 216, 229
Chekhov, Anton, 97
Chelčicky, Peter, 36–37, 49, 54, 252
Chrétien de Troyes, 31, 137, 140–41, 143, 157f, 169, 206
Christine de Pisan, 212

Chronicon Eberheimense, 178
Chronik van der hilligen stat van Coellen, 212
Cicero, 67, 72f
Ciompi, 63
Cistercians, 8, 25–27
Coll i Alentorn, Miquel, 108
Colmar Song Collection, 19, 223
Cologne, symbolism of, 211–12
Colonus, use of term, 10
"Combat des Trente," 40
Conrad of Eberbach, 26
Conrad II, Emperor, 81
Constable, Giles, 20
Consuetudines Cathaloniae, 117
Conversi, 25–26, 312n54
"Corner-Stone Speech," 96
Cosmas of Prague, 81, 210
Coulton, G. G., 3
Cowardice, as origin of serfdom, 110–20
Cresques, 93
Crónica de Espanya, 115
Crusade ideology, 273, 276–80, 298
Cullage, 146. See also *Droit de seigneur*
Cursor mundi, 99

Dante Alighieri, 64
Death Dance, 162
Deschamps, Eustache, 56
"Descriptio-Turpin," 111, 341n24
Dialogue between a Cluniac and a Cistercian,
   25
"Dit des Avocats," 40
Dithmarschen, 199–201
Dives and Pauper, 100
"Doctrine of the Holy Crown," 122–23, 125
Domesday Book, 106, 129–30, 264
Dominicans, 27, 48 *passim,* 99
Donnei des Amants, 138
Dózsa, György, 269–71, 273–77
Droit de seigneur, 243–45
Duby, Georges, 17, 20, 22–24, 41–45, 182,
   259, 311n37
Dudo of Saint-Quentin, 43
Dyer, Christopher, 262

Eating, as metaphor, 47–50 *passim*
Ebner, Herwig, 3

"Edelmannslehre," 38
Edward III, King of England, 129
Edwards, John, 299
Eike von Repgow, *see Sachsenspiegel*
Eiximenis, Francesc, 148, 151, 221
Elias, Norbert, 31
Engelmar of Bavaria, Saint, 222
Engels, Friedrich, 280
England: views of servitude in, 106, 126–30;
   and Rising of 1381, 260–67
Enikel, Jansen, 100
Ephraim of Syria, 333n15
Equality, 59–79
Erasmus, 252, 285, 293
Estout de Goz, 146–47
Euchcrius of Lyon, Saint, 33, 223
Eupolemius, 143, 184, 372n128
Euripides, 62

Farrier, Susan E., 356n96
Feierman, Steven, 297
Ferry de Rocourt, 243–44
Fiter, Antoni, 188, 190, 367n66
Foix, counts of, 185–88
Fontane, Theodor, 200
Foucault, Michel, 300
Francis, Saint, 9, 11
Franciscans, 8–9, 27, 51, 217–18, 230, 273–80
   passim
Franz, Günther, 281, 284
Frederick Barbarossa, Emperor, 181
Freedom: as result of courage, 109–10, 115,
   121, 194–202 *passim,* 277–78; through
   Christ's sacrifice, 77–78, 249–56
Frey, Peter, 224
Friedman, Albert B., 62
Fries, Lorenz, 37
Frisch, Max, 190
Froissart, Jean, 53ff, 63, 139, 265, 267

Gaismair, Michael, 258
Galceran of Meulan, Count, 242
Galpin, Stanley Leman, 3, 134, 138, 348n7
Garin le Loherain, 143, 178, 180
Gaudry, Saint, 222
Gautier de Coincy, 221
Gengenbach, Pamphilius, 100

Gerald of Wales, 50
Gerard de Barry, 161
Gerard of Cambrai, 17, 182, 328n87
Gesta comitum Barcinonensium, 115, 194
Gildas, 127
Giles of Rome, 83
Ginzburg, Carlo, 138
Goldonowski, Andrzej, 223
Gómez de Guzmán, Fernán, 183
Goswin of Villers, 26
Gower, John, 20, 41, 62, 93, 100, 143, 149
Gramsci, Antonio, 297
Gratian, 73, 77f, 82, 251
Gravdal, Kathryn, 134–35, 165, 348n7
"Great Rumor" of 1377, 266
Gregory IX, Pope, 142, 199, 278
Gregory of Tours, 221
Gregory the Great: use of metaphors by, 34,
    223f; on equality and slavery, 48, 76–79,
    81, 85, 98, 102, 248, 250–51, 253, 255, 268,
    299, 329n88
"Grobianism," 173–73, 362n80
Gruenbeck, Joseph, 232
Gui de Bourgogne, Chanson de, 111, 121
Guifre "the Hairy," Count of Barcelona, 109,
    115, 194
Guillaume de Saint Amour, 27
Guillaume Le Clerc, 219
Gurevich, Aaron, 23, 299
Guy of Anderlecht, Saint, 222

Hagen, Godefrit, 212
Haimo of Auxerre, 80, 311n37, 330n103
"Halbritter," 178
Ham, *see* Noah's curse
Hannemann, Johann Ludwig, 95, 335n46
Hartmann von Aue, 208–9, 224
Heald, David, 3
Heinrich "der Teichner," 19, 213, 223
Heinrich von Burgus, 217–18
Helmbrecht, 18, 179–81, 223
Hemmerli, Felix: on peasants, 38, 41, 63,
    100–101, 140f, 149, 293, 378n64, 398n13;
    on the Swiss, 142, 160, 191, 194f
Hemmingstedt, Battle of, 200–201
Henry I, King of England, 50
Henry of Huntingdon, 127

Henry II, King of England, 48, 319n43
Henry the Navigator, Prince, 94
Heraclitus, 72
Hesse, Hans, 162
Hilton, Rodney, 260
Hoffmann, Richard, 124, 126
Holkham Bible, 34, 223
Holy Lance, discovery of the, 220
Honorius Augustodunensis, 31–32, 99, 216,
    218, 228, 231, 250, 291, 337n76
Horace, 30, 215
Horns, as "mark of Cain," 90, 91, 92
Hrabanus Maurus, 80, 98, 221, 250
Hue de Saint-Quentin, 165
Hugh of Saint-Cher, 49
Hughes, Christopher, 191
Hügli, Hilde, 3
Hugo von Trimberg, 52, 63, 83, 91, 100–101,
    178, 218, 235, 290–92, 332n6
Huguccio, 82
Hugues Capet, Chanson de, 64
Huizinga, Johan, 59, 323n91, 325n17
Humbert of Romans, 28, 380n74
Hungarian Illuminated Chronicle, 122, 124
Hungary: legendary origins of, 118–26; Re-
    volt of 1514, 269–80

Ibn Khaldun, 89, 333n20
Ibn Qutayba, 89
Idungus (Cistercian monk), 25
Inequality, 72, 77
Innocent III, Pope, 48
Iolo Goch, 228
Isaac of Stella, 25
Isidore of Seville, 31, 76–81 *passim*, 89, 98,
    239, 255
Isidore the Farmer, Saint, 222
ius maletractandi, 240, 254, 256, 323n87
Ivo of Chartres, 82, 98

Jackson, W.T.H., 164
Jacob, Robert, 183
Jacquerie (1358), 51, 53, 139, 267
Jacques de Vitry, 28, 23–33, 49, 220, 318nn31,
    36
James I, King of Aragon, 184
James of Lausanne, 49

Jean Colombe, 31
Jean de Condé, 133–34
Jean, Duke of Berry, 31, 35, 144–45
Jerome, Saint, 89, 203, 217
Joan de Socarrats, 117, 311n30
Joan I, King of Aragon, 117, 254
Joan of Arc, 212, 376n44
Jocelin (poet), 167
Johannes de Rupescissa, 51
Johannes, Master, 111
Johannes von Tepl, 35, 228, 384n132
Johann von Jenštejn, 251
Johann von Viktring, 242
John Chrysostom, 23, 97–98
John, King of England, 127
John of Bromyard, 51–52, 138, 218
John of Marmoutier, 140–41
John of Worcester, 50
Jonas of Orléans, 80, 102, 248, 250
Josephus, 89
Juan del Encina, 160
Juan Manuel, Don, 219
Justice, Steven, 259, 265, 266
Justin Martyr, 88

Kecskés, Tamás, 277
Kempten, 54, 245–47, 282
Kinky hair, motif of, 91ff
Kirk, Elizabeth, 34, 227
Klaniczay, Gábor, 108
Knighton, Henry, 265, 267
Konrad von Ammenhausen, 83, 91ff, 100

Labor: value of, 16–20, 24–33, 36–37, 213–14,
    229, 232, 234, 294–5; as penance, 26–32
    passim, 219; as servile, 145–48
La Bruyére, Jean de, 1
Lacombe, Gilbert, 45f
Lactantius, 74, 216, 248
Ladislas "the Cuman," King of Hungary, 119
Lambert of Ardres, 50
Landes, Richard, 36
Langland, William, 34, 224–29, 232, 261, 266
Langtoft, Peter, 128
Langton, Stephen, 24, 45–49, 51, 60, 81, 204,
    250, 316–18nn.25–37, 319–20nn.46–48
Le Goff, Jacques, 8, 24, 27 *passim*, 141, 299

Leisure, 30–31, 144, 161
Leo X, Pope, 123, 276f
Le Roy Ladurie, Emmanuel, 36
Levi, Carlo, 1, 256
Liber Catonianus, 228
Libro de Buen Amor, 163, 169–70
*Lied von der Entstehung der Eidgenossen-
    schaft, Das*, 192
"Life of the Infidel, Wicked, and Rustic
    Villeins," 154
Limbourg brothers, 31
Linehan, Peter, 108
Locher, James, 231
Lope de Vega, 183, 222
Louis IX, King of France, 121
Lucan, 48
Ludovicus, Brother (Franciscan preacher),
    19, 32, 217, 219
Luther, Martin, 37, 103, 232–34, 248, 258,
    281, 284, 286
Luttrell Psalter, 140, 145

Machiavelli, Niccolò, 63
"Magister P.," 119
Malleus maleficarum, 194
Mandeville, John de, 89, 96
Mannyng, Robert, 108, 128f
Mansa Musa, King of Mali, 93
Map, Walter, 48 *passim*, 319n43
Marcabru, 167
Marchal, Guy, 192, 194
Maria de Luna, Queen of Aragon, 254
Marie de France, 206
Markus, Robert, 77, 329n88
Martin V, Pope, 245
Martin I, King of Aragon, 254
Martin of Braga, 137–38, 217
Martin, Tony, 332n3
Martini, Fritz, 3
Marx, Karl, 150
Massys, Cornelis, 160
Matazone de Calignano, 147–48
Matthew Paris, 128–29
Maximilian I, Emperor, 195
Melanchthon, Philipp, 62, 284
Mellinkoff, Ruth, 137
Menander, 62

Mészáros, Lörine, 277
Meyer, Paul, 147
Michael of Northgate, 218
Mieres, Tomàs, 54, 256, 323n87
Ministeriales, 178
Mirror of Justices, 99
Mittelalterliches Hausbuch, 31
Moffat, Douglas, 127ff
Mohács, Battle of, 125
Monstrelet, 19
Montaigne, Michel de, 270
Montaillou, 36, 49, 189
Mont-Saint-Michel, 145–47
Moore, Barrington, 286f, 298
"Mountain liberties," 189, 191
Müller, Walter, 252, 285
Müntzer, Thomas, 258
Murner, Thomas, 232
Muskatblut, 224
Mutuality among social orders, 20–24, 294.
　　See also Three Orders of Society

Neidhart corpus, 38, 135–36, 150–52, 158,
　　162–63, 164, 166, 171–72, 213, 292
"Neocorus," 200–201
Nibelungenlied, 119–20
Nicholas of Tournai, 77
Nicolas of Oresme, 83
Noah's curse, 86–104
Nuremberg Carnival plays, 154
Nykrog, Per, 134

Oberman, Heiko A., 284
Odo of Cheriton, 216
Oexle, Otto Gerhard, 20, 23, 42
Offa, King of Mercia, 130, 265
Ogier le Danois, 109
Ordericus Vitalis, 15, 242
Ordinance and Statute of Laborers, 226, 262
Origen, 88, 93
Osbert, Viscount of Fontenay-le-Pesnel,
　　146–47
Oswald of Lasko, 250, 279–80
Oswald von Wolkenstein, 20
"Otger Cataló," 109, 117
"Other," concept of the, 300–302
Ottokar of Styria, 178–79

Otto of Freising, 93, 181
Owst, G. R. 51

Paden, William, 164
Panofsky, Erwin, 144, 314n87
Pariatges of Andorra, 186–88
Paris, Gaston, 164
Pastourelle, 164–71
Patterson, Lee, 100
Paul, Saint, 33–34, 72, 239, 248
Peace and Truce of God, 182–83
"Peasant Catechism," 134, 348n4
Peasants: as Christians, 1, 15–16, 204–5;
　　non-marginality of, 2; as economically
　　necessary, 2, 15, 17–20, 144–45, 213–14;
　　discourse about, 3–5, 7, 295–300; defini-
　　tion of, 9–10; violence against, 38, 148–
　　49, 240–47; diet of, 44, 147, 149–50;
　　mistreatment of, 50–55; as animals,
　　53–54, 142–43; descended from Cain,
　　91–93; as comical, 133–37; as unreligious,
　　137–39; bodily deformity of, 139–41;
　　ugliness of, 139–41; "otherness" of, 141f,
　　300–302; as dirty, 143–44; associated
　　with excrement, 143, 151–54; as stupid,
　　150–51; male, 157–63, 171; ineptitude of
　　at love, 158, 160–63; military incapacity
　　of, 158, 178–81; as violent, 158, 183–84,
　　275–76; female, 159, 163–72; in the pas-
　　tourelle, 164–71; armies of, 181–85; free
　　communities of, 182, 185–202; piety of,
　　201–203, 208–13, 216–35; shrewdness of,
　　205–8; productivity of, 213–14; virtuous
　　simplicity of, 214–18; spiritual advantage
　　of, 217–23; and sainthood, 221–23; forms
　　of resistance by, 296–99; acceptance of
　　their situation among, 297–300; aware-
　　ness of their situation among, 297–300.
　　See also Rebellions
Pere Ribera of Perpignan, 115
Peringer, Diepold, 234
Peter Bartholomew, 220
Peter I, King of Aragon, 240
Peter of Blois, 220
Peter of Riga, 88
Peter the Chanter, 21, 48, 64, 77
Peter the Hermit, 278

Peter von Andlau, 211
Petrarch, Francesco, 66–71, 91, 216
"Petrarch Master," 67–71, 326n43
Petrus Comestor, 102, 339n100
Philip de Thaon, 206
Pierre de Beauvais, 111
Piers Plowman, see Langland, William
Pinelo, Léon, 94
Plato, 69, 72
Plow, symbolism of, 33–35, 66, 223–29
"Poem on the First Nobleman," 214, 216
Poor people, 11–13
Popplau, Nicholas von, 245
Přemysl, of Bohemia, 210
Proverbe au vilain, Li, 208
Prudentius, 91
Pseudo-Aethicus Ister, 89
Pseudo-Turpin Chronicle, 110 *passim,* 121,
    341n23
Ptolemy of Lucca, 83

Queen Mary Psalter, 144–45

Radbruch, Renate and Gustav, 69–71
Ragusa, Great Council of, 81–82
Rasted Chronicle, 199
Rather of Verona, 80–81, 98, 179, 250
Raupp, Hans-Joachim, 71
Raymond of Aguilers, 220
Rebellions, 20, 63, 259–60; Normandy
    (997), 43–44; Hungary (1514), 52–53,
    123–24, 269–80; England (1381), 129–30,
    260–67; Flanders (1323–28), 258; Catalo-
    nia (1462–86), 267–69; Germany (1525),
    280–86
Recchia, Vincenzo, 329n88
Reformatio Sigismundi, 52f, 78, 249, 252, 285,
    290, 293
Reformation, impact of, 283–87
Reich, Oskar, 3
remences, 267–78
Resnikow, Sylvia, 61ff
Reynolds, Susan, 107f
Richard II, King of England, 262
Rigord, 140
Robert of Courçon, 53
Robert of Gloucester, 127–28

Roger of Wendover, 127
Rolevinck, Werner, 50, 231
Romance of Claris and Laris, 140
Roman de la Rose, Le, 161
Roman de Renart le Contrefait, 111–12, 121, 135
Roman de Thèbes, 206
Rosenplüt, Hans, 18, 62f, 66, 213–14, 223,
    293, 399n19
Ruiz, Juan, 163, 169–70
Ruprecht von Freising, 148–49, 241, 355n86
Rusticitas, 217
Rusticus, use of term, 10, 137–38
Rutebeuf, 153

Sachsenspiegel, 102–3, 249, 251f, 255–56,
    285–86
Saint Gall, 246, 282
Salinas y Cordova, Buenaventura de, 94
Sallust, 274
Sánchez de Arévalo, Rodrigo, 144
Santillana, Marqués de, 171
Scheidig, Walter, 69
Scheiner, Irwin, 299
Schiller, Friedrich von, 190, 192
Schmidt, Karl, 243–44
Schmitt, Jean-Claude, 8, 138
Schüppert, Helga, 3
Schwabenspiegel, 182, 249, 251f, 255–56,
    285–86, 390n84
Scott, James, 205, 297–98
Seifried Helbling, 178
Seitz, Alexander, 252
Seneca, 73f
Sentence of Guadalupe, 245
Sepúlveda, Ginés de, 331n133
Serfdom: definition of, 9–10; as distinct
    from slavery, 82–83; as result of Noah's
    curse, 86, 91–94, 96–104; as result of
    cowardice, 105–26; incompatibility with
    Christianity, 235, 247–56; as violation of
    natural law, 248–49; as issue in rebel-
    lions, 288
Servus, use of term, 10, 79 *passim,* 99, 116,
    327n68
Ševčenko, Ihor, 307n15
Sewall, Samuel, 95
Sigena, 28f, 65f, 66

Simon d'Authie, 167
Simon of Kéza, 119–22, 124–25, 272, 278
Slavery: as result of nature, 72; as contrary to
    natural law, 73; as result of sin, 74–81,
    97–98; as result of misfortune, 75–76,
    79–80, 328n81; and serfdom, 79, 81–82;
    as result of Noah's curse, 88–104
Slaves, 81–82
Smalley, Beryl, 45
Smaragdus, 81, 248
Smith, Helmut, 295
Song of Roland, The, 93, 110, 141
Southern, R. W., 84
Specht, Henrik, 216
Spiegel, Gabrielle, 108
Spiel von dem alten und jungen Eidgenossen,
    196, 198
Spil von der Vasnacht, Ein, 64
Squattriti, Paolo, 308n18
Stauromachia, 273–74
Stedingen, 199
Stegmüller, Friedrich, 45
Stephen, King of Hungary, 119–20
Stephen of Fougères, 19, 24, 44, 48, 53, 219
Stephen of Tournai, 85
Stephens, Alexander, 96
Stewart, Alison, 362n81
Stoicism, 73, 312n47
Strauss, Gerald, 255
"Stricker, Der," 51, 184, 206
Strohm, Paul, 259, 266
Stühlingen, 283
Stürner, Wolfgang, 329n88
Sudbury, Simon, 260
Summerfield, Thea, 127
Switzerland, 190–99
Sylvester II, Pope, 119
Synod of Coblenz, 81
Synod of Westminster, 81
Szűcs, Jenő, 41, 121, 273, 278

Tabari, 89
Taborites, 255, 258, 285
Talmud, on Noah's curse, 87–88
Tauler, Johannes, 213
Taurinus, 273–74
TeBrake, William, 258

Tell, William, 190–94
Thibaut IV, Count of Champagne, 168
Thomas of Wimbledon, 15, 49
Thomasin von Zerclaere, 53
Three Orders of Society: use of as model,
    16, 20–24, 40; failure in practice, 24,
    40–55
"Three Swiss," story of the, 193–94
Thuróczy, János, 122, 124–25, 272
Tobias of Bechyne, 211
Tomich, Pere, 117–18
Traverse, Elizabeth, 171
Trees, as metaphors, 69–70
Très Riches Heures, 31, 35, 144
Tripartitum, 124–25, 273
Tschudi, Aegidius, 192
Tubero, Ludovicus, 274, 276
Tucker, George, 336n52
Turell, Gabriel, 118, 125
Turville-Petre, Thorlac, 127f
Twelve Articles of the Peasants of Swabia, 252,
    260, 283 *passim*
Tyler, Wat, 260

Ulpian, 73
Ulrich von Turheim, 169
Unibos, 206
Urgell, bishops of, 185–88
Urner Tellspiel, Das, 192–93
Usatges of Barcelona, 240

Vale Royal, Cheshire, 263–64
Vauchez, André, 221, 385n100
Vaux Saint-Cyr, M.-B. de, 46
Vegio, Maffeo, 142, 216
Venette, Jean de, 53
Verbeeck, Frans, 172
Verson, Normandy, 145–47
Vézelay, basilica of, 141–42
Viaticum, 161
Vidal de Canellas, 241
Vienna Genesis, 91, 97
Vilain, use of term, 10
Villein, use of term, 10
Villon, François, 169
Vincent of Beauvais, 85
"Violet Prank," story of the, 151–52

Virgil, 30, 214–15
Vitale, Giovanni, 275–76
Vita Sancti Neoti, 209
Vivó, Joan Belloch, 188
Vladislav II, King of Hungary, 20, 122–23, 273–76
"Vom Rechte," 51
Von der Artzney bayder Glück, 67–71
Vovelle, Michel, 5

Wace, 43–44, 55, 84, 128, 206
Waldeby, John, 51
Waldemar, King of Denmark, 199
Walsingham, Thomas, 60, 63, 261, 264
   passim
Walter von der Vogelweide, 59
Wasif Sah, Ibrahim ben, 89
Weber, Max, 24, 27
Weinstein, Donald, 221
Wenceslas IV, King of Bohemia, 211
Wenceslas, Saint, 210–11
Werbőczy, István, 124–25, 273
Wernher de Gartenaere, 18
Westminster Chronicle, 265

Wheatley, Edward, 227
White Book of Sarnen, 192
White, Christine Pelzer, 298
Wickham, Chris, 189
William, Count of Holland, 182
William, Duke of Normandy, 43
William I, King of England, 127–30
William of St. Thierry, 312n54
William II, King of England, 50
Wimpfeling, Jakob, 194
Wittenwiler, Heinrich, 63, 83, 101–2, 172, 191
Work, *see* Labor
Wulfstan, Archbishop of York, 17, 22, 329n93
Wulfstan, Saint, 222
Wyclif, John, 36, 54, 85, 103, 255, 261, 266, 285

Zápolya, János, 269, 274
Zeckel, George, *see* Dózsa, György
Zclivsky, John, 384n140
Zschelletzschky, Herbert, 69
Zumthor, Paul, 4, 300
Zwingli, Ulrich, 281, 284

Library of Congress Cataloging-in-Publication Data

Freedman, Paul H.

Images of the medieval peasant / Paul Freedman.

p.   cm. — Figurae (Stanford, Calif.)

Includes bibliographical references and index.

ISBN 0-8047-3372-4 (cloth : alk. paper). —

ISBN 0-8047-3373-2 (pbk. : alk. paper)

1. Literature, Medieval—History and criticism.

2. Peasants in literature.   3. Peasantry.

I. Title.   II. Series.

PN682.P35F74   1999

809'.9335208863—dc21   98-36596

                                                                          CIP

∞ This book is printed on acid-free, recycled paper.

Original printing 1999

Last figure below indicates year of this printing:

08   07   06   05   04   03   02   01   00   99